CENSUS OF INDIA 1891

Census of India 1871-1951, 9 Sets In 384 Bindings (9788121258876) Rs. 700000

Census of India 1891, 28 Vols. In 49 Bindings (978-81-212-7129-5) Rs. 125000

1. General Report (9788121269834) Rs. 1450
2. General Tables For British Provinces And Feudatory States (9788121269810) Rs. 2710 (Vol. I)
3. General Tables For British Provinces And Feudatory States (9788121269797) Rs. 950 (Vol. II)
4. Assam - Report (9788121269773) Rs. 2390 (Vol. I, V.1)
5. Assam - Tables (9788121269759) Rs. 2210 (Vol. II, V.2)
6. Assam - Provincial Tables (9788121269735) Rs. 1310 (Vol. II, V.3)
7. The Lower Provinces of Bengal and their Feudatories - The Report (9788121269711) Rs. 1660 (Vol. III)
8. The Lower Provinces of Bengal and their feudatories - The Administrative Tables (9788121269698) Rs. 4200 (Vol. IV)
9. The Lower Provinces of Bengal and their feudatories - The Caste Tables (9788121269674) Rs. 2600 (Vol. V, Pt. 1)
10. Lower Provinces of Bengal - The Provincial Tables (9788121269650) Rs. 1980 (Vol. V, Pt. 2)
11. Berar or the Hyderabad Assigned Districts (9788121269636) Rs. 3360 (Vol. VI)
12. Bombay and Its Feudatories - Report (9788121269612) Rs. 4010 (Vol. VII, Pt. 1)
13. Bombay And Its Feudatories - Imperial Tables (9788121269599) Rs. 790 (Vol. VIII, Pt. 2)
14. Imperial Series - Burma Report (9788121269575) Rs. 2320 (Vol. IX-V.1)
15. Imperial Tables - Burma Report (9788121269551) Rs. 3360 (Vol. X-V.2)
16. Provincial Tables Burma Report (9788121269537) Rs. 3510 (Vol. X-V.3)
17. Provincial Tables Burma Report (9788121269513) Rs. 3630 (Vol. X-V.4)
18. The Central Provinces And Feudatories - The Report (9788121269490) Rs. 2290 (Vol. XI, Pt. 1)
19. The Central Provinces And Feudatories - Imperial tables and supplementary returns (9788121268936) Rs. 2010 (Vol. XII)
20. Madras The Report On The Census (9788121269476) Rs. 2870 (Vol. XIII)
21. Madras - Tables I to XVII-C, British Territory (9788121269452) Rs. 3490 (Vol. XIV)
22. Madras - Tables A TO E, British Territory. Tables for feudatory States and A Caste Index (9788121269438) Rs. 2820 (Vol. XV)
23. The North Western Provinces and Outh - Report and Provincial Tables (9788121268912) Rs. 3100 (Vol. XVI, Pt. 1)
24. The North - Western Provinces and Oudh- Imperial Tables (9788121269414) Rs. 2000 (Vol. XVII, Pt. 2)
25. The North - Western Provinces and Oudh- Imperial Caste Tables (9788121269391) Rs. 3020 (Vol. XVIII, Pt. 3)
26. Punjab and Its Feudatories - The Report on the Census (9788121269377) Rs. 2710 (Vol. XIX, Pt. 1)
27. Punjab and Its Feudatories - Imperial Tables and Supplementary Returns for the British Territory (9788121269353) Rs. 1370 (Vol. XX, Pt. 2)
28. Punjab and Its Feudatories - Imperial Tables and Supplementary Returns for the Native States, Together With A Caste Index (9788121269339) Rs. 4910 (Vol. XXI, Pt. 3)
29. Report on The Census of The Districts of Ajmere-Merwara (9788121269056) Rs. 720 (Vol. XXII)
30. His Highness The Nizam's Dominions - Report (9788121269315) Rs. 2240 (Vol. XXIII, Pt. 1)
31. His Highness The Nizam's Dominions - Report (9788121269292) Rs. 2410 (Vol. XXIII, Pt. 2)
32. His Highness The Nizam's Dominions - Imperial And Supplementry Tables and Caste Index (9788121269278) Rs. 3390 (Vol. XXIII, Pt. 3)
33. Baroda - Report (9788121269254) Rs. 3810 (Vol. XXIV, Pt. 1)
34. Baroda - Tables (9788121269230) Rs. 2620 (Vol. XXIV, Pt. 2)
35. Mysore - Report (9788121269216) Rs. 2590 (Vol. XXV, Pt. 1)
36. Mysore - Imperial Tables (9788121269193) Rs. 1600 (Vol. XXV, Pt. 2)
37. Mysore - Tables (9788121269179) Rs. 5320 (Vol. XXV, Pt. 3)
38. Mysore - Supplementary Tables (9788121269155) Rs. 3590 (Vol. XXV, Pt. 4)
39. Mysore- Supplement to the Mysore census report of 1891 being a list of villages in the Mysore province and : comparing the population as per Censuses of 1891, 1881 & 1871 (9788121279024) Rs. 5350 (Vol. XXV, Pt. 5)
40. Rajputana - The Report, Imperial Tables And Supplementary Returns (9788121269131) Rs. 2330 (Vol. XXVI, Pt. 1)
41. Rajputna - The Provincial Tables and Remarks (9788121269117) Rs. 550 (Vol. XXVI, Pt. 2)
42. Central India (9788121269094) Rs. 2000 (Vol. XXVII)
43. Kashmir State - The Report on the census and Imperial and supplementary Tables (9788121269070) Rs. 2290 (Vol. XXVIII)
44. The Census of Calcutta (9788121269032) Rs. 890
45. Report on the census of Cochin (9788121269018) Rs. 790 (Pt. 1)
46. Report on the census of Cochin - The Final Census Tables with Appendices (9788121268998) Rs. 910 (Pt. 2)
47. Report on the Census of Coorg (9788121268974) Rs. 730
48. Report on the census of Travancore -Report (9788121274029) Rs. 4220 (Vol. I)
49. Report on the census of Travancore -Appendix (9788121268950) Rs. 5300 (Vol. II)

Owing to the antiquity and rarity of this book, certain pages are regrettably absent, and readability is compromised due to the blurring of the original text. If you possess any insights regarding the availability of these missing sections, kindly inform us. Your assistance is crucial in ensuring the completion of this significant work for the benefit of future generations.

CENSUS OF INDIA, 1891

BOOK-43: VOLUME XXVIII

KASHMIR STATE

THE REPORT ON THE CENSUS AND IMPERIAL AND SUPPLEMENTARY TABLES

RAI BAHADUR PANDIT BHAG RAM

GYAN

Published by

Gyan Publishing House
5, Ansari Road
Daryaganj, New Delhi-110002
Phone: 011-47034999, 9811692060
E-mail: books@gyanbooks.com

Distribution Network
gyanbooks.com
India, USA, Canada, UK, Australia

ISBN: 978-81-212-7129-5 (Set) 28 Vols. In 49 Bindings
978-81-212-6907-0 Book-43, (PB) Vol. XXVIII

First Published, 1893

2nd Impression 2024

Printed at: Gyan Press, Delhi.

CENSUS OF INDIA 1891

CENSUS OF INDIA, 1891.

VOLUME XXVIII.

THE

KASHMIR STATE.

THE REPORT ON THE CENSUS

AND

IMPERIAL AND SUPPLEMENTARY TABLES,

BY

RAI BAHADUR PANDIT BHAG RAM,
JUDICIAL MEMBER AND SECRETARY STATE COUNCIL,
SUPERINTENDENT OF CENSUS OPERATIONS, KASHMIR STATE.

Lahore:
PRINTED AT THE MUFID-I-AM PRESS.

1893.

CENSUS REPORT

OF

KASHMIR STATE,

1891.

CHAPTER I.

General description, physical and climatic divisions, rainfall, area, density, proximity of towns and villages, rural and urban population.

1. The Native State of Jammu and Kashmír is politically subordinate to the Government of India, and constitutes the territories of the Mahárája of Kashmír, extending from 32° 17′ to 36° 58′ North-latitude, and from 73° 26′ to 80° 30′ East-longitude. Its area is 80,900 square miles, with a population returned in 1891, of 25,43,952 persons. No previous Census appears to have been taken, the enumeration of 1873 being far from reliable. The State is bounded on the North by some petty semi-independent hill chiefships mostly subordinate to Kashmír, and by the Karakorum mountains, on the East by Chinese Tibet, on the South and West by the Panjab Districts of Ráwalpindi, Jhelam, Gujrát and Siálkot and the Hazára country.

2. For administrative purposes it is divided into the following Divisions :—

Jammu (including the feudatory Jágírs of Rámnagar, Bhadráwah and Punch).

Kashmír, Ladákh, Skardu and Gilgit.

3. The Provinces of Jammu and Kashmír form the more important part of the State, while Ladákh, Skardu and Gilgit owe their importance to their position on the Frontier.

4. The greater portion of the country is mountainous, and with the exception of a strip of plain on the south-west which is continuous with the great level of the Panjab, may be conveniently divided into the following regions :—

1st.—The outer hills and the middle mountains of Jammu District.

2nd.—Kashmír.

3rd.—The far side of the great watershed range.

(*a*). Semi-Tibetan climate including Astor and some parts of Gilgit and Baltistán.

(*b*). Tibetan or almost rainless climate taking in the rest of Gilgit, the greater part of Baltistán and all Ladákh.

5. The hills in the outer region begin with a height of 100 to 200 feet above the plain, followed by a tract of rugged country, including various ridges running nearly parallel to the first one, with long narrow valleys between them.

6. The average height of these ridges ranges from 3,000 to 4,000 feet.

7. The middle mountains are commonly 8,000 to 10,000 feet high, covered with pasture, or else with forest, then follow the more lofty mountain ranges, including the region of perpetual snow.

8. A great chain of snowy mountains running south-east and south-west, divides the drainage of the Chenáb and Jhelam rivers from that of the higher branches of the Indus.

9. What may be called branches from this, enclose the valley or plain of Kashmír.

10. All beyond that great range is a wide tract of mountainous country the whole of which is at a high level, it is the north-western part of Tibet, embracing Ladákh, Baltistán and Gilgit.

11. Here the mountain ranges are of heights of from 17,000 up to 22,000 feet and more.

12. The whole country abounds with valleys, varying in character, and in a few places with table-lands.

13. With these great variations of level the climate is necessarily different for every region.

14. The temperature ranges from the more than tropical heat of the Panjab summer, to such an intensity of cold as keeps perpetual snow on the mountains. In the inhabited places even the variation is such that in the parts the fashion of the poor of India, going almost unclad is followed, in the higher sheep skin coats are wanted for protection against the cold, and people are in places confined to their houses by snow for seven months in the year.

15. Besides temperature there is the element of moisture, which gives another variety to the climate.

(1)—The outer hills and the middle mountains of Jammu where the periodical rains prevail.

(2)—Kashmír, where the periodical rains reach partially, but there is rain-fall enough for all crops but rice without need of irrigation.

(3)—Astor with some parts of Gilgit and Baltistán, where no crops can be raised without irrigation and the hill sides are for the most part bare, but some forest grows on portions of the mountain slopes.

(4)—The rest of Gilgit and the greater portion of Baltistán where no crop can be raised without irrigation, and the whole country is bare both of forest and of pasture, this tract is nearly rainless.

16. The general aspect of the Valley of Kashmír is that of a basin, encircled on every side by lofty mountains. In the middle is an extensive alluvial tract intersected by the Jhelam and its numerous tributaries which flow down from the mountains and find their way by the sole channel of the Jhelam through the Bárámulá Pass to the plains of the Panjab. The elevation of this valley is about 5,200 feet above the sea.

17. Besides the low alluvial tract extending along the banks of the Jhelam, there occur extensive plateaux of slight elevation stretching from the mountains at various distances into the plains. These plateaux are known as Karewas. Their soil for the most part is a loam or loamy clay, containing remains of fresh water, fishes and molluscs, which indicate a locustrine or fluvial origin. They are divided from each other by ravines of from 100 to 300 feet in depth. Occasionally they are entirely surrounded by lower ground, but more generally they connect with some of the mountains that bound the valley. Over the surface of the Karewas, water has some times been brought for irrigation, and then a fertile tract is the result, but more commonly the cultivation depends on rain alone, and in that case the yield is precarious. The slopes of the hills between the flat ground and the limit of forest, are a mixture of cultivation, good grazing grounds, and forests of cedars, pines, firs, &c.

18. The southern and more inbabited portion of Kashmír includes the lower half of the Kishen Ganga Valley and the whole district south of the snowy range that separates the drainage of the Indus from that of the Jhelam and Chenáb. In this region the hills are covered with pine forests interspersed with pastures, the banks of the streams are green with cultivation; villages are connected with each other by roads, while the principal valley is crowded with objects of interest and is fertile and beautiful in a high degree.

19. The beauties of the Kashmír Valley have been so often celebrated in prose and verse that further allusion to them here would be out of place. The Pír Panjál range is said to have been the home of a Pír or Saint, who gave benediction to travellers passing northwards over the mountains. The belief is still current among Mohamedans in Kashmír that the Pír resides on one of the summits and the whole range is thus invested with peculiar sanctity.

20. The general direction of the range is from north-west to south-east.

21. The margs or mountain downs, which are numerous on the tops of the range of the hills immediately below the Pír Panjál, and also upon the northern slopes of those mountains which enclose the north-eastern side of the valley, are a peculiar feature of the country. They are covered with rich grass, and afford pasturage during the summer months to large herds of ponies, cattle, sheep and goats. The principal ones are Sunamarg (golden meadow) and Goolmarg (land of flowers), the latter a favorite refuge in the malarious months of July and August, both for Europeans and Natives of high rank.

22. Ladakh.—The district of Ladákh comprises the Valley of the Indus, and also of most of its tributaries from 32° to 35° North-latitude, and from 75° 29′ to 79° 29′ East-longitude. The different districts of Central Ladákh, Rupshu, and Neobra, besides the bleak and almost uninhabited plateaux of the Kuen-lun and Linzhithang plains together make up the province.

23. Lying as it does at the back of the great central range of the Himalayas, it may be readily understood that Ladákh is one of the loftiest of the inhabited regions of the globe. The valley and plateaux vary between 9,000 and 17,000 feet, while many of the peaks attain attitudes of 25,000 feet. The slopes of the mountains and the lofty table-lands in the north-east of the province are, with the exception of occasional forest growth, almost destitute of vegetation.

24. The common domestic goat of Ladákh is the well-known shawl goat the wool of which is exported to Kashmír, Nepál and British India.

25. The trade of the country in home produce is confined to four articles, *viz.*, wool, borax, sulphur, and dried fruits. But the fact of Leh being an important entrepot for trade between Kashmír and Hindustán on the south of Yárkand, Khotan, and Tibet on the north and east has probably contributed more to the wealth of the country. The chief imports from Chinese territories are wool (sheep and goats), tea, gold dust and coins, silver, silk and charas (an intoxicating preparation of hemp); while those from India consist of cotton goods, hides, skins and leathers, grain, guns, pistols, &c., brocades and tea.

26. The Ladákhís are a settled and cultivating people, living in villages, which vary from 9,500 to 13,500 feet above the sea. They are cheerful, willing, and not quarrelsome unless excited by their intoxicating drink, chang; simplicity and clumsiness are in a measure their chief characteristics. On the other hand, authorities agree in remarking that the Ladákhís far excel the Indian Munshís or learned men, in one point, *i. e.*, the understanding of a map. Almost all the Ladákhís are engaged in agriculture, and the area cultivated by one family is from 2 to 4 acres.

27. Except among the few richer people, polyandry or plurality of husbands, is quite general; the practice having no doubt arisen from the limited extent of cultivable land and the general inelasticity of the country's resources.

28. In nearly every village there is a monastery which sometimes holds but one or two Lámás or Monks, sometimes hundreds. These monasteries are, as a rule, conspicuously built on a spur of the mountain or isolated rock, and always somewhat apart from the village itself. The supply of priests is kept up by one boy in each family being usually devoted to the profession. The religious tone of the inhabitants is further exemplified by colossal figures of deities carved in the rock and stone-heaps on walls covered with inscriptions and miscellaneous sacred structures.

29. Baltistán or Skardu is composed of enormous mountain chains or masses of mountains, varying in height from 18,000 to 28,000 feet above sea level; of the valleys the most important are the Indus Valley and the valley of the Shazok that joins it and that of Shigár which combines with the united valley at Skardu.

30. By far, the most of the Skardu plain is uncultivated, it is a waste of sand and stones. Cultivation however is limited more by the supply of water than by the barrenness of the soil. The village of Skardu itself is out in the plain 7,440 feet above the sea, it is rather a scattered collection of houses and hamlets. It is the head-quarter of the district. The shop-keepers are Kashmír. settlers.

31. The district of Gilgit is situated in the centre of the most mountainous region of the Himalayas, lying on the southern slope of the Hindu Kush, or perhaps more correctly the Himalayas between Baltistán and Yásin. The village of Gilgit, which gives its present name to the valley, lies in latitude 35° 55′ North-longitude 74° 22′ East. The lower part of the valley of the Gilgit river, nearly 40 miles in length, forms the Gilgit district. The language spoken is Shiná, though the Shins are numerically inferior to the rest of the population.

32. The population of the Gilgit Valley must at one time have been large, as traces of cultivated terraces high up on the mountain sides to an elevation of 10,000 feet distinctly prove.

Nowhere else in the world, probably, is there to be found so great a number of deep valleys, and lofty mountains in so small an area. Within a radius of 65 miles from Gilgit village, the survey maps show, amidst innumerable smaller peaks, eleven varying from 18,000 to 20,000 feet, seven from 20,000 to 22,000 feet, six from 22,000 to 24,000 feet and eight from 24,000 to 26,000 feet, while half of the tract thus included still remains to be surveyed. A rival to mount Everest and Kanchanchanga may be found among the lofty mountains of these parts. A road from Srinagar to Gilgit is in course of construction; gold washing is only practised by the poorest in winter, but sometimes very remunerative, the best gold being of 20 carats. Nearly half way between Gilgit village and the Indus is the Bugrot Valley, which contains several flourishing villages. This valley is celebrated for the quantity and quality of its gold production, and there are many signs of mineral wealth. It was a favourite resort of the old Gilgit rulers, and was their last place of refuge, when hard pressed by external enemies. The Bugrot people are almost entirely the Shin caste or clan. In Gilgit itself there are a great number of Kashmíris, or as they are here called Kashirús whose fore-fathers settled in the place in the time of Ahmed Shah Abdállee, about A.D. 1760. They now form the largest section of the Gilgit population, and the shrewdness which forms so distinctive a part of the character of the ordinary Kashmírí has suffered little by transplanting; some are said to have penetrated into Chitrál where they have since become merged in the regular population. Those, in Gilgit, are weavers and carpenters and they are regarded with some contempt by the Shins and Yeshkuns.

33. The outer hill region is mostly occupied by Dográs and Chibbális, a well-featured race of rather slight build, the middle mountains by the Paháris, a stouter race. The Kashmírí, though allied to the Paháris, are a race possessing very marked characters, they are large made and robust and of a cast of features really fine, though largely confined to their own mountain bounded country of Kashmír, they have settled in the higher parts of the neighbouring valleys, and in outlying places.

34. The district of Gilgit and its surrounding is occupied by Dards. They are broad shouldered, moderately stout built, well proportioned men, and are active. Ladákh is inhabited by:—

Champas, Ladákhí, Balti, and Dard, the first three belong to the frontier race.

The Ladákhís have the Turanian cast of feature, they are short in stature, both sexes are broad made and strong and are generally an ugly race.

The Baltis of Skardu or Baltistán, are of the same stock as the Ladákhís. In stature they are less thick set than most Ladákhís.

The Kashmírís are quick, versatile and plausible, the Ladákhí including the Balti, slow, inapt, and much given to truth telling.

The Dards are as a race decidedly clever, but not so ingenious as the Kashmírís, yet they are both clear headed and quick.

The Dográs are Hindus and Mohamedans, Kashmírís mostly Mohamedans, the Dards and Baltis are all Mohamedans and the Ladákhís Budhists.

35. The languages of Kashmír are divided into thirteen separate dialects, of these Dográ and Chibbáli, which do not differ much from Hindustáni and Panjabi, are spoken in the hills and country of the Punch and Jammu Districts. Kashmírí is mostly used in Kashmír proper, and is rather curiously and closely related to the Sanskrit. It is not, however, the Court language and for the purpose of a traveller through Kashmír, either Hindustáni or Panjabi will serve. Five dialects are included under the term "Pahárí" a language spoken by the mountaineers in the east of Kashmír. Besides these, there are two dialects of Tibetan which are spoken in Baltistán, Ladákh and Champas, and in the north-west three or four varieties of the Dard dialects of Aryan origin.

36. Commerce and trade.—The principal commercial intercourse is with the Panjab, Ladákh and Afghánistán. The main routes by which the merchandise of Kashmír enters India are from Srinagar, by the Jhelam Valley Road, the Banihál Pass to Jammu and Amritsar by the Pír Panjál and Bhimbar to Gujrát, and also by Akhnúr and the Budil Pass. The great mart in the Panjab for the trade of Kashmír is Amritsar. Goods to a considerable amount pass through Kashmír from British India for the markets of Central Asia. Several main lines of road lead from the Panjab into Kashmír, the most important of which is the Jhelam Valley Road. There it also a Railway between Siálkot and Jammu.

37. The country is rich in minerals, but little or nothing has been done towards the development of its natural resources.

38. Malaria is very prevalent throughout the Kashmír Valley, and fevers and affections of the bowels are common, but the other diseases peculiar to India are seldom observed. Epidemics of small-pox and cholera are not unfrequent. In many villages the inhabitants suffer from goitre. In addition to the above diseases, phthisis, elephantiasis, syphilis and scrofula are common.

39. The following table gives a detail of the fiscal divisions of the State and results of the present Census :—

Name of Division.	Fiscal Sub-divisions.	Tehsíls.	Number of towns and villages.	Number of occupied houses.	Total Population. Both sexes.	Males.	Females.
JAMMU.	RANBIR SINGHPORA	Khás	208	20,404	1,03,295	60,104	43,191
		Ranbir Singhpora	292	14,573	73,772	39,287	34,485
		Samba	238	12,669	62,518	33,508	29,010
		Total	738	47,646	2,39,585	1,32,899	1,06,686
	JASROTA	Jasmergarh	259	8,576	41,956	22,490	19,466
		Kathua	153	8,122	39,425	22,227	17,198
		Basohli	145	14,941	70,137	36,717	33,420
		Total	557	31,639	1,51,518	81,434	70,084
	UDHAMPORE	Udhampore	220	10,825	53,886	28,706	25,180
		Chanaini	40	2,010	9,998	5,644	4,354
		Ramban	130	6,521	45,574	24,798	20,776
		Kishtwar	117	4,269	31,679	16,939	14,740
		Padar Jaskar	30	1,390	9,570	5,005	4,565
		Total	537	25,015	1,50,707	81,092	69,615
	REASI	Reasí	282	12,902	65,256	34,891	30,365
		Parat	215	11,110	57,726	30,558	27,168
		Akhnúr	199	13,103	68,385	36,514	31,871
		Total	696	37,115	1,91,367	1,01,963	89,404
	BHIMBAR	Bhimbar	104	13,973	70,756	37,807	32,949
		Mirpore	279	18,905	88,384	45,678	42,706
		Rámpore	181	7,874	53,227	28,715	24,512
		Noshehra	102	13,942	71,344	37,877	33,467
		Kotli	192	13,661	71,788	38,176	33,612
		Total	858	68,355	3,55,499	1,88,253	1,67,246
		GRAND TOTAL	3,386	2,09,770	10,88,676	5,85,641	5,03,035
	JAGIRS.						
	RAM NAGAR	Ram Nagar	129	9,263	49,826	25,880	23,946
	BHUDRAWAH	Nagar Khas	155	3,384	17,099	8,744	8,355
		Palesah	168	3,194	15,334	8,031	7,303
		Total	323	6,578	32,433	16,775	15,658
	PUNCH	Haveli	177	8,986	71,880	38,846	33,034
		Mendar	99	8,322	65,023	34,922	30,101
		Bagh	114	9,112	62,725	32,759	29,966
		Sodanti	99	10,415	68,980	35,418	33,562
		Total	489	36,835	2,68,608	1,41,945	1,26,663
		Total Jagirs	941	52,676	3,50 867	1,84,600	1,66,267
		Total Jammu Division	4,327	2,62,446	14,39,543	7.70,241	6,69,302

Name of Division.	Fiscal Sub-divisions.	Tehsíls.	Number of towns and villages.	Number of occupied houses.	Total Population. Both sexes.	Males.	Females.
KASHMIR.	Khas ...	Khás	109	27,076	1,46,267	77,369	68,898
		Ach and Nagam ...	221	6,984	48,524	25,705	22,819
		Dansú Machama ...	201	5,691	38,453	20,021	18,432
		Ular Víhú	171	5,596	37,880	20,213	17,667
		Charat	146	5,431	38,661	20,444	18,217
		Total ...	848	50,778	3,09,785	1,63,752	1,46,033
	Kamraj ...	Uttar Machipora ...	237	7,744	56,890	30,064	26,826
		Biroh Magam	240	6,748	46,239	24,323	21,916
		Kiroham	205	7,588	47,947	25,350	22,597
		Hamalzenagir ...	219	7,705	51,990	27,314	24,676
		Chob Chakal	26	1,482	10,454	5,524	4,930
		Lál	186	5,926	42,044	22,180	19,864
		Total ...	1,113	37,193	2,55,564	1,34,755	1,20,809
	Anantnag ...	Anantnág	134	6,735	43,069	22,975	20,094
		Sri Ranbir Singhpora ...	125	8,042	53,793	28,298	25,495
		Deosar	182	6,037	40,169	20,923	19,246
		Dachanpara	151	7,121	46,404	24,477	21,927
		Shopian	205	6,221	41,123	21,452	19,671
		Total ...	797	34,156	2,24,558	1,18,125	1,06,433
	Muzafferabad ...	Karnáh	105	3,618	29,342	15,481	13,861
		Uri-Chakar	358	8,351	53,967	29,021	24,946
		Muzafferabad	316	7,973	51,491	28,379	23,112
		Total ...	779	19,942	1,34,800	72,881	61,919
		Grand Total ...	3,537	1,42,069	9,24,707	4,89,513	4,35,194
	JAGIRS	Raja Amar Singh ...	80	2,069	14,470	7,664	6,806
		Raja Rám Singh ...	36	1,551	9,864	5,168	4,696
		Total Jágírs ...	116	3,620	24,334	12,832	11,502
		Total Kashmír Division ...	3,653	1,45,689	9,49,041	5,02,345	4,46,696
FRONTIER DISTS.	Ladakh ...	...	86	6,264	28,274	14,350	13,924
	Skardu ...	...	243	31,307	1,10,325	56,098	54,227
	Gilgit ...	...	110	2,287	16,769	10,195	6,574
		Total Frontier Districts ...	439	39,858	1,55,368	80,643	74,725
		Total Kashmír State ...	8,419	4,47,993	25,43,952	13,53,229	11,90,723

40. There are four towns in Jammu and the same number in Kashmír, *viz* :—

			Total Population.
Jammu District ...	Jammu	... ...	34,542
	Batála	... ...	5,206
	Mirpore	... ...	7,253
	Punch	... ...	7,489
		Total ...	54,490

		Total Population.
Kashmir District ...	Srinagar	... 1,18,960
	Anantnág	... 10,227
	Sopore	... 8,410
	Bárámula	... 5,656
	Total	... 1,43,253
	Grand Total	... 1,97,743

There are no towns in Ladákh, Skardu and Gilgit.

41. The city of Jammu is situated on the Tawí, a tributary of the Chenáb among the mountains of the outer Himalayan range. It is the seat of the Government. The town and palace stand upon the right bank of the river, the fort overhangs the left or eastern shore at an elevation of 150 feet above the stream. It is the largest city in the province.

42. Srinagar (or Surjyanagar, the city of the Sun) is picturesquely situated in the "Happy Valley" of Kashmír, about mid-way between its two ends, and close to the hills which bound its north-western side, on the banks of the River Jhelum in latitude 34° 5′ 31″ North and longitude 74° 51′ East. The city extends for about 2 miles along the banks of the river, which divides it into two nearly equal portions, connected by seven bridges.

43. Srinagar is built at an elevation of about 5,276 feet above the sea, but is surrounded by low swampy tracts, which render it unhealthy.

44. Fires are frequent, and often very destructive.

45. The public buildings are few. The principal of them are the Báràdari, palace, fort, gun-factory, dispensary, school and mint; also some ancient mosques, temples and cemeteries.

46. The streets are generally narrow, and some of them are paved with large and irregular masses of lime-stone. They are all, however, very dirty and unfit to be visited by ladies. There are several Bazars or market places in different parts of the city, one of which called the Mahárájganj, has been lately built for the convenience of visitors, in which all the manufactures peculiar to Kashmír can be readily obtained. There are several large mansions on its outskirts, chiefly occupied by the great shawl merchants and bankers; some of them exhibit beautiful specimens of trellised wood-work, and in other respects are very tastefully fitted up.

47. The Takht-i-Suleman, or throne of Solomon, is a hill over-looking the city from which a good view is obtained. On the top is a fine old stone temple called by Hindus, Shankar Ácharya; it was originally Budhist, and was built by Jaloka, son of Asoka, about 220 B. C.

48. The "Hari-parbat" or "Fort Hill," is an isolated hill on the northern outskirts of the city. It is about 250 feet high, and is crowned by the fort. A wall surrounds the hill, in which the principal gateway, called the Káti Darwázá, is surrounded by a Persian inscription. Both wall and fort were built by Akbar Shah about 1590 A. D., at a cost of a million sterling. The length of the wall is about 3 miles, its height 28 feet.

49. The Shergarhi, within the city, contains the city fort and the royal palace. It is 400 yards long by 200 wide; its walls are about 22 feet high, and the interior contains the State apartments, Government offices and barracks. The Juma Masjid or Cathedral Mosque, which is in the city, is a very large four-sided building, with an open square in the centre and a wooden steeple in the middle of each side, the roof of the surrounding cloister is supported by wooden pillars, each formed of a single deodar tree about 30 feet high.

50. The Dal or City lake of Kashmír which has been sung by Moore in Lalla-i-Rookh, lies on the north-eastern side of the city. It is about 5 miles long 2½ miles broad with an average depth of about 10 feet. Its surface in many parts is covered with the famous Kashmírian "floating gardens"—Shalimár Bágh well-known as the scene of Moore's Light of the Harem, is a beautiful pleasure ground laid out by Jahángír, the Nasim Bágh, or garden of bliss, another picturesque pleasure ground, is said to have been first planned by Akbar, and there are several other gardens of similar character in the environs of Srinagar.

51. A large population of the inhabitants are shawl weavers, with their usual complement of dyers, washers and brokers, the other ornamental arts are silver work, papier machí painting. There is every variety of handicraft usually found in an Indian city, but few of these either from superiority of skill or from the importance of numbers, require special mention.

52. The other towns are hardly of any importance to deserve special mention.

53. The total area of the Kashmír State is 80,900 square miles. The Provinces and Districts have never been brought under measurement, and it is under the circumstance impossible to determine the order in which the districts fall when arranged according to area, and to show the relationship between population and area.

54. The total population is 25,43,952 or 31 per square mile.

55. Arranged according to population the districts fall as below, but in the absence of a proper record of measurement this is mere guess work based on personal local knowledge of the country.

	Jammu.	*Kashmír.*	*Ladákh.*	*Skardu*	*Gilgit.*
Densely populated ...	Ranbir Singhpura ...	Khás	...	...	...
	Bhimbar	Kámráj	...	...	.
Fairly densely peopled ...	Jasrota	Anantnág	...	...	...
	Reasi and southern portion of Udhampore		...	...	...
Averagely thinly peopled ...	Northern portion of Udhampore	Muzafferabad		Skardu	...
Sparsely peopled ...	... ...	...	Ladákh	...	Gilgit.

56. Table I. deals with houses, towns, villages and population. There are 8 towns and 8,411 villages in the State distributed as follows :—

	Number of towns.	Number of villages.
Jammu	4	4,323
Kashmír	4	3,649
Ladákh	...	86
Skardu	...	243
Gilgit	...	110
Total ...	8	8,411

57. Occupied houses number 4,47,993, of which 36,252 or 8·1 per cent. belong to the urban, and 4,11,741 or 91·9 per cent. to the rural population. The detail of percentage by Provinces and Districts is as follows :—

(I).—PROVINCES.

	Urban Population.		Rural Population.	
	Number of houses.	Percentage.	Number of houses.	Percentage.
Jammu	9,895	2·3	2,52,551	56·5
Kashmír	26,357	5·8	1,19,332	26·6
Ladákh	...	...	6,264	1·4
Skardu	...	...	31,307	6·9
Gilgit	...	...	2,287	0·5

(2).—DISTRICTS.

	Urban Population.		Rural Population.	
	Number of houses.	Percentage.	Number of houses.	Percentage.
Jammu.				
Khálsa Districts. Ranbir Singhpora	6,194	1·6	41,452	9·3
Khálsa Districts. Jasrota	...	...	31,639	7·1
Khálsa Districts. Udhampore	...	...	25,015	5·5
Khálsa Districts. Reasi	...	...	37,115	8·4
Khálsa Districts. Bhimbar	2,544	0·5	65,811	14·7
Jágírs	1,157	0·2	51,519	11·5
Kashmir.				
Khás	22,448	5·0	28,330	6·2
Kámráj	2,289	0·5	34,904	7·7
Anantnág	1,620	0·3	32,536	7·2
Muzafferabad	...	...	19,942	4·7
Jágírs	...	...	3,620	0·8
Ladákh	...	...	6,264	1·4
Skardu	...	...	31,307	6·9
Gilgit	...	...	2,287	0·5

58. The following table shows the average number of houses and the average number of persons per house, for each town and village:—

(a).—RURAL POPULATION.

	Total number of villages.	Total number of houses.	Average number of houses per village.	Total. population.	Average number of persons per house.
Jammu Province.					
Sri Ranbir Singhpora	737	41,452	56	2,05,043	5
Jasrota	557	31,639	57	1,51,518	5
Udhampore	537	25,015	47	1,50,707	6
Reasi	696	37,115	53	1,91,367	5
Bhimbar	856	65,811	77	3,43,040	5
Jágírs	940	51,519	55	3,43,378	7
Total	4,323	2,52,551	58	13,85,053	5
Kashmir.					
Khás	847	28,330	33	1,90,825	7
Kámráj	1,111	34,904	31	2,41,498	7
Anantnág	796	32,536	41	2,14,331	6
Muzafferabad	779	19,942	26	1,34,800	7
Jágírs	116	3,620	31	24,334	7
Total	3,649	1,19,332	33	8,05,788	7
Ladákh	86	6,264	73	28,274	4
Skardu	243	31,307	129	1,10,325	3
Gilgit	110	2,287	21	16,769	7

(*b.*)—URBAN POPULATION.

	Total number of houses.	Total population.	Average number of persons per house.
Jammu	6,194	34,542	5
Batála	991	5,206	5
Mirpore	1,553	7,253	4
Punch	1,157	7,489	6
Total	9,895	54,490	5
Srinagar	22,448	1,18,960	5
Bárámula	1,063	5,656	5
Sopore	1,226	8,410	7
Anantnág	1,620	10,227	6
Total	26,357	1,43,253	5

59. The details for rural population of Jágírs in Jammu Province are given below :—

	Total number of villages.	Total number of houses.	Total population	Average number of persons per house.
Rámnagar...	129	9,263	49,826	5
Bhadrawah	323	6,578	32,433	5
Punch	488	35,678	2,61,119	7
Total	940	51,519	3,43,378	6

60. The following statement shows the average population for villages and towns :—

I.—VILLAGES.

	Total rural population.	Number of villages.	Average population per village.
Jammu	13,85,053	4,323	320
Kashmír	8,05,788	3,649	220
Ladákh	28,274	86	328
Skardu	1,10,325	243	454
Gilgit	16,769	110	152
Total	23,46,209	8,411	279

61. The average population of towns is 24,718, shown in order of memorial strength, the towns in the State are as noted below :—

II.—TOWNS.

	Total urban population.	Per cent.
Srinagar	1,18,960	60·2
Jammu	34,542	17·5
Anantnág	10,227	5·2
Sopore	8,410	4·3
Punch	7,489	3·8
Mirpore	7,253	3·6
Bárámula	5,656	2·8
Batála	5,206	2·6
Total	1,97,743	100·0

62. As regards collocation of the population in aggregates large and small, the results obtained from Tables III and IV are as follows :—

	1—199.		200—499.		500—999.		1,000—1,999.		2,000—2,999.		3,000—4,999.		5,000 & above.	
	Number.	Percentage.	Number.	Percentage.	Number.	Percentage.	Number.	Percentage.	Number.	Percentage.	Number.	Percentage.	Number.	Percentage.
Jammu	2,140	25·4	1,423	16·9	539	6·4	175	2·08	33	0·39	12	0·14	5	0·06
Kashmír	2,309	27·4	999	11·87	273	3·24	59	0·7	6	0·07	3	·03	4	0·04
Ladákh	36	0·5	35	0·41	13	0·15	1	0·01	1	0·01	...	...	...	...
Skardu	90	1·07	75	0·9	46	0·55	31	0·37	1	0·01	...	...	...	...
Gilgit	87	1·03	19	0·22	3	0·04	...	...	1	0·01	...	...	...	...
Total ...	4,662	55·4	2,551	30·3	74	10·38	266	3·16	42	0·49	15	0·17	9	0·10

Villages below 500, average about 86 per cent. above 500 but not exceeding 1,999, 13½ per cent.

63. These statistics, it must be confessed, are to a great extent misleading, except in the Kashmír Valley and the plains of Jammu Province, the unit known as a village could hardly be said as correctly representing collocation of the population in aggregates large and small. The division into villages is one made for fiscal purposes without any reference to collocation. In the hilly tracts every farmer or cultivator has his homestead in the immediate vicinity of his farm and is naturally secluded from his fraternity by intervening forests and waste-lands. A village with a population of 200 persons not unfrequently comprises 60 houses situated within a radius of 3 to 4 miles from each other, and are yet considered one village with special reference to the revenue area under their cultivation. The same remarks apply to nomadic villages of herdsmen, Gujars, &c., in the Udhampore, Punch and other districts where cattle breeding is the principal source of income.

64. Collocation of the population in large or small aggregates, practically exists in towns, and in villages where cultivation covers extensive areas divided among communities occupying holdings in close proximity to each other, or where such collocation has been made to ensure supplies for the outside population, as Udhampore and other marts of internal trade which are small townships for the exchange of commodities.

65. The relative proportion of the Urban and Rural population is given below :—

	Total Population.	Urban.	Rural.	Percentage.	
				Urban.	Rural.
Jammu	14,39,543	54,490	13,85,053	3·7	96·3
Kashmír	9,49,041	1,43,253	8,05,788	15·1	84·9
Ladákh	28,274	...	28,274	...	...
Skardu	1,10,325	...	1,10,325	...	...
Gilgit	16,769	...	16,769	...	...
Total	25,43,952	1,97,743	23,46,209	7·7	92·3

66. The towns in this State are the nucleus of trade.

Jammu owes its development to the fact of its being the Capital of the State, the head quarters of the Chief and Provincial Establishments and the principal mart of commerce with the hilly tracts comprising the high road to Kashmír *via* Banihál.

Srinagar, to influx of visitors to the Valley, and the Chief seat of the Hindu and Mohamedan gentry of the Province.

CHAPTER II.

Movement of the Population.

67. In the absence of any previous Census it is impossible to deal with the movement of the population, but advantage will be taken to discuss elsewhere the inequalities in sexes which throw some light on the subject.

CHAPTER III.

Religion.

68. The inhabitants of the State may, in regard to religion, be distinguished as Hindus, Jains, Sikhs, Mohamedans, Budhists, Christians and Parsís.

69. There were no Jews on the night of the Census.

70. The following table shows the number returned under each religion and its ratio to the total population :—

	Hindus.	Jains.	Sikhs.	Mohamedans.	Budhists.	Christians.	Parsís.	Unspecified.
Jammu	6,31,225	593	5,926	7,97,459	4,293	46	1	...
Kashmír	60,316	...	5,473	8,83,099	...	145	8	...
Ladákh	182	...	...	2,991	25,076	25	...	...
Skardu	64	...	...	1,10,022	239	...	...	...
Gilgit	13	...	...	139	...	2	...	16,615
Total ...	6,91,800	593	11,399	17,93,710	29,608	218	9	16,615

(II). Ratio of Hindus, Mohamedans and Budhists to total population :—

	Total population.	Hindus, including Jains & Sikhs	Mohamedans.	Budhists.	Unspecified.
Jammu	14,39,543	44·3	55·5	0·2	...
Kashmír	9,49,041	6·9	93·1	...	...
Ladákh	28,274	·6	10·5	88·9	...
Skardu	1,10,325	...	99·7	·3	...
Gilgit	16,769	·07	·83	...	99.1
Total ...	25,43,952	27·7	70·5	1·2	·6

71. The above figures prove:—

(1).—That the predominant religion of the State is Mohamedanism, representing 70 per cent. of the total population.

(2).—That next in order stand Hinduism, representing 27 per cent., Budhist 1·2 per cent., Sikhs ·4 per cent., and Jains ·02 per cent., of the total population.

(3).—That Christians number only 218 and Parsís 9, a very small minority.

(4).—That Hindus are mostly found in Jammu, and represent a very small minority in Kashmír, while in Ladákh, Skardu and Gilgit, their numbers are quite insignificant.

(5).—That Sikhs are found only in Jammu and Kashmír, and Jains only in Jammu ; that Mohamedans out-number Hindus almost in every part of the State.

(6).—That Skardu and Gilgit are solely Mohamedan tracts.

N.B.—The number shown as "unspecified" against Gilgit are mostly Mohamedans.

(7).—That Ladákh is the chief seat of Budhism.

(8).—That Christians are confined to Jammu, Kashmír and Ladákh, and Parsís to Jammu and Kashmír.

Thus out of every 10,000 inhabitants in the State, there are 2,770 Hindus, (including Jains and Sikhs), 7,050 Mohamedans and 120 Budhists. Christians and Parsís represent respectively 8 and ·3 to every 1,00,000 of the population.

72. Major Sub-division of Hindus.—The animistic or the religion of the forests and hill-tribes is unknown in this country, the prevailing religion being the Brahmanic orthodox Hinduism. A distinction may, however, be drawn between pure and impure Hindus, the former comprising Hindus of all denominations, excepting Bhangís and artisans of low castes, who though classed generally as Hindus are, in consequence of their trade and occuption, the inferiority of their social status and adherence to usages and customs prohibited in other orders, considered a quite distinct creed.

73. No persons have been returned as "Aryans" or Brahmos.

74. Barring a few Sayads, Moghals and Patháns of Non-Indian origin, the Mohamedan population of this State is either of Hindu or Budhist origin, and opportunity will be taken, when dealing with castes and their Sub-divisions, to furnish all the information contained in the statistics, but considering that no previous Census of the State has been taken, it would be premature from a statistical point of view either to collate communities of probably one origin but split up at the present time into Hindus, Musalmáns and Christians, or to draw conclusion from those figures. Hindus however might, as explained above, be sub-divided into :—

(1) Followers of the Brahmanic Religion.

(2) Impure castes, (3) Sikhs and (4) Jains, as the subjoined table will show.

	Jammu.			Kashmir.			Ladakh.			Skardu.			Gilgit.		
	Total.	Males.	Famales.	Total.	Males.	Females.	Total.	Males.	Females.	Total.	Males.	Females.	Total.	Males.	Females.
Brahmanical Religion ...	4,58,300	2,49,165	2,09,135	59,690	33,742	25,948	181	171	10	63	56	7	12	12	...
Impure castes	1,72,925	90,841	82,084	626	409	217	1	1	...	1	1	...	1	1	...
Total ...	6,31,225	3,40,006	2,91,219	60,316	34,151	26,165	182	172	10	64	57	7	13	13	...
Sikhs	5,926	3,321	2,605	5,473	2,937	2,536	...	...	...	...	...	...	...	...	...
Jains	593	339	254	...	...	...	...	...	...	...	...	...	...	...	...
Grand Total ...	6,37,744	3,43,666	2,94,078	65,789	37,088	28,701	182	172	10	64	57	7	13	13	...

Ratio per 1,000 of Males and Females to total population (Jammu and Kashmír).

	Jammu.		Kashmir.		Whole State.	
	Males.	Females.	Males.	Females.	Males.	Females.
Brahmanical Religion	543	457	565	435	546	454
Impure castes	525	475	653	347	525	475
Total ...	538	462	566	434	541	459
Sikhs	560	440	537	463	549	451
Jains	572	428	...	...	572	428
Grand Total ...	539	461	564	436	541	459

Average number of Females to 1,000 Males.

	Jammu.	Kashmír.	Ladákh.	Skardu.	Gilgit.	Whole State.
Brahmanical Religion...	839	769	58	125	...	830
Impure castes	903	530	...	...	...	901
Total ...	856	766	58	122	...	847
Sikhs	784	863	...	...	...	821
Jains	749	...	...	...	...	749
Grand Total ...	855	773	58	122	...	847

75. The district of Ladákh contains :—

	Total.	*Males.*	*Females.*
Brahmanical Religion	180	170	10
Impure castes	1	1	...
Unspecified	1	1	...
Total ...	182	172	10

76. These are mostly immigrants from the Panjab and the adjoining Province of Kashmír, including State employés, which circumstance accounts for the absence of Hindu females.

77. The majority of the Hindu population is confined to the village of Ladákh which is the entrepot of trade with Yárkand and Chinese Turkistán.

78. The same circumstances account for the inequality of sexes in Skardu where the Hindu population comprises 57 males and 7 females as detailed below :—

	Total.	*Males.*	*Females.*
Brahmanical Religion	63	56	7
Unspecified	1	1	...
Total ...	64	57	7

79. Traders and State employés proceeding to Ladákh and Skardu rarely take their families with them.

80. In Gilgit the figures represent coolies employed on the road, a detailed Census of the Civil District of Gilgit itself not having been taken.

81.—MOHAMEDANS.

	Total.	Males.	Females.	*Ratio per 1,000 to total population.*		Average number of females to 1,000 males.
				Males.	Females.	
Jammu	7,97,459	4,24,371	3,73,088	532	468	879
Kashmír	8,83,099	4,65,174	4,17,925	526	474	898
Ladákh	2,991	1,552	1,439	519	481	927
Skardu	1,10,022	55,893	54,129	508	492	968
Gilgit	139	136	3	978	22	22
Total ...	17,93,710	9,47,126	8,46,584	528	472	893

82. The Mohamedans of this State are with few exceptions, purely of Indian origin. About 1000 A. D. the population of Kashmír and Jammu Province was mostly Hindu, the majority being Brahmans, Rajpúts and Khatris. The Non-Indian or Asiatic Mohamedans consisted only of a few Sayads, Moghals and Pathans, who were imported by the local Mohamedan rulers of the country.

83. The population of the Frontier Provinces of Ladákh and Gilgit was Budhist, while Skardu was partly Budhistic and partly Brahmanic.

84. The Non-Indians though they can be hardly classed as such in consequence of intermarriages with the tribes of Indian origin are returned as follows :—

	Total.	Males.	Females.
Sayads	1,14,393	59,940	54,453
Moghals	16,588	8,757	7,831
Pathans	38,016	20,331	17,685
Total ...	1,68,997	89,028	79,969
Tribes of Indian origin... ...	16,24,713	8,58,098	7,66,615
Grand Total ...	17,93,710	9,47,126	8,46,584

85. The following traditional account of the development of Sunni and Shiah sects among the local Mohamedans, is as interesting as it is amusing.

There could be no doubt that originally, the local Mohamedans were Sunnis, believers in the Divine mission of Shah Hamdan, a Saint of Bukhara, whose pseudo mausoleum is situated in the heart of the city of Srinagar. In the reign of Zainulabdin, acting under the influence of their co-religionists in Badakhshan, the people of Hunza-Nagar and surroundings of Gilgit joined the Shiah sect believing in the Divine incarnation of Ali, in consequence of which they are called Ali-ullas. The Mohamedans of Gilgit of the present day are still Shiahs.

In 1450 A. D. Shams-ud-Din Iraki, a Shiah missionary, visited Kashmír, the Mohamedan population of which Province, as has been already described, were Sunnis followers of Shah Hamdan, and pretending to be a descendant of that Saint, easily attracted the simpletons of the day. His son Danial was the author of a work intended ostensibly to reconcile differences between the Sunnis and Shiah sects, but having for its ultimate object the propogation of the Shiah faith his followers are styled Nur Bakhshi, after the name of Nur Bakhsh, one of the disciples of Shah Hamdan. They are as a class devout followers of Islam and well versed in the philosophy of their religion, and are mostly found in Skardu and the adjoining Jammu District of Khishtwar.

In 939 (A. H.) corresponding to 1532 A. D. the Shiah system encountered a severe defeat at the hands of Mirza Haidar, the conqueror, who having obtained from the learned men of Delhi an edict denouncing Danial's philosophical work to be a piece of a blasphemy, deputed Mulla Kasim to Skardu, where he not only succeeded in restoring the Sunni system, but instigated his votaries to put Danial to death as an impostor. The victory, however, was not complete, a predilection for the Shiah sect again sprang up, and in 988 A. H. Kagarmusa, a Sunni missionary was assassinated by the revolting tribes. This incident roused the indignation of the Emperor Akbar who sent out an expedition to Kashmír, and again there was a revival of Sunnism.

The Nur Bakhshi Shiahs, unlike their fraternity in other part of the country, are not very strict in popular denounciation of the Divine mission of the three apostles of Mohamed, and recite their prayers according to the Sunni method. The Shiah are avowed enemies of the Sunnis, and not unfrequently quarrel with each other.

Mohamedanism in Ladákh dates from 1074 Hijri (1663 A. D.) and is said to owe its origin to an expedition headed by Saif Khan. The first Mohamedan convert was Duldul a rich influential zemindar who constructed a Mohamedan mosque. The prevailing sect in Ladákh and Tibet Kalan is Sunnism.

Two-thirds of the population of Skardu are Shiahs and one-third Sunnis.

86. The following table shows the proportion of males to females in the Urban and Rural population of Hindus and Mohamedans :—

	Hindus.				Mohamedans.			
	Total popula-tion.	Males.	Females.	Average number of females to 1,000 males.	Total popula-tion.	Males.	Females.	Average number of females to 1,000 males.
Jammu Province.								
Jammu	22,355	14,771	7,584	513	11,601	7,440	4,161	559
Mirpore	3,393	1,685	1,708	1,013	3,303	1,678	1,625	968
Batála	4,119	2,463	1,656	672	1,087	616	471	764
Punch	2,726	1,863	863	463	4,698	2,767	1,931	697
Total Urban population Jammu	32,593	20,782	11,811	568	20,689	12,501	8,188	654
Do. Rural do. ...	5,98,632	3,19,224	2,79,408	875	7,76,770	4,11,870	3,64,900	885
Grand Total ...	6,31,225	3,40,006	2,91,219	856	7,97,459	4,24,371	3,73,088	879
Kashmir Province.								
Srinagar	26,069	14,299	11,770	823	92,575	48,231	44,344	919
Anantnág	981	573	408	712	9,236	4,933	4,303	872
Sopore	858	472	386	817	7,550	3,886	3,664	942
Bárámula	787	441	346	784	4,809	2,528	2,281	902
Total Urban population Kashmír	28,695	15,785	12,910	817	1,14,170	59,578	54,592	916
Do. Rural do. ...	31,621	18,366	13,255	721	7,68,929	4,05,596	3,63,333	895
Grand Total ...	60,316	34,151	26,165	766	8,83,099	4,65,174	4,17,925	898
Rural population Ladákh	182	172	10	58	2,991	1,552	1,439	927
Do. Skardu	64	57	7	122	1,10,022	55,893	54,129	968
Do. Gilgit	13	13	...	...	139	136	3	22
Total Urban population whole State	61,288	36,567	24,721	676	1,34,859	72,079	62,780	871
Do. Rural do. do. ...	6,30,512	3,37,832	2,92,680	866	16,58,851	8,75,047	7,83,804	895
Grand Total Jammu and Kashmir State ...	6,91,800	3,74,399	3,17,401	847	17,93,710	9,47,126	8,46,584	893

87. The apparent deductions from these figures are ;—

(1).—That on the whole the average number of Mohamedan females to every 1,000 males is larger than the corresponding proportion of Hindu females, the only exception being in the city of Mirpore, where Hindu females, average 1,013 as against 968 Mohamedan females.

(2).—That the excess difference noted above (excluding Ladákh, Skardu and Gilgit which require special explanation) is abnormally large in the cities of Punch, Anantnág, Sopore and Bárámula, in the Rural population of Kashmír Province, and in the whole Province of Kashmír generally.

(3).—That it is lowest in the Rural population of Jammu Province and in the Urban and Rural population of Jammu Province combined.

(4).—That the Urban population of the whole State represents an excess difference of 195 and the Rural population 29.

88. Taking the Rural population as representing the normal standard of equality of sexes, the figures stand as follows :—

	Hindu females to every 1,000 males.	Mohamedan females to every 1,000 males.
Rural population, Jammu Province ...	875	885
Do. Kashmír do, ...	721	895
In Ajmere Merwara (1881) the proportions were	870	740

So that as a rule, the inequality of sexes in this State does not seem to call for special remark excepting of course the Province of Kashmír where Mohamedan females were 895 as against 721 Hindu females to every 1,000 males, which was apparently due to the absence of Mohamedan males who unlike Hindu males, largely seek employment as coolies in the Panjab.

89. Males as a rule undoubtedly outnumber females, the average standard being about 879 females to every 1,000 males throughout the State.

90. Full explanation of the abnormal inequalities of sexes between Hindus and Mohamedans, is reserved, till the statistics of age and religion are subjected to careful scrutiny and examination, but it would nevertheless be worth while to make a passing allusion to certain salient points suggested by local peculiarities.

(1).—That in the towns of Jammu and Punch the low ratio of females is accounted for by the presence of a considerable number of males, as members of the Military aud Police Forces and Civil Departments of the State.

(2).—That in the town of Mirpore the high ratio of Hindu females is due to the absence of males on employment in other parts of the country.

(3).—That while the Hindu of Kashmír Province are mostly Brahmans who employ themselves either in agriculture or service of the State, the Mohamedans in the towns of Srínagar, Anantnág, Báráṃula and Sopore, who are not well off, seek employment as coolies in the Panjab, notoriously during the cold season, when agricultural pursuits are temporarily suspended, this probably explains the reason why among the Mohamedans of Kashmír towns, the ratio of females is as high as 902, and 942 per thousand males.

(4).—It is noteworthy that in the rural population of Jammu Province, Hindu and Mohamedan females average 875 and 885 respectively per thousand males, the slight difference of 10 per mille being quite insignificant, while in the rural population of Kashmír the ratio of Hindu females is 721 as against 895 per mille returned for Mohamedan females.

91. Budhists.—The Budhists number 29,608 (males 14,942 and females 14,666) and are distributed as follows :—

	Total.	Males.	Females.	Proportion per mille to total population.		Average number of females to every 1,000 males.
				Males.	Females.	
Jammu Province	4,293	2,179	2,114	508	492	970
Ladákh...	25,076	12,615	12,461	504	496	987
Skardu...	293	148	91	619	381	614
Total ...	29,608	14,942	14,666	503	497	981

92. The relative proportion of Hindu and Mohamedan females as compared with Budhists is as follows :—

	Per mille to total population of		Average number of Females to every 1,000 males (excluding urban population.)
	Males.	Females.	
Hindu...	541	459	866
Mohamedan	528	472	895
Budhist	503	497	981

It is singular that Budhist females claim the highest proportion and the highest average.

93. Barring Skardu where the males outnumber females rather disproportionately, the females are almost equal in number to males, notwithstanding the fact that polyandry largely prevails in Ladákh, and that Lamás (priests) are celibates.

94 In the absence of statistics of civil condition, it is impossible to collect material for the solution of the difficult problem of inequality of sexes.

95. The system of polyandry is strictly confined to brothers; each family of brothers has only one wife in common, the most usual number of husbands is two, but three or even four husbands are not uncommon. The system prevails of course only among the poor classes, and is said to have originated from the smallness of the extent of land and the general inelasticity of the resources of the country, the isolation from the rest of the world, manners, language and religion, as well as geographical isolation accounting for absence of emigration. It was found impossible for the younger ones either to marry and settle or to go out for their living, and they naturally become more helpers in the household from servants to the elder brother. From that there came about the curious custom that when the elder brother married a wife she became a wife to all the brothers. The younger brothers remain in a very subordinate position in the family, but the wife is held in common. The children recognize all as father, speaking of their elder and then younger father. In addition to this form of polyandry there is liberty for the woman to choose yet another husband from a different family, a stranger.

96. The religion of Ladákh is a modified form of Indian Budhism. The modification is due to the introdction of the mystical system of the Tantrists, as evidenced by the pictures of the prevailing red and yellow sects which are filled with representations of the three eyed destroying Shiva, and of his blood drinking consort, the three eyed goddess Trilochna.

97. The great mass of the people of Ladákh are all of one race or caste, they intermarry and eat together and are all eligible as members of the national priesthood. But in the Northern Provinces of Ladákh numerous clans called Boni or low which include all the dancing women and their attendant musicians, all smiths and carpenters and in fact handicraftmen of every kind.

98. In Leh itself there are small colonies of Kashmíris whose connection with the native Bhots has produced a mixed race called Argon.

99. **Christians**.—Christians number 218, of whom 113 were males and 105 females—

	Total.	*Males.*	*Females*
Jammu	46	24	22
Kashmír	145	77	68
Ladákh	25	11	14
Gilgit	2	1	1
	218	113	105

of these the details for the urban and rural population are as follows :—

	Total.	*Males.*	*Females.*
Jammu (town)	14	7	7
Rural Population Jammu	32	17	15
Srínagar (town)	119	57	62
Anantnág (town)	2	1	1
Rural Population Kashmír	24	19	5
Ladákh (Rural Population)	25	11	14
Gilgit Road	2	1	1
Total Urban Population	135	65	70
Do. Rural do.	83	48	35

100. The details of the Rural population are given below :—

	Total.	*Males.*	*Females.*
JAMMU PROVINCE—			
Ránbir Singhpora District	23	13	10
Udhampore do.	1	1	...
Punch Jágír	8	3	5
Total Jammu Province ...	32	17	15
KASHMIR PROVINCE—			
Khás District	9	4	5
Kámráj District	2	2	...
Muzafferabad	13	13	...
Total Kashmír Province ...	24	19	5
Ladákh	25	11	14
Gilgit	2	1	1
GRAND TOTAL ...	83	48	35

101. The races of Christians are :—

	Total.			Jummu.			Kashmir.			Ladakh.			Gilgit.		
	Total.	Males.	Females.	Total.	Males.	Females.	Total.	Males.	Females.	Total.	Males.	Females.	Total.	Males.	Females.
Non-Asiatics ...	134	67	67	23	12	11	102	50	52	7	4	3	2	1	1
Eurasians ...	5	2	3	5	2	3	...	...	...	...	...	...	...	...	...
Natives ...	79	44	35	18	10	8	43	27	16	18	7	11	...	...	...
Total ...	218	113	105	46	24	22	145	77	68	25	11	14	2	1	1

102. The distribution by race and sect is given below :—

	Total.			*Church of England.*			*Roman Catholic.*			*Unsectarian.*			*Presbyterian.*			*Moravian.*			*Unspecified.*		
	Total.	Males.	Females.	Total.	Males.	Females.	Total.	Males.	Females.	Total.	Males.	Females.	Total.	Males.	Females.	Total.	Males.	Females.	Total.	Males.	Females.
Non-Asiatics ...	134	67	67	98	45	53	15	11	4	4	3	1	4	3	1	5	2	3	8	3	5
Eurasians ...	5	2	3	5	2	3	...	...	...	...	...	...	...	...	...	...	...	...	...	...	...
Natives ...	79	44	35	79	44	35	...	...	...	...	...	...	...	...	...	...	...	...	...	...	...
Total ...	218	113	105	182	91	91	15	11	4	4	3	1	4	3	1	5	2	3	8	3	5

103. Christians by race and age are :—

	Total.			0–14.			15–34.			35–49.			50 and over.		
	Total.	Males.	Females.	Total.	Males.	Females.	Total.	Males.	Females.	Total.	Males.	Females.	Total.	Males.	Females.
Non-Asiatics ...	134	67	67	37	17	20	51	24	27	35	18	17	11	8	3
Eurasians ...	5	2	3	3	1	2	2	1	1	...	...	...	...	...	...
Natives ...	79	44	35	28	17	11	31	15	16	17	11	6	3	1	2
Total ...	218	113	105	68	35	33	84	40	44	52	29	23	14	9	5

104. Non-Asiatics represent 62 per cent. Eurasians, 2 per cent. and Natives, 36 per cent. of the total Christian population, of these the Church of England represents 83 per cent. Roman Catholics 7 per cent. while the other sects do not call for special notice.

105. The proportion of age periods is as follows :—

	0—14.	15—34.	35—49.	50 and over.
Non-Asiatics	28 per cent.	38 per cent.	26 per cent.	8 per cent.
Eurasians	60 ,,	40 ,,	...	...
Natives	35 ,,	39 ,,	22 per cent.	4 per cent.
Total ...	31 per cent.	40 per cent.	23 per cent.	6 per cent.

106. The sexes of Non-Asiatics are equal, of Eurasians, males represent 40 and females 60 per cent. and of Natives 55 and 45 respectively.

107. The following statistics have been prepared for Europeans and Eurasians only :—

CIVIL CONDITION.

	Age Distribution.																	
	Total.			0—19.			20—29.			30—49.			50—59.			60 and over.		
	Total.	Males.	Females.	Total.	Males.	Females.	Total.	Males.	Females.	Total.	Males.	Females.	Total.	Males.	Females.	Total.	Males.	Females.
Unmarried ...	76	37	39	42	19	23	20	10	10	14	8	6	...	...	...	...	...	...
Married ...	58	30	28	...	...	...	10	1	9	40	22	18	7	6	1	1	1	...
Widowed ...	5	2	3	...	...	...	...	...	...	2	1	1	2	...	2	1	1	...
Total ...	139	69	70	42	19	23	30	11	19	56	31	25	9	6	3	2	2	...

108. The relative proportion of civil condition to total population is :—

Unmarried	54
Married	42
Widowed	4

Of 42 persons under 0—19 years, 36 or 85 per cent. were under 10 years, married life commences after 19, and the highest percentage is obtainable in 30—49, the number representing that age being 40 out of 58 the total of married persons.

109. Widowed persons numbered only 5, 2 males and 3 females, the former comprising one between 30 and 34 and the other, 60 and over, and the latter one between 35 and 39 and the remaining two between 50 and 59.

110. Education by Religion and Age.—Of the total population of Europeans and Eurasians, 14 or 10 per cent. are returned as learning, 104 or 75 per cent. as literate, and 21 or 15 per cent. as illiterate.

111. The illiterates are all under 0—14 years, learning also under 0—14, and literate above that age.

112. The age returns show 29 to be 0—4 years old, so that the number shown as illiterate, not only appears to be correct but affords *primâ facie* evidence of the fact, that education is not neglected.

113. Parent tongue.—With the exception of one female whose mother tongue is returned as Hindustáni, the group of languages exhibits the following results :—

English	124
English and French	1
English and Italian	2
French	5
Dutch	1
German	5
Total ...	138

The English speaking population being 91 per cent. of the whole.

114. Parsis.—Parsís represent a very small section of the community, their number being one male in Jammu, and six males and two females in Kashmír.

CHAPTER IV.

Ages of the Population.

115. I now proceed to examine the specified periods of the Census Returns. It is difficult to elicit from the people a correct return of age, more particularly, the ages of the female population. The Ladákhís are said to make use of the cycle of twelve years for common computations such as a man's age, and it is difficult to say if ages under 12 were correctly given to the enumerators. The Miáns and other high families whose women are subject to the Pardah system were naturally averse to any enquiry being made in respect of age of females. Some of them distinctly refused to help the enumerators, while others who were more complacent, gave information of questionable reliability. Again the age periods of 0—1 and 1 years, must have been confounded, because calculations in this respect are scarcely ever correct in an uneducated community.

116. The following tables show the Divisional periods of age for the whole State and its provincial rural and urban Sub-divisions :—

ALL RELIGIONS.

	Under 5.			5—9.			10—14.			15—19.			20—24.			25—29.			30—34.		
	Total.	Males.	Females.	Total.	Males.	Females.	Total.	Males.	Females.	Total.	Males.	Females.	Total.	Males.	Females.	Total.	Males.	Females.	Total.	Males.	Females.
Jammu Urban ...	6,578	3,622	2,956	5,444	3,150	2,294	4,489	2,855	1.634	4,362	2,675	1,687	5,575	3,485	2,090	6,111	3,959	2,152	5,645	3,667	1,978
Do. Rural ...	214,584	107,325	107,259	192,087	101,007	91,080	132,936	76,364	56,572	109,859	58,074	51,785	110,030	53,881	56,149	119,279	60,415	58,864	121,911	63,293	58,618
Total Jammu Province.	221,162	110,947	110,215	197,531	104,157	93,374	137,425	79,219	58,206	114,221	60,749	53,472	115,605	57,366	58,239	125,390	64,374	61,016	127,556	66,960	60,596
Kashmír Urban ...	22,848	11,402	11,446	19,393	10,047	9,346	12,238	7,257	4,981	11,868	6,504	5,364	14,884	7,371	7,513	11,945	6,000	5,945	13,410	6,780	6,630
Do. Rural ...	167,410	85,104	82,300	124,790	66,483	58,307	67,350	39,229	28,121	61,272	32,590	28,682	64,332	31,202	33,130	63,675	31,807	31,868	65,009	33,503	31,506
Total Kashmír Province.	190,258	96,506	93,752	144,183	76,530	67,653	79,588	46,486	33,102	73,140	39,094	34,046	79,216	38,573	40,643	75,620	37,807	37,813	78,419	40,283	38,136
Total Frontier Districts, Ladákh Skardu and Gilgit.	17,396	8,234	9,162	18,312	9,278	9,034	13,537	7,330	6,207	11,702	6,292	5,410	15,396	7,434	7,962	6,207	3,269	2,938	8,722	4,515	4,207
Whole State Urban ...	29,426	15,024	14,402	24,837	13,197	11,640	16,727	10,112	6,615	16,230	9,179	7,051	20,459	10,856	9,603	18,056	9,959	8,097	19,055	10,447	8,608
Do. Rural ...	399,390	200,663	198,727	335,189	176,768	158,421	213,823	122,923	90,900	182,833	96,956	85,877	189,758	92,517	97,241	189,161	95,491	93,670	195,642	101,311	94,331
Total whole State.	428,816	215,687	213,129	360,026	189,965	170,061	230,550	133,035	97,515	199,063	106,135	92,928	210,217	103,373	106,844	207,217	105,450	101,767	214,697	111,758	102,939

ALL RELIGIONS.—(*continued.*)

	35—39.			40—44.			40—49.			50—54.			55—59.			60 AND OVER.			UNSPECIFIED.		
	Total.	Males.	Females.	Total.	Males.	Females.	Total.	Males.	Females.	Total.	Males.	Females.	Total.	Males.	Females.	Total.	Males.	Females	Total	Males.	Females.
Jammu Urban ...	3,448	2,337	1,111	3,976	2,536	1,440	2,265	1,531	734	2,542	1,644	898	1,085	712	373	2,805	1,692	1,113	165	89	76
Do. Rural ...	78,159	43,501	34,658	89,577	48,029	41,548	46,404	27,345	19,059	61,299	34,718	26,581	19,504	11,468	8,036	89,350	50,828	38,522	74	39	35
Total Jammu Province ...	81,607	45,838	35,769	93,553	50,565	42,988	48,669	28,876	19,793	63,841	36,862	27,479	20,589	12,180	8,409	92,155	52,520	39,635	239	128	111
Kashmir Urban ...	7,428	4,138	3,290	10,679	5,331	5,348	4,577	2,773	1,804	6,936	3,927	3,009	1,575	1,053	522	5,472	3,015	2,457	...	...	...
Do. Rural ...	40,631	22,381	18,250	50,888	26,306	24,582	22,937	13,661	9,276	30,344	17,142	13,202	8,380	5,046	3,334	38,740	22,293	16,447	30	...	30
Total Kashmir Province ...	48,059	26,519	21,540	61,567	31,637	29,930	27,514	16,434	11,080	37,280	21,069	16,211	9,955	6,099	3,856	44,212	25,308	18,904	30	...	30
Total Frontier Districts, Ladákh, Skardu, and Gilgit.	12,721	6,299	6,422	6,316	3,319	2,997	8,770	4,233	4,537	4,041	2,223	1,818	2,673	1,462	1,211	12,938	6,698	6,240	16,637	10,057	6,580
Whole State Urban ...	10,876	6,475	4,401	14,655	7,867	6,788	6,842	4,304	2,538	9,478	5,571	3,907	2,660	1,765	895	8,277	4,707	3,570	165	89	76
Do. Rural ...	131,511	72,181	59,330	146,781	77,654	69,127	78,111	45,239	32,872	95,684	54,083	41,601	30,557	17,976	12,581	141,028	79,819	61,209	16,741	10,096	6,645
Total whole State ...	142,387	78,656	63,731	161,436	85,521	75,915	84,953	49,543	35,410	105,162	59,654	45,508	33,217	19,741	13,476	149,305	84,526	64,779	16,906	10,185	6,721

PROPORTION PER 10,000.—(ALL RELIGIONS.)

	Under 5.			5—9.			10—14.			15—19.			20—24.			25—29.			30—34.		
	Total.	Males.	Females.	Total.	Males.	Females.	Total.	Males.	Females.	Total.	Males.	Females.	Total.	Males.	Females.	Total.	Males.	Females.	Total.	Males.	Females.
Jammu Urban ...	1,207	1,067	1,439	999	927	1,117	824	841	796	808	788	821	1.023	1,027	1,018	1,121	1,166	1,048	1,037	1,080	963
Do. Rural ...	1,549	1,458	1,653	1,387	1,372	1,404	960	1,037	827	792	789	798	795	732	866	861	820	907	880	860	904
Total Jammu Province ...	1,536	1,440	1,647	1,372	1,352	1,395	955	1,028	869	793	789	798	803	745	870	871	836	912	886	869	905
Kashmír Urban ...	1,594	1,508	1,693	1,354	1,329	1,382	854	960	737	828	860	793	1,039	975	1,111	834	794	877	936	897	979
Do. Rural ...	2,078	1,994	2,172	1,549	1,558	1,538	836	919	742	760	761	757	798	732	874	790	744	841	807	785	831
Total Kashmír Province ...	2,005	1,921	2,099	1,519	1,523	1,514	839	925	741	770	778	762	835	768	909	797	753	847	826	802	854
Frontier Districts.																					
Total Frontier Districts, Ladákh, Skardu, and Gilgit.	1,119	1,021	1,226	1,178	1,152	1,209	871	908	831	753	780	724	991	920	1,065	400	405	394	562	559	563
Whole State Urban ...	1,488	1,371	1,633	1,256	1,205	1,320	846	923	750	821	838	800	1,034	991	1,089	913	909	918	964	954	976
Do. Rural ...	1,702	1,613	1,802	1,429	1,421	1,437	912	988	824	779	780	779	809	744	882	806	768	850	834	815	856
Total whole State ...	1,685	1,594	1,789	1,415	1,404	1,428	906	983	819	782	784	780	826	764	898	815	779	855	844	826	864

PROPORTION PER 10,000. (ALL RELIGIONS—*continued.*)

	35—39.			40—44.			45—49.			50—54.			55—59.			60 and over.			Unspecified.		
	Total.	Males.	Females.	Total.	Males.	Females.	Total.	Males.	Females.	Total.	Males.	Females.	Total.	Males.	Females.	Total.	Males.	Females.	Total.	Males.	Females.
Jammu Urban	633	688	541	731	747	701	416	451	357	462	484	437	199	210	182	515	498	542	30	26	37
Do. Rural	564	591	534	647	652	640	335	371	293	443	471	410	141	156	124	645	690	594	1	1	1
Total Jammu Province ...	567	595	535	650	657	642	338	375	296	444	472	411	143	158	126	640	682	592	2	2	2
Kashmir Urban	519	547	486	746	705	791	319	367	267	484	519	444	110	139	77	383	399	363	...	...	...
Do. Rural	504	524	481	632	616	648	285	321	245	377	402	348	104	119	88	480	542	434	...	...	1
Total Kashmir Province ...	506	528	482	649	630	670	290	327	248	393	419	363	105	121	86	466	504	424	...	...	1
Frontier Districts.																					
Total Frontier Districts, Ladákh, Skardu, and Gilgit.	819	781	859	406	412	401	565	525	607	260	276	242	172	182	162	833	831	835	1,071	1,248	882
Whole State Urban ...	550	591	499	741	718	769	546	393	288	479	509	443	135	161	102	419	429	405	8	8	8
Do. Rural ...	561	580	538	625	624	627	333	364	298	408	435	377	130	145	114	601	642	555	71	81	60
Total whole State ...	559	581	535	634	632	638	338	366	298	413	441	382	130	146	113	587	625	544	66	75	75

HINDUS INCLUDING SIKHS AND JAINS.

	Under 5.			5—9.			10—14.			15—19.			20—24.			25—29.			30—34.		
	Total.	Males.	Females.	Total.	Males.	Females.	Total.	Males.	Females.	Total.	Males.	Females.	Total.	Males.	Females.	Total.	Males.	Females.	Total.	Males.	Females.
Jammu Urban	3,843	2,164	1,679	3,244	1,944	1,300	2,745	1,789	956	2,721	1,710	1,011	3,429	2,155	1,274	3,839	2,552	1,287	3,518	2,294	1,224
Do. Rural	79,459	39,863	39,596	74,340	38,758	35,582	55,230	32,021	23,209	48,349	25,680	22,663	50,477	24,999	25,478	55,403	28,397	27,006	5,4363	28,529	55,834
Total Jammu Province ...	83,302	42,027	41,275	77,584	40,702	36,882	57,975	33,810	24,165	51,070	27,390	23,674	53,906	27,154	26,752	59,242	30,949	28,293	57,881	30,823	27,058
Kashmir Urban ...	3,451	1,738	1,713	3,462	1,854	1,608	2,594	1,621	973	2,596	1,484	1,112	3,062	1,607	1,455	2,595	1,343	1,252	2,760	1,441	1,319
Do. Rural ...	5,816	2,998	2,818	5,049	2,637	2,412	3,505	2,078	1,427	2,953	1,716	1,237	3,194	1,816	1,378	3,142	1,881	1,261	2,847	1,698	1,149
Total Kashmir Provinces ...	9,267	4,736	4,531	8,511	4,491	4,020	6,099	3,699	2,400	5,549	3,200	2,349	6,256	3,423	2,833	5,737	3,224	2,513	5,607	3,139	2,468
Ladákh	1	...	1	...	...	...	1	1	...	4	3	1	34	29	5	70	67	3	32	32	...
Skardu	...	...	...	...	...	...	...	...	...	6	4	2	4	4	...	12	11	1	8	7	1
Gilgit	...	...	...	...	...	...	...	...	...	2	2	...	2	2	...	2	2	...	1	1	...
Whole State Urban ...	7,294	3,902	3,392	6,706	3,798	2,908	5,339	3,410	1,929	5,317	3,194	2,123	6,491	3,762	2,729	6,434	3,895	2,539	6,278	3,735	2,543
Do. Rural ...	85,276	42,861	42,415	79,389	41,395	37,994	58,736	34,100	24,636	51,314	27,411	23,903	53,711	26,850	26,861	58,629	30,358	28,271	57,251	30,267	26,984
Total whole State ...	92,570	46,763	45,807	86,095	45,193	40,902	64,075	37,510	26,565	56,631	30,605	26,026	60,202	30,612	29,590	65,063	34,253	30,810	63,529	34,002	29,527

HINDUS INCLUDING SIKHS AND JAINS.—(*continued.*)

	35—39.			40—44.			45—49.			50—54.			55—59.			60 AND OVER.			UNSPECIFIED.		
	Total.	Males.	Females.	Total.	Males.	Females.	Total.	Males.	Females.	Total.	Males.	Females.	Total.	Males.	Females.	Total.	Males.	Females	Total	Males.	Females.
Jammu Urban ...	2,194	1,476	718	2,466	1,612	854	1,438	983	455	1,641	1,084	557	725	497	228	1,819	1,097	722	165	89	76
Do. Rural ...	35,975	19,893	16,082	42,155	22,436	19,719	22,644	13,225	9,419	30,287	16,889	13,398	10,229	6,049	4,180	44,972	25,436	19,536	74	39	35
Total Jammu Province ...	38,169	21,369	16,800	44,621	24,048	20,573	24,082	14,208	9,874	31,928	17,973	13 955	10,954	6,546	4,408	46,791	26,533	20,258	239	128	111
Kashmir Urban ...	1,665	1,027	638	2,253	1,199	1,059	1,069	677	392	1,512	828	684	477	323	154	1,453	814	639	...	...	...
Do. Rural ...	2,159	1,321	838	2,308	1,368	940	1,419	928	491	1,486	851	635	632	424	208	2,295	1,416	879	30	...	30
Total Kashmir Province ...	3,824	2,348	1,476	4,566	2,567	1,999	2,488	1,605	883	2,998	1,679	1,319	1,109	747	362	3,748	2,230	1,518	30	...	30
Ladákh ...	14	14	...	12	12	...	9	9	...	1	1	...	1	1	...	3	3	...	...	...	...
Skardu ...	11	11	...	8	5	3	3	3	...	6	6	...	2	2	...	4	4	...	...	...	...
Gilgit ...	3	3	...	2	2	...	1	1	...	...	...	...	...	...	...	...	...	...	...	...	...
Whole State Urban ...	3,859	2,503	1,356	4,724	2,811	1,913	2,507	1,660	847	3,153	1,912	1,241	1,202	820	382	3,272	1,911	1,361	165	89	76
Do. Rural ...	38,162	21,242	16,920	44,485	23,823	20,662	24,076	14,166	9,910	31,780	17,747	14,033	10,864	6,476	4,388	47,274	26,859	20,415	104	39	65
Total whole State ...	42,021	23,745	18,276	49,209	26,684	22,575	26,583	15,826	10,757	34,933	19,659	15,274	12,066	7,296	4,770	50,546	28,770	21,776	269	128	141

PROPORTION PER 10,000.—(HINDUS INCLUDING SIKHS AND JAINS.)

	Under 5.			5—9.			10—14.			15—19.			20—24.			25—29.			30—34.		
	Total.	Males.	Females.	Total.	Males.	Females.	Total.	Males.	Females.	Total.	Males.	Females.	Total.	Males.	Females.	Total.	Males.	Females.	Total.	Males.	Females.
Jammu Urban ...	1,137	1,009	1,361	961	906	1,053	812	834	775	805	797	819	1,015	1,005	1,032	1,136	1,190	1,042	1,041	1,070	991
Do. Rural ...	1,315	1,239	1,405	1,233	1,203	1,263	914	994	824	801	797	805	836	776	904	917	881	959	901	885	917
Total Jammu Province ...	1,306	1,222	1,404	1,216	1,184	1,254	909	984	822	801	797	805	845	790	909	929	900	962	908	897	920
Kashmir Urban ...	1,192	1,090	1,318	1,196	1,162	1,237	896	1,016	749	897	930	856	1,058	1,007	1,119	896	842	963	953	903	1,015
Do. Rural ...	1,579	1,418	1,794	1,368	1,248	1,536	952	983	909	802	812	788	868	860	878	853	890	803	773	804	732
Total Kashmir Province ...	1,409	1,276	1,578	1,294	1,211	1,402	927	997	836	843	863	818	950	923	987	872	869	876	852	846	861
Ladákh ...	55	...	1,000	...	...	...	55	58	...	220	175	1,000	1,868	1,686	5,000	3,846	3,395	3,000	1,758	1,860	...
Skardu ...	...	...	...	...	...	...	...	...	...	938	702	2,857	625	702	...	1,875	1,930	1,429	1,250	1,228	1,428
Gilgit ...	...	...	...	...	...	...	...	...	...	1,538	1,538	...	1,538	1,538	...	1,539	1,539	...	769	769	...
Whole State Urban ...	1,162	1,044	1,339	1,069	1,015	1,148	851	912	761	847	854	838	1,035	1,006	1,077	1,025	1,041	1,002	1,000	999	1,003
Do. Rural ...	1,330	1,247	1,426	1,238	1,205	1,277	916	992	828	800	798	804	838	781	903	915	884	950	898	881	907
Total whole State ...	1,315	1,227	1,419	1,223	1,186	1,267	910	986	828	805	808	806	855	808	917	925	899	955	903	898	915

PROPORTION PER 10,000. (HINDUS INCLUDING SIKHS AND JAINS—(*continued*.)

	35—39.			40—44.			45—49.			50—54.			55—59.			60 AND OVER.			UNSPECIFIED.		
	Total.	Males.	Females.	Total.	Males.	Females.	Total.	Males.	Females.	Total.	Males.	Females.	Total.	Males.	Females.	Total.	Males.	Females.	Total.	Males.	Females.
Jammu Urban	650	688	583	730	752	692	426	458	368	485	505	451	215	232	185	538	512	585	49	42	63
Do. Rural	594	617	571	698	696	700	875	410	334	501	524	476	169	188	148	745	789	693	1	1	1
Total Jammu Province ...	598	622	571	700	699	700	378	416	336	500	523	475	172	190	149	734	772	689	4	4	4
Kashmir Urban	575	644	491	780	751	815	369	424	302	522	519	526	164	202	118	502	510	491	...	...	...
Do. Rural	587	625	534	627	647	599	385	439	313	403	403	404	172	201	132	623	670	559	8	...	19
Total Kashmir Province,	583	634	514	694	693	696	378	433	307	456	453	460	168	201	126	569	601	529	5	...	10
Ladakh	769	814	...	659	698	...	495	523	...	55	58	...	55	58	...	165	175	...	...	...	...
Skardu	1,719	1,930	...	1,250	877	4,286	469	526	...	937	1,052	...	312	351	...	625	702	...	...	...	...
Gilgit	2,308	2,308	...	1,539	1,539	...	769	769	...	...	...	...	...	...	...	...	...	...	...	...	...
Whole State Urban ...	615	669	536	753	752	755	400	443	334	503	511	490	192	219	151	522	511	537	26	24	29
Do. Rural ...	595	618	569	694	693	695	376	412	333	496	517	472	170	189	148	737	782	686	2	1	2
Total whole State ...	597	623	566	699	699	699	378	415	333	496	516	473	172	192	148	718	755	675	4	3	4

MOHAMEDANS.

	Under 5.			5—9.			10—14.			15—19.			20—24.			25—29.			30—34.		
	Total.	Males.	Females.	Total.	Males.	Females.	Total.	Males.	Females.	Total.	Males.	Females.	Total.	Males.	Females.	Total.	Males.	Females.	Total.	Males.	Females.
Jammu Urban	2,731	1,455	1,276	2,200	1,206	994	1,744	1,066	678	1,639	965	674	2,144	1,330	814	2,271	1,407	864	2,124	1,370	754
Do. Rural	1,34,778	67,289	67,489	1,17,255	61,988	55,267	77,266	44,105	33,161	61,110	32,209	28,901	59,201	28,704	30,497	63,443	31,825	31,618	67,177	34,586	32,591
Total Jammu Province ...	1,37,509	68,744	68,765	1,19,455	63,194	56,261	79,010	45,171	33,839	62,749	33,174	29,575	61,345	30,034	31,311	65,714	33,232	32,482	69,301	35,956	33,345
Kashmir Urban	19,376	9,653	9,723	15,916	8,184	7,732	9,639	5,633	4,006	9,267	5,019	4,248	11,812	5,761	6,051	9,333	4,652	4,681	10,634	5,328	5,306
Do. Rural	1,61,594	82,106	79,488	1,19,739	63,844	55,895	63,843	37,151	26,692	58,319	30,874	27,445	61,184	29,382	31,752	60,530	29,925	30,605	62,156	31,799	30,357
Total Kashmir Province...	1,80,970	91,759	89,211	1,35,655	72,028	63,627	73,482	42,784	30,698	67,586	35,893	31,693	72,946	35,143	37,803	69,863	34,577	35,286	72,790	37,127	35,663
Ladákh	304	149	155	350	177	173	278	145	133	223	127	96	249	132	117	267	136	131	267	145	122
Skardu	14,937	7,037	7,900	15,417	7,818	7,599	11,240	6,149	5,091	9,687	5,252	4,435	13,159	6,258	6,901	3,824	2,008	1,816	6,521	3,361	3,160
Gilgit	2	...	2	...	...	...	2	2	...	5	5	...	37	37	...	29	28	1	23	93	...
Whole State Urban ...	22,107	11,108	10,999	18,116	9,390	8,726	11,383	6,699	4,684	10,906	5,984	4,922	13,956	7,091	6,865	11,604	6,069	5,545	12,758	6,698	6,060
Do. Rural ...	3,11,615	1,56,581	1,55,034	2,52,761	1,33,827	1,18,934	1,52,629	87,552	65,077	1,29,344	68,467	60,877	1,33,780	64,513	69,267	1,28,093	63,922	64,171	1,36,144	69,914	66,230
Total whole State ...	3,33,722	1,67,689	1,66,033	2,70,877	1,43,217	1,27,660	1,64,012	94,251	69,761	1,40,250	74,451	65,799	1,47,736	71,604	76,132	1,39,697	69,981	69,716	1,48,902	76,612	72,290

MOHAMEDANS.—(continued.)

	35—39.			40—44.			45—49.			50—54.			55—59.			60 AND OVER.			UNSPECIFIED.		
	Total.	Males.	Females.	Total.	Males.	Females.	Total.	Males.	Females.	Total.	Males.	Females.	Total.	Males.	Females.	Total.	Males.	Females.	Total.	Males.	Females.
Jammu Urban ...	1,254	861	393	1,509	923	586	826	548	278	901	560	341	360	215	145	986	595	391	...	...	...
Do. Rural ...	41,922	23,476	18,446	47,132	25,453	21,679	23,543	14,001	9,542	30,793	17,709	13,084	9,154	5,351	3,803	43,996	25,174	18,822	...	...	...
Total Jammu Province ...	43,176	24,337	18,839	48,641	26,376	22,265	24,369	14,549	9,820	31,694	18,269	13,425	9,514	5,566	3,948	44,982	25,769	19,213	...	...	...
Kashmír Urban ...	5,752	3,108	2,644	8,410	4,126	4,284	3,499	2,090	1,409	5,421	3,096	2,325	1,094	729	365	4,017	2,199	1,818	...	...	...
Do. Rural ...	38,468	21,057	17,411	48,579	24,937	23,642	21,518	12,733	8,785	28,858	16,291	12,567	7,748	4,622	3,126	36,443	20,875	15,568	...	...	...
Total Kashmír Province ...	44,220	24,165	20,055	56,989	29,063	27,926	25,017	14,823	10,194	34,279	19,387	14,892	8,842	5,351	3,491	40,460	23,074	17,386	...	...	...
Ladákh ...	231	116	115	211	108	103	145	72	73	151	77	74	72	42	30	243	126	117	...	...	...
Skardu ...	10,559	5,193	5,366	4,286	2,274	2,012	7,086	3,377	3,709	2,712	1,549	1,163	1,320	771	549	9,252	4,834	4,418	22	12	10
Gilgit ...	11	11	...	8	8	...	7	7	...	10	10	...	3	3	...	2	2	...	...	...	...
Whole State Urban ...	7,006	3,969	3,037	9,919	5,049	4,870	4,325	2,638	1,687	6,322	3,656	2,666	1,454	944	510	5,003	2,794	2,209	...	...	...
Do. Rural ...	91,191	49,853	41,338	1,00,216	52,780	47,436	52,299	30,190	22,109	62,524	35,636	26,888	18,297	10,789	7,508	89,936	51,011	38,925	22	12	10
Total whole State ...	98,197	53,822	44,375	1,10,135	57,829	52,306	56,624	32,828	23,796	68,846	39,292	29,554	19,751	11,733	8,018	94,939	53,805	41,134	22	12	10

PROPORTION PER 10,000. (MOHAMEDANS.)

	Under 5.			5—9.			10—14.			15—19.			20—24.			25—29.			30—34.		
	Total.	Males.	Females.	Total.	Males.	Females.	Total.	Males.	Females.	Total.	Males.	Females.	Total.	Males.	Females.	Total.	Males.	Females.	Total.	Males.	Females.
Jammu Urban ...	1,320	1,164	1,558	1,063	965	1,214	843	853	828	792	772	823	1,086	1,063	994	1,098	1,126	1,054	1,027	1,096	922
Do. Rural ...	1,735	1,634	1,849	1,510	1,505	1,515	995	1,071	909	787	782	792	782	697	836	817	773	867	865	840	893
Total Jammu Province ...	1,724	1,620	1,843	1,498	1,489	1,507	991	1,064	907	787	782	793	769	708	840	824	783	871	869	847	894
Kashmir Urban ...	1,697	1,620	1,781	1,394	1,374	1,416	804	946	734	812	842	778	1,035	966	1,108	817	780	857	931	894	973
Do. Rural ...	2,102	2,024	2,188	1,557	1,575	1,538	830	916	735	759	761	755	795	724	874	787	738	842	808	784	835
Total Kashmir Province ...	2,049	1,972	2,135	1,536	1,548	1,522	832	920	735	766	772	758	826	755	905	791	743	844	825	798	853
Ladákh ...	1,017	960	1,077	1,170	1,134	1,202	929	934	924	746	818	667	833	850	813	893	876	911	893	934	848
Skardu ...	1,357	1,259	1,459	1,401	1,399	1,403	1,022	1,100	945	880	940	819	1,196	1,220	1,275	348	359	335	593	601	583
Gilgit ...	144	...	6,667	...	...	...	144	147	...	360	368	...	2,662	2,721	...	2,086	2,059	3,333	1,655	1,691	...
Whole State Urban ...	1,639	1,541	1,751	1,343	1,302	1,390	844	929	746	809	830	784	1,035	984	1,093	860	842	883	946	929	965
Do. Rural ...	1,878	1,789	1,978	1,524	1,529	1,517	920	1,001	830	780	782	777	806	737	884	772	735	819	821	798	845
Total whole State ...	1,861	1,770	1,961	1,510	1,512	1,508	914	995	824	782	786	777	825	757	899	779	738	823	830	808	854

PROPORTION PER 10,000. (MOHAMEDANS—*continued.*)

	35—39.			40—44.			45—49.			50—54.			55—59.			60 AND OVER.			UNSPECIFIED.		
	Total.	Males.	Females.	Total.	Males.	Females.	Total.	Males.	Females.	Total.	Males.	Females.	Total.	Males.	Females.	Total.	Males.	Females.	Total.	Males.	Females.
Jammu Urban ...	606	689	480	729	738	716	399	438	340	436	448	416	174	172	177	477	476	478	...	...	...
Do. Rural ...	540	570	506	607	618	594	303	340	261	396	429	359	117	130	104	566	611	515	...	...	...
Total Jammu Province...	541	573	505	610	622	597	306	343	263	397	430	360	119	132	106	564	607	514	...	...	...
Kashmir Urban ...	504	522	484	737	693	785	306	352	258	475	520	426	96	122	67	352	369	333	...	...	...
Do. Rural ...	500	519	479	632	615	652	280	314	242	375	401	346	101	114	86	474	515	428	...	...	...
Total Kashmir Province...	501	520	480	645	625	668	283	319	244	388	417	356	100	115	84	458	496	416	...	...	...
Ladákh ...	771	748	799	704	696	716	485	464	507	505	503	514	241	271	209	813	812	813	...	...	...
Skardu ...	960	929	991	390	407	372	643	604	685	247	277	214	120	138	101	841	865	816	2	2	2
Gilgit ...	791	809	...	575	588	...	504	514	...	719	735	...	216	221	...	114	147	...	...	...	...
Whole State Urban ...	520	551	484	735	700	776	321	366	269	469	507	425	108	131	81	371	388	352	...	...	...
Do. Rural ...	550	566	528	604	603	605	315	345	282	377	408	343	110	123	95	542	583	496	1	1	1
Total whole State ...	547	568	524	614	611	618	315	347	281	384	415	349	110	124	95	529	568	486	...	1	1

BUDHISTS.

	Under 5.			5—9.			10—14.			15—19.			20—24.			25—29.			30—34.		
	Total.	Males.	Females.	Total.	Males.	Females.	Total.	Males.	Females.	Total.	Males.	Females.	Total.	Males.	Females.	Total.	Males.	Females.	Total.	Males.	Females.
Jammu Urban	...	...	...	...	...	...	...	...	...	...	...	...	...	...	...	...	...	...	...	...	...
Do. Rural	342	170	172	490	260	230	436	236	200	398	178	220	352	178	174	430	192	238	365	176	189
Total Jammu Province ...	342	170	172	490	260	230	436	236	200	398	178	220	352	178	174	430	192	238	365	176	189
Kashmir Urban	...	...	...	...	...	...	...	...	.	...	...	...	...	...	...	...	...	...	...	...	...
Do. Rural	...	...	...	...	...	...	...	...	...	...	...	...	...	...	...	...	...	...	...	...	...
Total Kashmir Province ...	...	...	...	...	...	...	...	...	...	...	...	...	...	...	...	...	...	...	...	...	...
Ladákh	2,130	1,041	1,089	2,524	1,269	1,255	1,989	1,018	971	1,760	890	870	1,892	959	933	1,981	1,006	975	1,853	933	920
Skardu	20	6	14	15	12	3	25	15	10	12	8	4	18	12	6	20	10	10	15	12	3
Gilgit	...	...	...	...	...	...	...	..	...	...	...	...	...	...	...	...	...	...	...	...	...
Whole State Urban ...	...	...	...	...	...	...	...	...	..	...	...	...	...	...	...	...	...	...	...	...	...
Do. Rural ...	2,492	1,217	1,275	3,029	1,541	1,488	2,450	1,269	1,181	2,170	1,076	1,094	2,262	1,149	1,113	2,481	1,208	1,223	2,233	1,121	1,112
Total whole State ...	2,492	1,217	1,275	3,029	1,541	1,488	2,450	1,269	1,181	2,170	1,076	1,094	2,262	1,149	1,113	2,481	1,208	1,223	2,233	1,121	1,112

BUDHISTS.—(*continued.*)

	35—39.			40—44.			45—49.			50—54.			55—59.			60 AND OVER.			UNSPECIFIED.		
	Total.	Males.	Females.	Total.	Males.	Females.	Total.	Males.	Females.	Total.	Males.	Females.	Total.	Males.	Females.	Total.	Males.	Females.	Total.	Males.	Females.
Jammu Urban	...	...	...	...	...	...	...	...	...	...	...	...	...	...	...	...	...	...	...	...	...
Do. Rural	258	130	128	287	137	150	214	116	98	218	120	98	121	68	53	382	218	164	...	...	...
Total Jammu Province. ...	258	130	128	287	137	150	214	116	98	218	120	98	121	68	53	382	218	164	...	...	...
Kashmír Urban ...	...	...	...	...	...	...	...	...	...	...	...	...	...	...	...	...	...	...	...	...	...
Do. Rural	...	...	...	...	...	...	...	...	...	...	...	...	...	...	...	...	...	...	...	...	...
Total Kashmír Province ...	...	...	...	...	...	...	...	...	...	...	...	...	...	...	...	...	...	...	...	...	...
Ladákh	1,870	937	933	1,772	903	869	1,498	752	746	1,146	568	578	1,269	638	631	3,392	1,701	1,691	...	...	...
Skardu	21	13	8	13	5	8	20	12	8	14	11	3	5	4	1	41	28	13	...	...	...
Gilgit	...	...	...	...	...	...	...	...	...	...	...	...	...	...	...	...	...	...	...	...	...
Whole State Urban ...	...	...	...	...	...	...	...	...	...	...	...	...	...	...	...	...	...	...	...	...	...
Do. Rural ...	2,149	1,080	1,069	2,072	1,045	1,027	1,732	880	852	1,378	699	679	1,395	710	685	3,815	1,947	1,868	...	...	...
Total whole State ...	2,149	1,080	1,069	2,072	1,045	1,027	1,732	880	852	1,378	699	679	1,395	710	685	3,815	1,947	1,868	...	...	...

PROPORTION PER 10,000. (BUDHISTS.)

	UNDER 5.			5—9.			10—14.			15—19.			20—24.			25—29.			30—34.		
	Total.	Males.	Females.	Total.	Males.	Females.	Total.	Males.	Females.	Total.	Males.	Females.	Total.	Males.	Females.	Total.	Males.	Females.	Total.	Males.	Females.
Jammu Urban ...	...	...	...	...	...	...	...	...	...	...	...	...	...	...	...	...	...	...	...	...	...
Do. Rural ...	797	780	813	1,141	1,193	1,088	1,017	1,083	946	927	817	1,041	817	817	823	1,002	881	1,126	850	808	894
Total Jammu Province ...	797	780	813	1,141	1,193	1,088	1,017	1,083	946	927	817	1,041	817	817	823	1,002	881	1,126	850	808	894
Kashmir Urban ...	...	...	...	...	...	...	...	...	...	...	...	...	...	...	...	...	...	...	...	...	...
Do. Rural ...	...	...	...	...	...	...	...	...	...	...	...	...	...	...	...	...	...	...	...	...	...
Total Kashmir Province ...	...	...	...	...	...	...	...	...	...	...	...	...	...	...	...	...	...	...	...	...	...
Ladákh ...	449	625	674	1,006	1,006	1,007	794	807	779	701	706	689	754	760	748	790	798	783	739	739	738
Skardu ...	838	405	1,538	628	811	330	1,046	1,014	1,099	503	541	440	753	810	660	838	676	1,098	628	811	330
Gilgit ...	...	...	...	...	...	...	...	...	...	...	...	...	...	...	...	...	...	...	...	...	...
Whole State Urban ...	...	...	...	...	...	...	...	...	...	...	...	...	...	...	...	...	...	...	...	...	...
Do. Rural ...	841	815	869	1,023	1,031	1,015	828	849	805	733	721	746	764	769	759	821	808	834	754	750	758
Total whole State ...	841	815	869	1,023	1,031	1,015	828	849	805	733	721	746	764	769	759	821	808	834	754	750	758

PROPORTION PER 10,000. (BUDHISTS—*continued.*)

	35—39.			40—44.			45—49.			50—54.			55—59.			60 AND OVER.			UNSPECIFIED.		
	Total.	Males.	Females.	Total.	Males.	Females.	Total.	Males.	Females.	Total.	Males.	Females.	Total.	Males.	Females.	Total.	Males.	Females.	Total.	Males.	Females.
Jammu Urban ...	...	...	...	...	...	...	...	...	...	...	...	...	...	...	...	...	...	...	...	...	...
Do. Rural ...	601	597	605	669	629	710	499	532	463	508	551	464	282	312	251	890	1,000	776	...	...	...
Total Jammu Province ...	601	597	605	669	629	710	499	532	463	508	551	464	282	312	251	890	1,000	776	...	...	...
Kashmir Urban ...	...	...	...	...	...	...	...	...	...	...	...	...	...	...	...	...	...	...	...	...	...
Do. Rural ...	...	...	...	...	...	...	...	...	...	...	...	...	...	...	...	...	...	...	...	...	...
Total Kashmir Province ...	...	...	...	...	...	...	...	...	...	...	...	...	...	...	...	...	...	...	...	...	...
Ladákh ...	746	743	748	706	716	698	797	596	598	460	450	475	506	506	506	1,352	1,348	1,357	...	...	...
Skardu ...	871	879	879	544	337	879	838	811	879	586	743	330	211	270	110	1,716	1,892	1,428	...	...	...
Gilgit ...	...	...	...	...	...	...	...	...	...	...	...	...	...	...	...	...	...	...	...	...	...
Whole State Urban ...	...	...	...	...	...	...	...	...	...	...	...	...	...	...	...	...	...	...	...	...	...
Do. Rural ...	726	723	729	700	699	700	585	589	581	465	468	463	471	475	467	1,289	1,303	1,274	...	...	...
Total whole State ...	726	723	729	700	699	700	585	589	581	465	468	463	471	475	467	1,289	1,303	1,274	...	...	...

CHRISTIANS.

	Under 5.			5—9.			10—14.			15—19.			20—24.			25—29.			30—34.		
	Total.	Males.	Females.	Total.	Males.	Females.	Total.	Males.	Females.	Total.	Males.	Females.	Total.	Males.	Females.	Total.	Males.	Females.	Total.	Males.	Females.
Jammu Urban ...	4	3	1	...	...	...	...	...	...	2	...	2	2	...	2	1	...	1	3	3	...
Do. Rural ...	5	3	2	2	1	1	4	2	2	2	1	1	...	...	...	3	1	2	6	2	4
Total Jammu Province	9	6	3	2	1	1	4	2	2	4	1	3	2	...	2	4	1	3	9	5	4
Kashmír Urban ...	20	10	10	15	9	6	4	2	2	4	...	4	9	3	6	17	5	12	15	10	5
Do. Rural ...	...	...	...	2	2	...	2	...	2	...	...	...	4	4	...	3	1	2	6	6	...
Total Kashmír Province	20	10	10	17	11	6	6	2	4	4	...	4	13	7	6	20	6	14	21	16	5
Ladákh ...	2	1	1	6	2	4	2	...	2	3	1	2	1	1	...	2	1	1	1	1	...
Skardu ...	...	...	...	...	...	...	...	...	...	...	...	...	...	...	...	...	...	...	...	...	...
Gilgit ...	...	...	...	...	...	...	...	...	...	...	...	...	...	...	...	...	...	...	1	...	1
Whole State Urban ...	24	13	11	15	9	6	4	2	2	6	...	6	11	3	8	18	5	13	18	13	5
Do. Rural ...	7	4	3	10	5	5	8	2	6	5	2	3	5	5	...	8	3	4	14	9	5
Total whole State ...	31	17	14	25	14	11	12	4	8	11	2	9	16	8	8	26	8	18	32	22	10

CHRISTIANS.—*(continued)*.

	35—39.			40—44.			45—49.			50—54.			55—59.			60 and over.			Unspecified.		
	Total.	Males.	Females.	Total.	Males.	Females.	Total.	Males.	Females.	Total.	Males.	Females.	Total.	Males.	Females.	Total.	Males.	Females.	Total.	Males.	Females.
Jammu Urban ...	...	...	...	1	1	...	1	...	1	...	...	...	...	...	...	...	...	...	...	...	...
Do. Rural ...	3	1	2	3	3	...	3	3	...	1	...	1	...	...	...	...	...	...	...	...	...
Total Jammu Province	3	1	2	4	4	...	4	3	1	1	...	1	...	...	...	...	...	...	...	...	...
Kashmír Urban ...	10	2	8	10	6	4	8	5	3	3	3	...	4	1	3	2	2	...	...	...	...
Do. Rural ...	4	3	1	1	1	...	...	...	...	...	...	...	...	...	...	2	2	...	...	...	...
Total Kashmír Province	14	5	9	11	7	4	8	5	3	3	3	...	4	1	3	4	4	...	...	...	...
Ladákh ...	1	1	...	3	1	2	1	...	1	1	1	...	1	1	...	1	...	1	...	...	...
Skardu ...	...	...	...	...	...	...	...	...	...	...	...	...	...	...	...	...	...	...	...	...	...
Gilgit ...	...	...	...	1	1	...	...	...	...	...	...	...	...	...	...	...	...	...	...	...	...
Whole State Urban ...	10	2	8	11	7	4	9	5	4	3	3	...	4	1	3	2	2	...	...	...	...
Do. Rural ...	8	5	3	8	6	2	4	3	1	2	1	1	1	1	...	3	2	1	...	...	...
Total whole State ...	18	7	11	19	13	6	13	8	5	5	4	1	5	2	3	5	4	1	...	...	...

PROPORTION PER 10,000. (CHRISTIANS).

	Under 5.			5—9.			10—14.			15—19.			20—24.			25—29.			30—34.		
	Total.	Males.	Females.	Total.	Males.	Females.	Total.	Males.	Females.	Total.	Males.	Females.	Total.	Males.	Females.	Total.	Males.	Females.	Total.	Males.	Females.
Jammu Urban ...	2,857	4,285	1,429	...	...	...	...	...	...	1,429	...	2,857	1,429	...	2,857	714	...	1,429	2,143	4,285	...
Do. Rural ...	1,563	1,765	1,333	625	588	667	1,250	1,176	1,333	625	588	666	...	...	...	937	588	1,334	1,875	1,177	2,666
Total Jammu Province	1,956	2,500	1,363	435	417	455	870	833	909	870	416	1,363	434	...	909	870	417	1,363	1,956	2,083	1,819
Kashmír Urban ...	1,663	1,724	1,587	1,240	1,552	952	331	345	317	330	...	636	744	517	952	1,405	862	1,904	1,240	1,724	793
Do. Rural ...	...	...	...	833	1,053	...	833	...	4,000	...	...	...	1,667	2,105	...	1,250	526	4,000	2,500	3,158	...
Total Kashmír Province	1,379	1,299	1,470	1,173	1,429	883	414	260	588	275	...	588	897	909	883	1,379	780	2,059	1,448	2,078	735
Ladákh ...	800	909	714	2,400	1,818	2,857	800	...	1,429	1,200	909	1,429	400	909	...	800	909	714	400	909	...
Skardu ...	...	...	...	...	...	...	...	...	...	...	...	...	...	...	...	...	...	...	...	...	...
Gilgit ...	...	...	...	...	...	...	...	...	...	...	...	...	...	...	...	...	...	...	500	...	10,000
Whole State Urban ...	1,778	2,000	1,571	1,111	1,385	857	296	308	286	245	...	857	815	461	1,143	1,333	769	1,857	1,333	2,000	714
Do. Rural ...	843	833	857	1,205	1,042	1,429	964	417	1,714	602	417	857	602	1,042	...	964	625	1,429	1,687	1,875	1,429
Total whole State ...	1,422	1,505	1,333	1,146	1,239	1,047	550	354	762	505	177	857	738	708	762	1,192	708	1,718	1,468	1,947	952

PROPORTION PER 10,000. (CHRISTIANS—*continued.*)

	35—39.			40—44.			45—49.			50—54.			55—59.			60 AND OVER.			UNSPECIFIED.		
	Total.	Males.	Females.	Total.	Males.	Females.	Total.	Males.	Females.	Total.	Males.	Females.	Total.	Males.	Females.	Total.	Males.	Females.	Total.	Males.	Females.
Jammu Urban ...	...	...	...	714	1,429	...	714	...	1,428	...	...	...	...	...	...	...	...	...	...	...	...
Do. Rural ...	938	588	1,334	938	1,765	...	937	1,765	...	312	...	667	...	...	...	...	...	...	...	...	...
Total Jammu Province	652	417	909	870	1,667	...	870	1,250	455	217	...	455	...	...	...	...	...	...	...	...	...
Kashmír Urban ...	826	345	1,271	826	1,035	636	661	862	476	248	517	...	331	172	476	165	345	...	...	...	...
Do. Rural ...	1,667	1,579	2,000	417	526	...	...	...	...	...	...	...	...	...	...	833	1,053	...	...	...	...
Total Kashmír Province	966	649	1,324	759	909	588	551	649	441	207	890	...	276	129	441	276	519	...	...	...	...
Ladákh ...	400	909	...	1,200	909	1,429	400	...	714	400	909	...	400	910	...	400	...	714	...	...	...
Skardu ...	...	...	...	...	...	...	...	...	...	...	...	...	...	...	...	...	...	...	...	...	...
Gilgit ...	...	...	...	500	1,000	...	...	...	...	...	...	...	...	...	...	...	...	...	...	...	...
Whole State Urban ...	741	308	1,143	815	1,077	572	667	769	571	222	461	...	296	154	429	148	308	...	...	...	...
Do. Rural ...	964	1,041	857	964	1,250	572	482	625	285	241	209	286	121	208	...	361	416	285	...	...	...
Total whole State ...	825	619	1,047	871	1,150	571	596	708	476	229	354	95	229	177	285	229	354	95	...	...	...

PARSIS.

	Under 5.			5—9.			10—14.			15—19.			20—24.			25—29.			30—34.		
	Total.	Males.	Females.	Total.	Males.	Females.	Total.	Males.	Females.	Total.	Males.	Females.	Total.	Males.	Females.	Total.	Males.	Females.	Total.	Males.	Females.
Jammu Urban ...	...	...	...	...	...	...	...	...	...	...	...	...	...	...	...	...	...	...	...	...	...
Do. Rural ...	...	...	...	...	...	...	...	...	...	...	...	...	...	...	...	...	...	...	...	...	...
Total Jammu Province	...	...	...	...	...	...	...	...	...	...	...	...	...	...	...	...	...	...	...	...	...
Kashmír Urban ...	1	1	...	...	...	...	1	1	...	1	1	...	1	...	1	...	...	...	1	1	...
Do. Rural ...	...	...	...	...	...	...	...	...	...	...	...	...	...	...	...	...	...	...	...	...	...
Total Kashmír Province	1	1	...	...	...	...	1	1	...	1	1	...	1	...	1	...	...	...	1	1	...
Ladákh ...	...	...	...	...	...	...	...	...	...	...	...	...	...	...	...	...	...	...	...	...	...
Skardu ...	...	...	...	...	...	...	...	...	...	...	...	...	...	...	...	...	...	...	...	...	...
Gilgit ...	...	...	...	...	...	...	...	...	...	...	...	...	...	...	...	...	...	...	...	...	...
Whole State Urban ...	1	1	...	...	...	...	1	1	...	1	1	...	1	...	1	...	...	...	1	1	...
Do. Rural ...	...	...	...	...	...	...	...	...	...	...	...	...	...	...	...	...	...	...	...	...	...
Total whole State ...	1	1	...	...	...	...	1	1	...	1	1	...	1	...	1	...	...	...	1	1	...

PARSIS.—(*continued.*)

	35—39.			40—44.			45—49.			50—54.			55—59.			60 and over.			Unspecified.		
	Total.	Males.	Females.	Total.	Males.	Females.	Total.	Males.	Females.	Total.	Males.	Females.	Total.	Males.	Females.	Total.	Males.	Females.	Total.	Males.	Females.
Jammu Urban ...	...	...	...	...	...	...	...	...	...	...	...	...	...	...	...	...	...	...	...	...	...
Do. Rural ...	1	1	...	...	...	...	...	...	...	...	...	...	...	...	...	...	...	...	...	...	...
Total Jammu Province	1	1	...	...	...	...	...	...	...	...	...	...	...	...	...	...	...	...	...	...	...
Kashmír Urban ...	1	1	...	1	...	1	1	1	...	...	...	...	...	...	...	...	...	...	...	...	...
Do. Rural ...	...	...	...	...	...	...	...	...	...	...	...	...	...	...	...	...	...	...	...	...	...
Total Kashmír Province	1	1	...	1	...	1	1	1	...	...	...	...	...	...	...	...	...	...	...	...	...
Ladákh ...	...	...	...	...	...	...	...	...	...	...	...	...	...	...	...	...	...	...	...	...	...
Skardu ...	...	...	...	...	...	...	...	...	...	...	...	...	...	...	...	...	...	...	...	...	...
Gilgit ...	...	...	...	...	...	...	...	...	...	...	...	...	...	...	...	...	...	...	...	...	...
Whole State Urban ...	1	1	...	1	...	1	1	1	...	...	...	...	...	...	...	...	...	...	...	...	...
Do. Rural ...	1	1	...	...	...	...	...	...	...	...	...	...	...	...	...	...	...	...	...	...	...
Total whole State ...	2	2	...	1	...	1	1	1	...	...	...	...	...	...	...	...	...	...	...	...	...

PROPORTION PER 10,000. (PARSIS.)

	Under 5.			5—9.			10—14.			15—19.			20—24.			25—29.			30—34.		
	Total.	Males.	Females.	Total.	Males.	Females.	Total.	Males.	Females.	Total.	Males.	Females.	Total.	Males.	Females.	Total.	Males.	Females.	Total.	Males.	Females.
Jammu Urban ...	...	...	...	...	...	...	...	...	...	...	...	...	...	...	...	...	...	...	...	...	...
Do. Rural ...	...	...	...	...	...	...	...	...	...	...	...	...	...	...	...	...	...	...	...	...	...
Total Jammu Province	...	...	...	...	...	...	...	...	...	...	...	...	...	...	...	...	...	...	...	...	...
Kashmír Urban ...	1,250	1,666	...	...	...	...	1,250	1,666	...	1,250	1,667	...	1,250	...	5,000	...	...	...	1,250	1,667	...
Do. Rural ...	...	...	...	...	...	...	...	...	...	...	...	...	...	...	...	...	...	...	...	...	...
Total Kashmír Province	1,250	1,666	...	...	...	...	1,250	1,666	...	1,250	1,667	...	1,250	...	5,000	...	...	...	1,250	1,667	...
Ladákh ...	...	...	...	...	...	...	...	...	...	...	...	...	...	...	...	...	...	...	...	...	...
Skardu ...	...	...	...	...	...	...	...	...	...	...	...	...	...	...	...	...	...	...	...	...	...
Gilgit ...	...	...	...	...	...	...	...	...	...	...	...	...	...	...	...	...	...	...	...	...	...
Whole State Urban ...	1,250	1,666	...	...	...	...	1,250	1,666	...	1,250	1,667	...	1,250	...	5,000	...	...	...	1,250	1,667	...
Do. Rural ...	...	...	...	...	...	...	...	...	...	...	...	...	...	...	...	...	...	...	...	...	...
Total whole State ...	1,111	1428	...	...	...	...	1,111	1,428	...	1,111	1,429	...	1,111	...	5,000	...	...	...	1,111	1,429	...

PROPORTION PER 10,000 PARSIS—(*continued.*)

	35—39.			40—44.			45—49.			50—54.			55—59.			60 AND OVER.			UNSPECIFIED.		
	Total.	Males.	Females.	Total.	Males.	Females.	Total.	Males.	Females.	Total.	Males.	Females.	Total.	Males.	Females.	Total.	Males.	Females.	Total.	Males.	Females.
Jammu Urban ...	...	...	...	...	...	...	...	...	...	...	...	...	...	...	...	...	...	...	...	...	...
Do. Rural ...	10,000	10,000	...	...	...	...	...	...	...	...	...	...	...	...	...	...	...	...	...	...	...
Total Jammu Province	10,000	10,000	...	...	...	...	...	...	...	...	...	...	...	...	...	...	...	...	...	...	...
Kashmír Urban ...	1,250	1,667	...	1,250	...	5,000	1,250	1,667	...	...	...	...	...	...	...	...	...	...	...	...	...
Do. Rural ...	...	...	...	...	...	...	...	...	...	...	...	...	...	...	...	...	...	...	...	...	...
Total Kashmír Province	1,250	1,667	...	1,250	...	5,000	1,250	1,667	...	...	...	...	...	...	...	...	...	...	...	...	...
Ladákh ...	...	...	...	...	...	...	...	...	...	...	...	...	...	...	...	...	...	...	...	...	...
Skardu ...	...	...	...	...	...	...	...	...	...	...	...	...	...	...	...	...	...	...	...	...	...
Gilgit ...	...	...	...	...	...	...	...	...	...	...	...	...	...	...	...	...	...	...	...	...	...
Whole State Urban ...	1,250	1,667	...	1,250	...	5,000	1,250	1,667	...	...	...	...	...	...	...	...	...	...	...	...	...
Do. Rural ...	10,000	10,000	...	...	...	...	...	...	...	...	...	...	...	...	...	...	...	...	...	...	...
Total whole State ...	2,223	2,857	...	1,111	...	5,000	1,111	1,429	...	...	...	...	...	...	...	...	...	...	...	...	...

ALL RELIGIONS.

	Under 5.			5—9.			10—14.			15—19.			20—24.			25—29.			30—34.		
	Total.	Males.	Females.	Total.	Males.	Females.	Total.	Males.	Females.	Total.	Males.	Females.	Total.	Males.	Females.	Total.	Males.	Females.	Total.	Males.	Females.
Urban Population Jammu.																					
Jammu ...	3,809	2,160	1,649	2,922	1,695	1,227	2,776	1,786	990	2,874	1,790	1,084	3,828	2,516	1,312	4,194	2,900	1,294	3,732	2,596	1,136
Batála ...	681	400	281	701	443	258	613	420	193	406	242	164	400	212	188	447	221	226	422	213	209
Mirpur ...	1,189	589	600	1,003	545	458	597	329	268	462	248	214	531	235	296	590	289	301	624	297	327
Punch ...	899	473	426	818	467	351	503	320	183	620	395	225	816	522	294	880	549	331	867	561	306
Total Jammu Urban ...	6,578	3,622	2,956	5,444	3,150	2,294	4,489	2,855	1,634	4,362	2,675	1,687	5,575	3,485	2,090	6,111	3,959	2,152	5,645	3,667	1,978
Urban Population Kashmir.																					
Srinagar ...	18,342	9,081	9,261	16,015	8,270	7,745	10,137	6,071	4,066	9,893	5,451	4,442	12,559	6,211	6,348	9,843	4,956	4,887	11,319	5,687	5,632
Anantnág ...	1,733	899	834	1,383	726	657	875	505	370	883	487	396	1,053	559	494	847	427	420	870	455	415
Sopore ...	1,713	856	857	1,218	630	588	742	406	336	641	340	301	759	369	390	728	333	395	694	371	323
Bárámula ...	1,060	566	494	777	421	356	484	275	209	451	226	225	513	232	281	527	284	243	527	267	260
Total Kashmir Urban ...	22,848	11,402	11,446	19,393	10,047	9,346	12,238	7,257	4,981	11,868	6,504	5,364	14,884	7,371	7,513	11,945	6,000	5,945	13,410	6,780	6,630
Total Urban whole State	29,426	15,024	14,402	24,837	13,197	11,640	16,727	10,112	6,615	16,230	9,179	7,051	20,459	10,856	9,603	18,056	9,959	8,097	19,055	10,447	8,608

ALL RELIGIONS—(*continued.*)

	35—39.			40—44.			45—49.			50—54.			55—59.			60 AND OVER.			UNSPECIFIED.		
	Total.	Males.	Females.	Total.	Males.	Females.	Total.	Males.	Females.	Total.	Males.	Females.	Total.	Males.	Females.	Total.	Males.	Females.	Total.	Males.	Females.
URBAN POPULATION JAMMU.																					
Jammu ...	2,175	1,574	601	2,618	1,768	850	1,460	1,028	432	1,605	1,076	529	740	500	240	1,644	1,067	577	165	89	76
Batála ...	295	158	137	326	176	150	201	119	82	242	165	77	62	49	13	410	261	149	...	...	...
Mirpur ...	407	209	198	502	251	251	304	165	139	394	194	200	175	86	89	475	218	257	..	...	...
Punch ...	571	396	175	530	341	189	300	219	81	301	209	92	108	77	31	276	146	130	...	...	...
Total Jammu Urban ...	3,448	2,337	1,111	3,976	2,536	1,440	2,265	1,531	734	2,542	1,644	898	1,085	712	373	2,805	1,692	1,113	165	89	76
URBAN POPULATION KASHMIR.																					
Srinagar ...	6,085	3,381	2,704	9,135	4,532	4,603	3,852	2,336	1,516	5,940	3,361	2,579	1,351	907	444	4,489	2,476	2,013	...	...	...
Anantnág ...	559	328	231	725	382	343	344	202	142	439	259	180	91	64	27	425	222	203	...	...	...
Sopore ...	478	271	207	470	239	231	235	132	103	331	177	154	89	53	36	312	183	129	...	...	...
Bárámula ...	306	158	148	349	178	171	146	103	43	226	130	96	44	29	15	246	134	112	...	...	...
Total Kashmír Urban ...	7,428	4,138	3,290	10,679	5,331	5,348	4,577	2,773	1,804	6,936	3,927	3,009	1,575	1,053	522	5,472	3,015	2,457	...	...	...
Total Urban whole State	10,876	6,475	4,401	14,655	7,867	6,788	6,842	4,304	2,538	9,478	5,571	3,907	2,660	1,765	895	8,277	4,707	3,570	165	89	76

PROPORTION PER 10,000 (ALL RELIGIONS).

	Under 5.			5—9.			10—14.			15—19.			20—24.			25—29.			30—34.		
	Total.	Males.	Females.	Total.	Males.	Females.	Total.	Males.	Females.	Total.	Males.	Females.	Total.	Males.	Females.	Total.	Males.	Females.	Total.	Males.	Females.
Urban Population Jammu.																					
Jammu ...	1,108	957	1,375	846	752	1,023	804	792	825	832	794	903	1,108	1,116	1,094	1,214	1,286	1,078	1,080	1,152	947
Batála ...	1,808	1,299	1,321	1,346	1,439	1,213	1,177	1,364	908	780	786	771	768	689	884	859	718	1,063	816	692	983
Mirpur ...	1,639	1,612	1,668	1,383	1,491	1,273	823	900	745	637	678	595	732	643	823	814	791	837	860	813	909
Punch ...	1,201	1,012	1,514	1,092	998	1,247	672	684	651	829	845	799	1,090	1,117	1,045	1,183	1,175	1,176	1,158	1,200	1,087
Total Jammu Urban ...	1,207	1,067	1,439	999	927	1,117	824	841	796	803	788	821	1,023	1,027	1,018	1,121	1,166	1,048	1,087	1,080	963
Urban Population Kashmir.																					
Srinagar ...	1,541	1,448	1,647	1,346	1,319	1,376	853	968	722	832	869	789	1,056	990	1,128	827	790	869	951	906	1,001
Anantnág ...	1,695	1,630	1,770	1,352	1,317	1,395	856	916	785	864	883	840	1,030	1,013	1,049	828	774	892	850	825	880
Sopore ...	2,037	1,963	2,116	1,448	1,445	1,452	882	931	830	762	780	743	902	846	964	866	764	975	825	851	798
Bárámula ...	1,874	1,885	1,862	1,374	1,402	1,342	856	916	787	797	752	848	907	772	1,059	981	946	919	982	889	980
Total Kashmir Urban...	1,594	1,508	1,693	1,354	1,329	1,382	854	960	737	828	860	793	1,039	975	1,111	834	794	877	936	897	979
Total Urban whole State	1,488	1,371	1,633	1,256	1,205	1,320	846	923	750	821	838	800	1,034	991	1,089	913	909	918	964	954	976

PROPORTION PER 10,000. (ALL RELIGIONS—*continued.*)

	35—39.			40—44.			45—49.			50—54.			55—59.			60 and over.			Unspecified.		
	Total.	Males.	Females.	Total.	Males.	Females.	Total.	Males.	Females.	Total.	Males.	Females.	Total.	Males.	Females.	Total.	Males.	Females.	Total.	Males.	Females.
Urban Population Jammu.																					
Jammu ...	630	698	500	758	784	709	423	456	361	465	477	441	214	222	200	476	474	480	47	40	64
Batála ...	566	513	644	626	572	705	384	386	385	464	536	362	119	159	61	787	847	700	...	...	...
Mirpur ...	561	572	550	692	687	698	419	451	386	543	531	555	242	235	247	655	596	714	...	...	...
Punch ...	763	848	622	708	729	672	401	468	288	402	447	327	132	165	110	369	312	462	...	...	...
Total Jammu Urban ...	633	688	541	731	747	701	416	451	357	462	484	437	199	210	182	515	498	542	30	26	37
Urban Population Kashmir.																					
Srinagar ...	512	539	488	768	723	818	324	372	269	499	536	458	114	145	78	377	395	357	...	...	...
Anantnág ...	546	595	490	709	692	728	336	366	301	429	470	382	89	116	57	416	403	431	...	...	...
Sopore ...	569	622	511	559	548	570	279	302	254	394	405	380	106	121	89	371	422	318	...	...	...
Bárámula ...	541	526	557	617	593	644	258	343	162	400	433	362	78	96	56	435	447	422	...	...	...
Total Kashmír Urban ...	519	547	486	746	705	791	319	367	267	484	519	444	110	139	77	383	399	363	...	...	...
Total Urban whole State	550	591	499	741	718	769	546	393	288	479	509	443	135	161	102	419	429	405	8	8	8

HINDUS INCLUDING JAINS AND SIKHS.

	Under 5.			5—9.			10—14.			15—19.			20—24.			25—29.			30—34.		
	Total.	Males.	Females.	Total.	Males.	Females.	Total.	Males.	Females.	Total.	Males.	Females.	Total.	Males.	Females.	Total.	Males.	Females.	Total.	Males.	Females.
Urban Population Jammu.																					
Jammu ...	2,477	1,404	1,073	1,910	1,152	758	1,801	1,169	632	1,910	1,209	701	2,498	1,634	864	2,781	1,956	825	2,497	1,740	757
Batála ...	523	322	201	553	364	189	488	345	143	329	198	131	313	167	146	346	166	180	336	163	173
Mirpur ...	602	304	298	551	289	262	294	169	125	243	136	107	289	128	161	332	161	171	359	159	200
Punch ...	241	134	107	230	139	91	162	106	56	239	167	72	329	226	103	380	269	111	326	232	94
Total Jammu Urban ...	3,843	2,164	1,679	3,244	1,944	1,300	2,745	1,789	956	2,721	1,710	1,011	3,429	2,155	1,274	3,839	2,552	1,287	3,518	2,294	1,224
Urban Population Kashmir.																					
Srinagar ...	3,055	1,528	1,527	3,130	1,674	1,456	2,355	1,488	867	2,372	1,367	1,005	2,815	1,454	1,361	2,336	1,211	1,125	2,537	1,322	1,215
Anantnág ...	130	69	61	111	55	56	84	50	34	88	44	44	100	71	29	85	42	43	95	52	43
Sopore ...	126	67	59	112	61	51	82	45	37	67	32	35	80	47	33	83	40	43	66	38	28
Bárámula ...	140	74	66	109	64	45	73	38	35	69	41	28	67	35	32	91	50	41	62	29	33
Total Kashmír Urban...	3,451	1,738	1,713	3,462	1,854	1,608	2,594	1,621	973	2,596	1,484	1,112	3,062	1,607	1,455	2,595	1,343	1,252	2,760	1,441	1,319
Total Urban whole State	7,294	3,902	3,392	6,706	3,798	2,908	5,339	3,410	1,929	5,317	3,194	2,123	6,491	3,762	2,729	6,434	3,895	2,539	6,278	3,735	2,543

HINDUS INCLUDING JAINS AND SIKHS—(*continued.*)

	35—39.			40—44.			45—49.			50—54.			55—59.			60 and over.			Unspecified.		
	Total.	Males.	Females.	Total.	Males.	Females.	Total.	Males.	Females.	Total.	Males.	Females.	Total.	Males.	Females.	Total.	Males.	Females.	Total.	Males.	Females.
Urban Population Jammu.																					
Jammu ...	1,516	1,077	489	1,723	1,182	541	992	709	283	1,065	720	345	524	367	157	1,068	690	378	165	89	76
Batála ...	222	113	109	254	134	120	165	99	66	200	134	66	52	40	12	338	218	120	...	...	...
Mirpur ...	217	108	109	293	148	145	154	72	82	243	127	116	97	50	47	276	126	150	...	...	...
Punch ...	239	178	61	196	148	48	127	103	24	133	103	30	52	40	12	137	63	74	...	...	...
Total Jammu Urban ...	2,194	1,476	718	2,466	1,612	854	1,438	983	455	1,641	1,084	557	725	497	228	1,819	1,097	722	165	89	76
Urban Population Kashmir.																					
Srinagar ...	1,472	895	577	2,096	1,099	997	971	613	358	1,377	751	626	433	296	137	1,309	728	581	...	...	...
Anantnág ...	75	60	15	63	41	22	46	31	15	52	30	22	15	12	3	45	24	21	...	...	...
Sopore ...	73	45	28	54	31	23	26	14	12	39	18	21	14	8	6	38	28	10	...	...	...
Bárámula ...	45	27	18	45	28	17	26	19	7	44	29	15	15	7	8	61	34	27	...	...	...
Total Kashmir Urban ...	1,665	1,027	638	2,258	1,199	1,059	1,069	677	392	1,512	828	684	477	823	154	1,453	814	639	...	...	...
Total Urban whole State	3,859	2,503	1,356	4,724	2,811	1,913	2,507	1,660	847	3,153	1,912	1,241	1,202	820	382	3,272	1,911	1,361	165	89	76

PROPORTION PER 10,000, (HINDUS INCLUDING JAINS AND SIKHS).

	Under 5.			5—9.			10—14.		
	Total.	Males.	Females.	Total.	Males.	Females.	Total.	Males.	Females.
Urban Population Jammu.									
Jammu ...	1,089	930	1,371	833	763	968	785	774	807
Batála ...	1,270	1,308	1,214	1,343	1,478	1,141	1,185	1,401	864
Mirpur ...	1,524	1,537	1,510	1,395	1,462	1,328	744	855	634
Punch ...	868	702	1,212	824	729	1,030	580	556	634
Total Jammu Urban ...	1,137	1,009	1,361	961	906	1,053	812	834	775
Urban Population Kashmir.									
Srinagar ...	1,163	1,059	1,291	1,192	1,160	1,231	897	1,031	733
Anantnág ...	1,315	1,188	1,495	1,122	947	1,373	850	860	833
Sopore ...	1,465	1,414	1,529	1,302	1,287	1,321	953	950	959
Bárámula ...	1,653	1,558	1,774	1,287	1,347	1,210	862	800	941
Total Kashmír Urban ...	1,192	1,090	1,318	1,196	1,162	1,237	896	1,016	749
Total Urban whole State	1,162	1,044	1,389	1,069	1,015	1,148	851	912	761

	15—19.			20—24.			25—29.			30—34.		
	Total.	Males.	Females.	Total.	Males.	Females.	Total.	Males.	Females.	Total.	Males.	Females.
Urban Population Jammu.												
Jammu ...	833	801	895	1,090	1,082	1,103	1,213	1,295	1,054	1,089	1,153	967
Batála ...	799	804	791	760	678	882	840	674	1,087	816	662	1,045
Mirpur ...	615	688	542	732	647	816	840	814	867	909	807	1,014
Punch ...	856	875	815	1,178	1,185	1,166	1,361	1,410	1,257	1,168	1,216	1,065
Total Jammu Urban ...	805	797	819	1,015	1,005	1,032	1,136	1,190	1,042	1,041	1,070	991
Urban Population Kashmir.												
Srinagar ...	903	948	849	1,072	1,008	1,150	890	840	951	967	916	1,027
Anantnág ...	890	757	1,078	1,011	1,222	711	859	723	1,054	960	895	1,054
Sopore ...	779	675	907	930	992	955	965	844	1,114	768	802	725
Bárámula ...	815	863	753	791	737	860	1,074	1,053	1,102	732	611	887
Total Kashmír Urban ...	897	930	856	1,058	1,007	1,119	896	842	963	953	903	1,015
Total Urban whole State	847	854	838	1,085	1,006	1,077	1,025	1,041	1,002	1,000	999	1,003

PROPORTION PER 10,000, (HINDUS INCLUDING JAINS AND SIKHS.—*continued*).

	35—39.			40—44.			45—49.			50—54.			55—59.			60 and over.			Unspecified.		
	Total.	Males.	Females.	Total.	Males.	Females.	Total.	Males.	Females.	Total.	Males.	Females.	Total.	Males.	Females.	Total.	Males.	Females.	Total.	Males.	Females.
Urban Population Jammu.																					
Jammu ...	661	713	561	751	783	691	433	470	361	465	477	441	229	243	201	466	457	483	72	59	97
Batála ...	538	458	658	616	544	725	401	402	398	485	544	399	126	162	72	821	885	724	...	...	...
Mirpur ...	549	546	552	742	748	735	390	364	416	615	642	588	246	253	238	699	637	760	...	...	...
Punch ...	856	932	691	702	775	544	455	540	272	476	540	340	186	210	136	490	330	838	...	...	...
Total Jammu Urban ...	650	688	583	730	752	692	426	458	368	485	505	451	215	232	185	538	512	585	49	42	63
Urban Population Kashmir.																					
Srinagar ...	561	620	488	797	762	842	370	425	302	524	521	529	165	205	116	499	505	491	...	...	...
Anantnág ...	758	1,033	368	637	706	539	465	533	368	526	516	539	152	207	73	455	413	515	...	...	...
Sopore ...	849	945	725	628	655	596	302	296	311	454	380	544	163	169	155	442	591	259	...	...	...
Bárámula ...	531	568	484	531	589	457	307	400	188	520	611	403	177	147	215	720	716	726	...	...	...
Total Kashmír Urban ...	575	644	491	780	751	815	369	424	302	522	519	526	164	202	118	502	510	491	...	...	...
Total Urban whole State	615	669	536	753	752	755	400	443	334	503	511	490	192	219	151	522	511	537	26	24	29

MOHAMEDANS.

	Under 5.			5—9.			10—14.			15—19.			20—24.			25—29.			30—34.		
	Total.	Males.	Females.	Total.	Males.	Females.	Total.	Males.	Females.	Total.	Males.	Females.	Total.	Males.	Females.	Total.	Males.	Females.	Total.	Males.	Females.
Urban Population Jammu.																					
Jammu ...	1,328	753	575	1,012	543	469	975	617	358	962	581	381	1,328	882	446	1,412	944	468	1,232	853	379
Batála	158	78	80	148	79	69	125	75	50	77	44	33	87	45	42	101	55	46	86	50	36
Mirpore	587	285	302	452	256	196	303	160	143	219	112	107	242	107	135	258	128	130	265	138	127
Punch	658	339	319	588	328	260	341	214	127	381	228	153	487	296	191	500	280	220	541	329	212
Total Jammu Urban ...	2,731	1,455	1,276	2,200	1,206	994	1,744	1,066	678	1,639	965	674	2,144	1,330	814	2,271	1,407	864	2,124	1,370	754
Urban Population Kashmir.																					
Srinagar ...	15,266	7,542	7,724	12,870	6,587	6,283	7,777	4,580	3,197	7,516	4,083	3,433	9,735	4,754	4,981	7,490	3,740	3,750	8,766	4,354	4,412
Anantnág ...	1,603	830	773	1,272	671	601	791	455	336	795	443	352	952	488	464	762	385	377	775	403	372
Sopore ...	1,587	789	798	1,106	569	537	660	361	299	574	308	266	679	322	357	645	293	352	628	333	295
Bárámula ...	920	492	428	668	357	311	411	237	174	382	185	197	446	197	249	436	234	202	465	238	227
Total Kashmír Urban ...	19,376	9,653	9,723	15,916	8,184	7,732	9,639	5,633	4,006	9,267	5,019	4,248	11,812	5,761	6,051	9,333	4,652	4,681	10,634	5,328	5,306
Total Urban whole State...	22,107	11,108	10,999	18,116	9,390	8,726	11,383	6,699	4,684	10,906	5,984	4,922	13,956	7,091	6,865	11,604	6,059	5,545	12,758	6,698	6,060

MOHAMEDANS.—(*continued.*)

	35—39.			40—44.			45—49.			50—54.			55—59.			60 AND OVER.			UNSPECIFIED.		
	Total.	Males.	Females.	Total.	Males.	Females.	Total.	Males.	Females.	Total.	Males.	Females.	Total.	Males.	Females.	Total.	Males.	Females.	Total.	Males.	Females.
URBAN POPULATION JAMMU.																					
Jammu ...	659	497	162	894	585	309	467	319	148	540	356	184	216	133	83	576	377	199	...	...	...
Batála ...	73	45	28	72	42	30	36	20	16	42	31	11	10	9	1	72	43	29	...	...	...
Mirpore ...	190	101	89	209	103	106	150	93	57	151	67	84	78	36	42	199	92	107	...	...	...
Punch ...	332	218	114	334	193	141	173	116	57	168	106	62	56	37	19	139	83	56	...	...	...
Total Jammu Urban ...	1,254	861	393	1,509	923	586	826	548	278	901	560	341	360	215	145	986	595	391	...	...	...
URBAN POPULATION KASHMIR.																					
Srinagar ...	4,602	2,483	2,119	7,029	3,428	3,601	2,872	1,717	1,155	4,560	2,607	1,953	914	610	304	3,178	1,746	1,432	...	...	...
Anantnág	484	268	216	661	340	321	298	171	127	387	229	158	76	52	24	380	198	182	...	...	...
Sopore	405	226	179	416	208	208	209	118	91	292	159	133	75	45	30	274	155	119	...	...	...
Bárámula	261	131	130	304	150	154	120	84	36	182	101	81	29	22	7	185	100	85	...	...	...
Total Kashmir Urban ...	5,752	3,108	2,644	8,410	4,126	4,284	3,499	2,090	1,409	5,421	3,096	2,325	1,094	729	365	4,017	2,199	1,818	...	...	...
Total Urban whole State...	7,006	3,969	3,037	9,919	5,049	4,870	4,325	2,638	1,687	6,322	3,656	2,666	1,454	944	510	5,003	2,794	2,209	...	...	...

PROPORTION PER 10,000 (MOHAMEDANS).

	UNDER 5.			5—9.			10—14.			15—19.			20—25.			25—29.			30—34.		
	Total.	Males.	Females.	Total.	Males.	Females.	Total.	Males.	Females.	Total.	Males.	Females.	Total.	Males.	Females.	Total.	Males.	Females.	Total.	Males.	Females.
URBAN POPULATION JAMMU.																					
Jammu	1,145	1,012	1,382	872	730	1,127	840	829	860	829	781	915	1,145	1,186	1,072	1,217	1,268	1,125	1,062	1,147	912
Batála	1,454	1,267	1,698	1,362	1,282	1,465	1,150	1,218	1,062	708	714	701	800	731	892	929	893	977	791	812	764
Mirpore	1,777	1,698	1,859	1,369	1,526	1,206	917	954	880	663	667	658	733	638	831	781	763	800	802	822	782
Punch	1,401	1,225	1,652	1,252	1,185	1,347	726	737	658	811	824	792	1,037	1,070	989	1,065	1,012	1,139	1,152	1,189	1,098
Total Jammu Urban ...	1,320	1,164	1,558	1,063	965	1,214	843	853	828	792	772	823	1,036	1,068	994	1,098	1,126	1,054	1,027	1,096	922
URBAN POPULATION KASHMIR.																					
Srinagar	1,649	1,564	1,740	1,390	1,366	1,417	840	949	720	812	846	773	1,052	985	1,123	809	776	846	947	903	995
Anantnág	1,736	1,682	1,797	1,377	1,360	1,397	856	923	781	861	898	819	1,031	989	1,079	825	781	876	839	817	865
Sopore	2,102	2,030	2,177	1,465	1,464	1,465	874	929	816	760	793	725	899	829	974	855	754	961	832	857	805
Bárámula	1,913	1,946	1,877	1,389	1,412	1,363	854	938	763	794	732	864	927	789	1,091	907	926	886	967	941	995
Total Kashmir Urban ...	1,697	1,620	1,781	1,394	1,374	1,916	804	946	734	812	842	778	1,035	966	1,108	817	780	857	931	894	973
Total Urban whole State...	1,639	1,541	1,751	1,343	1,302	1,890	844	929	746	809	830	784	1,035	984	1,093	860	842	883	946	929	963

PROPORTION PER 10,000 (MOHAMEDANS—*continued*).

	35—39.			40—44.			45—49.			50—54.			55—59.			60 AND OVER.			UNSPECIFIED.		
...	Total.	Males.	Females.	Total.	Males.	Females.	Total.	Males.	Females.	Total.	Males.	Females.	Total.	Males.	Females.	Total.	Males.	Females.	Total.	Males.	Females.
URBAN POPULATION JAMMU.																					
Jammu ...	568	668	389	771	786	743	403	429	356	465	478	442	186	179	199	497	507	478	...	...	...
Batála ..	672	731	594	662	682	637	331	325	340	387	502	233	92	146	21	662	698	616	...	...	...
Mirpore ...	575	602	548	633	614	652	454	554	351	457	399	517	236	215	258	603	548	658	...	...	...
Punch ...	707	788	591	712	698	730	364	419	295	358	383	321	119	134	98	296	300	290	...	...	...
Total Jammu Urban ...	606	689	480	729	738	716	399	438	340	436	448	416	174	172	177	477	476	478	...	...	...
URBAN POPULATION KASHMIR.																					
Srinagar ...	497	515	478	759	711	813	310	356	261	493	541	440	99	126	70	343	362	323	...	...	...
Anantnag ...	524	543	502	716	689	746	323	347	296	419	465	368	82	105	51	411	401	423	...	...	...
Sopore ...	536	581	489	551	535	570	277	304	249	387	409	363	99	116	81	363	399	325	...	...	...
Bárámula ...	543	518	570	630	598	675	249	332	157	378	400	355	62	87	31	385	396	377	...	...	...
Total Kashmir Urban ...	504	522	484	737	693	785	306	352	258	475	520	426	96	122	67	352	369	333	...	...	...
Total Urban whole State...	520	551	484	735	700	776	321	366	269	469	507	425	108	131	81	371	388	352	...	...	...

CHRISTIANS.

	Under 5.			5—9.			10—14.			15—19.			20—24.			25—29.			30—34.		
	Total.	Males.	Females.	Total.	Males.	Females.	Total.	Males.	Females.	Total.	Males.	Females.	Total.	Males.	Females.	Total.	Males.	Females.	Total.	Males.	Females.
Urban Population Jammu.																					
Jammu ...	4	3	1	...	...	...	...	...	...	2	...	2	2	...	2	1	...	1	3	3	...
Batála ...	...	...	...	...	...	...	...	...	...	...	...	...	...	...	...	...	...	...	...	...	...
Mirpur ...	...	...	...	...	...	...	...	...	...	...	...	...	...	...	...	...	...	...	...	...	...
Punch ...	...	...	...	...	...	...	...	...	...	...	...	...	...	...	...	...	...	...	...	...	...
Total Jammu Urban ...	4	3	1	...	...	...	...	...	...	2	...	2	2	...	2	1	...	1	8	3	...
Urban Population Kashmir.																					
Srinagar ...	20	10	10	15	9	6	4	2	2	4	...	4	8	3	5	17	5	12	15	10	5
Anantnág ...	...	...	...	...	...	...	...	...	...	...	...	...	1	...	1	...	...	...	...	...	...
Sopore ...	...	...	...	...	...	...	...	...	...	...	...	...	...	...	...	...	...	...	...	...	...
Bárámula ...	...	...	...	...	...	...	...	...	...	...	...	...	...	...	...	...	...	...	...	...	...
Total Kashmir Urban ...	20	10	10	15	9	6	4	2	2	4	...	4	9	3	6	17	5	12	15	10	5
Total Urban whole State	24	13	11	15	9	6	4	2	2	6	...	6	11	3	8	18	5	13	18	18	5

CHRISTIANS.—(*continued.*)

	35—39.			40—44.			45—49.			50—54.			55—59.			60 and over.			Unspecified.		
	Total.	Males.	Females.	Total.	Males.	Females.	Total.	Males.	Females.	Total.	Males.	Females.	Total.	Males.	Females.	Total.	Males.	Females.	Total.	Males.	Females.
Urban Population Jammu.																					
Jammu ...	...	...	...	1	1	...	1	...	1	...	...	...	...	...	...	...	...	...	...	...	...
Batála ...	...	...	...	...	...	...	...	...	...	...	...	...	...	...	...	...	...	...	...	...	...
Mirpur ...	...	...	...	...	...	...	...	...	...	...	...	...	...	...	...	...	...	...	...	...	...
Punch ...	...	...	...	...	...	...	...	...	...	...	...	...	...	...	...	...	...	...	...	...	...
Total Jammu Urban ...	...	...	...	1	1	...	1	...	1	...	...	...	...	...	...	...	...	...	...	...	...
Urban Population Kashmir.																					
Srinagar ...	10	2	8	9	5	4	8	5	3	3	3	...	4	1	3	2	2	...	...	...	...
Anantnág ...	...	...	...	1	1	...	...	...	...	...	...	...	...	...	...	...	...	...	...	...	...
Sopore ...	...	...	...	...	...	...	...	...	...	...	...	...	...	...	...	...	...	...	...	...	...
Bárámula ...	...	...	...	...	...	...	...	...	...	...	...	...	...	...	...	...	...	...	...	...	...
Total Kashmír Urban ...	10	2	8	10	6	4	8	5	3	3	3	...	4	1	3	2	2	...	...	...	...
Total Urban whole State	10	2	8	11	7	4	9	5	4	3	3	...	4	1	3	2	2	...	...	...	...

PROPORTION PER 10,000. (CHRISTIANS.)

	Under 5.			5—9.			10—14.			15—19.			20—24.			25—29.			30—34.		
	Total.	Males.	Females.	Total.	Males.	Females.	Total.	Males.	Females.	Total.	Males.	Females.	Total.	Males.	Females.	Total.	Males.	Females.	Total.	Males.	Females.
Urban Population Jammu.																					
Jammu ...	2,857	4,285	1,429	...	...	...	...	...	...	1,429	...	2,857	1,429	...	2,857	714	...	1,429	2,143	4,286	...
Batála ...	...	...	...	...	...	...	...	...	...	...	...	...	...	...	...	...	...	...	...	...	...
Mirpur ...	...	...	...	...	...	...	...	...	...	...	...	...	...	...	...	...	...	...	...	...	...
Punch ...	...	...	...	...	...	...	...	...	...	...	...	...	...	...	...	...	...	...	...	...	...
Total Jammu Urban ...	2,857	4,285	1,429	...	...	...	...	...	...	1,429	...	2,857	1,429	...	2,857	714	...	1,429	2,143	4,286	...
Urban Population Kashmir.																					
Srinagar ...	1,681	1,754	1,613	1,261	1,579	968	336	350	323	336	...	646	672	526	806	1,429	878	1,935	1,261	1,754	806
Anantnág ...	...	...	...	...	...	...	...	...	...	...	...	...	5,000	...	10,000	...	...	...	...	...	...
Sopore ...	...	...	...	...	...	...	...	...	...	...	...	...	...	...	...	...	...	...	...	...	...
Bárámula ...	...	...	...	...	...	...	...	...	...	...	...	...	...	...	...	...	...	...	...	...	...
Total Kashmír Urban ...	1,653	1,724	1,587	1,240	1,552	952	330	345	317	330	...	636	744	517	952	1,405	862	1,904	1,240	1,724	793
Total Urban whole State	1,778	2,000	1,571	1,111	1,385	857	296	308	286	444	...	857	815	461	1,148	1,834	769	1,857	1,834	2,000	714

PROPORTION PER 10,000. (CHRISTIANS.—*continued.*)

	35—39.			40—44.			45—49.			50—54.			55—59.			60 AND OVER.			UNSPECIFIED.		
	Total.	Males.	Females.	Total.	Males.	Females.	Total.	Males.	Females.	Total.	Males.	Females.	Total.	Males.	Females.	Total.	Males.	Females.	Total.	Males.	Females.
URBAN POPULATION JAMMU.																					
Jammu ...	...	...	...	714	1,429	...	714	...	1,428	...	...	...	...	...	...	...	...	...	...	...	...
Batála ...	...	...	...	...	...	...	...	...	...	...	...	...	...	...	...	...	...	...	...	...	...
Mirpur ...	...	...	...	...	...	...	...	...	...	...	...	...	...	...	...	...	...	...	...	...	...
Punch ...	...	...	...	...	...	...	...	...	...	...	...	...	...	...	...	...	...	...	...	...	...
Total Jammu Urban ...	...	...	...	714	1,429	...	714	...	1,428	...	...	...	...	...	...	...	...	...	...	...	...
URBAN POPULATION KASHMIR.																					
Srinagar ...	840	351	1,290	756	878	646	672	878	484	252	526	...	336	175	483	168	351	...	...	...	...
Anantnág ...	...	...	...	500°	10,000	...	...	...	...	...	...	...	...	...	...	...	...	...	...	...	...
Sopore ...	...	...	...	...	...	...	...	...	...	...	...	...	...	...	...	...	...	...	...	...	...
Bárámula ...	...	...	...	...	...	...	...	...	...	...	...	...	...	...	...	...	...	...	...	...	...
Total Kashmir Urban ...	627	345	1,271	827	1,035	636	661	862	476	248	517	...	330	172	476	165	345	...	...	...	...
Total Urban whole State	741	308	1,143	815	1,077	572	666	769	571	222	461	...	296	154	429	148	308	...	...	...	...

PARSIS.

	Under 5.			5—9.			10—14.			15—19.			20—24.			25—29.			30—34.		
	Total.	Males.	Females.	Total.	Males.	Females.	Total.	Males.	Females.	Total.	Males.	Females.	Total.	Males.	Females.	Total.	Males.	Females.	Total.	Males.	Females.
Urban Population Jammu.																					
Jammu ...	...	...	...	...	...	...	...	...	...	...	...	...	...	...	...	...	...	...	...	...	...
Batála ...	...	...	...	...	...	...	...	...	...	...	...	...	...	...	...	...	...	...	...	...	...
Mirpur ...	...	...	...	...	...	...	...	...	...	...	...	...	...	...	...	...	...	...	...	...	...
Punch ...	...	...	...	...	...	...	...	...	...	...	...	...	...	...	...	...	...	...	...	...	...
Total Jammu Urban ...	...	...	...	...	...	...	...	...	...	...	...	...	...	...	...	...	...	...	...	...	...
Urban Population Kashmir.																					
Srinagar ...	1	1	...	...	...	...	1	1	...	1	1	...	1	...	1	...	...	...	1	1	...
Anantnág ...	...	...	...	...	...	...	...	...	...	...	...	...	...	...	...	...	...	...	...	...	...
Sopore ...	...	...	...	...	...	...	...	...	...	...	...	...	...	...	...	...	...	...	...	...	...
Bárámula ...	...	...	...	...	...	...	...	...	...	...	...	...	...	...	...	...	...	...	...	...	...
Total Kashmir Urban ...	1	1	...	...	...	...	1	1	...	1	1	..	1	...	1	...	...	...	1	1	...
Total Urban whole State ...	1	1	...	...	...	...	1	1	...	1	1	...	1	...	1	...	...	...	1	1	...

PARSIS—(*continued*).

	35—39.			40—44.			45—49.			50—54.			55—59.			60 AND OVER.			UNSPECIFIED.		
	Total.	Males.	Females.	Total.	Males.	Females.	Total.	Males.	Females.	Total.	Males.	Females.	Total.	Males.	Females.	Total.	Males.	Females.	Total.	Males.	Females.
URBAN POPULATION JAMMU.																					
Jammu ...	...	...	...	...	...	...	...	...	...	...	...	...	...	...	...	...	...	...	...	...	...
Batála ...	...	...	...	...	...	...	...	...	...	...	...	...	...	...	...	...	...	...	...	...	...
Mirpur ...	...	...	...	...	...	...	...	...	...	...	...	...	...	...	...	...	...	...	...	...	...
Punch ...	—	...	...	...	...	...	...	...	...	...	...	...	...	...	...	...	...	...	...	...	...
Total Jammu Urban ...	...	...	...	...	...	...	...	...	...	...	...	...	...	...	...	...	...	...	...	...	...
URBAN POPULATION KASHMIR.																					
Srinagar ...	1	1	...	1	...	1	1	1	...	...	...	...	...	...	...	...	...	...	...	...	...
Anantnág ...	...	...	...	...	...	...	...	...	...	...	...	...	...	...	...	...	...	...	...	...	...
Sopore ...	...	...	...	...	...	...	...	...	...	...	...	...	...	...	...	...	...	...	...	...	...
Bárámula ...	...	...	...	...	...	...	...	...	...	...	...	...	...	...	...	...	...	...	...	...	...
Total Kashmír Urban ...	1	1	...	1	...	1	1	1	...	...	...	...	...	...	...	...	...	...	...	...	...
Total Urban whole State ...	1	1	...	1	...	1	1	1	...	...	...	...	...	...	...	...	...	...	...	...	...

PROPORTION PER 10,000 (PARSIS).

	Under 5.			5—9.			10—14.			15—19.			20—24.			25—29.			30—34.		
	Total.	Males.	Females.	Total.	Males.	Females.	Total.	Males.	Females.	Total.	Males.	Females.	Total.	Males.	Females.	Total.	Males.	Females.	Total.	Males.	Females.
Urban Population Jammu.																					
Jammu ...	...	...	...	...	...	...	...	...	...	...	...	...	...	...	...	...	...	...	...	...	...
Batála ...	...	...	...	...	...	...	...	...	...	...	...	...	...	...	...	...	...	...	...	...	...
Mirpore ...	...	...	...	...	...	...	...	...	...	...	...	...	...	...	...	...	...	...	...	...	...
Punch ...	...	...	...	...	...	...	...	...	...	...	...	...	...	...	...	...	...	...	...	...	...
Total Jammu Urban ...	...	...	...	...	...	...	...	...	...	...	...	...	...	...	...	...	...	...	...	...	...
Urban Population Kashmir.																					
Srinagar ...	1,250	1,666	...	...	...	...	1,250	1,666	...	1,250	1,667	...	1,250	...	500	...	...	...	1,250	1,667	...
Anantnág ...	...	...	...	...	...	...	...	...	...	...	...	...	...	...	...	...	...	...	...	...	...
Sopore ...	...	...	...	...	...	...	...	...	...	...	...	...	...	...	...	...	...	...	...	...	—
Bárámula ...	...	...	...	...	...	...	...	...	...	...	...	...	...	...	...	...	...	...	...	...	...
Total Kashmir Urban ...	1,250	1,666	...	...	...	...	1,250	1,666	...	1,250	1,667	...	1,250	...	500	...	...	...	1,250	1,667	...
Total Urban whole State	1,250	1,666	...	...	...	...	1,250	1,666	...	1,250	1,667	...	1,250	...	500	...	...	...	1250	1,667	...

PROPORTION PER 10,000 (PARSIS—*continued*).

	35—39.			40—44.			45—49.			50—54.			55—59.			60 AND OVER.			UNSPECIFIED.		
	Total.	Males.	Females.	Total.	Males.	Females.	Total.	Males.	Females.	Total.	Males.	Females.	Total.	Males	Females.	Total.	Males.	Females.	Total.	Males.	Females.
URBAN POPULATION JAMMU.																					
Jammu	...	...	...	...	...	...	...	...	...	...	...	...	...	...	...	...	...	...	...	...	...
Bátala	...	...	...	...	...	...	...	...	...	...	...	...	...	...	...	...	...	...	...	...	...
Mirpore	...	...	...	...	...	...	...	...	...	...	...	...	...	...	...	...	...	...	...	...	...
Punch	...	...	...	...	...	...	...	...	...	...	...	...	...	...	...	...	...	...	...	...	...
Total Jammu Urban ...	...	...	...	...	...	...	...	...	...	...	...	...	...	...	...	...	...	...	...	...	...
URBAN POPULATION KASHMIR.																					
Srinagar	1,250	1,667	...	1,250	...	500	1,250	1,667	...	...	...	...	...	...	...	...	...	...	...	...	...
Anantnág	...	...	...	...	...	...	...	...	...	...	...	...	...	...	...	...	...	...	...	...	...
Sopore	...	...	...	...	...	...	...	...	...	...	...	...	...	...	...	...	...	...	...	...	...
Bárámula	...	...	...	...	...	...	...	...	...	...	...	...	...	...	...	...	...	...	...	...	...
Total Kashmír Urban ...	1,250	1,667	...	1,250	...	500	1,250	1,667	...	...	...	...	...	...	...	...	...	...	...	...	...
Total Urban whole State...	1,250	1,667	...	1,250	...	500	1,250	1,667	...	...	...	...	...	...	...	...	...	...	...	...	...

116. Speaking generally it appears :—

(1).—That the ratio of females per 10,000 is higher than that of males in each of the age periods between 0-5.

(2).—That at the age of 5-9 the inequality between males and females is reduced to a minimum, while at the age of 10-14, there is an abrupt rise in the number of males with a corresponding decrease in females.

(3)—That between the age periods of 15 to 34, there is again a preponderance in the ratio of females, as compared with males, the only exception being in the Urban population of Jammu Province and the Rural Frontier Districts of Ladákh, Skardu and Gilgit, in which notably in the former, the proportion of males is in excess of females.

(4).—That between 35 and 44 the ratios vary most irregularly.

(5).—That in the subsequent age periods, the ratio of males again shows generally a marked increase, compared with that of females, the only exceptions being in the Urban population of Jammu and Frontier Districts of Ladákh, Skardu and Gilgit.

117. The subjoined table shows the difference between the proportions per 10,000 of males and females at each age period :—

Distribution of Age.	Whole State.						Jammu Province.						Kashmir Province.						Total Frontier Districts Ladakh, Skardu & Gilgit.	
	Total whole State.		Urban population.		Rural population.		Total.		Urban population.		Rural population.		Total.		Urban population.		Rural population.		Rural population.	
	Males.	Females.	Males.	Females.	Males.	Females.	Males	Females.	Males.	Females.	Males.	Females.	Males.	Females.	Males.	Females.	Males.	Females.	Males.	Females.
Under 1 year	...	59	...	60	...	59	...	61	...	82	...	59	...	55	...	42	...	58	...	57
1 do.	...	17	...	26	...	16	...	18	...	51	...	16	...	15	...	17	...	10	...	28
2 years	...	39	...	63	...	37	...	37	...	61	...	34	...	45	...	51	...	45	...	31
3 do.	...	53	...	67	...	52	...	55	...	83	...	53	...	48	...	47	...	49	...	61
4 do.	...	27	...	46	...	25	...	36	...	95	...	33	...	15	...	28	...	16	...	28
Total under 5 ...	...	195	...	262	...	189	...	207	...	372	...	195	...	178	...	185	...	178	...	205
5—9	...	24	...	115	...	16	...	43	...	190	...	32	9	...	...	53	20	...	...	57
10—14	164	...	173	...	164	...	159	...	45	...	165	...	184	...	223	...	177	...	77	...
15—19	4	...	38	...	1	...	...	9	...	33	...	9	16	...	67	...	4	...	56	...
20—24	...	134	...	98	...	138	...	125	9	...	...	134	...	141	...	136	...	142	...	145
25—29	...	76	...	9	...	82	...	76	118	...	...	87	...	94	...	83	...	97	11	...
30—34	...	38	...	22	...	41	...	36	117	...	...	44	...	52	...	82	...	46	...	4
35—39	46	...	92	...	42	...	60	...	147	...	57	...	46	...	61	...	43	...	...	78
40—44	...	6	...	51	...	3	15	...	46	...	12	...	...	40	...	86	...	32	11	...
45—49	68	...	105	...	66	...	79	...	94	...	78	...	79	...	100	...	76	...	...	82
50—54	59	...	66	...	58	...	61	...	47	...	61	...	56	...	75	...	54	...	34	...
55—59	33	...	59	...	31	...	32	...	28	...	32	...	35	...	62	...	31	...	20	...
60 and over	81	...	24	...	87	...	90	...	...	44	96	...	80	...	36	...	90	...	...	4
Unspecified	18	...	...	...	21	...	...	...	...	11	...	...	...	1	...	...	...	1	366	...

118. Difference in proportions per 10,000 of males and females at each age period.

COMPARISON WITH OTHER INDIAN PROVINCES.

Distribution of Age.	Kashmir State.		India.		Ajmere.		Assam.		Berar.		Sindh.		Central Provinces.	
	Males.	Females.	Males.	Females.	Males.	Females.	Males.	Females.	Males.	Females.	Males.	Females.	Males.	Females.
Under 1 year	...	59	...	12	...	49	...	37	...	32	...	37	...	8
1 do.	...	17	...	17	...	23	...	25	...	30	...	30	...	21
2 years	...	39	...	28	...	14	...	42	...	42	...	63	...	33
3 do.	...	53	...	34	...	34	...	49	...	49	...	50	...	40
4 do.	...	27	...	11	...	12	...	20	...	24	...	19	...	8
Total under 5 ...	...	195	...	102	...	132	...	173	...	177	...	199	...	110
5—9	...	24	49	...	...	7	98	...	...	96	99	...	59	...
10—14	164	...	208	...	155	...	162	...	142	...	220	...	196	...
15—19	4	...	32	...	61	...	...	61	...	82	58	...	17	...
20—24	...	134	...	106	...	36	...	83	...	223	...	91	...	154
25—29	...	76	...	29	37	...	...	114	24	...	...	25	...	68
30—34	...	38	4	...	...	...	66	...	107	...	...	25	60	...
35—39	46	...	60	...	65	...	86	...	154	...	78	...	46	...
40—44	...	6	...	3	...	74	47	...	66	...	...	52	67	...
45—49	68	...	27	...	31	...	53	...	56	...	38	...	28	...
50—54	59	...	...	28	...	47	...	2	29	...	4	...	...	...
55—59	33	...	4	...	27	...	19	...	23	...	16	...	...	4
60 and over	81	...	...	116	...	80	...	98	...	23	...	121	...	137
Unspecified	18	...	...	...	...	...	...	...	...	...	...	...	...	...

119. These figures prove that generally speaking, the condition of the population of the Kashmír State bears a normal comparison with other Indian Provinces.

120. The ratio per 10,000 of males and females at each age period in the Kashmír State, contrasted with other Provinces, stands as below :—

At each age period between 0—5 years, the Kashmír ratio as well as those of other Indian Provinces are similar so far that the ratio of females is generally higher than that of males, but Kashmír presents certain peculiarities which require special mention, *viz.* :—

At 0—1, the Kashmír ratio of females is higher than that of each of the Indian Provinces cited above, the nearest approach to it being in Ajmere.

At 1, it is lower than all the Indian Provinces.

At 2, it is higher than Ajmere and Central Provinces, extremely lower than Sindh, and slightly lower than Assam and Berar.

At 3 and 4, it is again higher than all the Indian Provinces.

121. The apparent deductions from these statistics are :—

(1).—That births in Kashmír are more numerous than in other Indian Provinces.

(2).—That deaths between 0—2 years in Kashmír are more numerous than in other Indian Provinces.

(3).—That the vitality of children between 2—4 years is more favorable in Kashmír than in other provinces.

(4).—That as in Kashmír, so in other provinces, the increase in the ratio of females is reduced to a minimum at the age of 4, accounted for by the admitted fact that female children are not properly taken care of, and therefore die in greater numbers than males ; at the age period of 5—9 the ratio of females in Kashmír is higher than that of males, being slightly lower than the age period immediately preceding it, but singularly enough, the corresponding ratios in other Provinces vary considerably, there being an abrupt rise in the ratio of males, in India, Assam, Sindh and Central Provinces, so that the only Provinces maintaining the increased proportion of females, are Ajmere and Berars. This is mainly attributed to climatic influences and the consequent ravages of small-pox, the effects of which are obviously more injurious to females than males. The abrupt rise in the ratio of males as compared with females at the age of 10—14 and its continuity at the subsequent age period of 15—19 which is perceptible throughout Kashmír and the Indian Provinces, is a problem well worth examination and solution. We have proved that there are greater female births than male births, that more or less, the increase in females continues uniformly till the age of 5, and that at the subsequent age period (5—9), there is a susceptibility of increase in the ratio of males, because that is the age when children are generally affected by small-pox and other fatal diseases, and the negligent treatment of female patients appear to account satisfactorily for the corresponding increase in proportion of males, but it is impossible to apply this proposition to the age periods of 10—14 and 15—19, at which female lives undoubtedly become as valuable as male lives. I have given the subject very careful consideration, but in the absence of the Census Reports of other Provinces, can only suggest that early consummation of marriage and premature child birth probably accounts for the loss of female life at these age periods.

The increase in the proportion of females at the age periods between 20—34 and 40—44 is attributed to absence of able bodied males on employment in the Punjab and elsewhere.

On the other hand, the increased ratio in males at age periods between 45 and 60 and over, is due to greater longevity in males than in females.

ALL RELIGIONS.

Territorial Sub-divisions.	Under one year.			One year.			Two years.			Three years.			Four years.			Total under five.		
	Both sexes.	Males.	Females.	Both sexes.	Males.	Females.	Both sexes.	Males.	Females.	Both sexes.	Males.	Females.	Both sexes.	Males.	Females.	Both sexes.	Males.	Females.
Jammu Urban	1,859	1,053	806	721	384	337	1,198	668	530	1,294	700	594	1,506	817	689	6,578	3,622	2,956
Do. Rural	57,194	28,369	28,825	20,998	10,591	10,407	40,326	20,254	20,072	48,716	24,079	24,637	47,350	24,032	23,318	2,14,584	1,07,325	1,07,259
Total Jammu Province ...	59,053	29,422	29,631	21,719	10,975	10,744	41,524	20,922	20,602	50,010	24,779	25,231	48,856	24,849	24,007	2,21,162	1,10,947	1,10,215
Kashmír Urban	6,544	3,303	3,241	1,742	860	882	4,999	2,460	2,539	5,328	2,644	2,684	4,235	2,135	2,100	22,848	11,402	11,446
Do. Rural	45,147	22,753	22,394	13,510	6,853	6,657	35,454	17,905	17,549	39,234	19,820	19,414	34,065	17,773	16,292	1,67,410	85,104	82,306
Total Kashmír Province ...	51,691	26,056	25,635	15,252	7,713	7,539	40,453	20,365	20,088	44,562	22,464	22,098	38,300	19,908	18,392	1,90,258	96,506	93,752
Total Frontier Districts (Ladákh, Skardu and Gilgit.)	3,476	1,583	1,893	2,711	1,299	1,412	3,365	1,625	1,740	4,186	1,936	2,250	3,658	1,791	1,867	17,396	8,234	9,162
Whole State Urban	8,403	4,356	4,047	2,463	1,244	1,219	6,197	3,128	3,069	6,622	3,344	3,278	5,741	2,952	2,789	29,426	15,024	14,402
Do. Rural	1,05,817	52,705	53,112	37,219	18,743	18,476	79,145	39,784	39,361	92,136	45,835	46,301	85,073	43,596	41,477	3,99,390	2,00,663	1,98,727
Total whole State ...	1,14,220	57,061	57,159	39,682	19,987	19,695	85,342	42,912	42,430	98,758	49,179	49,579	90,814	46,548	44,266	4,28,816	2,15,687	2,13,129

ALL RELIGIONS.

Territorial Sub-divisions.	Ratio per ten thousand.																	
	Under one year.			*One year.*			*Two years.*			*Three years.*			*Four years.*			*Total under five.*		
	Both sexes.	Males.	Females.	Both sexes.	Males.	Females.	Both sexes.	Males.	Females.	Both sexes.	Males.	Females.	Both sexes.	Males.	Females.	Both sexes.	Males.	Females.
Jammu Urban	341	310	392	132	113	164	220	197	258	238	206	289	276	241	336	1,207	1,067	1,439
Do. Rural	413	385	444	152	144	160	291	275	309	352	327	380	341	327	360	1,549	1,458	1,653
Total Jammu Province ...	410	382	443	151	142	160	289	271	308	347	322	377	339	323	359	1,536	1,440	1,647
Kashmír Urban	457	437	479	121	114	131	349	325	376	372	350	397	295	282	310	1,594	1,508	1,693
Do. Rural	560	533	591	168	166	176	440	418	463	487	463	512	423	414	430	2,078	1,994	2,172
Total Kashmír Province ...	545	519	574	160	154	169	426	405	450	470	447	495	404	396	411	2,005	1,921	2,099
Total Frontier Districts (Ladákh, Skardu and Gilgit.)	224	196	253	174	161	189	216	202	233	270	240	301	235	222	250	1,119	1,021	1,226
Whole State Urban	425	399	459	125	113	139	313	285	348	335	305	372	290	269	315	1,488	1,371	1,633
Do. Rural	451	423	482	159	151	167	337	320	357	393	368	420	362	351	376	1,702	1,613	1,802
Total whole State	449	422	481	156	148	165	335	317	356	388	363	416	357	344	371	1,685	1,594	1,789

122. Assuming the figures under one year as representing approximately the births during twelve months, the difference between each subsequent period shows approximately the ratio of deaths every year. This proposition is based on the theory that supposing the population to have remained stationary, those returned under 4—5 years ought to have been at least as numerous as those now under one year. The Census being taken in February 1891, and the State year commencing on 11th April, it follows that those returned under one year, were ten months old; add to this the average for two months obtained by dividing the figures under one year by five, we have the following, as representing approximately the average births that take place during a year of 12 months. Calculated at this rate, the ratio of births per ten thousand of the male and female population is :—

	Total Births.			Total under 5.			Average annual Population.			Average Deaths.		
	Both sexes.	Males.	Females.	Both sexes.	Males.	Females.	Both sexes.	Males.	Females.	Both sexes.	Males.	Females.
Jammu Urban	411	370	472	1,207	1,067	1,439	241	213	288	170	157	184
Do. Rural	493	460	532	1,549	1,458	1,653	309	291	330	184	169	202
Total Jammu Province ...	490	457	531	1,536	1,440	1,647	307	288	329	183	169	202
Kashmír Urban	547	524	575	1,594	1,508	1,693	319	301	338	228	223	237
Do. Rural	672	639	709	2,078	1,994	2,172	415	399	434	257	240	275
Total Kashmír Province ...	654	623	689	2,005	1,921	2,099	401	384	420	253	239	269
Frontier Districts	269	235	303	1,119	1,021	1,226	224	204	245	45	31	58
Urban whole State	510	478	551	1,488	1,371	1,633	299	274	326	211	204	225
Rural Do.	541	508	578	1,702	1,613	1,802	340	322	360	201	186	218
Total whole State	538	506	577	1,685	1,594	1,789	337	319	358	201	187	219

The above figures are by no means so reliable as could be desired, because in calculating the average births no allowance has been made for the deaths which must have taken place during the year of enumeration, the figures returned under one year representing the net results of the ten months immediately preceding the night of Census; yet they may be held as approximately giving an idea of the reductions which take place during the period of infancy from 1 to 5 years, and nothing more deserves the attention of the statistician than to observe with regret that more than half of our children after birth, and nearly one-third after attaining the age of one year, are annihilated from various causes, the majority of which it is within human energy and foresight to avoid with moderate yet certain success.

123. The averages returned above show as a fact that there are more deaths among female infants than among males, that the mortality is rather high in the Kashmír Province than in Jammu; compared with other Provinces in India we have :—

	Total Births.			Total under 5.			Average annual Population.			Average Deaths.		
	Both sexes.	Males.	Females.	Both sexes.	Males.	Females.	Both sexes.	Males.	Females.	Both sexes.	Males.	Females.
Kashmír State	538	506	577	1,685	1,594	1,789	337	319	358	201	187	219
Ajmere	489	463	522	1,491	1,431	1,563	298	286	312	191	177	219
Assam	336	314	358	1,734	1,652	1,825	346	330	365	—10	—16	—7
Berar	384	366	404	1,475	1,390	1,567	295	278	313	89	88	91
Sindh	370	356	401	1,582	1,492	1,691	316	298	338	54	58	63
Central Provinces	340	337	346	1,611	1,557	1,667	322	311	333	18	26	13
India	322	315	330	1,368	1,318	1,420	273	263	284	49	52	46

124. Comparing the ratios returned for the various divisions of the State there are fewer births and larger deaths in the Urban than in the Rural population, that the averages of Jammu Province are generally lower than those of Kashmír, that the lowest ratio is obtained in the Frontier Districts, but the vitality there appears to be better than that of any other part of the State.

HINDUS INCLUDING JAINS AND SIKHS.

Territorial Sub-divisions.	Under one year.			One year.			Two years.			Three years.			Four years.			Total under five.		
	Both sexes.	Males.	Females.	Both sexes.	Males.	Females.	Both sexes.	Males.	Females.	Both sexes.	Males.	Females.	Both sexes.	Males.	Females.	Both sexes.	Males.	Females.
Jammu Urban	1,059	605	454	426	240	186	705	414	291	765	425	340	888	480	408	3,843	2,164	1,679
Do. Rural	21,033	10,538	10,495	8,977	4,518	4,459	14,616	7,388	7,228	17,604	8,740	8,864	17,229	8,679	8,550	79,459	39,863	39,596
Total Jammu Province ...	22,092	11,143	10,949	9,403	4,758	4,645	15,321	7,802	7,519	18,369	9,165	9,204	18,117	9,159	8,958	83,302	42,027	41,275
Kashmír Urban	982	496	486	291	145	146	739	378	361	744	363	381	695	356	339	3,451	1,738	1,713
Do. Rural	1,745	892	853	369	199	170	1,199	599	600	1,320	688	632	1,183	620	563	5,816	2,998	2,818
Total Kashmír Province ...	2,727	1,388	1,339	660	344	316	1,938	977	961	2,064	1,051	1,013	1,878	976	902	9,267	4,736	4,531
Ladákh	...	...	...	...	...	...	...	...	...	1	...	1	...	...	...	1	...	1
Skardu	...	...	...	...	...	...	...	...	...	...	...	...	...	...	...	...	...	...
Gilgit	...	...	...	...	...	...	...	...	...	...	...	...	...	...	...	...	...	...
Whole State Urban	2,041	1,101	940	717	385	332	1,444	792	652	1,509	788	721	1,583	836	747	7,294	3,902	3,392
Do. Rural	22,778	11,430	11,348	9,346	4,717	4,629	15,815	7,987	7,828	18,925	9,428	9,497	18,412	9,299	9,113	85,276	42,861	42,415
Total whole State ...	24,819	12,531	12,288	10,063	5,102	4,961	17,259	8,779	8,480	20,434	10,216	10,218	19,995	10,135	9,860	92,570	46,763	45,807

HINDUS INCLUDING JAINS AND SIKHS.

Territorial Sub-divisions.	Ratio per ten thousand.																	
	Under one year			*One year.*			*Two years.*			*Three years.*			*Four years.*			*Total under five.*		
	Both sexes.	Males.	Females.	Both sexes.	Males.	Females.	Both sexes.	Males.	Females.	Both sexes.	Males.	Females.	Both sexes.	Males.	Females.	Both sexes.	Males.	Females.
Jammu Urban	313	282	368	126	112	151	209	193	236	226	198	275	263	224	331	1,137	1,009	1,361
Do. Rural	348	327	372	149	142	158	242	229	257	291	271	315	285	270	303	1,315	1,239	1,405
Total Jammu Province	346	324	372	148	139	158	240	227	256	288	267	313	284	265	305	1,306	1,222	1,404
Kashmír Urban	339	311	374	101	91	112	255	237	278	257	228	293	240	223	261	1,192	1,090	1,318
Do. Rural	474	422	543	101	94	109	325	283	382	358	326	402	321	293	358	1,579	1,418	1,794
Total Kashmír Province... ...	415	374	467	100	93	110	295	263	335	314	283	352	285	263	314	1,409	1,276	1,578
Ladákh	...	...	...	...	...	...	...	...	...	55	...	1,000	...	...	...	55	...	1,000
Skardu	...	...	...	...	...	...	...	...	...	...	...	...	...	...	...	...	...	...
Gilgit	...	...	...	...	...	...	...	...	...	...	...	...	...	...	...	...	...	...
Whole State Urban...	325	294	371	114	103	131	230	212	257	241	211	285	252	224	295	1,162	1,044	1,339
Do. Rural	355	333	382	146	137	156	247	232	263	295	274	319	287	271	306	1,330	1,247	1,426
Total whole State	353	329	381	143	134	154	245	230	263	290	268	316	284	266	305	1,315	1,227	1,419

MOHAMEDANS.

Territorial Sub-divisions.	Under one year.			One year.			Two years.			Three years.			Four years.			Total under five.		
	Both sexes.	Males.	Females.	Both sexes.	Males.	Females.	Both sexes.	Males.	Females.	Both sexes.	Males.	Females.	Both sexes.	Males.	Females.	Both sexes.	Males.	Females.
Jummu Urban	799	448	351	294	143	151	491	252	239	529	275	254	618	337	281	2,731	1,455	1,276
Do. Rural	36,058	17,792	18,266	12,016	6,070	5,946	25,647	12,825	12,822	31,015	15,293	15,722	30,042	15,309	14,733	1,34,778	67,289	67,489
Total Jummu Province ...	36,857	18,240	18,617	12,310	6,213	6,097	26,138	13,077	13,061	31,544	15,568	15,976	30,660	15,646	15,014	1,37,509	68,744	68,765
Kashmír Urban	5,560	2,806	2,754	1,448	714	734	4,255	2,079	2,176	4,575	2,277	2,298	3,538	1,777	1,761	19,376	9,653	9,723
Do. Rural	43,402	21,861	21,541	13,141	6,654	6,487	34,255	17,306	16,949	37,914	19,132	18,782	32,882	17,153	15,729	1,61,594	82,106	79,488
Total Kashmír Province ...	48,962	24,667	24,295	14,589	7,368	7,221	38,510	19,385	19,125	42,489	21,409	21,080	36,420	18,930	17,490	1,80,970	91,759	89,211
Ladákh	37	16	21	58	27	31	56	30	26	78	35	43	75	41	34	304	149	155
Skardu	3,045	1,383	1,662	2,315	1,109	1,206	2,940	1,417	1,523	3,552	1,622	1,930	3,085	1,506	1,579	14,937	7,037	7,900
Gilgit	1	...	1	...	...	...	1	...	1	...	...	...	...	...	...	2	...	2
Whole State Urban	6,359	3,254	3,105	1,742	857	885	4,746	2,331	2,415	5,104	2,552	2,552	4,156	2,114	2,042	22,107	11,108	10,999
Do. Rural	82,543	41,052	41,491	27,530	13,860	13,670	62,899	31,578	31,321	72,559	36,082	36,477	66,084	34,009	32,075	3,11,615	1,56,581	1,55,034
Total whole State	88,902	44,306	44,596	29,272	14,717	14,555	67,645	33,909	33,736	77,663	38,634	39,029	70,240	36,123	34,117	3,33,722	1,67,689	1,66,033

MOHAMEDANS.

Territorial distribution.	Ratio per ten thousand.																	
	Under one year.			*One year.*			*Two years.*			*Three years.*			*Four years.*			*Total under five.*		
	Both sexes.	Males.	Females.	Both sexes.	Males.	Females.	Both sexes.	Males.	Females.	Both sexes.	Males.	Females.	Both sexes.	Males.	Females.	Both sexes.	Males.	Females.
Jammu Urban	386	358	429	142	114	184	237	202	292	256	220	310	299	270	343	1,320	1,164	1,558
Do. Rural	464	433	501	155	147	163	330	311	351	399	371	431	387	372	403	1,735	1,634	1,849
Total Jammu Province ...	462	429	498	154	146	163	328	309	351	396	367	428	384	369	403	1,724	1,620	1,843
Kashmír Urban	487	471	504	127	120	134	373	349	398	401	382	421	309	298	324	1,697	1,620	1,781
Do. Rural	564	539	593	171	164	179	445	426	466	493	471	517	429	424	433	2,102	2,024	2,188
Total Kashmír Province ...	555	530	581	165	158	173	436	417	458	481	460	504	412	407	419	2,049	1,972	2,135
Ladákh	124	103	146	194	174	215	187	194	181	261	225	299	251	264	236	1,017	960	1,077
Skardu	277	248	307	210	198	223	267	254	281	323	290	357	280	269	291	1,357	1,259	1,459
Gilgit	72	...	3,333	...	...	...	72	...	3,334	...	...	...	...	...	...	144	...	6,667
Whole State Urban	472	451	494	129	119	140	352	323	385	378	354	406	308	294	326	1,639	1,541	1,751
Do. Rural	498	469	529	166	158	175	379	361	400	437	412	465	398	389	409	1,878	1,789	1,978
Total whole State ...	496	468	527	163	155	172	377	358	398	433	407	461	392	382	403	1,861	1,770	1,961

BUDHISTS.

Territorial Sub-divisions.	Under one year.			One year.			Two years.			Three years.			Four years.			Total under five.		
	Both sexes.	Males.	Females.	Both sexes.	Males.	Females.	Both sexes.	Males.	Females.	Both sexes.	Males.	Females.	Both sexes.	Males.	Females.	Both sexes.	Males.	Females.
Jammu Urban	...	...	...	...	...	...	...	...	...	...	...	...	...	...	...	...	...	...
Do. Rural	103	39	64	5	3	2	60	38	22	96	46	50	78	44	34	342	170	172
Total Jammu Province ...	103	39	64	5	3	2	60	38	22	96	46	50	78	44	34	342	170	172
Kashmír Urban	...	...	...	...	...	...	...	...	...	...	...	...	...	...	...	...	...	...
Do. Rural	...	...	...	...	...	...	...	...	...	...	...	...	...	...	...	...	...	...
Total Kashmír Province ...	...	...	...	...	...	...	...	...	...	...	...	...	...	...	...	...	...	...
Ladákh	390	183	207	338	163	175	366	177	189	548	275	273	488	243	245	2,130	1,041	1,089
Skardu	2	1	1	...	...	...	2	1	1	6	3	3	10	1	9	20	6	14
Gilgit	...	...	...	...	...	...	...	...	...	...	...	...	...	...	...	...	...	...
Whole State Urban	...	...	...	...	...	...	...	...	...	...	...	...	...	...	...	...	...	...
Do. Rural	495	223	272	343	166	177	428	216	212	650	324	326	576	288	288	2,492	1,217	1,275
Total whole State	495	223	272	343	166	177	428	216	212	650	324	326	576	288	288	2,492	1,217	1,275

BUDHISTS.

Territorial Sub-divisions.	Ratio per ten thousand.																	
	Under one year.			*One year.*			*Two years.*			*Three years.*			*Four years.*			*Total under five.*		
	Both sexes.	Males.	Females.	Both sexes.	Males.	Females.	Both sexes.	Males.	Females.	Both sexes.	Males.	Females.	Both sexes.	Males.	Females.	Both sexes.	Males.	Females.
Jammu Urban	...	...	...	...	...	...	...	...	...	...	...	...	...	...	...	...	...	...
Do. Rural	240	179	303	11	14	9	140	174	104	224	211	236	182	202	161	797	780	813
Total Jammu Province ...	240	179	303	11	14	9	140	174	104	224	211	236	182	202	161	797	780	813
Kashmír Urban	...	...	...	...	...	...	...	...	...	...	...	...	...	...	...	...	...	...
Do. Rural	...	...	...	...	...	...	...	...	...	...	...	...	...	...	...	...	...	...
Total Kashmír Province ...	...	...	...	...	...	...	...	...	...	...	...	...	...	...	...	...	...	...
Ladákh	156	145	166	135	129	140	146	140	152	218	218	219	194	193	197	849	825	874
Skardu	84	68	110	...	...	...	84	67	109	251	203	330	419	67	989	838	405	1,538
Gilgit	...	...	...	...	...	...	...	...	...	...	...	...	...	...	...	...	...	...
Whole State Urban...	...	...	...	...	...	...	...	...	...	...	...	...	...	...	...	...	...	...
Do. Rural	167	149	185	115	111	121	145	145	145	219	217	222	195	193	196	841	815	869
Total whole State	167	149	185	115	111	121	145	145	145	219	217	222	195	193	196	841	815	869

CHRISTIANS.

Territorial Sub-divisions.	Under one year.			One year.			Two years.			Three years.			Four years.			Total under five.		
	Both sexes.	Males.	Females.	Both sexes.	Males.	Females.	Both sexes.	Males.	Females.	Both sexes.	Males.	Females.	Both sexes.	Males.	Females.	Both sexes.	Males.	Females.
Jammu Urban	1	...	1	1	1	...	2	2	...	...	...	...	...	...	...	4	3	1
Do. Rural	...	...	...	...	...	...	3	3	...	1	...	1	1	...	1	5	3	2
Total Jammu Province ...	1	...	1	1	1	...	5	5	...	1	...	1	1	...	1	9	6	3
Kashmír Urban	2	1	1	3	1	2	5	3	2	9	4	5	1	1	...	20	10	10
Do. Rural	...	...	...	...	...	...	...	...	...	...	...	...	...	...	...	...	...	...
Total Kashmír Province ...	2	1	1	3	1	2	5	8	2	9	4	5	1	1	...	20	10	10
Ladákh	1	...	1	...	...	...	...	...	...	1	1	...	...	...	...	2	1	1
Skardu	...	...	...	...	...	...	...	...	...	...	...	...	...	...	...	...	...	...
Gilgit	...	...	...	...	...	...	...	...	...	...	...	...	...	...	...	...	...	...
Whole State Urban	3	1	2	4	2	2	7	5	2	9	4	5	1	1	...	24	13	11
Do. Rural	1	...	1	...	...	...	3	3	...	2	1	1	1	...	1	7	4	3
Total whole State	4	1	3	4	2	2	10	8	2	11	5	6	2	1	1	31	17	14

CHRISTIANS.

Territorial Sub-divisions.	Ratio per ten thousand.																	
	Under one year.			*One year.*			*Two years.*			*Three years.*			*Four years.*			*Total under five.*		
	Both sexes.	Males.	Females.	Both sexes.	Males.	Females.	Both sexes.	Males.	Females.	Both sexes.	Males.	Females.	Both sexes.	Males.	Females.	Both sexes.	Males.	Females.
Jammu Urban	714	...	1,429	714	1,428	...	1,429	2,857	...	...	...	...	...	...	...	2,857	4,285	1,429
Do. Rural	...	...	...	...	...	...	938	1,765	...	312	...	667	313	...	666	1,563	1,765	1,333
Total Jammu Province ...	217	...	455	217	417	...	1,088	2,083	...	217	...	454	217	...	454	1,956	2,500	1,363
Kashmír Urban	165	172	159	248	173	318	413	517	317	744	690	793	83	172	...	1,653	1,724	1,587
Do. Rural...	...	...	...	...	...	...	...	...	...	...	...	...	...	...	...	...	...	...
Total Kashmír Province ...	138	130	147	207	130	294	345	390	294	621	519	735	68	130	...	1,379	1,299	1,470
Ladákh	400	...	714	...	...	...	...	...	...	400	909	...	...	...	...	800	909	714
Skardu	...	...	...	...	...	...	...	...	...	...	...	...	...	...	...	...	...	...
Gilgit	...	...	...	...	...	...	...	...	...	...	...	...	...	...	...	...	...	...
Whole State Urban	222	154	286	296	308	286	519	769	285	667	615	714	74	154	...	1,778	2,000	1,571
Do. Rural	121	...	285	...	...	...	361	625	...	241	208	286	120	...	286	843	833	857
Total whole State ...	183	88	285	184	177	190	459	708	191	505	443	572	91	89	95	1,422	1,505	1,333

Christian infants have the highest percentage, but considering that they number only 218, it is rather premature to draw any conclusions regarding them.

PARSIS.

Territorial Sub-divisions.	Under one year.			One year.			Two years.			Three years.			Four years.			Total under five.		
	Both sexes.	Males.	Females.	Both sexes.	Males.	Females.	Both sexes.	Males.	Females.	Both sexes.	Males.	Females.	Both sexes.	Males.	Females.	Both sexes.	Males.	Females.
Jammu Urban	...	...	...	...	...	...	...	...	...	...	...	...	...	...	...	...	...	...
Do. Rural	...	...	...	...	...	...	...	...	...	...	...	...	...	...	...	...	...	...
Total Jammu Province ...	...	...	...	...	...	...	...	...	...	...	...	...	...	...	...	...	...	...
Kashmír Urban	...	...	...	...	...	...	...	...	...	...	...	...	1	1	...	1	1	...
Do. Rural	...	...	...	...	...	...	...	...	...	...	...	...	...	...	...	...	...	...
Total Kashmír Province ...	...	...	...	...	...	...	...	...	...	...	...	...	1	1	...	1	1	...
Ladákh	...	...	...	...	...	...	...	...	...	...	...	...	...	...	...	...	...	...
Skardu	...	...	...	...	...	...	...	...	...	...	...	...	...	...	...	...	...	...
Gilgit	...	...	...	...	...	...	...	...	...	...	...	...	...	...	...	...	...	...
Whole State Urban	...	...	...	...	...	...	...	...	...	...	...	...	1	1	...	1	1	...
Do. Rural	...	...	...	...	...	...	...	...	...	...	...	...	...	...	...	...	...	...
Total whole State ...	...	...	...	...	...	...	...	...	...	...	...	...	1	1	...	1	1	...

PARSIS.

Territorial Sub-divisions.	Ratio per ten thousand.																	
	Under one year.			*One year.*			*Two years.*			*Three years.*			*Four years.*			*Total under five.*		
	Both sexes.	Males.	Females.	Both sexes.	Males.	Females.	Both sexes.	Males.	Females.	Both sexes.	Males.	Females.	Both sexes.	Males.	Females.	Both sexes.	Males.	Females.
Jammu Urban	...	...	...	...	...	...	...	...	...	...	...	...	...	...	...	...	...	...
Do. Rural	...	...	...	...	...	...	...	...	...	...	...	...	...	...	...	...	...	...
Total Jammu Province ...	...	...	...	...	...	...	...	...	...	...	...	...	...	...	...	...	...	...
Kashmír Urban	...	...	...	...	...	...	...	...	...	...	...	...	1,250	1,666	...	1,250	1,666	...
Do. Rural	...	...	...	...	...	...	...	...	...	...	...	...	...	...	...	...	...	...
Total Kashmír Province ...	...	...	...	...	...	...	...	...	...	...	...	...	1,250	1,666	...	1,250	1,666	...
Ladákh	...	...	...	...	...	...	...	...	...	...	...	...	...	...	...	...	...	...
Skardu	...	...	...	...	...	...	...	...	...	...	...	...	...	...	...	...	...	...
Gilgit	...	...	...	...	...	...	...	...	...	...	...	...	...	...	...	...	...	...
Whole State Urban	...	...	...	...	...	...	...	...	...	...	...	...	1,250	1,666	...	1,250	1,666	...
Do. Rural	...	...	...	...	...	...	...	...	...	...	...	...	...	...	...	...	...	...
Total whole State ...	...	...	...	...	...	...	...	...	...	...	...	...	1,111	1,428	...	1,111	1,428	...

125. Before comparing the ratio returned for religious divisions, it may be remarked that there is only one Hindu infant of three years in Ladákh, and none in Skardu and Gilgit, that the population of Ladákh is generally Budhistic, while that of Skardu is almost Mohamedan, there being only 304 infant Mohamedans in Ladákh and 20 Budhist infants in Skardu. While therefore the normal standard of Hindu and Mohamedan population is obtainable for the purpose of comparison, only in Jammu and Kashmír, it would be as well to compare the Mohamedan and Budhist population of Ladákh and Skardu, leaving out Gilgit Road which represents the floating population brought about by the Public Works Department.

126. It will be seen :—

(1).—That in the case of both Hindus and Mohamedans the ratio of infants in the Urban population, is decidedly lower than the Rural population, and that the highest percentage is obtained in the Rural District of Kashmír.

(2).—That the ratio of Hindu infants is invariably lower than that of Mohamedan infants in both Jammu and Kashmír.

(3).—That the ratio of Mohamedan infants in Skardu is lower than that in the Rural District of Jammu and the whole Province of Kashmír.

(4).—That the ratio of Mohamedan infants in Skardu is more close to Hindu infants in Jammu District and lower than those in Kashmír Province.

(5).—That the ratio of Budhist infants in Ladákh is almost alike in Jammu and Skardu, and is the lowest, compared with that of Mohamedans.

(6).—That the ratio of Budhist infants in Ladákh and Skardu, is much lower than that of Mohamedans in those Districts.

(7).—That the above differences in ratios among Hindus and Mohamedans are due to climatic influences, to mode of life, and in the case of Budhists, to polyandry.

ALL RELIGIONS.

TOWNS.	Under one year.			One year.			Two years.			Three years.			Four years.			Total under five.		
	Both sexes.	Males.	Females.	Both sexes.	Males.	Females.	Both sexes.	Males.	Females.	Both sexes.	Males.	Females.	Both sexes.	Males.	Females.	Both sexes.	Males.	Females.
URBAN POPULATION JAMMU.																		
Jammú	1,030	590	440	512	290	222	703	399	304	735	412	323	829	469	360	3,809	2,160	1,649
Batála	197	119	78	61	34	27	108	62	46	138	81	57	177	104	73	681	400	281
Mirpore	307	154	153	104	44	60	246	138	108	235	111	124	297	142	155	1,189	589	600
Punch	325	190	135	44	16	28	141	69	72	186	96	90	203	102	101	899	473	426
Total Jammu Urban ...	1,859	1,053	806	721	384	337	1,198	668	530	1,294	700	594	1,506	817	689	6,578	3,622	2,956
URBAN POPULATION KASHMIR.																		
Srinagar	5,038	2,481	2,557	1,429	705	724	4,046	1,998	2,048	4,356	2,142	2,214	3,473	1,755	1,718	18,342	9,081	9,261
Anantnág	456	252	204	249	122	127	340	166	174	366	194	172	322	165	157	1,733	899	834
Sopore	647	334	313	61	31	30	356	163	193	363	187	176	286	141	145	1,713	856	857
Bárámula	403	236	167	3	2	1	257	133	124	243	121	122	154	74	80	1,060	566	494
Total Kashmír Urban ...	6,544	3,303	3,241	1,742	860	882	4,999	2,460	2,539	5,328	2,644	2,684	4,235	2,135	2,100	22,848	11,402	11,446
Do. Urban whole State ...	8,403	4,356	4,047	2,463	1,244	1,219	6,197	3,128	3,069	6,622	3,344	3,278	5,741	2,952	2,789	29,426	15,024	14,402

ALL RELIGIONS.

TOWNS.	Ratio per ten thousand.																	
	Under one year.			*One year.*			*Two years.*			*Three years.*			*Four years.*			*Total under five.*		
	Both sexes.	Males.	Females.	Both sexes.	Males.	Females.	Both sexes.	Males.	Females.	Both sexes.	Males.	Females.	Both sexes.	Males.	Females.	Both sexes.	Males.	Females.
Urban Population Jammu.																		
Jammu	298	261	367	148	129	185	204	177	253	213	182	270	240	208	300	1,103	957	1,375
Batála	378	387	367	117	110	127	208	201	216	265	263	268	340	338	343	1,308	1,299	1,321
Mirpore	423	421	425	143	120	167	339	378	300	324	304	345	410	389	431	1,639	1,612	1,668
Punch	434	407	480	59	34	99	188	147	256	249	206	320	271	218	359	1,201	1,012	1,514
Total Jammu Urban ...	341	310	392	132	113	164	220	197	258	238	206	289	276	241	336	1,207	1,067	1,439
Urban Population Kashmir.																		
Srinagar	423	396	455	120	112	129	340	318	364	366	342	394	292	280	305	1,541	1,448	1,647
Anantnág	446	457	433	244	221	270	333	301	369	358	352	365	314	299	333	1,695	1,630	1,770
Sopore	769	766	773	73	71	74	423	374	476	431	429	435	341	323	358	2,037	1,963	2,116
Bárámula	713	786	629	5	7	4	454	443	467	430	403	460	272	246	302	1,874	1,885	1,862
Total Kashmír Urban ...	457	437	479	121	114	131	349	325	376	372	350	397	295	282	310	1,594	1,508	1,693
Do. Urban whole State ...	425	399	459	125	113	139	313	285	348	335	305	372	290	269	315	1,488	1,371	1,633

The year immediately preceding the Census seems to have been a very bad one, for Batála and Punch in Jammu, and Sopore and Bárámula in Kashmír. The loss of infant life in these towns would appear to have been very considerable.

The birth rate of Jammu city appears to be nearly half of that of Srinagar; of all the towns in the State, Sopore and Bárámula have the highest birth rate, the increase being particularly in the Mohamedan population.

The desparity between males and females under 5 years is highest in Jammu representing an excess of 418 per 10,000 in females. It is chiefly in the population of Hindus, including Jains and Sikhs.

HINDUS INCLUDING JAINS AND SIKHS.

TOWNS.	Under one year.			One year.			Two years.			Three years.			Four years.			Total under five.		
	Both sexes.	Males.	Females.	Both sexes.	Males.	Females.	Both sexes.	Males.	Females.	Both sexes.	Males.	Females.	Both sexes.	Males.	Females.	Both sexes.	Males.	Females.
URBAN POPULATION JAMMU.																		
Jammu	639	359	280	327	185	142	461	271	190	493	285	208	557	304	253	2,477	1,404	1,073
Batála	146	98	48	48	28	20	86	51	35	109	66	43	134	79	55	523	322	201
Mirpore	174	90	84	45	24	21	121	71	50	114	50	64	148	69	79	602	304	298
Punch	100	58	42	6	3	3	37	21	16	49	24	25	49	28	21	241	134	107
Total Jammu Urban ...	1,059	605	454	426	240	186	705	414	291	765	425	340	888	480	408	3,843	2,164	1,679
URBAN POPULATION KASHMIR.																		
Srinagar	845	423	422	267	131	136	649	339	310	659	317	342	635	318	317	3,055	1,528	1,527
Anantnág	33	18	15	15	10	5	27	15	12	28	14	14	27	12	15	130	69	61
Sopore	48	26	22	8	3	5	27	8	19	25	14	11	18	16	2	126	67	59
Bárámula	56	29	27	1	1	...	36	16	20	32	18	14	15	10	5	140	74	66
Total Kashmír Urban ...	982	496	486	291	145	146	739	378	361	744	363	381	695	356	339	3,451	1,738	1,713
Do. Urban whole State ...	2,041	1,101	940	717	385	332	1,444	792	652	1,509	788	721	1,583	836	747	7,294	3,902	3,392

HINDUS INCLUDING JAINS AND SIKHS.

TOWNS.	RATIO PER TEN THOUSAND.																	
	Under one year.			*One year.*			*Two years.*			*Three years.*			*Four years.*			*Total under five*		
	Both sexes.	Males.	Females.	Both sexes.	Males.	Females.	Both sexes.	Males.	Females.	Both sexes.	Males.	Females.	Both sexes.	Males.	Females.	Both sexes.	Males.	Females.
URBAN POPULATION JAMMU																		
Jammu	278	238	358	143	122	181	201	180	243	215	189	266	243	201	323	1,080	930	1,371
Batála	354	398	290	117	114	122	209	207	211	265	268	259	325	321	332	1,270	1,308	1,214
Mirpore	441	455	426	114	121	106	306	359	253	288	253	324	375	349	401	1,524	1,537	1,510
Punch	358	304	476	21	15	34	133	110	181	178	126	283	178	147	238	868	702	1,212
Total Jammu Urban ...	313	282	368	126	112	151	209	193	236	226	198	275	263	224	331	1,137	1,009	1,361
URBAN POPULATION KASHMIR.																		
Srinagar	322	293	357	101	91	115	247	235	262	251	220	289	242	220	268	1,163	1,059	1,291
Anantnág	334	310	368	152	172	122	273	258	294	283	241	343	273	207	368	1,315	1,188	1,495
Sopore	558	549	570	93	63	130	314	169	492	291	295	285	209	338	52	1,465	1,414	1,529
Bárámula	661	611	726	12	21	...	425	337	538	378	379	376	177	210	134	1,653	1,558	1,774
Total Kashmír Urban ...	339	311	374	101	91	112	255	237	278	257	228	293	240	223	261	1,192	1,090	1,318
Do. Urban whole State ...	325	294	371	114	103	131	230	212	257	241	211	285	252	224	295	1,162	1,044	1,339

MOHAMEDANS.

TOWNS.	Under one year.			One year.			Two years.			Three years.			Four years.			Total under five.		
	Both sexes.	Males.	Females.	Both sexes.	Males.	Females.	Both sexes.	Males.	Females.	Both sexes.	Males.	Females.	Both sexes.	Males.	Females.	Both sexes.	Males.	Females.
URBAN POPULATION JAMMU.																		
Jammu	390	231	159	184	104	80	240	126	114	242	127	115	272	165	107	1,328	753	575
Batála	51	21	30	13	6	7	22	11	11	29	15	14	43	25	18	158	78	80
Mirpore	133	64	69	59	20	39	125	67	58	121	61	60	149	73	76	587	285	302
Punch	225	132	93	38	13	25	104	48	56	137	72	65	154	74	80	658	339	319
Total Jammu Urban ...	799	448	351	294	143	151	491	252	239	529	275	254	618	337	281	2,731	1,455	1,276
URBAN POPULATION KASHMIR.																		
Srinagar	4,191	2,057	2,134	1,159	573	586	3,392	1,656	1,736	3,688	1,821	1,867	2,836	1,435	1,401	15,266	7,542	7,724
Anantnág	423	234	189	234	112	122	313	151	162	338	180	158	295	153	142	1,603	830	773
Sopore	599	308	291	53	28	25	329	155	174	338	173	165	268	125	143	1,587	789	798
Bárámula	347	207	140	2	1	1	221	117	104	211	103	108	139	64	75	920	492	428
Total Kashmír Urban ...	5,560	2,806	2,754	1,448	714	734	4,255	2,079	2,176	4,575	2,277	2,298	3,538	1,777	1,761	19,376	9,653	9,723
Total Urban whole State ...	6,359	3,254	3,105	1,742	857	885	4,746	2,331	2,415	5,104	2,552	2,552	4,156	2,114	2,042	22,107	11,108	10,999

MOHAMEDANS.

TOWNS.	Ratio per ten thousand.																	
	Under one year.			*One year.*			*Two years.*			*Three years.*			*Four years.*			*Total under five.*		
	Both sexes.	Males.	Females.	Both sexes.	Males.	Females.	Both sexes.	Males.	Females.	Both sexes.	Males.	Females.	Both sexes.	Males.	Females.	Both sexes.	Males.	Females.
Urban Population Jammu.																		
Jammu	336	311	382	159	140	193	207	169	274	209	171	276	234	221	257	1,145	1,012	1,382
Batála	469	342	637	120	97	149	202	179	233	267	244	297	396	405	382	1,454	1,267	1,698
Mirpore	403	381	425	179	119	240	378	399	357	366	364	369	451	435	468	1,777	1,698	1,859
Punch	479	478	482	81	47	129	221	173	290	292	260	337	328	267	414	1,401	1,225	1,652
Total Jammu Urban ...	386	358	429	142	114	184	237	202	292	256	220	310	299	270	343	1,320	1,164	1,558
Urban Population Kashmir.																		
Srinagar	454	427	481	125	119	132	366	343	391	398	378	421	306	297	315	1,649	1,564	1,740
Anantnág	458	474	439	254	227	284	339	306	337	366	365	367	319	310	330	1,736	1,682	1,797
Sopore	793	793	794	70	72	68	436	398	475	448	445	450	355	322	390	2,102	2,030	2,177
Bárámula	721	819	614	4	4	4	460	463	456	439	407	474	289	253	329	1,913	1,946	1,877
Total Kashmír Urban ...	487	471	504	127	120	134	373	349	398	401	382	421	309	298	324	1,697	1,620	1,781
Total Urban whole State ...	472	451	494	129	119	140	352	323	385	378	354	406	308	294	326	1,639	1,541	1,751

CHRISTIANS.

TOWNS.	Under one year.			One year.			Two years.			Three years.			Four years.			Total under five.		
	Both sexes.	Males.	Females.	Both sexes.	Males.	Females.	Both sexes.	Males.	Females.	Both sexes.	Males.	Females.	Both sexes.	Males.	Females.	Both sexes.	Males.	Females.
URBAN POPULATION JAMMU.																		
Jammu	1	...	1	1	1	...	2	2	...	...	...	...	...	...	...	4	3	1
Batála	...	...	...	...	...	...	...	...	...	...	...	...	...	...	...	...	...	...
Mirpore	...	...	...	...	...	...	...	...	...	...	...	...	...	...	...	...	...	...
Punch	...	...	...	...	...	...	...	...	...	...	...	...	...	...	...	...	...	...
Total Jammu Urban ...	1	...	1	1	1	...	2	2	...	...	...	...	...	...	...	4	3	1
URBAN POPULATION KASHMIR.																		
Srinagar	2	1	1	3	1	2	5	3	2	9	4	5	1	1	...	20	10	10
Anantnág	...	...	...	...	...	...	...	...	...	...	...	...	...	...	...	...	...	...
Sopore	...	...	...	...	...	...	...	...	...	...	...	...	...	...	...	...	...	...
Bárámula	...	...	...	...	...	...	...	...	...	...	...	...	...	...	...	...	...	...
Total Kashmír Urban ...	2	1	1	3	1	2	5	3	2	9	4	5	1	1	...	20	10	10
Do. Urban whole State ...	3	1	2	4	2	2	7	5	2	9	4	5	1	1	...	24	13	11

CHRISTIANS.

TOWNS.	Ratio per ten thousand.																	
	Under one year.			*One year.*			*Two years.*			*Three years.*			*Four years.*			*Total under five.*		
	Both sexes.	Males.	Females.	Both sexes.	Males.	Females.	Both sexes.	Males.	Females.	Both sexes.	Males.	Females.	Both sexes.	Males.	Females.	Both sexes.	Males.	Females.
Urban Population Jammu.																		
Jammu	714	...	1,429	714	1,428	...	1,429	2,857	...	...	...	...	...	...	...	2,857	4,285	1,429
Batála	...	...	...	...	...	...	...	...	...	...	...	...	...	...	...	...	...	...
Mirpore	...	...	...	...	...	...	...	...	...	...	...	...	...	...	...	...	...	...
Punch	...	...	...	...	...	...	...	...	...	...	...	...	...	...	...	...	...	...
Total Jammu Urban ...	714	...	1,429	714	1,428	...	1,429	2,857	...	...	...	...	...	...	...	2,857	4,285	1,429
Urban Population Kashmir.																		
Srinagar	168	175	161	252	175	323	420	526	323	757	702	806	84	176	...	1,681	1,754	1,613
Anantnág	...	...	...	...	...	...	...	...	...	...	...	...	...	...	...	...	...	...
Sopore	...	...	...	...	...	...	...	...	...	...	...	...	...	...	...	...	...	...
Báramula	...	...	...	...	...	...	...	...	...	...	...	...	...	...	...	...	...	...
Total Kashmir Urban ...	165	172	159	248	178	318	413	517	317	744	690	793	83	172	...	1,653	1,724	1,587
Do. Urban whole State ...	222	154	286	296	308	286	519	769	285	667	615	714	74	154	...	1,778	2,000	1,571

PARSIS.

Towns.	Under one year.			One year.			Two years.			Three years.			Four years.			Total under five.		
	Both sexes.	Males.	Females.	Both sexes.	Males.	Females.	Both sexes.	Males.	Females.	Both sexes.	Males.	Females.	Both sexes.	Males.	Females.	Both sexes.	Males.	Females.
Urban Population, Jammu.																		
Jammu	...	...	...	...	...	...	...	...	...	...	...	...	...	...	...	...	...	...
Batála	...	...	...	...	...	...	...	...	...	...	...	...	...	...	...	...	...	...
Mirpore	...	...	...	...	...	...	...	...	...	...	...	...	...	...	...	...	...	...
Punch	...	...	...	...	...	...	...	...	...	...	...	...	...	...	...	...	...	...
Total Jammu Urban ...	...	...	...	...	...	...	...	...	...	...	...	...	...	...	...	...	...	...
Urban Population, Kashmir.																		
Srinagar	...	...	...	...	...	...	...	...	...	...	...	...	1	1	...	1	1	...
Anantnág	...	...	...	...	...	...	...	...	...	...	...	...	...	...	...	...	...	...
Sopore	...	...	...	...	...	...	...	...	...	...	...	...	...	...	...	...	...	...
Bárámula	...	...	...	...	...	...	...	...	...	...	...	...	...	...	...	...	...	...
Total Kashmír Urban ...	...	...	...	...	...	...	...	...	...	...	...	...	1	1	...	1	1	...
Do. Urban whole State ...	...	...	...	...	...	...	...	...	...	...	...	...	1	1	...	1	1	...

PARSIS.

Towns.	Ratio per Ten Thousand.																	
	Under one year.			*One year.*			*Two years.*			*Three years.*			*Four years.*			*Total under five.*		
	Both sexes.	Males.	Females.	Both sexes.	Males.	Females.	Both sexes.	Males.	Females.	Both sexes.	Males.	Females.	Both sexes.	Males.	Females.	Both sexes.	Males.	Females.
Urban Population, Jammu.																		
Jammu	...	...	...	...	...	...	...	...	...	...	...	...	...	...	...	...	...	...
Batála	...	...	...	...	...	...	...	...	...	...	...	...	...	...	...	...	...	...
Mirpore	...	...	...	...	...	...	...	...	...	...	...	...	...	...	...	...	...	...
Punch	...	...	...	...	...	...	...	...	...	...	...	...	...	...	...	...	...	...
Total Jammu Urban ...	...	...	...	...	...	...	...	...	...	...	...	...	...	...	...	...	...	...
Urban Population, Kashmir.																		
Srinagar	...	...	...	...	...	...	...	...	...	...	...	...	1,250	1,666	...	1,250	1,666	...
Anantnág	...	...	...	...	...	...	...	...	...	...	...	...	...	...	...	...	...	...
Sopore	...	...	...	...	...	...	...	...	...	...	...	...	...	...	...	...	...	...
Bárámula	...	...	...	...	...	...	...	...	...	...	...	...	...	...	...	...	...	...
Total Kashmír Urban ...	...	...	...	...	...	...	...	...	...	...	...	...	1,250	1,666	...	1,250	1,666	...
Do. Urban whole State ...	...	...	...	...	...	...	...	...	...	...	...	...	1,250	1,666	...	1,250	1,666	...

127. Repeating the process referred to in para. 122, the rates of births and deaths by religions are shown in the subjoined table:—

	Annual Births per 10,000.			Total under 5.			Average Annual Population.			Average Deaths.		
	Both sexes.	Males.	Females.	Both sexes.	Males.	Females.	Both sexes.	Males.	Females.	Both sexes.	Males.	Females.
Hindús, including Jains and Sikhs...	423	395	457	1,315	1,227	1,419	263	245	284	160	150	173
Mohamedans ...	596	561	632	1,861	1,770	1,961	372	354	392	224	207	240
Budhists ...	200	179	222	841	815	869	168	163	173	32	16	49

128. These figures show that the rates of births and deaths per 10,000 is largest among Mohamedans, that there are fewer births and fewer deaths among Hindús than among Mohamedans, that the lowest ratio of births is obtained in Budhists, but at the same time the rate of mortality there, is also extremely low.

129. Christians numbering only 218, the majority of whom were visitors to the valley, it is premature to draw any conclusions regarding them. The same remark applies to Parsís, who number only 9 in all.

URBAN POPULATION WHOLE STATE.

	Annual Births per 10,000.			Total under 5.			Average Annual Population.			Average Deaths.		
	Both sexes.	Males.	Females.	Both sexes.	Males.	Females.	Both sexes.	Males.	Females.	Both sexes.	Males.	Females.
Hindús, including Jains and Sikhs...	390	353	445	1,162	1,044	1,339	232	209	268	158	144	177
Mohamedans ...	566	541	594	1,639	1,541	1,751	328	308	350	238	233	244
Budhists ...	...	...	...	...	...	...	...	...	...	...	...	...

RURAL POPULATION WHOLE STATE.

	Annual Births per 10,000.			Total under 5.			Average Annual Population.			Average Deaths.		
	Both sexes.	Males.	Females.	Both sexes.	Males.	Females.	Both sexes.	Males.	Females.	Both sexes.	Males.	Females.
Hindús, including Jains and Sikhs ..	426	400	458	1,330	1,247	1,426	266	249	285	160	151	173
Mohamedans ...	598	563	635	1,878	1,789	1,978	377	358	395	221	205	240
Budhists ...	200	179	222	841	815	869	168	163	173	32	16	49

130. Taking the age periods under 5, 5—9 and 10—14 collectively, we have the following results. For sake of comparison all those under 15 are taken as children, and above 15 as adults.

	CHILDREN. 0—5. Both sexes.	0—5. Males.	0—5. Females.	5—14. Both sexes.	5—14. Males.	5—14. Females.	*Total.* Both sexes.	*Total.* Males.	*Total.* Females.	ADULTS. Both sexes.	ADULTS. Males.	ADULTS. Females.	EXCESS DIFFERENCE IN PROPORTION BETWEEN MALES AND FEMALES. *Children.* Males.	*Children.* Females.	*Adults.* Males.	*Adults.* Females.
Jammu Urban	1,207	1,067	1,439	1,823	1,768	1,913	3,030	2,835	3,352	6,970	7,165	6,647	...	517	518	...
Do. Rural	1,549	1,458	1,653	2,347	2,409	2,276	3,896	3,867	3,929	6,104	6,133	6,071	...	62	62	...
Total Jammu Province ...	1,536	1,440	1,647	2,327	2,380	2,264	3,863	3,820	3,911	6,137	6,180	6,089	...	91	91	...
Kashmír Urban	1,594	1,508	1,693	2,208	2,289	2,119	3,802	3,797	3,812	6,198	6,202	6,188	...	15	14	...
Do. Rural	2,078	1,994	2,172	2,385	2,477	2,280	4,463	4,471	4,452	5,537	5,528	5,548	19	...	...	20
Total Kashmír Province ...	2,005	1,921	2,099	2,358	2,448	2,255	4,363	4,369	4,354	5,637	5,630	5,646	15	...	...	16
Frontier Districts (Ladakh, Skardu and Gilgit Road.)	1,119	1,021	1,226	2,049	2,060	2,040	3,168	3,081	3,266	6,832	6,919	6,734	...	185	185	...
Whole State Urban	1,488	1,371	1,633	2,102	2,128	2,070	3,590	3,499	3,703	6,610	6,501	6,297	...	204	204	...
Do. Rural	1,702	1,613	1,802	2,341	2,409	2,261	4,043	4,022	4,063	5,957	5,978	5,936	...	41	42	...
Total Whole State ...	1,685	1,594	1,789	2,321	2,387	2,247	4,006	3,981	4,036	5,994	6,019	5,964	...	55	55	...
Ajmere	1,491	1,431	1,563	2,071	2,147	1,999	3,562	3,578	3,562	6,437	6,422	6,438	16	...	...	16
Assam	1,734	1,652	1,825	2,414	2,538	2,278	4,148	4,190	4,103	5,851	5,810	5,897	87	...	...	87
Berar	1,475	1,390	1,567	2,307	2,329	2,283	3,782	3,719	3,850	6,217	6,281	6,150	...	131	131	...
Sindh	1,582	1,492	1,691	2,509	2,654	2,335	4,091	4,146	4,026	5,909	5,854	5,974	120	...	...	120
Central Provinces	1,611	1,557	1,667	2,458	2,585	2,330	4,069	4,142	3,997	5,930	5,858	6,003	145	...	...	145
India	1,368	1,318	1,420	2,520	2,646	2,389	3,888	3,964	3,809	6,112	6,036	6,191	155	...	...	155

131. The proportion of children to the total population is largest in the rural population of Kashmír, being 4,463 per ten thousand and lowest in the urban population of Jammu. Contrasted with other provinces the figures are :—

Kashmír Rural	4,463
Do. Province	4,363
Assam	4,148
Sindh	4,091
Central Provinces	4,069
Whole State Kashmír (Rural)	4,043
Whole State, Kashmir	4,006
India	3,888
Jummu (Rural)	3,896
Jummu Province	3,863
Kashmír (Urban)	3,802
Berar	3,782
Whole State Kashmír (Urban)	3,590
Ajmere	3,562
Frontier Districts (Ladákh, Skardu and Gilgit)	3,168
Jummu (Urban)	3,030

132. The proportion of male children to total male population on the other hand is :—

Berar	3,719
Kashmír Rural	4,471
Kashmír Province	4,369
Urban population whole State Kashmír	3,499
Assam	4,190
Sindh	4,146
Central Provinces	4,142
Rural population whole State	4,022
Total population Kashmír State	3,981
India	3,964
Rural population Jammu Province	3,867
Jammu Province	3,820
Urban population Kashmír Province	3,797
Ajmere	3,578
Frontier Districts (Ladákh, Skardu and Gilgit)	3,081
Urban population Jummu Province	2,835

and of females—

Rural population, Kashmír	4,452
Total population, Kashmír Province	4,354
Assam	4,103
Rural population, whole State	4,063
Total do. do.	4,036
Sindh	4,026
Central Provinces	3,997
Rural population, Jammu Province	3,929
Total do. do. do.	3,911
Berar	3,850
Urban population, Kashmír	3,812
India	3,809
Urban population, whole State	3,703
Ajmere	3,562
Urban population, Jammu	3,352
Frontier Districts (Ladákh, Skardu and Gilgit) ...	3,266

133. Contrasting the proportions of boys with girls we find :—

Excess in proportion of females as compared with that of males.	Urban population, Jammu Province ...	517
	Total do. do. do. ...	91
	Rural do. do. do. ...	62
	Rural population, whole State ...	41
	Total do. do.	55
	Berar	131
	Urban population, Kashmír State ...	15
	Frontier Districts (Ladákh, Skardu and Gilgit)	185
	Urban population, whole State ...	204
Excess in proportion of males as compared with that of females.	India...	155
	Central Provinces	145
	Sindh	120
	Assam	87
	Rural population, Kashmír Province ...	19
	Ajmere	16
	Total population, Kashmír Province ...	15

134. The result of these statistics is :—

(1). That the ratio of children of both sexes per 10,000 of total population.

(*a*) for the whole state is lower than Assam, Sindh and the Central Provinces by 142, 85, and 63 respectively, and higher than India, Berar and Ajmere by 118, 224 and 444 respectively.

(*b*) for the whole Rural population, lower than Assam, Sindh and the Central Provinces by 105, 48, and 26 respectively, and higher than India, Berar and Ajmere by 155, 261 and 481 respectively.

(*c*) for the whole Urban population, lower than Assam, Sindh, Central Provinces, India and Berar by 558, 501, 479, 298 and 192 respectively, and higher only than Ajmere by 28.

(*d*) for Rural population Kashmir Province higher than :—

Assam	by	315
Sindh	,,	372
Central Provinces	,,	394
India	,,	575
Berar	,,	681
Ajmere	,,	901

and lower than none—

(*e*) for Rural population Jammu Province higher than :—

Berar	by	114
Ajmere	,,	334
India	,,	8

and lower than—

Assam	by	252
Sindh	,,	195
Central Provinces	,,	178

(*f*) for Frontier Rural Districts (Ladákh, Skardu and Gilgit), lower than :—

Assam	by	980
Sindh	,,	923
Central Provinces	,,	901
India	,,	720
Berar	,,	614
Ajmere	,,	394

(*g*) For Urban population Kashmir Province higher than :—

Berar	by	20
Ajmere	,,	240

and lower than—

Assam	by	346
Sindh	,,	289
Central Provinces	,,	267
India	,,	86

(*h*) For Urban population Jammu lower than :—

Assam	by	1,118
Sindh	,,	1,061
Central Provinces	,,	1,039
India	,,	858
Berar	,,	752
Ajmere	,,	532

135. The subjoined tables give the difference between the proportions for the internal divisions of the State.

(1.) For both sexes up to the age of 14.
(2.) For males.
(3.) For females.

BOTH SEXES (Children). Age Period 0-14.

Difference in proportions per Ten Thousand.

	Kashmír State.	Jammu Province.	Kashmír Province.	Frontier Districts.	Rural Population. Whole State.	Rural Population. Jammu. Province.	Rural Population. Kashmír. Province.	Urban Population. Whole State.	Urban Population. Jammu. Province.	Urban Population. Kashmír. Province.
Higher than										
Kashmír State	...	...	357	...	37	...	457	...	...	...
Jammu Province	143	...	500	...	180	33	600	...	...	...
Kashmír Province	...	...	...	...	...	...	100	...	...	...
Frontier Districts	838	695	1,195	...	875	728	1,295	422	...	634
Rural Population. Whole State	...	...	320	...	...	...	420	...	...	...
Rural Population. Jammu Province	110	...	467	...	147	...	567	...	...	...
Rural Population. Kashmír Province	...	...	...	...	...	...	...	...	...	...
Urban Population. Whole State	416	273	773	...	453	306	873	...	...	212
Urban Population. Jammu Province	976	833	1,333	138	1,013	866	1,433	560	...	772
Urban Population. Kashmír Do.	204	61	561	...	241	94	661	...	...	...
Lower than										
Kashmír State	...	143	...	838	...	110	...	416	976	204
Jammu Province	...	...	...	695	...	...	...	273	833	61
Kashmir do.	357	500	...	1,195	320	467	...	773	1,333	561
Frontier Districts	...	...	...	...	...	...	...	...	138	...
Rural Population. Whole State	37	180	...	875	...	147	...	453	1,013	241
Rural Population. Jammu Province	...	33	...	728	...	...	...	306	866	94
Rural Population. Kashmír do.	457	600	100	1,295	420	567	...	873	1,433	661
Urban Population. Whole State	...	...	...	422	...	...	...	...	560	...
Urban Population. Jammu Province	...	...	...	...	...	...	...	...	...	...
Urban Population. Kashmír do.	...	...	...	634	...	...	...	212	772	...

Males.—Age period 0—14.

Difference in proportions per Ten Thousand of Male Population.

	Kashmír State.	Jammu Province.	Kashmír Province.	Frontier Districts of Ladákh, Skardu and Gilgit.	Rural Population. Whole State.	Rural Population. Jammu Province.	Rural Population. Kashmír Province.	Urban Population. Whole State.	Urban Population. Jammu Province.	Urban Population. Kashmír Province.	Assam.	Sindh.	Central Provinces.	India.	Berar.	Ajmere.
Higher than																
Kashmír State	...	...	388	...	41	...	490	...	...	...	209	165	161	...	...	...
Jammu Province	161	...	549	...	202	47	651	...	...	...	370	326	322	144	...	...
Kashmír Province	...	...	...	...	...	...	102	...	...	...	...	...	...	...	...	...
Frontier Districts	900	739	1,288	...	941	786	1,390	418	...	716	1,109	1,065	1,061	883	638	497
Rural Population — Whole State	...	...	347	...	...	...	449	...	...	...	168	124	120	...	...	...
Rural Population — Jammu Province	114	...	502	...	155	...	604	...	...	...	323	279	275	97	...	...
Rural Population — Kashmír Province	...	...	...	...	...	...	...	...	...	...	...	...	...	...	...	...
Urban Population — Whole State	482	321	870	...	523	368	972	...	...	298	691	647	643	465	220	79
Urban Population — Jammu Province	1,146	985	1,534	246	1,187	1,032	1,636	664	...	962	1,355	1,311	1,307	1,129	884	743
Urban Population — Kashmír Province	184	23	572	...	225	70	674	...	...	...	393	349	345	167	...	...
Assam	...	...	179	...	...	...	281	...	...	...	...	...	...	...	...	...
Sindh	...	...	223	...	...	...	325	...	...	...	44	...	...	...	...	...
Central Provinces	...	...	227	...	...	...	329	...	...	...	48	4	...	...	...	...
India	17	...	405	...	58	...	507	...	...	...	226	182	178	...	...	...
Berar	262	101	650	...	303	148	752	...	...	78	471	427	423	245	...	...
Ajmere	403	242	791	...	444	289	893	...	...	219	612	568	564	386	141	...
Lower than																
Kashmír State	...	116	...	900	...	114	...	482	1,146	184	...	...	...	17	262	403
Jammu Province	...	...	...	739	...	...	...	321	985	23	...	...	...	...	101	242
Kashmír Do.	388	549	...	1,288	347	502	...	870	1,534	572	179	223	227	405	650	791
Frontier Districts	...	...	...	...	...	...	...	...	246	...	...	...	...	...	...	...
Rural Population — Whole State	41	202	...	941	...	155	...	523	1,187	225	...	...	...	58	303	444
Rural Population — Jammu Province	...	47	...	786	...	...	...	368	1,032	70	...	...	...	...	148	289
Rural Population — Kashmír Do.	490	651	102	1,390	449	604	...	972	1,636	674	281	325	329	507	752	893
Urban Population — Whole State	...	...	...	418	...	...	...	...	664	...	...	...	...	...	...	...
Urban Population — Jammu Province	...	...	...	...	...	...	...	...	...	...	...	...	...	...	...	...
Urban Population — Kashmír Do.	...	...	...	716	...	...	...	298	962	...	...	...	...	...	78	219
Assam	209	370	...	1,109	168	323	...	691	1,355	393	...	44	48	226	471	612
Sindh	165	326	...	1,065	124	279	...	647	1,311	349	...	...	4	182	427	568
Central Provinces	161	322	...	1,061	120	275	...	648	1,307	345	...	...	...	178	423	564
India	...	144	...	883	...	97	...	465	1,129	167	...	...	...	...	245	386
Berar	...	...	...	638	...	...	...	220	884	...	...	...	...	...	...	141
Ajmere	...	...	...	497	...	...	...	79	743	...	...	...	...	...	...	...

Females.—Age period 0—14.

Difference in proporations per Ten Thousand of Female population.

	Kashmír State.	Jammu Province.	Kashmír Province.	Frontier Districts of Ladákh Sakardu and Gilgit.	Rural Population. Whole State.	Rural Population. Jammu Province.	Rural Population. Kashmír Province.	Urban Population. Whole State.	Urban Population. Jammu Province.	Urban Population. Kashmír Province.	Assam.	Sindh.	Central Provinces.	India.	Berar.	Ajmere.
Higher than																
Kashmír State	...	...	318	...	27	...	416	...	...	...	67	...	...	...	...	...
Jammu Province	125	...	443	...	152	18	541	...	...	...	192	115	86	...	...	...
Kashmír Province	...	...	...	...	...	...	98	...	...	...	...	...	...	...	...	...
Frontier Districts...	770	645	1,088	...	797	663	1,186	437	86	546	837	760	731	543	584	296
Rural population ... Whole State	...	...	291	...	...	...	389	...	...	...	40	...	...	...	...	...
Rural population ... Jammu Province	107	...	425	...	134	...	523	...	...	...	174	97	68	...	...	...
Rural population ... Kashmír do.	...	...	...	...	...	...	...	...	...	...	...	...	...	...	...	...
Urban population ... Whole State	333	208	651	...	360	226	749	...	...	109	400	323	294	106	147	...
Urban population ... Jammu Province	684	559	1,002	...	711	577	1,100	351	...	460	751	674	645	457	498	210
Urban population ... Kashmír do.	224	99	542	...	251	117	640	...	...	...	291	214	185	...	38	...
Assam	...	...	251	...	...	...	349	...	...	...	...	...	...	...	...	...
Sindh...	10	...	328	...	37	...	426	...	...	...	77	...	...	...	...	...
Central Provinces	39	...	357	...	66	...	455	...	...	...	106	29	...	...	...	...
India	227	102	545	...	254	120	643	...	...	3	294	217	188	...	41	...
Berar	186	61	504	...	213	79	602	...	...	...	253	176	147	...	...	...
Ajmere	474	349	792	...	501	367	890	141	...	250	541	464	435	247	288	...
Lower than																
Kashmír State	...	125	...	770	...	107	...	333	684	224	...	10	39	227	186	474
Jammu Province	...	...	...	645	...	...	...	208	559	99	...	...	...	102	61	349
Kashmír Province	318	443	...	1,088	291	425	...	651	1,002	542	251	328	357	545	504	792
Frontier Districts	...	...	...	...	...	...	...	...	...	...	...	...	...	...	...	...
Rural population ... Whole State	27	152	...	797	...	134	...	360	711	251	...	37	66	254	213	501
Rural population ... Jammu Province	...	18	...	663	...	...	...	226	577	117	...	...	...	120	79	367
Rural population ... Kashmír do.	416	541	98	1,186	389	523	...	749	1,100	640	349	426	455	643	602	890
Urban population ... Whole State	...	...	...	437	...	...	...	...	351	...	...	...	...	...	...	141
Urban population ... Jammu Province	...	...	...	86	...	...	...	...	...	...	...	...	...	...	...	...
Urban population ... Kashmír do.	...	...	...	546	...	...	...	109	460	...	...	...	...	3	...	250
Assam	67	192	...	837	40	174	...	400	751	291	...	77	106	294	253	541
Sindh	...	115	...	760	...	97	...	323	674	214	...	...	29	217	176	464
Central Provinces	...	86	...	731	...	68	...	294	645	185	...	...	...	188	147	435
India	...	...	...	543	...	...	...	106	457	...	...	...	...	...	...	247
Berar	...	...	...	584	...	...	...	147	498	38	...	...	...	41	...	288
Ajmere	...	...	...	296	...	...	...	...	210	...	...	...	...	...	...	...

136. To sum up the ratio per ten thousand of both sexes, males and females under 15 years as compared with India, and the Indian Provinces of Assam, Sindh, Central Provinces, Berar and Ajmere stands as follows :—

	Higher than			Lower than		
	Both sexes.	Males.	Females.	Both sexes.	Males.	Females.
Kashmir State	Assam, Sindh and Central Provinces.	Assam, Sindh, and Central Provinces.	Assam	Ajmere, Berar and India ...	India, Berar and Ajmere ...	Sindh, Central Provinces, India, Berar and Ajmere.
Jammu Province	Assam, Sindh, Central Provinces and India.	Assam, Sindh, Central Provinces and India.	Assam, Sindh and Central Provinces.	Ajmere and Berar ...	Ajmere and Berar ...	India, Berar and Ajmere.
Kashmir do.	......	......	......	Ajmere, Assam, Berar, Sindh, Central Provinces and India.	Assam, Berar, Sindh, Central Provinces, India and Ajmere.	Assam, Sindh, Central Provinces, India, Berar and Ajmere.
Frontier Districts (Ladákh, Skardu and Gilgit).	Assam, Sindh, Central Provinces, India, Berar and Ajmere.	Assam, Sindh, Central Provinces, India, Berar and Ajmere.	Assam, Sindh, Central Provinces, India, Berar and Ajmere.	......	......	......
Rural Population whole State...	Assam, Sindh and Central Provinces.	Assam, Sindh and Central Provinces.	Assam	Ajmere, Berar and India ...	India, Berar and Ajmere ...	Sindh, Central Provinces, India, Berar and Ajmere.
Do. do. Jammu ...	Assam, Sindh and Central Provinces.	Assam, Sindh, Central Provinces and India.	Assam, Sindh and Central Provinces.	Ajmere, Berar and India ...	Ajmere and Berar ...	India, Berar and Ajmere.
Do. do. Kashmir ...	......	......	......	Assam, Sindh, Berar, Central Provinces, India and Ajmere.	Assam, Sindh, Berar, Central Provinces, India and Ajmere.	Assam, Sindh, Central Provinces, India, Berar and Ajmere.
Urban Population Whole State.	Assam, Berar, Sindh, Central Provinces and India.	Berar, Assam, Sindh, India, Central Provinces and Ajmere.	Assam, Sindh, Central Provinces India and Berar.	Ajmere	......	Ajmere.
Do. do. Jammu ...	Assam, Sindh, Central Provinces, India, Berar, and Ajmere.	Assam, Sindh, Central Provinces, India, Berar and Ajmere.	Assam, Sindh, Central Provinces, India, Berar and Ajmere.	......	......	......
Do. do. Kashmir ...	Assam, Berar, Sindh, Central Provinces and India.	Assam, Sindh, Central Provinces and India.	Assam, Sindh, Central Provinces and Berar.	Ajmere	Ajmere and Berar ...	India and Ajmere.

Adults both sexes.—Age period 15 and above.

Difference in proportions per Ten Thousand

	Kashmír State	Jammu Province.	Kashmír Province.	Frontier Districts of Ladákh, Skardu and Gilgit.	Rural Population. Whole State.	Rural Population. Jammu Province.	Rural Population. Kashmír Province.	Urban Population. Whole State.	Urban Population. Jammu Province.	Urban Population. Kashmír Province.	Assam.	Sindh.	Central Provinces.	India.	Berar.	Ajmere.
Higher than																
Kashmír State	...	143	...	838	...	110	...	616	976	204	...	...	...	118	223	443
Jammu Province	...	...	...	695	...	...	...	473	833	61	...	...	...	...	80	300
Kashmír Province	357	500	...	1,195	320	467	...	973	1,333	561	214	272	293	475	580	800
Frontier Districts	...	...	...	...	...	...	...	...	138	...	...	...	...	...	...	...
Rural ... Whole State	37	180	...	875	...	147	...	653	1,013	241	...	...	...	155	260	480
Rural ... Jammu	...	33	...	728	...	...	...	506	866	94	...	...	...	8	113	333
Rural ... Kashmír	457	600	100	1,295	420	567	...	1,073	1,433	661	314	372	393	575	680	900
Urban ... Whole State	...	...	...	222	...	...	...	...	360	...	...	...	...	...	...	...
Urban ... Jammu	...	...	...	...	...	...	...	...	...	...	...	...	...	...	...	...
Urban ... Kashmír	...	...	...	634	...	...	...	412	772	...	...	...	...	...	19	339
Assam	143	286	...	981	106	253	...	759	1,119	347	...	58	79	261	366	586
Sindh	85	228	...	923	48	195	...	701	1,061	289	...	...	21	203	308	528
Central Provinces	64	207	...	902	27	174	...	680	1,040	268	...	...	...	182	287	507
India	...	25	...	720	...	...	...	498	858	86	...	...	...	...	105	325
Berar	...	...	...	615	...	...	...	393	753	...	...	...	...	...	...	220
Ajmere	...	...	...	395	...	...	...	173	533	...	...	...	...	...	...	...
Lower than																
Kashmír State	...	...	357	...	37	...	457	...	...	...	143	85	64	...	...	...
Jammu Province	143	...	500	...	180	33	600	...	...	...	286	228	207	25	...	...
Kashmír Province	...	...	...	...	...	...	100	...	...	...	...	...	...	...	...	...
Frontier Districts	838	695	1,195	...	875	728	1,295	222	...	634	981	923	902	720	615	395
Rural ... Whole State	...	...	320	...	...	...	420	...	...	...	106	48	27	...	...	...
Rural ... Jammu	110	...	467	...	147	...	567	...	...	...	253	195	174	...	...	...
Rural ... Kashmír	...	...	...	...	...	...	...	...	...	...	...	...	...	...	...	...
Urban ... Whole State	616	473	973	...	653	506	1,073	...	...	412	759	701	680	498	393	173
Urban ... Jammu	976	833	1,333	138	1,013	866	1,433	360	...	772	1,119	1,061	1,040	858	753	533
Urban ... Kashmír	204	61	561	...	241	94	661	...	...	...	347	289	268	86	...	...
Assam	...	...	214	...	...	...	314	...	...	...	...	...	...	...	...	...
Sindh	...	...	272	...	...	...	372	...	...	...	58	...	...	...	...	...
Central Provinces	...	...	293	...	...	...	393	...	...	...	79	21	...	...	...	...
India	118	...	475	...	155	8	575	...	...	...	261	203	182	...	...	...
Berar	223	80	580	...	260	113	680	...	...	19	366	308	287	105	...	...
Ajmere	443	300	800	...	480	333	900	...	...	339	586	528	507	325	220	...

Adult Males.—Age 15 and above.

Difference in Proportions per Ten Thousand.

	Kashmír State.	Jammu Province.	Kashmír Province.	Frontier Districts of Ladákh, Skardu and Gilgit.	*Rural Population.* Whole State.	*Rural Population.* Jammu Province.	*Rural Population.* Kashmír Province.	*Urban Population.* Whole State.	*Urban Population.* Jammu Province.	*Urban Population.* Kashmír Province.	Assam.	Sindh.	Central Provinces.	India.	Berar.	Ajmere.
Higher than																
Kashmír State...	...	161	...	900	...	114	...	482	1,146	183	...	...	...	17	262	403
Jammu Province	...	...	...	739	...	...	...	321	985	22	...	...	...	...	101	242
Kashmír Province	389	550	...	1,289	348	503	...	871	1,535	572	180	224	228	406	651	792
Frontier Districts	...	...	...	...	...	...	...	...	246	...	...	...	...	...	...	...
Rural — Whole State	41	202	...	941	...	155	...	523	1,187	224	...	...	...	58	303	444
Rural — Jammu	...	47	...	786	...	...	...	368	1,032	69	...	...	...	...	148	289
Rural — Kashmír	491	652	102	1,391	450	605	...	973	1,637	674	282	326	330	508	753	894
Urban — Whole State	418	...	...	...	...	...	...	...	664	...	...	...	...	...	...	...
Urban — Jammu	...	...	...	...	...	...	...	...	...	...	...	...	...	...	...	...
Urban — Kashmír	...	...	...	717	...	...	...	299	963	...	...	...	...	...	79	220
Assam	209	370	...	1,109	168	323	...	691	1,355	392	...	44	48	226	471	612
Sindh	165	326	...	1,065	124	279	...	647	1,311	348	...	...	4	182	427	568
Central Provinces	161	322	...	1,061	120	275	...	643	1,307	344	...	...	...	178	423	564
India	...	144	...	883	...	97	...	465	1,129	166	...	...	...	...	245	386
Berar	638	...	...	...	...	...	...	220	884	...	...	...	...	...	...	141
Ajmere	...	...	...	497	...	...	...	79	743	...	...	...	...	...	...	...
Lower than																
Kashmír State...	...	...	389	...	41	...	491	418	...	...	209	165	161	...	638	...
Jammu Province	161	...	550	...	202	47	652	...	...	...	370	326	322	144	...	...
Kashmír Province	...	...	...	...	...	...	102	...	...	...	...	...	...	...	...	...
Frontier Districts	900	739	1,289	...	941	786	1,391	...	...	717	1,109	1,065	1,061	883	...	497
Rural — Whole State	...	...	348	...	...	...	450	...	...	...	168	124	120	...	...	...
Rural — Jammu	114	...	503	...	155	...	605	...	...	...	323	279	275	97	...	...
Rural — Kashmír	...	...	...	...	...	...	...	...	...	...	...	...	...	...	...	...
Urban — Whole State	482	321	871	...	523	368	973	...	...	299	691	647	643	466	220	79
Urban — Jammu	1,146	985	1,535	246	1,187	1,032	1,637	664	...	963	1,355	1,311	1,307	1,129	884	743
Urban — Kashmír	183	22	572	...	224	69	674	...	...	...	392	348	344	166	...	...
Assam	...	...	180	...	...	...	282	...	...	...	...	...	...	...	...	...
Sindh	...	...	224	...	...	...	326	...	...	...	44	...	...	...	...	...
Central Province	...	...	228	...	...	...	330	...	...	...	48	4	...	...	...	...
India	17	...	406	...	58	...	508	...	...	...	226	182	178	...	...	...
Berar	262	101	651	...	303	148	753	...	...	79	471	427	423	245	...	...
Ajmere	403	242	792	...	444	289	894	...	...	220	612	568	564	386	141	...

Adult Females.—Age period 15 and above.

Difference in proportions per Ten Thousand.

	Kashmír State.	Jammu Province.	Kashmír Province.	Frontier Districts of Ladákh, Skardu and Gilgit.	Rural Population. Whole State.	Rural Population. Jammu Province.	Rural Population. Kashmír Province.	Urban Population. Whole State.	Urban Population. Jammu Province.	Urban Population. Kashmír Province.	Assam.	Sindh.	Central Provinces.	India.	Berar.	Ajmere.
Higher than																
Kashmír State	...	125	...	770	...	107	...	333	683	224	...	10	39	227	186	474
Jammu Province	...	...	...	645	...	...	...	208	558	99	...	...	...	102	61	349
Kashmír Province	318	443	...	1,088	290	425	...	651	1,001	542	251	328	357	545	504	792
Frontier Districts	...	...	...	...	...	...	...	...	...	...	...	...	...	...	...	...
Rural ... Whole State ...	28	153	...	798	...	135	...	361	711	252	...	38	67	255	214	502
Rural ... Jammu ...	...	18	...	663	...	...	...	226	576	117	...	...	...	120	79	367
Rural ... Kashmír ...	416	541	98	1,186	388	523	...	749	1,099	640	349	426	455	643	602	890
Urban ... Whole State ...	...	...	...	437	...	...	...	...	350	...	...	...	...	...	...	141
Urban ... Jammu ...	...	...	...	87	...	...	...	...	...	...	...	...	...	...	...	...
Urban ... Kashmír ...	...	...	...	546	...	...	...	109	459	...	...	...	...	3	...	250
Assam	67	192	...	837	39	174	...	400	750	291	...	77	106	294	253	541
Sindh	...	115	...	760	...	97	...	323	673	214	...	...	29	217	176	464
Central Provinces	...	86	...	731	...	68	...	294	644	185	...	...	...	188	147	435
India	...	...	...	543	...	...	...	106	456	...	...	...	...	...	...	247
Berar	...	...	...	584	...	...	...	147	497	38	...	...	...	41	...	288
Ajmere	...	...	...	296	...	...	...	...	209	...	...	...	...	...	...	...
Lower than																
Kashmír State	...	...	318	...	28	...	416	...	...	...	67	...	...	...	...	...
Jammu Province	125	...	443	...	153	18	541	...	...	...	192	115	86	...	...	...
Kashmír Province	...	...	...	...	...	...	98	...	...	...	...	...	...	...	...	...
Frontier Districts	770	645	1,088	...	798	663	1,186	437	87	546	837	760	731	543	584	296
Rural ... Whole State ...	...	...	290	...	...	...	388	...	...	...	39	...	...	...	...	...
Rural ... Jammu ...	107	...	425	...	135	...	523	...	...	...	174	97	68	...	...	...
Rural ... Kashmír ...	...	...	...	...	...	...	...	...	...	...	...	...	...	...	...	...
Urban ... Whole State ...	333	208	651	...	361	226	749	...	...	109	400	323	294	106	147	...
Urban ... Jammu ...	683	558	1,001	...	711	576	1,009	350	...	459	750	673	644	456	497	209
Urban ... Kashmír ...	224	99	542	...	252	117	640	...	...	...	291	214	185	...	38	...
Assam	...	...	251	...	...	...	349	...	...	...	...	...	...	...	...	...
Sindh	10	...	328	...	38	...	426	...	...	...	77	...	...	...	...	...
Central Provinces	39	...	357	...	67	...	455	...	...	...	106	29	...	...	...	...
India	227	102	545	...	255	120	643	...	...	3	294	217	188	...	41	...
Berar	186	61	504	...	214	79	602	...	...	...	253	176	147	...	...	...
Ajmere	474	349	792	...	502	367	890	141	...	250	541	464	435	247	288	...

137. To sum up the ratio per ten thousand of both sexes, males and females, from 15 and above years of age, as compared with India and the Indian Provinces of Assam, Sindh, Central Provinces, Berar and Ajmere, stands as follows :—

	Higher than			Lower than		
	Both sexes.	Males.	Females.	Both sexes.	Males.	Females.
Kashmir State	India, Berar and Ajmere ...	India, Ajmere and Berar ...	Sindh, Central Provinces, India, Berar and Ajmere.	Assam, Sindh and Central Provinces.	Assam, Sindh and Central Provinces.	Assam.
Jammu Province	Berar and Ajmere ...	Ajmere and Berar ...	India, Berar and Ajmere ...	Assam, Sindh Central Provinces and India.	Assam, Sindh, Central Provinces and India.	Assam, Sindh and Central Provinces.
Kashmir Province	Assam, Sindh, Central Provinces, India, Berar and Ajmere.	Assam, Sindh, Central Provinces, India, Ajmere and Berar.	Assam, Sindh, Central Provinces, India, Berar and Ajmere.	......	......	......
Frontier Districts (Ladákh Skardu and Gilgit.)	......	......	......	Assam, Sindh, Central Provinces, India, Berar and Ajmere.	Assam, Sindh, Central Provinces, India, Berar and Ajmere.	Assam, Sindh, Central Provinces, India, Berar and Ajmere.
Rural Population Whole State.	India, Berar and Ajmere ...	India, Ajmere and Berar ...	Sindh, Central Provinces, India, Berar and Ajmere.	Assam, Sindh, and Central Provinces.	Assam, Sindh, and Central Provinces.	Assam.
Do. Jammu ...	Berar, Ajmere and India ...	Ajmere and Berar ...	India, Berar and Ajmere ...	Assam, Sindh, and Central Provinces.	Assam, Sindh, Central Provinces and India.	Assam, Sindh and Central Provinces.
Do. Kashmir ...	Assam, Sindh, Central Provinces, India, Berar and Ajmere.	Assam, Sindh, Central Provinces, India, Ajmere and Berar.	Assam, Sindh, Central Provinces, India, Berar and Ajmere.	......	......	......
Urban population Whole State.	......	......	Ajmere	Assam, Sindh, Central Provinces, India, Berar and Ajmere.	Assam, Sindh, Central Provinces, India, Berar and Ajmere.	Assam, Sindh, Central Provinces, India and Berar.
Do. Jammu ...	......	......	......	Assam, Sindh, Central Provinces, India, Berar and Ajmere.	Assam, Sindh, Central Provinces, India, Berar and Ajmere.	Assam, Sindh, Central Provinces, India, Berar and Ajmere.
Do. Kashmir ...	Berar and Ajmere ...	Ajmere and Berar ...	India and Ajmere ...	Assam, Sindh, Central Provinces and India.	Assam, Sindh, Central Provinces, India and Berar.	Assam, Sindh, Central Provinces and Berar.

138. Ratios per 10,000 (All Religions)—

(a).—Urban Population.

	Whole State.		Urban Population, Jammu.		Urban Population, Kashmir.		Jammu City.		Srinagar City.	
	Males.	Females.	Males.	Females.	Males.	Females.	Males.	Females.	Males.	Females.
Total under 5 years	1,371	1,633	1,067	1,439	1,508	1,693	957	1,375	1,448	1,647
5—9	1,205	1,320	927	1,117	1,329	1,382	752	1,023	1,319	1,376
10—14	923	750	841	796	960	737	792	825	968	722

(b).—Rural Population.

	Whole State.		Jammu.		Kashmir.		Jammu City.		Frontier Districts.	
	Males.	Females.	Males.	Females.	Males.	Females.	Males.	Females.	Males.	Females.
Total under 5 ...	1,613	1,802	1,458	1,653	1,994	2,172	...	...	1,021	1,226
5—9	1,421	1,437	1,372	1,404	1,558	1,538	...	...	1,152	1,209
10—14	988	824	1,037	872	919	742	...	...	908	831

BY RELIGION.—HINDUS (INCLUDING JAINS AND SIKHS) AND MOHAMEDANS PER 10,000.

(a).—Urban Population.

	Whole State.				Urban Population, Jammu.				Urban Population, Kashmir.				Jammu City.				Srinagar City.			
	Hindus.		Mohamedans.		Hindus.		Mohamedans.		Hindus.		Mohamedans.		Hindus.		Mohamedans.		Hindus.		Mohamedans.	
	Males.	Females.	Males.	Females.	Males.	Females.	Males.	Females.	Males.	Females.	Males.	Females.	Males.	Females.	Males.	Females.	Males.	Females.	Males.	Females.
Total under 5 ...	1,044	1,339	1,541	1,751	1,009	1,361	1,164	1,558	1,090	1,318	1,620	1.781	930	1,371	1,012	1,382	1,059	1,291	1,564	1,740
5-9 ..	1,015	1,148	1,302	1,390	906	1053	965	1,214	1,162	1,237	1,374	1416	763	968	730	1,127	1,160	1,231	1,366	1,417
10-14 ..	912	761	929	746	834	775	853	828	1016	749	946	734	774	807	829	860	1,031	733	949	720

(b).—Rural Population.

	Whole State.				Jammu.				Kashmir.				Frontier Districts.			
	Hindus.		Mohamedans.		Hindus.		Mohamedans.		Hindus.		Mohamedans.		Hindus.		Mohamedans.	
	Males.	Females.	Males.	Females.	Males.	Females.	Males.	Females.	Males.	Females.	Males.	Females.	Males.	Females.	Males.	Females.
Total under 5 ..	1,247	1,426	1,789	1,978	1,289	1,405	1,634	1,849	1,418	1.794	2,024	2,188	..	588	1.248	1,447
5—9 ..	1,205	1,277	1,529	1,517	1,203	1,263	1,505	1,515	1,248	1,536	1,575	1,538	..	..	1,888	1,390
10—14 ..	992	828	1,001	830	994	824	1,071	909	983	909	916	735	41	..	1,093	938

139. The inequality in the above ratios will be best understood from the following tables which give the difference between the ratios of males and females under each head.

(1).—Urban Population.

	Whole State.		Jammu Province.		Kashmir Province.		Jammu City.		Srinagar City.		
	Males.	Females.	Males.	Females.	Males.	Females.	Males.	Females.	Males.	Females.	
Total under 5	...	262	...	372	...	185	...	418	...	199	Urban population Whole State.
5—9	...	115	...	190	...	53	...	271	...	57	
10—14	173	...	45	...	223	...	...	33	246	...	

(2).—*Rural Population.*

	Whole State.		*Jammu Province.*		*Kashmír Province,*		*Frontier Districts.*		
	Males.	Females.	Males.	Females.	Males.	Females.	Males.	Females.	
Total under 5	...	189	...	195	...	178	...	205	Rural Population.
5—9	...	16	...	32	20	...	...	57	
10—14	164	...	165	...	177	...	77	...	

BY RELIGION.

(1).—*Urban Population.*

	Whole State.				Jammu Province.				Kashmir Province.				Jammu City.				Srinagar City.				
	Hindus.		Mohamedans.		Hindus.		Mohamedans.		Hindus.		Mohamedans		Hindus.		Mohamedans		Hindus.		Mohamedans		
	Males.	Females.	Males.	Females.	Males.	Females.	Males.	Females.	Males.	Females.	Males.	Females.	Males.	Females.	Males.	Females.	Males.	Females.	Males.	Females.	
Total under 5 ..	..	295	..	210	..	352	..	394	..	228	..	161	..	441	..	370	..	232	..	176	Urban Population, Hindus (including Sikhs and Jains) and Mohamedans.
5—9	..	133	..	88	..	147	..	249	..	75	..	42	..	205	..	397	..	71	..	51	
10—14	151	..	183	..	59	..	25	..	267	..	212	..	..	33	..	31	298	..	229	..	

(2).—*Rural Population.*

	Whole State.				Jammu Province.				Kashmir Province.				Frontier Districts.				
Total under 5 ..	..	179	..	189	..	166	..	215	..	376	..	164	..	588	..	199	Rural Population Hindus (including Sikhs and Jains) and Mohamedans
5—9	..	72	12	..	..	60	..	10	..	288	27	..	..	..	..	8	
10—14	164	..	171	..	70	..	162	..	74	..	181	..	41	..	155	..	

140. The disparity between the ratios of males and females, the excess difference being in favor of females, at 0—5—is more marked in Jammu City and in the Urban population of Jammu Province generally and is less marked in Srinagar City and in the Urban population of Kashmír Province generally. In the Rural population it is nearly half of the Urban population in Jammu Province, and on a par with the Urban population in Kashmír Province, and is more marked in the Frontier Districts.

141. By religions it is generally higher in Hindus than Mohamedans in the Urban population and lower in Hindus in the Rural population, excepting the Frontier Districts in Kashmír Province.

At 5—9.—It is nearly half of that in the preceding period in the Urban population, and is almost reduced to a minimum in the Rural population.

In the Urban population, Hindus show an excess in the whole State, Kashmír Province and Srinagar City; and Mohamedans in Jammu Province and Jammu City, and in the Rural population it is more marked in Hindus than in Mohamedans.

At 10—14.—The abrupt rise in the ratio of males, as compared with that of females, is more prominent in the Urban and Rural population of Kashmír, and less so in the Urban and Rural population of Jammu, the disparity between Hindus and Mohamedans not being very considerable.

INEQUALITY IN RATIOS.

(a). Urban Population.

	Whole State.		Jammu Province.		Kashmir Province.		Jammu City.		Srinagar City.	
	Males.	Females.	Males.	Females.	Males.	Females.	Males.	Females.	Males.	Females.
15—19	38	...	...	33	67	...	...	109	80	...
20—29	...	107	127	...	...	219	230	...	...	217
30—39	70	...	264	...	...	21	403	...	...	44
40—49	54	...	140	...	14	...	170	...	8	...
50—59	125	...	75	...	137	...	58	...	145	...
60 and over	24	...	...	44	36	...	...	6	38	...

(b). Rural Population.

							Frontier Districts.			
15—19	1	...	...	9	4	...	56	...	...	...
20—29	...	220	...	221	...	239	...	134	...	...
30—39	1	...	13	...	...	3	...	82	...	...
40—49	63	...	90	...	44	...	...	71	...	...
50—59	39	...	93	...	85	...	54	...	...	...
60 and over	87	...	96	...	90	...	...	4	...	...

BY RELIGION.

(a). Urban Population.

	Whole State.						Jammu Province.						Kashmir Province.						Jammu City.						Srinagar City.					
	Hindus.		Mohamedans.		Budhists.		Hindus.		Mohamedans.		Budhists.		Hindus.		Mohamedans.		Budhists.		Hindus.		Mohamedans.		Budhists.		Hindus.		Mohamedans.		Budhists.	
	Males.	Females.	Males.	Females.	Males.	Females.	Males.	Females.	Males.	Females.	Males.	Females.	Males.	Females.	Males.	Females.	Males.	Females.	Males.	Females.	Males.	Females.	Males.	Females.	Males.	Females.	Males.	Females.	Males.	Females.
15—19 ..	16	..	46	..	..	..	..	22	..	51	..	..	74	..	64	..	..	..	..	94	..	134	..	..	99	..	73	..	..	..
20—29 ..	..	32	..	150	..	..	121	..	141	..	..	..	..	233	..	219	..	..	220	..	257	..	..	..	..	258	..	208	..	..
30—39 ..	129	..	81	..	..	..	184	..	388	..	..	..	41	..	..	41	..	..	338	..	514	..	..	..	21	..	..	55	..	..
40—49 ..	106	..	21	..	..	..	150	..	120	..	..	..	58	..	2	..	..	..	201	..	116	..	..	..	43	..	..	7	..	..
50—59 ..	89	..	132	..	..	..	101	..	27	..	..	..	77	..	149	..	..	..	78	..	16	..	..	..	81	..	157	..	..	..
60 and over	..	26	36	..	..	..	..	73	..	2	..	..	10	..	36	..	..	..	..	26	29	..	..	..	14	..	39	..	..	..

(b). Rural Population.

																			Frontier Districts.					
15—19 ..	..	6	5	..	..	25	..	8	..	10	..	224	24	..	6	..	..	..	..	1,393	121	..	8	..
20—29 ..	..	188	..	231	..	16	..	206	..	233	..	251	69	..	..	254	..	..	..	541	..	117	24	..
30—39 ..	23	..	..	9	..	14	14	..	11	..	..	94	168	..	..	11	..	..	2,222	..	..	38	..	1
40—49 ..	77	..	61	..	7	..	72	..	103	..	..	12	174	..	35	..	..	..	..	443	..	62	10	..
50—59 ..	86	..	93	..	13	..	88	..	96	..	148	..	68	..	83	..	..	..	413	..	100	..	..	10
60 and over	96	..	87	..	29	..	96	..	96	..	224	..	111	..	87	..	..	..	269	..	47	..	..	8

INEQUALITY IN RATIOS.

Whole State.

	Whole State.		Jammu Province.		Kashmir Province.		Ladakh.		Skardu.		Gilgit.	
	Males.	Females.	Males.	Females.	Males.	Females.	Males.	Females.	Males.	Females.	Males.	Females.
15—19	4	...	...	9	16	...	16	...	119	...	467	...
20—29	...	210	...	201	...	235	69	...	...	130	2,100	...
30—39	8	...	24	...	...	6	16	...	...	42	2,600	...
40—49	62	...	94	...	39	...	5	...	...	47	...	1,300
50—59	92	...	93	...	91	...	...	16	102	...	867	...
60 and over	81	...	90	...	80	...	...	24	50	...	133	...

BY RELIGION.

	Whole State.						Jammu Province.						Kashmir Province.					
	Hindus.		Mohamedans.		Budhists.		Hindus.		Mohamedans.		Budhists.		Hindus.		Mohamedans.		Budhists.	
	Males.	Females.	Males.	Females.	Males.	Females.	Males.	Females.	Males.	Females.	Males.	Females.	Males.	Females.	Males.	Females.	Males.	Females.
15—19	..	3	9	..	..	25	..	8	..	11	..	224	45	..	14	..	..	..
20—29	..	170	..	227	..	16	..	181	..	220	..	251	..	71	..	251	..	..
30—39	35	..	..	2	..	14	28	..	21	...	..	94	105	..	..	15	..	..
40—49	62	..	59	..	7	..	79	..	105	..	..	12	123	..	32	..	..	..
50—59	87	..	95	..	18	..	89	..	96	..	148	..	68	..	92	..	..	..
60 and over	80	..	82	..	29	..	83	..	93	..	224	..	72	..	80	..	..	..

	Ladakh.						Skardu.						Gilgit.					
	Hindus.		Mohamedans.		Budhists.		Hindus.		Mohamedans.		Budhists.		Hindus.		Mohamedans.		Budhists.	
	Males.	Females.	Males.	Females.	Males.	Females.	Males.	Females.	Males.	Females.	Males.	Females.	Males.	Females.	Males.	Females.	Males.	Females.
15—19	..	825	151	..	17	..	..	2,155	121	..	101	..	1,538	..	368	..	..	..
20—29	..	2,419	2	..	27	..	1,303	..	..	31	..	272	3,077	..	1,447	..	..	..
30—39	2,674	..	35	..	..	4	1,730	..	..	44	481	..	3,077	..	2,500	..	..	..
40—49	1,221	..	..	63	16	..	..	2,883	..	46	..	610	2,308	..	1,102	..	..	..
50—59	116	..	51	..	..	26	1,403	..	100	..	573	..	..	..	956	..	..	..
60 and over	175	..	..	1	..	9	703	..	49	..	464	..	..	..	147	..	..	..

142. These statistics prove :—

(1).—That at the age of 15—19, and subsequent periods, female life is not subject to loss, at the high rates prevailing in anterior periods.

(2).—That the high ratios in males between the age periods (20—59) in the Urban Province of Jammu generally, is influenced by the resort to cities of adult males for purpose of trade, while in the city of Jammu which is the most important town in the Province, it might also be attributed to the presence of the Chief and his staff, as well as to troops and the Civil Establishments at head-quarters. This deduction is borne out by comparing the proportions returned for the Urban and Rural population of Jammu.

(3).—The proportions of Kashmír Province and Frontier Districts, notably Skardu on the other hand, (see age periods 20—39) show an excess in females, which is accounted for by the absence of adult males for employment in the Punjab during the winter. These remarks apply equally to the Urban and Rural population.

(4).—The high ratios in subsequent age periods in males, are due to longevity which is greater in males than females.

143. Average number of females to 1,000 males at each age period.

Comparison with other Indian Provinces.

	AGE DISTRIBUTION.																	
	Under one year.	One year.	Two years.	Three years.	Four years.	Total under five.	5—9.	10—14.	15—19.	20—24.	25—29.	30—34.	35—39.	40—44.	45—49.	50—54.	55—59.	60 and over.
Jammu and Kashmir State ..	1,001	986	991	1,008	951	988	895	733	876	1,033	965	921	810	888	716	768	683	767
Punjab	950	954	966	963	914	948	842	739	817	911	873	868	813	905	779	806	723	826
Ajmere	960	937	910	948	884	930	856	701	792	882	819	851	756	949	770	939	710	1,029
Assam	1,082	1,032	1,064	1,076	997	1,048	886	802	1,027	1,052	1,065	874	822	866	818	954	861	1,163
Berars	1,033	1,043	1,075	1,102	1,022	1,055	1,008	814	1,050	1,229	912	837	712	853	773	886	786	972
Central Provinces	1,013	1,056	1,090	1,096	1,007	1,054	923	809	960	1,183	1,058	923	895	893	875	984	1,028	1,260
Sindh	936	978	1,040	946	871	944	782	654	766	928	859	856	717	899	739	825	727	1,040
India	1,004	1,036	1,072	1,070	992	1,034	926	795	922	1,088	991	955	861	964	885	1,021	936	1,195

The Kashmir State compares favourably with the Punjab, Ajmere and Assam.

144.—CHILDREN (OMITTING GILGIT ROAD.)

	WHOLE STATE.			JAMMU PROVINCE.			KASHMIR PROVINCE.			Ladákh.	Skardu.
	Total.	Urban.	Rural.	Total.	Urban.	Rural.	Total.	Urban.	Rural.		
0—5 ...	988	959	990	993	816	999	971	1,004	967	1,046	1,124
5—9 ...	895	882	896	896	728	901	884	930	877	989	958

145. It is noteworthy that the disparity between males and females is, (excepting Urban population of Jammu) not very considerable at the age of 0—5 years, that in Jammu Rural there are 999 females to every 1,000 males, while in the Urban population of Kashmír and the Rural Districts of Ladákh and Skardu there are respectively 1,004, 1,046, and 1,124 females to every one thousand males.

BY RELIGIONS.

	WHOLE STATE.						JAMMU PROVINCE.						KASHMIR PROVINCE.						LADAKH.		SKARDU.	
	Total.		Urban.		Rural.		Total.		Urban.		Rural.		Total.		Urban.		Rural.					
	0—5	5—9	0—5	5—9	0—5	5—9	0—5	5—9	0—5	5—9	0—5	5—9	0—5	5—9	0—5	5—9	0—5	5—9	0—5	5—9	0—5	5—9
Hindus (including Jains and Sikhs) ..	980	905	870	766	980	920	982	915	776	669	993	918	957	895	1,071	867	940	915	1,000	..	..	..
Mohamedans	980	891	990	929	990	889	1,000	890	877	824	1,003	892	972	883	1,007	945	968	876	1,040	977	1,123	972
Budhists	1,048	966	..	..	1,048	966	1,012	886	..	..	1,012	885	..	..	..	..	..	..	1,046	988	2,333	250

146. At 0—5 years, the disparity between Mohamedan males and females, is not so considerable as it is among Hindu males and females, but the subsequent age period of 5—9 presents a quite contrary aspect.

147. The only place where the average of Hindu females to every 1,000 males exceeds one thousand at 0—5 years, is the Urban population of Kashmír and the Rural district of Ladákh. Mohamedan females on the other hand are equal to males in Jammu Province and higher than males in the Rural population of Jammu, Urban population of Kashmír, and in Ladákh and Skardu, the highest average being obtained in Skardu which returns 1,123 females to every one thousand males.

148. Compared with Hindus and Mohamedans, Budhist females have a very high average at 0—5 years, particularly in Skardu where there are 2,333 females to every 1,000 females:—

URBAN POPULATION.

	Jammu.	Batala.	Mirpore.	Punch.	Srinagar.	Anantnág.	Sopore.	Bárámula.
0—5 ...	763	702	1,019	922	1,020	927	1,001	873
5—9 ...	724	582	840	752	937	905	933	846

BY RELIGION.

	Jammu.		Batala.		Mirpore.		Punch.		Srinagar.		Anantnág.		Sopore.		Bárámula.	
	Hindus.	Mohamedans.	Hindus.	Mohamedans.	Hindus.	Mohamedans.	Hindus.	Mohamedans.	Hindus.	Mohamedans.	Hindus.	Mohamedans.	Hindus.	Mohamedans.	Hindus.	Mohamedans.
0—5 ...	764	764	627	1,026	980	1,060	798	941	999	1,024	884	931	881	1,111	892	870
5—9 ...	657	856	516	873	917	766	655	798	870	953	1,018	896	836	944	703	871

The towns of Mirpore, Srinagar and Sopore return a high average of females, the excess being particularly in the Mohamedan population:—

MARRIAGEABLE LIFE.

	Whole State.			Jammu Province.			Kashmir Province.			Ladákh.	Skardu.	Gilgit
	Total.	Urban.	Rural.	Total.	Urban.	Rural.	Total.	Urban.	Rural.			
10—14 ...	733	654	748	735	572	741	712	686	717	950	828	...
15—19 ...	876	768	881	880	630	882	871	825	880	949	844	...

BY RELIGION.

	Whole State.						Jammu Province.						Kashmir Province.						Ladakh.		Skardu.		Gilgit.	
	Total.		Urban.		Rural.		Total.		Urban.		Rural.		Total.		Urban.		Rural.							
	Hindus.	Mohamedans.	Hindus.	Mohamedans.	Hindus.	Mohamedans.	Hindus.	Mohamedans.	Hindus.	Mohamedans.	Hindus.	Mohamedans.	Hindus.	Mohamedans.	Hindus.	Mohamedans.	Hindus.	Mohamedans.	Hindus.	Mohamedans.	Hindus.	Mohamedans.	Hindus.	Mohamedans.
10—14	708	740	566	699	722	743	712	747	529	636	725	752	649	718	600	711	708	718	...	917	...	828	...	...
15—19	581	884	668	828	872	889	864	892	591	698	921	897	784	888	749	846	721	888	885	756	600	844	...	...

DETAILS OF URBAN POPULATION.

	Jammu.	Batala.	Mirpore.	Punch.	Srinagar.	Anantnág.	Sopore.	Bárámula.
10—14 ...	554	459	815	572	670	732	828	760
15—19 ...	606	678	863	569	814	813	885	996

BY RELIGION.

	Jammu.		Batála.		Mirpore.		Punch.		Srinagar.		Anantnág.		Sopore.		Bárámula.	
	Hindus.	Mohamedans.	Hindus.	Mohamedans.	Hindus.	Mohamedans.	Hindus.	Mohamedans.	Hindus.	Mohamedans.	Hindus.	Mohamedans.	Hindus.	Mohamedans.	Hindus.	Mohamedans.
10—14 ...	541	577	414	667	740	994	528	593	515	698	680	739	822	828	921	734
15—19 ...	580	656	662	750	787	955	431	671	735	841	1,000	795	1,094	864	683	1,065

149. It is difficult to fix the period of marriageable life, and the statistics of civil condition have not been prepared during the present Census, so as to give an idea of the number of single and married males and females at these age periods—marriages in the hilly tracts generally take place at or after the age of 9, and the numbers of the population at the two subsequent age periods at least, serve to show the extent to which wives are obtainable by the male population without resorting to other parts for matrimony.

150. It appears that young women are more numerous in Ladákh than in any other part of the State, that they are fewer in the Urban population of Jammu than in the Urban and Rural population of both Jammu and Kashmír.

151. For the whole State there appear to be about 300 males per mille in the Urban and 200 in the Rural population, whose condition of celibacy is due to want of females, the want being particularly traceable to Hindus in the towns of Jammu, Batála, Punch and Srinagar.

152. The figures for Budhists are given below :—

	Whole State.	Jammu.	Ladákh.	Skardu.
10—14	930	847	954	667
15—19	1,017	1,236	978	500

With the exception of Skardu, the Budhists are generally better off than Hindus and Mohamedans in their comparison of young women with young males.

ABLE BODIED.

	Whole State.			Jammu Province.			Kashmir Province.			Ladákh.	Skardu.	Gilgit.
	Total.	Urban.	Rural.	Total.	Urban.	Rural.	Total.	Urban.	Rural.			
20—24 ...	1,033	885	1,052	1,015	600	1,042	1,054	1,019	1,062	941	1,101	...
25—29 ...	965	813	982	948	544	974	1,000	991	1,002	917	900	33
30—34 ...	921	838	931	905	539	928	947	978	940	938	986	...
35—39 ...	810	680	734	780	885	797	812	796	815	981	1,030	...
40—44 ...	888	876	890	850	568	865	946	1,003	934	951	886	100
45—49 ...	715	590	727	685	479	693	674	651	679	984	1,096	...

BY RELIGION.

	Whole State.						Jammu Province.						Kashmir Province.						Ladákh.		Skardu.		Gilgit.	
	Total.		Urban.		Rural.		Total.		Urban.		Rural.		Total.		Urban.		Rural.							
	Hindus.	Mohamedans.	Hindus.	Mohamedans.	Hindus.	Mohamedans.	Hindus.	Mohamedans.	Hindus.	Mohamedans.	Hindus.	Mohamedans.	Hindus.	Mohamedans.	Hindus.	Mohamedans.	Hindus.	Mohamedans.	Hindus.	Mohamedans.	Hindus.	Mohamedans.	Hindus.	Mohamedans.
20—24 ..	967	1,063	725	968	1,000	1,073	985	1,024	591	612	1,019	1,062	828	1,076	905	1,050	759	1,080	175	886	..	1,103	..	..
25—29 ..	809	997	652	915	799	1,004	930	977	489	614	951	990	779	1,021	932	1,006	724	1,028	45	963	91	904	..	357
30—34 ..	868	944	681	905	892	947	878	927	534	550	906	942	786	961	915	996	677	955	..	841	148	940	..	..
35—39 ..	770	824	542	766	796	849	886	774	494	456	808	785	629	830	621	861	635	827	..	991	..	1,038	..	..
40—44 ..	848	904	681	763	867	899	853	845	530	635	878	852	779	981	888	1,088	687	948	..	954	600	885	..	..
45—49 ..	680	795	510	637	700	732	695	675	462	507	712	682	550	688	579	674	529	690	..	1,015	..	1,098	..	..

ABLE BODIED.

	Jammu.	Batála.	Mirpore.	Punch.	Srinagar.	Anantnág.	Sopore.	Bárámula.
20—24 ...	521	887	1,260	563	1,022	884	1,057	1,211
25—29 ...	446	1,023	1,042	603	986	578	1,186	856
30—34 ...	438	981	1,101	545	990	912	871	966
35—39 ...	395	867	947	289	800	704	764	937
40—44 ...	476	852	1,000	554	1,016	897	967	961
45—49 ...	420	689	841	370	649	703	780	417

BY RELIGION.

	Jammu.		Batála.		Mirpore.		Punch.		Srinagar.		Anantnág.		Sopore.		Bárámula.	
	Hindus.	Mohamedans.	Hindus.	Mohamedans.	Hindus.	Mohamedans.	Hindus.	Mohamedans.	Hindus.	Mohamedans.	Hindus.	Mohamedans.	Hindus.	Mohamedans.	Hindus.	Mohamedans.
20—24 ...	529	506	874	933	1,258	1,262	456	645	936	1,048	408	951	702	1,109	914	1,264
25—29 ...	429	496	1,084	836	1,063	1,016	413	786	929	1,003	1,024	979	1,075	1,201	820	863
30—34 ...	435	444	1,061	720	1,258	920	405	644	919	1,018	827	925	737	886	1,138	954
35—39 ...	408	326	965	622	1,009	881	344	523	646	853	250	806	622	792	519	992
40—44 ...	458	529	896	714	980	1,029	324	730	907	1,050	537	944	742	1,000	708	1,026
45—49 ...	399	463	667	800	1,139	618	233	491	584	678	484	743	857	814	368	429

153. An examination of these statistics establishes a remarkably interesting point in connection with the movement of the male population as will appear from the following facts :—

(1).—That for the whole State females outnumber males at the age of 20—24 by 33 per mille, and at subsequent periods show a gradual decrease till at the age of 45—49 ~~when there are only 715 females to every one~~ thousand males, the said gradual decrease being more marked in Hindus than Mohamedans.

(2).—That this irregular rise and fall in numbers is perceptible with rare exceptions throughout the Rural population of both Jammu and Kashmír and the Urban population of Kashmír, the highest figures at 20—24 being :—

1,052 Rural population Whole State.
1,042 Ditto Jammu Province.
1,062 Ditto Kashmír do.
1,019 Urban population Kashmír Province.

and the lowest at 45—49 being :—

727 Rural population Whole State.
693 Ditto Jammu Province.
679 Ditto Kashmír do.
651 Urban population Kashmír Province.

(3).—That the Urban population of Jammu Province with one exception at age period (35—39) shows a singular falling off in females, the highest number being only 600 at (20—24) and the lowest 479 at (45—49) to every one thousand males.

(4).—That there is no perceptible rise or fall in Ladákh, the average being 941 at 20—24 and 984 at 45—49.

(5).—That in Skardu the average number of females to every 1,000 males, shows a marked increase in females which is not met elsewhere at age periods 20—24, 35—39 and 45—49.

(6).—Contrasted by religions, the decrease in the average of females to every one thousand males, is found in both Hindus and Mohamedans, but more prominently in the former.

(7).—That the abnormal decrease in females in the Urban population of Jammu Province is conclusively traced to the towns of Jammu and Punch, the other towns keeping pace generally with the Rural population, notably the town of Mirpore the averages of which are generally higher than it.

154. The figures for Budhists are given below :—

	Whole State.	Jammu Province.	Ladákh.	Skardu.
20—24	967	977	973	500
25—29	1,012	1,240	967	1,000
30—34	992	1,074	986	250
35—39	990	984	996	615
40—44	983	1,095	963	1,600
45—49	968	845	992	667

and prove generally that the population is stationary.

155. The above affords convincing proof of the propositions stated in paragraph 90 of this report, *viz.* :—

(*a*) That an unusually large number of able-bodied males reside in the towns of Jammu and Punch as State employés in the Civil and Military Departments, and consequently the average number of females to every 1,000 males is extremely low.

(*b*) That in the town of Mirpore the high ratio of Hindu and Mohamedan females is due to the absence of males on employment in other parts of the country.

(*c*) That the Mohamedan population of Kashmír and Skardu seek employment in the Punjab during the winter months.

AGED PERSONS.

	Whole State.			Jammu Province.			Kashmir Province.			Ladákh.	Skardu.	Gilgit.
	Total.	Urban.	Rural.	Total.	Urban.	Rural.	Total.	Urban.	Rural.			
50—54 ...	763	689	769	756	545	766	769	766	770	1,008	745	...
55—59 ...	683	507	700	690	524	701	632	496	661	969	709	...
60 and over ...	767	758	766	755	658	758	747	815	738	989	911	...

BY RELIGION.

	Kashmir Province.						Jammu Province.						Whole State.						Ladákh.		Skardu.		Gilgit.	
	Total.		Urban.		Rural.		Total.		Urban.		Rural.		Total.		Urban.		Rural.							
	Hindus.	Mohamedans.	Hindus.	Mohamedans.	Hindus.	Mohamedans.	Hindus.	Mohamedans.	Hindus.	Mohamedans.	Hindus.	Mohamedans.	Hindus.	Mohamedans.	Hindus.	Mohamedans.	Hindus.	Mohamedans.	Hindus.	Mohamedans.	Hindus.	Mohamedans.	Hindus.	Mohamedans.
50—54 ...	777	452	649	729	791	755	776	735	515	609	800	740	811	768	826	751	748	771	...	961	...	751	..	...
55—59 ...	654	683	466	540	662	696	673	709	459	674	692	713	485	652	477	500	333	676	...	714	...	712	...	...
60 & over	757	765	712	791	760	763	764	746	658	657	768	748	681	735	785	826	620	746	...	929	...	914	...	...

AGED PERSONS.

	Jammu.	Batála.	Mirpore.	Punch.	Srinagar.	Anantnag.	Sopore.	Bárámula.
50—54 ...	492	467	1,031	440	767	695	871	932
55—59 ...	480	365	1,035	403	490	422	679	517
60 and over...	541	571	1,179	490	813	915	705	843

BY RELIGION.

	Jammu.		Batala.		Mirpore.		Punch.		Srinagar.		Anantnag.		Sopore.		Baramula.	
	H.	M.	H.	M.	H.	M.	H.	M.	H.	M.	H.	M.	H.	M.	H.	M.
50—54 ...	479	516	493	355	913	1,254	291	585	834	749	733	690	1,167	836	517	802
55—59 ...	427	541	300	111	940	1,167	300	513	462	498	250	462	750	667	1,143	318
60 and over	548	328	550	674	1,190	1,163	1,175	675	798	821	875	919	357	1,284	794	850

156. These figures show that the general vitality, and consequently the period of longevity of females in this State, is better in the Rural than in the Urban population, that it is more satisfactory in the cold climate of Ladákh than in any other part of the State, excepting of course the town of Mirpore where the average of Mohamedan females is the highest.

157.—The subjoined table elicits another interesting point in connection with age. Dividing the population equally, that division is made at the following age; the numbers under and over being nearly equal:—

	Males.	*Females.*
Whole State, Rural Population	21·63	20·96
Do. Urban do.	22·5	21·46
Jammu Province Urban	25.8	23·11
Do. do. Rural	22·27	21·45
Total Jammu	22·4	21·5
Kashmír Province, Urban	21·3	21·005
Do., Rural	20·11	19·19
Total Kashmír	20·26	19·9
Ladákh	28·96	28·76
Skardu	20·66	20·35
Gilgit	37·5	24·00

158. If we divide our people into classes, the results are found, as follows:—

Hindu males	23·97
Do. females	22·93
Mohamedan males	20·61
Do. females	20·1
Budhist males	28·67
Do. females	28·55

159. We have now to deduce an average age for our population.

In the following table are given the different periods, the average age for each, and the living numbers, with the sums of their years, and dividing the sums of all by 25,27,046 our total population, we get 24·26 years as the average age for each person in the Province. For males it is 24·26 and for females 22·48, higher in males by 1·78 of a year or 1 year 9·49 months:—

Age periods.	Mean age for each period.	Population enumerated.	Sum of years.
0—9	$4\frac{1}{2}$	7,88,842	35,49,789
10—24	17	6,39,830	1,08,77,110
25—39	32	5,64,301	1,80,57,632
40—44	42	1,61,436	67,80,312
45—59	52	2,23,332	1,16,13,264
60 and above.	70	1,49,305	1,04,51,350
		*25,27,046	6,13,29,457
		* excluding unspecified (16,906)	

6,13,29,457 ÷ 25,27,046 = 24·26.

160. In the North-Western Provinces the average age of the population is 23 years, in Madras it is 22·27, in Bombay 22·36, and in Central Provinces 21·59, the mean for the four Provinces approximates to that for this Province.

161. Compared with the English average (32·1) ours is lower by 7·84, which means that death-rate is higher in India in the advanced periods, and life is consequently of shorter duration.

162. For the Urban and Rural population the average age is as given below :—

	Total Population.		Average.	
	Males.	Females.	Males.	Females.
Urban Population, Jammu.				
Jammu City	22,545	11,997	27·19	22·99
Batála do.	3,079	2,127	21·51	23·55
Mirpore do.	3,655	3,598	22·53	23·51
Punch do.	4,675	2,814	25·76	22·83
Total Jammu, Urban	33,954	20,536	25·80	23·11
Urban Population, Kashmir.				
Srinagar City	62,720	56,240	21·45	21·18
Anantnág do.	5,515	4,712	20·83	20·55
Sopore do.	4,360	4,050	20·11	19·66
Bárámula do.	3,003	2,653	20·94	20·35
Total Urban, Kashmír	75,598	67,655	21·30	21·005
Total Urban, Whole State	1,09,552	88,191	22·50	21·46
Jammu (Rural)	7,36,287	6,48,766	22·27	21·45
Kashmír (Rural)	4,26,747	3,79,041	20·11	19·19
Frontier Districts	80,643	74,725	25·08	23·73
Total Rural, Whole State	12,43,677	11,02,532	21·63	20·96
Grand Total	13,53,229	11,90,723	21·70	20·99

163. There is another point which is equally interesting, *viz.*, that of life expectancy, or the average duration of Native life.

Age periods.	Duration of each period.	Population.	Average annual population.	Decrease per year.
0— 9 ...	9	7,88,842	87,649	41,947
10—24 ...	14	6,39,830	45,702	5,395
25—39 ...	14	5,64,301	40,307	—52
40—44 ...	4	1,61,436	40,359	24,407
45—59 ...	14	2,23,332	15,952	8,487
60 and over ...	20	1,49,305	7,465	7,465
Total ...	...	* 25,27,046 excluding unspecified (16,906)	...	87,701—52=87,649

164. The total annual mortality for the whole State is, therefore, 87,649, being highest at the age of 0—9 and 40—44.

The sum of the last column gives 34·68 as the death-rate per mille per annum on the total population of both sexes, for males 34·68, and for females 34·68, the average duration of life coming to 25·98 years, as will be seen from the subjoined table :—

Age periods.	Mean age for each period.	Computed deaths.	Sum of years.
0—9	4½	41,947	1,88,761
10—24	17	5,395	91,715
25—39	32	—52	—1,664
40—44	42	24,407	10,25,094
45—59	52	8,487	4,41,324
60 and over	70	7,465	5,22,550
	Total ...	87,701—52=87,649	22,67,780

$$\frac{22,67,780}{87,649} = 25{\cdot}98.$$

165. Our life expectancy is as follows:—

	Males.	*Females.*
Jammu	22·4	21·5
Kashmír	20·26	19·9
Ladákh	28·96	28·76
Skardu	20·66	20·35
Urban Population, Jammu	25·8	23·11
Do. do., Kashmír	21·3	21·005
Rural Population, Jammu	22·27	21·45
Do. do., Kashmír	20·11	19·19
Urban Population, Whole State	22·5	·21·46
Rural Population, Whole State	21·63	20·96

CHAPTER V.

Birth-place.

166. The subjoined table shows the distribution of the population according to Birth-place :—

	Total.	Males.	Females.	Percentage on total population.		
				Both sexes.	Males.	Females.
Within the State	24,57,799	13,08,748	11,49,051	96·6	51·4	45·1
Provinces and States in India ...	66,152	31,906	34,246	2·6	1·3	1·4
Asia beyond India	3,032	2,327	705	0·2	0·2	...
Europe	71	42	29	...	...	...
Africa	2	...	2	...	...	...
Unspecified	16,896	10,206	6,690	0·6	0·4	0·2
TOTAL ...	25,43,952	13,53,229	11,90,723	100·0	53·3	46·7

167. Persons born within the State represent 96·6 per cent. or including the unspecified population of Gilgit (16,615) 97 per cent. nearly.

168. The population due to immigration is 86,153, or 3.4 per cent., or excluding Gilgit 3 per cent., of whom 44,481 are males, and 41,672 females; of this the Punjab, and the adjoining Native States of Kapurthala, Patiála, Chamba, Sarmore and Biláspore contribute 65,108, or 2·56 per cent., the remainder being distributed as follows :—

	Total.	Males.	Females.
British India	1,027	799	228
Feudatory States	17	10	7
Yagistán (Chitral)	1,183	711	472
Nepál	1,001	904	97
Afghánistán	745	625	120
Other countries adjacent to India	61	50	11
Remote from India	42	37	5
Europe	71	42	29
Africa	2	...	2
Unspecified	16,896	10,206	6,690

169. The movement of the population from the Punjab into this State is more considerable in Jammu than in Kashmír, the figures in the former being 28,275 males and 32,598 females, total 60,873; and in the latter 2,501 males, 1,180 females, total 3,681. This is apparently due to the close proximity of Jammu Province to the Punjab Districts of Siálkot, Gujrát, Jhelam and Ráwalpindi, and to the consequent frequency of inter-marriages, trade and employment in the State.

170. The subjoined table gives proportion per mille to total population and the average number of females to every 1,000 males by provinces :—

	Males.	Females.	Average number of females to every 1,000 males.
Jammu	535	465	868
Kashmír	529	471	889
Ladákh	508	492	970
Skardu	508	492	966
Gilgit	608	392	644
Whole State	532	468	879

The disparity is prominently noticeable in Gilgit owing to the presence of troops, and to some extent in Jammu and Kashmír, in consequence of State Establishments and the floating population; but there could be no doubt that on the whole, there is an excess of 120 per mille in males over females. A comparison of the relative figures of the aboriginal population with immigrants from other countries, gives the following results :—

171. The aboriginal inhabitants, or in other words, those born within the State, muster 24,57,799, of whom 13,08,748 are males, and 11,49,051 females; the relative proportions being—

Males	533	per mille.
Females	467	"
Average number of females to every 1,000 males	877	"

172. The figures for the outside or Foreign population stand as below :—

Total.	Males.	Females.	*Proportion per mille.* Males.	Females	*Average number of females of every* 1,000 *males*
86,153	44,481	41,672	516	484	937

173. The details by provinces are as follows :—

	Aboriginals.			*Outside Population.*			PROPORTION PER MILLE. *Aboriginals.*		*Foreign.*		*Average number of females to 1,000 males.*	
	Total.	Males.	Females.	Total.	Males.	Females.	Males.	Females.	Males.	Females.	Aboriginals.	Foreign.
Jammu ...	13,76,183	7,40,118	6,36,065	63,360	30,123	33,237	537	463	476	524	859	1,103
Kashmír ..	9,43,273	4,98,424	4,44,849	5,768	3,921	1,847	528	472	680	320	892	471
Ladákh ...	28,087	14,176	13,911	187	174	13	505	495	930	70	981	75
Skardu ...	1,10,123	55,899	54,224	202	199	3	507	493	985	15	970	15
Gilgit ...	Statistics not collected.											

The disparity in Ladákh and Skardu compared with Jammu and Kashmír, is comparatively slight owing to scanty migration to other parts of the country. The foreign element in the State is largest in Jammu, representing 46 per mille. In Kashmír and Ladákh it is only 6 per mille, and in Skardu nearly two per mille. The coldness of the climate, difference in social and religious ceremonies and the hardship caused by intervening mountains, accounts for the fact that native immigrants to Ladákh and Skardu are not accompanied by their families. The immigrants in Ladákh are mostly traders and missionaries, not to speak of a few State servants, while in Skardu they are mostly servants of the State.

174. The total number of Europeans, including those born in Africa, is returned as 42 males and 31 females, of whom 31 males and 28 females were British-born, as detailed below:—

	Total.	Males.	Females.
England	50	27	23
Scotland	5	3	2
Wales	1	...	1
Ireland	3	1	2
Total	59	31	28

175. The details for other European countries are as follows:—

	Total.	Males.	Females.
France	3	3	...
Holland	1	1	...
Italy	3	3	...
Portugal	2	2	...
Germany	3	2	1
Cape Colony	1	...	1
Africa (unspecified)	1	...	1
Total	14	11	3

176. The Asiatic element comprises 99·997, and the non-Asiatic ·0003 per cent. of the total population.

CHAPTER VI.

Castes.

177. The following information is taken from the standard form prescribed by the Census Commissioner :—

Class.	Hindus.	Sikhs.	Jains.	Total.	Mohamedans.	Gilgit district not enumerated.	Total strength.
A. Agricultural	3,07,049	370	...	3,07,419	6,48,915	...	9,56,334
B. Professional	2,39,619	9,412	...	2,49,031	4,18,787	...	6,67,818
C. Commercial	45,885	1,178	593	47,656	52,492	...	1,00,148
D. Artisans and Village Menials	97,095	317	...	97,412	2,11,622	...	3,09,034
E. Vagrant Minor Artisans and Performers.	1,065	...	...	1,065	3,569	...	4,634
F. Races and Nationalities ...	...	...	...	...	4,54,739	...	4,54,739
Unspecified	1,087	122	...	1,209	3,586	16,615	21,410
Total ...	6,91,800	11,399	593	7,03,792	17,93,710	16,615	25,14,117

178. Divided by Districts the figures stand as below :—

(1).—HINDUS (INCLUDING JAINS AND SIKHS).

Districts.	Agricultural.	Professional.	Commercial.	Artisans and Village Menials.	Vagrant Minor Artisans and Performers.	Races and Nationalities.	Unspecified.	Total.
Jammu Urban	10,711	8,112	8,016	6,282	184	...	482	33,787
Do. Rural	2,93,946	1,82,594	35,444	90,588	837	...	548	6,03,957
Total ...	3,04,657	1,90,706	43,460	96,870	1,021	...	1,030	6,37,744
Kashmir Urban	408	26,903	1,363	211	34	...	35	28,954
Do. Rural	2,255	31,325	2,788	315	10	...	142	36,835
Total ...	2,663	58,228	4,151	526	44	...	177	65,789
Ladakh	62	69	35	15	...	...	1	182
Skardu	36	25	2	...	...	...	1	64
Gilgit	1	8	3	1	...	...	...	13
Grand Total ...	3,07,419	2,49,031	47,656	97,412	1,065	...	1,209	7,03,792

(2).—MOHAMEDANS.

Districts.	Agricultural.	Professional.	Commercial.	Artisans and Village Menials.	Vagrant-Minor Artisans and Performers.	Races and Nationalities.	Unspecified.	Total strength.
Jammu Urban	4,398	1,871	48	5,372	96	8,814	90	20,689
Do. Rural	4,88,341	38,256	8,415	1,22,546	3,090	1,14,918	1,204	7,76,770
Total ...	4,92,739	40,127	8,463	1,27,918	3,186	1,23,732	1,294	7,97,459
Kashmir Urban	6,067	38,166	1,861	15,283	5	52,611	177	1,14,170
Do. Rural	1,49,344	3,38,315	41,665	67,529	378	1,69,584	2,114	7,68,929
Total ...	1,55,411	3,76,481	43,526	82,812	383	2,22,195	2,291	8,83,099
Ladákh	8	455	6	38	...	2,489	...	2,991
Skardu	758	1,721	496	854	...	1,06,193	...	1,10,022
Gilgit	4	3	1	...	...	130	1	139
Grand Total ..	6,48,915	4,18,787	52,492	2,11,622	3,569	4,54,739	3,586	17,93,710

179. The same details for Sikhs and Jains separately are given below :—

(1).—SIKHS.

Districts.	Agricultural.	Professional.	Commercial.	Artisans and Village Menials.	Vagrant-Minor Artisans and Performers.	Races and Nationalities.	Unspecified.	Total strength.
Jammu Urban	6	110	438	88	...	...	8	650
Do. Rural	77	4,522	506	73	...	...	98	5,276
Total ...	83	4,632	944	161	...	...	106	5,926
Kashmir Urban	38	87	28	106	...	...	...	259
Do. Rural	249	4,693	206	50	...	...	16	5,214
Total ...	287	4,780	234	156	...	...	16	5,473
Ladákh	...	...	...	...	...	...	...	...
Skardu	...	...	...	...	...	...	...	...
Gilgit	...	...	...	...	...	...	...	...
Grand Total ...	370	9,412	1,178	317	...	...	122	11,399

(2).—JAINS.

Districts.	Agricultural.	Professional.	Commercial.	Artisans and Village Menials.	Vagrant Minor Artisans and Performers,	Races and Nationalities.	Unspecified.	Total strength.
Jammu Urban	...	...	544	...	...	...	...	544
Do. Rural	...	...	49	...	...	...	...	49
Total ...	...	...	593	...	...	...	...	593
Kashmir Urban	...	...	...	...	...	...	...	...
Do. Rural	...	...	...	...	...	...	...	...
Total ...	...	...	...	...	...	...	...	...
Ladákh	...	...	...	...	...	...	...	...
Skardu	...	...	...	...	...	...	...	...
Gilgit	...	...	...	...	...	...	...	...
Grand Total ...	...	...	593	...	...	...	...	593

180. The total population of Hindus (including Sikhs and Jains), Mohamedans and Budhists being 25,27,110, the relative proportions of castes are :—

Class.	Total percentage.	Hindus, including Jains and Sikhs.	Budhists.	Mohamedans.
A. Agricultural	38·00	12·20	...	25·8
B. Professional	26·46	9·8	...	16·66
C. Commercial	3·94	1·88	...	2·06
D. Artisans and Village Menials	12·24	3·84	...	8·4
E. Vagrant Minor Artisans and Performers	·18	·04	...	·14
F. Races and Nationalities	19·00	...	1	18
G. Unspecified	·18	·04	...	·14
Total ...	100	27·8	1	71·2

181. The above classification of castes is by no means accurate. The occupation tables return 17,62,843 as agriculturists, whereas the caste returns show only 9,56,334. The anomaly is attributed to the fact, that in the Rural population, all classes whether professional or others, with few exceptions, devote themselves to agriculture, either as their sole occupation, or in addition to other occupations. The following gives a detail of castes generally employed in agriculture, with special reference to the figures returned in the occupation tables. It would be more convenient and accurate, if the standard form of the Imperial return of castes was modified, as at present the classification of castes by occupation appears to be grossly misleading, while in a statistical point of view, such classification hardly gives a clear insight into the complicated system of castes, its origin, and development.

Agricultural Castes.	Total Population. Hindus and Sikhs.	Mohamedans.	Total.
(a.)—Traditional—			
Rájputs	150,647	252,271	402,918
Ját	24,150	118,445	142,595
Arain	...	22,243	22,243
Seni	728	...	728
Gujar	883	247,906	248,789
Total (a.)	176,408	640,865	817,273
(b.)—Brahman castes of Kashmír, who by change of religion, have adopted agriculture as their principal occupation—			
Pandit	...	2,895	2,895
Sufi	...	11,003	11,003
Bat	...	94,144	94,144
Aitu	...	6,345	6,345
Tantre	...	5,478	5,478
Dár	...	68,949	68,949
Rathar	...	23,801	23,801
Rishi	...	6,290	6,290
Raina	...	1,286	1,286
Khande	...	6,093	6,093
Ganai	...	37,987	37,987
Total (b.)	...	264,271	264,271
(c.)—Khatrís who by embracing Mohamedanism, have turned agriculturists—			
Khoja	...	8,580	8,580
Magre	...	5,811	5,811
Malik	...	21,887	21,887
Total (c.)	...	36,278	36,278
(d.)—Religious Devotees—			
Jogi	3,610	2,589	6,199
(e.)—Professional Priests who have taken to cultivation—			
Brahmans (Hindus) in rural population ...	206,174	...	206,174
Sayads, in rural population, Jammu and Kashmír and in Frontier Districts	...	103,669	103,669
Mírs, an agricultural caste of Sayads ...	...	59,827	59,827
Total (d.)	206,174	163,496	369,670
(f.)—Sheikhs, in rural population	...	347,667	347,667
Budhists do. do.	...	29,608	29,608
Total (f.)	...	377,275	377,275
(g.)—Barwála, Basith, Batwál, Dhyar, Gen, Saryara, Sepi, Megh, Ratyál, Begári, Gomsa, Pakhiwár } Field laborers	96,528	13	96,541
Grand Total	482,720	1,484,787	1,967,507
Deduct Class B., Agriculture			1,762,843
General Labor			74,235
Total			1,837,078
Difference			130,429

which comprises other castes who have adopted agriculture as their occupation.

182. The following details of Castes peculiar to the several Provinces are not devoid of interest :—

(*A.*)—ONLY HINDUS.

A. Agricultural.	B. Professional.	C. Commercial.	D. Artisans and Village Menials.	E. Vagrant Minor Artisans and Performers.	F. Races and Nationalities.
DUM. *Sub-divisions of Dum* { Basith. Batwál. Sarvara. Sepi. Megh. Barwála. Ratyál. Begári. Gen. Gomsa. Dhyár. NEPALESE AND OTHER HILL TRIBES. Sudar. Gola. Goran. MAKARKONI ALIAS NAGARKOTI. Nobahar. Bodar. Garti. Heku. Majithia. Doni. Dagori. Kagar. Godurz. Hotaberi. *Sub-divisions of Rajput.* { Ahlia. Shahi. Thappa. *Seni.*	Beragi. BRAHMAN. *Sub-divisions of Brahman* { Bhatre. Bedangi. Pati. SANYASI. *Sub-divisions of Sanyasi.* { Bharti. Gorya. Jangam. Bramhohari. Nirmala. *Sub-divisions of Mirasi.* { Rawabia. Kathak. Sarnain. Gardi. KAYASTH.	AROBA. Bania. Bhatya. KHATRI. *Sub-divisions of Khatri* { Kurgi. Kaur. Bohar.	Chamar. CHURA. *Sub-divisions of Chura.* { Charu. Ramdasi or Mazhabi. *Sub-division of Darzi.* { Sochi. *Sub-division of Jhiwar.* { Ghirath. *Sub-division of Julaha.* { Kuch-band. KALAL.	Dasali. Sansi.	

(*B.*)—ONLY MOHAMEDANS.

A. Agricultural.	B. Professional.	C. Commercial.	D. Artisans and Village Menials.	E. Vagrant Minor Artisans and Performers.	F. Races and Nationalities.
Araín. Awán. *Sub-division of Gujar.* { Choupan. *Nepalese and other hill tribes.* } Bokru. Pakhiwár. *Sub-divisions of Rajput.* { Pare. Lon.	*Sub-divisions of Brahman.* { Pandit. Sufi. Dár. Bat. Aitu. Tantre. Rathar. Rishi. Raina. Khande. Ganai. *Dervesh.* *Sub-divisions of Dervesh.* { Chishti. Said-Makar. Kádri. Miskin. Madári. Tamburi. Musáfir. Kalandar. Noshahi. Rawal. Vagi. SAYAD. *Sub-divisions of Sayad.* { Pír. Mír. MIRASI. *Sub-divisions of Mírási.* { Bharai. Beda. Nikarchi. Malakhan. Mon. Doom (watchman) KANJAR. *Sub-division of Kanjar.* { Perna.	*Sub-divisions of Bania.* { Wain. Vani. *Sub-divisions of Khatri.* { Khoja. Magre. Malik.	BANGI. *Sub-division of Chura.* { Vatal. Hanji. *Sub-division of Jhiwar.* { Bhishti. Julaha. Kassab. Memar. *Sub-division of Manyar.* { Kamangar. MOCHI. *Sub-divisions of Mochi.* { Saraj. Khatik. Dabgar. Musalli. Naddáf. Niyaria. Rangrez. Teli.	*Sub-division of Batehra.* { Beldár. Changar. Shakhsaz.	BUDHIST CONVERTS:— Argon. Tang. Jáju. Champa. Dokpa. Brokpa. Chon. Deo. Kharpon. Nospun. Gonkpa. Kafalpa. Churankpa. Ofpa. Karimpa. Narankzapa. Charnaupa. Arkabakpa. Monkeypa. Aliarpa. Tarsarpa. Kanopa. Chaupon. Dasokharampa. Pahapa. Abdulpa. Galudanpa. Asarpa. Stapa. Kachapa. Dachapa. Samplepa. Dolupa. Mahvapa. Malakpa. Lakhbakpa. MOGHAL. PATHAN. SHEIKH. *and its Sub-divisions:*— Hakim. Nanbai. Malla. Balti. Bazdar. Raodi. Soni. Sagar. Kangu. Ganarak. Kamakhu. Gashu. Geri. Mangrak. Meva. Makh. Shaban. Miai. Hanghi. Doru. Turanj. Hajia. Chedeva. Sambava. Nanva. Balida. Harsakhia. Homan Chirmal. Kashna.

(*C.*)—BOTH HINDUS AND MOHAMEDANS.

A. Agricultural.	B. Professional.	C. Commercial.	D. Artisans and Village Menials.	E. Vagrant Minor Artisans and Performers.	F. Races and Nationalities.
Gujar.	Jogi.	Kambo.	Darzi.	Batehra.	
Ját.	*Sub-divisions of Sanyasi.* Sadhu.	Labana.	Dhobi.	Bázigar.	
Rájput.	Gusáin.		Jhiwar.		
	Fakír.		Kumhar.		
	Sain.		Lohár.		
	Udasi.		*Sub-division of Lohár*—Saikalgar.		
	Suthra.		Manyar.		
			Nái.		
			Sunár.		
			Tarkhán.		
			Thatyár.		

(D).—CASTES FOUND GENERALLY IN THE SEVARAL PROVINCES.

A. Agricultural.		B. Professional.		C. Commercial.		D. Artisans and Village Menials.		E. Vagrant Minor Artisans and Performers.		F Races and Nationalities.	
Hindus.	Mohamedans.	Hindus.	Mohamedans.	Hindus.	Mohamedans.	Hindus.	Mohamedans.	Hindus.	Mohamedans.		Mohamedans.
Dum.	Arain.	Berági.	*Sub-divisions of Brahman.* Sufi.	Arora.	*Sub-division of Bania.* Wain.	Chamar.	Hanji.	Dasali.	*Sub-division of Batehra.* Beldar	Christians.	Moghal.
Sub-divisions of Dum. Basith.	Awán.	Brahman.	Bat.	Bania.		Chura.	Julaha.	Sansi.			Pathán.
Batwal.	*Sub-division of Rajput.* Lon.	Sanyasi.	Dar.	Khatri.	*Sub-divisions of Khatri.* Khoja. Malik. Magre.	*Sub-division of Chura.* Ramdasi or Mazhabi.	Kassab.	BOTH HINDUS AND MOHAMEDANS.			Sheikh.
Saryara.		*Sub-division of Sanyasi.* Bramhchari.	Bathar.				Memar.	Batehra.			*Sub-divisions of Sheikh.* Balti. Hakim
Megh.			Ganai.			Kalal.	Mochi				
Dhyar.		*Sub-division of Mirasi.* Gardi.	DERVESH.	BOTH HINDUS AND MOHAMEDANS.			Naddáf.				
BOTH HINDUS AND MOHAMEDANS.			*Sub-divisions of Dervesh.* Chishti.	Labána.			Rangrez.				
Gujar.			Madari.				*Sub-division of Manyar.* Kamangar.				
Jat.			Kalandar.				Teli.				
Rajput.			SAYAD.			BOTH HINDUS AND MOHAMEDANS.					
			Sub-divisions of Sayad. Pir. Mir.			Darzi.					
			Sub-divisions of Mirasi. Doom. (Watchman.)			Dhobi.					
			KANJAR.			Jhiwar.					
		BOTH HINDUS AND MOHAMEDANS.				Kumhár.					
		JOGI.				Nai.					
		Sub-divisions of Sanyasi. Udási.				Sunar.					
		Sadhu.				Tarkhán.					
		Suthra.				Lohár.					
		Gusain.				*Sub-division of Lohar.*—Saikalgar.					
		Fakir.									

E.—CASTES PECULIAR TO JAMMU.

A. Agricultural.		B. Professional.		C. Commercial.		D. Artisans and Village Menials.		E. Vagrant Minor Artisans and Performers.		F. Races and Nationalities.	
Hindus.	Mohamedans.	Hindus.	Mohamedans.	Hindus.	Mohamedans.	Hindus.	Mohamedans.	Hindus.	Mohamedans.	Hindus.	Mohamedans.
Sub-divisions of Dum. { Barwals. Batyal. Begari. Gen. Gomsa. Sepi.	Pakhiwar.	*Sub-division of Brahman* } Bhatre. *Sub-divisions of Sanyasi* { Gorya. Jangam. Bharti. *Sub-divisions of Mirasi.* { Rawabia. Kathak. Sarnain. Kayasth.	*Sub-divisions of Dervesh.* { Noshahi. Rawal. Vagi. *Sub-division of Mirasi.* } Bharai. *Sub-division of Kanjar.* } Perna.	Bhatya.	...	*Sub-division of Jhiwar.* } Ghirath. *Sub-division of Chura.* } Charu. *Sub-division of Julaha.* } Kuchband.	Musalli. *Sub-division of Jhiwar.* } Bhishti. *Sub-divisions of Mochi.* { Saraj. Khatik. Dabgar. Niyaria.	...	Changar.	...	...
		BOTH HINDUS AND MOHAMEDANS. *Sub-division of Sanyasi.* } Sáin.		BOTH HINDUS AND MOHAMEDANS. Kambo.		BOTH HINDUS AND MOHAMEDANS. Thatyar. Manyar.		BOTH HINDUS AND MOHAMEDANS. Bazigar.			

(F.)—CASTES PECULIAR TO KASHMIR.

A. Agricultural.		B. Professional.		C. Commercial.		D. Artisans and Village Menials.		E. Vagrant Minor Artisans and Performers.		F. Races and Nationalities.	
Hindus.	Mohamedans.	Hindus.	Mohamedans.	Hindus.	Mohamedans.	Hindus.	Mohamedans.	Hindus.	Mohamedans.		Mohamedans.
...	*Sub-division of Rajput.* } Pare.	...	*Sub-divisions of Brahman.* { Pandit. Aitu. Tantre. Rishi. Raina. Khande. *Sub-divisions of Dervesh.* { Saidmakar. Kadri. Miskin. Tamburi. Musafir. *Sub-division of Mirasi.* } Doom (Watchman.)	...	...	...	*Sub-division of Chura.* } Vatal.	...	...	Parsis.	...

(G).—CASTES PECULIAR TO LADAKH.

A. Agricultural.		B. Professional.		C. Commercial.		D. Artisans and Village Menials.		E. Vagrant Minor Artisans and Performers.		F. Races and Nationalities.	
Hindus.	Mohamedans.	Hindus.	Mohamedans.	Hindus.	Mohamedans.	Hindus.	Mohamedans.	Hindus.	Mohamedans.		Mohamedans.
Sub-divisions of Rajput.: Ahlia. Shahi. Thappa.	*Nepalese and other hill tribes.*: BOKRU.	*Sub-divisions of Brahman.*: Bedangi. Pati.	PIR. (*Sub-division of Sayad.*)	*Sub-divisions of Khatri.*: Kurgi. Kaur. Bohar.	VANI. (*Sub-division of Bania.*)	SOCHI. (*Sub-division of Darzi.*)	Bangi.			*Budhists.*	*Sub-divisions of Sheikh.*: Raodi. Soni. Sagar. Kangu. Ganark. Kamakhu. Gashu. Geri. Mangrak. Meva. Makh. Miai. Hanghi. Hakim. Nanbai. Bazdar.
Nepalese aud other hill tribes.			*Sub-divisions of Mirasi-*: Mon. Beda. Malakhan.								*Budhist Converts.*: Kharpon. Nospun. Tang. Jaju. Champa. Dokpa. Chon. Deo. Argon.
Doni.											
Dagori.											
Sudar.											
Gola											
Goran.											
Godurs.											
Garti.											
Makarkoni *alias* Nagarkoti.											
Nobahar.											
Bodar.											
Kagar.											

(H.)—CASTES PECULIAR TO SKARDU.

A. Agricultural.		B. Professional.		C. Commercial.		D. Artisans and Village Menials.		E. Vagrant Minor Artisans and Performers.		F. Races and Nationalities.	
Hindus.	Mohamedans.	Hindus.	Mohamedans.	Hindus.	Mohamedans.	Hindus.	Mohamedans.	Hindus.	Mohamedans.	Hindus.	Mohamedans.
Nepalese and other hill tribes. Hotaberi. Majithia. Heku.			PIR. (*Sub-division of Sayad.*) NIKARCHI. (*Sub-division of Mirási.*)								*Budhist Converts.* Brokpa. Chaupon. *Sub-divions of Sheikh.* Shabán. Doru. Hakim. Malla.

(I.)—CASTES PECULIAR TO GILGIT.

A. Agricultural.		B. Professional.		C. Commercial.		D. Artisans and Village Menials.		E. Vagrant Minor Artisans and Performers.		F. Races and Nationalities.
Hindus.	Mohamedans.	Hindus.	Mohamedans.	Hindus.	Mohamedans.	Hindus.	Mohamedans.	Hindus.	Mohamedans.	Mohamedans.
...	...	...	...	...	...	...	...	...	...	*Sub-divisions of Sheikh.* Turanj. Hajia. Chedva. Sambava. Nanva. Balida. Harsakhia. Homan-Chirmal. Kashna. *Budhist Converts.* Gonkpa. Kafalpa. Churankpa. Ofpa. Karimpa. Narankzapa. Charnanpa. Arkabakpa. Monkeypa. Aliarpa. Tarsarpa. Kanopa. Dasokharampa. Pahapa. Abdulpa. Galudanpa. Asarpa. Stapa. Kachapa. Dachapa. Samplepa. Dolupa. Mahvapa. Malakpa. Lakhbakpa.

183. I now proceed to deal with each caste separately.

1. Brahmans (also Agricultural)	505,086
Jammu	182,643
Kashmír	321,985
Ládákh	184
Skardu	271
Gilgít Road	3

184. The main sub-divisions of Brahmans have not been returned for want of the necessary column in the Enumerator's Schedule, but in a future census of the Kashmír State an enquiry on the lines hereinafter laid down will be interesting, not only in a statistical, but also in an ethnological point of view.

185. The Brahmans in this State are divided into three classes, *viz.* :—

1.—Immigrants from Panjab and other parts of India strictly following their ancient regulations as regards marriage, social union, &c.

2.—The aboriginal Brahmans of the hills known as "Dográs."

3.—The Brahmans of Kashmír.

186. The immigrants from the Panjab and other parts of India are mostly Saraswat and Gour Brahmans who are strictly governed by the rules and regulations of their caste and clan, and nothing further need be said about them, except that they neither eat with the other two classes nor inter-marry with them.

187. The aboriginal or Dográ Brahmans of the hills comprise the following principal sub-divisions :—

Acharjí.	Pandit.
Bhatt.	Gulwadhe.
Bhadyal.	Gujrate.
Banotri.	Mangotri.
Phalgotri.	Kohol.
Parohit.	Raina.

With the exception of Acharjís and Gujrátís, who have suffered degradation by their avocation of presiding over funeral ceremonies, these castes stand on an equal footing with one another, but compared with Panjábi Brahmans, the Dográ Brahmans decidedly occupy an inferior status. Singularly enough the Kashmír Raina Brahmans have severed their connection with the Brahmans of Kashmír and intermixed with the Dográs, and are now considered a sub-division of Dográs. The local sub-divisions mentioned in the margin, are not found among the Brahmans of the Panjab.

188. The present population of Kashmír is composed of Hindus and Mohamedans, but the former have not, as a fact, the four *Varans* or caste sub-divisions prevailing in the Panjab ; they consist only of Pandits, Bohras, Jinsi-Sikhs and Dográs.

189. The Province of Kashmír excluding the District of Muzafferabad, has been the most remarkable seat, if not of the first, at any rate of the ancient colony of Aryan immigrants from Central Asia.

190. The popular tradition is that the Brahmans of Kashmír are in the direct line of descent from Kashap. They are divided into 133 *gotras*, named after the divine sages or ascetics by whom their clans are represented, though, as a matter of fact, the original *gotras* did not exceed 6, as noted in the margin, the remaining 127 *gotras* being due to inter-marriages or intermixture with other Brahmans. Some authorities give the principal divisions as only three, *viz.* :—Bhatt, Pandit and Rázdán from which are derived the distinctive appellations of Koul, Sopuri Pandit, and Raina. The Koul *gotra* is Dattatrye, the Sopuri Pandit, Pathdev Vasgargey, and the Rázdán (Raina) (1) Kanth Dhumayan, and (2) Sáman Mudhgale. From these three families gradually as each took to a distinct and particular trade or occupation or by adoption and inter-marriage, farther *gotras* came into existence and new castes were formed. According to another authority, the parent stock is represented by three brothers, Kayitachari, Mammatachari, and Ubbatachari. History further records that between the year 1435 and 1442 A. D., consequent on the slaughter by the Mohamedan conqueror of all but

Dattatrye.	Pathdev.
Bhardwaj.	Upmani.
Mudhgale.	Dhum.

eleven families of Kashmírí Pandits, excepting those who managed to escape from the country, those left behind assumed the tribal distinction of Malmas, while those who subsequently returned from the flight were called Banamasis. These two surnames, however, have reference to the astrological calendar observed by the two races, Malmas meaning the lunar and Banamas the solar months of the year, and it is difficult under the circumstances to regard these as race distinctions, unless the new settlers into the valley after the wholesale slaughter of 1435 A. D., observed the solar month as contra-distinguished from the aborigines whose calculations were based on the phases of the moon. This account may be taken for what it is worth, but there could be no doubt that the above distinctions did not interfere with inter-marriage or social position, till the reign of Sultan Zain-ul-Abdin, when the withdrawal of the interdiction against employment of Hindus in the State, encouraged the study of Persian, and enabled the Brahmans to aspire to high offices in the administration. It was then that they divided off into two parties known as *Karkun* and *Bachabat*, the former forming the laity, and the latter the priesthood. To enable this arrangement to be carried out, as all were equally Brahmans of the same status, the *Karkuns* made their daughters' sons their *Bachabats*. Later on, such of the *Karkuns* as relinquished the study of Persian and took to Sanskrit literature, began to be called "Pandits," but were not, for that particular reason, estranged from their fraternity. Among the *Karkuns* there is a class known as Bhattaraks who are said to be descended from royal blood, and the Rázdániks from the nobility.

The *Karkuns* strictly refrain from *Dan* (receiving charity), and do not, as a rule, take a wife from the *Bachabats*, in all other respects, irrespective of *gotra*, clan, caste or sub-division, they observe the same customs, religious rites, and are otherwise on perfect equality with one another. If any of them commit himself, or take up a lowering occupation, he is called *Dági* (or stained), but does not forfeit any of his caste privileges. Trade and agriculture are looked upon as low, but this idea is gradually losing ground.

All Kashmírí Brahmans conduct their funeral and religious ceremonies according to the Nilmat Puran and according to the Vedas of Langak Rishi.

The Kashmírí Pandits are mostly *Shaktikas* or *Tantrikas*, their favorite goddesses being the *Khir Bhawani* and *Jawala Mukhi*, but they are also known as *Shaivas* and *Vaishnavs*. They unscrupulously eat food cooked in a boat rowed by Mohamedan boatmen, employ Mohamedans as water-bearers, and invariably wear a white turban on their head.

191. The subjoined statement gives an exhaustive list of the Kashmír *gotras* and clan subdivisions of *Karkun* and *Bachabat* Pandits :—

No.	Gotras.	Banamas or Malmas.	Castes.
1	Dattatrye (Koul)	Banamas ...	Koul, Nagari, Jinsi, Jalali, Watal, Nika, Sultan, Ugra, Aima, Moza, Bamzai, Dont, Tota, Sabih, Kissoo, Mandal, Singari, Rafiz, Babu, Darabi.
2	Upman	Malmas ...	Reyu.
3	Dhum	Do. ...	Rázdán.
4	Kanth Dhumáyan	Banamas ...	Rázdán, Wangani, Mujjoo, Sháir.
5	Sáman Mudhgale	Malmas ...	Zaba Rázdán, Mushran, Chana, Kanth. Khazanchi, Hastwalu, Monga, Dewani, Zittoo, Zotan, Poot, Shora.
6	Sáman Gotam	Do. ...	Gurtu, Rázdán, Thapal, Naqib, Thalachar, Kak, Labru, Parman, Zari, Padora, Langar, Charangu, Khosa, Kakapuri, Badam, Raina, Kasi, Chilmu.
7	Sáman Gotam Logakhyi	Do. ...	Chokku, Rázdán.
8	Sáman Bhardwáj	Banamas ...	Tikku, Munshi, Khar, Miskin, Gharyáli, Bazari, Khan.
9	Paldeo Wasgargey	Malmas ...	Sopuripandit, Mala, Poot, Mirakhur, Kadlabajjoo, Kokru, Bangru, Baqáyá, Khashu, Kichlu, Misri, Khar, Mam.

No.	Gotras.	Banamas or Malmas.	Castes.
10	Patsaman Koshak	Banamas ...	Mattoo, Fotadár, Ganjoo, Kachru, Suloo, Mam, Zittoo, Anbárdár, Kalli, Vaishnavi, Bararoo, Pandit, Musalman, Kayan, Vauchu, Miyan, Jawánsher, Jálá, Panzu.
11	Deapat Sáman Upmanikoshak	Malmas ...	Sopuri.
12	Deo Upmani	Do. ...	Khoshu, Meva, Pandit.
13	Bhava Kapishtal Upmani	Banamas ...	Wanyikhan.
14	Sámanwas Upmani	Malmas ...	Walloo.
15	Sáman Upmani	Do. ...	Giggoo.
16	Bhút Upmani Shalan Kayan	Do. ...	Gaira.
17	Sámanwas Upmani	Do. ...	Batt.
18	Kash Upmani	Do. ...	Batt.
19	Bhutwas Upmani Logákh	Do. ...	Peshin, Zalpuri, Thákur.
20	Ráj Bhút Logakh Déval	Do. ...	Bhán.
21	Rátra Bhargawa	Do. ...	Zitshu.
22	Bhut Logakhyi Dhumayan Gotam ...	Do. ...	Hundú.
23	Deo Sáman Gotam Koshak Mudhgale Bhardwaj	Do. ...	Kukil Pandit.
24	Sáman Mudhgale Parashar	Do. ...	Gairu.
25	Sámanwas	Do. ...	Tufchi.
26	Sáman Koshak	Do. ...	Thakur, Watal.
27	Sáman Bhargawa	Do. ...	Báli Battoo.
28	Sáman Koshak Bhardwaj	Banamas ...	Batt, Kakru.
29	Sáman Shándley	Malmas ...	Pandit, Vas.
30	Sámanwas Atrey	Do. ...	Thussoo, Ghasi, Wáza.
31	Sáman Gotam Atrey Shalan Kotch ...	Do. ...	Rainá.
32	Sáman Gotam Atrey	Do. ...	Cholu.
33	Sáman Bhargawa Bhardwaj Was Atrey ...	Do. ...	Kalloo.
34	Sáman Kanth Kashap	Do. ...	Lábru.
35	Sáman Gargey	Do. ...	Machána.
36	Sáman Gan Bhúshak	Do. ...	Padey.
37	Sáman Gotam Bhardwaj	Do. ...	Kemdar.
38	Sámanwas Logakh	Banamas ...	Toor.
39	Dar Bhardwaj	Do. ...	Dar, Trachhal, Misri, Jawansher, Kandhári, Tháiachur, Uthoo, Turku, Waguzari, Bangi.
40	Waisisht Bhardwaj	Malmas ...	Batt, Hukku, Hundu.
41	Deo Bhardwaj	Do. ...	Batt, Gadar, Kalloo.
42	Sharman Bhardwaj	Do. ...	Batt.
43	Deo Bhardwaj Koshak	Do. ...	Dewa.
44	Shandley Bhardwaj	Do. ...	Batt.
45	Nanda Koshak Bhardwaj	Do. ...	Batt.
46	Koshak Bhardwaj	Do. ...	Batt.
47	Shandley	Do. ...	Kár.
48	Chand Shandley	Do. ...	Sadhoo.
49	Dar Shandley	Do. ...	Jogi.
50	Dar Vasak Shandley	Banamas ...	Safáyá.
51	Dar Deo Shalan Kapi	Malmas ...	Mots.
52	Mitra Shándley	Do. ...	Sayad.

No.	Gotras.	Banamas or Malmas.	Caste.
53	Deo Shándley	Do. ...	Batapholu.
54	Raj Shándley	Do. ...	Dooru.
55	Sam Shándley	Do. ...	Batt.
56	Sáman Rishi Kanyi Gargey	Do. ...	Koul (Akulun).
57	Shalan Kotch	Banamas ...	Tulwan Kol-Mukkoo.
58	Kotch Atrey	Malmas ...	Batt.
59	Rájdat Atrey Shalan Kotch	Do. ...	Batt.
60	Sharman Atrey	Do. ...	Gaddoo.
61	Bhava Atrey	Do. ...	Warkoo.
62	Sáman Warshagan	Do. ...	Katjoo, Kavj, Clotháyi.
63	Bhava Kapishtal	Banamas ...	Kavj.
64	Rátra Bishwamitra Agast	Malmas ...	Trakru, Muttoo.
65	Dar Varshagan	Banamas ...	Safaya, Bakhshi, Kuchru, Shali.
66	Dar Kapishtal	Malmas ...	Liddu, Batt.
67	Kanth Kashap	Do. ...	Dássoo, Rázdán, Batt.
68	Mitra Kashap	Do. ...	Batt.
69	Dat Sharman Kanth Kashap	Do. ...	Raina.
70	Deo Kashap Mudhgale Kashap	Do. ...	Braddoo.
71	Deo Kashap Mudhgale Gotam	Do. ...	Akhoon.
72	Deo Gargey	Do. ...	Bhán.
73	Deo Waisisht	Do. ...	Ukhlu.
74	Deo Kotch Atrey	Do. ...	Badgámí.
75	Deo Bishwamitra Warshagan	Do. ...	Wangú.
76	Deo Gotam	Do. ...	Batt.
77	Deo Kanth Kashap	Do. ...	Kár.
78	Deo Logakhyi	Do. ...	Pandit Mántapuri.
79	Deo Koshak	Do. ...	Batt.
80	Arth Warshagan Shándal	Do. ...	Choudri.
81	Koshak	Do. ...	Batt.
82	Pat Sáman Koshak Deo Ratra Parwara ...	Banamas ...	Pandit Watal.
83	Waisisht	Malmas ...	Batt, Rangataing.
84	Rátra Bishwamitra Agast	Do. ...	Pandit.
85	Kárchanda Shándley	Do. ...	Chandru Kár.
86	Mitra Koshak	Do. ...	Pandit.
87	Sharman Kotch	Do. ...	Batt, Sas.
88	Datwas	Do. ...	Khár.
89	Waisisht Sáman Mudhgale	Do. ...	Bhandárí.
90	Eishur Shandal Koshak	Do. ...	Rával, Nakhasi.
91	Dat Dat Shalan Kotch	Do. ...	Batt, Sathoo, Kasab, Malik, Khaumushu.
92	Rátra Warshagan	Do. ...	Katar.
93	Parashar	Do. ...	Yachh.
94	Atra Bhargawa	Do. ...	Hapa.
95	Bhút Logakhyi	Do. ...	Pandit.
96	Raj Waisisht	Do. ...	Shonglu.
97	Dat Warshagan	Do. ...	Sazá[illegible].
98	Rishi Koshak	Do. ...	Kashkari.

No.	Gotras.	Banamas or Malmas.	Castes.
99	Rishi Kavigarg	Malmas ...	Zárú.
100	Samwasgarg	Do. ...	Batt Sum.
101	Nanda Koshak	Do. ...	Batt.
102	Sáman Mudhgale	Do. ...	Madan.
103	Sáman Hása Dasay	Do. ...	Khánakattoo.

Statement of Gotras and Castes of Bachabat Pandits.

No.	Gotras.	Banamas or Malmas.	Castes.
1	Bhava Kapishtal	Banamas ...	Zádú, Kala, Sapun, Lattú, Kattu, Wántú Char Chandar, Geru, Hakim, Wángnú, Siv.
2	Bhava Kapishtal Upmani	Do. ...	Kharú.
3	Sámanwas Logakh	Do. ...	Chotoo.
4	Kanth Dhumayan	Do. ...	Kávj, Brith.
5	Dar Bhardwáj	Do. ...	Zangam.
6	Deo Bhardwáj	Do. ...	Jattoo.
7	Bhút Upmani	Malmás ...	Revu, Khobri, Braru, Sida, Upal.
8	Bhút Upmani Shalan Kayáná	Do. ...	Ganju, Ganzu.
9	Sáman Atrey	Do. ...	Shál, Haudu, Jadwali, Sikh, Chaka.
10	Shándley	Do. ...	Sháir.
11	Sámanwasgarg	Do. ...	Sum, Langú.
12	Sáman Goshawas Upmani	Do. ...	Chokao.
13	Sharman Koteh Atrey	Do. ...	Raggu, Nand, Gadwa, Datt, Halmat.
14	Deo Parashar	Do. ...	Yachh.
15	Sáman Gotam	Do. ...	Kalloo.
16	Deo Parashar	Do. ...	Tulsi, Thogan.
17	Dar Kapishtal Upmani	Do. ...	Meech.
18	Mitra Saman Koshak Atrey	Do. ...	Pandit.

OTHER KASHMIR CASTES.

192. Bohras.—This is a caste of Hindus, not being Brahmans, descended from the *Chhatri* stock, whose principal business is trade and shop-keeping. Having adopted the rites and ceremonies of the Brahmans, they are excluded from relationship with the Panjabi Khatris, and therefore inter-marry among themselves. It is not known when they originally settled in Kashmír, but from their customs and habits, it appears probable that they came into the country prior to the advent of the Mohamedans. There is evidence to show that in times gone by, they were freely admitted to caste among Pandits, as for instance, the reputable family of Chaudhri Mohesh, the builder of the nine masonry bridges in the Srinagar Dal and of the dry causeway across it nearly four miles in length, on which these bridges are situated. But with this notable exception, the Bohras do not appear to have been admitted to fellow-casteship in any manner with the Pandits. The Bohra woman, unlike the Pandits, does not wear a waist-girdle, while also unlike her, she does wear a nose-ring. In all other respects, the habiliments of the Bohra of both sexes, are undistinguishable from those of the ordinary Pandit. In general disposition they are closely assimilated with the *Dogra* and *Bakal* castes. The local *Purabeahs* are an off-shoot of this caste, whose general occupation is personal service.

193. Jinsi-Sikhs.—The Jinsi-Sikhs are Panjabi Brahmans. During the years 1751 to 1762 A. D., in the reign of the Emperor Ahmad Shah Durrani, Raja Sukhjiwan Subah of the Emperor, brought the Jinsi-Sikhs from Potowar and the adjoining hills to assist him in asserting his independence against his master. As these mercenaries were paid in kind, and had, in the time of the Maharaja Ranjit Singh, embraced Sikhism, they began to be called Jinsi-Sikhs, or Sikhs in receipt of rations. The Jinsi-Sikh is mostly found in the following portions of Kashmír territory, *viz.*, Parganahs-Tral, Hamal, Kirohan, Biroh and Ranbirsinghpora. They live by agriculture and personal service.

194. The Mians.—The settlement of Mians is due to *jagirs* conferred by Maharaja Gulab Singh on the *Dográ* Mians of Jammu, in Parganah Deosar, as a measure necessary for the preservation of peace in his newly-acquired territory.

195. Mohamedans.—Up to 1340 A. D. there was not a single Mohamedan in Kashmír. In 1341 Bulbul Shah, a Mohamedan ascetic of renown, came here from Turkistan *viá* Ladákh, and took up his habitation in a spot just below the Ali Kadal (fifth bridge of city Srinagar) where his mausoleum is held in great veneration. In those days Reinchan Shah, a Thibetan and Budhist whose original name was Ratanjbu, had been banished from his country while yet a youth, and sought the protection of Raja Udiandev king of Kashmír, who gave him an asylum, and assigned him a *jagir* to live in Parganah Lal. Meanwhile an expedition headed by Zukdar Khan marched into Kashmír, and Udiandev escaped the general slaughter which followed, by relinquishing his kingdom. Reinchan Shah who remained behind, forcibly married his Rani (known as the Kut Rani) and took possession of the kingdom.

Having been expelled from the fatherland in tender years, Reinchan Shah was naturally ignorant of the doctrine and ritual of his original faith, he offered to become a Hindu, but on his application being rejected by the Brahmans, Bulbul Shah prevailed on him to embrace Mohamedanism. It was in this manner that the Mohamedan faith first found its converts and adherents in Kashmír, who, under the auspices of a line of Mohamedan kings in general, and Sikandar (idol-destroyer) in particular, increased so steadily, that the country may now be said to be almost Mohamedan, the resuscitation of the Hindu community dating only from the days of Zain-ul-Abdin. The proselytes to Islamism in Kashmír were mostly from the original Hindu population, strangers and foreigners being but few, and this is the more patent from the fact that the present Mohamedan population is divided and sub-divided in accordance with the distinctions observable among their fellow-countrymen, though the lapse of years has slightly modified particular caste derivations, so as to make them unrecognizable by the light of previous custom. It has come to be recognized as a sort of analogy, that as the trade, occupation, or *habitat* of the person, so the peculiar affix to his name, as for instance, Aziz *Khar*, the *Khar* referring to the occupation of blacksmith, Sobhan *Chan*, or carpenter, then again Ramzan *Kakpura*, from *Kakpur*, the name of the ancestral home, &c., &c.

Of course it must be expected that a certain proportion of the resident Mohamedan population comprise families whose progenitors or common ancestors had been foreigners, and although, as already observed, these are remarkably few, it is significant that they are up to the present even known as *bahar se ae hue*, or foreigners.

196. The *Sheikhs* who are the convert class of Kashmír Mohamedans, as distinguished from the *Sayad*, *Moghal* or *Pathan* are the following castes, *viz.* :—

(1) *Pirzadas*, the descendants of *fakirs* (holy mendicants) and others of religious worth or sanctity, quite irrespective of their descent.

(2) *Baba Zadas*, or descendants of the *Khalifas* of Makhdum Sahib, whose shrine is considered the most sacred in the country.

(3) *Vains*, the original Mohamedans of Srinagar city, considered also the purest and of the best descent. These are sub-divided into castes, as follows :—

(1) Kánth, (2) Gúndrú, (3) Bachh, (4) Bándi, (5) Gúneh, (6) Gáni, (7) Dár, (8) Pakshivál, (9) Vakil, (10) Ashái, (11) Shál, (12) Kunru, (13) Ishlú, (14) Diwáni.

Of a lesser status among Mohamedans of Kashmír are the shawl-weavers and embroiderers and the zemindars of the country, and it must be remembered that those from among them who know Arabic are, in addition to their names, styled *Mullan*, *Vaiz* and *Maulvi*.

197. The principal Rajput sub-divisions returned are :—

			Hindus.	*Mohamedans.*	*Total.*
Hindus and Mohamedans	Manas	...	3,235	3,680	6,915
	Chibb	...	4,865	6,891	11,756
	Charak	...	2,163	...	2,163
	Langeh	...	1,891	...	1,891
	Bhau	...	2,345	2,134	4,479
	Rakwal	...	602	...	602
	Thakkar	...	109,912	13,908	123,820
Mohamedans ...	Bhatti	...	...	5,852	5,852
	Khokhar	...	...	5,498	5,498
	Bambhe	...	...	999	999
	Khakhe	...	...	4,046	4,046
	Turand	...	...	130,998	130,998

198. The principal and most important section of the Rajput community is that of Jamwal Rajputs, the clan to which the ruling family of the Jammu and Kashmír State belongs. The founder of the tribe was Jámulochan, the sixth in descent from Agnigir, one of the reigning Rajput princes of Oudh, who is said to have acquired vast tracts of territory in the Jammu Province by conquest. The following genealogical table shows the subsequent development of caste in this tribe :—

AGNIGIR.

- Bajulochan, 6th generation
- Jámulochan (6th generation) — 5th generation.
  - Shaktkaran, Kings of Jammu. — 70th generation
    - Jasdeo, Raja, founded Jasrota and the clan of Jasrota Mians. — 5th generation.
      - Narsinghdeo. Raja of Jammu.
        - Arjandeo. 2nd generation.
          - Sameldeo. Manas of Samelpore.
          - Bhamaldeo. Manas of Suhanjna Thub (Jammu District.)
            - Bharat. Bhalwal Manas tribe.
            - Mulo. Bhalwal, lower.
            - Saru. Sarwal Gudha Muthi Manas.
            - Kasu. Bhadwal Manas.
            - Malu. Childless.
          - Jankardeo. Manas, cultivators in Sialkot District (Panjab.)
          - Maldeo. 2nd generation.
            - Jey Singhdeo. Manas, cultivators.
              - Palchaldeo.
              - Achaldeo.
                - Sanju.
                - Parkashdeo.
                  - Parkashdeo had 23 sons, of whom Nathudeo killed a Brahman on suspicion of a criminal intrigue with his wife (Mussummat Bajyál) and suffered the penalty of excommunication from caste, and subsequently died childless. The remaining 22 were the founders of Rajput, Manas, Jat, Darzi, (Tailors) Goldsmiths and Thakkars as detailed on the other page.
                - Peju.
            - Jabdeo. Raja of Jammu.
        - Kalyandeo. Cultivator of soil, hereafter known as Manas of Palohra and Akalpore, &c., (Jammu).
        - Pehladdeo. Settled in Samba and known as Sambyal Mians.
      - Rai Jaggú. 3rd generation.
        - Manju. Took to cultivation and became patriarch of the tribe of Manas, residing in Ghamrola, a village in Sialkot District (Panjab)
        - Bhimdeo. 5th generation. Ahmaldeo became Manas by resorting to agriculture. His descendants reside in villages of Gakhral, Jajwal, Sudardan in Akhnúr Tehsil (Jammu.)
  - Balkand, Raja of Kashmir. This clan became extinct by embracing the religion of Mohamed.
  - Udepat. Family of Bhau Rajputs, now regarded as a separate clan.

- 1 Nathudeo died childless.
- 2 Jamrathdeo.
  - Sadhu. 1
  - Bharat. 2
  - Billú. 3
  - Sandh. 4
  - Meansaid. 5
    - Gangwal, Beli, Zinda, Kalyal, Thalyala, villages in British District of Sialkot.

  Descendants of Nos. 1, 3 and 4 reside in Hamirpore, those of Bharat No. 2 in Sidhar Hamirpore.
- 3 Pahlwandeo.
  - Bandwal. Deyawra. Dhungi. Hail. Phagwari. Pindi. Pagwal villages.
- 4 Udiandeo, died childless.
- 5 Beramdeo.
  - Birak Jats, in Sialkot and Gujranwala Districts.
- 6 Ranu.
  - Jhiwars.
- 7 Lehri.
  - Mallah (boatmen.)
- 8 Sardeo.
  - Goldsmith, Sunar.
- 9 Majasdeo, } died childless.
- 10 Muleput, } died childless.
- 11 Dhartha.
  - Darzis. (Tailors.)
- 12 Gambhaju, died childless.
- 13 Gangu.
  - Rajputs in Nowshera (Jammu.)
- 14 Balgu.
  - Balangan Jats in Sialkot District.
- 15 Kamla.
  - Thakkars in Reasi.
- 16 Dhayaru.
  - Jats of Tara Got in Gujrat District (Panjab.)
- 17 Rabú.
  - Fakeers, particulars not known.
- 18 Singhú.
  - Saugwal, Thakkars in Reasi.
- 19 Dhangu.
  - Mohamedan Manas in Punch.
- 20 Phaggar, childless.
- 21 Galu.
  - Galotra, Rajputs, in Nowshera, mostly Mohamedans.
- 22 Gakhu.
  - Ghagrial in Nowshera.
- 23 Amolakdeo.
  - Manas of Pargwal and Silalyara villages.

The above affords data for the conclusion that the inferior castes of Hindus have generally emanated from the superior castes, owing their separation from the parent-stock to unauthorized marriages and recourse to prohibited occupations. An ethnological enquiry into the castes, which at the present day prevails in the Hindu community, is most desirable, and in a state like Kashmír abounding as it does with the greatest variety, it will, if vigorously pushed at the future census, prove highly interesting and useful.

199. Jamwals.—The Jamwals are divided into three main sub-divisions, *viz.*, Jasroteas, Mankoteas and Jamwals, which are again sub-divided into the following clans :—

Clan			
Jandi Panj Gerain Thalwal	...	Descents of Kansardeo, second son of Dhrivdeo.	
Serohin	...	Do.	of Balwantdeo.
Raipurye Panjorye Kanachakye	...	Do.	of Maharaja Gajey Singh.
Khal-ki-Mandi Sohl Khas Mandi Chani	...	Do.	of Amar Singh.
Agorye Hamsali Jagti	...	Do.	of Mahárája Hari Deo.
Ramgarhye Kapur Dyaliye	...	Do.	of Kapur Deo.
Narainye	...	Do.	of Narain Deo.
Salhatye Sherkhanye	...	Do.	of Mian Hásil Deo.
Dalpatye	...	Do.	of Sangram Deo.
Manhálye	...	Do.	of Dingi Man.
Bal Bhadryi	...	Do.	of Balbhadra Deo.

200. Chibbs.—Chibbs number 4,865 Hindus, and 6,891 Mohamedans. They represent a clan of Katoch Rajpúts, so called after the name of its founder Chib Chand, who settled in Bhimbar, marrying the daughter of the Rajpút Chieftain Bhopal Singh.

In the seventh generation Raja Dharm Chand *alias* Shadi Khan embraced Mohamedanism, and his descendants are also called *Chibb* Rajpúts. The territory known as Chibbal (Gujrat District and its surroundings) is generally occupied by Hindu and Mohamedan Chibbs.

201. Charaks.—The Charaks numbering 2,163 are so called from their progenitor being a professional *Chábuk Sawar* (horse-breaker).

They claim descent from Surajbansi Rajpúts, and are good cultivators.

They occupy the villages of Mahin, Lollarh, Makhanpore, Laswara, Jagatpore, Pachal and Ala in Jammu Province.

202. Katals.—Katals are an offshoot of Khokhar Rajpúts. Kelan, the founder of the clan, extended his predatory excursions to Samba, a parganah of Jammu, and was a source of extreme annoyance to the local Rajpúts who got rid of him by causing him to be murdered by his own wife, a Thakkar girl ; his son Sahi, settled in the village of Katal whence the clan derives its name. They occupy eleven villages in Jammu, as detailed in the margin. The Katals are mostly cultivators.

Ragbal.	Chak Puroja.
Bhathiari.	Mawa.
Mator.	Nandwal.
Gungit.	Philora.
Ghaink.	Sahal.
Salari.	

203. Chaudhris of Kathua and Padol.—These clans belong to the Anadotra *alias* Allotra section of the lunar race. They are professional cultivators. They occupy 18 villages in the Jammu Province :—

Saidpore.	Bagwan Kala.	Pathu, lower.
Khakharyal.	Khokhanyal.	Padhri, upper and lower.
Mator.	Kirpalpore.	Lankot.
Godand.	Taraf Sanjhi.	Phaknot.
Mirpore Ram.	Taraf, upper and lower.	
Mirpore Jaggu.	Pathu, upper.	

204. Rakwal.—The founder of the clan was Malkhu, a Surajbansi Rajpút of Oudh, whose son held high offices in the Jammu State, and eventually took to agriculture. They occupy 5 villages, *viz.* :—

Chak Rakwal. Taror. Chak Malhore. Thathar. Bhatror.

205. Jaj.—Surajbansi Rajpúts claiming descent from Kushu, son of Ramchandra.

The founder of the clan was Trilochan who obtained the Chireahi *ilaqa* (Udhampore District) in *jagir*. The grant was resumed by Maháraja Gulab Singh, but the Jajs still own proprietary rights in the villages which number five in all. The clan derives its name from Jajot, a village in Reási, that being the original residence of Trilochan. The Jaj Thakkars are an offshoot of this clan.

Pata. Motal.
Dhanu. Samol.
Kotli.

206. Langeh.—The Jammu Langehs are mostly Hindus, and are said to have migrated from Ghazni, to escape conversion to Mohamedanism.

The Langeh community is divided into 7 clans, named after the seven villages noted in the margin, which were granted, about 800 years ago, to the original Rajpút immigrants from Ghazni. The clan now occupies nine more villages (see margin), all in the Jammu Tehsil, and have agriculture for their principal occupation.

Ghurota. Jandyal.
Amb. Malpore.
Ghaink. Lalyal.
Aranjan.

Samachak. Suhi.
Halka. Gudha.
Jaswan. Dammi.
Paryal Gaitha.
Kolasachak.

Their fraternity in Kabul, who are all Mohamedans, still retain the distinctive appellation of Langeh Pathans.

The Langehs occupy a subordinate position among semi-Rajpút clans, giving their daughters in marriage to Mians, Manas, and sometimes to Chibbs, and taking wives from the inferior clan of Thakkars.

207. Thakkars.—Thakkars number 109,912 Hindus, and 13,908 Mohamedans.

No Hindu caste is, in its details, more complicated than that of the Thakkars of Jammu.

Judging by the test of the sacred thread Thakkars undoubtedly rank with castes of good social position, but residence in the Himalayas, and the consequent exclusion of intercourse with the plains, have largely contributed to their degradation in a social and religious point of view. The majority of Thakkars are of Rajpút blood, but not uncommonly the clan has unscrupulously received among it, Brahmans and people of unknown parentage or doubtful origin, and it is difficult to say without an exhaustive inquiry, whether Thakkars are still Rajpúts, or comprise an independent agricultural caste inferior to Rajpúts, and superior to Jats and Gujars. The latter theory is probably the correct one, as Rajpúts of the lower orders do marry Thakkar girls, while the Thakkars themselves are not allowed the privilege of marrying in the lowest of Rajpút families.

208. The following is an ethnological account of some of the principal sub-divisions of Thakkars :—

1. *Dangereyi.*—Descended from the Senpal clan of Surajbansi Rajpúts.
2. *Bijeyi.*—Descended from Katoch Rajpúts, the founder of the clan receiving the epithet of Bijju in proving himself an exemplary cultivator of the soil.
3. *Gunge.*—Rajpúts of the Taj clan, so called after the name of their progenitor Ganga.
4. *Salhotre.*—Kharar Khatris of Salor.
5. *Jagyotre.*—Bhau Rajpúts.
6. *Jarrihal.*—Descended from a man of unknown parentage, and called after the name of the village in which he was born.
7. *Kúl.*—So called from Kulúr, the village of residence.
9. *Ladh.*—Manas Rajpúts, the word "Ladh" signifying "found" from the fact of the settler having selected land in the bed of a *nalla* (torrent) in Chanaini *jagir*, for cultivation.
12. *Chulanyal.*—So called from *Chula* (hearth) made in an outlying locality, by a lonely pregnant woman who settled in a village in Jammu, and gave birth to the founder of the clan.
13. *Gulyotre.*—Amba Ram Rajpúts.
14. *Agre.*—Sumbri Rajpúts.
15. *Kalas.*—Bhatyal Rajpúts.

16. *Bhaggu.*—Lakhan Brahman, became Thakkar by marrying a Thakkar girl.

17. *Nar.*—Katoch Rajpúts, the founder being a careless and ignorant cultivator, was surnamed *Anari* (unskilled) hence the clan name *Nar.*

209. In the hilly tracts of Bhaddu, the Thakkars have assimilated themselves with the zemindari clans of Satarmal, Rajwal, Nagwar and Jameri, and inter-marriage between them is freely allowed.

210. The various degrees of Rajpúts as regards inter-marriages and social position, are given below :—

I. Full Rajpúts representing ruling Rajpút families :—

Solar.

Jamwal.
Jasrotye.
Mankotye.
} Mians.

Lunar.

CIS-RAVI.

Bandral.
Bhadwal.
Bilorye.
} One family.
Hantal.
Bhotyal.
Bhadrawah.
Kishtwar.

TRANS-RAVI.

Katoch.
Guler.
Siba.
Jaswal.
Dadwal.
} One family, kings of Kangra.
Suket.
Mandi.
Kúlú.
} One family.
Kulurye (Bilaspore).
Guler.
Sarmore.

All these stand on an equal footing as regards inter-marriages between the Solar and Lunar races. The Lunar races also inter-marry among themselves, members of the same family excepted.

II. Half Rajpúts of the second degree, who give their daughters in marriage to full Rajpúts but who take wives from Rajpúts of the third degree—

Solar.

Manas Clans.

Lunar.

Amba Rai.
Chibb.
Jaral.
Bhaú.

NOTE.—These also inter-marry among themselves.

III. Half Rajpúts who give daughters in marriage to Rajpúts of the first and second degrees, but who take wives from the 4th degree.

Lunar Race.

Rakwal. (These generally give daughters in marriage to Mians and Manas).
Salarye.
Charak.
Bágal.
} One family.
Langeh.
Bijial.
Chaudhris of Kathúa.
Chaudhris of Padol.
} One family of Bhadwals.
Jaj.

These do not inter-marry among themselves.

IV. **Half Rajpúts who give daughters in marriage to Rajpúts of the third degree, but who take wives from Thakkars, besides inter-marrying among themselves—**

Mándle.	Bhalwal.
Rasial.	Hans.
Kharar Khatri.	Bajju.
Samsal.	Balwal.
Jaggi.	Gaure.
Lalotri.	Seroch.
Katal.	

NOTE.—These clans are now regarded as Thakkars of a superior order.

Mándle, Bhalwal, Bajju, Hans and Seroch generally give their daughters in marriage to Rakwals and the Chaudhris of Kathúa and Padol.

V. Those who give daughters in marriage to Rajpúts of the fourth degree and also inter-marry among themselves—

Thakkars.

NOTE.—With the exception of Turands all wear the sacred thread.

The *Chádar dálná* system of re-marriage of widows prevails among Thakkars.

The Khas clans of Thakkars, or in other words, Thakkars of the snowy range inter-marry among themselves, they are considered inferior to other Thakkars.

211. To return to an examination of the return of castes we have—

(*A*.)—AGRICULTURAL—

I.—Military and Dominant—

Rajpúts (also agricultural)		361,989
Ahlia		1
Pare		9,573
Lon		31,350
Shahi		2
Thappa		3
Total I ...		402,918

II.—Other Agricultural—

(*a*) *Cultivators—*		
Arain	22,243	
Awan	8,034	
Ját	142,595	
Seni	728	173,600
(*b*) *Cattle Breeders and Graziers—*		
Gujar (also agricultural)	245,796	
Choupan	2,993	248,789
(*c*) *Field Laborers—*		
Dum (also agricultural)	34,457	
Basith	5,929	
Batwal	5,848	
Saryara	2,277	
Sepi	828	
Megh	75,500	
Barwala	5,310	
Ratyal	653	
Begari	16	
Gen	57	
Comsa	6	
Dhyar	104	
Pakhiwar	13	130,998
Total II ...		553,387

III.—Nepalese and other Hill Tribes—

Nepalese ...	*Sudar*	2
	Gola	1
	Goran	3
	Makarkoni alias *Nagarkoti*	9
	Nobahar	1
	Bodar	1
	Bokru	3
	Garti	1
Other Hill Tribes.	*Heku*	1
	Majithia	2
	Doni	1
	Dagori	1
	Kagar	1
	Godurz	1
	Hotaberi	1
	Total III	29
	TOTAL CLASS A ...	956,334

Of the Rajpút sub-divisions, Ahlia is Nepali Rajpút of low degree; Pare and Lon, Kashmir caste of Mohamedan Rajpút converts, and Sháhi and Thappa, Nepalese Rajpút caste.

Ját, Seni, Arain, Arain, Awan, are well-known agricultural castes, and do not require any special comment.

Choupans, sub-division of Gujar, are peculiar to Kashmir. The majority of Gujars are Mohamedans and constitute one of the principal nomadic tribes of the hills. They are immigrants from Punch and certain parts of the Panjab, and, in spite of their long and continued residence in the remotest and inaccessible parts of the State, still retain their primitive costume, language, and tribal sections.

(*B.*)—PROFESSIONAL—

V.—Priests—

Brahmans (also agricultural)	240,765	
Pandit	2,895	
Sufi	11,003	
Bat	94,144	
Aitw	6,345	
Tantre	5,478	
Dar	68,949	
Rathar	23,801	
Rishi	6,290	
Raina	1,286	
Khande	6,093	
Ganai	37,987	
Bhatre	46	
Bedangi	1	
Pati	3	505,086
Sayad	54,187	
Pir	379	
Mir	59,827	114,393
	Carried over ...	619,479

	Carried forward ...	619,479
VI.—Devotees—		
Beragi	910	
Dervesh	89	
Chishti	180	
Said-Makar	20	
Kadri	14	
Miskin	64	
Madari	30	
Tamburi	158	
Musafir	6	
Kalandar	117	
Noshahi	14	
Rawal	9	
Vagi	7	
Jogi	6,199	
Sanyas	437	
Sadhu	835	
Gusain	1,833	
Bharti	28	
Fakir	12,775	
Sain	139	
Gorya	181	
Jangam	2	
Bramhchari	9	
Udasi	60	
Nirmala	7	
Suthra	69	24,192
IX.—Writers—		
Kayasth		12
XI.—Musicians and Ballad Reciters—		
Mirasi	9,629	
Rawabia	5	
Kathak	11	
Bharai	857	
Beda	220	
Nikarchi	5	
Malakhan	35	
Mon	71	
Sarnain	2	
Gardi	139	
Doom (watchmen)	12,386	23,360
XII.—Dancers and Singers—		
Kanjar	525	
Perna	250	775
Total Class B	667,818	

Of the Brahman sub-divisions, Pandit, Safi, Bat, Aitu, Tantre, Dar, Rathar, Rishi, Raina, Khande, Ganai are Brahman converts to Mohamedanism; Bhatre are palmisters, and Bedangi and Pati, Brahmans of Nepal.

The sword of Islam was so prominent in Kashmír during the reign of Sikandar, the notorious idol-destroyer (*But Shikan*) that the majority of the population embraced that religion.

Mir is an agricultural caste of Sayads.

Devotees number 8,046 Hindus, 1 Sikh, and 16,145 Mohamedans. There are, of course, no Sanyasi, Beragi and Bramhchari Mohamedans. The Jogis and other Hindu ascetics who return males and females, comprise regular tribal section of communities in full enjoyment of secular and social rights and privileges, with the nominal distinctive appellation of sects merely because their progenitors happened at one time to be religious mendicants who subsequently renouncing the condition of celibacy and reclusion imposed on them by custom, resumed their worldly pursuits.

Of the Mohamedan Fakirs, Chishti, Kadri, Madari, Kalandar, Noshahi and Rawal, are found throughout Rajputana and Upper India. Said-Makars, Miskin and Tamburi, are local Kashmírí appellations, the first named being a set of mock Fakirs who are professional cheats and swindlers.

Beda, Malakhan and Mon sub-divisions of Mirasi are peculiar to Ladákh.

(*C.*)—COMMERCIAL.

xiv.—*Traders*—	
Arora	3,731
Bania	22,184
Wain	16,148
Vani	4
Bhatya	41
Kambo	531
Khatri	16,106
Khoja	8,580
Magre...	5,811
Kurgi	1
Kaur	3
Bohar	4
Malik	21,887
Total, XIV	95,031
xv.—*Carriers*—	
Labana	5,117
Total Class C	100,148

Wain and Vani are Banias of Kashmír and Ladákh respectively. Khoja, Magre Mohamedan Khatris of Kashmír, Malik a Kashmír caste of Khatris or Rajpúts converted to Mohamedanism, Kurgi, Kaur and Bohar, Khatri castes of Nepal.

(*D.*)—ARTISANS AND VILLAGE MENIALS—

xvii.—Goldsmiths	Sunár	7,892
xviii.—Barbers	Nái	29,192
xix.—Blaksmiths	Lohár	27,827
...	*Saikalgar* ...	272
xx.—Carpenters and Turners ...	Tarkhan	28,710
xx (*a*).—Masons	Memar	440
xxi.—Brass and Coppersmiths ...	Thatyar	864
xxii.—Tailors	Darzi	4,851
...	*Soohi* ...	1
xxii (*b*).—Drug Preparers ...	Bangi	1
xxiii.—Weavers and Dyers ...	Julaha	29,001
...	*Kuchband* ...	12
...	Rangrez	2,024
xxiv.—Washermen	Dhobi	14,446
xxv.—Cotton Cleaners ...	Naddaf	787
xxvii.—Oil-pressers	Teli	20,124
xxviii.—Potters	Kumhar	22,507
xxix.—Glass-workers ...	Manyar	541
...	*Kamangar* ...	667
xxxii.—Goldsmith's refuse collectors.	Niyaria	75
	Carried over ...	190,184

	Brought forward	...	190,184
xxxv.—Fishermen, boatmen Palki-bearers and Cooks	Hánji ...	...	33,870
	Jhiwar ...	...	12,929
...	*Ghirath*	...	293
...	*Bhishti*	...	2,849
xxxvi.—Distillers	Kalál ...	...	121
xxxvii.—Butchers	Kassab ...	...	1,126
xxxviii.—Leather workers ...	Chamar ...	...	33,679
...	Mochi ...	...	13,626
...	*Saraj*	...	81
...	*Khatik*	...	1,057
...	*Dabgar*	...	20
xxxix.—Scavengers	Chura ...	...	8,257
...	*Vatal*	...	8,152
...	*Charu*	...	47
...	*Ramdasi or Mazhabi*		165
...	Musalli ...	...	2,578
Total Class D	...	...	3,090,034

Artisans and Village Menials in the State of Kashmír are generally those found in other parts of India, with the exception of Sochi and Bangi castes of Ladákh, Kuch-band and Kamangar of Jammu, and Hanji and Vatal of Kashmír.

It is noteworthy that there are no Jhiwars (water-bearers) in Ladákh, Skardu and Gilgit, while those in Kashmír belong to the Rural District of Muzafferábád, the office of water-bearer in Srinagar city being performed by Mohamedans.

The absence of Artisans and Village Menials in Ladákh is accounted for by each household being its own barber, carpenter, &c., as will be proved by the following, the existence of which is mainly due to immigration from Kashmír for the benefit of the foreign population in Leh.

Goldsmiths ...	... Sunar	...	... 1
Barbers ...	... Nai	...	... 11
Tailors ...	... Darzi	...	... 9
Drug-preparers ...	... Bangi	...	... 1
Oil-pressers ...	... Teli	...	... 16
Potters ...	... Kumhar	...	... 8
Butchers ...	... Kassab	...	... 6
Leather-workers ...	... Mochi	...	... 1
	Total	...	... 53

The Artisans and Village Menials in Skardu are :—

Goldsmiths ...	... Sunar ...	...	79
Barbers	... Nai ...	...	134
Blacksmiths ...	... Lohar ...	...	291
Carpenters ...	... Tarkhan	...	129
Oil-pressers ...	... Teli ...	...	19
Potters	... Kumhar	...	51
Leather-workers ...	... Mochi ...	...	151
	Total	...	854

The following Artisans and Village Menials are :—

(1).—*Peculiar to Jammu.*

Brass and Coppersmiths ...	Thatyar	...	864
Weavers	Kuch-band	...	12
Glass-workers	Manyar	...	541
Goldsmith's refuse collectors ...	Niyaria	...	75
Fishermen, boatmen, palki-bearers and cooks.	Ghirath	...	293
	Bhishti	...	2,849
	Carried over	...	4,634

	Brought forward	...	4,634
Leather-workers	Saraj ...	...	81
	Khatik	...	1,057
	Dabgar	...	20
Scavengers	Charu	...	47
	Musalli	...	2,578
	TOTAL		8,417
(2).—*Peculiar to Kashmír.*			
Scavengers	Vatal ...	...	8,152
(*E.*)—VAGRANT MINOR ARTISANS AND PERFORMERS—			
xli.—Earth-workers and Stone-dressers	Batehra	...	429
	Beldar	...	2,091
xliii—Cane-splitters, mat and leaf-plate makers.	Shakhsaz	...	306
	Dasali	...	369
xlv.—Miscellaneous and disreputable livers.	Changar	...	176
	Sansi ...	...	268
xlvi.—Tumblers and Acrobats ...	Bazigar	...	995
	TOTAL CLASS E	...	4,634
(*F.*)—RACES AND NATIONALITIES—			
xlviii.—Non-Indian Asiatic races ...	Budhists	...	29,608
	Budhist converts to Mohamedanism.		
...	*Argon*	...	706
...	*Tang*	...	3
...	*Jaju*	...	4
...	*Champa*	...	1
...	*Dokpa*	...	21
...	*Brokpa*	...	274
...	*Chon* ...	...	5
...	*Deo* ...	...	2
...	*Kharpon*	...	5
...	*Nospun*	...	1
...	*Gonkpa*	...	1
...	*Kafalpa*	...	2
...	*Churankpa*	...	1
...	*Ofpa* ...	...	1
...	*Karimpa*	...	1
...	*Narankzapa*	...	1
...	*Charnanpa*	...	1
...	*Arkabakpa*	...	1
...	*Monkeypa*	...	1
...	*Aliarpa*	...	1
...	*Tarsarpa*	...	2
...	*Kanopa*	...	1
...	*Chaupon*	...	2
...	*Dasokharampa*	...	1
...	*Pahapa*	...	1
...	*Abdulpa*	...	1
...	*Galudanpa*	...	1
...	*Asarpa*	...	1
...	*Stapa*	...	1
	Carried over		30,652

	Brought forward...	...	30,652
	Budhist converts—continued.		
...	*Kachapa*	...	4
...	*Dachapa*	...	5
...	*Samplepa*	...	1
...	*Dolupa*	...	5
...	*Mahvapa*	...	2
...	*Malakpa*	...	2
...	*Lakhbakpa*	...	1
		TOTAL	30,672

NOTE.—The Brokpa caste is peculiar to Skardu, and deserves special mention in consequence of their total abstinence from beef and even cow's milk.

	...	Moghal	...	16,588
	...	Pathan	...	38,016
	...	Parsi ...	...	9
	...	Sheikhs (including non-Musalmans of Indian origin.)		373,633
	...	*Hakim*	...	22
	...	*Nanbai*	...	2
	...	*Malla*	...	228
	...	*Balti*	...	25,024
	...	*Bazdar*	...	12
	...	*Raodi*	...	27
	...	*Soni*	...	5
	...	*Sagar*	...	3
	...	*Kangu*	...	7
	...	*Ganarak*	...	1
	...	*Kamakhu*	...	7
	...	*Gashu*	...	1
	...	*Geri*	...	2
	...	*Mangrak*	...	23
	...	*Meva*	...	1
	...	*Makh*	...	4
	...	*Shaban*	...	19
	...	*Miai*	...	6
	...	*Hanghi*	...	3
	...	*Doru*	...	16
	...	*Turanj*	...	13
	...	*Hajia*	...	2
	...	*Chedeva*	...	1
	...	*Sambava*	...	1
	...	*Nanva*	...	1
	...	*Balida*	...	1
	...	*Harsakhia*	...	4
	...	*Homan Chirmal*		1
	...	*Kashna*	...	1
l.—Non-Asiatic races ...	...	*Europeans*	...	132
	...	*Africans*	...	2
li.—Eurasians ...	...	*Eurasians*	...	5
lii.—Christian converts ...	...	*Christians*	...	79
		TOTAL CLASS F	...	484,574

CHAPTER VII.

Occupation.

212. The most laborious part of the work of compiling the Census Returns has been the preparation of the Returns of Occupation.

213. Separate statements have been prepared, showing for each district and the principal towns the occupations of the male and female population, distinguishing actual workers from dependents, while an attempt has been made to obtain more detailed information regarding Europeans and Eurasians by classifying the population by age.

214. Being a country where natural resources have not yet been at all developed, where difficulties of communication have impeded trade with British India, where the hills are inhabited either by agriculturists or by nomadic tribes, the Kashmír State cannot boast of any considerable variety in the occupations of its people. We find in Srinagar, however, traces of occupations owing their existence to an advanced stage of society, but in the rural population, there is none besides the agriculturist, the herdsmen, and the usual complement of village menials.

215. The total population of the State is 2,543,952.

Males ... 1,353,229 } of whom the ages of 10,185 males and 6,721 females are unspecified.
Females ... 1,190,723 }

Of the remainder, according to the statistics of age 538,687 males and 480,705 females are under15 years, and 84,526 males and 64,779 females 60 and above, making a total of 623,213 males and 545,484 females, who, being physically incapable of doing any work, might be said to be dependent on their relatives. We have, therefore, 623,213* males and 545,484* females, whose means of livelihood should be accounted for.

216. The subjoined table shows the results obtained from the Returns of Occupation :—

	Total strength.	Males.	Females.	According to Occupation Statistics.					
				Workers.		*Dependents.*		*Total.*	
				Males.	Females.	Males.	Females.	Males.	Females.
Whole State	2,543,952	1,353,229	1,190,723	676,545	73,442	676,684	1,117,281	1,353,229	1,190,723
Jammu	1,439,543	770,241	669,302	431,068	38,280	339,173	631,022	770,241	669,302
Kashmír	949,041	502,345	446,696	208,961	26,981	293,384	419,715	502,345	446,696
Ladákh	28,274	14,350	13,924	5,855	900	8,495	13,024	14,350	13,924
Skardu	110,325	56,098	54,227	20,466	711	35,632	53,516	56,098	54,227
Gilgit	16,769	10,195	6,574	10,195	6,570	...	4	10,195	6,574

217. It appears that all adult males generally follow some occupation or other, workers in males representing 49 per cent. and dependents 51 per cent. The percentage for each district is as follows :—

	Workers.		*Dependents.*	
	Males.	Females.	Males.	Females.
Jammu	56	5	44	95
Kashmír	41	6	59	94
Ladákh	40	6	60	94
Skardu	36	1	64	99
Gilgit	100	100		

218. The figures for the Urban and Rural population are :—

	Workers.		Dependents.	
	Males.	*Females.*	*Males.*	*Females.*
Urban population, Whole State ...	66,009	5,197	48,543	82,994
Rural ditto ...	610,536	68,245	633,141	1,034,287

* Omitting "Unspecified."

Class.	ORDER.	Whole State. Total.	Whole State. Males.	Whole State. Females.	Jammu. Total.	Jammu. Males.	Jammu. Females.	Kashmir. Total.	Kashmir. Males.	Kashmir. Females.	Ladakh. Total.	Ladakh. Males.	Ladakh. Females.	Skardu. Total.	Skardu. Males.	Skardu. Females.	Gilgit. Total.	Gilgit. Males.	Gilgit. Females.
	(1).—Workers.																		
A.	Administration	20,134	19,630	504	12,743	12,297	446	7,194	7,136	58	78	78	...	118	118	...	1	1	...
	Defence	6,946	6,946	...	5,466	5,466	...	1,097	1,097	...	163	163	...	220	220	...	...	...	...
	Foreign and Feudatory Service	289	272	17	173	169	4	115	102	13	1	1	...	...	...	...	...	...	...
B.	Live Stock	9,043	8,347	696	4,349	3,929	420	4,285	4,020	265	353	342	11	56	56	...	...	...	...
	Agriculture	446,795	426,105	20,690	308,375	291,252	17,123	114,207	111,504	2,703	4,791	4,210	581	19,421	19,138	283	1	1	...
C.	Personal and Household Services	34,015	30,677	3,338	21,109	18,505	2,604	12.519	11,914	605	98	76	22	278	171	107	11	11	...
D.	Preparation and supply of material substances	16,896	15,881	1,015	6,759	6,175	584	10,114	9,684	430	9	8	1	14	14	...	...	...	...
	Light Firing and Forage	3,793	3,574	219	1,840	1,676	164	1,948	1,894	54	2	1	1	3	3	...	...	...	...
	Buildings	935	928	7	337	330	7	591	591	...	1	1	...	...	...	...	6	6	...
	Supplementary requirements	1,368	1,354	14	335	334	1	1,032	1.019	13	1	1	...	...	...	...	...	...	...
	Textile Fabrics and Dress...	58.594	35,973	22,621	15,842	12,434	3,408	42,566	23,353	19,213	14	14	...	172	172	...	...	...	...
	Metals and Precious Stones	7,090	6,946	144	4,416	4,302	114	2,582	2,560	22	44	36	8	48	48	...	...	...	...
	Glass, Pottery and Stone-ware	3,683	3,417	241	2.255	2,039	216	1,432	1,407	25	...	...	...	1	1	...	...	...	...
	Wood, Cane and Leaves, &c.	7,568	7,272	296	4,334	4,185	149	3,200	3,053	147	12	12	...	16	16	...	6	6	...
	Drugs, Gums, Dyes, &c.	281	282	2	42	42	...	242	240	2	...	...	...	...	...	...	...	...	...
	Leather, Horns, Bones and Grease, &c. ...	9,032	8,552	480	6,481	6,036	445	2,542	2,507	35	2	2	...	7	7	...	...	...	...
E.	Commerce	21,164	20.179	985	18,647	17,693	954	2.452	2,421	31	50	50	...	15	15	...	...	...	...
	Transport and Storage	6,257	5,893	364	1,861	1,805	56	4,396	4,088	308	...	...	...	...	...	...	...	...	...
F.	Learned and Artistic Professions	13,871	13,008	863	7,930	7,260	670	5,336	5,192	144	577	529	48	17	16	1	11	11	...
	Sport and Amusements	490	474	16	123	107	16	346	346	...	1	1	...	20	20	...	...	...	...
G.	Indefinite	55,756	38,591	17,165	29,563	21,628	7,935	8,869	6,513	2,356	316	174	142	279	117	162	16,729	10,159	6,570
	Independent of work	25,979	22,214	3,765	16,368	13,404	2,964	8,877	8,320	557	242	156	86	492	334	158	...	...	...
	Total	749,987	676,545	73,442	469,348	431,068	38,280	235,942	208,961	26,981	6,755	5,855	900	21,177	20,466	711	16,765	10,195	6,570

Class.	ORDER.	Whole State. Total.	Whole State. Males.	Whole State. Females.	Jammu. Total.	Jammu. Males.	Jammu. Females.	Kashmir. Total.	Kashmir. Males.	Kashmir. Females.	Ladakh. Total.	Ladakh. Males.	Ladakh. Females.	Skardu. Total.	Skardu. Males.	Skardu. Females.	Gilgit. Total.	Gilgit. Males.	Gilgit. Females.
	(2).—Dependents.																		
A.	Administration	37,171	14,349	22,822	17,770	6,531	11,239	19,032	7,669	11,363	121	34	87	248	115	133	...	...	...
	Defence	3,667	1,116	2,551	2,426	721	1,705	1,122	363	759	62	20	42	57	12	45	...	...	...
	Foreign and Feudatory Service	528	171	357	244	69	175	274	99	175	10	3	7	...	...	...	...	...	...
B.	Live Stock	20,914	8,608	12,306	5,662	2,197	3,465	13,929	5,875	8,054	1,106	441	665	217	95	122	...	...	...
	Agriculture	1,286,091	489,991	796,100	732,064	256,610	475,454	449,545	191,868	257,677	18,433	7,117	11,316	86,049	34,396	51,653	...	...	...
C.	Personal and Household Services	50,758	19,296	31,462	19,842	6,993	12,849	30,292	12,024	18,268	186	88	98	438	191	247	...	...	...
D.	Preparation and supply of material substances	43,557	16,758	26,799	12,866	4,543	8,323	30,631	12,187	18,444	16	5	11	44	23	21	...	...	...
	Light Firing and Forage	11,302	4,461	6,841	3,747	1,298	2,449	7,545	3,162	4,383	2	1	1	8	...	8	3	...	3
	Buildings	2,157	789	1,368	711	258	453	1,440	528	912	3	3	...	...	...	...	...	...	...
	Supplementary requirements	2,756	869	1,887	618	188	430	2,137	681	1,456	1	...	1	...	...	...	...	...	...
	Textile Fabrics and Dress...	87,189	29,933	57,256	30,162	10,329	19,833	56,480	19,389	37,091	31	9	22	516	206	310	...	...	...
	Metals and Precious Stones	18,426	6,769	11,657	9,559	3,335	6,224	8,539	3,303	5,236	76	29	47	252	102	150	...	...	...
	Glass, Pottery and Stone-ware	9,521	3,611	5.910	4,573	1,603	2,970	4,943	2,007	2,936	...	...	...	5	1	4	...	...	...
	Wood, Cane and Leaves, &c.	18,402	6,764	11,638	8,647	2,911	5,736	9,702	3,833	5,869	11	3	8	42	17	25	...	...	...
	Drugs, Gums, Dyes, &c.	780	302	478	83	25	58	697	277	420	...	...	...	...	...	...	...	...	...
	Leather, Horns, Bones and Grease... ...	23,367	8,608	14,759	14,699	5,039	9,660	8,631	3,552	5,079	4	3	1	33	14	19	...	...	...
E.	Commerce	40,298	14,097	26,201	33,269	11,305	21,964	6,936	2,746	4,190	41	28	13	52	18	34	...	...	...
	Transport and Storage	16,059	6,274	9,785	3,389	1,212	2,177	12,670	5,062	7,608	...	...	...	...	...	...	...	...	...
F.	Learned and Artistic Professions	31,596	11,706	19,890	14,923	5,019	9,904	15,896	6,184	9,712	726	484	242	50	19	31	1	...	1
	Sport and Amusements	1,518	616	902	210	98	112	1,214	482	732	7	3	4	87	33	54	...	...	...
G.	Indefinite	46,210	16,058	30,152	35,388	12,052	23,336	10,198	3,846	6,352	441	120	321	183	40	143	...	...	...
	Independent of work	41,698	15,538	26,160	19,343	6,837	12,506	21,246	8,247	12,999	242	104	138	867	350	517	...	...	...
	Total	1,793,965	676,684	1,117,281	970,195	339,173	631,022	713,099	293,384	419,715	21,519	8,495	13,024	89,148	35,632	58,516	4	...	4
	Total Whole State	2,543,952	1,353,229	1,190,723	1,439,548	770,241	669,302	949,041	502,345	446,696	28,274	14,350	13,924	110,325	56,098	54,227	16,769	10,195	6,574

Class.	ORDER.	URBAN POPULATION.						RURAL POPULATION.						TOTAL.								
		Workers.			*Dependents.*			*Workers.*			*Dependents.*			*Workers.*			*Dependents.*			*Total.*		
		Total.	Males.	Females.	Total.	Males.	Females.	Total.	Males.	Females.	Total.	Males.	Females.	Total.	Males.	Females.	Total.	Males.	Females.	Total.	Males.	Females.
A.	Administration	7,535	7,474	61	12,608	4,627	7,981	12,599	12,156	443	24,563	9,722	14,841	20,134	19,630	504	37,171	14,349	22,822	57,305	33,979	23,326
A.	Defence	4,360	4,360	...	1,893	568	1,325	2,586	2,586	...	1,774	548	1,226	6,946	6,946	...	3,667	1,116	2,551	10,613	8,062	2,551
A.	Foreign and Feudatory Service ...	91	78	13	185	56	129	198	194	4	343	115	228	289	272	17	528	171	357	817	443	374
B.	Live Stock	452	448	4	1,564	485	1,079	8,591	7,899	692	19,350	8,123	11,227	9,043	8,347	696	20,914	8,608	12,306	29,957	16,955	13,002
B.	Agriculture	3,119	2,993	126	5,792	2,134	3,658	443,676	423,112	20,564	1,280,299	487,857	792,442	446,795	426,105	20,690	1,286,091	489,991	796,100	1,732,886	916,096	816,790
C.	Personal and Household Services ...	7,316	6,835	481	11,498	4,041	7,457	26,699	23,842	2,857	39,260	15,255	24,005	34,015	30,677	3,338	50,758	19,296	31,462	84,773	49,973	34,800
D.	Preparation and supply of material substances	5,927	5,562	365	13,910	5,104	8,806	10,969	10,319	650	29,647	11,654	17,993	16,896	15,881	1,015	43,557	16,758	26,799	60,453	32,639	27,814
D.	Light, Firing and Forage	655	618	37	2,163	869	1,294	3,138	2,956	182	9,139	3,592	5,547	3,793	3,574	219	11,302	4,461	6.841	15,095	8,035	7,060
D.	Buildings	597	597	...	1,350	464	886	338	331	7	807	325	482	935	928	7	2,157	789	1,368	3,092	1,717	1,375
D.	Supplementary requirements ...	1,093	1,085	8	2,087	630	1,457	275	269	6	669	239	430	1,368	1,354	14	2,756	869	1,887	4,124	2,223	1,901
D.	Textile Fabrics and Dress	17,073	14,779	2,294	29,674	9,216	20,458	41,521	21,194	20,327	57,515	20,717	36,798	58,594	35,973	22,621	87,189	29,933	57,256	145,783	65,906	79,877
D.	Metals and Precious Stones ...	1,626	1,612	14	3,776	1,227	2,549	5,464	5,334	130	14,650	5,542	9,108	7,090	6,946	144	18,426	6,769	11,657	25,516	13,715	11,801
D.	Glass, Pottery and Stone-ware ...	192	189	3	562	189	373	3,496	3,258	238	8,959	3,422	5,537	3,688	3,447	241	9,521	3,611	5,910	13,209	7,058	6,151
D.	Wood, Cane and Leaves, &c. ...	1,183	1,125	58	2,219	727	1,492	6,385	6,147	238	16,183	6,037	10,146	7,568	7,272	296	18,402	6,764	11,638	25,970	14,036	11,934
D.	Drugs, Gums, Dyes, &c. ...	232	230	2	626	253	373	52	52	...	154	49	105	284	282	2	780	302	478	1,064	584	480
D.	Leather, Horns, Bones and Grease, &c.	898	887	11	2,109	719	1,390	8,134	7,665	469	21,258	7,889	13,369	9,032	8,552	480	23,367	8,608	14,759	32,399	17,160	15,239
E.	Commerce	3,625	3,586	39	7,891	2,800	5,091	17.539	16,593	946	32,407	11,297	21,110	21,164	20,179	985	40,298	14,097	26,201	61,462	34,276	27,186
E.	Transport and Storage	2,229	2,129	100	6,135	2,356	3,779	4,028	3,764	264	9,924	3,918	6,006	6,257	5,893	364	16,059	6,274	9,785	22,316	12,167	10,149
F.	Learned and Artistic Professions...	3,474	3,292	182	8,020	2,813	5,207	10,397	9,716	681	23,576	8,893	14,683	13,871	13,008	863	31,596	11,706	19,890	45,467	24,714	20,753
F.	Sport and Amusements	14	14	...	34	15	19	476	460	16	1,484	601	883	490	474	16	1,518	616	902	2,008	1,090	918
G.	Indefinite	5,796	4,634	1,162	6,623	2,105	4,518	49,960	33,957	16,003	39,587	13,953	25,634	55,756	38,591	17,165	46,210	16,058	30,152	101,966	54,649	47,317
G.	Independent of work	3,719	3,482	237	5,818	2,145	3,673	22,260	18,732	3,528	35,880	13.393	22,487	25,979	22,214	3,765	41,698	15,538	26,160	67,677	37,752	29,925
	Total	71,206	66,009	5,197	126,537	43,543	82,994	678,781	610,536	68,245	1,667,428	633,141	1,034,287	749,987	676,545	73,442	1,793,965	676,684	1,117,281	2,543,952	1,353,229	1,190,723

Class.	ORDER.	Proportion of Workers per mille on Total Population.			Proportion of Dependents on Total Population.			Proportion of Workers and Dependents on Total Population.		
		Both sexes.	Males.	Females.	Both sexes.	Males.	Females.	Both sexes.	Males.	Females.
A.	Administration	7·91	14·506	·42	14·61	10·6	19·16	22·52	25·106	19·58
	Defence	2·72	5·13	......	1·44	·82	2·14	4·16	5·95	2·14
	Foreign and Feudatory Service	·11	·201	·04	·207	·12	·29	·317	·321	·33
B.	Live Stock	3·55	6·16	·58	8·22	6·36	10·33	11·77	12·52	10·91
	Agriculture	175·63	314·8	17·37	505·58	362·09	668·58	681·21	676·89	685·95
C.	Personal and Household Services	13·37	22·6	2·8	19·95	14·28	26·42	33·32	36·88	29·22
	Preparation and supply of material substances	6·64	11·73	·85	17·12	12·38	22·506	23·76	24·11	23·356
D.	Light, Firing, Forage	1·49	2·64	·18	4·44	3·29	5·74	5·93	5·93	5·92
	Buildings	·36	·685	·006	·84	·58	1·14	1·2	1·265	1·146
	Supplementary requirements	·53	1·0005	·01	1·08	·64	1·58	1·61	1·64	1·59
	Textile Fabrics and Dress	23·03	26·58	18·99	34·27	22·11	48·08	57·3	48·69	67·07
	Metals and Precious Stones	2·78	5·13	·12	7·24	5·002	9·78	10·02	10·132	9·9
	Glass, Pottery and Stone-ware	1·44	2·54	·202	3·74	2·66	4·96	5·18	5·2	5·162
	Wood, Cane and Leaves, &c.	2·97	5·45	·24	7·23	4·9	9·77	10·2	10·35	10·01
	Drugs, Gums and Dyes	·11	·208	·001	·306	·22	·4	·416	·428	.401
	Leather, Horns, Bones and Grease, &c.	3·55	6·31	·404	9·18	6·36	12·39	12·73	12·67	12·794
E.	Commerce	8·31	14·91	·82	15·84	10·41	22·004	24·15	25·32	22·824
	Transport and Storage	2·45	4·35	·305	6·31	4·63	8·21	8·76	8·98	8·515
F.	Learned and Artistic Professions	5·45	9·61	·72	12·42	8·65	16·62	17·87	18·26	17·34
	Sport and Amusements	·19	·35	·01	·59	·45	·75	·78	·8	·76
G.	Indefinite	21·95	28·51	14·41	18·16	11·86	25·33	40·11	40·37	39·74
	Independent of work	10 21	16·41	3·16	16·29	11·48	21·91	26·5	27·89	25·07
	Total	294·75	499·8105	61·678	705·063	499·892	938·09	999·813	999·702	999·768

Class.	Order.	Jammu.									Kashmir.								
		Proportion of Workers per mille on Total Population.			Proportion of Dependents on Total Population.			Proportion of Workers and Dependents on Total Population.			Proportion of Workers per mille on Total Population.			Proportion of Dependents on Total Population.			Proportion of Workers and Dependents on Total Population.		
		Both sexes.	Males.	Females.	Both sexes.	Males.	Females.	Both sexes.	Males.	Females.	Both sexes.	Males.	Females.	Both sexes.	Males.	Females.	Both sexes.	Males.	Females.
A.	Administration	8·8	15·96	·66	12·34	8·47	16·78	21·14	24·43	17·44	7·58	14·2	·13	20·05	15·27	25·44	27·63	29·47	25·57
	Defence	3·79	7·09	...	1·67	·93	2·54	5·46	8·02	2·54	1·15	2·18	...	1·18	·52	1·7	2·33	2·7	1·7
	Foreign and Feudatory Service	·12	·21	·005	·16	·08	·26	·28	29	·265	·11	·2	·03	·28	·19	·4	·39	·39	·43
B.	Live Stock	3·02	5·1	·62	3·97	2·85	5·17	6·99	7·95	5·79	4·51	8·00	·59	14·6	11·6	18·03	19·11	19·6	18·62
	Agriculture	214·22	378·13	25·58	508·53	333·15	710·37	722·75	711·28	735·95	120·34	221·98	5·91	473·68	381·94	576·85	593·02	603·92	582·76
C.	Personal and Household Services ...	14·67	24·02	3·88	13·78	9·07	19·19	28·45	33·09	23·07	13·19	23·71	1·35	31·91	23·93	40·89	45·1	47·64	42·24
D.	Preparation and supply of material substances	4·7	8·01	·87	8·93	5·89	12·43	13·63	13·9	13·3	10·66	19·27	·96	32·27	24·26	41·29	42·93	43·53	42·25
	Light, Firing, Forage	1·28	2·17	·22	2·6	1·68	3·65	3·88	3·85	3·87	2·05	3·77	·12	7·95	6·5	9·81	10	10·27	9·93
	Buildings...	·23	·43	·01	·49	·32	·67	·72	·75	·68	·62	1·17	...	1·51	1·05	2·04	2·13	2·22	2·04
	Supplementary requirements	·23	·43	·001	·42	·23	·63	·65	·66	·631	1·09	2·02	·03	2·25	1·3	3·26	4·34	3·32	3·29
	Textile Fabrices and Dress	11·00	16·14	5·09	20·95	13·4	29·63	31·95	29·54	34·72	44·85	46·49	43·01	59·51	38·6	83·03	104·36	85·09	126·04
	Metals and Precious Stones	3·06	5·58	·17	6·64	4·32	9·29	9·70	9·9	9·46	2·72	5·09	·05	8·99	6·5	11·72	11·71	11·59	11·77
	Glass, Pottery and Stone-ware	1·56	2·64	·32	3·17	2·08	4·43	4·73	4·72	4·75	1·5	2·8	·05	5·3	3·99	6·57	6·8	6·79	6·62
	Wood, Cane, and Leaves, &c.	3·01	5·43	·22	6·00	3·78	8·57	9·01	9·21	8·79	3·37	6·07	·33	10·22	7·63	13·14	13·59	13·7	13·47
	Drugs, Gums, and Dyes	·02	·05	...	·05	·03	·08	·07	·08	·08	·25	·47	·004	·73	·53	·94	·98	1·00	·944
	Leather, Horns, Bones and Grease, &c. ...	4·5	7·83	·66	10·21	6·54	14·43	14·71	14·37	15·09	2·68	4·99	·08	9·09	7·07	11·37	11·77	12·06	11·45
E.	Commerce	12·95	22·93	1·42	23·11	14·68	32·81	36·06	37·61	34·23	2·58	4·81	·07	7·2	5·5	9·38	9·78	10·31	9·45
	Transport and Storage	1·29	2·34	·08	2·28	1·58	3·25	3·57	3·92	3·33	4·63	8·14	·69	13·35	10·07	17·03	17·98	18·21	17·72
F.	Learned and Artistic Professions ...	5·5	9·42	1·001	10·36	6·51	14·79	15·86	15·93	15·791	5·62	10·55	·32	16·75	12·51	21·74	22·37	23·06	22·06
	Sport and Amusements	·08	·13	·02	·13	·12	·16	·21	·25	·18	36	·7	...	1·28	·96	1·64	1·64	1·66	1·64
G.	Indefinite...	20·55	28·08	11·85	24·58	15·64	34·86	45·13	43·72	46·71	9·34	12·29	5·27	10·82	7·66	14·22	20·16	19·95	19·49
	Independent of work	11·37	17·4	4·44	13·43	8·88	18·68	24·80	26·28	23·12	9·35	16·56	1·24	22·38	16·4	29·1	31·73	32·96	30·34
	Total ...	325·95	559·52	57·117	673·8	440·23	942·67	999·75	999·75	999·78	248·55	415·46	60·234	751·3	583·98	939·59	999·85	999·44	999·824

Class.	ORDER.	Ladakh. Proportion of Workers per mille on Total Population. Both sexes.	Males.	Females.	Proportion of Dependents on Total Population. Both sexes.	Males.	Females.	Proportion of Workers and Dependents on Total Population. Both sexes.	Males.	Females.	Skardu. Proportion of Workers per mille on Total Population. Both sexes.	Males.	Females.	Proportion of Dependents on Total Population. Both sexes.	Males.	Females.	Proportion of Workers and Dependents on Total Population. Both sexes.	Males.	Females.
A.	Administration	2·76	5·43	...	4·21	2·37	6·25	6·97	7·8	6·25	1·06	2·1	...	2·24	2·05	2·55	3·3	4·15	2·55
	Defence	5·76	11·36	...	2·19	1·39	3·02	7·95	12·75	3·02	1·9	3·92	...	·51	·21	·83	2·41	4·13	·83
	Foreign and Feudatory Service	·03	·07	...	·35	·21	·5	·38	·28	·5	...	...	...	...	...	...	...	...	...
B.	Live Stock	12·48	23·83	·8	39·11	30·73	47·76	51·59	54·56	48·56	·5	·99	...	1·96	1·69	2·25	2·46	2·68	2·25
	Agriculture	169·44	293·38	41 73	651·93	495·95	812·69	821·37	789·33	854·42	176·03	341·11	5·21	779·95	613·14	952·62	955·98	954·25	957·78
C.	Personal and Household Services	3·46	5·29	1·58	6·57	6·11	7·04	10·03	11·4	8·62	2·51	3·04	1·97	3·97	3·44	4·55	6·48	6·48	6·52
D.	Preparation and supply of material substances	·31	·56	·07	·56	·35	·8	·87	·91	·87	·12	·24	...	·39	·4	·38	·51	·64	·38
	Light, Firing, Forage	·07	·07	·07	·07	·07	·07	·14	·14	·14	·02	·05	...	·07	...	·14	·09	·05	·14
	Buildings	·03	·07	...	·1	·21	...	·13	·28	...	...	...	...	...	...	...	...	...	...
	Supplementary requirements	·03	·07	...	·03	...	·07	·06	·07	·07	...	...	...	...	...	...	...	...	...
	Textile Fabrics and Dress	·49	·97	...	1·1	·62	1·6	1·59	1·59	1·6	1·55	3·06	...	4 67	3·63	5 71	6·22	6·69	5·71
	Metals and Precious Stones	1·55	2·5	·57	2·7	2·02	3·38	4·25	4·52	3·95	·43	·85	...	2·28	1·81	2·77	2·71	2·66	2·77
	Glass, Pottery and Stone-ware	...	...	...	...	...	...	...	...	...	·009	·01	...	·04	·01	·07	·049	·02	·07
	Wood, Cane and Leaves, &c.	·41	·83	...	·39	·21	·6	·8	1·04	·6	·14	·28	...	·38	·3	·46	·52	·58	·46
	Drugs, Gums and Dyes	...	...	...	...	...	...	...	...	...	...	...	...	...	...	...	...	...	...
	Leather, Horns, Bones and Grease, &c.	·07	·14	...	·16	·21	·07	·23	·35	·07	·06	·12	...	·29	·24	·35	·35	·36	·35
E.	Commerce	1·77	3·49	...	1·45	1·95	·93	3·22	5·44	·93	·13	·26	...	·47	·32	·62	·6	·58	·62
	Transport and Storage	...	...	...	...	...	...	...	...	...	...	...	...	...	...	...	...	...	...
F.	Learned and Artistic Professions	20·41	36·86	3·44	25·7	33·72	17·37	46·11	70·58	20·81	·15	·28	·01	·45	·33	·57	·6	·61	·58
	Sport and Amusements	·03	·07	..	·24	·21	·28	·27	·28	·28	·18	·35	...	·78	·58	·62	·96	·93	·62
G.	Indefinite	11·17	12·12	10.2	15·6	8·36	23·05	26·77	20·48	33·25	2·52	2·08	2·98	1·65	·71	2·63	4 17	2·79	5·61
	Independent of work	8·55	10·9	6.2	8·56	7·24	9·9	17·11	18·14	16·1	4·45	5·95	2·93	7·85	6·24	9·55	12·3	12·19	12·48
	Total	238·82	408·01	64·66	761·02	591·93	935·38	999·84	999·04	1000·04	191·759	364·69	13·1	807·95	635·1	986·57	999·7	999·79	999·67

Class.	Order.	GILGIT. Proportion of Workers per mille on Total Population.			Proportion of Dependents on Total Population.			Proportion of Workers and Dependents on Total Population.		
		Both sexes.	Males.	Females.	Both sexes.	Males.	Females.	Both sexes.	Males.	Females.
A.	Administration	·059	·098	...	...	...	...	·059	·098	...
	Defence	...	...	...	...	...	...	...	...	...
	Foreign and Feudatory Service	...	...	...	...	...	...	...	...	...
B.	Live Stock	...	...	...	...	...	...	...	...	...
	Agriculture	·059	·098	...	...	...	...	·059	·098	...
C.	Personal and Household Services	·65	1·049	...	...	...	...	·65	1·049	...
D.	Preparation and supply of material substances	...	...	...	...	...	...	...	...	...
	Light, Firing, Forage	...	...	...	...	...	...	...	...	...
	Buildings	·35	·59	...	·17	...	·46	·52	·59	·46
	Supplementary requirements	...	...	...	...	...	...	...	...	...
	Textile Fabrics and Dress	...	...	...	...	...	...	...	...	...
	Metals and Precious Stones	...	...	...	...	...	...	...	...	...
	Glass, Pottery and Stoneware	...	...	...	...	...	...	...	...	...
	Wood, Cane and Leaves, &c.	·35	·59	...	...	...	...	·35	·59	...
	Drugs, Gums and Dyes &c.	...	...	...	...	...	...	...	...	...
	Leather, Horns, Bones and Grease	...	...	...	...	...	...	...	...	...
E.	Commerce	...	...	...	...	...	...	...	...	...
	Transport and Storage	...	...	...	...	...	...	...	...	...
F.	Learned and Artistic Professions	·65	1·049	...	·059	...	·15	·709	1·049	·15
	Sport and Amusements	...	...	...	...	...	...	...	...	...
G.	Indefinite	997·6	996·4	999·39	...	...	...	997·6	996·4	999·39
	Independent of work	...	...	...	...	...	...	...	...	...
	Total	999·718	999·87	999·39	·229	...	·61	999·947	999·87	1000

Class.	ORDER.	PROPORTION PER MILLE.																				
		URBAN POPULATION.						RURAL POPULATION.						TOTAL.								
		Workers.			*Dependents.*			*Workers.*			*Dependents.*			*Workers.*			*Dependents.*			*Total.*		
		Both sexes.	Males.	Females.	Both sexes.	Males.	Females.	Both sexes.	Males.	Females.	Both sexes.	Males.	Females.	Both sexes.	Males.	Females.	Both sexes.	Males.	Females.	Both sexes.	Males.	Females.
A.	Administration	38,1	68	.66	63.9	42	90.49	6	9·7	·4	10·4	7·92	13·47	7·9	14	·42	14·6	10·6	19·1	22	25	20
	Defence	22,04	40	...	9,5	5	15,74	1·1	2·07	...	·75	·046	1·11	2·7	5	...	1·4	·8	2·1	4	6	2
	Foreign and Feudatory Service	.46	,71	.13	.9	,511	1.46	·08	·1	·03	·14	·09	·206	·1	·2	·014	·27	·12	·29	1	1	...
B.	Live Stock	2,28	4	.04	7.9	4	12.24	3·7	6·3	·6	8·25	6·63	10·18	3·3	6·3	·58	8·2	6·3	10·3	12	12	11
	Agriculture	15,77	27	1.42	29,2	19	41,35	189·1	340·2	18·6	545·6	393·3	718·74	175·5	315	17·37	505·5	362·9	668·6	681	678	686
C.	Personal and Household Services	36,99	62	5.45	58.1	37	84.55	11·3	19·1	2·5	16·73	12·2	21·77	13	23	2·80	19·9	14·2	26·4	33	37	29
D.	Preparation and Supply of material substances	29,97	51	4·12	70.4	47	99.85	4·6	8·3	·5	12·63	9·03	16·31	7·5	12	·85	17·1	12·3	22·5	23	24	23
	Light, Firing, Forage	3.31	6	·41	10.8	8	14,68	1·3	2·4	·1	3·89	2·08	5·03	1·4	3	·18	4·4	3·2	5·7	5	6	6
	Buildings	3,01	5	...	6,8	4	10.04	·14	·2	·006	·34	·3	·43	·35	·7	·0058	·84	·5	1·1	1	1	1
	Supplementary requirements	5.52	10	.09	10.5	6	16.53	·12	·2	·005	·28	1·12	·39	·54	1	·011	1·08	·6	1·6	1	2	2
	Textile Fabrics and Dress	86.33	135	26.02	150,06	84	231.47	17·7	17·04	18·4	24·51	16·8	33·37	23·3	27	18·99	34·3	22	48·08	57	49	67
	Metals and Precious Stones	8,22	15	.15	18.4	11	28,68	2·3	4·2	·1	6·24	4·5	8·26	2·7	5	·12	7·3	5·002	9·8	10	10	10
	Glass, Pottery and Stoneware	.97	2	.03	2.8	2	4,23	1·5	2·6	·2	3·43	2·8	5·02	1·5	3	·202	3·8	2·7	4·9	5	5	5
	Wood, Cane and Leaves &c.	5,98	10.3	.65	11.2	7	16.8	2·7	4·9	·2	6·9	4·9	9·20	2·9	5	·24	7·2	4·9	9·8	10	10	10
	Drugs, Gums and Dyes	1,17	2	·02	3.2	2	4.23	·019	·04	...	·47	·03	·09	·11	·2	·0016	·306	·3	·405	1	...	1
	Leather, Horns, Bones and Grease	4,54	8	.12	10.6	7	15.76	3·5	6·1	·4	9·07	6·42	12·12	3·6	6	·403	9·1	6·3	12·4	13	13	13
E.	Commerce	18.33	33	.44	40.2	26	57.74	7·4	13·3	·8	13·82	9·08	19·14	8·3	15	·82	15·9	10·5	22·1	25	25	23
	Transport and Storage	11.27	19	1.13	31.02	22	42.85	1·7	3·02	·2	4·23	3·11	5·44	2·4	4	·305	6·3	5·3	8·8	9	9	8
F.	Learned and Artistic Professions	17,56	30	2.06	40,8	26	59.54	4·4	7·8	·6	10·05	7·1	13·31	5·3	10	·72	12·4	8·6	16·7	18	18	17
	Sport and Amusements	.07	.13	...	.1	.136	.22	·202	·3	·01	·63	·4	·80	·19	·3	·013	·6	·45	·8	1	1	1
G.	Indefinite	29.31	42	13.17	33.4	19	51.23	21·2	27·3	14·5	16·87	11·2	23·25	22·6	28	14·41	18·2	11·8	25·3	41	40	40
	Independent of work	18,8	32	2,68	29,4	19	41.65	9·4	15·06	3·1	15·29	10·7	20·39	10·2	16	3·16	16·5	11·4	21·9	27	28	25
	Total	360,5	602,55	58.79	639.5	397.45	941.21	289·3	490·9	61·8	710·7	509·1	938·2	295	499·8	61·67	705	500·2	938·33	1000	1000	1000

219. It is impossible to obtain correct statistics in this country regarding commercial occupations. The figures given for grain-dealers, general merchants and shop-keepers may be simply said to be misleading. Every shop-keeper is a general merchant, a grain-dealer and banker in his own way, and unless the enumerator is thoroughly intelligent and discriminating, he would certainly be guilty of some error or other, if he merely puts down the evasive reply given to his query. This explains the reason why 3,336 grain-dealers have been returned in Kashmír, against only 17 in Jammu, why there are only 281 general merchants in Kashmír against 4,591 in Jammu, and why other shop-keepers in Kashmír number only 1,419 against 11,578 in Jammu. Again, there are no blanket-weavers in Jammu, and no cotton-weavers in Kashmír, while, in fact, all weavers in both places work in both cotton and wool, and the enumerators apparently used their discretion in classifying one in contra-distinction of the other.

220. The province of Jammu cannot boast of any industrial occupations beyond the ordinary occupations of village menials. The towns in this Province of which that of Jammu is the seat of government, carry on an extensive trade in ghi, oil, grains and other necessaries with the hilly tracts in the interior, while Jammu answers besides, the requirements of the royal family and the civil and military establishments at the seat of government.

221. The province of Kashmír, or rather urban population of Kashmír, is more advanced in industrial occupations, the principal of which are :—

Shawl-weaving, &c.
Blanket-weaving.
Woollen Yarn spinning and carding.
Gold and Silver work.
Carpenter.

222. The Kashmír shawls and blankets are largely exported to British India, while carpenter's work and metal work find favor with the European visitors to the valley.

223. The principal occupations in the rural districts of Jammu and Kashmír are agricultural and tending of cattle and sheep.

224. The population of Ladákh which is effectively checked by polyandry is from natural causes, precluded from cultivating the more profitable industrial occupations, being content either with cultivation of the soil the proceeds of which are sufficient for their immediate requirements, or enjoying seclusion from worldly affairs by being ordained as Lamas. This explains the reason why the numerous occupations returned in Jammu and Kashmír are absent in Ladákh. Circumstanced by nature the Ladákhi is trained in all the avocations necessary for his existence and personal comfort. He is himself his own menial, barber, tailor, butcher and anything else. The same remarks apply to Skardu.

225. The following Comparative Statement, which has been prepared from the Occupation Tables, shows the number of workers in each district, with separate details for the urban and rural population. Advantage has also been taken to give approximately the average number of dependents on each worker :—

Number.	Occupations.	Workers. Jammu.	Workers. Kashmir.	Workers. Ladákh.	Workers. Skardu.	Workers. Gilgit.	Workers. Total Whole State.	Workers. Urban Population.	Workers. Rural Population.	Workers. Europeans and Eurasians.	Dependents. Jammu Urban.	Dependents. Kashmir Urban.	Dependents. Jammu Rural.	Dependents. Kashmir Rural.	Dependents. Ladákh.	Dependents. Skardu.	Dependents. Gilgit.	Dependents. Whole State Urban.	Dependents. Whole State Rural.	Dependents. Total Whole State.	Dependents. Europeans and Eurasians.
1	Maharaja and Rajas and their families	3	...	...	...	...	3	3	...	...	26	...	...	...	...	...	...	26	...	26	...
2	Officers	163	8	...	...	...	171	167	4	1	1	1	D	D	...	...	...	1	D	1	2
3	State Servants	10,886	5,718	78	117	...	16,799	6,246	10,553	...	1	3	2	2	2	2	...	2	2	2	...
4	Police Constables, Orderlies and Bandukies	950	353	...	...	...	1,303	940	363	...	W	2	1	2	...	...	...	1	1	1	...
5	Inspecting and Supervising Officials	1	..	...	...	...	1	1	...	1	4	...	...	...	...	...	...	4	...	4	4
9	Patwaries	11	653	...	1	...	665	82	583	...	...	4	W	4	...	1	...	4	4	4	...
11	Chowkidars	729	462	...	...	1	1,192	96	1,096	...	2	2	2	5	...	...	D	3	2	2	...
12	Military Officers	3	...	...	...	...	3	3	...	3	3	...	...	...	...	...	...	3	...	3	3
13	Military Servants	5,463	1,097	163	220	...	6,943	4,357	2,586	...	W	2	W	W	W	W	...	W	W	W	...
20 & 21	Residency Clerks and other Menials	173	107	1	...	...	281	83	198	...	D	2	1	3	10	...	...	2	2	2	...
22	Officers Foreign British ...	...	8	...	...	...	8	8	...	8	...	3	...	...	...	...	...	3	...	3	3
25	Cattle breeders and dealers...	...	891	347	44	...	1,282	313	969	...	...	4	...	2	3	4	...	4	3	3	...
26	Herdsmen	...	1,898	...	...	...	1,898	47	1,851	...	...	W	...	4	...	...	...	W	4	4	...
31	Sheep and goat breeders ...	4,319	1,410	6	12	...	5,747	11	5,736	...	2	...	1	3	3	2	...	2	2	2	...
34	Farriers and Gelders ...	18	27	...	...	...	45	29	16	...	D	2	4	D	...	...	...	2	4	3	...
35	Horse and elephant breakers and trainers	12	59	...	...	...	71	52	19	...	3	2	1	2	...	...	...	2	2	2	...
37	Land occupants, not cultivating	12,789	...	4,783	19,058	1	36,631	...	36,631	...	...	...	2	...	4	4	...	...	3	3	...
38	Land occupants, cultivating	135,289	83,329	6	3	...	218,627	1,224	217,403	...	1	3	2	4	5	6	...	2	3	3	...
39	Lessees of villages	935	531	1	3	...	1,470	56	1,414	...	2	5	2	4	4	16	...	4	3	3	...
41	Tenants and sharers, cultivating	158,966	30,202	...	357	...	189,525	1,671	187,854	...	2	2	2	4	...	4	...	2	3	3	...
44	Tea planters	...	1	...	...	...	1	...	1	1	...	...	...	D	...	...	.	...	D	...	D
47	Waternut growers	...	64	...	...	...	64	61	3	...	...	1	...	4	...	...	...	1	4	1	...
52	Gardners, seedsmen, &c. ...	267	77	1	...	...	345	81	264	...	2	2	2	5	1	...	...	2	3	2	...
54	Forest Officers	1	...	...	...	...	1	1	...	...	4	X	...	...	...	...	...	7	...	7	X
55	Forest Rangers, Guards, &c.,	128	...	...	...	...	128	22	106	...	1	...	1	...	...	...	...	1	2	2	...
56	Directors of Agriculture ...	...	3	...	...	...	3	3	...	3	...	D	...	...	...	...	...	D	...	...	D
59	Barbers	2,171	1,971	5	13	...	4,160	632	3,528	...	2	2	2	3	3	3	...	2	3	3	...

63	Washermen	1,079	648	1	6	...	1,734	498	1,236	...	2	2	2	4	2	4	...	2	2	2	...
64	Water Carriers	1,355	291	...	...	...	1,646	440	1,206	...	1	2	2	W	...	...	...	2	2	2	...
65	Cooks	24	266	...	...	...	290	253	37	...	1	2	4	4	...	...	...	2	4	3	...
66	In-door Servants	15,656	9,072	92	259	11	25,090	5,289	19,801	5	1	2	W	2	2	1	D	1	1	1	D
67	Grooms	69	...	...	...	...	69	51	18	...	W	...	W	...	...	...	...	W	W	W	...
68	Door Keepers	16	8	...	...	...	24	22	2	...	2	2	7	1	...	...	...	2	4	2	...
70	Rest-house, Sarai, Bath-house, Owners and Managers ...	14	143	...	...	...	157	16	141	...	...	1	W	5	...	...	...	1	5	5	...
74	Sweepers and Scavengers ...	725	102	...	...	...	827	97	730	...	4	W	2	2	...	...	...	2	2	2	...
75	Dust and Sweepings Contractors	...	18	...	...	...	18	18	...	...	...	2	...	...	...	...	...	2	...	2	...
76	Cow and buffalo keepers, and milk and butter sellers ...	2,535	2,695	...	...	...	5,230	915	4,315	...	3	2	2	4	...	...	...	2	3	3	...
77	Ghee preparers and sellers ...	781	...	...	...	...	781	34	747	...	W	...	2	...	...	...	...	W	3	2	...
79	Butchers	282	665	4	2	...	953	600	353	...	2	3	1	4	2	3	...	3	3	3	...
81	Fishermen and fish curers ...	8	394	...	...	...	402	133	269	...	2	3	2	4	...	...	...	3	4	4	...
83	Grain dealers	17	3,336	...	...	...	3,353	1,522	1,831	...	...	3	W	3	...	...	...	3	3	3	...
84	Grain parchers	46	32	...	...	...	78	40	38	...	1	2	W	...	...	...	...	2	1	1	...
86	Flour mill service	1,870	248	1	12	...	2,131	151	1,980	...	1	4	2	2	3	3	...	2	2	2	...
87	Bakers	318	826	4	...	...	1,148	607	541	...	1	2	2	W	1	...	...	2	3	3	...
89	Vegetable sellers	308	773	...	...	...	1,081	715	366	...	2	2	2	3	...	...	...	2	2	2	...
90	Fruit sellers	15	573	...	...	...	588	474	114	...	1	2	3	4	...	...	...	2	4	3	...
92	Confectioners and sweetmeat makers and sellers and cooks, &c.	230	187	...	...	...	417	305	112	...	2	2	2	W	...	...	...	2	2	2	...
97	Country spirit distillers and sellers	25	12	...	...	...	37	26	11	...	W	W	W	...	...	...	...	W	W	W	...
105	Salt sellers	97	...	...	...	...	97	...	97	...	...	...	W	...	...	...	...	...	W	W	...
109	Grocers	190	...	...	...	...	190	61	129	...	2	...	2	...	...	...	...	2	2	2	...
112	Tobacco and Snuff sellers ...	33	361	...	...	...	394	328	66	...	1	2	4	2	...	...	...	2	3	2	...
114	Opium sellers	1	...	...	...	...	1	1	...	...	D	...	...	...	...	...	...	D	...	D	...
115	Bhang, Ganja, &c., sellers ...	3	12	...	...	...	15	15	...	...	1	W	...	X	...	...	...	2	X	2	...
116	Oil pressers	1,452	1,574	...	...	...	3,026	296	2,730	...	3	2	2	4	...	...	...	3	3	3	...
119	Candle makers, &c.	...	2	...	...	...	2	2	...	...	...	W	...	...	...	...	...	W	...	W	...
120	Torch makers and sellers ...	5	11	...	...	...	16	15	1	...	3	3	...	5	...	...	...	3	5	3	...
125	Firewood sellers	331	240	2	3	...	576	274	302	...	1	4	2	2	1	3	...	4	2	3	...
	Grass do.	42	121	...	...	...	163	68	95												
131	Hay, &c., dealers	10	...	...	...	...	10	...	10	...	...	...	W	...	...	...	...	...	W	W	...
132	Brick and tile burners and sellers	28	69	...	...	...	97	75	22	...	3	3	2	...	...	...	...	3	2	3	...
133	Lime, chunam burners and sellers	...	73	...	...	...	73	...	73	...	...	...	...	3	...	...	...	...	3	3	...
136	Building Contractors ...	...	199	1	...	...	200	94	106	...	...	3	...	2	3	...	...	3	2	3	...
137	Stone-workers	72	15	...	...	...	87	48	39	...	2	3	4	8	...	...	...	2	4	3	...
138	Masons	237	235	...	...	6	478	380	98	...	2	2	2	W	...	...	W	2	2	2	...

NOTE.—W. Workers outnumber Dependents D. No Dependenst X. No Workers.

Number.	Occupations.	Workers. Jammu.	Workers. Kashmír.	Workers. Ladákh.	Workers. Skardu.	Workers. Gilgit.	Workers. Total Whole State.	Workers. Urban population.	Workers. Rural population.	Workers. Europeans and Eurasians.	Dependents. Jammu Urban.	Dependents. Kashmír Urban.	Dependents. Jammu Rural.	Dependents. Kashmír Rural.	Dependents. Ladákh.	Dependents. Skardu.	Dependents. Gilgit.	Dependents. Whole State Urban.	Dependents. Whole State Rural.	Dependents. Total Whole State.	Dependents. Europeans and Eurasians.
		Workers.									**Average number of Dependents on every Worker.**										
153	Paper-makers and sellers ...	...	147	...	...	...	147	145	2	...	...	3	...	5	...	...	...	3	5	3	...
157	Press Proprietors, &c. ...	27	1	...	...	...	28	28	...	...	1	3	...	...	...	...	...	1	...	1	...
158	Book-binders	21	34	...	...	...	55	45	10	...	2	2	2	7	...	...	...	2	3	2	...
159	Book-sellers	2	...	...	...	...	2	...	2	...	...	...	D	...	...	...	...	...	D	D	...
163	Watch and Clock makers and sellers	5	11	...	...	...	16	16	...	...	1	2	...	...	...	...	...	2	...	2	...
172	Turners and Lacquerers ...	15	28	...	...	...	43	37	6	...	2	3	7	...	...	...	...	3	6	3	...
173	Die Sinkers and Seal Engravers	2	93	...	...	...	95	91	4	...	D	2	...	2	...	...	...	2	2	2	...
178	Hukka Stem makers and sellers	28	22	1	...	...	51	48	3	...	1	2	2	...	1	...	...	2	2	2	...
179	Papier-maché workers and sellers	31	211	...	...	...	242	230	12	...	2	2	1	3	...	...	...	2	2	2	...
183	Music and Musical Instrument dealers	4	2	...	...	...	6	6	...	...	2	3	...	...	...	...	...	3	...	3	...
185	Bangle makers and sellers in lac	98	125	...	...	...	223	101	122	...	...	2	2	2	...	...	...	2	2	2	...
194	Flower garland makers and sellers	...	5	...	...	...	5	4	1	...	...	3	...	D	...	...	...	3	D	2	...
201	Saddlery and harness makers and sellers	6	274	...	...	...	280	252	28	...	4	1	2	2	...	...	...	1	2	2	...
205	Knife and tool grinders ...	28	32	...	...	...	60	23	37	...	1	3	2	3	...	...	...	2	3	2	...
210	Ammunition and cap dealers	1	...	...	...	...	1	1	...	...	D	...	...	...	...	...	...	D	...	D	...
212	Firework makers and sellers	27	47	...	...	...	74	29	45	...	3	2	3	3	...	...	...	3	3	3	...
215	Bow and arrow workers and sellers	40	...	...	...	...	40	37	3	...	1	...	3	...	...	...	...	1	3	1	...
217	Carpet weavers and sellers...	7	339	...	...	...	346	339	7	...	W	1	X	1	...	...	...	1	1	1	...
218	Shawl weavers and sellers ...	74	9,491	...	57	...	9,622	5,452	4,170	...	W	2	2	2	...	4	...	2	2	2	...
219	Felt and Pashm workers, &c.	2	161	...	...	...	163	163	...	...	4	3	...	...	...	...	...	3	...	3	...
220	Blanket weavers and sellers	...	4,423	8	113	...	4,544	936	3,608	...	...	2	...	3	2	2	...	2	3	3	...
221	Woollen cloth manufacturers and dealers	183	301	...	...	...	484	350	134	...	2	2	2	5	...	...	...	2	3	3	...
222	Woollen yarn spinners and sellers	2,633	19,110	...	...	...	21,743	2,195	19,548	...	1	W	W	W	...	...	...	W	W	W	...

223	Wool carders...	...	188	...	...	...	188	188	...	...	...	3	...	...	...	...	...	3	...	3	...
224	Wool dyers	527	355	...	...	...	882	362	520	...	2	2	2	4	...	...	...	2	2	3	...
226	Silk worm rearers and cacoon gatherers	...	94	...	...	...	94	26	68	...	...	3	...	4	...	...	...	3	3	3	...
229	Silk printers and dyers ...	10	...	...	...	...	10	4	6	...	3	...	2	...	...	...	...	3	2	3	...
230	Braid and ribbon makers and sellers	111	325	...	...	...	436	388	48	...	1	2	2	2	...	...	...	2	2	2	...
231	Cotton cleaners	481	601	...	...	...	1,082	163	919	...	1	2	2	3	...	...	...	2	2	3	...
232	Cotton carpet and rug makers and sellers	...	45	...	...	...	45	45	...	...	...	2	...	...	...	...	...	2	...	2	...
234	Cotton weavers	10,248	...	...	...	...	10,248	433	9,815	...	2	...	2	...	...	...	...	2	2	2	...
236	Calenderers	21	70	...	...	...	91	50	41	...	1	3	1	3	...	...	...	3	2	3	...
237	Cotton dyers...	18	...	...	...	...	18	...	18	...	...	...	4	...	...	...	...	...	3	3	...
241	Hemp rope makers and sellers	4	...	...	...	...	4	...	4	...	...	...	2	...	...	...	...	...	2	2	...
243	Sacking makers and sellers	1	...	...	...	...	1	...	1	...	...	...	5	...	...	...	...	...	5	5	...
247	Tailors	1,519	6,654	6	2	...	8,181	5,570	2,611	...	2	2	2	3	3	5	...	2	2	2	...
254	Embroiderers...	3	409	...	...	...	412	409	3	...	...	1	2	...	...	...	...	2	2	2	...
260	Gold and Silver workers ...	1,523	881	23	12	...	2,439	891	1,548	...	2	3	2	4	1	5	...	2	3	3	...
261	Gold beaters	2	...	...	2	...	4	...	4	...	...	...	2	...	...	9	...	...	6	6	...
262	Goldsmith's dust washers ...	9	...	...	1	...	10	1	9	...	2	...	2	...	...	11	...	2	3	3	...
265	Electro-platers	6	...	...	...	...	6	...	6	...	...	...	1	...	...	...	...	...	1	1	...
266	Gold and Silver wire drawers	3	...	...	...	...	3	...	3	...	...	...	3	...	...	...	...	...	3	3	...
277	Brass pot makers and sellers	131	39	...	...	...	170	56	114	...	4	2	1	...	...	...	...	3	1	2	...
279	Copper workers and sellers	73	213	...	3	...	289	211	78	...	2	2	2	4	...	7	...	2	3	3	...
284	Tin workers and sellers ...	140	6	...	...	...	146	12	134	...	1	3	3	...	...	...	...	2	3	3	...
290	Blacksmiths	2,529	1,443	21	30	...	4,023	455	3,568	...	2	2	2	4	2	4	...	2	3	3	...
297	Glass and Chinaware dealers	5	...	...	...	...	5	...	5	...	...	...	W	...	...	...	...	...	W	W	...
298	Potters	2,245	1,432	...	1	...	3,678	192	3,486	...	3	3	2	3	...	5	...	3	3	3	...
299	Grindstone makers and sellers	5	...	...	...	...	5	...	5	...	...	...	2	...	...	...	...	...	2	2	...
302	Timber dealers	668	3	...	...	...	671	7	664	...	1	3	2	...	...	...	...	2	2	2	...
303	Wood cutters and sawyers ...	3	318	...	...	...	321	138	183	...	...	2	1	3	...	...	...	2	3	3	...
304	Carpenters	2,830	2,179	12	16	6	5,043	848	4,195	...	1	2	2	4	1	2	D.	2	3	3	...
306	Bamboo and rattan splitters, workers, &c.	298	438	...	...	...	736	85	651	...	...	2	2	3	...	...	...	2	3	3	...
307	Basket weavers, &c. ...	454	56	...	...	...	510	29	481	...	W	...	2	3	...	...	...	2	3	2	...
308	Mat makers and sellers ...	7	200	...	...	...	207	69	138	...	1	1	5	W	...	...	...	...	1	W	...
310	Leaf plate makers and sellers	42	...	...	...	...	42	1	41	...	4	...	1	...	...	...	...	1	1	1	...
313	Brush and comb makers and sellers	32	...	...	...	...	32	...	32	...	...	...	2	...	...	...	...	4	1	1	...
315	Pith and bark collectors, workers and sellers ...	...	6	...	...	...	6	6	...	...	...	3	...	...	...	...	...	...	2	2	...
324	Druggists	19	159	...	...	...	178	155	23	...	...	3	3	7	...	...	...	3	...	3	...

NOTE.—W. Workers outnumber Dependents D. No Dependents X. No Workers.

Number.	Occupations.	Workers. Jammu.	Workers. Kashmír.	Workers. Ladákh.	Workers. Skardu.	Workers. Gilgit.	Workers. Total Whole State.	Workers. Urban population.	Workers. Rural population.	Workers. Europeans and Eurasians.	Average number of Dependents on every Worker. Jammu Urban.	Kashmír Urban.	Jammu Rural.	Kashmír Rural.	Ladákh.	Skardu.	Gilgit.	Whole State Urban.	Whole State Rural.	Total whole State.	Europeans and Eurasians.
328	Soap makers and sellers ...	5	60	...	...	...	65	38	27	...	...	3	3	2	...	...	...	3	4	3	...
330	Indigo workers and dealers	1	...	...	...	...	1	1	...	...	D.	...	...	...	...	...	...	D.	...	D.	...
332	Ink makers and sellers ...	4	22	...	...	...	26	26	...	...	1	3	...	...	...	...	...	3	...	3	...
337	Perfume preparers and sellers	13	1	...	...	...	14	12	2	...	1	...	D	D	...	...	...	1	D	1	...
338	Tanners and hide sellers ...	83	...	...	...	...	83	42	41	...	3	...	3	...	...	...	...	3	3	3	...
339	Shoe makers and sellers ...	6,361	2,542	2	7	...	8,912	843	8,069	...	2	2	2	4	2	5	...	2	3	3	...
340	Leather dyers	36	...	...	...	...	36	13	23	...	2	...	2	...	...	...	...	2	2	2	...
341	Ghee pot makers and sellers	1	...	...	...	...	1	...	1	...	...	...	D	...	...	...	...	...	D	D	...
346	Bankers and Bank managers	1,825	1	...	...	...	1,826	349	1,477	1	2	D	2	...	...	...	...	2	2	2	D
350	Money changers and testers	127	460	...	...	...	587	535	52	...	3	3	3	...	...	...	...	3	3	3	...
352	General Merchants	4,591	281	...	...	...	4,872	171	4,701	2	1	3	2	3	...	...	...	2	2	2	1
353	Merchant's Managers ...	...	25	...	...	...	25	25	...	...	...	5	...	...	...	...	...	5	...	5	...
356	Shop Keepers	11,578	1,419	50	12	...	13,059	2,086	10,973	...	2	3	2	2	W	4	...	2	2	2	...
357	Pedlars and Hawkers ...	96	93	...	3	...	192	114	78	...	6	2	2	7	...	1	...	3	2	3	...
358	Brokers	5	156	...	...	...	161	150	11	...	D	3	W	3	...	...	...	3	2	3	...
359	House Agents	...	1	...	...	...	1	...	1	1	...	...	...	D	...	...	...	...	D	D	D
360	Farmers of Tolls Ferries ...	107	12	...	...	...	119	75	44	...	1	3	2	...	...	...	...	2	2	2	...
361	Farmers of liquor, opium, &c.	16	...	...	...	...	16	...	16	...	...	...	1	...	...	...	...	...	1	1	...
362	Lessees of markets, &c. ...	1	...	...	...	...	1	...	1	...	...	...	D	...	...	...	...	...	D	D	...
363	Contractors	301	3	...	...	...	304	119	185	...	2	...	2	3	...	...	...	2	3	2	...
364	Contractors for labor ...	...	1	...	...	...	1	1	...	...	...	4	...	...	...	...	...	4	...	4	...
371	Station Masters and Assistants, Inspectors, &c. ...	25	...	...	...	...	25	25	...	...	W	...	...	...	...	...	...	W	...	W	...
375	Cart owners and drivers &c.	7	3	...	...	...	10	...	10	...	...	...	3	D	...	...	...	...	2	2	...
377	Drivers and stable boys ...	10	...	...	...	...	10	10	...	...	1	...	...	...	...	...	...	1	...	1	...
378	Palki owners and bearers ...	...	186	...	...	...	186	148	38	...	...	2	...	5	...	...	...	2	3	2	...
379	Pack bullock owners and drivers	93	...	...	...	...	93	...	93	...	...	...	2	...	...	...	...	...	2	2	...
380	Pack camel owners & drivers	43	...	...	...	...	43	...	43 }												
	" mule " " ...	7	...	...	...	...	7	...	7 }	...	2	2	2	3	...	...	...	2	2	2	...
	" horse " " ...	849	977	...	...	...	1,826	306	1,520 }												
385	Boat and barge men ...	680	2,592	...	...	...	3,272	1,557	1,715	...	1	3	2	2	...	...	...	3	2	2	...
390	Postal Directors, Post Masters and Clerks	140	1	...	...	...	141	48	93	1	2	8	W	...	...	...	...	2	W	1	8

392	Messengers (unspecified) ...	2	3	...	...	...	5	3	2	...	...	6	1	...	...	...	...	6	1	4	...
394	Signallers and Messengers ...	4	...	...	...	...	4	...	4	...	...	...	D	...	...	...	...	...	D	D	...
398	Porters (general)	...	8	...	...	...	8	8	...	...	...	4	...	...	...	...	...	4	...	4	...
399	Weighmen and Measurers ...	1	171	...	...	...	172	124	48	...	...	3	3	4	...	...	...	3	4	3	...
400	Watchmen (not village) ...	...	455	...	...	...	455	...	455	...	...	...	...	4	...	...	...	...	4	4	...
401	Priests	5,054	1,454	1	...	...	6,509	1,707	4,802												
	Ministers	483	1,270	...	...	...	1,753	546	1,207	12	2	2	2	3	W	...	...	2	2	2	W
	Missionaries	...	4	4	...	...	8	4	4												
402	Readers and Zenana Mission Service	...	76	...	...	...	76	69	7	...	...	2	...	4	...	...	...	3	4	3	...
404	Religious Mendicants ...	...	24	...	...	...	24	13	11	...	...	W	...	2	...	...	...	W	2	1	...
405	Temple Service	581	49	553	...	...	1,183	17	1,166												
	Masjid Do.	264	1,099	3	...	...	1,366	225	1,141												
	Burial Ground service ...	1	14	...	...	...	15	1	14	...	1	3	2	4	1	...	...	3	2	2	...
	Pilgrim Contractors, &c. ...	9	...	5	...	...	14	...	14												
	Burning Ground service ...	...	15	...	...	...	15	8	7												
406	Inspecting Officials	1	...	...	...	...	1	1	...	...	2	...	...	...	...	...	...	2	...	2	...
407	Teachers in Schools, &c. ...	905	677	...	9	...	1,591	253	1,338	...	1	3	2	3	...	3	...	2	3	3	...
409	Authors, editors, ballad makers, &c.	...	135	...	...	...	135	75	60	...	...	3	...	4	...	...	...	3	4	3	...
412	Copyists	...	49	...	...	...	49	49	...	...	...	2	...	...	...	...	...	2	...	2	...
413	Pleaders, &c.	27	13	...	...	...	40	37	3	1	2	4	...	2	...	...	...	2	2	2	2
418	Stamp Vendors	13	25	...	...	...	38	36	2	...	1	4	2	...	...	...	...	3	3	4	...
419	Petition Writers	24	...	...	...	...	24	12	12	...	3	...	2	...	...	...	...	3	2	3	...
421	Practitioner by Diploma ...	3	1	1	...	...	5	1	4	...	...	2	5	...	1	...	...	2	4	3	...
422	Hakims, &c.	271	300	6	1	...	578	223	355	...	2	3	2	4	1	D	...	3	3	3	...
426	Midwifery	6	74	...	...	...	80	74	6	...	...	W	W	...	...	...	...	W	...	W	...
428	Compounders, Nurses and Hospital Asylum and Dispensary service	24	...	...	...	...	24	24	...	...	1	...	...	...	...	...	...	1	...	1	...
429	Administrating and Inspecting Staff	1	12	...	...	1	14	4	10	14	...	W	23	W	...	...	1	W	1	1	1
432	Draughtsmen, Surveyors, &c.	3	...	...	...	...	3	3	...	...	4	...	...	...	...	...	...	4	...	4	...
433	Clerks, &c., in offices of the above	3	...	...	...	10	13	3	10	2	2	...	...	...	...	...	D	2	D	W	1
437	Astrologers and Horoscope Casters	17	...	1	...	...	18	4	14	...	3	...	1	...	D	...	...	3	1	2	...
444	Band Masters, &c., (not military)	80	27	3	6	...	116	19	97	...	5	3	2	2	...	4	...	3	3	3	...
446	Singers, &c.	160	18	...	1	...	179	66	113	...	1	...	2	4	...	D	...	1	2	2	...
448	Shikari	7	46	1	20	...	74	9	65	...	...	3	2	4	7	4	...	3	4	4	...
453	Buffoons	22	299	...	...	...	321	2	319	...	...	2	2	3	...	...	...	2	3	3	...
454	Ballad Reciters	2	...	...	...	...	2	...	2	...	...	...	1	...	...	...	...	...	1	1	...
457	Tumblers	89	1	...	...	...	90	...	90												
	Professional Wrestlers ...	3	...	...	...	...	3	3	...	...	D	...	2	8	...	...	...	D	2	2	...

NOTE.—W. Workers outnumber Dependents. D. No Dependents. X. No Workers.

Number.	Occupations.	Workers. Jammu.	Workers. Kashmír.	Workers. Ladákh.	Workers. Skardu.	Workers. Gilgit.	Workers. Total Whole State.	Workers. Urban Population.	Workers. Rural Population.	Workers. Europeans and Eurasians.	Average number of Dependents on every Worker. Jammu Urban.	Kashmír Urban.	Jammu Rural.	Kashmír Rural.	Ladákh.	Skardu.	Gilgit.	Whole State Urban.	Whole State Rural.	Total Whole State.	Europeans and Eurasians.
461	Well sinkers	...	53	...	...	...	53	43	10	...	...	3	...	5	...	...	...	3	5	3	...
462	Tank diggers and excavators	11	...	...	...	...	11	1	10	...	1	...	D	...	...	...	...	1	D	W	...
466	Rice huskers	85	...	...	...	...	85	28	57	...	1	...	2	...	...	...	...	2	2	2	...
467	General labor	23,324	4,641	308	130	114	28,517	4,581	23,936	...	1	2	2	2	1	1	D	2	2	2	...
468	Kanjar	137	368	1	...	...	506	448	58	...	1	W	W	1	D	D	D	W	W	W	...
468	Unspecified	6,006	3,807	7	149	16,615	26,584	695	25,889	4	D	D	D	D	D	D	D	D	D	D	D
469	House-rent sharers	66	1,117	...	...	...	1,183	1,095	88	4	1	3	W	2	...	...	...	3	2	3	W
471	Dharmarth stipend holders	1,314	185	17	48	...	1,564	500	1,064	...	W	3	1	2	W	4	...	1	2	2	...
472	Mendicancy	14,481	7,431	225	444	...	22,581	1,849	20,732	...	W	1	1	2	1	1	...	1	1	1	...
473	Pension Civil Service ...	375	14	...	...	...	389	15	374	1	6	1	1	7	...	...	...	3	1	1	D
474	Do. Military	...	2	...	...	...	2	...	2	2	...	...	...	D	...	...	...	...	D	D	D
476	Prisoners under trial ...	21	5	...	...	...	26	26	...	...	D	D	...	...	...	...	...	D	...	D	...
477	Do. for debt	...	1	...	...	...	1	1	...	...	...	D	...	...	...	...	...	D	...	D	...
478	Do. Convicted ...	111	122	...	...	...	233	233	...	...	D	D	...	...	...	...	...	D	...	D	...

Note.—W. Workers outnumber Dependents. D. No Dependents. X. No Workers.

226. This information is interesting in the first place, as giving an idea of the general condition of the people, their principal means of livelihood, the extent to which they have succeeded in combining natural resources with industry and the tendency for improvement in the future.

227. Barring the Kashmír valley and that portion of the Jammu District, which immediately adjoins British territory, the rest of the country is intersected by lofty mountain ranges, is practically cut off from communication with the most favored parts of British India and constitutes the tranquil home of the agriculturist, the priest and the herdsman.

228. The average number of dependents on every worker is 3 for agriculturists, and nearly 2 for others, which is by no means excessive; in the urban population it is 2, in the rural population nearly 3.

229. There is no ground for the theory advanced by certain critics that the majority of the people are starving. It might be said with certainty about the natives of the State that they are fairly solvent and well to do.

230. The agriculturists here comprising 69 per cent. of the total population are remarkably free from debt. The mode of living is very simple, provisions in the interior are cheap and the people live in peace and harmony. The Kashmíri is extremely careless about his livelihood, he has been of late dependent on the State godowns for his food supply, always managing to get it at a trifling cost, but the increasing demand on the State exchequer has necessitated the making of revenue collections in cash and the agricultural classes will, it is hoped, under an improved system of administration of the land, make more profit out of their property than they have hitherto done.

231. Out of a total population of 2,543,952, 1,762,843, or 69 per cent. are agriculturists, below :—

	Jammu.	Kashmír.	Ladákh.	Skardu.	Gilgit.	Total.
Live Stock	10,011	18,214	1,459	273	...	29,957
Land occupants, not cultivating ...	35,682	...	23,180	103,522	1	162,385
Ditto, cultivating ...	462,216	419,230	37	22	...	881,505
Lessees of villages	3,333	2,743	5	52	...	6,133
Tenants and sharers cultivating ..	538,001	141,365	...	1,874	...	681,240
Growers of special products and trees	1,207	411	2	...	...	1,620
Directors of agriculture and their assistants.	...	3	...	...	...	3
Total ...	1,050,450	581,966	24,683	105,743	1	1,762,843

232. In the absence of a well-defined system of tenures, it is unsafe to accept the sub-divisions of the land owning communities as reliable. The enumerators of Ladákh and Skardu appear to have put down all land occupants as " not cultivating;" the mistake, however, is an excusable one, there could be no doubt that however faulty the internal details may be, agriculturists, as a class, have not escaped enumeration and record, and, considering that the present is the first census ever held in the State, and that the districts of Ladákh and Skardu were beyond the pale of provincial superintendence, it is gratifying that the general out-turn and quality of the work was fairly satisfactory.

233. The following is a record of occupations other than agriculture and State service followed by 1,000 workers and above, in Jammu and Kashmír :—

Occupations.	Total Whole State.	Jammu.	Kashmír.	Ladákh.	Skardu.	Gilgit.	Urban population.	Rural population.
Barbers	4,160	2,171	1,971	5	13	...	632	3,528
Washermen	1,734	1,079	648	1	6	...	498	1,236
Water Carriers	1,646	1,355	291	...	...	...	440	1,206
In-door Servants	25,090	15,656	9,072	92	259	11	5,289	19,801
Cow and buffalo keepers, &c. ...	5,230	2,535	2,695	...	...	...	915	4,315
Grain dealers	3,353	17	3,336	...	...	...	1,522	1,831
Flour mill service	2,131	1,870	248	1	12	...	151	1,980
Bakers	1,148	318	826	4	...	...	607	541
Vegetable sellers	1,081	308	773	...	...	...	715	366
Oil pressers	3,026	1,452	1,574	...	...	...	296	2,730
Shawl weavers and sellers ...	9,622	74	9,491	...	57	...	5,452	4,170
Blanket weavers and sellers ...	4,544	...	4,423	8	113	...	936	3,608
Woollen yarn spinners and sellers.	21,743	2,633	19,110	...	...	...	2,195	19,548
Cotton cleaners	1,082	481	601	...	...	...	163	919
Cotton weavers	10,248	10,248	...	...	...	...	433	9,815
Tailors	8,181	1,519	6,654	6	2	...	5,570	2,611
Gold and Silver workers ...	2,439	1,523	881	23	12	...	891	1,548
Blacksmiths	4,023	2,529	1,443	21	30	...	455	3,568
Potters	3,678	2,245	1,432	...	1	...	192	3,486
Carpenters	5,043	2,830	2,179	12	16	6	848	4,195
Shoe-makers and sellers ...	8,912	6,361	2,542	2	7	...	843	8,069
Bankers	1,826	1,825	1	...	...	...	349	1,477
General merchants	4,872	4,591	281	...	...	...	171	4,701
Shop keepers	13,059	11,578	1,419	50	12	...	2,086	10,973
Pack horse owners and drivers...	1,876	899	977	...	...	...	306	1,570
Boatmen	3,272	680	2,592	...	...	...	1,557	1,715
Priests, Ministers, &c.	8,270	5,537	2,728	5	...	...	2,257	6,013
Temple Service	1,183	581	49	553	...	...	17	1,166
Masjid Service	1,366	264	1,099	3	...	...	225	1,141
School Teachers	1,591	905	677	...	9	...	253	1,338
General labor	28,517	23,324	4,641	308	130	114	4,581	23,936
House rent Sharers, &c. ...	1,183	66	1,117	...	...	...	1,095	88
Dharmarth stipend-holders ...	1,564	1,314	185	17	48	...	500	1,064
Mendicants	22,581	14,481	7,431	225	444	...	1,849	20,732
Unspecified	26,584	6,006	3,807	7	149	16,615	695	25,889

234. The natives of India are, as a rule, extremely conservative in occupations, each tribe or section following the occupation handed to them by their ancestors, occupation being an important factor in the determination of social position among both Hindus and Mohamedans.

235. There are certain occupations which belong exclusively to certain tribes and would not under any circumstance be followed by others, and there are occupations peculiar to Hindus and peculiar to Mohamedans, to the exclusion of one another.

236. The impure castes, *viz.*, Churas, Sepi, Batwal and others, named in the return of Caste as "field laborers," are either scavengers, vagrants, or field-laborers and do not and cannot follow other occupations, because they are void of any social position and are considered unclean by the other castes of Hindus. Their occupations are, therefore, restricted to things which are considered unclean by the other Hindus.

237. The inferior castes comprise those tribal sections of the Hindu community as are admitted to the general platform of Hindus, or in other words, those whose water could be legally drunk by the higher classes. These are mostly castes by traditional occupation, and though their specific occupations could not be assumed by the superior castes without detriment to social position, yet they are at liberty to follow any other occupation of a higher order, without the risk of expulsion from caste.

238. Brahmans and other castes of good social position, generally engage themselves in a variety of occupations without loss of caste, but Rajputs incur degradation by one step, by taking to cultivation of the soil.

239. The Kashmírí Brahman is very strict about his occupation. A *karkun* would never dream of becoming a *Bachabatt*, nor would a *Bachabatt* aspire to a karkunship. The favorite occupation of the Kasmírí Pandits are trade and commerce, State service and the minor occupation of cooks, tailors, bakers, confectioners. They consider it beneath their dignity to work with the plough, or to follow any other occupation.

240. The favorite occupation of Kashmír Mohamedans is agriculture, but they are without any attempt at exaggeration credited with monopolizing all the occupations (excluding State service) of Kashmír.

241. An attempt is made in the subjoined table to compare the caste return with the corresponding entries in the Occupation Tables, to show what occupations are restricted to particular classes of the people and which are open to all, excluding of course the impure castes who are obviously restricted to their special avocation.

CLASS.	Group.	Strength. Total.	Strength. Males.	Strength. Females.	Religion.	Strength.	Corresponding entries in Return of Occupation. Total.	Males.	Females.	Castes to which Occupation is traditionally restricted to the exclusion of others. Hindus, including Jains and Sikhs.	Mohamedans.	Occupation open to all castes. Hindus, including Jains and Sikhs.	Mohamedans.
A.—Agricultural* ...	I.—Military and Dominant ...	402,918	215,602	187,316	Hindus ... Mohamedans.	150,647 252,271				Rajpúts	Rajputs	All castes of good social position.	All Mohamedans.
	I.—Other Agricultural— (a) Cultivators ...	173,600	92,338	81,262	Hindus ... Sikhs ... Mohamedans.	24,508 370 148,722				Jat, Seni	Arain, Awan, Jat	All castes ...	Do.
	(b) Cattle breeders and graziers	248,789	133,685	115,104	Hindus ... Mohamedans.	883 247,906	included in military.			Gujar	Gujar ... Choupan ...	...	...
	(c) Field Laborers ...	130,998	68,866	62,132	Hindus ... Mohamedans.	130,985 13				Barwala, Basith, Batwal, Gen, Sepi, Saryara, Dhyar, Megh, Ratyal, Begari Gomsa, Dum.	Pakhiwar ...	Impure castes ...	All.
	IV.—Forest and hill tribes ...	29	27	2	Hindus ... Mohamedans.	26 3							
	Total Class A. ...	956,334	510,518	445,816	Hindus ... Sikhs ... Mohamedans.	307,049 370 648,915	1,762,843	933,051	829,792				
B.—Professional* ...	V.—Priests	619,479	328,773	290,706	Hindus ... Sikhs ... Mohamedans.	231,411 9,404 378,664	26,623	14,111	12,512	Brahmans ...	Brahman converts to Mohamedanism. Sayads, Pirs, Pirzadas.	...	...
	VI.—Devotees	24,192	13,372	10,820	Hindus ... Sikhs ... Mohamedans.	8,046 1 16,145	66,756	37,263	29,493	Jogi, Sanyasi ...	Dervesh, Jogi ...	All ...	All.
	IX.—Writers	12	10	2	Hindus ...	All	included in Brahmans.			...	...	All ...	All.
	XI.—Musicians and Ballad Reciters	23,360	12,356	11,004	Hindus ... Sikhs ... Mohamedans.	150 7 23,203	912	476	436	...	Mirasi	...	...
	XII.—Dancers and Singers ...	775	394	381	Mohamedans...	All	1,160	484	676	...	Kanjar, Perna ...	...	...
	Total Class B. ...	667,818	354,905	312,913	Hindus ... Sikhs .. Mohamedans.	239,619 9,412 418,787	95,451	52,334	43,117				
C.—Commercial ...	XIV.—Traders	95,031	51,773	43,258	Hindus ... Sikhs ... Jains ... Mohamedans.	40,808 1,146 593 52,484	61,462	34,276	27,186	Arora, Banya, Bhatya, Khatri, Kambo	Kambo	All Hindus, except impure castes.	All Mohamedans.
	XV.—Carriers	5,117	2,712	2,405	Hindus ... Sikhs ... Mohamedans.	5,077 32 8	6,650	3,773	2,877	Labana ...	Labana	...	...
	Total Class C. ...	100,148	54,485	45,663	Hindus ... Sikhs ... Jains ... Mohamedans.	45,885 1,178 593 52,492	68,112	38,049	30,063				

* For correct detail of agriculturists see page 125 of report.

Class.	Group.	Strength. Total	Strength. Males.	Strength. Females.	Religion.	Strength.	Corresponding entries in Return of Occupation. Total.	Males.	Females.	Castes to which Occupation is traditionally restricted to the exclusion of others. Hindus, including Jains and Sikhs.	Mohamedans.	Occupation open to all castes. Hindus, including Jains and Sikhs.	Mohamedans.
D.—Artisans and Village Menials.	XVII.—Goldsmiths	7,892	4,265	3,627	Hindus ... Sikhs — Mohamedans.	5,528 107 2,257	8,734	4,622	4,112	Sunar ...	Sunár	...	Kashmír Mohamedans.
	XVIII.—Barbers	29,192	15,482	13,710	Hindus ... Mohamedans.	5,442 23,750	15,548	8,296	7,252	Nai ...	Nai ...	...	...
	XIX.—Blacksmiths	28,099	15,098	13,001	Hindus ... Sikhs Mohamedans.	11,663 1 16,435	15,259	8,294	6,965	Lohar ...	Lohar ...	...	...
	XX.—Carpenters and Turners	28,710	15,489	13,221	Hindus ... Mohamedans.	10,620 18,090	19,114	10,390	8,724	Tarkhan ...	Tarkhan ...	...	...
	XX (a).—Masons	440	252	188	Mohamedans.	All	1,404	779	625	...	Memar ...	...	...
	XXI.—Brass and Coppersmiths	864	439	425	Hindus .. Mohamedans.	786 78	1,427	749	678	Thatyar ...	Thatyar ...	...	All Mohamedans
	XXII.—Tailors	4,852	2,552	2,300	Hindus ... Mohamedans.	702 4,150	24,063	13,169	10,894	Darzi, Sochi ...	Darzi	All Hindus, except impure castes	Do.
	XXII (b).—Drug preparers...	1	1	...	Mohamedans.	All	Not enumerated as a separate occupation.			...	Bangi ...	...	...
	XXIII.—Weavers	29,013	15,401	13,612	Hindus ... Mohamedans.	12 29,001	33,436	17,583	15,863	Kuch-band ...	Julaha ...	...	...
	& Dyers	2,024	1,038	986	Mohamedans.	All	3,058	1,582	1,476	...	Rangrez ...	...	...
	XXIV.—Washermen... ...	14,446	7,668	6,778	Hindus ... Mohamedans.	1,273 13,173	5,455	2,936	2,519	Dhobi ...	Dhobi ...	...	...
	XXV.—Cotton cleaners ...	737	358	379	Mohamedans.	All	3,638	1,965	1,673	...	Naddaf ...	...	...
	XXVII.—Oil pressers ...	20,124	10,598	9,526	Do.	All	12,219	6,501	5,718	...	Teli ...	...	...
	XXVIII.—Potters	22,507	12,047	10,460	Hindus ... Sikhs ... Mohamedans	5,757 26 16,724	13,184	7,045	6,139	Kumhar ...	Kumhar ...	...	...
	XXIX.—Glass workers ...	1,208	689	519	Hindus ... Mohamedans.	39 1,169	681	351	330	Manyar ...	Manyar ...	...	...
	XXXII.—Goldsmith's refuse collectors ...	75	37	38	Mohamedans.	All	43	20	23	...	Niyaria ...	...	...
	XXXV.—Fishermen, boatmen, Palkibearers, Cooks, &c.	33,870 16,071	17,911 8,659	15,959 7,412	Do. Hindus ... Sikhs ... Mohamedans.	All 13,174 13 2,884	15,139	8,095	7,044	Jhiwar ... Ghirath ...	Hanji, Jhiwar ... Bhishti ...	...	All Mohamedans.
	XXXVI.—Distillers	121	60	61	Hindus ... Sikhs ...	87 34	57	43	14	Kalal ...	...	...	...
	XXXVII.—Butchers... ...	1,126	614	512	Mohamedans.	All	3,470	1,859	1,611	...	Kassab ...	...	...
	XXXVIII.—Leather workers	48,463	25,602	22,861	Hindus ... Mohamedans.	33,679 14,784	32,399	17,160	15,239	Chamar ...	Dabgar, Khatik, Mochi.	...	...
	XXXIX.—Scavengers ...	19,199	10,219	8,980	Hindus ... Sikhs ... Mohamedans.	8,333 136 10,730	2,463	1,308	1,155	Chura, Ramdasi or Mazhabi.	Vatal, Musalli ...	...	...
	Total Class D. ...	309,034	164,479	144,555	Hindus ... Sikhs ... Mohamedans.	97,095 317 211,622	210,791	112,747	98,044				

Class.	Group.	Strength. Total.	Strength. Males.	Strength. Females.	Religion.	Strength.	Corresponding entries in Return of Occupation Total.	Males.	Females.	Castes to which Occupation is traditionally restricted to the exclusion of others. Hindus, including Jains and Sikhs.	Mohamedans.	Occupation open to all castes. Hindus, including Jains and Sikhs.	Mohamedans.
E.—Vagrant Minor Artisans and Performers.	XLI.—Earth workers and stone dressers ...	2,520	1,315	1,205	Hindus ... Mohamedans.	355 2,165	325	186	139	Batehra	Batehra ... Beldar	...	...
	XLIII.—Cane-splitters ...	306	152	154	Mohamedans.	All	2,562	1,348	1,214	...	Shakhsaz ...	...	...
	Mat-makers and leaf-plate makers	369	161	208	Hindus ...	All	464	195	269	Dasali	...	...	...
	XLV.—Miscellaneous and disreputable livers ...	444	220	224	Hindus ... Mohamedans.	268 176	Not enumerated as a separate occupation.			Sansi	Changar	All	All
	XLVI.—Tumblers and acrobats	995	532	463	Hindus ... Mohamedans.	73 922	248	143	105	Bazigar	Bazigar	...	...
	Total Class E. ...	4,634	2,380	2,254	Hindus ... Mohamedans.	1,065 3,569	3,599	1,872	1,727	...	...		
F.—Races and Nationalities.	XLVIII.—Non-Indian Asiatic Races	484,356	253,585	230,771	Budhists ... Mohamedans. Parsis ...	29,608 454,739 9	See agriculturists.				Moghal, Pathan Sheikh ...		
	L.—Non-Asiatic Races ...	134	67	67	Christians ...	All	Various occupations especially service.						
	LI.—Eurasians	5	2	3	Do. ...	All							
	LII.—Christian Converts ...	79	44	35	Do. ...	All							
	Total Class F. ...	484,574	253,698	230,876	Budhists ... Mohamedans. Parsis ... Christians ...	29,608 454,739 9 218							
	Unspecified	21,410	12,764	8,646	Hindus ... Sikhs ... Mohamedans. Unspecified ...	1,087 122 3,586 16,615							

242. Occupations common to Hindus and Mohamedans.

AGRICULTURE

AND

CIVIL AND MILITARY SERVICE—TRADE AND COMMERCE.

Occupations peculiar to Hindus.	*Occupations peculiar to Mohamedans.*
Writers of Sanskrit.	Dancers and Singers.
Leaf-plate makers.	Masons.
	Dyers.
	Cotton dressers.
	Oil-pressers.
	Goldsmiths' dust-washers.
	Butchers.
	Cane splitters.
	Leather-workers.
	Boatmen.

Occupations peculiar to certain particular Hindu castes to the exclusion of all others—

Occupations peculiar to certain Mohamedan castes to the exclusion of all others—

Occupation.		
Field Laborers ...	Barwála, Basith, Batwal, Gen, Dhyar, Saryara, Sepi, Megh, Ratyal, Begari, Gomsa.	
Priests, &c. ...	Brahmans. (Devotees.)	Sayads. (Devotees.)
Musicians and Ballad Reciters ...	...	Mirási.
Dancers and Singers ...	...	Kanjar, Perna.
Carriers ...	Labana.	Labana.
Goldsmiths ...	Sunár.	Sunar.
Barbers ...	Nái.	Nái.
Blacksmiths ...	Lohár.	Lohár.
Carpenters, Turners, &c.	Tarkhan.	Tarkhan.
Brass and Coppersmiths ...	Thatyar.	Thatyar.
Washermen ...	Dhobi	Dhobi.
Weavers ...	Kuch-band.	Julaha.
Cotton-cleaners ...		Naddáf.
Oil-pressers ...	...	Teli.
Potters ...	Kumhár.	Kumhar.
Glass-workers ...	Manyar.	Manyar.
Goldsmiths' dust-washers	...	Niyaria.
Fisher-man, Boatman, Pálki-bearers, Cooks, &c. ...	Jhiwar, Ghirath.	Hanji (boatmen).
Distillers ...	Kalál.	...
Leather-workers ...	Chamar.	Dabgar, Khatik, Mochi.
Scavengers ...	Chura, Ramdasi, or Mazhabi ...	Vatal, Musalli.

CHAPTER VIII.

Administration of the Census Operations.

243. On 19th March 1890, the orders about taking a Census of the Jammu and Kashmír State, contained in Census Commissioner's No. 19, dated March, 1890, were communicated to the State Council by the Resident in Kashmír, for report as to what the Council proposed doing in regard to preliminary arrangements, registration of houses, instruction of enumerators and supervisors, the provision of Census Schedules and the character in which they should be printed or lithographed, and finally, the arrangements for abstraction and compilation, as also the general question of the superintendence of the operations.

Resident's endorsement No. 346, dated 19th March, 1890, to the Secretary State Council.

244. By Resolution No.1, dated 25th April, 1890, Rae Bahadur Pandit Bhag Ram, Judicial Member, was appointed Superintendent of Census for the whole State.

245. On taking charge of my duties, I at once addressed the Resident, requesting to be favored with the form of the house-lists, &c.

246. Meanwhile, certain circulars issued by the Census Commissioner were received, which enabled me to submit my proposals for future action.

247. The Circulars issued by me, which were generally approved by the Resident and the Census Commissioner, will be found in the Appendices to this Report.

248. The Rajputana and Central India Schedule of eight columns was adopted.

249. My experience of the dilatoriness which characterised the despatch of business by district Officers and Tehsildars in all administrative matters, prompted the necessity for very stringent and energetic action. It was hardly sufficient to issue instructions and wait for reports of compliance without one's satisfying himself by personal observation or otherwise, whether the work said to have been done was a reality. My first care, therefore, was to appeal to the President of the Council who issued a proclamation under his hand, inviting the co-operation of all officers in Census work. This had some effect on the local officers, but the introduction of a system of close supervision nevertheless appeared necessary, particularly in Jammu, where the District Officers displayed utter indifference, submitted false reports of progress, and did not care to move about within their respective jurisdiction, to see how the work was getting on.

250. For purposes of the Census, the whole State, excluding the frontier districts of Ladákh, Skardu and Gilgit, was divided into two Provinces, *viz.*, Jammu and Kashmír, each presided over by a Provincial Superintendent. The Provincial Governors being unable to accept this office, it was entrusted to the Chief Judges.

251. Each Wazir-Wazarat was made responsible for the work of his district, while Tehsildars were appointed Superintendents of charges in their respective Tehsils. Progress Reports were called for, but for sometime none were received. The Chief Judges were then ordered to make periodical tours which had the effect of bringing the local officers to a sense of their duty and since August 1890, thanks to the great interest taken by the President of the Council, Raja Sir Amar Singh, the work proceeded with exemplary regularity and promptitude. The enumerators were generally non-officials and with some exceptions, did their work willingly and cheerfully.

252. The Census Superintendent personally examined the house-lists of the Srinagar and Anantnag districts in Kashmír and the Udhampore and Reasi districts in Jammu and was satisfied with the result.

253. In Jammu special officers had to be deputed to see to Census work, as the Reports of Progress were considered totally unreliable. These officers constantly moved about in the districts to which they were attached, while each district was also visited by the Provincial Superintendent just about the time, when the house-lists had been prepared and the preliminary record was taken in hand.

254. In Srinagar, the local Municipality and their President, Dr. A. Mitra, did the work admirably.

255. No previous census having been taken, the task of preliminary operations connected with the registration of houses, determination of blocks, supervisors' circles and charges of superintendents, was a most difficult one. The officials in the mofassil hardly took an interest in this work, and though the preliminary lists of villages and houses were very simple, yet the orders issued at first regarding their preparation were entirely ignored, and recourse was had to the issue of a proclamation under the signature of the President of the Council, warning all concerned of the penalties to be incurred by wilful procrastination and indifference to Census work. This produced very little effect, and as the samples received from out-stations, were replete with errors too numerous to mention, a general order was again issued, inviting active co-operation of the staff, a series of simple rules drafted by the Census Superintendent were translated in the prevailing languages, and the work was entrusted to high paid Moharrirs specially trained at head-quarters. I particularly insisted on the preliminary operations being conducted with energy and exactitude, because from personal experience of the staff, I was fully conscious that the slightest divergence from established procedure would lead to endless confusion, and, therefore, with the greatest possible anxiety, I used all the means available for careful scrutiny of the work in progress.

256. In the absence of an organized settlement of land revenue, the distinction of parent villages from Dakhili hamlets was attended with difficulties, and the surest course was to rely on the judgment of Wazir-Wazarats, but as regards preparation of house-lists, determination of blocks, circles and charges, I may assert with confidence that our work was as successful as in any other part of British India.

257. The definition of house was very clearly explained and readily understood, there being very few big enclosures containing a number of separate dwelling-houses in the Rural Districts, while in the more important towns of Jammu and Srinagar, the presence of the Superintendent ensured the correct preparation of the house-lists. Rough maps, giving the relative position of each house on main site, were duly prepared and particular care was taken to check them. Then followed the determination of blocks, supervisors' circles, &c., which was done by local district officers under the immediate guidance of the Provincial Superintendents, strictly in conformity to the rules issued by me.

258. A sketch map of each charge was prepared and sub-divided into circles, every supervisor was also furnished with a block map to guide him into every corner of his circle.

259. The whole area having been divided into blocks and duly mapped out, the house numbering was begun, but again the Wazir-Wazarats and local officials in the interior displayed an unpardonable want of energy. A circular order was accordingly issued (Circular No. 3, dated 7th August, 1890) warning them, and an example was also made of notorious delinquents by summary dismissal from office.

260. The Chief Judges of Jammu and Kashmir made an extensive tour within their respective jurisdictions and spared no pains to keep the establishments up to their work.

261. Before taking in hand the preparation of the preliminary record, training schools for instruction of enumerators were established in each Tehsil. Great care was taken in selecting the best men available to serve as enumerators. A *parwana* of appointment was given to every enumerator, the blocks were determined with special reference to the nature of the work required, every enumerator being furnished with an extract from the house-list, index register and block map and particularly required to acquaint himself with the position of the houses in his block.

262. Similarly every supervisor and superintendent was furnished with the records appertaining to their circles and charges respectively.

263. The subjoined table shows the agency employed in Census :—

Province.	Enumerators.						Supervisors.						Superintendents.						Special Superintendents.						
	Non-officials.	Military employés.	Police.	Revenue.	Judicial.	Total.	Non-officials.	Military employés.	Police.	Revenue.	Judicial.	Total.	Non-officials.	Military employés.	Police.	Revenue	Judicial.	Total.	Non-officials.	Military employés.	Police.	Revenue.	Judicial.	Total.	Total persons.
Jammu	6,937	1	40	76	15	7,069	484	1	61	19[illegible]	35	774	19	..	1	24	1	45	..	..	..	7	..	7	*7,895
Kashmír	2,312	..	1	32	1	2,346	229	1	12	29	6	277	22	..	..	31	5	58	..	..	..	.	..	..	2,681
Ladákh	100	..	..	5	..	105	18	..	..	..	..	18	10	..	..	4	..	14	..	..	..	..	..	..	137
Skardu	76	..	..	..	..	76	27	..	..	3	..	30	10	..	..	2	..	12	..	..	..	..	..	..	118
Gilgit	..	..	..	..	..	..	..	..	..	..	..	..	..	..	..	..	..	..	..	..	..	..	..	..	..
Total ..	9,425	1	41	11[illegible]	16	9,596	758	2	73	226	41	1,099	61	..	1	61	6	129	..	..	..	7	..	7	10,881

*The Non-officials were :—

Lambardars of Villages 177

Shop-keepers 460

264. The final enumeration took place on the following dates :—

Jammu Province, 26th February 1891.

Kashmír Province, ditto ditto.

Padar, Jaskar, Kishtwar, and Ramban in Udhampore district, 20th December 1890.

Reasi, 20th December 1890.

Ladákh, 30th October 1890.

265. In Gilgit, with the concurrence of the Census Commissioner, the house-lists were only prepared and no detailed census was taken.

266. The only tract, where unpaid enumerators could not be had, was the district of Muzafferabad in the province of Kashmír, where 20 enumerators were employed at a total cost of Rs. 265-5-0.

267. The characters used by the Enumerators were :—

	Urdu.	Persian.	Dogri.	Ladákhí.
Jammu	5,333	...	3,600	...
Kashmír	...	4,808	...	...
Ladákh	137	...	...	571
Skardu	686	...	...	...
Total ...	6,156	4,808	3,600	571

268. For the convenience of the tabulating staff, the Ladákhí books had to be translated into Urdu, at a cost of Rs. 70.

269. The following Statement shows the distribution of printed papers, circulars, schedules, &c. :—

No.	Place.	Instructions for preparation of— House List (Register B.)	Instructions for preparation of— Register A.	Circular No. 3.	Circular No. 4.	Circular No. 5.	Circular No. 6.	Enumerators' Schedules.	Code for Supervisors.	Code for Superintendents.	Sanads to Enumerators.	Loose Schedule forms for Enumerators.	Supervisors' Diaries.	Remarks.
1	Jammu	92	9,000	Published in State *Gazette.*	Published in State *Gazette.*	624	Published in State *Gazette.*	10,051	707	144	6,322	10,896	674	Register B, printed in— Urdu ... ... 12,000 Bhootia 400
2	Kashmír	70	2,430			600		6,591	900	150	7,100	25,000	700	Register A, printed in— Urdu 200
3	Gilgit	...	...			..		Forms	supplied	by Judge	Sadar A	dalat Ka	shmír.	Enumerators' Schedule printed in— Urdu ... ... 12,550 Persian ... ... 10,000 Dogra ... ... 3,550 English 200
4	Ladákh	...	700			...		650	...	...	...	500	...	
5	Skardu	...	...			40		600	100	30	400	3,000	50	Circular No. 5— Urdu ... ... 700 Persian 1,000
6	Bhadrawah	5	200			20		466	41	21	401	2,000	40	Code for Superintendents— Urdu ... ... 400 Persian 250
7	Ramnagar	7	200			50		425	20	20	120	1,200	20	Code for Supervisors— Urdu ... ... 2,000 Persian 1,000
8	Punch	1	...			...		14	3	...	...	...	...	Supervisors' Diaries— Urdu ... ... 1,200 Persian 750
9	Miscellaneous	...	70			8		5	8	8	8	...	4	Sanads to Enumerators— Urdu ... ... 10,200 Persian 7,200

270. The printing of the Urdu Schedules was done in the *Mufid-i-Am Press,* that of Hindi and Dogra books, and of Circulars, &c., at the State Press. In both places the work was done promptly and expeditiously.

271. With the exception of Punch, the Jagirdar of which place had his Schedules printed at his own cost, the other Jagirs received their supply from the Census Superintendent.

272. The preliminary record, generally speaking, was prepared with the greatest care and no pains were spared to exercise the necessary supervision.

273. Every Tehsildar visited all the villages in his Tehsil and checked the house-lists and Enumerator's Schedules appertaining thereto. Every Wazir-Wazarat examined the work of the Tehsildars under him and submitted periodical reports to the Provincial Superintendents who also visited every District and Tehsil and satisfied themselves by personal examination of the records that they had been correctly prepared while special experts were also deputed, particularly in Jammu territory, to see that every thing was done carefully.

274. On the 3rd February 1891, the Census Commissioner visited Jammu, and his opinion regarding the quality of the work done may be gathered from the subjoined extract from a memorandum furnished by him to the Resident in Kashmír:—

"The map of Jammu town and of the blocks into which it has been divided are very clear, and apparently care has been taken not to omit any thing that will help the enumerator and supervisor in their work. The books of the town, too, which I have seen, as well as those of the Dehát of Rambir Singh, have been well written up, and generally in accordance with the instructions. Considering that this is the first attempt to obtain such a record, and that the books shown me had not been fully scrutinised by the Superintendents, the results are decidedly creditable, and if the outlying portions of this large State are as carefully done, the Census should be one of considerable value. The few defects I found were pointed out at the time of inspection, and were none of sufficient importance to require special notice here."

275. Special arrangements were made for counting the boat population in Kashmír by the appointment of Special Enumerators and Supervisors. The boat population amounted to 2,967 males, and 2,547 females. The railway population amounted to 144 males and 40 females, and was confined exclusively to residents within railway limits, as no trains arrived at Jammu on the night of the Census.

276. The enumerating staff was generally well-behaved and attentive to their work; of the seven cases of petty illegal exaction reported by the Police, conviction was had in all with the following result :—

1. Sher Singh, Enumerator, fined Rs. 25, or in default two months' imprisonment.
2. Nikka Doom, Chowkidar, sentenced to two weeks' imprisonment, and Rs. 3 fine.
3. Mohammed Bakhsh, Enumerator, fined Rs. 25.
4. Sohan Singh, Patwari, and Abbas Ali, fined Rs. 4 and 1 respectively.
5. Manohar, Enumerator, and Nabbir Mattu, fined Rs. 7 and 5 respectively.
6. Nabi Bakhsh, Enumerator, fined Rs. 15.
7. Samda, Enumerator, fined Rs. 5.

277. The revision of the Schedules on the night of the Census was conducted strictly according to the rules.

278. The procedure observed in regard to the disposal of the books after the final enumeration is laid down in Circular No. 8. There was some delay in the receipt of books from snowy tracts, but, on the whole, the work of tabulation had a fair start in the month of April 1891.

279. The Central Office was organized at Jammu under the immediate supervision and control of the Census Superintendent, while a branch of the same office was also established in Kashmír with a view to its eventual amalgamation with the Central Office, when the Census Superintendent proceeded to Srinagar during the hot season.

280. Before commencing the actual work of abstraction Moharrirs in Jammu and Srinagar were employed in checking and re-preparing the enumerators abstracts at a total cost of Rs. 406-12-0.

281. The Strength of the Central Office was :—

1. *Abstraction*—

62 Abstractors	2,625	10	9	for 5 months.
29 Re-abstractors	1,181	1	3	" "
6 Room Inspectors	1,124	13	6	for 7 months.
Contingencies	779	7	6	
Total...	5,711	1	0	

2. *Tabulation*—

Superintendent, *ex-officio.*				
Tabulating Moharrirs	1,853	12	6	for 6 months.
Contingencies	193	9	0	
Total...	2,047	5	6	

3. *Compilation*—

Superintendent, *ex-officio.*				
Moharrirs	830	1	3	for 8 months.
Contingencies	456	0	0	
Total ...	1,286	1	3	
GRAND TOTAL ...	9,044	7	9	

282. The *modus operandi* was precisely the same as that laid down by the Census Commissioner. No abstractor was allowed to communicate with any member of another gang or make notes of his totals.

283. The re-abstraction was conducted independently, and care was taken to prevent the re-abstracting establishment having access to the original working sheets. In every case, the original and re-abstracted sheets were passed by the Room Inspector and the Superintendent who invariably satisfied himself of their accuracy by personal examination, one-fourth of the working sheets were re-abstracted, and of these 85 per cent. tallied with the original, and where discrepancies were found, they were chiefly in internal details, without affecting the totals.

284. The Tabulation and Compilation was entrusted to trained clerks, and was under the immediate control and supervision of the Census Superintendent who personally checked every entry posted from the working sheets and registers.

285. The total cost of the Census was as detailed below :—

Census Officers attached to Districts ...	3,967	9	9
Office of Census Superintendent	1,415	5	0
Preparation of Enumerator's Abstracts	406	12	0
Central Office of Abstraction	4,931	9	6
Tabulation and Compilation	2,683	13	9
Contingencies including printing	11,404	6	6
Travelling Allowances	843	13	0
Total ...	25,653	5	6

or about Rs. 10 per thousand on a total population of 2,543,952. Calculated on the expenditure incurred on enumeration, the cost was only annas 2-6.

286. The enumerators' books were generally well-written, but owing to the variety of languages in which they were written, the establishment employed in abstraction was rather heavier than in British Districts. The Enumerators did not specify birth-place within the State by particularizing the district of birth. In the standard questions to be asked by the enumeration, the question regarding birth-place was—"In what State or Province were you born?" and the reply recorded was "born within the State."

287. In the column of Caste, the main tribe was only given, there being no column in the Schedule for minor sub-divisions. I think in a future Census of the State the full British India Schedule should be introduced, as the State presents a wide field for ethnological research.

288. In column 8, Occupations besides agriculture, were rarely recorded, and the words owner or tenant, owing to the absence of well-defined land tenures, were generally misunderstood, with these exceptions, the entries in the Schedules, thanks to the pains taken by the Subordinate Supervising Staff, were as correct as could be desired.

289. The difficulties attending the successful completion of Census operations in a Native State can be imagined rather described, and in Kashmír, these difficulties were particularly aggravated by the notorious incapability, want of energy and apathy of the local officials; while last but not least, the vast extent of territory, the remoteness of the frontier districts of Ladákh, Skardu and Gilgit and certain parts of the Jammu Province from head-quarters, the interruption caused by snow, and the sheer want of trained men, were by no means impediments which could be easily overcome.

290. No previous Census having been taken, the officials entrusted with the work, regarded it as a thinkless task and apparently hardly took any interest in it, repeated orders and instructions were ignored with impunity, and though the instructions issued were simple and clear, yet in several places the work had to be done twice over. The regular staff of supervisors and superintendents was found to be careless, untruthful, and non-persevering and special officers had to be deputed to set matters right by personal and close supervision.

291. The work which thus devolved on the Census Superintendent and the Provincial Superintendents of Jammu and Kashmír was a very heavy one, special arrangements were made for submission of periodical reports and keeping the establishment to their work, the least draw-back being effectively noticed and punished, and the greatest care taken to ensure the preparation of a correct record.

292. If any future Census of the State is taken, I may be permitted to state as the result of my personal experience, that the Census Superintendent and the Provincial Superintendents of Jammu and Kashmír be entirely relieved of other official duties, and placed solely in charge of Census work, that they be invested with full power of punishing their subordinates, and that, if possible, the highest revenue authority should have the final control of Census Operations. I do not mean to convey the impression that my control of Census Operations has, by reason of my being the head of the Judicial Department, met with any opposition from other Departments; on the contrary, I feel it my duty to publicly acknowledge the friendly support which was accorded to me by my colleagues and the Provincial Governors generally, but I cannot refrain from remarking that the Subordinate Staff not unfrequently displayed a spirit of indifference to my orders, and in answer to my stringent reminders generally pleaded press of their legitimate departmental work, and often gave cause for serious anxiety.

293. If therefore, after making due allowances for the numerous difficulties which blocked the way, the preliminary census operations could be pronounced to be on the whole successful, I would take the liberty to bring to the notice of the State Council the conspicuous services rendered by the chief Judges of Jammu and Kashmír, and the President of the Srinagar Municipality, to whose untiring zeal and energy in carrying out my orders, in frequently visiting their charges, in promptly detecting errors and shortcomings, and in according to me their most hearty co-operation in all matters too numerous to mention, was due the successful completion of this work, and I trust that these gentlemen will be substantially rewarded for their labors.

294. The District Officers generally worked well, and I think their services should receive due acknowledgment.

295. In Jammu the President (Provincial Governor) not being able to spare time for the exercise of close supervision, a special officer, namely, Bakhshi Parmanand, the Deputy Governor was deputed, and the work was done expeditiously and correctly. The Bakhsi desserves great credit for bringing up arrears.

CIRCULAR ORDER BY PRESIDENT OF COUNCIL.

Whereas the Government of India desires that a Census of the population of the Kashmír State should be taken, all Civil Officers, in the service of the State in the Revenue, Police, Judicial and other Departments, are hereby invited to co-operate with Rae Bahadur Pandit Bhag Ram, Judicial Member of the State Council, who has been nominated Superintendent of Census for the whole State, and by whom all instructions regarding the Census will be issued from time to time.

2. The undersigned desires to impress on all officers who may be employed on Census work, the desirability of performing the same with the utmost expedition and promptitude, and it is needless for him to state that any public officer who is found to be disloyal in carrying out instructions, or is proved to be negligent in the performance of Census duties entrusted to him, will be visited with severe punishment.

3. Officers in executive charge of duties must see that the objects of the Census are clearly understood by the people, and that all false rumours and reports which usually take place in connection with the work of enumeration must be duly checked. They must at the same time make it as widely known as possible that every person is legally bound to furnish such information as is necessary for the complete and accurate filling up of the Census Schedules, and see that unnecessary obstacles are not thrown in the way of the working staff.

4. Officials should, as a rule, be employed in the work of enumeration, but where they are not available, voluntary non-official agency should be obtained as far as possible, the men being assigned duties which do not take them away from their ordinary abode. Where special and paid agency is necessary, a special report should be submitted for the orders of the Superintendent.

5. Any person detected in extorting money on any pretext connected with the Census, shall be punished under the Penal Code of the State.

Crcular No. 1, dated 19th July 1890.

From—Rai Bahadur Pandit Bhag Ram, Judicial Member of State Council.

To—The Wazir-Wazarat of——

You have received official intimation that a Census of the population of the Kashmír State will be taken under the orders of the Imperial Government. The date proposed for the Census is the night of the 26th February 1891, when the final enumeration will take place, but the registration of houses and the distribution of circles and blocks, must be taken in hand at once. The State Council has sanctioned the entertainment of a Moharrir who will be attached to your office on duty connected with the Census, but you must remember that he is to be employed solely on clerical duty which will by no means be light, and that the State Council look to you as the officer responsible for the efficient control and supervision of Census Operations in your District. Under the Circular Order issued by the Prime Minister and President of the State Council, all Civil Officers employed in your department will co-operate with you, and you are particularly requested to avail yourself of their services without jeopardizing their legitimate work.

2. Having carefully studied the circulars and instructions issuing from this office, you must explain them to your subordinates and satisfy yourself that they are thoroughly understood before action is taken on them. With this object you might hold a conference of the officers nominated by you on Census duty as often as you may consider it necessary. If you are in doubt on any point you must unreservedly refer it to me for orders.

3. With regard to the operations themselves, the first step is to secure the preparation of Register (B) showing the name of each village, with those of its outlying hamlets, or other detached quarters.

4. The form of the Register accompanies herewith. It should be prepared separately for each village borne on the revenue list, Dakhili Mauzas being of course shown in the register of the parent village.

5. The preparation of the list of houses must be entrusted to official agency. It might be advantageously entrusted to the village Patwari or Mukaddam, the Kanugo or the Naib Tehsildar being told off to supervise the work. In outlying tracts situated at a distance from the Tehsil, the task of supervision might be undertaken by the officer in charge of the Police Station.

6. You must very carefully study the note of instructions accompanying this circular, and before starting work, submit to this office a detailed report of the arrangements made by you and the probable date by which they will be completed.

7. I am to invite your particular attention to Rule 4, which requires that the houses should not be marked with numbers till the lists have been finally revised and corrected.

8. On this point I will have the honor to communicate with you at an early date.

9. I am disposed to think that if proper arrangements are made by you, the preparation of the house-list ought not to take more than a month.

CENSUS REGISTER B (House-List).

(To be printed on reverse of outer sheet of Register.)

INSTRUCTIONS.

Columns of Register B.
Column 1. Name of village.
" 2. Name of sub-division.
" 3. Serial number of house.
" 4. Description of house.
" 5. Name of principal occupant of house.
" 6. Number of habitual residents of house.
" 7. Remarks.

1. In rural tracts the preparation of the list (B) should be taken in hand at once. The entries must be made in the order in which the sub-divisions can be visited in succession. The houses must be entered in columns 3, 4, 5 and 6, in corresponding order, and a separate series of house numbers must be kept for each village. For the purposes of the Census, "*House*" means a building inhabited either by day or by night, whether by a single individual or family, or by more than one person or family, but having a separate entrance on to a road, street, lane, or public place, or *open space used in common by the inhabitants of the building but which is not a mere court-yard forming a part of the house itself*. It is the duty of the supervising officer to see that this description of a house is duly explained and made intelligible to the *village officers,* and that the latter apply it correctly in drawing up their lists. No single house, shop, temple, *Sarai* and *Dharmsala,* must be omitted wherever it may be situated in the area of the village, and the supervisor should prepare a rough map giving the relative position of each house in main site, hamlets or landing places, &c., within the Mauza. After entering the house, space should be left for encampment of wanderers and cowherds, for travellers at wells or under trees, or for boats at the mooring places which may have to be visited at the Census.

2. Ruined houses, houses that are not likely to be completely built and inhabited by February 1891, stables, cow-sheds, ware-houses, store-sheds, &c., not being inhabited, should not be entered in the list, though a space or two must be left at the end of each village list to admit of the entry of any such building found casually tenanted at the time of Census, as also for entry of places of encamping, mooring boats, and similar localities, in which any body may be found on the Census night, other than a watchman, &c., who lives elsewhere and is counted as present at his residence; dispensaries and other public institutions should have a single number, but if there are separate and independent buildings, as quarters for the officials in charge or servants attached to the institutions, every one of such buildings should be counted as a house, and be shown under a separate number. As a general rule, each building must be shown as a house, in which any person resides, that is, habitually dwells and cooks. In the case of buildings such as shops or schools, which are only used in the day time, a note to that effect must be made in column 7 of the list. The serial numbers entered in column 3 must not be considered as final until the village has been visited and the entries tested by the supervisor or charge superintendent.

3. Where there are Havalats and Hospitals, the whole building should receive a single number, and detached quarters for the officials, &c., must be numbered separately. Police lines should be treated under the general definition as well as large *Sarais* and *Dharmsalas* or other buildings for the convenience of travellers, and column 5 need show only the permanent residents of such buildings, whilst column 6 should be left blank. Harbours, too, will be treated when large enough to form a separate charge in a special register. In the case of special buildings to which this definition does not, in the opinion of the charge Superintendent, correctly apply, he should draw a rough plan of the building, and point out his difficulties with regard to it.

4. When List (B), has been finally revised, the *village officers* or other persons appointed for the purpose should have the number corresponding to that in the list, affixed to each house, so that enumerators who are not residents of the place, may have no difficulty in finding every building down on the list attached to their schedule book. These numbers should be painted in the cheapest material in common use in the locality for that purpose, either on the wall of the

building or on a board or plate fixed to the wall. These numbers will be checked with the list by the supervising and Superintending Officers of the charge as well as by the District Officer when he makes his tour of inspection of the arrangements for the Census.

TOWNS.

5. The instructions laid down for rural tracts apply *mutatis mutandis* to towns, the second column of the Register (B) showing the name of sub-division, ward, mohalla and suburbs, in the order in which they can be conveniently visited in succession. The serial numbers should be separate for each ward or for such a division of a quarter, as the District Officer, or in the case of a municipality the President, may prescribe. Both in villages and towns, a copy of the block list should form part of each schedule book.

Circular No. 2, dated 23rd July 1890.

From—Rai Bahadur Pandit Bhag Ram, Judicial Member of State Council.

To—All Wazir-Wazarats, Kashmír State.

In my Circular No. 1 of 19th July 1890, I had the honor to lay down detailed instructions for the preparation of the village Register and list of houses (Form B). These lists will be prepared and checked by official agency. As soon as the number of houses is known, you should proceed at once to divide your District for Census purposes into blocks, circles, and charges.

2. By *'Block'* is meant the beat of an enumerator, comprising such number of houses as can be conveniently visited by him in the course of a day. In a country like Kashmír, it is impossible to prescribe a standard block, you will therefore use your own discretion in determining the enumerator's blocks in your district.

3. By *'Circle'* is meant the blocks entrusted to a supervisor. This officer ought to be able to check and supervise the work performed by enumerators, and unless for special local reasons to the contrary, a supervisor can be conveniently placed in charge of ten blocks.

4. By *'Charge'* is meant the jurisdiction of a superintendent who will under your orders supervise and control the work performed by supervisors and enumerators.

5. The enumerator must be able to read and write. He must thoroughly understand the columns of the schedule and the way of filling them, and must visit every house in his block, making the entries after personal enquiry.

6. The supervisor must ordinarily be a State official thoroughly conversant with the rules and instructions. He should not only train the enumerators in his circle in Census work, but must see that the work is properly done.

7. The Superintendent of a charge is the controlling officer subordinante to the Wazir-Wazarat.

8. Detailed instructions for the guidance of these officers will be issued in due course, but in the meanwhile, it is essential that the most fit and competent persons should be selected for the duties required of them, and this could not be better done than by making enquiries, while the house-lists are under preparation, in order that on their completion, the division into blocks, circles, and charges may be made at once.

9. In making your sub-divisions for Census purposes, I would suggest that you will probably consider it advisable to confine yourself to the existing territorial divisions for administrative purposes. For instance, you might advantageously nominate the Tehsildar as Superintendent of a charge comprising the whole of his Tehsil, unless it comprises too large an area to be satisfactorily handled by one person, in which case, a Police officer not below the rank of an Inspector of Police or the Naib-Tehsildar, might be associated with him. The Police Thanadar could more usefully act as supervisor for the village within his Police Station, while the village Patwari, such Headmen as are literate, and the non-official agency available, should be appointed enumerators of blocks of which their local knowledge and experience will prevent the possibility of errors creeping in the statistics.

10. The above is only a suggestion and is not intended to fetter your action in any way, which, I daresay, will be taken with due regard to the importance of the work and its usefulness.

11. This division. as finally determined by you, should be entered in Register (A), a form of which accompanies, a copy of this register for the whole district being furnished to this office, in order that due arrangement may be made for the supply of printed forms of Enumerator's Schedules.

12. I take this opportunity to invite your very careful attention to the extreme importance of getting through these stages of the work with promptitude and correctness. If the house-lists are correctly prepared, and the division into Blocks, Circles, and Charges, and the nomination of qualified agency, is made with proper exercise of judgment and discretion, you may safely look to the successful completion of the more onerous task of enumeration.

13. You should, therefore, spare no pains to make a tour in your district and satisfy yourself of the work of your subordinates. The rules regarding the preparation of Register (A) will be found in the accompanying note.

CENSUS REGISTER A (Rural Tracts).

Instructions.

(To be printed on the back of the outer sheet of the Register).

Columns of Register A.

Column		
Col. 1, No. of village on Revenue List.		
2. Name of village (or ward).		
3. Sub-divisions of village (or ward).		
4. Estimated population.	In each sub-division.	
5. Total No. of houses.	In each sub-division.	
6. First Serial No. of houses.	In each sub-division.	
7. Last Serial No. of houses.	In each sub-division.	
8. First Serial No. of houses.	In each block.	
9. Last Serial No. of houses.	In each block.	
10. Total No. of houses.	In each block.	
11. No. or letter of block.	In each block.	
12. Name, designation and residence of enumerator.	In each block.	
13. No. and Head-Quarter.	In each block.	
14. Name, designation and residence of supervisor.	Of each circle.	

[Size of Register page 18½ by 8½ in.]

1. The object of this register is to secure the inclusion in the Census Block of every village, hamlet, street, lane, encampment, landing-place, boat, house or hut in the charge, so that the enumerator may have no excuse for leaving unvisited any building, boat or other place in which any person may be stopping at the time of the Census, and that no traveller or wanderer may be likely to escape enumeration, wherever he may be at that time.

2. The Superintendent of a rural charge should fill in this register from the information contained in Form B entering the sub-divisions of each village in column 3. He must begin with the main village site, where there is one, and proceed to enter in the order, in which they can be most conveniently visited, the quarters occupied by the village menials, and other low castes, the hamlets, landing places of boats, *Sarais*, *Dharamsalas*, wells, &c., where travellers usually stop the night, and detached houses, farms and settlements in the fields, forests, or grazing grounds, marking the position of each on a rough map of the *locality*.

3. He should ascertain the number of persons usually residing in each of these sub-divisions and enter it in column 4. He should also enter in column 5 the number of houses in each, as recorded in Register B; at the same time he should find out what persons, officials or others in his charge, are competent and probably willing to act as supervisors and enumerators respectively, at the Census, and enter their names, designations and residences on a separate list.

4. He must then take or send this list and the register filled in as far as column 5 to the officer of the district to whom he is subordinate, communicating to that official the suggestions he has to make about the distribution of the places named in columns 2 and 3 into blocks and circles, He may enter these proposals in pencil in columns 11 to 14 and even on the map which should accompany his remarks; but until the approval of the District Officer has been communicated, they must not be considered as final.

5. In making the above proposals the charge Superintendent should take into consideration the distance between each of the sub-divisions, apart from the number of houses and people in them; and no block should be proposed in which an enumerator will not be able to visit each house and make the necessary inquiries at the time of Census within the space of about 5 hours. In the main site of a village an enumerator will probably be able to thus complete about sixty

houses or three hundred entries, but where there are detached hamlets and landing places, the block must be made much smaller.

6. When the blocks and circles have been finally determined as herein before provided, columns 6 to 12 of Register A should be filled in under the immediate guidance of the District Officer. A fair copy of the portion *relating* to each block must then be made and stitched into the book of schedules under the immediate eye of the supervisor with whom rests the responsibility of seeing that every enumerator is thoroughly acquainted with his block before the morning preceding the Census.

Towns.

7. In towns, the District Officer or the President of the Municipal Committee where there is one, will be responsible for the preparation of these lists. The work must be done in more detail than in rural charges, a sketch map of each charge should be prepared and sub-divided into circles. The supervisors should also be furnished with a block map to guide them into every corner of their circles. The ward (or *mohalla*) will ordinarily form the main sub-division, and its name should be entered in column 2 of list A, whilst in column 3 should be entered the name of every street, alley, court, lane and other sub-divisions in the order in which they can most conveniently be traversed at the Census. When the whole area has been divided into blocks and duly mapped out, the house numbering should begin. The Census numbering moreover, must be based on convenience in visiting each house in succession, as by traversing one side of the street or lane completely before crossing to visit the other. It is these Census numbers that must be entered in columns 6, 7, 8, 9 and 10 of list A, after list B has been completed. Columns 4 and 5, are for guidance in distributing the blocks, the municipal records, if any, may be used in filling them up.

8. In sub-dividing towns into blocks it must be borne in mind that though the population is closer-packed, and the enumerators have therefore an easier task on the Census night, the variety of caste, religion and occupation is much greater than in a village, so that to facilitate abstraction, when the Census is over, it is advisable to make the blocks small.

9. Supervisors must provide themselves with the extracts from list A, relating to their circles, and should also have a rough map of that area prepared by them showing the relative position of each village, hamlet, landing place, or detached home-steads.

Nos. 530—531, dated 7th August 1890.

From—Rai Bahadur Pandit Bhag Ram, Judical Member of State Council.

To—The Provincial Governors, Jammu and Kashmír.

I have the honor to enclose copies of the Circulars issued by me regarding the Census of the Kashmír State for your information and take the opportunity to bring to your notice that while the brunt of the work falls on Wazir-Wazarats, the Judges of the Sadar Adalats and Presidents of Municipal Committees, you are nevertheless primarily responsible for the successful and efficient control of the operations, and should with that view, adopt such measures as you may consider necessary to see that the instructions are promptly and correctly acted upon, and that the work in all its stages is most promptly and expeditiously performed.

2. The State Council trust that having regard to the paramount importance of Census work and the responsibility devolving on you as the Executive Head of the Province, you will give the subject your most serious attention, and accord to it your hearty co-operation. It is needless for me to add that on your prompt and energetic action alone will depend the successful completion of the work by your subordinates, and that you should lose no time and spare no pains to keep yourself acquainted with the progress which is being made and the manner in which the work is done by your subordinates.

Circular No. 3, dated 7th August 1890.

From—RAI BAHADUR PANDIT BHAG RAM, Judicial Member of State Council,

To—Governor and Judges, Sadar Adalats.

No. 535, dated 9th August 1890, to Governor, Jammu.
No. 534, dated 9th August 1890, to Governor, Srinagar.
No. 537, dated 9th August 1890, to Judge, Jammu.
No. 536, dated 9th August 1890, to Judge, Srinagar.

It appears to me that the Wazir-Wazarats as usual have taken no steps up to this time to ensure the preparation of the house-lists, and in certain instances, I understand that my Circular No. 1, of 19th July 1890, has been treated as a dead letter. The delays which ordinarily take place in this State in the disposal of ordinary business, may to a certain extent be excusable, but I think in the case of the Census, all officers must clearly understand that the slightest lukewarmness, want of energy and dilatoriness on their part, will render them liable to the severest displeasure of the State Council.

2. You should, therefore, make enquiries and let me know at the earliest practicable date, which of the Wazir-Wazarats were particularly dilatory in complying with the orders issued, in order that their conduct may be brought to the notice of the State Council.

3. Every officer entrusted with Census work must reply references made to him within 24 hours of their receipt by him. The Census work in all its stages must be performed with the greatest expedition possible, and on no excuse whatever, the making of periodical tours, instruction of subordinates and supervision of the work, should be delayed or put off to suit one's personal convenience.

4. The Government of India has called for a Progress Report by the 1st week of September 1890 regarding which I have addressed you separately, and I have every reason to hope that you will be able to submit it by the prescribed date.

5. You should in future direct every Wazir-Wazarat to submit a fortnightly Progress Report to you, so that you might be kept informed of the manner in which the work is progressing.

Circular No. 4, dated 22nd August 1890.

From—RAI BAHADUR PANDIT BHAG RAM, Judicial Member of State Council,

To—Wazir-Wazarats, Kashmir State.

1. You have now been furnished with detailed instructions regarding the preparation of the house-list (Register B) a specimen form of the house-list filled in for an imaginary village, and a sample of the rough village map, and I await a detailed report from you on the following points:—

1st.—What agency has been employed on the preparation of the house-lists,

2nd.—What arrangement has been made for supervision ?

(*a*) Checking by Supervisors.

(*b*) Checking by Superintendents.

3rd.—What places in your district were visited by yourself ? And with what result ?

4th.—Are the house-lists in your district in course of completion ? if so, by what date they will be completed ? Give number of villages completed, and those in course of completion.

5th.—Have the houses been numbered ?

6th.—Have rough maps been made out as required under the rules ?

7th.—Are there any villages in which the work has not yet been commenced, if so, why ?

2. This report should be submitted to me direct, within a week of the receipt of this letter, a copy being at the same time furnished to the Judge Sadar Adalat and the Provincial Governor.

Standard Questions to be asked by the Census Officer who fills up the Schedules.

Note.—These questions indicate the main points on which enquiries are to be made, but the instructions and rules must be carefully studied before the person filling up the schedules begins his task, so that if the answers first given to these questions do not contain the information required according to the rules, additional questions must be asked until the answers furnish that information.

Part I.—QUESTIONS ON THE FIRST ROUND.

1. Who is the head of this family, residing here?
2. (Column 2)—What is your name?
3. (Column 3)—What is your religion?
4. (Column 4)—What is your caste (tribe, race, &c.)?
5. (Column 6)—How old are you, that is how many years have you completed?
6. (Column 7)—In what State or Province were you born? If not in State, in what Province of British Territory? If not in India, in what country?
7. (Column 8)—How do you get your living? If from the land, are you owner or tenant? Have you any other occupation besides agriculture? If you have, what is it? If you have several occupations, which do you say is the principal one? If you have no occupation, what is the occupation of your supporter?
8. Now tell me the names of all who are ordinarily living or taking their meals with you? First, the members of your family in order of age, next, your servants who live with you; lastly, visitors likely to be here on the 26th of February?
9. Now answer each question from 2 to 8 above, about each of the persons you have mentioned.

Part II.—QUESTIONS ON THE FINAL ROUND.

10. Listen while I read out the names of the persons entered as living in your house.
11. Are all these persons alive? Has any one of them gone away or died, so that he is not living in or taking his meals from the house?
12. Has any child been born in your house since the entries were made?

If any person has come who was not entered before, answer all the questions from 2 to 8 about each of such persons.

Circular No. 5, dated 22nd August 1890.

From—RAI BAHADUR PANDIT BHAG RAM, Judicial Member of State Council,

To—Governors, Judges of Sadar Adalats, Presidents of Municipal Committees, and Wazir-Wazarats, Jammu and Kashmir State.

In my Circular No. 2, dated 23rd July 1890, I had the honor to furnish you with detailed instructions regarding the nomination of Superintendents, Supervisors and Enumerators, and the preparation of Register A.

2. Since then a copy of the enumerator's schedule, as finally settled, has also been furnished to you, and I have now the pleasure to enclose a copy of the code of instructions to supervisors. The enumerator's schedule and the codes will be printed at the *Mufid-i-'Am Press*, Lahore, and printed copies will be duly supplied to you for distribution in due course.

3. Meanwhile I again take the opportunity to invite your serious attention to the necessity for selecting the best men available. From a perusal of the enumerator's schedule you will find that the enumerator must not only be able to read and write, but must combine energy and intelligence to be able to carry on his work with regularity and precision. As the enumerators will be generally selected from non-officials, the appointment might be made attractive by giving each enumerator an *Irshad* in the accompanying form under the signature of the Wazir-Wazarat.

4. Printed forms of this *Irshad* will be furnished to you in due course. You must particularly impress on the enumerators that the *Irshad* shall be deemed to be a certificate of service to the State, and that it shall also be considered a qualification for future employment in the establishments of the State.

5. In regard to supervisors, it is needless for me to repeat that the Revenue, Judicial, Police, Education, &c., employés in the district, could be advantageously told off for this duty. The selection will, of course, be made by District Officers, but Judges of Sadar Adalats are particularly requested to see that the codes of instructions are thoroughly understood by the supervisors. You will see that the position of a supervisor carries with it great responsibility. He must himself be thoroughly conversant with the rules and orders, able to answer questions put to him by the enumerators, and must take an interest in his work.

6. You should so arrange that every supervisor must have his head-quarters within his circle, so that he may be readily accessible to the enumerators and might be able to visit the blocks subordinate to him as often as may be necessary.

7. The charge Superintendents of Census will be high officers, *viz.*, Tehsildars, Naib-Tehsildars, or in some cases Police Inspectors, who are already conscious of their personal responsibility, and will, it is hoped, perform their share of the work as ably as they can.

8. You should at the same time adopt a system of submission of Progress Reports by your subordinates. To keep the supervisors on their duty you must require them to report promptly to the charge Superintendent while the latter should report to you and the District Officer the progress that is being made in the various stages of Census work. I await a detailed report from you at your earliest convenience as to the measures taken by you in this respect.

9. I shall also be obliged by your issuing stringent orders to the District Officers that they must make a tour in their districts and personally scrutinize the papers under preparation.

Code for Supervisors.

1. You shall provide yourself with a rough map of your circle showing the position of the blocks, an extract from Register A containing detailed particulars regarding the enumerators' blocks in your circle, and a complete set of the intructions to enumerators.

2. You shall make a tour with the view of acquainting yourself with the position of the blocks in your circle, and in the course of your visit to each block furnish each enumerator with an extract from Register A, appertaining to his block, and direct him to acquaint himself with the relative position of the houses which he will have to deal with; you should also see that each enumerator is furnished with a block map, at the same time you should satisfy yourself by personal examination that each enumerator is sufficiently educated to fill the entries in the book; if you find him to be unfit for his duty you should at once submit a report to the charge Superintendent, with a view to the nomination of a better and qualified person in his place.

3. When you are satisfied that the enumerators in your circle are all thoroughly fit and qualified, and that each of them is intimately acquainted with his block, you shall summon them to your head-quarters and furnish them with the books which they have to fill in. Before delivery of these books it shall be your duty to fill in the blank pages intended for the house-list of the block. No enumerator shall be allowed to leave, until he has in your presence mastered the code of instructions, the specimen schedule and the set of questions contained in the book, and you must be particularly careful in clearing all doubtful points and in giving the enumerators the training neccessary for an efficient discharge of their duty. The training of enumerators must be completed by the first week of November.

4. You shall then direct the enumerators to proceed to their blocks and make entries on loose sheets for, say, 5 or 10 houses as may be determined by you. Every such entry must be carefully checked by you and if you find it to be correct in every particular, you should submit a report to the charge Superintendent in order that he may also satisfy himself by personal examination that no difficulty will be experienced in the preparation of the preliminary record.

5. You will note that the preliminary enumeration is not to be taken in hand before the 1st of January 1891.

6. If the rough entries made by an enumerator are not commendable, you shall stay in his block till the mistakes are thoroughly explained to him and till he has in your presence made fresh entries with accuracy and in conformity to the instructions.

7. You shall freely communicate with the enumerators in your circle and afford them every facility to seek your instructions, when they stand in need of them.

8. You shall keep a diary in the accompanying form showing the result of your visits to the blocks in your circle and submit copies thereof to the charge Superintendent once a week.

9. If any enumerator is dilatory in the performance of his duty, neglects to respond promptly to your call, or otherwise misbehaves himself, you will at once report him to the charge Superintendent who will take such notice of his conduct as he may consider necessary.

Preliminary Record.

10. The preliminary record will be commenced from 1st January 1891, when you must constantly move in your circle visiting the blocks within your jurisdiction and seeing that the work is promptly and accurately performed.

11. You must check all the entries made by the enumerators in your circle in each block.

12. You must at the same time satisfy yourself that all the houses borne on the house-list for the block are duly entered in the schedule.

13. When the preliminary record is completed, you shall report its completion to the charge Superintendent who shall then make his own examination of the entries made by the enumerators.

14. You shall initial the house schedules verified by you under your signature, noting below the date of such verification.

15. You shall warn your enumerators that the books should be written out legibly and that they are to remain in their custody till the day of the final enumeration.

Final Enumeration.

16. Not later than a fortnight before the date of the final enumeration, you should after personal examination ascertain and report to the charge Superintendent that the preliminary record of your circle is complete in every respect.

17. You must then visit each block and explain to the enumerator the way of conducting the final enumeration.

18. On the night of the Census and the following morning, you should pay a visit to each block in your circle, and in a summary manner watch the progress of work.

19. You must arrange that the enumerators are present in their respective blocks, and are duly provided with red ink to enable them to make corrections and alterations in the schedule.

20. If there are any special gatherings in your circle, in any *Sarai*, encamping grounds or other place on the night of the Census, you must appoint special enumerators to fill in the schedule.

21. Wandering tribes should be counted at the place where they are found on the night of the Census, special arrangements being made to ensure a correct record.

22. On the following morning you shall examine carefully the corrections and additions, &c., made on the previous night, and see that the rules have been strictly conformed to.

23. Separate rules will be issued regarding the action to be taken in regard to the enumerator's books after the final enumeration.

Code of Instructions for Superintendents of Census.

1. You are, subject to the orders of Wazir-Wazarat, primarily responsible for the successful completion of Census operations in your charge.

2. You shall provide yourself with (*a*) a rough map showing the circles and blocks in your charge (*b*) the detailed Register A of blocks and circles, and (*c*) a copy of the register of houses.

3. Under your immediate guidance and supervision, the supervisors of circles shall be furnished with the block map and Register A for their respective circles.

4. You shall, subject to the sanction of the District Officer, appoint supervisors and enumerators in your charge, arrange for the distribution of Census papers and before starting work, see that the rules and instructions are understood.

5. You must see that no illegal exactions or malpractices are made by your subordinates employed on Census.

6. You must see that the objects of the Census are understood by the people.

7. You must move about within your charge, on a tour of inspection of the work being done, and must by personal examination, satisfy yourself of its correctness. With this object you may check as many entries in each block as you may think fit, not less than 10 per cent. of the whole.

8. You shall carefully study the rules and instructions, and explain them to your subordinates.

9. You shall submit such periodical reports to the District Officer, the Judge Sadar Adalat and the Provincial Governor, as may be prescribed in this behalf.

DIARY OF SUPERVISOR CIRCLE NO. DISTRICT.

Three pages should be set apart for each Block, and as each Block is visited the result should be briefly noted in its proper place. The pages should be ruled and provided with the following headings :—

________________ ENUMERATOR BLOCK NO. 1.

Month and date of arrival of supervisor.	Date of departure.	Number of entries checked by supervisor.	REMARKS : Explaining further particulars, relating to the quality and quantity of work done.

FORM OF IRSHAD TO BE GRANTED TO AN ENUMERATOR.

________________ *District.*

________________ *Circle.*

1. The State Council has learnt with pleasure that you have volunteered to serve as an enumerator.

2. You are therefore appointed Enumerator of Block No.——and this Sanad is hereby granted to you in recognition of the service you have agreed to render to the State Council.

3. You shall keep this document in your possession, and perform your duties to the satisfaction of your superiors.

Circular No. 6, dated 12th September 1890.

I have the honor to request that as soon as Register B (house-list) has been completed and finally checked, you will be good enough to prepare and submit to this office an abstract statement in the accompanying form—

District.	Tehsil.	Name of village or town.	No of houses.	No. of permanent residents.	REMARKS.
1	2	3	4	5	6

2. The statement should be totalled for each Tehsil and District separately.

3. You should at the same time compile and submit a statement for the whole province in the following form, for villages and towns separately :—

Name of District.	No of Tehsils.	No of villages.	Total No of houses.	Total No. of residents.	REMARKS.
1	2	3	4	5	6

Name of District.	Name of town.	Number of houses.	Number of residents.	REMARKS.
1	2	3	4	5

Circular No. 8.

Census Department.

Immediately after the Census the supervisor shall take charge of the books brought in by the enumerators, and verify them with the circle register of blocks and books issued. The supervisor must see that no books are kept back by the enumerators and that in each case the enumerator's abstract is duly prepared and checked. He shall then prepare and compile the "abstract" for the whole circle, after which the books must be tied up in serial order of registration and brought to the Tehsil office.

2. The Tehsildar shall prepare a *chalan* in the form hereinto annexed for the whole Tehsil, and send it with the books to the Wazir-Wazarat who shall prepare an index register of the whole consignment for his district and forward it to the Provincial Superintendent of Census to whom he is subordinate. The Provincial Superintendent shall cause the consignments received from districts to be thoroughly examined and delivered to the record-keeper who shall be responsible for their custody and verification.

FORM OF CHALAN REFERRED TO IN RULE II.

____________________*District.*

____________________*Tehsil.*

1	2	3
Name of Supervisor.	Number of Blocks in Circle.	Number of books.
TOTAL ...		

FORM OF INDEX REGISTER.

———————— *District.*

1	2	3	4	5	6
Tehsil.	Name of Supervisor.	Serial number of blocks.	Number of Enumerator's books.	Serial number of books 1 to—	REMARKS.

The register should be totalled for each Tehsil, and for the whole district the number should be noted on the block book in red ink for purpose of identification.

Circular order by President of Council.

Dated 10th December 1890.

It has come to notice that in spite of repeated orders issued by this office and the Superintendent of Census operations in Jammu and Kashmír, Revenue Officers generally have displayed utter indifference and apathy in the discharge of Census duty. A number of Wazir-Wazarats and Tehsildars have absolutely done nothing and are said to have not even taken the trouble of acquainting themselves with the rules and instructions.

2. They must know that Census operations are conducted under the orders of the Government of India, and that undersigned will feel himself bound to visit with condign punishment such of the delinquents as are found guilty of wilful relaxation of duty.

3. On receipt of this Circular it shall be the duty of every Tehsildar and Wazir-Wazarat to make a tour in his jurisdiction and satisfy himself that the enumerators and supervisors are all present and willing to discharge their respective functions.

4. Every officer engaged in Census work must keep a diary of his proceedings and forward a copy of the same to the Provincial Superintendent for information.

Extract from Proceedings of a meeting of the Jammu and Kashmír State Council, held at Jammu, on Wednesday, the 26th March 1890.

Read Census Commissioner for India letter No. 19, dated March 1890, received under Resident's endorsement No. 346, dated 19th March 1890, regarding a Census of the population of the Kashmír State, the Resident enquiring what the Council propose doing in the matter.

VI. Resolved unanimously that the Member in charge of General Department be appointed Superintendent of Census for the whole State, and that he be requested to prepare a reply to the queries of the Census Commissioner for the consideration of the Council.

Extract from Proceedings of a meeting of the Jammu and Kashmír State Council, held at Jammu, on Wednesday, the 9th April 1890.

Read proposals of General Member regarding Census operations in compliance with Resolution No. 6, dated 26th March 1890.

XXII. Approved, reply to be sent to Resident accordingly.

Extract from Proceedings of a meeting of the Jammu and Kashmír State Council, held at Jammu, on Wednesday, the 16th April 1890.

Read General Department Memo. in connection with Census operations in 1891.

XXV. Resolved that proposals of the General Department be sanctioned, the cost to be debited to miscellaneous Foreign Department.

Extract from Proceedings of a meeting of the Jammu and Kashmír State Council, held at Jammu, on Friday the 25th April 1890.

Read Resident in Kashmír letter No. 443, dated 18th April 1890 proposing to transfer the management of Census operations in the Kashmír State from Khan Bahadur Sheikh Gulam Mohy-ud-din Khan to Rai Bahadur Pandit Bhag Ram and to ask the Settlement Officer to give his best assistance as his establishment will be utilized to a great extent in the matter.

I. Resolved that the suggestion of the Resident be approved.

Extract from Proceedings of a meeting of the Jammu and Kashmír State Council, held at Srinagar, on Tuesday the 28th August 1890.

Read Judicial Member's Memorandum bringing to notice that for the present a monthly expenditure of Rs. 500 on account of Census establishment employed throughout the State, and a lump sum of Rs. 1,000 for Jammu, and Rs. 1,000 for Kashmír, on account of contingencies, paper, &c., be sanctioned, debitable to the General Revenues of the State.

58. Resolved that the proposal of the Judicial Member be sanctioned.

Extract from Proceedings of a meeting of the Jammu and Kashmír State Council, held at Srinagar, on Thursday the 28th August 1890.

Read Judicial Member's Memorandum, submitting for information, the rules and instructions issued by him in connection with the approaching Census—

(1) Circular laying down instructions for registration of houses, &c.

(2) Rules regarding the preparation of Index Register A.

(3) Specimen forms of house-list and block map.

(4) Enumerator's Schedule, code of instructions and set of questions, &c.

(5) A code of instructions for supervisors and Superintendents of charges.

(6) Circulars issued to Governors, Judges Sadar Adalats, regarding supervision and control of Census arrangements.

Judicial Member brings to notice that the Wazir-Wazarat of Ladákh has not started work up to date for want of forms in the Tibetian character, although with the sanction of the President he was informed that entries in Tibetian characters might be made in manuscript.

IX.—Recorded.

Extract from the Proceedings of a meeting of the Jammu and Kashmír State Council, held at Jammu, on Tuesday the 16th December 1890.

Read Judicial Member's Memo. bringing to notice that in the absence of any information it is impossible to express an opinion on the result of Census operations in Gilgit and Skardu and the Feudatory States excepting Bhadrawah.

1st.—The house-lists of Kashmír and Jammú Provinces have all been finished, but in spite of repeated telegrams the Wazirs of Gilgit and Skardu have not yet submitted the abstract statements called for in Circular No. 6.

XXXVIII.—Resolved that necessary action in the matter be taken by the Prime Minister.

2nd.—The Wazir of Udhampore made false reports regarding completion of house-lists, while that of Manawar has been grossly dilatory in the discharge of his duties. The Jasrota man contravened orders by leaving his District for Jammu.

Resolved that the Wazir-Wazarats be warned that a recurrence of such conduct shall render them liable to summary dismissal. Further that the President of the Council be authorised to inflict punishment on delinquents without reference to State Council.

3rd.—The Census Superintendent regrets to observe that considering the dilatoriousness of the Local Revenue Officers in the preparation of the house-lists, the more important work of enumeration could hardly be expected to be pushed through, if such a state of things continues, and he begs that an example be made of the delinquents whose conduct has been specially reported by the Judge Sadar Adalat, and that power be given to the President of the Council to inflict immediate punishment on those who may be reported to His Highness in future.

4th.—Tehsildar Kashi Nath of Reasi has addressed a most improper and impertinent communication to the Judge, Sadar Adalat, which is specially laid before the Council in order that the controlling authority of the Judge be maintained by visiting the culprit with condign punishment.

Resolved that Pandit Kashi Nath be dismissed forthwith.

5th.—It should be definitely declared that the Census Superintendent has no concern with the operations in Punch and other feudatory jagirs, as he has practiclly no control over those parts.

The Council note that the feudatory jagirdars are by their own engagements personally responsible for Census arrangements within their jagirs, but the Census Superintendent may specially depute his nominees whose pay will be defrayed by the jagirs concerned, with a view to ascertain the quality and quantity of work which has been performed.

6th.—That villages of Jammu and Kashmír proper held by feudatory dependent chiefs in farm, mortgage or otherwise, ought to be supervised so far as Census operations are concerned, by the State officials, but the agents of these chiefs would not allow this to be done and the consequence is that those villages have been for the present excluded. Does the Council desire that they be deemed portions of the feudatory Jagirs and their Census incorporated with that of the main jagirs.

The Census of these villages must be supervised by State officials.

7th.—Great difficulty is experienced in respect of villages inhabited by Mians and the Census Superintendent is afraid that the final enumeration of these villages will not be so accurate as is deseired. This requires the special attention of the Council.

Resolved that Prime Minister be requested to make suitable arrangements.

Extract from Proceedings of a meeting of the Jammu and Kashmir State Council, held at Jammu, on Tuesday the 16th December 1890.

Read Census Superintendent's Memorandum laying before the State Council the final results of the house-lists of the Jummu and Kashmir Provinces as reported by Provincial Superintendents.

The figures for Gilgit, Skardu and Ladákh have not yet been received. The Ladákh papers are said to be in transit, but as regards Gilgit and Skardu no satisfactory replies to the repeated telegraphic reminders sent to the District Officers have been received. The house-lists, it may be said, have been prepared strictly in conformity to instructions but were it not for the cordial support accorded by Raja Amar Singh, President of the State Council, their completion, considering the absolute apathy and indifference displayed by the local Revenue Officers, was almost hopeless. The Judges of the Sadar Adalats of Jammu and Srinagar as well as Dr. A. Mitra, the President of the Srinagar Municipality, were most energetic and zealous in the performance of their duties, the two first named made an extensive tour in their respective jurisdiction and supervised the work of the local Officers and staff with care and expedition.

The Provincial Governors of Jammu and Srinagar did all in their power to help the Provincial Superintendents whenever their assistance was needed to rouse the District Officers and Tehsildars from their characteristically dormant state.

The preparation of the preliminary record and final enumeration is a task of no less difficulty, and the Census Superintendent trusts that the District Officers will be enjoined to carry it out with care and ability, and that power will be given to the President to punish any officer who is guilty of carelessness or neglect.

XLVI. Resolved that a copy of the Memorandum and its accompaniments be submitted to the Resident.

Resolved further that the services of the Judges of Sadar Adalats and Dr. A. Mitra, President of Srinagar Municipality, be acknowledged in suitable terms by an *Irshad* bearing the signature of the President of the Council.

Extract from Proceedings of a meeting of the Jammu and Kashmir State Council, held at Jammu, on Wednesday the 7th January 1890.

Read Prime Minister's letter No. 1488, dated 22nd December 1890 enclosing Mehta Sher Singh Wazir-Wazarat, Gilgit, letter No. 83, dated 22nd Katak 1947 setting forth the difficulties in successfully carrying out Census operations in Gilgit.

V.—Resolved that the Wazir-Wazarat be authorised to use his discretion in consultation with the British Agent at Gilgit to prepare the returns as correctly as possible under the circumstances.

The Council hope that the Resident will kindly advise Colonel Durand to help Mehta Sher Singh.

Extract from the Proceedings of a meeting of the Jammu and Kashmir State Council, held at Jammu, on Tuesday the 21st January 1891.

Read Census Superintendent's Memo. bringing to notice :—

(1) That the house-lists prescribed by Census Circular No. 6 have not yet been received from Gilgit and the feudatory jagirs of Punch and Ramnagar.

(2) That the Raja of Punch has not yet indented for any Census forms, nor submitted his Progress Report of the operations.

(3) That the abstract statement of houses and permanent residents is now over due and should be obtained from him without delay.

(4) That notwithstanding issue of repeated telegraphic reminders the Wazir-Wazarat of Gilgit has not submitted the house-lists of his district.

XX.—Resolved that a report be made to the Resident regarding the indifference of the Raja of Punch to the repeated calls of the Prime Minister, and that as regards Gilgit and Ramnagar, the President be requested to arrange for the prompt submission of the abstract of the house-lists.

BHAG RAM, PANDIT,

RAI BAHADUR,

Superintendent of Census, Kashmir State.

IMPERIAL AND SUPPLEMENTARY
TABLES.

CENSUS 1891.

KASHMIR STATE.

TABLE I.—*Area, Houses and Population.*

Province.	Area in square miles.	Number of		Occupied Houses.			Population.								
							Total.			*Males.*			*Females.*		
		Towns.	Villages.	Total.	Towns.	Villages.	Total.	Towns.	Villages.	Total.	Towns.	Villages.	Total.	Towns.	Villages.
Jammu including Jagirs ...	...	4	4,323	262,446	9,895	252,551	1,439,543	54,490	1,385,053	770,241	33,954	736,287	669,302	20,536	648,766
Kashmír	...	4	3,649	145,689	26,357	119,332	949,041	143,253	805,788	502,345	75,598	426,747	446,693	67,655	379,041
Ladákh	...	...	86	6,264	...	6,264	28,274	...	28,274	14,350	...	14,350	13,924	...	13,924
Skardu	...	...	243	31,307	...	31,307	110,325	...	110,325	56,098	...	56,098	54,227	...	54,227
Gilgit	...	...	110	2,287	...	2,287	16,769	...	16,769	10,195	...	10,195	6,574	...	6,574
Total ...	80,900	8	8,411	447,993	36,252	411,741	2,543,952	197,743	2,346,209	1,353,229	109,552	1,243,677	1,190,723	88,191	1,102,532

JAMMU:
Dated the 17th December 1891.

BHAG RAM,
Census Superintendent, Kashmír State.

CENSUS 1891.

KASHMIR STATE.

TABLE II.—*Variation in the enumerated Population since last Census.*

Province.	Total.			Males.			Females.		
	1891.	1873.	Variation.	1891.	1873.	Variation.	1891.	1873.	Variation.
Jammu	1,439,543	938,641	500,902	770,241	480,170	290,071	669,302	458,471	210,831
Kashmír	949,041	491,846	457,195	502,345	259,927	242,418	446,696	231,919	214,777
Ladákh	28,274	20,621	7,653	14,350	11,106	3,244	13,924	9,515	4,409
Skardu	110,325	58,030	52,295	56,098	29,881	26,217	54,227	28,149	26,078
Gilgit	16,769	25,834	— 9,065	10,195	14,310	—4,115	6,574	11,524	— 4,950
Total ...	2,543,952	1,534,972	1,008,980	1,353,229	795,394	557,835	1,190,723	739,578	451,145

JAMMU :
Dated the 17th December 1891.

BHAG RAM,
Census Superintendent, Kashmír State.

CENSUS 1891.

KASHMIR STATE.

TABLE III.—*Towns and Villages classified by Population.*

Province.	Total number of towns and villages.	Total Population.	1—199		200—499		500—999		1000—1999		2000—2999		3000—4999		5000—9999		10000—14999		15000—19999		20000—49999		50000 and over.	
			Number.	Population.	Number.	Population.	Number.	Population.	Number.	Population.	Number.	Population.	Number.	Population.	Number.	Population.	Number.	Population.	Number.	Population.	Number.	Population.	Number.	Population.
Jammu ...	4,327	1,439,543	2,140	207,832	1,423	447,382	539	373,402	175	234,847	33	79,298	12	37,179	4	25,061	...	...	...	...	1	34,542	...	...
Kashmír	3,653	949,041	2,309	212,292	999	311,275	273	183,043	59	74,704	6	17,308	3	10,291	3	21,168	...	...	...	...	...	...	1	118,960
Ladákh ...	86	28,274	36	4,146	35	11,899	13	8,331	1	1,253	1	2,645	...	...	...	...	...	...	...	...	...	...	...	...
Skardu ...	243	110,325	90	10,030	75	24,555	46	32,419	31	41,158	1	2,163	...	...	...	...	...	...	...	...	...	...	...	...
Gilgit ...	110	16,769	87	6,771	19	5,256	3	1,754	...	...	1	2,988	...	...	...	...	...	...	...	...	...	...	...	...
TOTAL ...	8,419	2,543,952	4,662	441,071	2,551	800,367	874	598,949	266	351,962	42	104,402	15	47,470	7	46,229	...	...	...	...	1	34,542	1	118,960

NOTE.—Gilgit Road treated as a village.

SRINAGAR:
Dated the 9th October 1891.

BHAG RAM,
Census Superintendent, Kashmír State.

CENSUS 1891.

KASHMIR STATE.

TABLE IV.—*Towns according to Population compared with the preceding Census.*

Towns.	District.	Municipality, Suburb or Cantonment.	Total Population.			Males.			Females.		
			1891	1881	Variation.	1891	1881	Variation.	1891	1881	Variation.
KASHMIR PROVINCE.											
Srinagar ...	Khas ...	Municipality ...	118,960	No Census taken.	...	62,720	No Census taken.	...	56,240	No Census taken.	...
Baramula ...	Kamraj ...	Town ...	5,656	Do.	...	3,003	Do.	...	2,653	Do.	...
Sopore ...	Do. ...	Do. ...	8,410	Do.	...	4,360	Do.	...	4,050	Do.	...
Anantnag ...	Anantnag ...	Do. ...	10,227	Do.	...	5,515	Do.	...	4,712	Do.	...
JAMMU PROVINCE.											
Jammu ...	Sri Ranbir Singhpora	Municipality ...	34,542	Do.	...	22,545	Do.	...	11,997	Do.	...
Batala ...	Bhimbar ...	Town ...	5,206	Do.	...	3,079	Do.	...	2,127	Do.	...
Mirpore ...	Do. ...	Do. ...	7,253	Do.	...	3,655	Do.	...	3,598	Do.	...
Punch ...	Punch Jagir ...	Do. ...	7,489	Do.	...	4,675	Do.	...	2,814	Do.	...

JAMMU:
Dated the 17th December 1891.

BHAG RAM,
Census Superintendent, Kashmir State.

CENSUS 1891.

KASHMIR STATE.

TABLE V.—*Towns arranged territorially, with population by religion.*

District.	Towns.	Total Population.			Hindu.			Mussalman.			Christian.			Budhist.			Jain.			Sikh.			Parsi.		
		Total.	Males.	Females.	Total.	Males.	Females.	Total.	Males.	Females.	Total.	Males.	Females.	Total.	Males.	Females.	Total.	Males.	Females.	Total.	Males.	Females.	Total.	Males.	Females.
JAMMU PROVINCE.																									
Sri Ranbir Singhpora	Jammu ...	34,542	22,545	11,997	22,355	14,771	7,584	11,601	7,440	4,161	14	7	7	...	...	...	513	287	226	59	40	19	...	...	...
Bhimbar	Mirpore ...	7,253	3,655	3,598	3,393	1,685	1,708	3,303	1,678	1,625	..	...	...	...	...	...	4	2	2	553	290	263	...	...	...
Do.	Batala ...	5,206	3,079	2,127	4,119	2,463	1,656	1,087	616	471	...	...	...	...	...	...	...	...	...	...	...	...	...	...	...
Punch Jagir	Punch ...	7,489	4,675	2,814	2,726	1,863	863	4,698	2,767	1,931	...	...	...	...	...	...	27	22	5	38	23	15	...	...	...
TOTAL URBAN POPULATION, JAMMU PROVINCE.	...	54,490	33,954	20,536	32,593	20,782	11,811	20,689	12,501	8,188	14	7	7	...	...	...	544	311	233	650	353	297	...	...	...
KASHMIR PROVINCE.																									
Wazarat Khas	Srinagar ...	118,960	62,720	56,240	26,069	14,299	11,770	92,575	48,231	44,344	119	57	62	...	...	...	...	...	...	189	127	62	8	6	2
Anantnag	Anantnag ...	10,227	5,515	4,712	981	573	408	9,236	4,933	4,303	2	1	1	...	...	...	...	...	...	8	8	...	...	...	...
Kamraj	Sopore ...	8,410	4,360	4,050	858	472	386	7,550	3,886	3,664	...	...	...	...	...	...	...	...	...	2	2	...	...	...	...
Do.	Baramula ...	5,656	3,003	2,653	787	441	346	4,809	2,528	2,281	...	...	...	...	...	...	...	...	...	60	34	26	...	...	...
TOTAL URBAN POPULATION, KASHMIR PROVINCE	...	143,253	75,598	67,655	28,695	15,785	12,910	114,170	59,578	54,592	121	58	63	...	...	...	...	...	...	259	171	88	8	6	2
GRAND TOTAL URBAN POPULATION, KASHMIR STATE	...	197,743	109,552	88,191	61,288	36,567	24,721	134,859	72,079	62,780	135	65	70	...	...	...	544	311	233	909	524	385	8	6	2

JAMMU:
Dated the 17th December 1891

BHAG RAM,
Census Superintendent, Kashmir State.

CENSUS 1891.

KASHMIR STATE.

TABLE VI.—*Religion.*

Province.	Total Population.			Hindu.			Mussalman.			Christian.			Budhist.			Jain.			Sikh.			Parsi.			Unspecified.		
	Total.	Males.	Females.	Total.	Males.	Females.	Total.	Males.	Females.	Total.	Males.	Females.	Total.	Males.	Females.	Total.	Males.	Females.	Total.	Males.	Females.	Total.	Males.	Females.	Total.	Males.	Females.
Jammu ...	1,439,543	770,241	669,302	631,225	340,006	291,219	797,459	424,871	373,088	46	24	22	4,293	2,179	2,114	593	339	254	5,926	3,321	2,605	1	1	...	...	...	...
Kashmír ...	949,041	502,345	446,696	60,316	34,151	26,165	883,099	465,174	417,925	145	77	68	...	...	...	...	...	...	5,473	2,937	2,536	8	6	2	...	...	...
Ladákh ...	28,274	14,350	13,924	182	172	10	2,991	1,552	1,439	25	11	14	25,076	12,615	12,461	...	...	...	...	...	...	...	...	...	...	...	...
Skardu ...	110,325	56,098	54,227	64	57	7	110,022	55,893	54,129	...	...	...	239	148	91	...	...	...	...	...	...	...	...	...	...	...	...
Gilgit ...	16,769	10,195	6,574	13	13	...	139	136	3	2	1	1	...	...	...	...	...	...	...	...	...	...	...	...	16,615	10,045	6,570
TOTAL ...	2,543,952	1,353,229	1,190,723	691,800	374,399	317,401	1,793,710	947,126	846,584	218	113	105	29,608	14,942	14,666	593	339	254	11,399	6,258	5,141	9	7	2	16,615	10,045	6,570

JAMMU:
Dated the 17th December 1891.

BHAG RAM,
Census Superintendent, Kashmír State.

CENSUS 1891.

KASHMIR STATE.

TABLE VII.—PART A. *Population by Age. All religions.*

Province.	Population.			Age Distribution.																					
	Total.	Males.	Females.	*Under one year.*		1—2.		2—3.		3—4.		4—5.		*Total under five.*		5—9.		10—14.		15—19.		20—24.	
				Males.	Females.	Males.	Females.	Males.	Females.	Males.	Females.	Males.	Females.	Males.	Females.	Males.	Females.	Males.	Females.	Males.	Females.	Males.	Females.
Jammu ...	1,439,543	770,241	669,302	29,422	29,631	10,975	10,744	20,922	20,602	24,779	25,231	24,849	24,007	110,947	110,215	104,157	93,374	79,219	58,206	60,749	53,472	57,366	58,239
Kashmír ...	949,041	502,345	446,696	26,056	25,635	7,713	7,539	20,365	20,088	22,464	22,098	19,908	18,392	96,506	93,752	76,530	67,653	46,486	33,102	39,094	34,046	38,573	40,643
Ladákh ...	28,274	14,350	13,924	199	229	190	206	207	215	311	317	284	279	1,191	1,246	1,448	1,432	1,164	1,106	1,021	969	1,121	1,055
Skardu ...	110,325	56,098	54,227	1,384	1,663	1,109	1,206	1,418	1,524	1,625	1,933	1,507	1,588	7,043	7,914	7,830	7,602	6,164	5,101	5,264	4,441	6,274	6,907
Gilgit ...	16,769	10,195	6,574	...	1	...	...	...	1	...	...	...	...	...	2	...	...	2	...	7	...	39	...
TOTAL ...	2,543,952	1,353,229	1,190,723	57,061	57,159	19,987	19,695	42,912	42,430	49,179	49,579	46,548	44,266	215,687	213,129	189,965	170,061	133,035	97,515	106,135	92,928	103,373	106,844

CENSUS 1891.

KASHMIR STATE.

TABLE VII.—PART A. *Population by Age. All religions.*

Province.	Population.			Age Distribution.																	
				25—29.		30—34.		35—39.		40—44.		45—49.		50—54.		55—59.		*60 and over.*		*Unspecified.*	
	Total.	Males.	Females.	Males.	Females.	Males.	Females.	Males.	Females.	Males.	Females.	Males.	Females.	Males.	Females.	Males.	Females.	Males.	Females.	Males.	Females.
Jammu	1,439,543	770,241	669,302	64,374	61,016	66,960	60,596	45,838	35,769	50,565	42,988	28,876	19,793	36,362	27,479	12,180	8,409	52,520	39,635	128	111
Kashmír	949,041	502,345	446,696	37,807	37,813	40,283	38,136	26,519	21,540	31,637	29,930	16,434	11,080	21,069	16,211	6,099	3,856	25,308	18,904	...	30
Ladákh	28,274	14,350	13,924	1,210	1,110	1,111	1,042	1,068	1,048	1,024	974	833	820	647	652	682	661	1,830	1,809	...	...
Skardu	110,325	56,098	54,227	2,029	1,827	3,380	3,164	5,217	5,374	2,284	2,023	3,392	3,717	1,566	1,166	777	550	4,866	4,431	12	10
Gilgit	16,769	10,195	6,574	30	1	24	1	14	...	11	...	8	...	10	...	3	...	2	...	10,045	6,570
TOTAL	2,543,952	1,353,229	1,190,723	105,450	101,767	111,758	102,939	78,656	63,731	85,521	75,915	49,543	35,410	59,654	45,508	19,741	13,476	84,526	64,779	10,185	6,721

SRINAGAR:
Dated the 3rd November 1891.

BHAG RAM,
Census Superintendent, Kashmír State.

CENSUS 1891.

KASHMIR STATE.

Table VII.—Part B. *Population by Age. Hindus.*

Province.	Population.			Age Distribution.																			
				Under one year.		1—2.		2—3.		3—4.		4—5.		*Total under five.*		5—9.		10—14.		15—19.		20—24.	
	Total.	Males.	Females.	Males.	Females.	Males.	Females.	Males.	Females.	Males.	Females.	Males.	Females.	Males.	Females.	Males.	Females.	Males.	Females.	Males.	Females.	Males.	Females.
Jammu ...	631,225	340,006	291,219	10,968	10,813	4,713	4,612	7,687	7,428	9,031	9,079	9,029	8,863	41,428	40,795	40,200	36,440	33,421	23,869	27,123	23,462	26,937	26,539
Kashmír ...	60,316	34,151	26,165	1,258	1,200	310	292	893	859	922	880	881	809	4,264	4,040	4,043	3,626	3,371	2,142	2,940	2,105	3,191	2,610
Ladákh ...	182	172	10	...	...	...	...	...	...	...	1	...	...	...	1	...	...	1	...	3	1	29	5
Skardu ...	64	57	7	...	...	...	...	...	...	...	...	...	...	...	...	...	...	...	...	4	2	4	...
Gilgit ...	13	13	...	...	...	...	...	...	...	...	...	...	...	...	...	...	...	...	...	2	...	2	...
Total ...	691,800	374,399	317,401	12,226	12,013	5,023	4,904	8,580	8,287	9,953	9,960	9,910	9,672	45,692	44,836	44,243	40,066	36,793	26,011	30,072	25,570	30,163	29,154

CENSUS 1891.

KASHMIR STATE.

TABLE VII.—PART B. *Population by Age. Hindus.*

Province.	Population.			Age Distribution.																	
				25—29.		30—34.		35—39.		40—44.		45—49.		50—54.		55—59.		60 *and over.*		*Unspecified.*	
	Total.	Males.	Females.	Males.	Females.	Males.	Females.	Males.	Females.	Males.	Females.	Males.	Females.	Males.	Females.	Males.	Females.	Males.	Females.	Males.	Females.
Jammu	631,225	340,006	291,219	30,676	28,095	30,535	26,825	21,148	16,628	23,822	20,389	14,058	9,771	17,773	13,836	6,475	4,367	26,282	20,092	128	111
Kashmír	60,316	34,151	26,165	2,975	2,320	2,937	2,237	2,204	1,381	2,376	1,863	1,516	845	1,558	1,229	706	348	2,070	1,389	...	30
Ladákh	182	172	10	67	3	32	...	14	...	12	...	9	...	1	...	1	...	3	...	...	...
Skardu	64	57	7	11	1	7	1	11	...	5	3	3	...	6	...	2	...	4	...	...	...
Gilgit	13	13	...	2	...	1	...	3	...	2	...	1	...	...	...	...	...	...	...	...	...
TOTAL ...	691,800	374,399	317,401	33,731	30,419	33,512	29,063	23,380	18,009	26,217	22,255	15,587	10,616	19,338	15,065	7,184	4,715	28,359	21,481	128	141

SRINAGAR:
Dated the 3rd November 1891.

BHAG RAM,
Census Superintendent, Kashmír State.

x

CENSUS 1891.

KASHMIR STATE.

TABLE VII.—PART C. *Population by Age. Mohamedans.*

Province.	Population.			Age Distribution.																			
				Under one year.		1—2.		2—3.		3—4.		4—5.		*Total under five.*		5—9.		10—14.		15—19.		20—24.	
	Total.	Males.	Females.	Males.	Females.	Males.	Females.	Males.	Females.	Males.	Females.	Males.	Females.	Males.	Females.	Males.	Females.	Males.	Females.	Males.	Females.	Males.	Females.
Jammu	797,459	424,371	373,088	18,240	18,617	6,213	6,097	13,077	13,061	15,568	15,976	15,646	15,014	68,744	68,765	63,194	56,261	45,171	33,839	33,174	29,575	30,034	31,311
Kashmir	883,099	465,174	417,925	24,667	24,295	7,368	7,221	19,385	19,125	21,409	21,060	18,930	17,490	91,759	89,211	72,028	63,627	42,784	30,698	35,893	31,693	35,143	37,803
Ladákh	2,991	1,552	1,439	16	21	27	31	30	26	35	43	41	34	149	155	177	173	145	133	127	96	132	117
Skardu	110,022	55,893	54,129	1,383	1,662	1,109	1,206	1,417	1,523	1,622	1,930	1,506	1,579	7,037	7,900	7,818	7,599	6,149	5,091	5,252	4,435	6,258	6,901
Gilgit	139	136	3	...	1	...	...	...	1	...	...	...	...	...	2	...	...	2	...	5	...	37	...
TOTAL ...	1,793,710	947,126	846,584	44,306	44,596	14,717	14,555	33,909	33,736	38,634	39,029	36,123	34,117	167,689	166,033	143,217	127,660	94,251	69,761	74,451	65,799	71,604	76,132

CENSUS 1891.

KASHMIR STATE.

TABLE VII.—PART C. *Population by Age. Mohamedans.*

Province.	Population.			Age Distribution.																	
				25—29		30—34		35—39		40—44		45—49		50—54		55—59		60 and over.		Unspecified.	
	Total.	Males.	Females.	Males.	Females.	Males.	Females.	Males.	Females.	Males.	Females.	Males.	Females.	Males.	Females.	Males.	Females.	Males.	Females.	Males.	Females.
Jammu	797,459	424,371	373,088	33,232	32,482	35,956	33,345	24,337	18,839	26,376	22,265	14,549	9,820	18,269	13,425	5,566	3,948	25,769	19,213	...	...
Kashmír	883,099	465,174	417,925	34,577	35,286	37,127	35,663	24,165	20,055	29,063	27,926	14,823	10,194	19,387	14,892	5,351	3,491	23,074	17,386	...	...
Ladákh	2,991	1,552	1,439	136	131	145	122	116	115	108	103	72	78	77	74	42	30	126	117	...	...
Skardu	110,022	55,893	54,129	2,008	1,816	3,361	3,160	5,193	5,366	2,274	2,012	3,377	3,709	1,549	1,163	771	549	4,834	4,418	12	10
Gilgit	139	136	3	28	1	23	...	11	...	8	...	7	...	10	...	3	...	2	...	...	...
TOTAL ...	1,793,710	947,126	846,584	69,981	69,716	76,612	72,290	53,822	44,375	57,829	52,306	32,828	23,796	39,292	29,554	11,733	8,018	53,805	41,134	12	10

SRINAGAR:
Dated the 3rd November, 1891.

BHAG RAM,
Census Superintendent, Kashmir State.

CENSUS 1891.

KASHMIR STATE.

TABLE VII.—PART D.—*Population by Age. Christians.*

Province.	Population.			Age Distribution.																	
				Under one year.		1—2.		2—3.		3—4.		4—5.		*Total under five.*		5—9.		10—14.		15—19.	
	Total.	Males.	Females.	Males.	Females.	Males.	Females.	Males.	Females.	Males.	Females.	Males.	Females.	Males.	Females.	Males.	Females.	Males.	Females.	Males.	Females.
Jammu ...	46	24	22	...	1	1	...	5	...	...	1	...	1	6	3	1	1	2	2	1	3
Kashmír ...	145	77	68	1	1	1	2	3	2	4	5	1	...	10	10	11	6	2	4	...	4
Ladákh ...	25	11	14	...	1	...	...	...	...	1	...	...	...	1	1	2	4	...	2	1	2
Skardu ...	...	...	...	...	...	...	...	...	...	...	...	...	...	...	...	...	...	...	...	...	...
Gilgit ...	2	1	1	...	...	...	...	...	...	...	...	...	...	...	...	...	...	...	...	...	...
TOTAL ...	218	113	105	1	3	2	2	8	2	5	6	1	1	17	14	14	11	4	8	2	9

CENSUS 1891.

KASHMIR STATE.

TABLE VII.—PART D. *Population by Age. Christians.*

Province.	Population.			Age Distribution.																			
				20—24.		25—29.		30—34.		35—39.		40—44.		45—49.		50—54.		55—59.		60 *and over.*		*Unspecified.*	
	Total.	Males.	Females.	Males.	Females.	Males.	Females.	Males.	Females.	Males.	Females.	Males.	Females.	Males.	Females.	Males.	Females.	Males.	Females.	Males.	Females.	Males.	Females.
Jammu ...	46	24	22	...	2	1	3	5	4	1	2	4	...	3	1	...	1	...	...	...	...	...	...
Kashmír ...	145	77	68	7	6	6	14	16	5	5	9	7	4	5	3	3	...	1	3	4	...	...	...
Ladákh ...	25	11	14	1	...	1	1	1	...	1	...	1	2	...	1	1	...	1	...	...	1	...	...
Skardu ...	...	...	...	...	...	...	...	...	...	...	...	...	...	...	...	...	...	...	...	...	...	...	...
Gilgit ...	2	1	1	...	...	...	...	...	1	...	...	1	...	...	...	...	...	...	...	...	...	...	...
TOTAL ...	218	113	105	8	8	8	18	22	10	7	11	13	6	8	5	4	1	2	3	4	1	...	...

SRINAGAR:
Dated the 3rd November 1891.

BHAG RAM,
Census Superintendent, Kashmír State.

CENSUS 1891.

KASHMIR STATE.

TABLE VII.—PART E.—*Population by Age. Budhists.*

Province.	Population.			Age Distribution.																					
				Under one year.		1—2.		2—3.		3—4.		4—5.		*Total under five.*		5—9.		10—14.		15—19.		20—24.	
	Total.	Males.	Females.	Males.	Females.	Males.	Females.	Males.	Females.	Males.	Females.	Males.	Females.	Males.	Females.	Males.	Females.	Males.	Females.	Males.	Females.	Males.	Females.
Jammu ...	4,293	2,179	2,114	39	64	3	2	38	22	46	50	44	34	170	172	260	230	236	200	178	220	178	174
Kashmír ...	...	...	...	...	...	...	...	...	...	...	...	...	...	...	...	...	...	...	...	...	...	...	...
Ladákh ...	25,076	12,615	12,461	183	207	163	175	177	189	275	273	243	245	1,041	1,089	1,269	1,255	1,018	971	890	870	959	933
Skardu ...	239	148	91	1	1	...	...	1	1	3	3	1	9	6	14	12	3	15	10	8	4	12	6
Gilgit ...	...	...	...	...	...	...	...	...	...	...	...	...	...	...	...	...	...	...	...	...	...	...	...
TOTAL ...	29,608	14,942	14,666	223	272	166	177	216	212	324	326	288	288	1,217	1,275	1,541	1,488	1,269	1,181	1,076	1,094	1,149	1,113

CENSUS 1891.

KASHMIR STATE.

TABLE VII.—PART E.—*Population by Age. Budhists.*

Province.	Population.			Age Distribution.																	
				25—29.		30—34.		35—39.		40—44.		45—49.		50—54		55—59.		60 *and over.*		*Unspecified.*	
	Total.	Males.	Females.	Males.	Females.	Males.	Females.	Males.	Females.	Males.	Females.	Males.	Females.	Males.	Females.	Males.	Females.	Males.	Females.	Males.	Females.
Jammu	4,293	2,179	2,114	192	238	176	189	130	128	137	150	116	98	120	98	68	53	218	164	...	...
Kashmír	...	...	...	...	...	...	...	...	...	...	...	...	...	...	...	...	...	...	...	...	...
Ladákh	25,076	12,615	12,461	1,006	975	933	920	937	933	903	869	752	746	568	578	638	631	1,701	1,691	...	...
Skardu	239	148	91	10	10	12	3	13	8	5	8	12	8	11	3	4	1	28	13	...	...
Gilgit	...	...	...	...	...	...	...	...	...	...	...	...	...	...	...	...	...	...	...	...	...
TOTAL ...	29,608	14,942	14,666	1,208	1,223	1,121	1,112	1,080	1,069	1,045	1,027	880	852	699	679	710	685	1,947	1,868	...	...

SRINAGAR:
Dated the 3rd November 1891.

BHAG RAM,
Census Superintendent, Kashmir State.

CENSUS 1891.

KASHMIR STATE.

TABLE VII.—PART F.—*Population by Age. Jains.*

Province.	Population.			Age Distribution.																					
	Total.	Males.	Females.	*Under one year.*		1—2.		2—3.		3—4.		4—5.		*Total under five.*		5—9.		10—14.		15—19.		20—24.	
				Males.	Females.	Males.	Females.	Males.	Females.	Males.	Females.	Males.	Females.	Males.	Females.	Males.	Females.	Males.	Females.	Males.	Females.	Males.	Females.
Jammu	593	339	254	9	7	10	7	9	6	5	10	7	3	40	33	30	26	30	26	33	23	33	22
Kashmír	...	...	...	...	...	...	...	...	...	...	...	...	...	...	...	...	...	...	...	...	...	...	...
Ladákh	...	...	...	...	...	...	...	...	...	...	...	...	...	...	...	...	...	...	...	...	...	...	...
Skárdu	...	...	...	...	...	...	...	...	...	...	...	...	...	...	...	...	...	...	...	...	...	...	...
Gilgit	...	...	...	...	...	...	...	...	...	...	...	...	...	...	...	...	...	...	...	...	...	...	...
TOTAL	593	339	254	9	7	10	7	9	6	5	10	7	3	40	33	30	26	30	26	33	23	33	22

CENSUS 1891.

KASHMIR STATE.

TABLE VII.—PART F.—*Population by Age. Jains.*

Province.	Population.			Age Distribution.																	
				25—29.		30—34.		35—39.		40—44.		45—49.		50—54.		55—59.		60 *and over.*		*Unspecified.*	
	Total.	Males.	Females.	Males.	Females.	Males.	Females.	Males.	Females.	Males.	Females.	Males.	Females.	Males.	Females.	Males.	Females.	Males.	Females.	Males.	Females.
Jammu	593	339	254	26	24	34	25	29	19	21	17	16	14	23	15	13	7	11	3	...	...
Kashmír		...	...	...	...	...	...	...	...	...	...	...	...	...	...	...	...	...	..	...	...
Ladákh	...	...	...	...	...	...	...	...	...	...	...	...	...	...	...	...	...	...	...	...	...
Skardu	...	...	...	...	...	...	...	...	...	...	...	...	...	...	...	...	...	...	...	...	...
Gilgit	...	...	...	...	...	...	...	...	...	...	...	...	...	...	...	...	...	...	...	...	...
TOTAL ...	593	339	254	26	24	34	25	29	19	21	17	16	14	23	15	13	7	11	3	...	...

SRINAGAR:
Dated the 3rd November, 1891.

BHAG RAM,
Census Superintendent, Kashmír State.

CENSUS 1891.

KASHMIR STATE.

TABLE VII.—PART G.—*Population by Age.—Sikhs.*

Province.	Population.			Age Distribution.																			
				Under one year.		1—2		2—3.		3—4.		4—5.		*Total under five.*		5—9.		10—14.		15—19.		20—24.	
	Total.	Males.	Females.	Males.	Females.	Males.	Females.	Males.	Females.	Males.	Females.	Males.	Females.	Males.	Females.	Males.	Females.	Males.	Females.	Males.	Females.	Males.	Females.
Jammu	5,926	3,321	2,605	166	129	35	26	106	85	129	115	123	92	559	447	472	416	359	270	240	189	184	191
Kashmír	5,473	2,937	2,536	130	139	34	24	84	102	129	133	95	93	472	491	448	394	328	258	260	244	232	223
Ladákh	...	...	...	...	...	...	...	...	...	...	...	...	...	...	...	...	...	...	...	...	...	...	...
Skardu	...	...	...	...	...	...	...	...	...	...	...	...	...	...	...	...	...	...	...	...	...	...	...
Gilgit	...	...	...	...	...	...	...	...	...	...	...	...	...	...	...	...	...	...	...	...	...	...	...
TOTAL ...	11,399	6,258	5,141	296	268	69	50	190	187	258	248	218	185	1,031	938	920	810	687	528	500	433	416	414

CENSUS 1891.

KASHMIR STATE.

TABLE VII.—PART G.—*Population by Age.—Sikhs.*

Province.	Population.			Age Distribution.																	
				25—29.		30—34.		35—39.		40—44.		45—49.		50—54.		55—59.		60 *and over.*		*Unspecified.*	
	Total.	Males.	Females.	Males.	Females.	Males.	Females.	Males.	Females.	Males.	Females.	Males.	Females.	Males.	Females.	Males.	Females.	Males.	Females.	Males.	Females.
Jammu	5,926	3,321	2,605	247	174	254	208	192	153	205	167	134	89	177	104	58	34	240	163	...	...
Kashmir	5,478	2,987	2,536	249	193	202	231	144	95	191	136	89	38	121	90	41	14	160	129	...	...
Ladákh	...	...	...	...	...	...	...	...	...	...	...	...	...	...	...	...	...	...	...	...	...
Skardu	...	...	...	...	...	...	...	...	...	...	...	...	...	...	...	...	...	...	...	...	...
Gilgit	...	...	...	...	...	...	...	...	...	...	...	...	...	...	...	...	...	...	...	...	...
TOTAL ...	11,399	6,258	5,141	496	367	456	439	336	248	396	303	223	127	298	194	99	48	400	292	...	...

SRINAGAR :
Dated the 3rd November, 1891.

BHAG RAM,
Census Superintendent, Kashmir State.

CENSUS 1891.

KASHMIR STATE.

TABLE VII.—PART H.—*Population by Age.—Parsis.*

Province.	Population.			Age Distribution.																			
				Under one year.		1—2.		2—3.		3—4.		4—5.		*Total under five.*		5—9.		10—14.		15—19.		20—24.	
	Total.	Males.	Females.	Males.	Females.	Males.	Females.	Males.	Females.	Males.	Females.	Males.	Females.	Males.	Females.	Males.	Females.	Males.	Females.	Males.	Females.	Males.	Females.
Jammu	1	1	...	...	...	...	...	...	...	...	...	...	...	...	...	...	...	...	...	...	...	...	...
Kashmír	8	6	2	...	...	...	...	...	...	...	...	1	...	1	...	...	...	1	...	1	...	...	1
Ladákh	...	...	...	...	...	...	...	...	...	...	...	...	...	...	...	...	...	...	...	...	...	...	...
Skardu	...	...	...	...	...	...	...	...	...	...	...	...	...	...	...	...	...	...	...	...	...	...	...
Gilgit	...	...	...	...	...	...	...	...	...	...	...	...	...	...	...	...	...	...	...	...	...	...	...
TOTAL ...	9	7	2	...	...	...	...	...	...	...	...	1	...	1	...	...	...	1	...	1	...	...	1

CENSUS 1891.

KASHMIR STATE.

TALBE VII.—PART H.—*Population by Age. Parsis.*

Province.	Population.			Age Distribution.																	
	Total.	Males.	Females.	25—29.		30—34.		35—39.		40—44.		45—49.		50—54.		55—59.		60 *and over.*		*Unspecified.*	
				Males.	Females.	Males.	Females.	Males.	Females.	Males.	Females.	Males.	Females.	Males.	Females.	Males.	Females.	Males.	Females.	Males.	Females.
Jammu	1	1	...	...	...	...	...	1	...	...	...	...	...	...	...	...	...	...	...	...	...
Kashmír	8	6	2	...	...	1	...	1	...	...	1	1	...	...	...	...	...	...	...	...	...
Ladákh	...	...	...	...	...	...	...	...	...	...	...	...	...	...	...	...	...	...	...	...	...
Skardu	...	...	...	...	...	...	...	...	...	...	...	...	...	...	...	...	...	...	...	...	...
Gilgit	...	...	...	...	...	...	...	...	...	...	...	...	...	...	...	...	...	...	...	...	...
TOTAL ...	9	7	2	...	...	1	...	2	...	...	1	1	...	...	...	...	...	...	...	...	...

SRINAGAR :
Dated the 3rd November 1891.

BHAG RAM,
Census Superintendent, Kashmir State.

CENSUS 1891.

KASHMIR STATE.

TABLE VII.—PART A.—*Population by Age—All religions.*—*(Provincial Summary.)*

Province.	Population.			Age Distribution.																	
				Under one year.		1—2.		2—3.		3—4.		4—5.		*Total under five.*		5—9.		10—14.		15—19.	
	Total.	Males.	Females.	Males.	Females.	Males.	Females.	Males.	Females.	Males.	Females.	Males.	Females.	Males.	Females.	Males.	Females.	Males.	Females.	Males.	Females.
JAMMU.																					
(*a*)—DISTRICTS.																					
Sri Ranbir Singhpora	239,585	132,899	106,686	4,687	4,451	2,182	2,102	3,261	3,139	3,681	3,444	4,048	3,596	17,859	16,732	15,450	13,399	13,095	9,536	10,602	8,673
Jasrota	151,518	81,434	70,084	2,572	2,586	1,146	1,117	1,866	1,850	2,164	2,164	2,084	2,106	9,832	9,823	9,757	8,886	8,221	5,730	6,879	5,893
Udhampore	150,707	81,092	69,615	3,263	3,105	1,031	1,083	1,940	1,834	2,421	2,435	2,325	2,208	10,980	10,665	10,287	8,961	7,503	5,519	6,122	5,686
Reasi	191,367	101,963	89,404	3,099	3,310	1,581	1,512	2,466	2,543	3,036	3,101	2,933	2,910	13,118	13,376	13,106	11,896	10,379	7,719	8,030	7,087
Bhimbar	355,499	188,253	167,246	8,010	7,987	1,801	1,766	5,408	5,090	6,562	6,643	6,741	6,403	28,522	27,889	28,130	24,931	20,664	15,529	14,667	13,485
TOTAL DISTRICTS (*a*) ...	1,088,676	585,641	503,035	21,631	21,439	7,744	7,580	14,941	14,456	17,864	17,787	18,131	17,223	80,311	78,485	76,730	68,073	59,862	44,033	46,300	40,824
(*b*)—JAGIRS.																					
Ramnagar	49,826	25,880	23,946	685	782	437	459	628	596	719	730	646	718	3,115	3,285	3,098	3,030	2,531	1,867	2,041	1,920
Bhadrawah...	32,433	16,775	15,658	426	360	387	382	428	500	449	492	425	436	2,115	2,170	1,990	1,918	1,649	1,363	1,423	1,574
Punch	268,608	141,945	126,663	6,680	7,050	2,407	2,323	4,925	5,050	5,747	6,222	5,647	5,630	25,406	26,275	22,339	20,353	15,177	10,943	10,985	9,154
TOTAL JAGIR (*a*) ...	350,867	184,600	166,267	7,791	8,192	3,231	3,164	5,981	6,146	6,915	7,444	6,718	6,784	30,636	31,730	27,427	25,301	19,357	14,173	14,449	12,648
TOTAL JAMMU PROVINCE ...	1,439,543	770,241	669,302	29,422	29,631	10,976	10,744	20,922	20,602	24,779	25,231	24,849	24,007	110,947	110,215	104,157	93,374	79,219	58,206	60,749	53,472

CENSUS 1891.

KASHMIR STATE.

TABLE VII.—PART A.—*Population by Age—All religions.—(Provincial Summary.)*

Province.	Population.			Age Distribution.																	
	Total.	Males.	Females.	*Under one year.*		1—2.		2—3.		3—4.		4—5.		*Total under five.*		5—9.		10—14.		15—19.	
				Males.	Females.	Males.	Females.	Males.	Females.	Males.	Females.	Males.	Females.	Males.	Females.	Males.	Females.	Males.	Females.	Males.	Females.
KASHMIR.																					
(*c*)—DISTRICTS.																					
Khas	309,785	163,752	146,033	7,927	7,764	2,349	2,297	6,159	6,038	6,861	6,784	5,803	5,500	29,099	28,383	23,346	20,892	14,997	10,442	13,002	11,087
Kamraj	255,564	134,755	120,809	8,068	7,908	2,083	2,052	6,203	6,112	6,791	6,609	5,706	5,146	28,851	27,827	20,706	18,618	11,718	8,504	9,906	8,886
Anantnag	224,558	118,125	106,433	6,302	6,010	1,887	1,889	4,616	4,567	5,027	4,898	4,714	4,326	22,546	21,690	17,761	15,906	11,642	8,605	9,491	8,212
Muzafferabad	134,800	72,881	61,919	3,157	3,319	1,077	975	2,826	2,868	3,153	3,211	3,179	2,962	13,392	13,335	12,603	10,442	6,955	4,651	5,704	4,963
TOTAL DISTRICTS.—(*c*) ...	924,707	489,513	435,194	25,454	25,001	7,396	7,213	19,804	19,585	21,832	21,502	19,402	17,934	93,888	91,235	74,416	65,858	45,312	32,202	38,103	33,148
(*d*).—JAGIRS																					
Raja Amar Singh	14,470	7,664	6,806	294	330	232	236	338	316	426	397	295	257	1,585	1,536	1,285	1,097	685	509	582	536
Raja Ram Singh	9,864	5,168	4,696	308	304	85	90	223	187	206	199	211	201	1,033	981	829	698	489	391	409	362
TOTAL JAGIRS (*d*) ...	24,334	12,832	11,502	602	634	317	326	561	503	632	596	506	458	2,618	2,517	2,114	1,795	1,174	900	991	898
TOTAL KASHMIR PROVINCE ...	949,041	502,345	446,696	26,056	25,635	7,713	7,539	20,365	20,088	22,464	22,098	19,908	18,392	96,506	93,752	76,530	67,653	46,486	33,102	39,094	34,046
(*e*).—FRONTIER DISTRICTS.																					
Ladákh	28,274	14,350	13,924	199	229	190	206	207	215	311	317	284	279	1,191	1,246	1,448	1,432	1,164	1,106	1,021	969
Skardu	110,325	56,098	54,227	1,384	1,663	1,109	1,206	1,418	1,524	1,625	1,933	1,507	1,588	7,043	7,914	7,830	7,602	6,164	5,101	5,264	4,441
Gilgit	16,769	10,195	6,574	...	1	...	...	...	1	...	...	...	...	...	2	...	...	2	...	7	...
TOTAL DISTRICTS (*e*) ...	155,368	80,643	74,725	1,583	1,893	1,299	1,412	1,625	1,740	1,936	2,250	1,791	1,867	8,234	9,162	9,278	9,034	7,330	6,207	6,292	5,410
GRAND TOTAL KASHMIR STATE ...	2,543,952	1,353,229	1,190,723	57,061	57,159	19,987	19,695	42,912	42,430	49,179	49,579	46,548	44,266	215,687	213,129	189,965	170,061	133,035	97,515	106,135	92,928

CENSUS 1891.

KASHMIR STATE.

TABLE VII.—PART A.—*Population by age—All religions.*—(*Provincial Summary.*)

Province.	Age Distribution.																			
	20—24.		25—29.		30—34.		35—39.		40—44.		45—49.		50—54.		55—59.		60 *and over.*		*Unspecified.*	
	Males.	Females.	Males.	Females.	Males.	Females.	Males.	Females.	Males.	Females.	Males.	Females.	Males.	Females.	Males.	Females.	Males.	Females.	Males.	Females.
JAMMU.																				
(*a*).—DISTRICTS.																				
Sri Ranbir Singhpora	11,521	9,983	13,051	10,284	12,224	9,283	7,922	5,687	8,706	6,933	5,294	3,659	6,343	4,869	2,652	1,765	8,091	5,807	89	76
Jasrota	6,780	6,512	7,824	6,964	7,247	6,190	5,089	4,008	5,601	4,908	3,377	2,379	3,962	3,297	1,359	1,036	5,506	4,448	...	10
Udhampore	5,984	6,190	6,632	6,475	7,179	6,692	4,349	3,692	6,048	5,063	2,961	1,890	4,268	3,014	1,183	751	7,057	5,017	39	...
Reasi...	7,812	7,982	8,556	8,154	9,040	8,239	6,020	4,821	6,986	6,046	3,859	2,756	5,264	3,995	1,806	1,203	7,987	6,105	...	25
Bhimbar	13,044	14,697	14,842	15,334	16,161	15,076	10,727	8,631	11,646	9,916	6,586	4,681	8,337	6,121	2,796	1,995	12,131	8,961	...	...
TOTAL DISTRICTS (*a*) ...	45,141	45,364	50,905	47,211	51,851	45,480	34,607	26,839	38,987	32,866	22,077	15,366	28,174	21,296	9,796	6,750	40,772	30,338	128	111
(*b*).—JAGIRS.																				
Ramnagar	1,837	2,081	2,186	2,186	2,265	2,123	1,600	1,435	1,826	1,660	1,042	739	1,504	1,224	528	355	2,307	2,041	...	...
Bhadrawah	1,196	1,463	1,352	1,509	1,434	1,429	1,050	880	1,211	1,130	656	464	977	725	290	158	1,432	875	...	...
Punch	9,192	9,331	9,931	10,110	11,410	11,564	8,581	6,615	8,541	7,332	5,101	3,225	5,707	4,234	1,566	1,146	8,009	6,381	...	...
TOTAL JAGIRS (*b*). ...	12,225	12,875	13,469	13,805	15,109	15,116	11,231	8,930	11,578	10,122	6,799	4,428	8,188	6,183	2,384	1,659	11,748	9,297	...	...
TOTAL JAMMU PROVINCE ...	57,366	58,239	64,374	61,016	66,960	60,596	45,838	35,769	50,565	42,988	28,876	19,793	36,362	27,479	12,180	8,409	52,520	39,635	128	111

CENSUS 1891.

KASHMIR STATE.

TABLE VII.—PART A.—*Population by Age—All religions.—(Provincial Summary.)*

Province.	Age Distribution.																			
	20—24.		25—29.		30—34.		35—39.		40—44.		45—49.		50—54.		55—59.		*60 and over.*		*Unspecified.*	
	Males.	Females.	Males.	Females.	Males.	Females.	Males.	Females.	Males.	Females.	Males.	Females.	Males.	Females.	Males.	Females.	Males.	Females.	Males.	Females.
KASHMIR.																				
(c).—DISTRICTS.																				
Khas	13,567	14,299	12,537	12,455	13,501	12,837	8,972	7,170	10,450	10,841	5,999	4,114	7,784	6,026	2,326	1,287	8,172	6,200	...	...
Kamraj	9,666	10,494	10,268	10,209	10,477	10,156	7,182	5,802	8,350	7,696	4,157	2,633	5,269	4,048	1,381	886	6,824	5,050	...	...
Anantnag	9,041	9,431	8,448	8,723	8,803	8,373	6,214	5,418	7,131	6,872	4,247	3,181	4,729	3,886	1,689	1,257	6,383	4,819	...	30
Muzafferabad	5,345	5,369	5,608	5,443	6,539	5,846	3,517	2,546	4,903	3,836	1,656	867	2,821	1,891	561	333	3,277	2,397	...	...
TOTAL DISTRICTS (c) ...	37,619	39,593	36,861	36,830	39,320	37,212	25,885	20,966	30,834	29,245	16,059	10,795	20,603	15,851	5,957	3,763	24,656	18,466	...	30
(d).—JAGIRS.																				
Raja Amar Singh	529	594	569	585	568	583	393	313	501	418	203	145	274	187	92	49	398	254	...	...
Raja Ram Singh	425	456	377	398	395	341	241	261	302	267	172	140	192	173	50	44	254	184	...	...
TOTAL JAGIRS (d) ...	954	1,050	946	983	963	924	634	574	803	685	375	285	466	360	142	93	652	438	...	...
TOTAL KASHMIR PROVINCE ...	38,573	40,643	37,807	37,813	40,283	38,136	26,519	21,540	31,637	29,930	16,434	11,080	21,069	16,211	6,099	3,856	25,308	18,904	...	30
(e).—FRONTIER DISTRICTS.																				
Ladákh	1,121	1,055	1,210	1,110	1,111	1,042	1,068	1,048	1,024	974	833	820	647	652	682	661	1,830	1,809	...	...
Skardu	6,274	6,907	2,029	1,827	3,380	3,164	5,217	5,374	2,284	2,023	3,392	3,717	1,566	1,166	777	550	4,866	4,431	12	10
Gilgit	39	...	30	1	24	1	14	...	11	...	8	...	10	...	3	...	2	...	10,045	6,570
TOTAL DISTRICTS (e) ...	7,434	7,962	3,269	2,938	4,515	4,207	6,299	6,422	3,319	2,997	4,233	4,537	2,223	1,818	1,462	1,211	6,698	6,240	10,057	6,580
GRAND TOTAL KASHMIR STATE ...	103,373	106,844	105,450	101,767	111,758	102,939	78,656	63,731	85,521	75,915	49,543	35,410	59,654	45,508	19,741	13,476	84,526	64,779	10,185	6,721

SRINAGAR :
Dated the 3rd November, 1891.

BHAG RAM,
Census Superintendent, Kashmir State.

CENSUS 1891.

KASHMIR STATE.

TABLE VII.—PART B.—*Population by Age.—Hindus.—(Provincial Summary).*

Province.	Population.			Age Distribution.																	
				Under one year.		1—2.		2—3.		3—4.		4—5.		*Total under five.*		5—9.		10—14.		15—19.	
	Total.	Males.	Females.	Males.	Females.	Males.	Females.	Males.	Females.	Males.	Females.	Males.	Females.	Males.	Females.	Males.	Females.	Males.	Females.	Males.	Females.
JAMMU.																					
(*a*).—DISTRICTS.																					
Sri Ranbir Singhpora ...	145,006	80,915	64,091	2,704	2,617	1,307	1,253	1,962	1,799	2,203	1,999	2,407	2,211	10,583	9,879	8,944	7,697	7,810	5,516	6,479	5,144
Jasrota	124,109	66,233	57,876	1,987	1,990	914	906	1,471	1,456	1,639	1,737	1,650	1,634	7,661	7,723	7,751	7,172	6,650	4,589	5,555	4,717
Udhampore	86,795	46,673	40,122	1,706	1,492	499	532	913	842	1,239	1,252	1,090	1,084	5,447	5,202	5,298	4,726	4,034	2,934	3,325	3,190
Reasi	124,749	66,194	58,555	1,854	1,918	945	870	1,410	1,461	1,749	1,804	1,701	1,726	7,659	7,779	8,040	7,442	6,733	4,898	5,200	4,574
Bhimbar	60,587	32,709	27,878	1,331	1,300	280	247	753	703	918	908	978	921	4,260	4,079	4,342	3,831	3,583	2,473	2,715	2,274
TOTAL DISTRICTS (*a*) ...	541,246	292,724	248,522	9,582	9,317	3,945	3,808	6,509	6,261	7,748	7,700	7,826	7,576	35,610	34,662	34,375	30,868	28,810	20,410	23,274	19,899
(*b*).—JAGIRS.																					
Ramnagar	44,398	22,970	21,428	582	664	381	419	564	521	621	632	553	627	2,701	2,863	2,729	2,665	2,226	1,631	1,815	1,702
Bhadrawah	21,269	10,831	10,438	287	246	217	224	259	301	258	316	247	259	1,268	1,346	1,262	1,222	1,015	859	910	1,010
Punch	24,312	13,481	10,831	517	586	170	161	355	345	404	431	403	401	1,849	1,924	1,834	1,685	1,370	969	1,124	851
TOTAL JAGIRS (*b*) ...	89,979	47,282	42,697	1,386	1,496	768	804	1,178	1,167	1,283	1,379	1,203	1,287	5,818	6,133	5,825	5,572	4,611	3,459	3,849	3,563
TOTAL JAMMU PROVINCE ...	631,225	340,006	291,219	10,968	10,813	4,713	4,612	7,687	7,428	9,031	9,079	9,029	8,863	41,428	40,795	40,200	36,440	33,421	23,869	27,123	23,462

CENSUS 1891.

KASHMIR STATE.

TABLE VII.—PART B.—*Population by Age.—Hindus.—(Provincial Summary.)*—(Continued).

Province.	Population.			Age Distribution.																			
				Under one year.		1—2.		2—3.		3—4.		4—5.		*Total under five.*		5—9.		10—14.		15—19.	
	Total.	Males.	Females.	Males.	Females.	Males.	Females.	Males.	Females.	Males.	Females.	Males.	Females.	Males.	Females.	Males.	Females.	Males.	Females.	Males.	Females.
KASHMIR.																					
(c).—DISTRICTS.																					
Khas	32,799	18,386	14,413	556	545	159	159	428	409	402	450	390	394	1,935	1,957	2,074	1,858	1,848	1,079	1,665	1,194
Kamraj	7,492	4,368	3,124	198	194	32	29	112	128	138	104	120	104	600	559	512	430	389	298	350	217
Anantnag	11,327	6,335	4,992	298	259	60	63	188	187	201	177	187	171	934	857	747	725	628	436	538	374
Muzafferabad	7,740	4,509	3,231	183	178	56	37	144	126	158	132	161	131	702	604	646	552	452	283	344	291
TOTAL DISTRICTS (c) ...	59,358	33,598	25,760	1,235	1,176	307	288	872	850	899	863	858	800	4,171	3,977	3,979	3,565	3,317	2,096	2,897	2,076
(d.)—JAGIRS.																					
Raja Amar Singh	411	251	160	8	10	3	2	6	5	9	9	12	2	38	28	24	25	21	13	22	13
Raja Ram Singh	547	302	245	15	14	...	2	15	4	14	8	11	7	55	35	40	36	33	33	21	16
TOTAL JAGIRS (d) ...	958	553	405	23	24	3	4	21	9	23	17	23	9	93	63	64	61	54	46	43	29
TOTAL KASHMIR PROVINCE ...	60,316	34,151	26,165	1,258	1,200	310	292	893	859	922	880	881	809	4,264	4,040	4,043	3,626	3,371	2,142	2,940	2,105
(e).—FRONTIER DISTRICTS.																					
Ladákh	182	172	10	...	...	...	...	...	...	...	1	...	...	...	1	...	...	1	...	3	1
Skardu	64	57	7	...	...	...	...	...	...	...	...	...	...	...	...	...	...	...	...	4	2
Gilgit	13	13	...	...	...	...	...	...	...	...	...	...	...	...	...	...	...	...	...	2	...
TOTAL DISTRICTS (e) ...	259	242	17	...	...	...	...	...	...	...	1	...	...	...	1	...	...	1	...	9	3
GRAND TOTAL KASHMIR STATE ...	691,800	374,399	317,401	12,226	12,013	5,023	4,904	8,580	8,287	9,953	9,960	9,910	9,672	45,692	44,836	44,243	40,066	36,793	26,011	30,072	25,570

CENSUS 1891.

KASHMIR STATE.

Table VII.—Part B.—*Population by Age.—Hindus.—(Provincial Summary.)*—(Continued).

Province.	Age Distribution.																			
	20—24.		25—29.		30—34.		35—39.		40—44.		45—49.		50—54.		55—59.		60 *and over.*		*Unspecified.*	
	Males.	Females.	Males.	Females.	Males.	Females.	Males.	Females.	Males.	Females.	Males.	Females.	Males.	Females.	Males.	Females.	Males.	Females.	Males.	Females.
JAMMU.																				
(*a*).—Districts.																				
Sri Ranbir Singhpora ...	7,160	6,152	8,068	6,226	7,443	5,615	4,945	3,549	5,369	4,261	3,357	2,253	3,955	3,031	1,717	1,111	4,996	3,581	89	76
Jasrota	5,540	5,372	6,359	5,864	5,894	5,218	4,266	3,422	4,638	4,138	2,873	2,060	3,266	2,846	1,168	894	4,612	3,851	...	10
Udhampore	3,379	3,599	3,947	3,852	4,313	4,092	3,034	2,332	3,691	3,106	1,891	1,247	2,706	1,930	789	488	4,780	3,424	39	...
Reasi	5,109	5,281	5,660	5,566	5,895	5,474	4,043	3,328	4,699	4,146	2,673	1,966	3,573	2,796	1,277	884	5,633	4,396	...	25
Bhimbar	2,390	2,564	2,670	2,651	2,908	2,581	1,887	1,544	2,158	1,812	1,304	896	1,622	1,146	599	400	2,271	1,627	...	...
Total Districts (*a*) ...	23,578	22,968	26,704	24,159	26,453	22,980	18,175	14,175	20,555	17,463	12,098	8,422	15,122	11,749	5,550	3,777	22,292	16,879	128	111
(*b*).—Jagirs.																				
Ramnagar	1,617	1,853	1,925	1,981	2,023	1,932	1,426	1,311	1,633	1,495	940	676	1,361	1,113	479	339	2,095	1,867	...	...
Bhadrawah	726	944	869	1,007	920	972	692	615	788	764	459	349	655	539	224	113	1,043	698	...	...
Punch	1,016	774	1,178	948	1,139	941	855	527	846	667	561	324	635	435	222	138	852	648	...	...
Total Jagirs (*b*) ...	3,359	3,571	3,972	3,936	4,082	3,845	2,973	2,453	3,267	2,926	1,960	1,349	2,651	2,087	925	590	3,990	3,213	...	...
Total Jammu Province ...	26,937	26,539	30,676	28,095	30,535	26,825	21,148	16,628	23,822	20,389	14,058	9,771	17,773	13,836	6,475	4,367	26,282	20,092	128	111

CENSUS 1891.

KASHMIR STATE.

TABLE VII.—PART B.—*Population by Age.—Hindus.—(Provincial Summary.*—(Concluded).

Province.	Age Distribution.																			
	20—24.		25—29.		30—34.		35—39.		40—44.		45—49.		50—54.		55—59.		*60 and over.*		*Unspecified.*	
	Males.	Females.	Males.	Females.	Males.	Females.	Males.	Females.	Males.	Females.	Males.	Females.	Males.	Females.	Males.	Females.	Males.	Females.	Males.	Females.
KASHMIR.																				
(*c*).—DISTRICTS.																				
Khas	1,816	1,560	1,631	1,365	1,669	1,406	1,208	726	1,359	1,148	817	465	925	732	389	180	1,050	743	...	...
Kamraj	395	277	427	259	325	211	287	199	300	179	188	126	208	134	85	49	302	186	...	...
Anantnag	549	437	476	400	474	315	438	297	373	309	338	189	242	226	156	97	442	300	...	30
Muzafferabad	369	294	411	280	436	278	237	126	308	206	145	48	157	117	66	14	236	138	...	...
TOTAL DISTRICTS (*c*) ...	3,129	2,568	2,945	2,304	2,904	2,210	2,170	1,348	2,340	1,842	1,488	828	1,532	1,209	696	340	2,030	1,367	...	30
(*d*).—JAGIRS.																				
Raja Amar Singh	33	17	16	5	17	13	15	9	14	7	10	7	11	8	6	4	24	11	...	...
„ Ram Singh	29	25	14	11	16	14	19	24	22	14	18	10	15	12	4	4	16	11	...	...
TOTAL JAGIRS (*d*) ...	62	42	30	16	33	27	34	33	36	21	28	17	26	20	10	8	40	22	...	...
TOTAL KASHMIR PROVINCE ...	3,191	2,610	2,975	2,320	2,937	2,237	2,204	1,381	2,376	1,863	1,516	845	1,558	1,229	706	348	2,070	1,389	...	30
(*e*).—FRONTIER DISTRICTS.																				
Ladákh	29	5	67	3	32	...	14	...	12	...	9	...	1	...	1	...	3	...	...	...
Skardu	4	...	11	1	7	1	11	...	5	3	3	...	6	...	2	...	4	...	...	...
Gilgit	2	...	2	...	1	...	3	...	2	...	1	...	...	...	...	...	...	...	...	...
TOTAL DISTRICTS (*e*) ...	35	5	80	4	40	1	28	...	19	3	13	...	7	...	3	...	7	...	...	...
GRAND TOTAL KASHMIR STATE ...	30,163	29,154	33,731	30.419	33,512	29,063	23,380	18,009	26,217	22,255	15,587	10,616	19,338	15,065	7,184	4,715	28,359	21,481	128	141

SRINAGAR :
Dated the 3rd November 1891.

BHAG RAM,
Census Superintendent, Kashmir State.

CENSUS 1891.

KASHMIR STATE.

TABLE VII.—PART C.—*Population by Age. Mohamedans. (Provincial Summary).*

Province.	Population.			Age Distribution.																			
				Under one year.		1—2.		2—3.		3—4.		4—5.		*Total under five.*		5—9.		10—14.		15—19.	
	Total.	Males.	Females.	Males.	Females.	Males.	Females.	Males.	Females.	Males.	Females.	Males.	Females.	Males.	Females.	Males.	Females.	Males.	Females.	Males.	Females.
JAMMU.																					
(a).—DISTRICTS.																					
Sri Ranbir Singhpora	93,705	51,475	42,230	1,969	1,824	864	841	1,277	1,330	1,465	1,432	1,633	1,380	7,208	6,807	6,457	5,665	5,245	3,976	4,074	3,496
Jasrota	27,388	15,186	12,202	583	595	232	211	394	394	525	427	434	472	2,168	2,099	2,005	1,714	1,570	1,140	1,324	1,176
Udhampore	59,591	32,220	27,371	1,518	1,548	529	549	989	970	1,136	1,131	1,191	1,090	5,363	5,288	4,728	4,004	3,233	2,384	2,618	2,275
Reasi	66,590	35,751	30,839	1,244	1,392	689	642	1,055	1,082	1,287	1,296	1,231	1,184	5,456	5,596	5,064	4,452	3,645	2,820	2,829	2,513
Bhimbar	294,014	155,025	138,989	6,658	6,670	1,513	1,516	4.627	4,375	5,627	5,717	5,743	5,467	24,168	23,745	23,738	21,063	17,043	13,031	11,916	11,187
TOTAL DISTRICTS (a) ...	541,288	289,657	251,631	11,972	12,029	3,777	3,759	8,342	8,151	10,040	10,003	10,232	9,593	44,363	43,535	41,992	36,888	30,736	23,351	22,761	20,647
(b).—JAGIRS.																					
Ramnagar	5,423	2,906	2,517	103	118	56	40	64	75	98	98	93	91	414	422	369	364	305	236	226	218
Bhadrawah	11,163	5,943	5,220	139	114	170	158	169	199	191	176	178	177	847	824	728	696	634	504	513	564
Punch	239,585	125,865	113,720	6,026	6,356	2,210	2,140	4,502	4,636	5,239	5,699	5,143	5,153	23,120	23,984	20,105	18,313	13,496	9,748	9,674	8,146
TOTAL JAGIRS (b) ...	256,171	134,714	121,457	6,268	6,588	2,436	2,338	4,735	4,910	5,528	5,973	5,414	5,421	24,381	25,230	21,202	19,373	14,435	10,488	10,413	8,928
TOTAL JAMMU PROVINCE ...	797,459	424,371	373,088	18,240	18,617	6,213	6,097	13,077	13,061	15,568	15,976	15,646	15,014	68,744	68,765	63,194	56,261	45,171	33,839	33,174	29,575

CENSUS 1891.

KASHMIR STATE.

Table VII.—Part C.—*Population by Age.—Mohamedans.* (*Provincial Summary.*)—(Continued).

Province.	Population.			Age Distribution.																	
				Under one year.		1—2.		2—3.		3—4.		4—5.		*Total under five*		5—9.		10—14.		15—19.	
	Total.	Males.	Females.	Males.	Females.	Males.	Females.	Males.	Females.	Males.	Females.	Males.	Females.	Males.	Females.	Males.	Females.	Males.	Females.	Males.	Females.
KASHMIR.																					
(*c*).—Districts.																					
Khas	275,233	144,441	130,792	7,337	7,191	2,174	2,120	5,695	5,605	6,412	6,290	5,381	5,072	26,999	26,278	21,136	18,922	13,053	9,275	11,267	9,813
Kamraj	245,988	129,302	116,686	7,814	7,649	2,040	2,021	6,062	5,941	6,611	6,449	5,547	5,010	28,074	27,070	20,029	18,030	11,201	8,100	9,463	8,575
Anantnag	212,838	111,587	101,251	5,993	5,743	1,827	1,826	4,424	4,374	4,817	4,711	4,524	4,149	21,585	20,803	16,980	15,147	10,993	8,151	8,936	7,821
Muzafferabad	125,666	67,567	58,099	2,944	3,102	1,013	932	2,664	2,711	2,960	3,051	2,995	2,810	12,576	12,606	11,838	9,794	6,417	4,318	5,279	4,615
Total Districts (*c*) ...	859,725	452,897	406,828	24,088	23,685	7,054	6,899	18,845	18,631	20,800	20,501	18,447	17,041	89,234	86,757	69,978	61,893	41,664	29,844	34,945	30,824
(*d*).—Jagirs.																					
Raja Amar Singh	14,057	7,411	6,646	286	320	229	234	332	311	417	388	283	255	1,547	1,508	1,261	1,072	664	496	560	523
Raja Ram Singh	9,317	4,866	4,451	293	290	85	88	208	183	192	191	200	194	978	946	789	662	456	358	388	346
Total Jagirs (*d*) ...	23,374	12,277	11,097	579	610	314	322	540	494	609	579	483	449	2,525	2,454	2,050	1,734	1,120	854	948	869
Total Kashmir Province ...	883,099	465,174	417,925	24,667	24,295	7,368	7,221	19,385	19,125	21,409	21,080	18,930	17,490	91,759	89,211	72,028	63,627	42,784	30,698	35,893	31,693
(*e*)—Frontier Districts.																					
Ladákh	2,991	1,552	1,439	16	21	27	31	30	26	35	43	41	34	149	155	177	173	145	133	127	96
Skardu	110,022	55,893	54,129	1,383	1,662	1,109	1,206	1,417	1,523	1,622	1,930	1,506	1,579	7,037	7,900	7,818	7,599	6,149	5,091	5,252	4,435
Gilgit	139	136	3	...	1	...	...	...	1	...	...	...	...	...	2	...	...	2	...	5	...
Total Districts (*e*) ...	113,152	57,581	55,571	1,399	1,684	1,136	1,237	1,447	1,550	1,657	1,973	1,547	1,613	7,186	8,057	7,995	7,772	6,296	5,224	5,384	4,531
Grand Total Kashmir State ...	1,793,710	947,126	846,584	44,306	44,596	14,717	14,555	33,909	33,736	38,634	39,029	36,123	34,117	167,689	166,033	143,217	127,660	94,251	69,761	74,451	65,799

CENSUS 1891.

KASHMIR STATE.

TABLE VII.—PART C.—*Population by Age.—Mohamedans.* (*Provincial Summary.*)—(Continued).

Province.	Age Distribution.																			
	20—24.		25—29.		30—34.		35—39.		40—44.		45—49.		50—54.		55—59.		60 *and over.*		*Unspecified.*	
	Males.	Females.	Males.	Females.	Males.	Females.	Males.	Females.	Males.	Females.	Males.	Females.	Males.	Females.	Males.	Females.	Males.	Females.	Males.	Females.
JAMMU.																				
(*a*).—DISTRICTS.																				
Sri Ranbir Singhpora	4,320	3,795	4,940	4,027	4,733	3,629	2,945	2,116	3,297	2,648	1,910	1,391	2,357	1,815	919	646	3,070	2,219	...	...
Jasrola	1,239	1,140	1,465	1,100	1,351	972	821	584	962	770	502	319	696	451	191	141	892	596	...	...
Udhampore	2,423	2,417	2,488	2,385	2,689	2,411	1,684	1,232	2,216	1,806	954	544	1,441	986	325	210	2,058	1,429	...	...
Reasi	2,699	2,699	2,895	2,587	3,144	2,765	1,975	1,490	12,287	1,900	1,185	790	1,690	1,199	529	319	2,353	1,709	...	...
Bhimbar	10,624	12,097	12,121	12,657	13,210	12,467	8,810	7,063	9,457	8,077	5,256	3,767	6,678	4,951	2,183	1,584	9,821	7,310	...	...
TOTAL DISTRICTS (*a*). ...	21,305	22,148	23,909	22,756	25,127	22,244	16,235	12,485	18,219	15,201	9,807	6,811	12,862	9,402	4,147	2,900	18,194	13,263	...	...
(*b*).—JAGIRS.																				
Ramnagar	219	228	260	205	242	191	173	124	193	165	102	63	143	111	49	16	211	174	...	...
Bhadrawah	470	519	483	502	514	457	358	265	423	366	197	115	322	186	66	45	388	177	...	...
Punch	8,040	8,416	8,580	9,019	10,073	10,453	7,571	5,965	7,541	6,533	4,443	2,831	4,942	3,726	1,304	987	6,976	5,599	...	...
TOTAL JAGIRS (*b*) ...	8,729	9,163	9,323	9,726	10,829	11,101	8,102	6,354	8,157	7,064	4,742	3,009	5,407	4,023	1,419	1,048	7,575	5,950	...	...
TOTAL JAMMU PROVINCE ...	30,034	31,311	33,232	32,482	35,956	33,345	24,337	18,839	26,376	22,265	14,549	9,820	18,269	13,425	5,566	3,948	25,769	19,213	...	...

CENSUS 1891.

KASHMIR STATE.

TABLE VII.—PART C.—*Population by Age.—Mohamedans. (Provincial Summary.)*—(Concluded).

Province.	Age Distribution.																			
	20—24.		25—29.		30—34.		35—39.		40—44.		45—49.		50—54.		55—59.		60 *and over.*		*Unspecified.*	
	Males.	Females.	Males.	Females.	Males.	Females.	Males.	Females.	Males.	Females.	Males.	Females.	Males.	Females.	Males.	Females.	Males.	Females.	Males.	Females.
KASHMIR.																				
(*c*).—DISTRICTS.																				
Khas	11,688	12,657	10,822	11,014	11,755	11,360	7,723	6,403	9,034	9,653	5,148	3,635	6,825	5,266	1,924	1,103	7,067	5,413	...	...
Kamraj	9,186	10,187	9,752	9,869	10,075	9,853	6,843	5,561	7,975	7,466	3,931	2,492	5,018	3,886	1,284	828	6,471	4,819	...	...
Anantnag	8,476	8,975	7,953	8,310	8,316	8,044	5,766	5,144	6,742	6,548	3,902	2,988	4,476	3,652	1,531	1,159	5,931	4,509	...	...
Muzafferabad	4,901	5,026	5,134	5,126	6,051	5,509	3,233	2,406	4,546	3,595	1,495	811	2,629	1,748	480	316	2,993	2,229	...	...
TOTAL DISTRICTS (*c*) ...	34,251	36,795	33,661	34,319	36,197	34,766	23,565	19,514	28,297	27,262	14,476	9,926	18,948	14,552	5,219	3,406	22,462	16,970	...	...
(*d*).—JAGIRS.																				
Raja Amar Singh	496	577	553	580	551	570	378	304	486	411	193	138	262	179	86	45	374	243	...	...
Raja Ram Singh	396	431	363	387	379	327	222	237	280	253	154	130	177	161	46	40	238	173	...	...
TOTAL JAGIRS (*d*) ...	892	1,008	916	967	930	897	600	541	766	664	347	268	439	340	132	85	612	416	...	...
TOTAL KASHMIR PROVINCE ...	35,143	37,803	34,577	35,286	37,127	35,663	24,165	20,055	29,063	27,926	14,823	10,194	19,387	14,892	5,351	3,491	23,074	17,386	...	...
(*e*).—FRONTIER DISTRICTS.																				
Ladákh	132	117	136	131	145	122	116	115	108	103	72	73	77	74	42	30	126	117	...	...
Skardu	6,258	6,901	2,008	1,816	3,361	3,160	5,193	5,366	2,274	2,012	3,377	3,709	1,549	1,163	771	549	4,834	4,418	12	10
Gilgit	37	...	28	1	23	...	11	...	8	...	7	...	10	...	3	...	2	...	...	...
TOTAL DISTRICTS (*e*) ...	6,427	7,018	2,172	1,948	3,529	3,282	5,320	5,481	2,390	2,115	3,456	3,782	1,636	1,237	816	579	4,962	4,535	12	10
GRAND TOTAL KASHMIR STATE ...	71,604	76,132	69,981	69,716	76,612	72,290	53,822	44,375	57,829	52,306	32,828	23,796	39,292	29,554	11,733	8,018	53,805	41,134	12	10

SRINAGAR :
Dated the 3rd November, 1891.

BHAG RAM,
Census Superintendent, Kashmír State.

CENSUS 1891.

KASHMIR STATE.

TABLE VII.—PART D.—*Population by Age. Christians.* (*Provincial Summary.*)

Province.	Population.			Age Distribution.																			
				Under one year.		1—2.		2—3.		3—4.		4—5.		*Total under five.*		5—9.		10—14.		15—19.	
	Total.	Males.	Females.	Males.	Females.	Males.	Females.	Males.	Females.	Males.	Females.	Males.	Females.	Males.	Females.	Males.	Females.	Males.	Females.	Males.	Females.
JAMMU.																					
(*a*).—DISTRICTS.																					
Sri Ranbir Singhpora ...	37	20	17	...	1	1	...	5	...	...	1	...	...	6	2	1	1	...	1	1	3
Jasrota	...	...	...	...	...	...	...	...	...	...	...	...	...	...	...	...	...	...	...	...	...
Udhampore	1	1	...	...	...	...	...	...	...	...	...	...	...	...	...	...	...	...	...	...	...
Reasi	...	...	...	...	...	...	...	...	...	...	...	...	...	...	...	...	...	...	...	...	...
Bhimbar	...	...	...	...	...	...	...	...	...	...	...	...	...	...	...	...	...	...	...	...	...
TOTAL DISTRICTS (*a*) ...	38	21	17	...	1	1	...	5	...	...	1	...	...	6	2	1	1	...	1	1	3
(*b*).—JAGIRS.																					
Ramnagar	...	...	...	...	...	...	...	...	...	...	...	...	...	...	...	...	...	...	...	...	...
Bhadrawah	...	...	...	...	...	...	...	...	...	...	...	...	...	...	...	...	...	...	...	...	...
Punch	8	3	5	...	...	...	...	...	...	...	...	...	1	...	1	...	...	2	1	...	...
TOTAL JAGIRS (*b*) ...	8	3	5	...	...	...	...	...	...	...	...	...	1	...	1	...	...	2	1	...	...
TOTAL JAMMU PROVINCE ...	46	24	22	...	1	1	...	5	...	...	1	...	1	6	3	1	1	2	2	1	3

CENSUS 1891.

KASHMIR STATE.

PABLE VII.—PART D.—*Population by Age. Christians. (Provincial Summary).*—(Continued.)

Province.	Population.			Age Distribution.																	
				Under one year.		1—2.		2—3.		3—4.		4—5.		*Total under five.*		5—9.		10—14.		15—19.	
	Total.	Males.	Females.	Males.	Females.	Males.	Females.	Males.	Females.	Males.	Females.	Males.	Females.	Males.	Females.	Males.	Females.	Males.	Females.	Males.	Females.
KASHMIR.																					
(c).—DISTRICTS.																					
Khas	128	61	67	1	1	1	2	3	2	4	5	1	...	10	10	10	6	2	4	...	4
Kamraj	2	2	...	...	...	...	...	...	...	...	...	...	...	...	...	...	...	...	...	...	...
Anantnag	2	1	1	...	...	...	...	...	...	...	...	...	...	...	...	...	...	...	...	...	...
Muzafferabad	13	13	...	...	...	...	...	...	...	...	...	...	...	...	...	1	...	...	...	...	...
TOTAL DISTRICTS (c) ...	145	77	68	1	1	1	2	3	2	4	5	1	...	10	10	11	6	2	4	...	4
(d).—JAGIRS.																					
Raja Amar Singh	...	...	...	...	...	...	...	...	...	...	...	...	...	...	...	...	...	...	...	...	...
Raja Ram Singh	...	...	...	...	...	...	...	...	...	...	...	...	...	...	...	...	...	...	...	...	...
TOTAL JAGIRS (d) ...	...	...	...	...	...	...	...	...	...	...	...	...	...	...	...	...	...	...	...	...	...
TOTAL KASHMIR PROVINCE ...	145	77	68	1	1	1	2	3	2	4	5	1	...	10	10	11	6	2	4	...	4
(e).—FRONTIER DISTRICTS.																					
Ladákh	25	11	14	...	1	...	...	...	...	1	...	...	...	1	1	2	4	...	2	1	2
Skardu	...	...	...	...	...	...	...	...	...	...	...	...	...	...	...	...	...	...	...	...	...
Gilgit	2	1	1	...	...	...	...	...	...	...	...	...	...	...	...	...	...	...	...	...	...
TOTAL DISTRICTS (e) ...	27	12	15	...	1	...	...	...	...	1	...	...	...	1	1	2	4	...	2	1	2
GRAND TOTAL KASHMIR STATE ...	218	113	105	1	3	2	2	8	2	5	6	1	1	17	14	14	11	4	8	2	9

CENSUS 1891.

KASHMIR STATE.

TABLE VII.—PART D.—*Population by Age. Christians.*—(*Provincial Summary.*)—(Continued.)

PROVINCE.	AGE DISTRIBUTION.																			
	20—24.		25—29.		30—34.		35—39.		40—44.		45—49.		50—54.		55—59.		60 *and over.*		*Unspecified.*	
	Males.	Females.	Males.	Females.	Males.	Females.	Males.	Females.	Males.	Females.	Males.	Females.	Males.	Females.	Males.	Females.	Males.	Females.	Males.	Females.
JAMMU.																				
(*a*).—DISTRICTS.																				
Sri Ranbir Singhpora	...	2	1	3	4	2	1	2	3	...	8	1	...	...	...	...	...	...	...	...
Jasrota	...	...	...	...	...	...	...	...	...	...	...	...	...	...	...	...	...	...	...	...
Udhampore	...	...	...	...	...	...	...	...	1	...	...	...	...	...	...	...	...	...	...	...
Reasi	...	...	...	...	...	...	...	...	...	...	...	...	...	...	...	...	...	...	...	...
Bhimbar	...	...	...	...	...	...	...	...	...	...	...	...	...	...	...	...	...	...	...	...
TOTAL DISTRICTS (*a*) ...	...	2	1	3	4	2	1	2	4	...	8	1	...	...	...	...	...	...	...	...
(*b*).—JAGIRS.																				
Ramnagar	...	...	...	...	...	...	...	...	...	...	...	...	...	...	...	...	...	...	...	...
Bhadrawah	...	...	...	...	...	...	...	...	...	...	...	...	...	...	...	...	...	...	...	...
Punch	...	...	...	...	1	2	...	...	...	...	...	...	...	1	...	...	...	...	...	...
TOTAL JAGIRS (*b*) ...	...	...	...	...	1	2	...	...	...	...	...	...	...	1	...	...	...	...	...	...
TOTAL JAMMU PROVINCE ...	...	2	1	3	5	4	1	2	4	...	8	1	...	1	...	...	...	...	...	...

CENSUS 1891.

KASHMIR STATE.

TABLE VII.—PART D.—*Population by Age—Christians—(Provincial Summary.)*—(Concluded).

PROVINCE.	AGE DISTRIBUTION.																			
	20—24.		25—29.		30—34.		35—39.		40—44.		45—49.		50—54.		55—59.		60 *and over.*		*Unspecified.*	
	Males.	Females.	Males.	Females.	Males.	Females.	Males.	Females.	Males.	Females.	Males.	Females.	Males.	Females.	Males.	Females.	Males.	Females.	Males.	Females.
KASHMIR.																				
(*c*).—DISTRICTS.																				
Khas	4	5	5	14	12	5	2	9	5	4	5	3	3	...	1	3	2	...	...	...
Kamraj	1	...	...	...	1	...	...	...	...	...	...	...	...	...	...	...	...	...	...	...
Anantnag	...	1	...	...	...	...	...	...	1	...	...	...	...	...	...	...	...	...	...	...
Muzafferabad	2	...	1	...	3	...	3	...	1	...	...	...	...	...	...	...	2	...	...	...
TOTAL DISTRICTS (*c*) ...	7	6	6	14	16	5	5	9	7	4	5	3	3	...	1	3	4	...	...	...
(*d*).—JAGIRS.																				
Raja Amar Singh	...	...	...	...	...	...	...	...	...	...	...	...	...	...	...	...	...	...	...	...
Raja Ram Singh	...	...	...	...	...	...	...	...	...	...	...	...	...	...	...	...	...	...	...	...
TOTAL JAGIRS (*d*) ...	...	...	...	...	...	...	...	...	...	...	...	...	...	...	...	...	...	...	...	...
TOTAL KASHMIR PROVINCE ...	7	6	6	14	16	5	5	9	7	4	5	3	3	...	1	3	4	...	...	...
(*e*).—FRONTIER DISTRICTS.																				
Ladákh	1	...	1	1	1	...	1	...	1	2	...	1	1	...	1	...	...	1	...	...
Skardu	...	...	...	...	...	...	...	...	...	...	...	...	...	...	...	...	...	...	...	...
Gilgit	...	...	...	...	...	1	...	...	1	...	...	...	...	...	...	...	...	...	...	...
TOTAL DISTRICTS (*e*) ...	1	...	1	1	1	1	1	...	2	2	...	1	1	...	1	...	...	1	...	...
GRAND TOTAL KASHMIR STATE ...	8	8	8	18	22	10	7	11	13	6	8	5	4	1	2	3	4	1	...	...

SRINAGAR:
Dated the 3rd November 1891.

BHAG RAM,
Census Superintendent, Kashmir State.

CENSUS 1891.

KASHMIR STATE.

TABLE VII.—PART E.—*Population by Age.—Buddhists.*—(*Provincial Summary.*)

Province.	Population.			Age Distribution.																	
				Under one year.		1—2.		2—3.		3—4.		4—5.		*Total under five.*		5—9.		10—14.		15—19.	
	Total.	Males.	Females.	Males.	Females.	Males.	Females.	Males.	Females.	Males.	Females.	Males.	Females.	Males.	Females.	Males.	Females.	Males.	Females.	Males.	Females.
JAMMU.																					
(*a*).—DISTRICTS.																					
Sri Ranbir Singhpora	...	...	...	...	...	...	...	...	...	...	...	...	...	...	...	...	...	...	...	...	...
Jasrota	...	...	...	...	...	...	...	...	...	...	...	...	...	...	...	...	...	...	...	...	...
Udhampore	4,293	2,179	2,114	39	64	3	2	38	22	46	50	44	34	170	172	260	230	236	200	178	220
Reasi	...	...	...	...	...	...	...	...	...	...	...	...	...	...	...	...	...	...	...	...	...
Bhimbar	...	...	...	...	...	...	...	...	...	...	...	...	...	...	...	...	...	...	...	...	...
TOTAL DISTRICTS (*a*) ...	4,293	2,179	2,114	39	64	3	2	38	22	46	50	44	34	170	172	260	230	236	200	178	220
(*b*).—JAGIRS.																					
Ramnagar	...	...	...	...	...	...	...	...	...	...	...	...	...	...	...	...	...	...	...	...	...
Bhadrawah	...	...	...	...	...	...	...	...	...	...	...	...	...	...	...	...	...	...	...	...	...
Punch	...	...	...	...	...	...	...	...	...	...	...	...	...	...	...	...	...	...	...	...	...
TOTAL JAGIRS (*b*) ...	...	...	...	...	...	...	...	...	...	...	...	...	...	...	...	...	...	...	...	...	...
TOTAL JAMMU PROVINCE ...	4,293	2,179	2,114	39	64	3	2	38	22	46	50	44	34	170	172	260	230	236	200	178	220

CENSUS 1891.

KASHMIR STATE.

TABLE VII.—PART E.—*Population by Age.—Buddhists.—(Provincial Summary.)*—(Continued).

Province.	Population.			Age Distribution.																			
				Under one year.		1—2.		2—3.		3—4.		4—5.		*Total under five.*		5—9.		10—14.		15—19.	
	Total.	Males.	Females.	Males.	Females.	Males.	Females.	Males.	Females.	Males.	Females.	Males.	Females.	Males.	Females.	Males.	Females.	Males.	Females.	Males.	Females.
KASHMIR.																							
(c).—DISTRICTS.																							
Khas	...	...	...	...	...	...	...	...	...	...	...	...	...	...	...	...	...	...	...	...	...
Kamraj	...	...	...	...	...	...	...	...	...	...	...	...	...	...	...	...	...	...	...	...	...
Anantnag	...	...	...	...	...	...	...	...	...	...	...	...	...	...	...	...	...	...	...	...	...
Muzafferabad	...	...	...	...	...	...	...	...	...	...	...	...	...	...	...	...	...	...	...	...	...
TOTAL DISTRICTS (c) ...	...	...	...	...	...	...	...	...	...	...	...	...	...	...	...	...	...	...	...	...	...
(d).—JAGIRS.																					
Raja Amar Singh	...	...	...	...	...	...	...	...	...	...	...	...	...	...	...	...	...	...	...	...	...
„ Ram Singh	...	...	...	...	...	...	...	...	...	...	...	...	...	...	...	...	...	...	...	...	...
TOTAL JAGIRS (d) ...	...	...	...	...	...	...	...	...	...	...	...	...	...	...	...	...	...	...	...	...	...
TOTAL KASHMIR PROVINCE ...	...	...	...	...	...	...	...	...	...	...	...	...	...	...	...	...	...	...	...	...	...
(e).—FRONTIER DISTRICTS.																					
Ladákh	25,076	12,615	12,461	183	207	163	175	177	189	275	273	243	245	1,041	1,089	1,269	1,255	1,018	971	890	870
Skardu	239	148	91	1	1	...	...	1	1	3	3	1	9	6	14	12	3	15	10	8	4
Gilgit	...	...	...	...	...	...	...	...	...	...	...	...	...	...	...	...	...	...	...	...	...
TOTAL DISTRICTS (e) ...	25,315	12,763	12,552	184	208	163	175	178	190	278	276	244	254	1,047	1,103	1,281	1,258	1,033	981	898	874
GRAND TOTAL KASHMIR STATE ...	29,608	14,942	14,666	223	272	166	177	216	212	324	326	288	288	1,217	1,275	1,541	1,488	1,269	1,181	1,076	1,094

CENSUS 1891.

KASHMIR STATE.

TABE VII.—PART E.—*Population by Age.—Buddhists.*—(*Provincial Summary.*)—(Continued).

Province.	Age Distribution.																			
	20—24.		24—29.		30—34.		35—39.		40—44.		45—49.		50—54.		55—59.		60 *and over.*		*Unspecified.*	
	Males.	Females.	Males.	Females.	Males.	Females.	Males.	Females.	Males.	Females.	Males.	Females.	Males.	Females.	Males.	Females.	Males.	Females.	Males.	Females.
JAMMU.																				
(*a*).—DISTRICTS.																				
Sri Ranbir Singhpora	...	...	...	...	...	...	...	...	...	...	...	...	...	...	...	...	...	...	...	...
Jasrota	...	...	...	...	...	...	...	...	...	...	...	...	...	...	...	...	...	...	...	...
Udhampore	178	174	192	238	176	189	130	128	137	150	116	98	120	98	68	53	218	164	...	...
Reasi	...	...	...	...	...	...	...	...	...	...	...	...	...	...	...	...	...	...	...	...
Bhimbar	...	...	...	...	...	...	...	...	...	...	...	...	...	...	...	...	...	...	...	...
TOTAL DISTRICTS (*a*) ...	178	174	192	238	176	189	130	128	137	150	116	98	120	98	68	53	218	164	...	...
(*b*).—JAGIRS.																				
Ramnagar	...	...	...	...	...	...	...	...	...	...	...	...	...	...	...	...	...	...	...	...
Bhadrawah	...	...	...	...	...	...	...	...	...	...	...	...	...	...	...	...	...	...	...	...
Punch	...	...	...	...	...	...	...	...	...	...	...	...	...	...	...	...	...	...	...	...
TOTAL JAGIRS (*b*) ...	...	...	...	...	...	...	...	...	...	...	...	...	...	...	...	...	...	...	...	...
TOTAL JAMMU PROVINCE ...	178	174	192	238	176	189	130	128	137	150	116	98	120	98	68	53	218	164	...	...

CENSUS 1891.

KASHMIR STATE.

TABLE VII.—PART E.—*Population by Age.—Buddhists.—(Provincial Summary.)*—(Concluded).

PROVINCE.	AGE DISTRIBUTION.																			
	20—24.		25—29.		30—34.		35—39.		40—44.		45—49.		50—54.		55—59.		*60 and over.*		*Unspecified.*	
	Males.	Females.	Males.	Females.	Males.	Females.	Males.	Females.	Males.	Females.	Males.	Females.	Males.	Females.	Males.	Females.	Males.	Females.	Males.	Females.
KASHMIR PROVINCE.																				
(c)—DISTRICTS.																				
Khas	...	...	...	...	...	...	...	...	...	...	...	...	...	...	...	...	...	...	...	...
Kamraj	...	...	...	...	...	...	...	...	...	...	...	...	...	...	...	...	...	...	...	...
Anantnag	...	...	...	...	...	...	...	...	...	...	...	...	...	...	...	...	...	...	...	...
Muzafferabad	...	...	...	...	...	...	...	...	...	...	...	...	...	...	...	...	...	...	...	...
TOTAL DISTRICTS (c) ...	...	...	...	...	...	...	...	...	...	...	...	...	...	...	...	...	...	...	...	...
(d)—JAGIRS.																				
Raja Amar Singh	...	...	...	...	...	...	...	...	...	...	...	...	...	...	...	...	...	...	...	...
„ Ram Singh	...	...	...	...	...	...	...	...	...	...	...	...	...	...	...	...	...	...	...	...
TOTAL JAGIRS (d) ...	...	...	...	...	...	...	...	...	...	...	...	...	...	...	...	...	...	...	...	...
TOTAL KASHMIR PROVINCE ...	...	...	...	...	...	...	...	...	...	...	...	...	...	...	...	...	...	...	...	...
(e)—FRONTIER DISTRICTS.																				
Ladákh	959	933	1,006	975	938	920	937	933	903	869	752	746	568	578	638	631	1,701	1,691	...	...
Skardu	12	6	10	10	12	3	13	8	5	8	12	8	11	3	4	1	28	13	...	...
Gilgit	...	...	...	...	...	...	...	...	...	...	...	...	...	...	...	...	...	...	...	...
TOTAL DISTRICTS (e) ...	971	939	1,016	985	945	923	950	941	908	877	764	754	579	581	642	632	1,729	1,704	...	...
GRAND TOTAL KASHMIR STATE ...	1,149	1,113	1,208	1,223	1,121	1,112	1,080	1,069	1,045	1,027	880	852	699	679	710	685	1,947	1,868	...	...

SRINAGAR :
Dated the 3rd November, 1891.

BHAG RAM,
Census Superintendent, Kashmír State.

CENSUS 1891.

KASHMIR STATE.

TABLE VII.—PART F.—*Population by Age.—Jains.—(Provincial Summary.)*

Province.	Population.			Age Distribution.																	
				Under one year.		1—2.		2—3.		3—4.		4—5.		*Total under five.*		5—9.		10—14.		15—19.	
	Total.	Males.	Females.	Males.	Females.	Males.	Females.	Males.	Females.	Males.	Females.	Males.	Females.	Males.	Females.	Males.	Females.	Males.	Females.	Males.	Females.
JAMMU.																					
(*a*).—DISTRICTS.																					
Sri Ranbir Singhpora	517	289	228	6	5	9	7	7	6	5	8	4	3	31	29	30	25	28	24	29	21
Jasrota	...	...	...	...	...	...	...	...	...	...	...	...	...	...	...	...	...	...	...	...	...
Udhampore	1	1	...	...	...	...	...	...	...	...	...	...	...	...	...	...	...	...	...	...	...
Reasi	10	6	4	...	...	...	...	1	...	...	...	...	...	1	...	...	1	...	...	...	...
Bhimbar	36	19	17	1	1	1	...	...	...	...	1	3	...	5	2	...	...	...	2	4	1
TOTAL DISTRICTS (*a*) ...	564	315	249	7	6	10	7	8	6	5	9	7	3	37	31	30	26	28	26	33	22
(*b*).—JAGIRS.																					
Ramnagar	1	1	...	...	...	...	...	...	...	...	...	...	...	...	...	...	...	...	...	...	...
Bhadrawah	...	...	...	...	...	...	...	...	...	...	...	...	...	...	...	...	...	...	...	...	...
Punch	28	23	5	2	1	...	...	1	...	...	1	...	...	3	2	...	...	2	...	...	1
TOTAL JAGIRS (*b*) ...	29	24	5	2	1	..	...	1	...	...	1	...	...	3	2	...	...	2	...	...	1
TOTAL JAMMU PROVINCE ...	593	339	254	9	7	10	7	9	6	5	10	7	3	40	33	30	26	30	26	33	23

xliv

CENSUS 1891.

KASHMIR STATE.

TABLE VII.—PART F.—*Population by Age.—Jains.*—(*Provincial Summary.*)—(Continued.)

PROVINCE.	POPULATION.			AGE DISTRIBUTION.																	
				Under one year.		1—2.		2—3.		3—4.		4—5.		*Total under five.*		5—9.		10—14.		15—19.	
	Total.	Males.	Females.	Males.	Females.	Males.	Females.	Males.	Females.	Males.	Females.	Males.	Females.	Males.	Females.	Males.	Females.	Males.	Females.	Males.	Females.
KASHMIR.																					
(*c*)—DISTRICTS.																					
Khas	...	...	...	...	...	...	...	...	...	...	...	...	...	...	...	...	...	...	...	...	...
Kamraj	...	...	...	...	...	...	...	...	...	...	...	...	...	...	...	...	...	...	...	...	...
Anantnag	...	...	...	...	...	...	...	...	...	...	...	...	...	...	...	...	...	...	...	...	...
Muzafferabad	...	...	...	...	...	...	...	...	...	...	...	...	...	...	...	...	...	...	...	...	...
TOTAL DISTRICTS (*c*) ...	...	...	...	...	...	...	...	...	...	...	...	...	...	...	...	...	...	...	...	...	...
(*d*).—JAGIRS.																					
Raja Amar Singh	...	...	...	...	...	...	...	...	...	...	...	...	...	...	...	...	...	...	...	...	...
Raja Ram Singh	...	...	...	...	...	...	...	...	...	...	...	...	...	...	...	...	...	...	...	...	...
TOTAL JAGIRS (*d*). ...	...	...	...	...	...	...	...	...	...	...	...	...	...	...	...	...	...	...	...	...	...
TOTAL KASHMIR PROVINCE ...	...	...	...	...	...	...	...	...	...	...	...	...	...	...	...	...	...	...	...	...	...
(*e*).—FRONTIER DISTRICTS.																					
Ladákh	...	...	...	...	...	...	...	...	...	...	...	...	...	...	...	...	...	...	...	...	...
Skardu	...	...	...	...	...	...	...	...	...	...	...	...	...	...	...	...	...	...	...	...	...
Gilgit	...	...	...	...	...	...	...	...	...	...	...	...	...	...	...	...	...	...	...	...	...
TOTAL DISTRICTS (*e*) ...	...	...	...	...	...	...	...	...	...	...	...	...	...	...	...	...	...	...	...	...	...
GRAND TOTAL KASHMIR STATE ...	593	339	254	9	7	10	7	9	6	5	10	7	3	40	33	30	26	30	26	33	23

CENSUS 1891.

KASHMIR STATE.

TABLE VII.—PART F.—*Population by Age.—Jains.—(Provincial Summary.)*—(Continued.)

Province.	Age Distribution.																			
	20—24.		25—29.		30—34.		35—39.		40—44.		45—49.		50—54.		55—59.		60 *and over.*		*Unspecified.*	
	Males.	Females.	Males.	Females.	Males.	Females.	Males.	Females.	Males.	Females.	Males.	Females.	Males.	Females.	Males.	Females.	Males.	Females.	Males.	Females.
JAMMU.																				
(*a*).—DISTRICTS.																				
Sri Ranbir Singhpora	27	19	22	23	26	20	21	16	19	15	15	11	19	15	13	7	9	3	...	...
Jasrota	...	...	...	...	...	...	...	...	...	...	...	...	...	...	...	...	...	...	...	...
Udhampore	...	...	...	...	1	...	...	...	...	...	...	...	...	...	...	...	...	...	...	...
Reasi	3	...	...	1	...	...	2	2	...	...	...	...	...	...	...	...	...	...	...	...
Bhimbar	3	3	...	...	2	4	...	1	2	2	...	2	3	...	...	...	...	...	...	...
TOTAL DISTRICTS (*a*) ...	33	22	22	24	29	24	23	19	21	17	15	13	22	15	13	7	9	3	...	...
(*b*).—JAGIRS.																				
Ramnagar	...	...	...	...	...	...	1	...	...	...	...	...	...	...	...	...	...	...	...	...
Bhadrawah	...	...	...	...	...	...	...	...	...	...	...	...	...	...	...	...	...	...	...	...
Punch	...	...	4	...	5	1	5	...	...	...	1	1	1	...	...	...	2	...	...	...
TOTAL JAGIRS (*b*) ...	...	...	4	...	5	1	6	...	...	...	1	1	1	...	...	...	2	...	...	...
TOTAL JAMMU PROVINCE ...	33	22	26	24	34	25	29	19	21	17	16	14	23	15	13	7	11	3	...	...

CENSUS 1891.

KASHMIR STATE.

TABLE VII.—PART F.—*Population by Age.—Jains.—(Provincial Summary.)*—(Concluded.)

Province.	Age Distribution.																			
	20—24.		25—29.		30—34.		35—39.		40—44.		45—49.		50—54.		55—59.		60 *and over.*		*Unspecified.*	
	Males.	Females.	Males.	Females.	Males.	Females.	Males.	Females.	Males.	Females.	Males.	Females.	Males.	Females.	Males.	Females.	Males.	Females.	Males.	Females.
KASHMIR.																				
(*c*).—DISTRICTS.																				
Khas	...	...	...	...	...	...	...	...	...	...	...	...	...	...	...	...	...	...	...	...
Kamraj	...	...	...	...	...	...	...	...	...	...	...	...	...	...	...	...	...	...	...	...
Anantnag	...	...	...	...	...	...	...	...	...	...	...	...	...	...	...	...	...	...	...	...
Muzafferabad	...	...	...	...	...	...	...	...	...	...	...	...	...	...	...	...	...	...	...	...
TOTAL DISTRICTS (*c*) ...	...	...	...	...	...	...	...	...	...	...	...	...	...	...	...	...	...	...	...	...
(*d*).—JAGIRS.																				
Raja Amar Singh	...	...	...	...	...	...	...	...	...	...	...	...	...	...	...	...	...	...	...	...
Raja Ram Singh	...	...	...	...	...	...	...	...	...	...	...	...	...	...	...	...	...	...	...	...
TOTAL JAGIRS (*d*) ...	...	...	...	...	...	...	...	...	...	...	...	...	...	...	...	...	...	...	...	...
TOTAL KASHMIR PROVINCE ...	...	...	...	...	...	...	...	...	...	...	...	...	...	...	...	...	...	...	...	...
(*e*).—FRONTIER DISTRICTS.																				
Ladákh	...	...	...	...	...	...	...	...	...	...	...	...	...	...	...	...	...	...	...	...
Skardu	...	...	...	...	...	...	...	...	...	...	...	...	...	...	...	...	...	...	...	...
Gilgit	...	...	...	...	...	...	...	...	...	...	...	...	...	...	...	...	...	...	...	...
TOTAL DISTRICTS (*e*) ...	...	...	...	...	...	...	...	...	...	...	...	...	...	...	...	...	...	...	...	...
GRAND TOTAL KASHMIR STATE ...	33	22	26	24	34	25	29	19	21	17	16	14	23	15	13	7	11	3	...	...

SRINAGAR:
Dated the 3rd November, 1891.

BHAG RAM,
Census Superintendent, Kashmir State.

CENSUS 1891.

KASHMIR STATE.

TABLE VII.—PART G.—*Population by Age. Sikhs—(Provincial Summary.)*

Province.	Population. Total.	Population. Males.	Population. Females.	Under one year. Males.	Under one year. Females.	1—2. Males.	1—2. Females.	2—3. Males.	2—3. Females.	3—4. Males.	3—4. Females.	4—5. Males.	4—5. Females.	Total under five. Males.	Total under five. Females.	5—9. Males.	5—9. Females.	10—14. Males.	10—14. Females.	15—19. Males.	15—19. Females.
JAMMU.																					
(*a*)—DISTRICTS.																					
Sri Ranbir Singhpora	319	199	120	8	4	1	1	10	4	8	4	4	2	31	15	18	11	12	19	19	9
Jasrota	21	15	6	2	1	...	...	1	...	...	...	...	...	3	1	1	...	1	1	...	...
Udhampore	26	18	8	...	1	...	...	...	...	...	2	...	...	...	3	1	1	...	1	1	1
Reasi	18	12	6	1	...	...	...	...	...	...	1	1	...	2	1	2	1	1	1	1	...
Bhimbar	862	500	362	20	16	7	3	28	12	17	17	17	15	89	63	50	47	38	23	32	23
TOTAL DISTRICTS (*a*) ...	1,246	744	502	31	22	8	4	39	16	25	24	22	17	125	83	72	60	52	45	53	33
(*b*)—JAGIRS.																					
Ramnagar	4	3	1	...	...	...	...	...	...	...	...	...	...	...	...	...	1	...	...	...	...
Bhadrawah...	1	1	...	...	...	...	...	...	...	...	...	...	...	...	...	...	...	...	...	...	...
Punch	4,675	2,573	2,102	135	107	27	22	67	69	104	91	101	75	434	364	400	355	307	225	187	156
TOTAL JAGIRS (*a*) ...	4,680	2,577	2,103	135	107	27	22	67	69	104	91	101	75	434	364	400	356	307	225	187	156
TOTAL JAMMU PROVINCE ...	5,926	3,321	2,605	166	129	35	26	106	85	129	115	123	92	559	447	472	416	359	270	240	189

CENSUS 1891.

KASHMIR STATE.

TABLE VII.—PART G.—*Population by Age.—Sikhs.—(Provincial Summary.)*—(Continued.)

Province.	Population.			Age Distribution.																	
				Under one year.		1—2.		2—3.		3—4.		4—5.		*Total under five.*		5—9.		10—14.		15—19.	
	Total.	Males.	Females.	Males.	Females.	Males.	Females.	Males.	Females.	Males.	Females.	Males.	Females.	Males.	Females.	Males.	Females.	Males.	Females.	Males.	Females.
KASHMIR.																					
(*c*)—DISTRICTS.																					
Khas	1,617	858	759	33	27	15	16	33	22	43	39	30	34	154	138	126	106	93	84	69	76
Kamraj	2,082	1,083	999	56	65	11	2	29	43	42	56	39	32	177	198	165	158	128	106	93	94
Anantnag	391	202	189	11	8	...	...	4	6	9	10	3	6	27	30	34	34	21	18	17	17
Muzafferabad	1,381	792	589	30	39	8	6	18	31	35	28	23	21	114	125	123	96	86	50	81	57
TOTAL DISTRICTS.—(*c*) ...	5,471	2,935	2,536	130	139	34	24	84	102	129	133	95	93	472	491	448	394	328	258	260	244
(*d*).—JAGIRS																					
Raja Amar Singh	2	2	...	...	...	...	...	...	...	...	...	...	...	...	...	...	...	...	...	...	...
Raja Ram Singh	...	...	...	...	...	...	...	...	...	...	...	...	...	...	...	...	...	...	...	...	...
TOTAL JAGIRS (*d*) ...	2	2	...	...	...	...	...	...	...	...	...	...	...	...	...	...	...	...	...	...	...
TOTAL KASHMIR PROVINCE ...	5,473	2,937	2,536	130	139	34	24	84	102	129	133	95	93	472	491	448	394	328	258	260	244
(*e*).—FRONTIER DISTRICTS.																					
Ladákh	...	...	...	...	...	...	...	...	...	...	...	...	...	...	...	...	...	...	...	...	...
Skardu	...	...	...	...	...	...	...	...	...	...	...	...	...	...	...	...	...	...	...	...	...
Gilgit	...	...	...	...	...	...	...	...	...	...	...	...	...	...	...	...	...	...	...	...	...
TOTAL DISTRICTS (*e*) ...	...	...	...	...	...	...	...	...	...	...	...	...	...	...	...	...	...	...	...	...	...
GRAND TOTAL KASHMIR STATE ...	11,399	6,258	5,141	296	268	69	50	190	187	258	248	218	185	1,031	938	920	810	687	528	500	433

CENSUS 1891.

KASHMIR STATE.

TABLE VII.—PART G.—*Population by Age.—Sikhs.—(Provincial Summary.)*—(Continued.)

Province.	20—24. Males.	20—24. Females.	25—29. Males.	25—29. Females.	30—34. Males.	30—34. Females.	35—39. Males.	35—39. Females.	40—44. Males.	40—44. Females.	45—49. Males.	45—49. Females.	50—54. Males.	50—54. Females.	55—59. Males.	55—59. Females.	60 *and over.* Males.	60 *and over.* Females.	*Unspecified.* Males.	*Unspecified.* Females.
JAMMU.																				
(*a*).—DISTRICTS.																				
Sri Ranbir Singhpora	14	15	20	5	18	17	9	4	18	9	9	3	12	8	3	1	16	4	...	...
Jasrota	1	...	...	...	2	...	2	2	1	...	2	...	...	...	...	1	2	1	...	...
Udhampore	4	...	5	...	...	...	1	...	3	1	...	1	1	...	1	...	1	...	...	...
Reasi...	1	2	1	...	1	...	...	1	...	...	1	...	1	...	...	...	1	...	...	...
Bhimbar	27	33	51	26	41	24	30	23	29	25	26	16	34	24	14	11	39	24	...	...
TOTAL DISTRICTS (*a*) ...	47	50	77	31	62	41	42	30	51	35	38	20	48	32	18	13	59	29	...	...
(*b*).—JAGIRS.																				
Ramnagar	1	...	1	...	...	...	...	...	...	...	...	...	...	...	...	...	1	...	...	...
Bhadrawah	...	...	...	...	...	...	...	...	...	...	...	...	...	...	...	...	1	...	...	...
Punch	136	141	169	143	192	167	150	123	154	132	96	69	129	72	40	21	179	134	...	...
TOTAL JAGIRS (*b*) ...	137	141	170	143	192	167	150	123	154	132	96	69	129	72	40	21	181	134	...	...
TOTAL JAMMU PROVINCE ...	184	191	247	174	254	208	192	153	205	167	134	89	177	104	58	34	240	163	...	...

CENSUS 1891.

KASHMIR STATE.

TABLE VII.—PART G.—*Population by Age—Sikhs.—(Provincial Summary.)*—(Concluded.)

Province.	Age Distribution. 20—24. Males.	20—24. Females.	25—29. Males.	25—29. Females.	30—34. Males.	30—34. Females.	35—39. Males.	35—39. Females.	40—44. Males.	40—44. Females.	45—49. Males.	45—49. Females.	50—54. Males.	50—54. Females.	55—59. Males.	55—59. Females.	60 *and over.* Males.	60 *and over.* Females.	*Unspecified.* Males.	*Unspecified.* Females.
KASHMIR.																				
(c).—DISTRICTS.																				
Khas	59	76	79	62	64	66	38	32	52	35	28	11	31	28	12	1	53	44	...	...
Kamraj	84	80	89	81	76	92	52	42	75	51	38	15	43	28	12	9	51	45	...	...
Anantnag	16	18	19	13	13	14	10	7	15	15	7	4	11	8	2	1	10	10	...	...
Muzafferabad	73	49	62	37	49	59	44	14	48	35	16	8	35	26	15	3	46	30	...	...
TOTAL DISTRICTS (c) ...	232	223	249	193	202	231	144	95	190	136	89	38	120	90	41	14	160	129	...	...
(d).—JAGIRS.																				
Raja Amar Singh	...	...	...	...	...	...	...	...	1	...	...	...	1	...	...	...	...	...	...	...
Raja Ram Singh	...	...	...	...	...	...	...	...	...	...	...	...	...	...	...	...	...	...	...	...
TOTAL JAGIRS (d) ...	...	...	...	...	...	...	...	...	1	...	...	...	1	...	...	...	...	...	...	...
TOTAL KASHMIR PROVINCE ...	232	223	249	193	202	231	144	95	191	136	89	38	121	90	41	14	160	129	...	...
(e).—FRONTIER DISTRICTS.																				
Ladákh	...	...	...	...	...	...	...	...	...	...	...	...	...	...	...	...	...	...	...	...
Skardu	...	...	...	...	...	...	...	...	...	...	...	...	...	...	...	...	...	...	...	...
Gilgit	...	...	...	...	...	...	...	...	...	...	...	...	...	...	...	...	...	...	...	...
TOTAL DISTRICTS (e) ...	...	...	...	...	...	...	...	...	...	...	...	...	...	...	...	...	...	...	...	...
GRAND TOTAL KASHMIR STATE ...	416	414	496	367	456	439	336	248	396	303	223	127	298	194	99	48	400	292	...	...

SRINAGAR :
Dated the 3rd November, 1891.

BHAG RAM,
Census Superintendent, Kashmir State.

CENSUS 1891.

KASHMIR STATE.

TABLE VII.—PART H.—*Population by Age.—Parsis—(Provincial Summary).*

Province.	Population.			Age Distribution.																	
				Under one year.		1—2.		2—3.		3—4.		4—5.		*Total under five.*		5—9.		10—14.		15—19.	
	Total.	Males.	Females.	Males.	Females.	Males.	Females.	Males.	Females.	Males.	Females.	Males.	Females.	Males.	Females.	Males.	Females.	Males.	Females.	Males.	Females.
JAMMU.																					
(*a*).—DISTRICTS.																					
Sri Ranbir Singhpora ...	1	1	...	...	...	...	...	...	...	...	...	...	...	...	...	...	...	...	...	...	...
Jasrota	...	...	...	...	...	...	...	...	...	...	...	...	...	...	...	...	...	...	...	...	...
Udhampore	...	...	...	...	...	...	...	...	...	...	...	...	...	...	...	...	...	...	...	...	...
Reasi	...	...	...	...	...	...	...	...	...	...	...	...	...	...	...	...	...	...	...	...	...
Bhimbar	...	...	...	...	...	...	...	...	...	...	...	...	...	...	...	...	...	...	...	...	...
TOTAL DISTRICTS (*a*) ...	1	1	...	...	...	...	...	...	...	...	...	...	...	...	...	...	...	...	...	...	...
(*b*).—JAGIRS.																					
Ramnagar	...	...	...	...	...	...	...	...	...	...	...	...	...	...	...	...	...	...	...	...	...
Bhadrawah	...	...	...	...	...	...	...	...	...	...	...	...	...	...	...	...	...	...	...	...	...
Punch	...	...	...	...	...	...	...	...	...	...	...	...	...	...	...	...	...	...	...	...	...
TOTAL JAGIRS (*b*) ...	...	...	...	...	...	...	...	...	...	...	...	...	...	...	...	...	...	...	...	...	...
TOTAL JAMMU PROVINCE ...	1	1	...	...	...	...	...	...	...	...	...	...	...	...	...	...	...	...	...	...	...

CENSUS 1891.

KASHMIR STATE.

TABLE VII.—PART H.—*Population by Age.—Parsis.—(Provincial Summary.)*—(Continued).

Province.	Population.			Age Distribution.																	
				Under one year.		1—2.		2—3.		3—4.		4—5.		*Total under five.*		5—9.		10—14.		15—19.	
	Total.	Males.	Females.	Males.	Females.	Males.	Females.	Males.	Females.	Males.	Females.	Males.	Females.	Males.	Females.	Males.	Females.	Males.	Females.	Males.	Females.
KASHMIR.																					
(*c*).—DISTRICTS.																					
Khas	8	6	2	...	...	...	...	...	...	...	...	1	...	1	...	...	...	1	...	1	...
Kamraj	...	...	...	...	...	...	...	...	...	...	...	...	...	...	...	...	...	...	...	...	...
Anantnag	...	...	...	...	...	...	...	...	...	...	...	...	...	...	...	...	...	...	...	...	...
Muzafferabad	...	...	...	...	...	...	...	...	...	...	...	...	...	...	...	...	...	...	...	...	...
TOTAL DISTRICTS (*c*) ...	8	6	2	...	...	...	...	...	...	...	...	1	...	1	...	...	...	1	...	1	...
(*d*.)—JAGIRS.																					
Raja Amar Singh	...	...	...	...	...	...	...	...	...	...	...	...	...	...	...	...	...	...	...	...	...
Raja Ram Singh	...	...	...	...	...	...	...	...	...	...	...	...	...	...	...	...	...	...	...	...	...
TOTAL JAGIRS (*d*) ...	...	...	...	...	...	...	...	...	...	...	...	...	...	...	...	...	...	...	...	...	...
TOTAL KASHMIR PROVINCE ...	8	6	2	...	...	...	...	...	...	...	...	1	...	1	...	...	...	1	...	1	...
(*e*).—FRONTIER DISTRICTS.																					
Ladákh	...	...	...	...	...	...	...	...	...	...	...	...	...	...	...	...	...	...	...	...	...
Skardu	...	...	...	...	...	...	...	...	...	...	...	...	...	...	...	...	...	...	...	...	...
Gilgit	...	..	...	...	...	...	...	...	...	...	...	...	...	...	...	...	...	...	...	...	...
TOTAL DISTRICTS (*e*) ...	...	...	...	...	...	...	...	...	...	...	...	...	...	...	...	...	...	...	...	...	...
GRAND TOTAL KASHMIR STATE ...	9	7	2	...	...	...	...	...	...	...	...	1	...	1	...	...	...	1	...	1	...

CENSUS 1891.

KASHMIR STATE.

TABLE VII.—PART H.—*Population by Age.—Parsis.—(Provincial Summary.)*—(Continued.)

PROVINCE.	AGE DISTRIBUTION.																			
	20—24.		25—29.		30—34.		35—39.		40—44.		45—49.		50—54.		55—59.		60 *and over.*		*Unspecified.*	
	Males.	Females.	Males.	Females.	Males.	Females.	Males.	Females.	Males.	Females.	Males.	Females.	Males.	Females.	Males.	Females.	Males.	Females.	Males.	Females.
JAMMU.																				
(*a*).—DISTRICTS.																				
Sri Ranbir Singhpora ...	...	...	...	...	...	...	1	...	...	...	...	...	...	...	...	...	...	...	...	...
Jasrota	...	...	...	...	...	...	...	...	...	...	...	...	...	...	...	...	...	...	...	...
Udhampore	...	...	...	...	...	...	...	...	...	...	...	...	...	...	...	...	...	...	...	...
Reasi	...	...	...	...	...	...	...	...	...	...	...	...	...	...	...	...	...	...	...	...
Bhimbar	...	...	...	...	...	...	...	...	...	...	...	...	...	...	...	...	...	...	...	...
TOTAL DISTRICTS (*a*) ...	...	...	...	...	...	...	1	...	...	...	...	...	...	...	...	...	...	...	...	...
(*b*).—JAGIRS.																				
Ramnagar	...	...	...	...	...	...	...	...	...	...	...	...	...	...	...	...	...	...	...	...
Bhadrawah	...	...	...	...	...	...	...	...	...	...	...	...	...	...	...	...	...	...	...	...
Punch	...	...	...	...	...	...	...	...	...	...	...	...	...	...	...	...	...	...	...	...
TOTAL JAGIRS (*b*) ...	...	...	...	...	...	...	...	...	...	...	...	...	...	...	...	...	...	...	...	...
TOTAL JAMMU PROVINCE ...	...	...	...	...	...	...	1	...	...	...	...	...	...	...	...	...	...	..	...	...

CENSUS 1891.

KASHMIR STATE.

TABLE VII.—PART H.—*Population by Age.—Parsis.—(Provincial Summary.*—(Concluded).

Province.	Age Distribution.																			
	20—24.		25—29.		30—34.		35—39.		40—44.		45—49.		50—54.		55—59.		60 *and over.*		*Unspecified.*	
	Males.	Females.	Males.	Females.	Males.	Females.	Males.	Females.	Males.	Females.	Males.	Females.	Males.	Females.	Males.	Females.	Males.	Females.	Males.	Females.
KASHMIR.																				
(c).—DISTRICTS.																				
Khas	...	1	...	...	1	...	1	...	...	1	1	...	...	...	...	...	...	...	...	...
Kamraj	...	...	...	...	...	...	...	...	...	...	...	...	...	...	...	...	...	...	...	...
Anantnag	...	...	...	...	...	...	...	...	...	...	...	...	...	...	...	...	...	...	...	...
Muzafferabad	...	...	...	...	...	...	...	...	...	...	...	...	...	...	...	...	...	...	...	...
TOTAL DISTRICTS (c) ...	...	1	...	...	1	...	1	...	...	1	1	...	...	...	...	...	...	...	...	...
(d).—JÁGIRS.																				
Raja Amar Singh	...	...	...	...	...	...	...	...	...	...	...	...	...	...	...	...	...	...	...	...
„ Ram Singh	...	...	...	...	...	...	...	...	...	...	...	...	...	...	...	...	...	...	...	...
TOTAL JAGIRS (d) ...	...	...	...	...	...	...	...	...	...	...	...	...	...	...	...	...	...	...	...	...
TOTAL KASHMIR PROVINCE ...	...	1	...	...	1	...	1	...	...	1	1	...	...	...	...	...	...	...	...	...
(e).—FRONTIER DISTRICTS.																				
Ladákh	...	...	...	...	...	...	...	...	...	...	...	...	...	...	...	...	...	...	...	...
Skardu	...	...	...	...	...	...	...	...	...	...	...	...	...	...	...	...	...	...	...	...
Gilgit	...	...	...	...	...	...	...	...	...	...	...	...	...	...	...	...	...	...	...	...
TOTAL DISTRICTS (e) ...	...	...	...	...	...	...	...	...	...	...	...	...	...	...	...	...	...	...	...	...
GRAND TOTAL KASHMIR STATE ...	...	1	...	...	1	...	2	...	...	1	1	...	...	...	...	...	...	...	...	...

SRINAGAR:
Dated the 3rd November, 1891.

BHAG RAM,
Census Superintendent, Kashmír State.

CENSUS 1891.

KASHMIR STATE.

TABLE VIII.—PART A.—UNMARRIED.—*Civil condition by Religion and Age.* (*Europeans and Eurasians*).

PROVINCE.	TOTAL UN-MARRIED.			(1.) UN-MARRIED. Age period.																									
				0—4.		5—9.		10—14.		15—19.		20—24.		25—29.		30—34.		35—39.		40—44.		45—49.		50—54.		55—59.		60 *and over.*	
	Total.	Males.	Females.	Males.	Females.	Males.	Females.	Males.	Females.	Males.	Females.	Males.	Females.	Males.	Females.	Males.	Females.	Males.	Females.	Males.	Females.	Males.	Females.	Males.	Females.	Males.	Females.	Males.	Females.
Jammu	14	7	7	5	5	1	...	...	1	1	...	...	...	...	1	...	...	...	...	...	...	...	...	...	...	...	...	...	...
Kashmír	59	28	31	5	8	7	4	...	3	...	1	4	1	4	8	6	1	2	2	...	1	...	2	...	...	...	...	...	...
Ladákh	3	2	1	...	...	...	1	...	...	...	...	1	...	1	...	...	...	...	...	...	...	...	...	...	...	...	...	...	...
Skardu	...	...	...	...	...	...	...	...	...	...	...	...	...	...	...	...	...	...	...	...	...	...	...	...	...	...	...	...	...
Gilgit	...	...	...	...	...	...	...	...	...	...	...	...	...	...	...	...	...	...	...	...	...	...	...	...	...	...	...	...	...
TOTAL ...	76	37	39	10	13	8	5	...	4	1	1	5	1	5	9	6	1	2	2	...	1	...	2	...	...	...	...	...	...

JAMMU:
Dated the 17th December 1891.

BHAG RAM,
Census Superintendent, Kashmír State.

CENSUS 1891.

KASHMIR STATE.

TABLE VIII.—PART B.—MARRIED.—*Civil condition by Religion and Age.* (*Europeans and Eurasians*).

PROVINCE.	TOTAL MARRIED.			(2.) MARRIED. — *Age period.*																									
				0—4.		5—9.		10—14.		15—19.		20—24.		25—29.		30—34.		35—39.		40—44.		45—49.		50—54.		55—59.		60 *and over.*	
	Total.	Males.	Females.	Males.	Females.	Males.	Females.	Males.	Females.	Males.	Females.	Males.	Females.	Males.	Females.	Males.	Females.	Males.	Females.	Males.	Females.	Males.	Females.	Males.	Females.	Males.	Females.	Males.	Females.
Jammu	14	7	7	...	...	...	...	...	...	...	...	...	1	...	3	3	2	1	...	2	...	1	...	...	1	...	...	...	...
Kashmír	38	20	18	...	...	...	...	...	...	...	...	1	1	...	3	3	5	2	5	5	2	4	2	4	...	...	...	1	...
Ladákh	4	2	2	...	...	...	...	...	...	...	...	...	...	...	1	...	...	...	...	...	1	...	...	2	...	...	...	...	...
Skardu	...	...	...	...	...	...	...	...	...	...	...	...	...	...	...	...	...	...	...	...	...	...	...	...	...	...	...	...	...
Gilgit	2	1	1	...	...	...	...	...	...	...	...	...	...	...	...	...	...	1	1	...	...	...	...	...	...	...	...	...	...
TOTAL ...	58	30	28	...	...	...	...	...	...	...	...	1	2	...	7	6	7	4	6	7	3	5	2	6	1	...	...	1	...

JAMMU:
Dated the 17th December, 1891.

BHAG RAM,
Census Superintendent, Kashmir State.

CENSUS 1891.

KASHMIR STATE.

TABLE VIII.—PART C.—WIDOWED.—*Civil condition by Religion and Age.* *(Europeans and Eurasians.)*

PROVINCE.	TOTAL WIDOWED.			(3.) WIDOWED. Age period.																									
				0—4.		5—9.		10—14.		15—19.		20—24.		25—29.		30—34.		35—39.		40—44.		45—49.		50—54.		55—59.		60 *and over.*	
	Total.	Males.	Females.	Males.	Females.	Males.	Females.	Males.	Females.	Males.	Females.	Males.	Females.	Males.	Females.	Males.	Females.	Males.	Females.	Males.	Females.	Males.	Females.	Males.	Females.	Males.	Females.	Males.	Females.
Jammu	...	...	...	...	...	...	...	...	...	...	...	...	...	...	...	...	...	...	...	...	...	...	...	...	...	...	...	...	...
Kashmír	5	2	3	...	...	...	...	...	...	...	...	...	...	...	...	1	...	...	1	...	...	...	...	...	...	...	2	1	...
Ladákh	...	...	...	...	...	...	...	...	...	...	...	...	...	...	...	...	...	...	...	...	...	...	...	...	...	...	...	...	...
Skardu	...	...	...	...	...	...	...	...	...	...	...	...	...	...	...	...	...	...	...	...	...	...	...	...	...	...	...	...	...
Gilgit	...	...	...	...	...	...	...	...	...	...	...	...	...	...	...	...	...	...	...	...	...	...	...	...	...	...	...	...	...
TOTAL ...	5	2	3	...	...	...	...	...	...	...	...	...	...	...	...	1	...	...	1	...	...	...	...	...	...	...	2	1	...

JAMMU :
Dated the 17th December 1891.

BHAG RAM,
Census Superintendent, Kashmír State.

CENSUS 1891.

KASHMIR STATE.

Table IX.—*Education by Religion and Age.* (*Europeans and Eurasians*).

Province.	Total Population.			Total by Education.						Age Period.																							
				Learning.		Literate.		Illiterate.		0—14								15—24								25 and over.							
										Total.		Learning.		Literate.		Illiterate.		Total.		Learning.		Literate.		Illiterate.		Total.		Learning.		Literate.		Illiterate.	
	Total.	Males.	Females.	Males.	Females.	Males.	Females.	Males.	Females.	Males.	Females.	Males.	Females.	Males.	Females.	Males.	Females.	Males.	Females.	Males.	Females.	Males.	Females.	Males.	Females.	Males.	Females.	Males.	Females.	Males.	Females.	Males.	Females.
Jammu ...	28	14	14	2	2	8	8	4	4	6	6	2	2	...	...	4	4	1	1	...	...	1	1	...	...	7	7	...	...	7	7	...	...
Kashmír ...	102	50	52	6	4	40	39	4	9	12	15	6	4	2	2	4	9	5	3	...	...	5	3	...	...	33	34	...	...	33	34	...	...
Ladákh ...	7	4	3	...	...	4	3	...	...	...	1	...	...	...	1	...	...	1	...	...	...	1	...	...	...	3	2	...	...	3	2	...	...
Skardu ...	...	...	...	...	...	...	...	...	...	...	...	...	...	...	...	...	...	...	...	...	...	...	...	...	...	...	...	...	...	...	...	...	...
Gilgit ...	2	1	1	...	...	1	1	...	...	...	...	...	...	...	...	...	...	...	...	...	...	...	...	...	...	1	1	...	...	1	1	...	...
Total ...	139	69	70	8	6	53	5	8	13	18	22	8	6	2	3	8	13	7	4	...	...	7	4	...	...	44	44	...	...	44	44	...	...

Jammu:
Dated the 17th December 1891.

BHAG RAM,
Census Superintendent, Kashmír State.

CENSUS 1891.

KASHMIR STATE.

TABLE X.—*Parent Tongue.* (*Europeans and Eurasians.*)

PROVINCE.		TOTAL POPULATION.			GROUP OF LANGUAGES.																				
					English.			*French.*			*Italian and English.*			*Hindustani.*			*English and French.*			*Dutch.*			*German.*		
		Total.	Males.	Females.	Total.	Males.	Females.	Total.	Males.	Females.	Total.	Males.	Females.	Total.	Males.	Females.	Total.	Males.	Females.	Total.	Males.	Females.	Total.	Males.	Females.
Jammu	...	28	14	14	28	14	14	...	...	...	...	...	...	...	...	...	...	...	...	...	...	...	...	...	...
Kashmír	...	102	50	52	93	44	49	5	3	2	2	2	...	1	...	1	1	1	...	...	...	...	...	...	...
Ladákh	...	7	4	3	1	1	...	...	...	...	...	...	...	...	...	...	...	...	...	1	1	...	5	2	3
Skardu	...	...	...	...	...	...	...	...	...	...	...	...	...	...	...	...	...	...	...	...	...	...	...	...	...
Gilgit	...	2	1	1	2	1	1	...	...	...	...	...	...	...	...	...	...	...	...	...	...	...	...	...	...
TOTAL	...	139	69	70	124	60	64	5	3	2	2	2	...	1	...	1	1	1	...	1	1	...	5	2	3

JAMMU:
Dated the 17th *December*, 1891.

BHAG RAM,
Census Superintendent, Kashmír State.

CENSUS 1891.

KASHMIR STATE.

Table XI.—*Birth-place.*

Birth-place.		Total Kashmir State.			Province. Jammu.			Kashmir.			Ladákh.			Skardu.			Gilgit.		
		Total.	Males.	Females.	Total.	Males.	Females.	Total.	Males.	Females.	Total.	Males.	Females.	Total.	Males.	Females.	Total.	Males.	Females.
	Within the State ...	2,457,799	1,308,748	1,149,051	1,376,183	740,118	636,065	943,273	498,424	444,849	28,087	14,176	13,911	110,123	55,899	54,224	133	131	2
A.—Province and States in India.	I.—British Territory.																		
	Ajmere Merwara ...	1	1	...	1	1	...	...	...	...	...	...	...	...	...	...	...	...	...
	Bengal ...	111	93	18	89	75	14	22	18	4	...	...	...	...	...	...	...	...	...
	Bombay ...	34	28	6	17	15	2	17	13	4	...	...	...	...	...	...	...	...	...
	Burma ...	4	1	3	3	1	2	1	...	1	...	...	...	...	...	...	...	...	...
	Central Provinces ...	1	...	1	...	...	...	1	...	1	...	...	...	...	...	...	...	...	...
	Madras ...	16	11	5	13	11	2	3	...	3	...	...	...	...	...	...	...	...	...
	North-Western Provinces ...	836	650	186	530	429	101	300	216	84	...	...	...	1	1	...	5	4	1
	Oudh ...	24	15	9	8	7	1	16	8	8	...	...	...	...	...	...	...	...	...
	Punjab ...	64,614	30,833	33,781	60,873	28,275	32,598	3,681	2,501	1,180	43	41	2	2	2	...	15	14	1
	Total ...	65,641	31,632	34,009	61,534	28,814	32,720	4,041	2,756	1,285	43	41	2	3	3	...	20	18	2
	II.—Feudatory States.																		
	Jeypore ...	1	1	...	1	1	...	...	...	...	...	...	...	...	...	...	...	...	...
	Gawaliar ...	1	1	...	...	...	...	1	1	...	...	...	...	...	...	...	...	...	...
	Rampore ...	15	8	7	...	...	...	15	8	7	...	...	...	...	...	...	...	...	...
	Kapurthala ...	12	9	3	9	6	3	2	2	...	1	1	...	...	...	...	...	...	...
	Patiala ...	3	2	1	3	2	1	...	...	...	...	...	...	...	...	...	...	...	...
	Chamba ...	476	251	225	476	251	225	...	...	...	...	...	...	...	...	...	...	...	...
	Sarmore ...	1	...	1	1	...	1	...	...	...	...	...	...	...	...	...	...	...	...
	Bilaspore ...	2	2	...	2	2	...	...	...	...	...	...	...	...	...	...	...	...	...
	Total ...	511	274	237	492	262	230	18	11	7	1	1	...	...	...	...	...	...	...
	Total A ...	66,152	31,906	34,246	62,026	29,076	32,950	4,059	2,767	1,292	44	42	2	3	3	...	20	18	2

CENSUS 1891.

KASHMIR STATE.

TABLE XI.—*Birth-place.*

Birth-place.	Total Kashmir State.			Province. Jummu.			Kashmír.			Ladákh.			Skardu.			Gilgit.		
	Total.	Males.	Females.	Total.	Males.	Females.	Total.	Males.	Females.	Total.	Males.	Females.	Total.	Males.	Females.	Total.	Males.	Females.
B.—Asia beyond India. I.—Adjacent to India.																		
Belochistan ...	9	7	2	...	...	...	9	7	2	...	...	...	...	...	...	...	...	...
Afghanistan ...	745	625	120	340	264	76	302	259	43	3	3	...	100	99	1	...	...	...
Yaghistan (Chitral)	1,183	711	472	158	114	44	929	503	426	...	...	...	96	94	2	...	...	...
Turkistan ...	28	24	4	...	...	...	28	24	4	...	...	...	...	...	...	...	...	...
Nepal ...	1,001	904	97	568	519	49	336	291	45	96	93	3	1	1	...	...	...	...
China ...	24	19	5	7	5	2	...	...	...	17	14	3	...	...	...	...	...	...
Total ...	2,990	2,290	700	1,073	902	171	1,604	1,084	520	116	110	6	197	194	3	...	...	...
II.—Remote from India.																		
Persia ...	4	4	...	1	1	...	2	2	...	...	...	...	1	1	...	...	...	...
Turkey in Asia ...	7	7	...	...	...	...	7	7	...	...	...	...	...	...	...	...	...	...
Arabia ...	4	4	...	3	3	...	...	...	...	...	...	...	1	1	...	...	...	...
Chinese Tartary ...	27	22	5	6	4	2	...	...	...	21	18	3	...	...	...	...	...	...
Total ...	42	37	5	10	8	2	9	9	...	21	18	3	2	2	...	...	...	...
Total B ...	3,032	2,327	705	1,083	910	173	1,613	1,093	520	137	128	9	199	196	3	...	...	...
C.—Europe.																		
England and Wales ...	51	27	24	11	6	5	38	19	19	1	1	...	...	...	...	1	1	...
Scotland ...	5	3	2	...	...	...	5	3	2	...	...	...	...	...	...	...	...	...
Ireland ...	3	1	2	...	...	...	3	1	2	...	...	...	...	...	...	...	...	...
France ...	3	3	...	...	...	...	3	3	...	...	...	...	...	...	...	...	...	...
Holland ...	1	1	...	...	...	...	...	...	...	1	1	...	...	...	...	...	...	...
Italy ...	3	3	...	...	...	...	3	3	...	...	...	...	...	...	...	...	...	...
Portugal ...	2	2	...	...	...	...	2	2	...	...	...	...	...	...	...	...	...	...
Germany ...	3	2	1	...	...	...	...	...	...	3	2	1	...	...	...	...	...	...
Total C ...	71	42	29	11	6	5	54	31	23	5	4	1	...	...	...	1	1	...
D.—Africa.																		
Cape Colony ...	1	...	1	...	...	...	...	...	...	1	...	1	...	...	...	...	...	...
Unspecified ...	1	...	1	...	...	...	1	...	1	...	...	...	...	...	...	...	...	...
Total D ...	2	...	2	...	...	...	1	...	1	1	...	1	...	...	...	...	...	...
E.—Unspecified.	16,896	10,206	6,690	240	131	109	41	30	11	...	...	...	...	...	...	16,615	10,045	6,570
Grand Total ...	2,543,952	1,353,229	1,190,723	1,439,543	770,241	669,302	949,041	502,345	446,696	28,274	14,350	13,924	110,325	56,098	54,227	16,769	10,195	6,574

Srinagar:
Dated the 17th December, 1891.

BHAG RAM,
Census Superintendent, Kashmír State.

CENSUS 1891.

KASHMIR STATE.

TABLE XI.—*Birth-place.* (*Europeans and Eurasians.*)

Birth-place.	Total Population.			Province.														
				Jammu.			*Kashmír.*			*Ladákh.*			*Skardu.*			*Gilgit.*		
	Total.	Males.	Females.	Total.	Males.	Females.	Total.	Males.	Females.	Total.	Males.	Females.	Total.	Males.	Females.	Total.	Males.	Females.
Within the State	12	4	8	5	2	3	7	2	5	...	...	...	...	...	...	...	...	...
Punjab	19	10	9	4	...	4	14	10	4	1	...	1	...	...	...	...	...	...
North-Western Provinces	23	10	13	4	4	...	18	6	12	...	...	...	...	...	...	1	...	1
Central Provinces	1	...	1	...	...	...	1	...	1	...	...	...	...	...	...	...	...	...
Bengal	3	1	2	2	1	1	1	...	1	...	...	...	...	...	...	...	...	...
Bombay and Deccan	6	3	3	1	...	1	5	3	2	...	...	...	...	...	...	...	...	...
Madras	1	...	1	...	...	...	1	...	1	...	...	...	...	...	...	...	...	...
Burmah	1	...	1	...	...	...	1	...	1	...	...	...	...	...	...	...	...	...
Great Britain and Ireland	59	31	28	11	6	5	46	23	23	1	1	...	...	...	...	1	1	...
Italy	3	3	...	...	...	...	3	3	...	...	...	...	...	...	...	...	...	...
Germany	3	2	1	...	...	...	...	...	...	3	2	1	...	...	...	...	...	...
France	3	3	...	...	...	...	3	3	...	...	...	...	...	...	...	...	...	...
Holland	1	1	...	...	...	...	...	...	...	1	1	...	...	...	...	...	...	...
Portugal	1	1	...	1	1	...	...	...	...	...	...	...	...	...	...	...	...	...
Africa	2	...	2	...	...	...	1	...	1	1	...	1	...	...	...	...	...	...
Unspecified	1	...	1	...	...	...	1	...	1	...	...	...	...	...	...	...	...	...
TOTAL ...	139	69	70	28	14	14	102	50	52	7	4	3	...	...	...	2	1	1

SRINAGAR :
Dated the 17th December 1891.

BHAG RAM,
Census Superintendent, Kashmír State.

Supplement to Table XI.

CENSUS 1891.

KASHMIR STATE.

PART A.—TABLE XI.—*Birth-place (British born).*

Birth-place.	Total Population.			Province.														
				Jammu.			*Kashmír.*			*Ladákh.*			*Skardu.*			*Gilgit.*		
	Total.	Males.	Females.	Total.	Males.	Females.	Total.	Males.	Females.	Total.	Males.	Females.	Total.	Males.	Females.	Total.	Males.	Females.
England	50	27	23	11	6	5	37	19	18	1	1	...	...	...	...	1	1	...
Scotland	5	3	2	...	...	...	5	3	2	...	...	...	...	...	...	...	...	...
Wales	1	...	1	...	...	...	1	...	1	...	...	...	...	...	...	...	...	...
Ireland	3	1	2	...	...	...	3	1	2	...	...	...	...	...	...	...	...	...
TOTAL ...	59	31	28	11	6	5	46	23	23	1	1	...	...	...	...	1	1	...

JAMMU:
Dated the 17th December, 1891.

BHAG RAM,
Census Superintendent, Kashmír State.

CENSUS 1891.

KASHMIR STATE.

TABLE XII.—*Persons of unsound mind, by Age.—(Europeans and Eurasians).*

Province.	Total Afflicted.			Age Distribution.																									
				0—4		5—9		10—14		15—19		20—24		25—29		30—34		35—39		40—44		45—49		50—54		55—59		60 & over.	
	Total.	Males.	Females.	Males.	Females.	Males.	Females.	Males.	Females.	Males.	Females.	Males.	Females.	Males.	Females.	Males.	Females.	Males.	Females.	Males.	Females.	Males.	Females.	Males.	Females.	Males.	Females.	Males.	Females.
Jammu	...	...	...	...	...	...	...	...	...	...	...	...	...	...	...	...	...	...	...	...	...	...	...	...	...	...	...	...	...
Kashmír	...	...	...	...	...	...	...	...	...	...	...	...	...	...	...	...	...	...	...	...	...	...	...	...	...	...	...	...	...
Ladákh	...	...	...	...	...	...	...	...	...	...	...	...	...	...	...	...	...	...	...	...	...	...	...	...	...	...	...	...	...
Skardu	...	...	...	...	...	...	...	...	...	...	...	...	...	...	...	...	...	...	...	...	...	...	...	...	...	...	...	...	...
Gilgit	...	...	...	...	...	...	...	...	...	...	...	...	...	...	...	...	...	...	...	...	...	...	...	...	...	...	...	...	...
TOTAL ...	...	...	...	...	...	...	...	...	...	...	...	...	...	...	...	...	...	...	...	...	...	...	...	...	...	...	...	...	...

JAMMU :
Dated the 17th December, 1891.

BHAG RAM,
Census Superintendent, Kashmir State.

CENSUS 1891.

KASHMIR STATE.

Table XVI.—*Caste Index.*

No.	Caste	Religion	Number
1.	Arain	Mohamedan	22,243
2.	Arora	Hindu	3,510
		Sikh	221
3.	Awan	Mohamedan	8,034
4.	Bangi	Do.	1
5.	Bania	Hindu	21,556
		Sikh	35
		Jain	593
	Wain	Mohamedan Kashmír caste	16,148
	Vani	Do. Ladákh	4
6.	Batehra	Hindu	355
		Mohamedan	74
	Beldar	Mohamedan	2,091
7.	Bhatya	Hindu	23
		Sikh	18
8.	Bazigar	Hindu	73
		Mohamedan	922
9.	Beragi (Hindu ascetic)	Hindu	910
10.	Brahmans	Hindu	231,381
		Sikh	9,384
Mohomedan Converts and originally Brahmans, Kashmír Caste.	*Pandit*		2,895
	Sufi		11,003
	Bat		94,144
	Aitu		6,345
	Tantre		5,478
	Dár		68,949
	Rathar		23,801
	Rishi		6,290
	Raina		1,286
	Khande		6,093
	Ganai		37,987
	Bhatre	Hindu	26
		Sikh	20
	Bedangi (Nepali Brahman)	Hindu	1
	Pati Do.	do. do.	8
11.	Buddhist		29,608
12.	Do. Converts to Mohamedanism—		
	Argon	Mohamedan	706
	Tang	Do.	3
	Jaju	Do.	4
	Champa	Do.	1
	Dokpa	Do.	21
	Brokpa	Do.	274
	Chon	Do.	5
	Deo	Do.	2
	Kharpon	Do.	5
	Nospún	Do.	1
	Gonkpa	Do.	1
	Kafalpa	Do.	2

CENSUS 1891.

KASHMIR STATE.

TABLE XVI.—*Caste Index.*—(Continued.)

Budhist Converts to Mohamedanism.—(*Concluded.*)—

Churankpa	...	Mohamedan	...	...	1
Ofpa ...	...	Do.	...	...	1
Karimpa	...	Do.	...	...	1
Narankzapa	...	Do.	...	...	1
Charnanpa	...	Do.	...	...	1
Arkabakpa	...	Do.	...	...	1
Monkeypa	...	Do.	...	...	1
Aliarpa	...	Do.	...	...	1
Tarsarpa	...	Do.	...	...	2
Kanopa	...	Do.	...	...	1
Chaupon	...	Do.	...	...	2
Dasokharampa	...	Do.	...	...	1
Pahapa ...	...	Do.	...	...	1
Abdulpa ...	...	Do.	...	...	1
Galudanpa	...	Do.	...	...	1
Asarpa	...	Do.	...	...	1
Satapa	...	Do.	...	...	1
Kachapa	...	Do.	...	...	4
Dachapa	...	Do.	...	...	5
Samplepa	...	Do.	...	...	1
Dolupa	...	Do.	...	...	5
Mahvapa	...	Do.	...	...	2
Malakpa	...	Do.	...	...	2
Lakhbakpa	...	Do.	...	...	1

NOTE.—The above are Buddhist clans to which these people belonged before conversion to Mohamedanism.

13.	Chamar	...	Hindu	...	...	33,679
14.	Changar	...	Mohamedan	...	...	176
15.	Christians	...		...	...	218
16.	Chura	...	Hindu	...	...	8,257
	Vatal	...	Mohamedan	...	...	8,152
	Charu	...	Hindu	...	...	47
	Ramdasi or Mazhabi		Hindu	...	...	29
			Sikh	...	...	136
17.	Dervesh (Mohamedan ascetic)			...	...	89
	Chishti	...	Mohamedan	...	...	180
	Said-Makár	...	Do.	...	...	20
	Kadri	...	Do.	...	...	14
	Miskin	...	Do.	...	...	64
	Madari	...	Do.	...	...	30
	Tamburi	...	Do.	...	...	158
	Musafir	...	Do.	...	...	6
	Kalandar	...	Do.	...	...	117
	Noshahi	...	Do.	...		14
	Rawal	...	Do.	...	...	9
	Vagi	...	Do.	...	...	7
18.	Darzi	...	Hindu	...	...	701
			Mohamedan	...	...	4,150
	Sochi	...	Hindu	...	...	1

CENSUS 1891.

KASHMIR STATE.

TABLE XVI.—*Caste Index*.—(Continued.)

No.	Caste	Religion	Number
19.	Dhobi	Hindu	1,273
		Mohamedan	13,173
20.	Dum	Hindu	34,457
	Basith	Do.	5,929
	Batwal	Do.	5,848
	Saryara	Do.	2,277
	Sepi	Do.	828
	Megh	Do.	75,500
	Barwala	Do.	5,310
	Ratyal	Do.	653
	Begari	Do.	16
	Gen	Do.	57
	Gomsa	Do.	6
	Dhyar	Do.	104
21.	Dasali	Do.	369
22.	Gujar	Hindu	883
		Mohamedan	244,913
	Choupan	Mohamedan	2,993
23.	Hanji	Do.	33,870
24.	Jat	Hindu	23,780
		Sikh	370
		Mohamedan	118,445
25.	Jhiwar	Hindu	12,881
		Sikh	13
		Mohamedan	35
	Ghirath	Hindu	293
	Bhishti	Mohamedan	2,849
26.	Jogi (An agricultural tribe of Hindu Fakirs)	Hindu	3,610
		Mohamedan	2,589
27.	Julaha	Mohamedan	29,001
	Kuchband	Hindu	12
28.	Kalal	Hindu	87
		Sikh	34
29.	Kanjar	Mohamedan	525
	Perna	Do.	250
30.	Kambo	Hindu	477
		Mohamedan	54
31.	Kassab	Mohamedan	1,126
32.	Kayasth	Hindu	12
33.	Khatri	Hindu	15,234
		Sikh	872
	Khoja (Mohamedan Kashmír caste)	Mohamedan	8,580
	Magre Do.	Do.	5,811
	Kurgi (Nepalese caste)	Hindu	1
	Kaur Do.	Do.	3
	Bohar Do.	Do.	4

CENSUS 1891.

KASHMIR STATE.

TABLE XVI.—*Caste Index.*—Continued.)

No.	Caste	Religion	Number
	Malik (Kashmír caste of Hindus converted to Mohamedanism) ...	Mohamedan	21,887
34.	Kumhar	Hindu	5,757
		Sikh	26
		Mohamedan	16,724
35.	Labana	Hindu	5,077
		Sikh	32
		Mohamedan	8
36.	Lohar	Hindu	11,473
		Sikh	1
		Mohamedan	16,353
	Saikalgar ...	Hindu	190
		Mohamedan	82
37.	Memar	Mohamedan	440
38.	Manyar	Hindu	39
		Mohamedan	502
	Kamangar ...	Mohamedan	667
39.	Mirasi	Do.	9,629
	Rawabia ...	Hindu	5
	Kathak ...	Do.	11
	Bharai ...	Mohamedan	857
	Beda (Ladákh) ...	Do.	220
	Nikarchi ...	Do.	5
	Malakhan (Ladákh),	Do.	35
	Mon do. ...	Do.	71
	Sarnain ...	Hindu	2
	Gardi ...	Hindu	132
		Sikh	7
	Doom (village watchman) ...	Mohamedan	12,386
40.	Mochi	Do.	13,626
	Saraj ...	Do.	81
	Khatik ...	Do.	1,057
	Dabgar ...	Do.	20
41.	Moghal	Do.	16,588
42.	Musalli ...	Do.	2,578
43.	Naddaf	Do.	737
44.	Nai	Hindu	5,442
		Mohamedan	23,750
45.	Nepalese and other hill tribes—		
	Nepalese. *Sudar* ...	Hindu	2
	Gola ...	Do.	1
	Goran ...	Do.	3
	Makarkoni alias *Nagarkoti* ...	Do.	9
	Nobahar ...	Do.	1
	Bodar ...	Do.	1
	Bokru ...	Mohamedan	3
	Garti ...	Hindu	1

CENSUS 1891.

KASHMIR STATE.

TABLE XVI.—*Caste Index.*—(Continued.)

No.	Caste	Religion	Number
	Nepalese and other hill tribes—*Concluded*)—		
	Other hill tribes. *Heku* ...	Hindu	1
	Majithia	Do.	2
	Doni ...	Do.	1
	Dagori ...	Do.	1
	Kagar ...	Do.	1
	Godurz...	Do.	1
	Hota-beri	Do.	1
46.	Niyaria	Mohamedan	75
47.	Pakhiwar	Do.	13
48.	Pathan	Do.	38,016
49.	Parsi		9
50.	Rajputs	Hindu	150,641
		Mohamedan	211,348
	Ahlia (Nepalese Rajput of low degree)	Hindu	1
	Pare } Kashmír caste of Mohamedan Rajputs	Mohamedan	9,573
	Lon }	Do.	31,350
	Shahi } Nepalese Rajput ...	Hindu	2
	Thappa } Caste ...	Do.	3
51.	Rangrez	Mohamedan	2,024
52.	Sanyasi (Hindu ascetic)	Hindu	437
	Sadhu ...	Hindu	788
		Mohamedan	46
		Sikh	1
	Gusain ...	Hindu	1,805
		Mohamedan	28
	Bharti ...	Hindu	28
	Fakir ...	Hindu	37
		Mohamedan	12,738
	Sain ...	Hindu	116
		Mohamedan	23
	Gorya ...	Hindu	181
	Jangam ...	Do.	2
	Bramhchari ...	Do.	9
	Udasi ...	Hindu	56
		Mohamedan	4
	Nirmala ...	Hindu	7
	Suthra ...	Hindu	60
		Mohamedan	9
53.	Sansi	Hindu	268
54.	Sayad	Mohamedan	54,187
	Pir (Priests)	Do.	379
	Mir (an agricultural caste of Sayad)	Do.	59,827
55.	Seni ...	Hindu	728
56.	Shakhsaz	Mohamedan	306
57.	Sheikh...	Do.	373,633
	Hakim	Do.	22

CENSUS 1891.

KASHMIR STATE.

TABLE XVI.—*Caste Index.*—(Concluded).

Sheikh—(*Contd.*)			
	Nanbai ...	Mohamedan	2
	Malla ...	Do.	228
	Balti	Do.	25,024
	Bazdar	Do.	12
	Raodi	Do.	27
	Soni	Do.	5
	Sagar	Do.	8
	Kangu ...	Do.	7
	Ganarak ...	Do.	1
	Kamakhu ...	Do.	7
	Gashu	Do.	1
	Geri	Do.	2
	Mangrak ...	Do.	23
	Meva	Do.	1
	Makh	Do.	4
	Shaban ...	Do.	19
	Miai	Do.	6
	Hanghi ...	Do.	8
	Doru	Do.	16
	Turanj ...	Do.	13
	Hajia	Do.	2
	Chedeva ...	Do.	1
	Sambava ...	Do.	1
	Nanva ...	Do.	1
	Balida	Do.	1
	Harsakhia ...	Do.	4
	Homan Chirmal ...	Do.	1
	Kashna ...	Do.	1
58.	Sunar ...	Hindu	5,528
		Sikh	107
		Mohamedan	2,257
59.	Tarkhan ...	Hindu	10,620
		Mohamedan	18,090
60.	Teli	Mohamedan	20,124
61.	Thatyar ...	Hindu	786
		Mohamedan	78
62.	Unspecified ...	Hindu	1,087
		Sikh	122
		Mohamedan	3,586
		Unspecified	16,615

JAMMU:
Dated the 14th May 1892.

BHAG RAM,
Census Superintendent, Kashmir State.

CENSUS 1891.

KASHMIR STATE.

TABLE XVI.—*Caste Return.*

Class.	Group.	Caste, Tribe, &c.	Number of recorded Sub-divisions, clans, &c.	Strength.			Religion.	Strength.
				Total.	Males.	Females.		
A.—Agricultural	I.—Military and Dominant ...	Rajpúts (also agricultural) ...	5	402,918	215,602	187,316	Hindus ... ... Mohamedans	150,647 252,271
	II.—Other Agricultural— (*a*) Cultivators	Aráin	...	22,243	11,730	10,513	Mohamedans	All
		Awán	...	8,034	4,277	3,757	Do.	All
		Ját	...	142,595	75,950	66,645	Hindus ... ... Sikhs ... ... Mohamedans	23,780 370 118,445
		Seni	...	728	381	347	Hindus	All
		Total Group II (*a*) ...	...	173,600	92,338	81,262	Hindus ... ... Sikhs ... ... Mohamedans	24,508 370 148,722
	(*b*) Cattle Breeders and Graziers	Gujar (also agricultural) ...	1	248,789	133,685	115,104	Hindus ... ... Mohamedans	888 247,906
	(*c*) Field Laborers	Dum do. ...	11	130,985	68,862	62,123	Hindus	All
		Pakhiwar	...	13	4	9	Mohamedans	All
		Total Group II (*c*) ...	11	130,998	68,866	62,132	Hindus ... ... Mohamedans	130,985 13
		Total Group II ...	12	553,387	294,889	258,498	Hindus ... ... Sikhs ... ... Mohamedans	156,376 370 396,641
	IV.—Forest and hill-tribes ...	Nepalese and other hill-tribes ...	15	29	27	2	Hindus ... ... Mohamedans	26 3
		TOTAL CLASS A ...	32	956,334	510,518	445,816	Hindus ... ... Sikhs ... ... Mohamedans	307,019 370 648,915

CENSUS 1891.

KASHMIR STATE.

TABLE XVI.—*Caste Return.*—(Continued.)

Class.	Group.	Caste, tribe, &c.	Number of recorded Sub-divisions, clans, &c.	STRENGTH.			Religion.	Strength.
				Total.	Males.	Females.		
B.—Professional	V.—Priests	Brahmans (also agricultural) ...	14	505,086	268,833	236,253	Hindus	231,411
							Sikhs	9,404
							Mohamedans	264,271
		Sayad do. ...	2	114.393	59,940	54,453	Do.	All
		Total Group V ...	16	619,479	328,773	290,706	Hindus	231,411
							Sikhs	9,404
							Mohamedans	378,664
	VI.—Devotees	Beragi (Hindu ascetic)	...	910	575	335	Hindus	All
		Dervesh (Mohamedan ascetic) ...	11	708	384	324	Mohamedans	All
		Jogi (an agricultural tribe of Hindu Fakirs.)	...	6,199	3,347	2,852	Hindus	3,610
							Mohamedans	2,589
		Sanyasi (Hindu ascetic)	11	16,375	9,066	7,309	Hindus	3,526
							Sikhs	1
							Mohamedans	12,848
		Total Group VI ...	22	24,192	13,372	10,820	Hindus	8,046
							Sikhs	1
							Mohamedans	16,145
	IX.—Writers	Káyasth	...	12	10	2	Hindus	All
	XI.—Musicians and Ballad Reciters...	Mirasi	10	23,360	12,356	11,004	Do.	150
							Sikhs	7
							Mohamedans	23,203
	XII.—Dancers and Singers ...	Kanjar	1	775	394	381	Do.	All
		TOTAL CLASS B ...	49	667,818	354,905	312,913	Hindus	239,619
							Sikhs	9,412
							Mohamedans	418,787

CENSUS 1891.

KASHMIR STATE.

TABLE XVI.—*Caste Return.*—(Continued.)

Class.	Group.	Caste, Tribe, &c.	Number of recorded Sub-divisions, clans, &c.	Strength. Total.	Strength. Males.	Strength. Females.	Religion.	Strength.
C.—Commercial	XIV.—Traders	Arora	...	3,731	2,148	1,583	Hindus	3,510
							Sikhs	221
		Bania	2	38,336	20,781	17,605	Hindus	21,556
							Sikhs	35
							Jains	593
							Mohamedans	16,152
		Bhátya	...	41	29	12	Hindus	23
							Sikhs	18
		Kambo	...	531	274	257	Hindus	477
							Mohamedans	54
		Khatri	6	52,392	28,591	23,801	Hindus	15,242
							Sikhs	872
							Mohamedans	36,278
		Total Group XIV ...	8	95,031	51,773	43,258	Hindus	40,808
							Sikhs	1,146
							Jains	593
							Mohamedans	52,484
	XV.—Carriers	Labana	...	5,117	2,712	2,405	Hindus	5,077
							Sikhs	32
							Mohamedans	8
		TOTAL CLASS C. ...	8	100,148	54,485	45,663	Hindus	45,885
							Sikhs	1,178
							Jains	593
							Mohamedans	52,492

CENSUS 1891.

KASHMIR STATE.

TABLE XVI.—*Caste Return.*—(Continued.)

Class.	Group.	Caste, Tribe, &c.	Number of recorded Sub-divisions, clans, &c.	Strength. Total.	Strength. Males.	Strength. Females.	Religion.	Strength.
D—Artisans and Village Menials	XVII.—Goldsmiths	Sunár	...	7,892	4,265	3,627	Hindus ... ... Sikhs ... ... Mohamedans	5,528 107 2,257
	XVIII.—Barbers	Nái	...	29,192	15,482	13,710	Hindus ... ... Mohamedans	5,442 23,750
	XIX.—Blacksmiths	Lohar	1	28,099	15,098	13,001	Hindus ... ... Sikhs ... ... Mohamedans	11,663 1 16,435
	XX.—Carpenters and Turners ...	Tarkhan	...	28,710	15,489	13,221	Hindus ... ... Mohamedans	10,620 18,090
	XX—(*a*) Masons	Memar	...	440	252	188	Mohamedans	All
	XXI.—Brass and Coppersmiths ...	Thatyar	...	864	439	425	Hindus ... ... Mohamedans	786 78
	XXII.—Tailors	Darzi	1	4,852	2,552	2,300	Hindus ... ... Mohamedans	702 4,150
	XII—(*b*) Drug Preparers	Bangi	...	1	1	...	Mohamedans	All
	XXIII.—Weavers and	Julaha	1	29,013	15,401	13,612	Hindus ... ... Mohamedans	12 29,001
	Dyers	Rangrez	...	2,024	1,036	986	Mohamedans	All
		Total Group XXIII ...	1	31,037	16,439	14,598	Hindus ... ... Mohamedans	12 31,025

CENSUS 1891.

KASHMIR STATE.

TABLE XVI.—*Caste Return.*—(Continued.)

Class.	Group.	Caste, Tribe, &c.	Number of recorded Sub-divisions, clans, &c.	Strength. Total.	Strength. Males.	Strength. Females.	Religion.	Strength.
D.—Artisans and Village Menials—(*contd.*)	XXIV.—Washermen	Dhobi	...	14,446	7,668	6,778	Hindus	1,273
							Mohamedans	13,173
	XXV.—Cotton Cleaners	Naddaf	...	737	358	379	Mohamedans	All
	XXVII.—Oil Pressers	Teli	...	20,124	10,598	9,526	Do.	All
	XXVIII.—Potters	Kumhar	...	22,507	12,047	10,460	Hindus	5,757
							Sikhs	26
							Mohamedans	16,724
	XXIX.—Glass workers	Manyar	1	1,208	689	519	Hindus	39
							Mohamedans	1,169
	XXXII.—Goldsmith's refuse collectors	Niyaria	...	75	37	38	Mohamedans	All
	XXXV.—Fishermen, boatmen ...	Hanji	...	33,870	17,911	15,959	Do.	All
	Palkibearers, Cooks, &c. ...	Jhiwar	2	16,071	8,659	7,412	Hindus	13,174
							Sikhs	13
							Mohamedans	2,884
	XXXVI.—Distillers	Kalal	...	121	60	61	Hindus	87
							Sikhs	34
	XXXVII.—Butchers	Kassab	...	1,126	614	512	Mohamedans	All
	XXXVIII.—Leather Workers ...	Chamar	...	33,679	17,650	16,029	Hindus	All
		Mochi	3	14,784	7,952	6,832	Mohamedans	All
		Total Group XXXVIII ...	3	48,463	25,602	22,861	Hindus	33,679
							Mohamedans	14,784
	XXXIX.—Scavengers	Chura	3	16,621	8,811	7,810	Hindus	8,333
							Sikhs	136
							Mohamedans	8,152
		Musalli	...	2,578	1,408	1,170	Mohamedans	All
		Total Group XXXIX ...	3	19,199	10,219	8,980	Hindus	8,333
							Sikhs	136
							Mohamedans	10,730
		TOTAL CLASS D ...	12	309,034	164,479	144,555	Hindus	97,095
							Sikhs	317
							Mohamedans	211,622

CENSUS 1891.

KASHMIR STATE.

TABLE XVI.—*Caste Return.*—(Continued.)

Class.	Group.	Caste, Tribe, &c.	Number of recorded Sub-divisions, clans, &c.	Strength. Total.	Strength. Males.	Strength. Females.	Religion.	Strength.
E.—Vagrant Minor Artisans and Performers.	XLI.—Earth workers and stone dressers	Batehra	1	2,520	1,315	1,205	Hindus	355
							Mohamedans	2,165
	XLIII.—Cane Splitters	Shakhsaz	...	306	152	154	Mohamedans	All
	Mat-makers and leaf plate makers ...	Dasali	...	369	161	208	Hindus	Do.
		Total Group XLIII ...	...	675	313	362	Hindus	369
							Mohamedans	306
	XLV.—Miscellaneous and disreputable livers ...	Changar	...	176	90	86	Mohamedans	All
		Sansi	...	268	130	138	Hindus	Do.
		Total Group XLV ...	...	444	220	224	Hindus	268
							Mohamedans	176
	XLVI.—Tumblers and Acrobats ...	Bazigar	...	995	532	463	Hindus	73
							Mohamedans	922
		TOTAL CLASS E ...	1	4,634	2,380	2,254	Hindus	1,065
							Mohamedans	3,569
F.—Races and Nationalities ...	XLVIII.—Non-Indian Asiatic Races ...	Budhist	...	29,608	14,942	14,666	Budhists	All
		Budhist Converts to Mohamedanism	36	1,064	516	548	Mohamedans	Do.
		Moghal	...	16,588	8,757	7,831	Do.	Do.
		Pathan	...	38,016	20,331	17,685	Do.	Do.
		Parsi	...	9	7	2	Parsis	Do.
		Sheikh (including non-Musalmins of Indian origin).	29	399,071	209,032	190,039	Mohamedans	Do.
		Total Group XLVIII ...	65	484,356	253,585	230,771	Budhists	29,608
							Mohamedans	454,739
							Parsis	9

CENSUS 1891.

KASHMIR STATE.

TABLE XVI.—*Caste Return.*—(Continued.)

Class.	Group.	Caste, Tribe, &c.	Number of recorded Sub-divisions, clans, &c.	Strength. Total.	Strength. Males.	Strength. Females.	Religion.	Strength.
F.—Races and Nationalities —(*contd.*)	L.—Non-Asiatic Races	Europeans	...	132	67	65	Christians	All
		Africans	...	2	...	2	Do. ...	Do.
		Total Group L ...	...	134	67	67	Christians	All
	LI.—Eurasians	Eurasians	...	5	2	3	Christians	All
	LII.—Christian Converts ...	Christians	...	79	44	35	Do. ...	Do.
		TOTAL CLASS F ...	65	484,574	253,698	230,876	Budhists ... ... Mohamedans ... ... Parsis ... ... Christians	29,608 454,739 9 218
		Unspecified ...	...	21,410	12,764	8,646	Hindus ... ... Sikhs ... ... Mohamedans ... ... Unspecified	1,087 122 3,586 16,615

CENSUS 1891.

KASHMIR STATE.

TABLE XVI.—*Caste Return*.—(Concluded).

Tribe, &c.	Number of recorded Sub-divisions, clans, &c.	Strength. Total.	Strength. Males.	Strength. Females.	Religion.	Strength.
ABSTRACT.						
TOTAL CLASS A.	32	956,334	510,518	445,816	Hindus	307,049
					Sikhs	370
					Mohamedans	648,915
Do. B.	49	667,818	354,905	312,913	Hindus	239,619
					Sikhs	9,412
					Mohamedans	418,787
Do. C.	8	100,148	54,485	45,663	Hindus	45,885
					Sikhs	1,178
					Jains	593
					Mohamedans	52,492
Do. D.	12	309,034	164,479	144,555	Hindus	97,095
					Sikhs	317
					Mohamedans	211,622
Do. E.	1	4,634	2,380	2,254	Hindus	1,065
					Mohamedans	3,569
Do. F.	65	484,574	253,698	230,876	Budhists	29,608
					Mohamedans	454,739
					Parsis	9
					Christians	218
UNSPECIFIED	...	21,410	12,764	8,646	Hindus	1,087
					Sikhs	122
					Mohamedans	3,586
					Unspecified	16,615
GRAND TOTAL KASHMIR STATE ...	167	2,543,952	1,353,229	1,190,723	Hindus	691,800
					Sikhs	11,399
					Mohamedans	1,793,710
					Jains	593
					Christians	218
					Budhists	29,608
					Parsis	9
					Unspecified	16,615

JAMMU:
Dated the 14th May 1892.

BHAG RAM,
Census Superintendent, Kashmir State.

TABLE XVI.

Caste Return for Jammu Province.

CENSUS

KASHMIR

TABLE XVI.—*Caste Return for*

Class.	Group.	Caste, Tribe, &c.	Number of recorded Sub-divisions, Clans, &c.	Jammu.			Mirpore.			Batala.		
				Total.	Males.	Females.	Total.	Males.	Females.	Total.	Males.	Females.
A.—Agricultural.	I.—Military and Dominant.	Rajput	...	4,594	3,754	840	216	120	96	2,071	1,306	768
	II.—Other Agricultural—											
	(a) Cultivators ...	Arain	...	93	71	22	10	8	2	...	...	...
		Awan	...	73	57	16	7	3	4	3	2	1
		Jat	...	878	687	191	128	93	35	661	383	278
		Seni	...	2	2	...	...	...	...	...	...	...
		Total Group II (a) ...	...	1,046	817	229	145	104	41	664	385	279
	(b) Cattle Breeders and Graziers.	Gujar (also agricultural)	...	560	413	147	13	9	4	16	9	7
	(c) Field Laborers ...	Dum do.	...	3,648	2,448	1,200	1	1	...	427	245	182
		Pakhiwar	...	...	...	...	...	...	...	...	...	...
		Total Group II (c) ...	...	3,648	2,448	1,200	1	1	...	427	245	182
		Total Group II ...	...	5,254	3,678	1,576	159	114	45	1,107	639	468
		TOTAL CLASS A ...	...	9,848	7,432	2,416	375	234	141	3,178	1,947	1,231
B.—Professional.	V.—Priests	Brahmans (also agricultural.)	...	5,496	3,729	1,767	1,059	504	555	396	222	174
		Sayad do. ...	...	584	359	225	94	45	49	10	5	5
		Total Group V ...	...	6,080	4,088	1,992	1,153	549	604	406	227	179
	VI.—Devotees ...	Beragi (Hindu ascetic)...	...	60	52	8	8	5	3	17	14	3
		Dervesh (Mohamedan ascetic.)	...	...	...	...	...	...	...	9	5	4
		Jogi (an agricultural tribe of Hindu Fakirs.)	...	43	30	13	1	1	...	23	14	9
		Sanyasi (Hindu ascetic),	...	189	153	36	70	47	23	5	3	2
		Total Group VI ...		292	235	57	79	53	26	54	36	18
	IX.—Writers	Kayasth	...	12	10	2	...	...	...	...	...	...
	XI.—Musicians and Ballad Reciters.	Mirasi	...	382	231	151	93	40	53	15	10	5
	XII.—Dancers & Singers.	Kanjar	...	154	65	89	42	18	24	...	...	...
		TOTAL CLASS B ...	...	6,920	4,629	2,291	1,367	660	707	475	278	202

1891.

STATE.

the Jummu Province.

Punch.			Total Urban population.			Total Rural population.			Grand Total.			Religion.	Strength.
Total.	Males.	Females.	Total.	Males.	Females.	Total.	Males.	Females.	Total.	Males.	Females.		
1,186	870	816	8,067	6,052	2,015	309,874	164,224	145,650	317,941	170,276	147,665	Hindus ... Mohamedans ...	149,121 168,820
29	15	14	132	94	38	21,345	11,227	10,118	21,477	11,321	10,156	Mohamedans ...	All
18	14	4	101	76	25	7,906	4,186	3,720	8,007	4,262	3,745	Do. ...	All
108	72	36	1,775	1,235	540	135,489	71,816	63,673	137,264	73,051	64,213	Hindus ... Sikhs ... Mohamedans ...	23,243 83 113,938
...	...	...	2	2	...	726	379	347	728	381	347	Hindus ...	All
155	101	54	2,010	1,407	603	165,466	87,608	77,858	167,476	89,015	78,461	Hindus ... Sikhs ... Mohamedans ...	23,971 83 143,422
306	184	122	895	615	280	180,469	97,132	83,337	181,364	97,747	83,617	Hindus ... Mohamedans ...	880 180,484
61	30	31	4,137	2,724	1,413	126,465	65,866	60,599	130,602	68,590	62,012	Hindus ...	All
...	...	...	...	...	...	13	4	9	13	4	9	Mohamedans ...	All
61	30	31	4,137	2,724	1,413	126,478	65,870	60,608	130,615	68,594	62,021	Hindus ... Mohamedans ...	130,602 13
522	315	207	7,042	4,746	2,296	472,413	250,610	221,803	479,455	255,356	224,099	Hindus ... Sikhs ... Mohamedans ...	155,453 83 323,919
1,708	1,185	523	15,109	10,798	4,311	782,287	414,834	367,453	797,396	425,632	371,764	Hindus ... Sikhs ... Mohamedans ...	304,574 83 492,739
826	580	246	7,777	5,035	2,742	174,866	92,774	82,092	182,643	97,809	84,834	Hindus ... Sikhs ...	178,019 4,624
310	186	124	998	595	403	16,127	8,547	7,580	17,125	9,142	7,983	Mohamedans ...	All
1,136	766	370	8,775	5,630	3,145	190,993	101,321	89,672	199,768	106,951	92,817	Hindus ... Sikhs ... Mohamedans ...	178,019 4,624 17,125
4	3	1	89	74	15	791	475	316	880	549	331	Hindus ...	All
...	...	...	9	5	4	295	153	142	304	158	146	Mohamedans ...	All
8	6	2	75	51	24	6,056	3,254	2,802	6,131	3,305	2,826	Hindus ... Mohamedans ...	3,590 2,541
40	29	11	304	232	72	13,228	7,358	5,870	13,532	7,590	5,942	Hindus ... Sikhs ... Mohamedans ...	3,426 1 10,105
52	38	14	477	362	115	20,370	11,240	9,130	20,847	11,602	9,245	Hindus ... Sikhs ... Mohamedans ...	7,896 1 12,950
...	...	...	12	10	2	...	...	...	12	10	2	Hindus ...	All
33	19	14	523	300	223	9,134	4,824	4,310	9,657	5,124	4,533	Hindus ... Sikhs ... Mohamedans ...	147 7 9,503
...	...	...	196	83	113	353	193	160	549	276	273	Do. ...	All
1,221	823	398	9,983	6,385	3,598	220,850	117,578	103,272	230,833	123,963	106,870	Hindus ... Sikhs ... Mohamedans ...	186,027 4,632 40,127

CENSUS

KASHMIR

TABLE XVI.—*Caste Return for*

Class.	Group.	Caste, Tribe, &c.	Number of recorded Sub-divisions, Clans, &c.	JUMMU. Total.	JUMMU. Males.	JUMMU. Females.	MIRPORE. Total.	MIRPORE. Males.	MIRPORE. Females.	BATALA. Total.	BATALA. Males.	BATALA. Females.
C.—Commercial	XIV.—Traders ...	Arora	...	1,272	766	506	131	83	48	16	11	5
		Bania	...	1,831	1,093	738	1,369	662	707	1	1	...
		Bhatya	...	...	...	...	18	9	9	...	...	...
		Kambo	...	12	7	5	...	...	...	...	...	...
		Khatri	...	2,031	947	1,084	705	359	346	75	54	21
		Total Group XIV ...	...	5,146	2,813	2,333	2,223	1,113	1,110	92	66	26
	XV.—Carriers ...	Labana	...	11	11	...	...	...	...	...	...	...
		TOTAL CLASS C ...	...	5,157	2,824	2,333	2,223	1,113	1,110	92	66	26
D.—Artisans and Village Menials	XVII.—Goldsmiths ...	Sunar	...	527	306	221	191	102	89	38	19	19
	XVIII.—Barbers ...	Nai	...	527	303	224	83	41	42	100	59	41
	XIX.—Blacksmiths ...	Lohar	...	241	165	76	40	18	22	90	60	30
	XX.—Carpenters and Turners ...	Tarkhan	...	475	333	142	32	17	15	119	66	53
	XX(a).—Masons ...	Memar	...	129	86	43	...	...	...	...	...	...
	XXI.—Brass and Coppersmiths ...	Thatyar	...	19	12	7	...	...	...	...	...	...
	XXII.—Tailors ...	Darzi	...	200	113	87	130	62	68	...	...	...
	XXIII.—Weavers and	Julaha	...	384	195	189	588	289	299	...	...	...
	Dyers ...	Rangrez	...	57	37	20	51	...	51	6	6	...
	XXIV.—Washermen ...	Dhobi	...	237	140	97	89	39	50	189	96	93
	XXV.—Cotton Cleaners,	Naddaf	...	1	1	...	...	...	...	...	...	...
	XXVII.—Oil Pressers ...	Teli	...	106	72	34	147	80	67	53	22	31
	XXVIII.—Potters ...	Kumhar	...	255	166	89	329	158	171	60	27	33
	XXIX.—Glass-workers...	Manyar	...	36	27	9	...	...	...	93	50	43
	XXXII.—Goldsmiths refuse collectors...	Niyaria	...	75	37	38	...	...	...	...	...	...
	XXXV.—Fishermen, boatmen, palki, bearers, &c.	Hanji	...	16	15	1	16	10	6	13	7	6
		Jhiwar	...	1,973	1,201	772	180	105	75	118	74	44
		Total Group XXXV ...	...	1,989	1,216	773	196	115	81	131	81	50
	XXXVI.—Distillers ...	Kalal	...	10	9	1	6	3	3	...	...	...
	XXXVII.—Butchers ...	Kassab	...	177	94	83	55	25	30	...	...	...
	XXXVIII.—Leather	Chamar	...	279	155	124	6	1	5	402	205	197
	workers ...	Mochi	...	262	155	107	192	98	94	10	8	2
		Total Group XXXVIII	...	541	310	231	198	99	99	412	213	199

1891.

STATE.

the Jummu Province.—(Continued).

Punch.			Total Urban population.			Total Rural population.			Grand Total.			Religion.	Strength.
Total.	Males.	Females.	Total.	Males.	Females.	Total.	Males.	Females.	Total.	Males.	Females.		
24	12	12	1,443	872	571	2,143	1,188	955	3,586	2,060	1,526	Hindus ... Sikhs ...	3,393 193
217	161	56	3,418	1,917	1,501	18,591	10,177	8,414	22,009	12,094	9,915	Hindus ... Sikhs ... Jains ...	21,381 35 593
...	...	...	18	9	9	23	20	3	41	29	12	Hindus ... Sikhs ...	23 18
...	...	...	12	7	5	519	267	252	531	274	257	Hindus ... Mohamedans ...	477 54
351	240	111	3,162	1,600	1,562	18,060	10,426	7,634	21,222	12,026	9,196	Hindus ... Sikhs ... Mohamedans ...	12,155 666 8,401
592	413	179	8,053	4,405	3,648	39,336	22,078	17,258	47,389	26,483	20,906	Hindus ... Sikhs ... Jains ... Mohamedans ...	37,429 912 593 8,455
...	...	...	11	11	...	4,523	2,385	2,138	4,534	2,396	2,138	Hindus ... Sikhs ... Mohamedans ...	4,494 32 8
592	413	179	8,064	4,416	3,648	43,859	24,463	19,396	51,923	28,879	23,044	Hindus ... Sikhs ... Jains ... Mohamedans ...	41,923 944 593 8,463
248	140	108	1,004	567	437	5,513	2,977	2,536	6,517	3,544	2,973	Hindus ... Sikhs ... Mohamedans ...	5,459 107 951
81	48	33	791	451	340	16,098	8,566	7,532	16,889	9,017	7,872	Hindus ... Mohamedans ...	5,434 11,455
59	34	25	430	277	153	23,877	12,753	11,124	24,307	13,030	11,277	Hindus ... Sikhs ... Mohamedans ...	11,598 1 12,708
68	35	33	694	451	243	23,383	12,536	10,847	24,077	12,987	11,090	Hindus ... Mohamedans ...	10,567 13,510
1	1	...	130	87	43	136	73	63	266	160	106	Mohamedans ...	All
6	4	2	25	16	9	839	423	416	864	439	425	Hindus ... Mohamedans ...	786 78
8	7	1	338	182	156	3,655	1,933	1,722	3,993	2,115	1,878	Hindus ... Mohamedans ...	685 3,308
39	24	15	1,011	508	503	26,258	13,940	12,318	27,269	14,448	12,821	Hindus ... Mohamedans ...	12 27,257
8	5	3	122	48	74	1,700	884	816	1,822	932	890	Mohamedans ...	All
18	15	3	533	290	243	11,902	6,310	5,592	12,435	6,600	5,835	Hindus ... Mohamedans ...	1,255 11,180
2	2	...	3	3	...	422	191	231	425	194	231	Mohamedans ...	All
40	29	11	346	203	143	14,650	7,770	6,880	14,996	7,973	7,023	Mohamedans ...	All
68	37	31	712	388	324	15,884	8,600	7,284	16,596	8,988	7,608	Hindus ... Sikhs ... Mohamedans ...	5,744 26 10,826
...	...	...	129	77	52	1,032	585	447	1,161	662	499	Hindus ... Mohamedans ...	39 1,122
...	...	...	75	37	38	...	...	...	75	37	38	Mohamedans ...	All
...	...	...	45	32	13	938	505	433	983	537	446	Do.	Do.
298	179	119	2,569	1,559	1,010	13,411	7,044	6,367	15,980	8,603	7,377	Hindus ... Mohamedans ...	13,131 2,849
298	179	119	2,614	1,591	1,023	14,349	7,549	6,800	16,963	9,140	7,823	Hindus ... Mohamedans ...	13,131 3,832
5	2	3	21	14	7	66	26	40	87	40	47	Hindus ... Sikhs ...	81 6
...	...	...	232	119	113	303	193	110	535	312	223	Mohamedans ...	All
27	15	12	714	376	338	32,954	17,265	15,689	33,668	17,641	16,027	Hindus ...	All
27	17	10	491	278	213	10,503	5,648	4,855	10,994	5,926	5,068	Mohamedans ...	All
54	32	22	1,205	654	551	43,457	22,913	20,544	44,662	23,567	21,095	Hindus ... Mohamedans ...	33,668 10,994

KASHMIR

TABLE XVI.—*Caste Return for*

Class.	Group.	Caste, Tribe, &c.	Number of recorded Sub-divisions, Clans, &c.	JUMMU. Total.	JUMMU. Males.	JUMMU. Females.	MIRPORE. Total.	MIRPORE. Males.	MIRPORE. Females.	BATALA. Total.	BATALA. Males.	BATALA. Females.
D.—Artisans & Village Menials—Contd.	XXXIX.—Scavengers ...	Chura	...	893	486	407	215	107	108	2	2	...
		Musalli	...	...	...	...	...	...	...	...	...	...
		Total Group XXIX ...	...	893	486	407	215	107	108	2	2	...
		TOTAL CLASS D ...	...	6,879	4,108	2,771	2,350	1,155	1,195	1,293	701	592
E.—Vagrant Minor Artisans and Performers.	XLI.—Earth workers & stone dressers	Batehra	...	25	16	9	...	...	...	...	...	...
	XLIII.—Cane Splitters ...	Dasali	...	151	84	67	...	...	...	...	...	...
	XLV.—Miscellaneous and disreputable livers	Changar	...	38	19	19	...	...	...	...	...	...
		Sansi	...	...	...	...	...	...	...	...	...	...
		Total Group XLV ...	...	38	19	19	...	...	...	...	...	...
	XLVI.—Tumblers and Acrobats ...	Bazigar	...	...	...	...	...	...	...	...	...	...
		TOTAL CLASS E ...	...	214	119	95	...	...	...	...	..	...
F.—Races and Nationalities.	XLVIII.—Non Indian ...	Buddhist	...	...	...	...	...	...	...	...	...	...
	Asiatic Races	Moghal	...	391	224	167	28	17	11	...	...	...
		Pathan	...	759	509	250	20	11	9	23	13	10
		Parsi	...	...	...	...	...	...	...	...	...	...
		Sheikh	...	3,866	2,349	1,517	884	459	425	145	79	66
		Total Group XLVIII ...	...	5,016	3,082	1,934	932	487	445	168	92	76
	L.—Non Asiatic Races ...	Europeans	...	4	2	2	...	...	...	...	...	...
	LI.—Eurasians ...	Eurasians	...	5	2	3	...	...	...	...	...	...
	LII.—Christian converts	Christians	...	5	3	2	...	...	...	...	...	...
		TOTAL CLASS F ...	...	5,030	3,089	1,941	932	487	445	168	92	76
	...	Unspecified ...	...	494	344	150	6	6	...	...	...	...

1891.

STATE.

***the Jummu Province.*—(Continued).**

Punch.			Total Urban population.			Total Rural population.			Grand Total.			Religion.	Strength.
Total.	Males.	Females.	Total.	Males.	Females.	Total.	Males.	Females.	Total.	Males.	Females.		
129	74	55	1,239	669	570	7,032	3,727	3,305	8,271	4,396	3,875	Hindus ... Sikhs ...	8,250 21
...	...	...	...	...	...	2,578	1,408	1,170	2,578	1,408	1,170	Mohamedans ...	All
129	74	55	1,239	669	570	9,610	5,135	4,475	10,849	5,804	5,045	Hindus ... Sikhs ... Mohamedans ...	8,250 21 2,578
1,132	668	464	11,654	6,632	5,022	213,134	113,357	99,777	224,788	119,989	104,799	Hindus ... Sikhs ... Mohamedans ...	96,709 161 127,918
46	29	17	71	45	26	2,372	1,229	1,143	2,443	1,274	1,169	Hindus ... Mohamedans ...	355 2,088
20	15	5	171	99	72	188	56	132	359	155	204	Hindus ...	All
...	...	...	38	19	19	138	71	67	176	90	86	Mohamedans ...	All
...	...	...	...	...	...	234	117	117	234	117	117	Hindus ...	All
...	...	...	38	19	19	372	188	184	410	207	203	Hindus ... Mohamedans ...	234 176
...	...	...	...	...	...	995	532	463	995	532	463	Hindus ... Mohamedans ...	73 922
66	44	22	280	163	117	3,927	2,005	1,922	4,207	2,168	2,039	Hindus ... Mohamedans ...	1,021 3,186
...	...	...	...	...	...	4,293	2,179	2,114	4,293	2,179	2,114	Buddhists ...	All
84	47	37	503	288	215	5,302	2,794	2,508	5,805	3,082	2,723	Mohamedans ...	All
293	167	126	1,095	700	395	8,167	4,327	3,840	9,262	5,027	4,235	Do. ...	All
...	...	...	...	...	...	1	1	...	1	1	...	Parsis ...	All
2,321	1,300	1,021	7,216	4,187	3,029	101,449	53,719	47,730	108,665	57,906	50,759	Mohamedans ...	All
2,698	1,514	1,184	8,814	5,175	3,639	119,212	63,020	56,192	128,026	68,195	59,831	Mohamedans ... Buddhists ... Parsis ...	123,732 4,293 1
...	...	...	4	2	2	19	10	9	23	12	11	Christians ...	All
...	...	...	5	2	3	...	...	...	5	2	3	Do. ...	All
...	...	...	5	3	2	13	7	6	18	10	8	Do. ...	All
2,698	1,514	1,184	8,828	5,182	3,646	119,244	63,037	56,207	128,072	68,219	59,853	Buddhists ... Mohamedans ... Parsis ... Christians ...	4,293 123,732 1 46
72	28	44	572	378	194	1,752	1,013	739	2,324	1,391	933	Hindus ... Sikhs ... Mohamedans ...	924 106 1,294

CENSUS

KASHMIR

TABLE XVI.—*Caste Return for*

	Number of recorded Sub-divisions Clans, &c.	Jummu.			Mirpore.			Batala.		
		Total.	Males.	Females.	Total.	Males.	Females.	Total.	Males.	Females.
ABSTRACT.										
Total Class A	...	9,848	7,432	2,416	375	234	141	3,178	1,947	1,231
Do. B	...	6,920	4,629	2,291	1,367	660	707	475	273	202
Do. C	...	5,157	2,824	2,333	2,223	1,113	1,110	92	66	26
Do. D	...	6,879	4,108	2,771	2,350	1,155	1,195	1,293	701	592
Do. E	...	214	119	95	...	...	...	...	...	...
Do. F	...	5,030	3,089	1,941	932	487	445	168	92	76
Unspecified	...	494	344	150	6	6	...	...	...	...
GRAND TOTAL JAMMU PROVINCE ...	...	34,542	22,545	11,997	7,253	3,655	3,598	5,206	3,079	2,127

JAMMU:
Dated 14th May 1892.

1891.

STATE.

the Jammu Province.

Baramula.			Total Urban population.			Total Rural population.			Grand Total.			Religion.	Strength.
Total.	Males.	Females.	Total.	Males.	Females.	Total.	Males.	Females.	Total.	Males.	Females.		
1,708	1,185	523	15,109	10,798	4,311	782,287	414,834	367,453	797,396	425,632	371,764	Hindus ... Sikhs ... Mohamedans ...	304,574 83 492,739
1,221	823	398	9,983	6,385	3,598	220,850	117,578	103,272	230,833	123,963	106,870	Hindus ... Sikhs ... Mohamedans ...	186,074 4,632 40,127
592	413	179	8,064	4,416	3,648	43,859	24,463	19,396	51,923	28,879	23,044	Hindus ... Sikhs ... Jains ... Mohamedans ...	41,923 944 593 8,463
1,132	668	464	11,654	6,632	5,022	213,134	113,357	99,777	224,788	119,989	104,799	Hindus ... Sikhs ... Mohamedans ...	96,709 161 127,918
66	44	22	280	163	117	3,927	2,005	1,922	4,207	2,168	2,039	Hindus ... Mohamedans ...	1,021 3,186
2,698	1,514	1,184	8,828	5,182	3,646	119,244	63,037	56,207	128,072	68,219	59,853	Buddhists ... Mohamedans ... Parsis ... Christians ...	4,293 123,732 1 46
72	28	44	572	378	194	1,752	1,013	739	2,324	1,391	933	Hindus ... Sikhs ... Mohamedans ...	924 106 1,294
7,489	4,675	2,814	54,490	33,954	20,536	1,385,053	736,287	648,766	1,439,543	770,241	669,302	Hindus ... Sikhs ... Mohamedans ... Buddhists ... Parsis ... Christians ... Jains ...	631,225 5,926 797,459 4,293 1 46 593

BHAG RAM,

Census Superintendent, Kashmír State.

CENSUS

KASHMIR

TABLE XVI.—*Caste Return for*

Class.	Group.	Caste, Tribe, &c.	Number of recorded Sub-divisions, Clans, &c.	Srinagar. Total.	Srinagar. Males.	Srinagar. Females.	Anantnag. Total.	Anantnag. Males.	Anantnag. Females.	Sopore. Total.	Sopore. Males.	Sopore. Females.
A.—Agricultural.	I.—Military and Dominant	Rajput	...	2,408	1,305	1,103	414	228	186	390	151	239
	II.—Other Agricultural—											
	(a) Cultivators ...	Arain	...	...	...	...	74	41	33	7	3	4
		Awan	...	25	13	12	...	...	...	...	...	...
		Jat	...	263	167	96	20	10	10	...	...	...
		Total Group II (a) ...	...	288	180	108	94	51	43	7	3	4
	(b) Cattle Breeders and Graziers ...	Gujar (also agricultural)	...	1,369	716	653	180	92	88	551	289	262
	(c) Field Laborers ...	Dum (Do.) ...	...	146	104	42	...	...	...	...	...	...
		TOTAL CLASS A ...	...	4,211	2,305	1,906	688	371	317	948	443	505
B.—Professional.	V.—Priests ...	Brahman (also agricultural)	...	47,515	25,131	22,384	2,997	1,639	1,358	2,415	1,279	1,136
		Sayad Do. ...	...	8,170	4,160	4,010	808	433	375	287	159	128
		Total Group V. ...	...	55,685	29,291	26,394	3,805	2,072	1,733	2,702	1,438	1,264
	VI.—Devotees ...	Beragi	...	12	10	2	...	...	...	...	...	...
		Dervesh (Mohamedan ascetic)	...	137	71	66	...	...	...	...	...	...
		Jogi (an agricultural tribe of Hindu Fakirs) ...	...	16	7	9	...	...	...	...	...	...
		Sanyasi (Hindu ascetic),	...	151	97	54	44	23	21	116	57	59
		Total Group VI ...	...	316	185	131	44	23	21	116	57	59
	XI.—Musicians and Ballad Reciters ...	Mirasi	...	27	21	6	...	..	...	...	...	...
	XII.—Dancers and Singers ...	Kanjar	...	24	13	11	...	...	...	...	...	...
		TOTAL CLASS B ...	...	56,052	29,510	26,542	3,849	2,095	1,754	2,818	1,495	1,323

1891.

STATE.

the Kashmir Province.

Baramula.			Total Urban population.			Total Rural population.			Grand Total.			Religion.	Strength.
Total.	Males.	Females.	Total.	Males.	Females.	Total.	Males.	Females.	Total.	Males.	Females.		
391	203	188	3,603	1,887	1,716	80,547	43,004	37,543	84,150	44,891	39,259	Hindus ... Mohamedans ...	1,455 82,695
8	8	...	89	52	37	677	357	320	766	409	357	Mohamedans ...	All.
...	...	...	25	13	12	1	1	...	26	14	12	Do. ...	Do.
64	35	29	347	212	135	4,984	2,687	2,297	5,331	2,899	2,432	Hindus ... Sikhs ... Mohamedans ...	537 287 4,507
72	43	29	461	277	184	5,662	3,045	2,617	6,123	3,322	2,801	Hindus ... Sikhs ... Mohamedans ...	537 287 5,299
164	99	65	2,264	1,196	1,068	65,156	34,740	30,416	67,420	35,936	31,484	Hindus ... Mohamedans ...	3 67,417
1	1	...	147	105	42	234	165	69	381	270	111	Hindus ...	All.
628	346	282	6,475	3,465	3,010	151,599	80,954	70,645	158,074	84,419	73,655	Hindus ... Sikhs ... Mohamedans ...	2,376 287 155,411
1,868	1,069	794	54,790	29,118	25,672	267,195	141,625	125,570	321,985	170,743	151,242	Hindus ... Sikhs ... Mohamedans ...	53,298 4,780 263,967
461	235	226	9,726	4,987	4,739	86,197	45,140	41,057	95,923	50,127	45,796	Mohamedans ...	All.
2,324	1,304	1.020	64,516	34,105	30,411	353,392	186,765	166,627	417,908	220,870	197,038	Hindus ... Sikhs ... Mohamedans ...	53,298 4,780 359,830
...	...	...	12	10	2	18	16	2	30	26	4	Hindus ...	All.
...	...	...	137	71	66	267	155	112	404	226	178	Mohamedans ...	Do.
...	...	...	16	7	9	52	35	17	68	42	26	Hindus ... Mohamedans ...	20 48
1	1	...	312	178	134	2,389	1,218	1,171	2,701	1,396	1,3[illegible]5	Hindus ... Mohamedans ...	97 2,604
1	1	...	477	266	211	2,726	1,424	1,302	3,203	1,690	1,513	Hindus ... Mohamedans ...	147 3,056
...	...	...	27	21	6	13,845	7,044	6,301	13,372	7,065	6,307	Hindus ... Mohamedans ...	3 13,369
25	13	12	49	26	23	177	92	85	226	118	108	Mohamedans ...	All.
2,350	1,318	1,032	65,069	34,418	30,651	369,640	195,325	174,315	434,709	229,743	204,966	Hindus ... Sikhs ... Mohamedans ...	53,448 4,780 376,481

CENSUS

KASHMIR

TABLE XVI.—*Caste Return for*

Class.	Group.	Caste, Tribe, &c.	Number of recorded Sub-divisions Clans, &c.	Srinagar. Total.	Srinagar. Males.	Srinagar. Females.	Anantnag. Total.	Anantnag. Males.	Anantnag. Females.	Sopore. Total.	Sopore. Males.	Sopore. Females.
C.—Commercial.	XIV.—Traders ...	Arora	...	19	14	5	6	5	1	...	...	...
		Bania	...	40	29	11	...	...	...	...	...	...
		Khatri	...	2,702	1,568	1,134	164	82	82	258	122	131
		Total Group XIV ...	...	2,761	1,611	1,150	170	87	83	258	122	131
	XVI.—Carrier ...	Labana	...	3	3	...	...	...	...	...	...	...
		TOTAL CLASS C ...	...	2,764	1,614	1,150	170	87	83	253	122	131
D.—Artisans and Village Menials.	XVII.—Goldsmiths ...	Sunar	...	166	88	78	63	31	32	16	6	10
	XVIII.—Barbers ...	Nai	...	981	542	439	151	76	75	77	37	40
	XIX.—Blacksmiths ...	Lohar	...	76	50	26	...	...	...	...	...	...
	XX.—Carpenters and Turners ...	Tarkhan	...	70	33	37	143	76	67	...	...	...
	XX.—(a) Masons ...	Memar	...	25	12	13	13	5	8	...	...	...
	XXII.—Tailors ...	Darzi	...	358	188	170	12	6	6	9	5	4
	XXIII.—Weavers and	Julaha	...	45	26	19	3	2	1	...	...	...
	Dyers ...	Rangrez	...	73	32	41	12	6	6	...	...	...
		Total Group XXVII ...	...	118	58	60	15	8	7	...	...	...
	XXIV.—Washermen ...	Dhobi	...	274	142	132	46	24	22	42	28	19
	XXV.—Cotton Cleaners	Naddaf	...	64	19	45	39	24	15	...	...	...
	XXVII.—Oil Pressers ...	Teli	...	212	110	102	126	66	60	...	...	...
	XXVIII.—Potters ...	Kumhar	...	252	127	125	7	5	2	49	30	19
	XXIX.—Glass-workers...	Manyar	...	...	...	...	...	...	...	...	...	...
	XXXV.—Fishermen, boatmen.	Hanji	...	10,675	5,596	5,079	108	57	46	...	...	...
	Palki Bearers, Cooks, &c.	Jhiwar	...	22	14	8	...	...	...	...	...	...
		Total Group XXXV ...	...	10,697	5,610	5,087	103	57	46	...	...	...

1891.

STATE.

the Kashmir Province.—(Continued.)

Baramula.			Total Urban Population.			Total Rural Population.			Grand Total.			Religion.	Strength.
Total.	Males.	Females.	Total.	Males.	Females.	Total.	Males.	Females.	Total.	Males.	Females.		
...	...	...	25	19	6	117	67	50	142	86	56	Hindus ... Sikhs ...	114 28
3	2	1	43	31	12	16,247	8,581	7,666	16,290	8,612	7,678	Hindus ... Mohamedans ...	163 16,127
34	20	14	3,153	1,792	1,361	27,509	14,485	13,024	30,662	16,277	14,385	Hindus ... Sikhs ... Mohamedans ...	3,057 206 27,899
37	22	15	3,221	1,842	1,379	43,873	23,133	20,740	47,094	24,975	22,119	Hindus ... Sikhs ... Mohamedans ...	3,334 234 43,526
...	...	...	3	3	...	580	313	267	583	316	267	Hindus ...	All
37	22	15	3,224	1,845	1,379	44,453	23,446	21,007	47,677	25,291	22,386	Hindus ... Sikhs ... Mohamedans ...	3,917 234 43,526
...	...	...	245	125	120	1,050	549	501	1,295	674	621	Hindus ... Mohamedans ...	68 1,227
33	16	17	1,242	671	571	10,916	5,714	5,202	12,158	6,385	5,773	Hindus ... Mohamedans ...	8 12,150
...	...	...	76	50	26	3,425	1,851	1,574	3,501	1,901	1,600	Hindus ... Mohamedans ...	65 3,436
...	...	...	213	109	104	4,291	2,309	1,982	4,504	2,418	2,086	Hindus ... Mohamedans ...	53 4,451
19	10	9	57	27	30	117	65	52	174	92	82	Mohamedans ...	All
...	...	...	379	199	180	471	229	242	850	428	422	Hindus ... Mohamedans ...	11 839
...	...	...	48	28	20	1,696	925	771	1,744	953	791	Mohamedans ...	All
...	...	...	85	38	47	117	68	49	202	106	96	Do. ...	All
...	...	...	133	66	67	1,813	993	820	1,946	1,059	887	Mohamedans ...	All
...	...	...	362	189	173	1,649	879	770	2,011	1,068	943	Hindus ... Mohamedans ...	18 1,993
...	...	...	103	43	60	209	121	88	312	164	148	Mohamedans ...	All
65	36	29	403	212	191	4,690	2,402	2,288	5,093	2,614	2,479	Do. ...	All
1	1	...	309	163	146	5,543	2,860	2,683	5,852	3,023	2,829	Hindus ... Mohamedans ...	5 5,847
...	...	...	...	...	...	47	27	20	47	27	20	Mohamedans ...	All
...	...	...	10,778	5,653	5,125	22,109	11,721	10,388	32,887	17,374	15,513	Mohamedans ...	All
...	...	...	22	14	8	69	42	27	91	56	35	Hindus ... Sikhs ... Mohamedans ...	43 13 35
...	...	...	10,800	5,667	5,133	22,178	11,763	10,415	32,978	17,430	15,548	Hindus ... Sikhs ... Mohamedans ...	43 13 32,922

CENSUS

KASHMIR

TABLE XVI.—*Caste Return for*

Class.	Group.	Caste, Tribe, &c.	Number of recorded Sub-divisions, Clans, &c.	Srinagar. Total	Srinagar. Males.	Srinagar. Females.	Anantnag. Total.	Anantnag. Males.	Anantnag. Females.	Sopore. Total.	Sopore. Males.	Sopore. Females.
D.—Artisans and Village Menials.—(Contd.)	XXXVI.—Distillers ...	Kalal	...	6	3	3	...	...	...	...	...	...
	XXXVII.—Butchers ...	Kassab	...	...	...	...	...	...	...	...	...	...
	XXXVIII.—Leather Workers.	Chamar	...	...	...	...	...	...	...	...	...	...
		Mochi	...	338	177	161	...	...	...	121	67	54
		Total Group XXXVIII...	...	338	177	161	...	...	...	121	67	54
	XXXIX.—Scavengers ...	Chura	...	581	341	240	120	55	65	...	...	...
		Total Class D ...	...	14,218	7,500	6,718	838	433	405	314	168	146
E—Vagrant Minor Artisans and Performers.	XLI.—Earth workers ...	Batehra	...	5	1	4	...	...	...	...	...	...
	XLIII.—Cane Splitters &	Shakhsaz	...	...	...	...	...	...	...	...	...	...
	Leaf plate makers.	Dasali	...	...	...	...	...	...	...	...	...	...
		Total Group XLII ...	...	...	...	...	...	...	...	...	...	...
	XLV.—Miscellaneous and Disreputable Livers.	Sansi	...	34	13	21	...	...	...	...	...	...
		Total Class E ...	...	39	14	25	...	...	...	...	...	...
F.—Races and Nationalities.	XLVIII.—Non Indian Asiatic Races.	Moghal	...	1,742	890	852	136	67	69	13	8	5
		Pathan	...	5,902	3,078	2,824	287	155	132	229	116	113
		Parsi	...	8	6	2	...	...	...	...	...	...
		Sheikh	...	33,815	17,690	16,125	4,219	2,282	1,937	3,757	1,960	1,797
		Total Group XLVIII ...	...	41,467	21,664	19,803	4,642	2,504	2,138	3,999	2,084	1,915
	L.—Non Asiatic Races ...	Europeans	...	81	36	45	2	1	1	...	...	...
		Africans	...	1	...	1	...	...	...	...	...	...
		Total Group L ...	...	82	36	46	2	1	1	...	...	...
	LII.—Christian Converts	Christian	...	37	21	16	...	...	...	...	...	...
		Total Class F ...	...	41,586	21,721	19,865	4,644	2,505	2,139	3,999	2,084	1,915
		Unspecified ...	...	90	56	34	38	24	14	78	48	30

1891.

STATE.

the Kashmir Province—(Continued.)

Punch.			Total Urban population.			Total Rural population.			Grand Total.				
Total.	Males.	Females.	Total.	Males.	Females.	Total.	Males.	Females.	Total.	Males.	Females.	Religion.	Strength.
...	...	...	6	3	3	28	17	11	34	20	14	Hindus ... Sikhs ...	6 28
...	...	...	...	...	...	585	297	288	585	297	288	Mohamedans ...	All.
...	...	...	...	...	...	11	9	2	11	9	2	Hindus ...	Do.
6	4	2	465	248	217	3,178	1,697	1,476	3,638	1,945	1,693	Mohamedans ...	Do.
6	4	2	465	248	217	3,184	1,706	1,478	3,649	1,954	1,695	Hindus ... Mohamedans ...	11 3,638
...	...	...	701	396	305	7,648	4,018	3,630	8,349	4,414	3,935	Hindus ... Sikhs ... Mohamedans ...	82 115 8,152
124	67	57	15,494	8,168	7,326	67,844	35,800	32,044	83,338	43,968	39,370	Hindus ... Sikhs ... Mohamedans ...	370 156 82,812
...	...	...	5	1	4	72	40	32	77	41	36	Mohamedans ...	All.
...	...	...	...	...	...	306	152	154	306	152	154	Do. ...	Do.
...	...	...	...	...	...	10	6	4	10	6	4	Hindus ...	Do.
...	...	...	...	...	...	316	158	158	316	158	158	Hindus ... Mohamedans ...	10 306
...	...	...	34	13	21	...	...	...	34	13	21	Hindus ...	All.
...	...	...	39	14	25	388	198	190	427	212	215	Hindus ... Mohamedans ...	44 383
47	24	23	1,938	989	949	8,845	4,686	4,159	10,783	5,675	5,108	Mohamedans ...	All
67	40	27	6,485	3,389	3,096	22,223	11,875	10,348	28,708	15,264	13,444	Do. ...	All
...	...	...	8	6	2	...	...	...	8	6	2	Parsis ...	All
2,397	1,182	1,215	44,188	23,114	21,074	138,516	73,251	65,265	182,704	96,365	86,339	Mohamedans ...	All
2,511	1,246	1,265	52,619	27,498	25,121	169,584	89,812	79,772	222,203	117,310	104,893	Mohamedans ... Parsis ...	222,195 8
...	...	...	83	37	46	18	13	5	101	50	51	Christians ...	All
...	...	...	1	...	1	...	...	...	1	...	1	Do. ...	All
...	...	...	84	37	47	18	13	5	102	50	52	Christians ...	All
...	...	...	37	21	16	6	6	...	43	27	16	Christians ...	All
2,511	1,246	1,265	52,740	27,556	25,184	169,608	89,831	79,777	222,348	117,387	104,961	Mohamedans ... Parsis ... Christians ...	222,195 8 145
6	4	2	212	132	80	2,256	1,193	1,063	2,468	1,325	1,143	Hindus ... Sikhs ... Mohamedans ...	161 16 2,291

CENSUS

KASHMIR

TABLE XVI.—*Caste Return for*

	Number of recorded Sub-divisions, Clans, &c.	Srinagar. Total.	Srinagar. Males.	Srinagar. Females.	Anantnag. Total.	Anantnag. Males.	Anantnag. Females.	Sopore. Total.	Sopore. Males.	Sopore. Females.
ABSTRACT.										
Total Class A	...	4,211	2,305	1,906	688	371	317	948	443	505
Do. B	...	56,052	29,510	26,542	3,849	2,095	1,754	2,818	1,495	1,323
Do. C	...	2,764	1,614	1,150	170	87	83	253	122	131
Do. D	...	14,218	7,500	6,718	838	433	405	314	168	146
Do. E	...	39	14	25	...	...	...	...	...	...
Do. F	...	41,586	21,721	19,865	4,644	2,505	2,139	3,999	2,084	1,915
Unspecified ...	...	90	56	34	38	24	14	78	48	30
GRAND TOTAL ...	...	118,960	62,720	56,240	10,227	5,515	4,712	8,410	4,360	4,050

JAMMU :
Dated 14*th May* 1892.

1891.

STATE.

the Kashmir Province.—(Concluded).

Baramula.			Total Urban Population.			Total Rural population.			Grand Total.			Religion.	Strength.
Total.	Males.	Females.	Total.	Males.	Females.	Total.	Males.	Females.	Total.	Males.	Females.		
628	346	282	6,475	3,465	3,010	151,599	80,954	70,645	158,074	84,419	73,655	Hindus ... Sikhs ... Mohamedans ...	2,376 287 155,411
2,350	1,318	1,032	65,069	34,418	30,651	369,640	195,325	174,315	434,709	229,743	204,966	Hindus ... Sikhs ... Mohamedans ...	53,448 4,780 376,481
37	22	15	3,224	1,845	1,379	44,453	23,446	21,007	47,677	25,291	22,386	Hindus ... Sikhs ... Mohamedans ...	3,917 234 43,526
124	67	57	15,494	8,168	7,326	67,844	35,800	32,044	83,338	43,968	39,370	Hindus ... Sikhs ... Mohamedans ...	370 156 82,812
...	...	...	39	14	25	388	198	190	427	212	215	Hindus ... Mohamedans ...	44 383
2,511	1,246	1,265	52,740	27,556	25,184	169,608	89,831	79,777	222,348	117,387	104,961	Mohamedans ... Parsis ... Christians ...	222,195 8 145
6	4	2	212	132	80	2,256	1,193	1,063	2,468	1,325	1,143	Hindus ... Sikhs ... Mohamedans ...	161 16 2,291
5,656	3,003	2,653	143,253	75,598	67,655	805,788	426,747	379,041	949,041	502,345	446,696	Hindus ... Sikhs ... Mohamedans ... Parsis ... Christians ...	60,316 5,473 883,099 8 145

BHAG RAM,

Census Superintendent, Kashmir State.

CENSUS 1891.

KASHMIR STATE.

TABLE XVI.—*Caste Return for the Frontier Districts.*

Class.	Group.	Caste, Tribe, &c.	Number of recorded sub-divisions, clans, &c.	Ladakh. Total.	Ladakh. Males.	Ladakh. Females.	Skardu. Total.	Skardu. Males.	Skardu. Females.	Gilgit. Total.	Gilgit. Males.	Gilgit. Females.	Total Population. Total.	Total Population. Males.	Total Population. Females.	Religion.	Strength.
A.—Agricultural.	I. Military & Dominant	Rajput (also agricultural)	...	39	36	3	784	395	389	4	4	...	827	435	392	Hindus ... Mohamedans ...	71 756
	II. Other Agricultural— (a) Cultivators ...	Awan ...	...	...	...	...	...	...	...	1	1	...	1	1	...	Mohamedans ...	All.
	(b) Cattle Breeders and Graziers.	Gujar (also agricultural)	...	...	...	...	5	2	3	...	...	...	5	2	3	Do. ...	Do.
	(c) Field Laborers ...	Dum (Do.) ...	...	1	1	...	1	1	...	...	...	...	2	2	...	Hindus ...	Do.
		TOTAL GROUP II ...	...	1	1	...	6	3	3	1	1	...	8	5	3	Hindus ... Mohamedans ...	2 6
	IV. Forest & hill tribes	Nepalese & other hill tribes	...	25	23	2	4	4	...	...	...	...	29	27	2	Hindus ... Mohamedans ...	26 3
		TOTAL CLASS A ...	...	65	60	5	794	402	392	5	5	...	864	467	397	Hindus ... Mohamedans ...	99 765
B.—Professional.	V. Priests ...	Brahman (also agricultural)	...	184	130	54	271	148	123	3	3	...	458	281	177	Hindus ... Mohamedans ...	94 364
		Syad (Do.) ...	...	14	5	9	1,328	663	665	3	3	...	1,345	671	674	Mohamedans ...	All.
		TOTAL GROUP V ...	...	198	135	63	1,599	811	788	6	3	...	1,803	952	851	Hindus ... Mohamedans ...	94 1,709
	VI. Devotees ...	Sanyasi (ascetic Hindu) ..	...	...	...	...	142	80	62	...	...	...	142	80	62	Hindus ... Mohamedans ...	3 139
	XI. Musicians & Ballad Reciters.	Mirasi ...	...	326	164	162	5	3	2	...	...	...	331	167	164	Mohamedans ...	All.
		TOTAL CLASS B ...	...	524	299	225	1,746	894	852	6	6	...	2,276	1,199	1,077	Hindus ... Mohamedans ...	97 2,179

CENSUS 1891.

KASHMIR STATE.

TABLE XVI.—*Caste Return for the Frontier Districts.*—(Continued).

Class.	Group.	Caste, Tribe, &c.	Number of recorded sub-divisions, clans, &c.	Ladakh.			Skardu.			Gilgit.			Total Population.			Religion.	Strength.
				Total.	Males.	Females.	Total.	Males.	Females.	Total.	Males.	Females.	Total.	Males.	Females.		
C.—Commercial.	XIV. Traders ...	Arora ...	...	2	1	1	...	...	...	1	1	...	3	2	1	Hindus ...	All.
		Bania ...	...	8	6	2	21	11	10	8	8	...	37	25	12	Hindus ... Mohamedans...	12 25
		Khatri ...	...	31	31	...	477	257	220	...	...	...	508	288	220	Hindus ... Mohamedans...	30 478
		Total Class C ...	...	41	38	3	498	268	230	9	9	...	548	315	233	Hindus ... Mohamedans...	45 503
D.—Artisans & Village Menials.	XVII. Goldsmiths ...	Sunar ...	...	1	1	...	79	46	33	...	...	...	80	47	33	Hindus ... Mohamedans...	1 79
	XVIII. Barbers ...	Nai ...	...	11	3	8	134	77	57	...	...	...	145	80	65	Mohamedans ...	All
	XIX. Blacksmiths ...	Lohar ...	...	...	...	...	291	167	124	...	...	...	291	167	124	Do. ...	Do.
	XX. Carpenters & Turners.	Tarkhan ...	...	...	...	...	129	84	45	...	...	...	129	84	45	Do. ...	Do.
	XXII. Tailors ...	Darzi ...	...	9	9	...	...	...	...	...	...	...	9	9	...	Hindus ... Mohamedans...	6 3
	XXII (b). Drug-preparers	Bangi ...	...	1	1	...	...	...	...	...	...	...	1	1	...	Mohamedans ...	All.
	XXVII. Oil-pressers ...	Teli ...	...	16	5	11	19	6	13	...	...	...	35	11	24	Do. ...	Do.
	XXVIII. Potters ...	Kumhar ...	...	8	8	...	51	28	23	...	...	...	59	36	23	Hindus ... Mohamedans...	8 51
	XXXVII. Butchers ...	Kassab ...	...	6	5	1	...	...	...	...	...	...	6	5	1	Mohamedans ...	All.
	XXXVIII. Leather workers.	Mochi ...	...	1	1	...	151	80	71	...	...	...	152	81	71	Do. ...	Do.
	XXXIX. Scavengers ...	Chura ...	...	...	...	...	...	...	...	1	1	...	1	1	...	Hindus ...	Do.
		Total Class D ...	...	53	33	20	854	488	360	1	1	...	908	522	386	Hindus ... Mohamedans...	16 892

CENSUS 1891.

KASHMIR STATE.

TABLE XVI.—*Caste Return for the Frontier Districts.*—(Continued).

Class.	Group.	Caste, Tribe, &c.	Number of recorded sub-divisions, clans, &c.	Ladakh.			Skardu.			Gilgit.			Total Population.			Religion.	Strength.
				Total.	Males.	Females.	Total.	Males.	Females.	Total.	Males.	Females.	Total.	Males.	Females.		
F.—Races & Nationalities.	XLVIII.—Non-Indian Asiatic Races.	Budhist ...	...	25,076	12,615	12,461	239	148	91	...	...	...	25,315	12,763	12,552	Budhists ...	All.
		Do. Converts to Mohamedanism.	...	748	343	405	276	133	143	40	40	...	1,064	516	548	Mohamedans ...	Do.
		Pathan ...	...	14	8	6	25	25	...	7	7	...	46	40	6	Do. ...	Do.
		Sheikh ...	...	1,727	942	785	105,892	53,739	52,153	83	80	3	107,702	54,761	52,941	Do. ...	Do.
		TOTAL GROUP XLVIII ...	...	27,565	13,908	13,657	106,432	54,045	52,387	130	127	3	134,127	68,080	66,047	Budhists ... Mohamedans...	25,315 108,812
	L.—Non-Asiatic Races ...	Europeans ...	...	6	4	2	...	...	...	2	1	1	8	5	3	Christians ...	All.
		Africans ...	...	1	...	1	...	...	...	...	...	...	1	...	1	Do. ...	Do.
		TOTAL GROUP L ...	...	7	4	3	...	...	...	2	1	1	9	5	4	Christians ...	All.
	LII.—Christian Converts	Christians ...	...	18	7	11	...	...	...	...	...	...	18	7	11	Christians ...	All.
		TOTAL CLASS F ...	...	27,590	13,919	13,671	106,432	54,045	52,387	132	128	4	134,154	68,092	66,062	Budhists ... Mohamedans... Christians ...	25,315 108,812 27
		Unspecified ...	...	1	1	...	1	1	...	16,616	10,046	6,570	16,618	10,048	6,570	Hindus ... Mohamedans... Unspecified ...	2 1 16,615

CENSUS 1891.

KASHMIR STATE.

TABLE XVI.—*Caste Return for the Frontier Districts.*—(Concluded).

	Number of recorded sub-divisions, clans, &c.	Ladakh.			Skardu.			Gilgit.			Total Population.			Religion.	Strength.
		Total.	Males.	Females.	Total.	Males.	Females.	Total.	Males.	Females.	Total.	Males.	Females.		
ABSTRACT.															
Total Class A	...	65	60	5	794	402	392	5	5	...	864	467	397	Hindus ... Mohamedans...	99 765
„ „ B	...	524	299	225	1,746	894	852	6	6	...	2,276	1,199	1,077	Hindus ... Mohamedans...	97 2,179
„ „ C	...	41	38	3	498	268	230	9	9	...	548	315	233	Hindus ... Mohamedans...	45 503
„ „ D	...	53	33	20	854	488	366	1	1	...	908	522	386	Hindus ... Mohamedans...	16 892
„ „ E	...	...	...	...	...	...	...	...	...	...	...	...	...	...	...
„ „ F	...	27,590	13,919	13,671	106,432	54,045	52,387	132	128	4	134,154	68,092	66,062	Budhists ... Mohamedans... Christians ...	25,315 108,812 27
Unspecified	...	1	1	...	1	1	...	16,616	10,046	6,570	16,618	10,048	6,570	Hindus ... Mohamedans... Unspecified ...	2 1 16,615
GRAND TOTAL	...	28,274	14,350	13,924	110,325	56,098	54,227	16,769	10,195	6,574	155,368	80,643	74,725	Hindus ... Mohamedans... Budhists ... Christians ... Unspecified ...	259 113,152 25,315 27 16,615

JAMMU:
Dated 14th *May* 1892.

BHAG RAM,

Census Superintendent, Kashmir State.

CENSUS 1891.

KASHMIR STATE.

TABLE XVII.—*Occupations.*—PART A.

Class.	Order.	Sub-order and Group.	Occupation.	Urban Population.						Rural Population.					
				Workers.			*Dependents.*			*Workers.*			*Dependents.*		
				Total.	Males.	Females.	Total.	Males.	Females.	Total.	Males.	Females.	Total.	Males.	Females.
CLASS A.	I.—Administration	1. Service of the State ...	1. Maharaja and Rajas and their Families	3	3	...	77	1	76	...	...	...	...	...	...
			2. Officers	167	167	...	231	104	127	4	4	...	...	...	...
			3. Office Superintendents and Clerical Establishments. Police and Excise Inspectors, Sub-Registrars, &c.	6,246	6,193	53	10,922	4,014	6,908	10,553	10,243	310	19,097	7,508	11,589
			4. Messengers, Constables, Bailiffs, Warders, Menials, &c. ...	940	939	1	796	271	525	363	363	...	436	191	245
		2. Service of Local and Municipal Bodies.	5. Inspecting and Supervising Officials	1	1	...	4	1	3	...	...	...	...	...	...
		3. Village Service	9. Accountants	82	82	...	331	147	184	583	583	...	2,299	978	1,321
			11. Watchmen and other Menials ...	96	89	7	247	89	158	1,096	963	133	2,731	1,045	1,686
	II.—Defence ...	4. Army	12. Officers	3	3	...	8	3	5	...	...	...	...	...	...
			13. Non-Commissioned Officers and Privates	4,357	4,357	...	1,885	565	1,320	2,586	2,586	...	1,774	548	1,226
	III.—Foreign and Feudatory State Service.	6. Administrative Service ...	20. Clerical Establishments and 21. Menials, &c. ...	83	70	13	163	50	113	198	194	4	343	115	228
		7. Army and Marine	22. Officers	8	8	...	22	6	16	...	...	...	...	...	...
			TOTAL CLASS A ...	11,986	11,912	74	14,686	5,251	9,435	15,383	14,936	447	26,680	10,385	16,295

CENSUS 1891.

KASHMIR STATE.

TABLE XVII.—*Occupations.*—PART A.—(Continued.)

Class.	Order.	Sub-order and Group.	Occupation.	TOTAL.								
				Workers.			*Dependents.*			*Total.*		
				Total.	Males.	Females.	Total.	Males.	Females.	Total.	Males.	Females.
CLASS A.	I.—Administration	1. Service of the State ...	1. Maharaja and Rajas and their Families	3	3	...	77	1	76	80	4	76
			2. Officers	171	171	...	231	104	127	402	275	127
			3. Office Superintendents and Clerical Establishments. Police and Excise Inspectors, Sub-Registrars, &c.	16,799	16,436	363	30,019	11,522	18,497	46,818	27,958	18,860
			4. Messengers, Constables, Bailiffs, Warders, Menials, &c. ...	1,303	1,302	1	1,232	462	770	2,535	1,764	771
		2. Service of Local and Municipal Bodies.	5. Inspecting and Supervising Officials	1	1	...	4	1	3	5	2	3
		3. Village Service	9. Accountants	665	665	...	2,630	1,125	1,505	3,295	1,790	1,505
			11. Watchmen and other Menials ...	1,192	1,052	140	2,978	1,134	1,844	4,170	2,186	1,984
	II.—Defence ...	4. Army	12. Officers	3	3	...	8	3	5	11	6	5
			13. Non-Commissioned Officers and Privates	6,943	6,943	...	3 659	1,113	2,546	10,602	8,056	2,546
	III.—Foreign and Feudatory State Service.	6. Administrative Service ...	20. Clerical Establishments and 21. Menials, &c.	281	264	17	506	165	341	787	429	358
		7. Army and Marine	22. Officers	8	8	...	22	6	16	30	14	16
			TOTAL CLASS A ...	27,369	26,848	521	41,366	15,636	25,730	68,735	42,484	26,251

CENSUS 1891

KASHMIR STATE.

TABLE XVII.—*Occupations.*—PART A—(Continued.)

Class.	Order.	Sub-order and Group.		Occupation.	Urban Population. Workers. Total.	Urban Workers. Males.	Urban Workers. Females.	Urban Dependents. Total.	Urban Dependents. Males.	Urban Dependents. Females.	Rural Population. Workers. Total.	Rural Workers. Males.	Rural Workers. Females.	Rural Dependents. Total.	Rural Dependents. Males.	Rural Dependents. Females.
CLASS B.	IV.—Live stock ...	8. Stock breeding and dealing.	(a.) Horses and horned cattle...	25. Cattle breeders and dealers and Commissariat Farm Establishment	313	310	3	1,328	402	926	969	950	19	2,640	1,201	1,439
				26. Herdsmen	47	46	1	32	21	11	1,851	1,794	57	7,112	3,033	4,079
			(c.) Small stock ...	31. Sheep and Goat breeders and dealers	11	11	...	24	4	20	5,736	5,120	616	9,497	3,854	5,643
		9. Subsidiary services to stock.	(a.) Training and doctoring live stock...	34. Farriers and Gelders ...	29	29	...	60	17	43	16	16	...	68	24	44
				35. Horse and Elephant breakers and trainers, &c.	52	52	...	120	41	79	19	19	...	33	11	22
	V.—Agriculture ...	10. Interest in Land		37. Land occupants, not cultivating,	...	...	...	...	...	...	36,631	35,292	1,339	125,754	47,384	78,370
				38. Land occupants, cultivating ...	1,224	1,178	46	2,551	1,025	1,526	217,403	208,589	8,814	660,327	258,635	401,692
				39. Lessees of Villages, &c. ...	56	55	1	204	84	120	1,414	1,325	89	4,459	1,770	2,689
				41. Tenants and sharers, cultivating	1,671	1,626	45	2,772	934	1,838	187,854	177,561	10,293	488,943	179,757	309,186
		12. Growers of special products and trees		44. Tea, Coffee and Cinchona Planters, Managers and Assistants.	...	...	...	...	...	...	1	1	...	...	...	...
				47. Waternut growers	61	37	24	78	28	50	3	3	...	11	5	6
				52. Gardeners, seedsmen, &c. ...	81	71	10	154	52	102	264	235	29	632	259	373
				54. Forest Officers	1	1	...	7	1	6	...	...	...	...	...	...
				55. Forest Rangers, Guards, Peons ...	22	22	...	26	10	16	106	106	...	173	47	126
		13. Agricultural training and supervision.		56. Directors of agriculture and their Assistants	3	3	...	...	...	...	...	...	...	...	...	...
				TOTAL CLASS B ...	3,571	3,441	130	7,356	2,619	4,737	452,267	[illegible]1,011	21,256	1,299,649	495,980	803,669

CENSUS 1891.

KASHMIR STATE.

TABLE XVII.—*Occupations.*—PART A.—(Continued.)

Class.	Order.	Sub-order and Group.		Occupation.	Workers. Total.	Workers. Males.	Workers. Females.	Dependents. Total.	Dependents. Males.	Dependents. Females.	Total. Total.	Total. Males.	Total. Females.
CLASS B.	IV.—Live stock ...	8. Stock breeding and dealing.	(a.) Horses and horned cattle	25. Cattle breeders and dealers and Commissariat Farm Establishment	1,282	1,260	22	3,968	1,603	2,365	5,250	2,863	2,387
				26. Herdsmen	1,898	1,840	58	7,144	3,054	4,090	9,042	4,894	4,148
			(c.) Small stock ...	31. Sheep and Goat breeders and dealers	5,747	5,131	616	9,521	3,858	5,663	15,268	8,989	6,279
		9. Subsidiary services to stock.	(a) Training and doctoring live stock ...	34. Farriers and Gelders ...	45	45	...	128	41	87	173	86	87
				35. Horse and Elephant breakers and trainers, &c.	71	71	...	153	52	101	224	123	101
	V.—Agriculture ...	10. Interest in Land		37. Land occupants, not cultivating	36,631	35,292	1,339	125,754	47,384	78,370	162,385	82,676	79,709
				38. Land occupants, cultivating ...	218,627	209,767	8,860	662,878	259,660	403,218	881,505	469,427	412,078
				39. Lessees of Villages, &c. ...	1,470	1,380	90	4,663	1,854	2,809	6,133	3,234	2,899
				41. Tenants and sharers, cultivating	189,525	179,187	10,338	491,715	180,691	311,024	681,240	359,878	321,362
		12. Growers of special products and trees		44. Tea, Coffee and Cinchona Planters, Managers and Assistants	1	1	...	...	...	...	1	1	...
				47. Waternut growers ...	64	40	24	89	33	56	153	73	80
				52. Gardeners, seedsmen, &c. ...	345	306	39	786	311	475	1,131	617	514
				54. Forest Officers	1	1	...	7	1	6	8	2	6
				55. Forest Rangers, Guards, Peons...	128	128	...	199	57	142	327	185	142
		13. Agricultural training and supervision.		56. Directors of Agriculture and their Assistants ...	3	3	...	...	...	...	3	3	...
				TOTAL CLASS B ...	455,838	434,452	21,386	1,307,005	498,599	808,406	1,762,843	933,051	829,792

CENSUS 1891.

KASHMIR STATE.

TABLE XVII.—*Occupations.*—PART A.—(Continued.)

Class.	Order.	Sub-order and Group.	Occupation.	Urban Population.						Rural Population.					
				Workers.			*Dependents.*			*Workers.*			*Dependents.*		
				Total.	Males.	Females.	Total.	Males.	Females.	Total.	Males.	Females.	Total.	Males.	Females.
CLASS C.	VI.—Personal and household services.	14. Personal and domestic services...	59. Barbers	632	632	...	1,372	467	905	3,528	3,528	...	10,016	3,669	6,347
			63. Washermen (*sometimes also dyers*)	498	441	57	905	314	591	1,236	1,102	134	2,816	1,079	1,737
			64. Water-carriers	440	379	61	841	275	566	1,206	961	245	2,097	755	1,342
			65. Cooks	253	253	...	555	172	383	37	37	...	145	58	87
			66. Indoor servants	5,289	4,942	347	7,478	2,685	4,793	19,801	17,484	2,317	22,053	8,814	13,239
			67. Grooms, coachmen and dog-boys, &c.	51	51	...	21	5	16	18	18	...	13	3	10
			68. Door-keepers, &c.	22	22	...	47	17	30	2	2	...	8	1	7
		15. Non-domestic Establishment ...	70. Rest-house, Serai, Bath-house, &c., owners and Managers ...	16	16	...	22	4	18	141	138	3	692	307	385
		16. Sanitation	74. Sweepers and scavengers ...	97	84	13	216	83	133	730	572	158	1,420	569	851
			75. Dust and sweepings contractors	18	15	3	41	19	22	...	...	...	...	...	...
			TOTAL CLASS C ...	7,316	6,835	481	11,498	4,041	7,457	26,699	23,842	2,857	39,260	15,255	24,005
CLASS D.	Preparation and supply of material substances.	VII. Food and drink. 17. Animal Food	76. Cow and buffalo-keepers and milk and butter sellers ...	915	848	67	2,151	778	1,373	4,315	4,025	290	12,755	5,125	7,630
			77. Ghee preparers and sellers ...	34	34	...	12	4	8	747	732	15	1,879	723	1,156
			79. Butchers	600	598	2	1,502	515	987	353	348	5	1,015	398	617
			81. Fishermen and fish curers (*many are also boatmen and palki bearers*)	133	127	6	361	126	235	269	262	7	1,099	493	606
			Carried over Class D ...	1,682	1,607	75	4,026	1,423	2,603	5,684	5,367	317	16,748	6,739	10,009

CENSUS 1891.

KASHMIR STATE.

TABLE XVII.—*Occupations.*—PART A.—(Continued.)

Class.	Order.	Sub-order and Group.	Occupation.	TOTAL. Workers. Total.	Workers. Males.	Workers. Females.	Dependents. Total.	Dependents. Males.	Dependents. Females.	Total. Total.	Total. Males.	Total. Females.
CLASS C.	VI.—Personal and household services.	14. Personal and domestic services ...	59. Barbers	4,160	4,160	...	11,388	4,136	7,252	15,548	8,296	7,252
			63. Washermen (*sometimes also dyers*)	1,734	1,543	191	3,721	1,393	2,328	5,455	2,936	2,519
			64. Water-carriers	1,646	1,340	306	2,938	1,030	1,908	4,584	2,370	2,214
			65. Cooks	290	290	...	700	230	470	990	520	470
			66. Indoor servants	25,090	22,426	2,664	29,531	11,499	18,032	54,621	33,925	20,696
			67. Grooms, coachmen and dog-boys, &c.	69	69	...	34	8	26	103	77	26
			68. Door-keepers, &c.	24	24	...	55	18	37	79	42	37
		15. Non-domestic Establishment ...	70. Rest-house, Serai, Bath-house, &c., owners and Managers ...	157	154	3	714	311	403	871	465	406
		16. Sanitation	74. Sweepers and scavengers ...	827	656	171	1,636	652	984	2,463	1,308	1,155
			75. Dust and sweepings contractors	18	15	3	41	19	22	59	34	25
			TOTAL CLASS C ...	34,015	30,677	3,338	50,758	19,296	31,462	84,773	49,973	34,800
CLASS D.	Preparation and supply of material substances.	VII. Food & drink — 17. Animal Food	76. Cow and buffalo-keepers and milk and butter sellers ...	5,230	4,873	357	14,906	5,903	9,003	20,136	10,776	9,360
			77. Ghee preparers and sellers ...	781	766	15	1,891	727	1,164	2,672	1,493	1,179
			79. Butchers	953	946	7	2,517	913	1,604	3,470	1,859	1,611
			81. Fishermen and fish curers (*many are also boatmen and palki bearers*) ...	402	389	13	1,460	619	841	1,862	1,008	854
			Carried over Class D ...	7,366	6,974	392	20,774	8,162	12,612	28,140	15,136	13,004

CENSUS 1891.

KASHMIR STATE.

TABLE XVII.—*Occupations.*—PART A.—(Continued.)

Class.	Order.	Sub-order and Group.		Occupation.	Urban Population. Workers. Total.	Urban Workers. Males.	Urban Workers. Females.	Urban Dependents. Total.	Urban Dependents. Males.	Urban Dependents. Females.	Rural Population. Workers. Total.	Rural Workers. Males.	Rural Workers. Females.	Rural Dependents. Total.	Rural Dependents. Males.	Rural Dependents. Females.
				Brought forward Class D ...	1,682	1,607	75	4,026	1,423	2,603	56,84	5,367	317	16,748	6,739	10,009
CLASS D.—(*Continued.*)	Preparation and supply of material substances.—(*Contd*).	VII. Food & drink	18. Vegetable Food.	83. Grain dealers	1,522	1,489	33	4,140	1,526	2,614	1,831	1,799	32	6,184	2,539	3,645
				84. Grain parchers	40	30	10	66	28	38	38	30	8	23	8	15
				86. Flour-mill service and management	151	120	31	296	120	176	1,980	1 801	179	3,214	1,086	2,128
				87. Bakers	607	557	50	1,345	531	814	541	514	27	1,569	621	948
				89. Vegetable sellers ...	715	629	86	1,662	602	1,060	366	320	46	709	260	449
				90. Fruit sellers	474	406	68	1,023	388	635	114	111	3	437	172	265
				92. Confectioners and sweetmeat makers and sellers, and cooks who are also sometimes fishermen and water-carriers ...	305	300	5	529	206	323	112	112	...	249	74	175
			19. Drink condiments and narcotics.	97. Country spirits distillers & sellers	26	24	2	12	5	7	11	11	...	8	3	5
				105. Salt preparers and sellers ...	...	...	...	...	...	...	97	65	32	74	15	59
				109. Grocers and general condiment dealers	61	57	4	108	31	77	129	124	5	263	75	188
				112. Tobacco and snuff manufacturers and sellers	328	327	1	679	237	442	66	65	1	168	62	106
				114. Opium, &c., manufacturers and sellers	1	1	...	...	...	...	...	...	...	...	...	...
				115. Bhang, ganja, &c, preparers and sellers	15	15	...	24	7	17	...	...	...	1	...	1
				Carried over Class D ...	5,927	5,562	365	13,910	5,104	8,806	10,969	10,319	650	29,647	11,654	17,993

CENSUS 1891.

KASHMIR STATE.

TABLE XVII.—*Occupations.*—PART A.—(Continued.)

Class.	Order.	Sub-order and Group.		Occupation.	TOTAL. Workers. Total.	Workers. Males.	Workers. Females.	Dependents. Total.	Dependents. Males.	Dependents. Females.	Total. Total.	Total. Males.	Total. Females.
				Brought forward Class D.	7,366	6,974	392	20,774	8,162	12,612	28,140	15,136	13,004
CLASS D.—(*Continued.*)	Preparation and supply of material substances.—(*Contd.*)	VII. Food & drink	18. Vegetable Food.	83. Grain dealers	3,353	3,288	65	10,324	4,065	6,259	13,677	7,358	6,324
				84. Grain parchers	78	60	18	89	36	53	167	96	71
				86. Flour-mill service and management	2,131	1,921	210	3,510	1,206	2,304	5,641	3,127	2,514
				87. Bakers	1,148	1,071	77	2,914	1,152	1,762	4,062	2,223	1,889
				89. Vegetable sellers	1,081	949	132	2,371	862	1,509	3,452	1,811	1,641
				90. Fruit sellers	588	517	71	1,460	560	900	2,048	1,077	971
				92. Confectioners and sweetmeat makers and sellers, and cooks who are also sometimes fishermen and water carriers ...	417	412	5	778	280	498	1,195	692	503
			19. Drink condiments and narcotics.	97. Country spirits distillers & sellers	37	35	2	20	8	12	57	43	14
				105. Salt preparers and sellers ...	97	65	32	74	15	59	171	80	91
				109. Grocers and general condiment dealers	190	181	9	371	106	265	561	287	274
				112. Tobacco and snuff manufacturers and sellers	394	392	2	847	299	548	1,241	691	550
				114. Opium, &c., manufacturers and sellers	1	1	...	...	...	...	1	1	...
				115. Bhang, ganja, &c, preparers and sellers	15	15	...	25	7	18	40	22	18
				Carried over Class D ...	16,896	15,881	1,015	43,557	16,758	26,799	60,453	32,639	26,814

CENSUS 1891.

KASHMIR STATE.

Table XVII.—*Occupations.*—Part A.—(Continued.)

Class.	Order.	Sub-order and Group.	Occupation.	Urban Population. Workers. Total.	Urban Workers. Males.	Urban Workers. Females.	Urban Dependents. Total.	Urban Dependents. Males.	Urban Dependents. Females.	Rural Population. Workers. Total.	Rural Workers. Males.	Rural Workers. Females.	Rural Dependents. Total.	Rural Dependents. Males.	Rural Dependents. Females.
			Brought forward Class D ...	5,927	5,562	365	13,910	5,104	8,806	10,969	10,319	650	29,647	11,654	17,993
Class D.—(*Continued.*)	VIII. Light, firing, and forage.	20. Lighting	116. Oil-pressers and sellers ...	296	277	19	754	276	478	2,730	2,602	128	8,439	3,346	5,093
			119. Candle makers and sellers ...	2	2	...	1	...	1	...	...	...	...	...	...
			120. Torch makers and sellers ...	15	15	...	49	17	32	1	1	...	5	2	3
		21. Fuel and Forage	125. Firewood and grass gatherers and sellers	342	324	18	1,359	576	783	397	343	54	693	242	451
			131. Hay, &c., contractors and dealers	...	...	...	...	...	...	10	10	...	2	2	...
	IX. Buildings ...	22. Building materials	132. Brick and tile burners and sellers	75	75	...	201	69	132	22	15	7	42	16	26
			133. Lime chunam and shell burners and sellers	...	...	...	...	...	...	73	73	...	245	91	154
		23. Artificers in Buildings ...	136. Building contractors ...	94	94	...	282	117	165	106	106	...	223	96	127
			137. Stone and marble workers ...	48	48	...	99	33	66	39	39	...	189	66	73
			138. Masons	380	380	...	768	245	523	98	98	...	158	56	102
	XI. Supplementary requirements.	27. Paper, &c.	153. Paper makers and sellers and palm leaf binders	145	145	...	398	147	251	2	2	...	11	3	8
		28. Books and Prints, &c. ...	157. Press Proprietors, Lithographers and Printers	28	28	...	33	6	27	...	...	...	...	...	...
			158. Book-binders	45	45	...	92	30	62	10	10	...	27	6	21
			159. Book-sellers and publishers ...	...	...	...	...	...	...	2	2	...	...	...	...
			Carried over Class D ...	7,397	6,995	402	17,946	6,620	11,326	14,459	13,620	839	39,631	15,580	24,051

CENSUS 1891.

KASHMIR STATE.

TABLE XVII.—*Occupations.*—PART A.—(Continued).

Class.	Order.	Sub-order and Group.	Occupation.	TOTAL. Workers. Total.	Workers. Males.	Workers. Females.	Dependents. Total.	Dependents. Males.	Dependents. Females.	Total. Total.	Total. Males.	Total. Females.
CLASS D.—(Continued).			*Brought forward Class D* ...	16,896	15,881	1,015	43,557	16,758	26,799	60,453	32,639	27,814
	VIII. Light, firing, and forage.	20. Lighting ...	116. Oil-pressers and sellers ...	3,026	2,879	147	9,193	3,622	5,571	12,219	6,501	5,718
			119. Candle makers and sellers ...	2	2	...	1	...	1	3	2	1
			120. Torch makers and sellers ...	16	16	...	54	19	35	70	35	35
		21. Fuel and Forage ...	125. Firewood and grass gatherers and sellers ...	739	667	72	2,052	818	1,234	2,791	1,485	1,306
			131. Hay, &c, contractors and sellers	10	10	...	2	2	...	12	12	...
	IX. Buildings ...	22. Building materials ...	132. Brick and tile burners and sellers	97	90	7	243	85	158	340	175	165
			133. Lime chunam and shell burners and sellers ...	73	73	...	245	91	154	318	164	154
		23. Artificers in Buildings ...	136. Building contractors ...	200	200	...	505	213	292	705	413	292
			137. Stone and marble workers ...	87	87	...	238	99	139	325	186	139
			138. Masons	478	478	...	926	301	625	1,404	779	625
	XI. Supplementary requirements.	27. Paper, &c. ...	153. Paper makers and sellers and palm leaf binders ...	147	147	...	409	150	259	556	297	259
		28. Books and Prints, &c. ...	157. Press Proprietors, Lithographers and Printers ...	28	28	...	33	6	27	61	34	27
			158. Book-binders ...	55	55	...	119	36	83	174	91	83
			159. Book-sellers and publishers ...	2	2	...	...	...	...	2	2	...
			Carried over Class D ...	21,856	20,615	1,241	57,577	22,200	35,377	79,433	42,815	35,618

CENSUS 1891.

KASHMIR STATE.

TALBE VII.—*Occupations.*—PART A.—(Continued.)

Class.	Order.	Sub-order and Group.	Occupation.	Urban Population. Workers. Total.	Urban Population. Workers. Males.	Urban Population. Workers. Females.	Urban Population. Dependents. Total.	Urban Population. Dependents. Males.	Urban Population. Dependents. Females.	Rural Population. Workers. Total.	Rural Population. Workers. Males.	Rural Population. Workers. Females.	Rural Population. Dependents. Total.	Rural Population. Dependents. Males.	Rural Population. Dependents. Females.
			Brought forward Class D ...	7,397	6,995	402	17,946	6,620	11,326	14,459	13,620	839	39,631	15,580	24,051
CLASS D.—(*Continued.*)	XI. Supplementary requirements.—*Concld.*	29. Watches, Clocks and scientific instruments	163. Watch and Clock makers and sellers	16	16	...	29	10	19	...	...	...	...	...	...
		30. Carving, engraving, &c. ...	172. Turners and lacquerers ...	37	37	...	97	32	65	6	6	...	39	14	25
			173. Die-sinkers and seal, &c., engravers	91	91	...	150	40	110	4	4	...	9	3	6
		31. Toys, curiosities &c.	178. Hukka stem makers and sellers	48	48	...	92	35	57	3	3	...	6	1	5
			179. Papier-mache workers and sellers	230	230	...	463	122	341	12	10	2	21	9	12
		32. Music and Musical Instruments ...	183. Music and Musical Instrument dealers	6	6	...	16	7	9	...	...	...	...	...	...
		33. Necklaces, Bracelets, beads, sacred threads, &c.	185. Bangle makers and sellers in lac	101	93	8	203	63	140	122	119	3	247	71	176
			194. Flower garland makers and sellers	4	4	...	12	3	9	1	1	...	...	...	...
		35. Harness	201. Saddlery and Harness makers and sellers	252	252	...	352	86	266	28	28	...	65	35	30
		36. Tools and Machinery ...	205. Knife and tool grinders ...	23	23	...	47	13	34	37	37	...	101	34	67
		37. Arms and ammunition ...	210. Ammunition and Cap dealers ...	1	1	...	...	...	...	...	...	...	...	...	...
			212. Fire-work makers and sellers ...	29	29	...	76	34	42	45	44	1	134	58	76
			215. Bow and arrow makers and sellers	37	37	...	27	2	25	3	3	...	9	5	4
			Carried over Class D ...	8,272	7,862	410	19,510	7,067	12,443	14,720	13,875	845	40,262	15,810	24,452

CENSUS 1891.

KASHMIR STATE.

TABLE VII.—*Occupations.*—PART A.—(Continued.)

Class.	Order.	Sub-order and Group.	Occupation.	Workers. Total.	Workers. Males.	Workers. Females.	Dependents. Total.	Dependents. Males.	Dependents. Females.	Total. Total.	Total. Males.	Total. Females.
			Brought forward Class D ...	21,856	20,615	1,241	57,577	22,200	35,377	79,433	42,815	36,618
CLASS D.—(*Continued.*)	XI. Supplementary requirements.—(*Concld.*)	29. Watches, Clocks and scientific instruments	163. Watch and Clock makers and sellers	16	16	...	29	10	19	45	26	19
		30. Carving, engraving, &c. ...	172. Turners and lacquerers ...	43	43	...	136	46	90	179	89	90
			173. Die-sinkers and seal, &c., engrávers	95	95	...	159	43	116	254	138	116
		31. Toys, curiosities &c.	178. Hukka stem makers and sellers ...	51	51	...	98	36	62	149	87	62
			179. Papier-mache workers and sellers	242	240	2	484	131	353	726	371	355
		32. Music and Musical Instruments ...	183. Music and Musical Instrument dealers	6	6	...	16	7	9	22	13	9
		33. Necklaces, Bracelets, beads, sacred threads, &c.	185. Bangle makers and sellers in lac	223	212	11	450	134	316	673	346	327
			194. Flower garland makers and sellers	5	5	...	12	3	9	17	8	9
		35. Harness	201. Saddlery and Harness makers and sellers	280	280	...	417	121	296	697	401	296
		36. Tools and Machinery ...	205. Knife and tool grinders ...	60	60	...	148	47	101	208	107	101
		37. Arms and ammunition ...	210. Ammunition and Cap dealers ...	1	1	...	...	...	...	1	1	...
			212. Fire-work makers and sellers ...	74	73	1	210	92	118	284	165	119
			215. Bow and arrow makers and sellers	40	40	...	36	7	29	76	47	29
			Carried over Class D ...	22,992	21,737	1,255	59,772	22,877	36,895	82,764	44,614	38,150

CENSUS 1891.

KASHMIR STATE.

TABLE XVII.—*Occupations.*—PART A.—(Continued.)

Class.	Order.	Sub-order and Group.	Occupation.	Urban Population. Workers. Total.	Urban Workers. Males.	Urban Workers. Females.	Urban Dependents. Total.	Urban Dependents. Males.	Urban Dependents. Females.	Rural Population. Workers. Total.	Rural Workers. Males.	Rural Workers. Females.	Rural Dependents. Total.	Rural Dependents. Males.	Rural Dependents. Females.
			Brought forward Class D ...	8,272	7,862	410	19,510	7,067	12,443	14,720	13,875	845	40,262	15,810	24,452
CLASS D.—(*Continued.*)	XII.—Textile Fabrics and dress ...	38. Wool and Fur	217. Carpet weavers and sellers ...	339	338	1	412	104	308	7	7	...	8	1	7
			218. Shawl weavers and sellers ..	5,452	5,449	3	10,758	3,180	7,678	4,170	4,170	...	9,928	3,645	6,283
			219. Felt and pashm workers and sellers	163	163	...	443	130	313	...	...	...	...	...	...
			220. Blanket weavers and sellers (*often also shepherds*)	936	936	...	2,178	748	1,430	3,608	3,570	38	10,822	4,167	6,655
			221. Woollen cloth manufacturers and dealers	350	332	18	860	300	560	134	134	...	385	157	228
			222. Woollen yarn spinners and sellers	2,195	32	2,163	974	380	594	19,548	51	19,497	4,110	1,565	2,545
			223. Wool carders	188	188	...	538	177	361	...	...	...	...	...	...
			224. Wool dyers	362	358	4	803	256	547	520	476	44	1,286	460	826
		39. Silk	226. Silk-worm rearers and cocoon gatherers	26	26	...	76	23	53	68	68	...	190	68	122
			229. Silk printers and dyers ...	4	4	...	13	4	9	6	6	...	12	6	6
			230. Braid and ribbon makers and sellers	388	333	55	622	210	412	48	47	1	88	32	56
		40. Cotton	231. Cotton cleaners, pressers and ginners	163	162	1	360	124	236	919	874	45	2,196	805	1,391
			232. Cotton carpet and rug makers and sellers	45	45	...	105	29	76	...	...	...	...	...	...
			Carried over Class D ...	18,883	16,228	2,655	37,652	12,732	24,920	43,748	23,278	20,470	69,287	26,716	42,571

CENSUS 1891.

KASHMIR STATE.

TABLE XVII.—*Occupations.*—PART A.—(Continued.)

Class.	Order.	Sub-order and Group.	Occupation.	TOTAL. Workers. Total.	Workers. Males.	Workers. Females.	Dependents. Total.	Dependents. Males.	Dependents. Females.	Total. Total.	Total. Males.	Total. Females.
			Brought forward Class D ...	22,992	21,737	1,255	59,772	22,877	36,895	82,764	44,614	38,150
CLASS D.—(*Continued.*)	XII.—Textile Fabrics and dress.	38. Wool and Fur	217. Carpet weavers and sellers ...	346	345	1	420	105	315	766	450	316
			218. Shawl weavers and sellers ...	9,622	9,619	3	20,686	6,825	13,861	30,308	16,444	13,864
			219. Felt and pashm workers and sellers	163	163	...	443	130	313	606	293	313
			220. Blanket weavers and sellers (*often also shepherds*)	4,544	4,506	38	13,000	4,915	8,085	17,544	9,421	8,123
			221. Woollen cloth manufacturers and dealers	484	466	18	1,245	457	788	1,729	923	806
			222. Woollen yarn spinners and sellers	21,743	83	21,660	5,084	1,945	3,189	26,827	2,028	24,799
			223. Wool carders	188	188	...	538	177	361	726	365	361
			224. Wool dyers	882	834	48	2,089	716	1,373	2,971	1,550	1,421
		39. Silk	226. Silk-worm rearers and cocoon gatherers	94	94	...	266	91	175	360	185	175
			229. Silk printers and dyers ...	10	10	...	25	10	15	35	20	15
			230. Braid and ribbon makers and sellers	436	380	56	710	242	468	1,146	622	524
		40. Cotton	231. Cotton cleaners, pressers and ginners	1,082	1,036	46	2,556	929	1,62[illegible]	3,638	1,965	1,673
			232. Cotton carpet and rug makers and sellers	45	45	...	105	29	76	150	74	76
			Carried over Class D. ...	62,631	39,506	23,125	106,939	39,448	67,491	169,570	78,954	90,616

CENSUS 1891.

KASHMIR STATE.

TABLE XVII.—Occupations.—Part A.—(Continued).

Class.	Order.	Sub-order and Group.	Occupation.	Urban Population. Workers. Total.	Urban Workers. Males.	Urban Workers. Females.	Urban Dependents. Total.	Urban Dependents. Males.	Urban Dependents. Females.	Rural Population. Workers. Total.	Rural Workers. Males.	Rural Workers. Females.	Rural Dependents. Total.	Rural Dependents. Males.	Rural Dependents. Females.
Class D.—(Continued.)			*Brought forward Class D* ...	18,883	16,228	2,655	37,652	12,732	24,920	43,748	23,278	20,470	69,287	26,716	42,571
	XII.—*Concld.* ...	40. Cotton—(*contd.*)	234. Cotton weavers, Mill-owners and Managers	433	426	7	1,069	367	702	9,815	9,273	542	22,119	7,517	14,602
			236. Calenderers, fullers and printers	50	50	...	147	55	92	41	41	...	101	36	65
			237. Cotton dyers	...	...	...	...	...	...	18	18	...	69	14	55
		41. Jute, flax, coir, &c.	241. Hemp rope makers and sellers ...	...	...	...	...	...	...	4	4	...	7	...	7
			243. Sacking, tarpaulin and gunny makers and sellers	...	...	...	...	...	...	1	1	...	5	2	8
		42. Dress	247. Tailors and darners	5,570	5,528	42	9,698	2,945	6,753	2,611	2,454	157	6,184	2,242	3,942
			254. Embroiderers and lace and muslin makers	409	409	...	618	184	434	3	...	3	5	...	5
	XIII.—Metals and precious stones.	43. Gold, silver, and precious stones	260. Gold and silver workers ...	891	888	3	2,214	733	1,481	1,548	1,540	8	4,081	1,461	2,620
			261. Gold beaters	...	...	...	...	...	...	4	4	...	24	12	12
			262. Goldsmiths' dust washers ...	1	1	...	2	1	1	9	9	...	31	9	22
			265. Electro-platers	...	...	...	...	...	...	6	6	...	6	1	5
			266. Gold and silver wire drawers, and braid makers	...	...	...	...	...	...	3	3	...	10	4	6
		44. Brass, copper and bell metal ...	277. Brass pot makers and sellers ...	56	45	11	151	64	87	114	99	15	143	44	99
			279. Copper workers and sellers ...	211	211	...	464	186	328	78	78	...	210	72	138
			Carried over Class D ...	26,504	23,786	2,718	52,015	17,217	34,798	58,003	36,808	21,195	102,282	38,130	64,152

CENSUS 1891.

KASHMIR STATE.

TABLE XVII.—*Occupations*.—PART A.—(Continued.)

Class.	Order.	Sub-Order and Group.	Occupation.	TOTAL. Workers. Total.	Workers. Males.	Workers. Females.	Dependents. Total.	Dependents. Males.	Dependents. Females.	Total. Total.	Total. Males.	Total. Females.
			Brought forward Class D ...	62,631	39,506	23,125	106,939	39,448	67,491	169,570	78,954	90,616
CLASS D.—(*Continued.*)	XII.—*Concld.* ...	40. Cotton—(*contd.*)	234. Cotton weavers, Mill-owners and Managers	10,248	9,699	549	23,188	7,884	15,304	33,43	17,583	15,853
			236. Calenderers, fullers and printers	91	91	...	248	91	157	339	182	157
			237. Cotton dyers	18	18	...	69	14	55	87	32	55
		41. Jute, flax, coir, &c.	241. Hemp rope makers and sellers ...	4	4	...	7	...	7	11	4	7
			243. Sacking, tarpaulin and gunny makers and sellers ...	1	1	...	5	2	3	6	3	3
		42. Dress	247. Tailors and darners	8,181	7,982	19	15,882	5,187	10,695	24,063	13,169	10,894
			254. Embroiderers and lace and muslin makers	412	40	3	623	184	439	1,035	593	442
	XIII.—Metals and precious stones.	43. Gold, silver, and precious stones	260. Gold and silver workers ...	2,439	2,428	11	6,295	2,194	4,101	8,734	4,622	4,112
			261. Gold beaters	4	4	...	24	12	1	28	16	12
			262. Goldsmiths' dust washers ...	10	10	...	33	10	2	43	20	23
			265. Electro-platers	6	6	...	6	1	5	12	7	5
			266. Gold and silver wire drawers, and braid makers	3	3	...	1	4	6	13	7	6
		44. Brass, copper and bell metal ...	277. Brass pot makers and sellers ...	170	144	2	294	108	186	464	252	212
			279. Copper workers and sellers ...	28	289	...	67	208	466	963	497	466
			Carried over Class D ...	84,507	60,594	23,91	154,297	55,347	98,950	238,804	115,941	122,863

CENSUS 1891.

KASHMIR STATE.

TABLE XVII.—*Occupations.*—PART A.—(Continued.)

Class.	Order.	Sub-order and Group.	Occupation.	Urban Population. Workers. Total.	Urban Workers. Males.	Urban Workers. Females.	Urban Dependents. Total.	Urban Dependents. Males.	Urban Dependents. Females.	Rural Population. Workers. Total.	Rural Workers. Males.	Rural Workers. Females.	Rural Dependents. Total.	Rural Dependents. Males.	Rural Dependents. Females.
Class D.—(*Continued.*)			*Brought forward Class D* ...	26,504	23,786	2,718	52,015	17,217	34,798	58,003	36,808	21,195	102,282	38,130	64,152
	XIII.—*Concld.* ...	45. Tin, zinc, mercury and lead ...	284. Tin workers and sellers ...	12	12	...	22	5	17	134	134	...	413	147	266
		46. Iron and steel	290. Blacksmiths	455	455	...	923	288	635	3,568	3,461	107	9,732	3,792	5,940
	XIV.—Glass, pottery and stone ware.	47. Glass and Chinaware ...	297. Glass and Chinaware dealers ...	...	...	...	...	...	...	5	4	1	3	1	2
		48. Earthen and stone ware ...	298. Potters and pot and pipe-bowl-makers and sellers. (*Some are brick and tile makers also*) ...	192	189	3	562	189	373	3,486	3,249	237	8,944	3,418	5,526
			299. Grindstone and millstone makers, menders and sellers ...	...	...	...	...	...	...	5	5	...	12	3	9
	XV.—Wood cane and leaves, &c.	49. Timber and wood	302. Timber and bamboo agents and dealers	7	7	...	14	4	10	664	628	36	1,446	540	906
			303. Wood cutters and sawyers ...	138	188	...	303	92	211	183	183	...	631	275	356
			304. Carpenters	848	848	...	1,655	551	1,104	4,195	4,195	...	111,61	4,108	7,053
		50. Canework, matting and leaves &c.	306. Bamboo and rattan splitters, workers and sellers ...	85	73	12	143	50	93	651	599	52	1,683	626	1,057
			307. Basket weavers and winnowing pan makers and sellers ...	29	29	...	20	5	15	481	413	68	1,087	406	681
			308. Mat makers and sellers ...	69	23	46	61	16	45	138	64	74	101	39	62
			310. Leaf-plate makers and sellers. (*Are also often temple servants*) ...	1	1	...	4	...	4	41	33	8	49	19	30
			Carried over Class D ...	28,340	25,561	2,779	55,722	18,417	37,305	71,554	49,776	21,778	137,494	51,504	85,990

CENSUS 1891.

KASHMIR STATE.

TABLE XVII.—*Occupations.*—PART A.—(Continued.)

Class.	Order.	Sub-order and Group.	Occupation.	TOTAL.								
				Workers.			*Dependents.*			*Total.*		
				Total.	Males.	Females.	Total.	Males.	Females.	Total.	Males.	Females
CLASS D.—(*Continued.*)			*Brought forward Class D* ...	84,507	60,594	23,913	154,297	55,347	98,950	238,804	115,941	122,863
	XIII.—*Concld.*	45. Tin, zinc, mercury and lead ...	284. Tin workers and sellers ...	146	146	...	435	152	283	581	298	283
		46. Iron and steel	290. Blacksmiths	4,023	3,916	107	10,655	4,080	6,575	14,678	7,996	6,682
	XIV.—Glass, pottery and stone ware.	47. Glass and Chinaware ...	297. Glass and Chinaware dealers ...	5	4	1	3	1	2	8	5	3
		48. Earthen and stone ware ...	298. Potters and pot and pipe-bowl-makers and sellers. (*Some are brick and tile makers also*) ...	3,678	3,438	240	9,506	3,607	5,899	13,184	7,045	6,139
			299. Grindstone and millstone makers, menders and sellers ...	5	5	...	12	3	9	17	8	9
	XV.—Wood cane and leaves, &c.	49. Timber and wood	302. Timber and bamboo agents and dealers	671	635	36	1,460	544	916	2,181	1,179	952
			303. Wood cutters and sawyers ...	321	321	...	934	367	567	1,255	688	567
			304. Carpenters	5,043	5,048	...	12,816	4,659	8,157	17,859	9,702	8,157
		50. Canework, matting and leaves &c.	306. Bamboo and rattan splitters, workers and sellers ...	736	672	64	1,826	676	1,150	2,562	1,348	1,214
			307. Basket weavers and winnowing pan makers and sellers ...	510	442	68	1,057	411	646	1,567	853	714
			308. Mat makers and sellers ...	207	87	120	162	55	107	369	142	227
			310. Leaf-plate makers and sellers. (*Are also often temple servants*) ...	42	34	8	53	19	34	95	53	42
			Carried over Class D ...	99,894	75,337	24,557	193,216	69,921	123,295	293,110	145,258	147,853

CENSUS 1891.

KASHMIR STATE.

TABLE XVII.—*Occupations.*—PART A.—(Continued.)

Class.	Order.	Sub-order and Group.	Occupation.	Urban Population. Workers. Total.	Urban Workers. Males.	Urban Workers. Females.	Urban Dependents. Total.	Urban Dependents. Males.	Urban Dependents. Females.	Rural Population. Workers. Total.	Rural Workers. Males.	Rural Workers. Females.	Rural Dependents. Total.	Rural Dependents. Males.	Rural Dependents. Females.
			Brought forward Class D ...	28,340	25,561	2,779	55,722	18,417	37,305	71,554	49,776	21,778	137,494	51,504	85,990
CLASS D.—(*Concluded.*)	XV.—*Concld.* ...	50.—*Concld.*	313. Brush and comb makers and sellers	...	...	...	...	...	...	32	32	...	75	24	51
			315. Pith and bark collectors, workers and sellers	6	6	...	19	9	10	...	...	...	...	...	...
	XVI.—Drugs, gums, dyes, &c.	52. Drugs, dyes, pigments, &c. ...	324. Chemists and druggists ...	155	153	2	402	172	230	23	23	...	83	26	57
			328. Soap makers and sellers ...	38	38	...	131	51	80	27	27	...	71	23	48
			330. Indigo workers and dealers (not planters)	1	1	...	...	...	...	...	...	...	...	...	...
			332. Ink-makers and sellers ...	26	26	...	84	27	57	...	...	...	...	...	...
			337. Perfume preparers and sellers ...	12	12	...	9	3	6	2	2	...	...	...	...
	XVII.—Leather, horns, bones, and grease.	53. Leather, &c.	338. Tanners, curriers and hide sellers (*many also shoe-makers*) ...	42	42	...	131	55	76	41	41	...	128	38	90
			339. Shoe, sandals, boot-makers and sellers	843	832	11	1,953	656	1,297	8,069	7,600	469	21,090	7,841	13,249
			340. Leather dyers	13	13	...	25	8	17	23	23	...	40	10	30
			341. Water bag, well-bag, bucket and ghee pot makers and sellers ...	...	...	...	...	...	...	1	1	...	...	...	...
			TOTAL CLASS D ...	29,476	26,684	2,792	58,476	19,398	39,078	79,772	57,525	22,247	158,981	59,466	99,515

CENSUS 1891.

KASHMIR STATE.

TABLE XVII.—*Occupations*.—PART A.—(Continued.)

Class.	Order.	Sub-order and Group.	Occupation.	TOTAL. Workers. Total.	Workers. Males.	Workers. Females.	Dependents. Total.	Dependents. Males.	Dependents. Females.	Total. Total.	Total. Males.	Total. Females.
			Brought forward Class D ...	99,894	75,337	24,557	193,216	69,921	123,295	293,110	145,258	147,852
CLASS D.—(*Concluded.*)	XV.—*Concld.* ...	50.—*Concld.*	313. Brush and comb makers and sellers	32	32	...	75	24	51	107	56	51
			315. Pith and bark collectors, workers and sellers	6	6	...	19	9	10	25	15	10
	XVI.—Drugs, gums, dyes, &c.	52. Drugs, dyes, pigments, &c. ...	324. Chemists and druggists ...	178	176	2	485	198	287	663	374	289
			328. Soap makers and sellers ...	65	65	...	202	74	128	267	139	128
			330. Indigo workers and dealers (not planters)	1	1	...	...	...	...	1	1	...
			332. Ink-makers and sellers ...	26	26	...	84	27	57	110	53	57
			337. Perfume preparers and sellers ...	14	14	...	9	3	6	23	17	6
	XVII.—Leather, horns, bones and grease.	53. Leather, &c.	338. Tanners, curriers, and hide sellers (*many also shoe-makers*) ...	83	83	...	259	93	166	342	176	166
			339. Shoe, sandals, boot-makers and sellers	8,912	8,432	480	23,043	8,497	14,546	31,955	16,929	15,026
			340. Leather dyers	36	36	...	65	18	47	101	54	47
			341. Warter bag, well-bag, bucket and ghee-pot makers and sellers ...	1	1	...	...	...	...	1	1	...
			TOTAL CLASS D ...	109,248	84,209	25,039	217,457	78,864	138,593	326,705	163,073	163,632

CENSUS 1891.

KASHMIR STATE.

TABLE XVII.—*Occupations.*—PART A.—(Continued.)

Class.	Order.	Sub-order and Group.	Occupation.	Urban Population. Workers. Total.	Urban Workers. Males.	Urban Workers. Females.	Urban Dependents. Total.	Urban Dependents. Males.	Urban Dependents. Females.	Rural Population. Workers. Total.	Rural Workers. Males.	Rural Workers. Females.	Rural Dependents. Total.	Rural Dependents. Males.	Rural Dependents. Females.
CLASS E.—Commerce, Transport, Storage.	XVIII.—Commerce	54. Dealers in money and securities...	346. Bankers and Bank Managers ...	349	342	7	691	234	457	1,477	1,368	109	3,171	991	2,180
			350. Money changers and testers ...	535	535	...	1,618	583	1,035	52	52	...	140	41	99
		55. General Merchandise ...	352. General Merchants	171	166	5	399	168	231	4,701	4,452	249	7,823	2,612	5,211
			353. Merchants' Managers, Accountants, Clerks, Assistants, &c. ...	25	25	...	129	62	67	...	...	...	...	...	...
		56. Dealing unspecified	356. Shopkeepers, otherwise unspecified	2,086	2,063	23	3,913	1,350	2,563	10,973	10,386	587	20,489	7,401	13,088
			357. Pedlars, Hawkers, &c. ...	114	110	4	357	121	236	78	78	...	181	62	119
		57. Middlemen, &c. (a) Brokers, &c.	358. Brokers, Agents, Dubash ...	150	150	...	438	160	278	11	11	...	27	11	16
			359. Auctioneers, Auditors, Actuaries, Notaries public, Appraisers, House-Agents, &c. ...	...	...	...	...	...	...	1	...	1	...	...	...
		57. Middlemen, &c. (b) Contractors and farmers.	360. Farmers of Tolls, ferries ...	75	75	...	116	45	71	44	44	...	97	24	73
			361. Farmers of liquor, opium, &c. ...	...	...	...	...	...	...	16	16	...	15	14	1
			362. Lessees and Superintendents of markets, stalls, &c. ...	...	...	...	...	...	...	1	1	...	...	...	...
			363. Contractors, otherwise unspecified	119	119	...	226	77	149	185	185	...	464	141	323
			364. Contractors for labour, Emigration Agents, &c.	1	1	...	4	...	4	...	...	...	...	...	...
			Carried over Class E ...	3,625	3,586	39	7,891	2,800	5,091	17,539	16,593	946	32,407	11,297	21,110

CENSUS 1891.

KASHMIR STATE.

TABLE XVII.—*Occupations.*—PART A.—(Continued).

Class.	Order.	Sub-order and Group.	Occupation.	TOTAL. Workers. Total.	Workers. Males.	Workers. Females.	Dependents. Total.	Dependents. Males.	Dependents. Females.	Total. Total.	Total. Males.	Total. Females.
CLASS E.—Commerce, Transport, Storage.	XVIII.—Commerce	54. Dealers in money and securities ...	346. Bankers and Bank Managers ...	1,826	1,710	116	3,862	1,225	2,637	5,688	2,935	2,753
			350. Money changers and testers ...	587	587	...	1,758	624	1,134	2,345	1,211	1,134
		55. General Merchandise ...	352. General Merchants	4,872	4,618	254	8,222	2,780	5,442	13,094	7,398	5,696
			353. Merchants' Managers, Accountants, Clerks, Assistants, &c. ...	25	25	...	129	62	67	154	87	67
		56. Dealing unspecified	356. Shopkeepers, otherwise unspecified	13,059	12,449	610	24,402	8,751	15,651	37,461	21,200	16,261
			357. Pedlars, Hawkers, &c. ...	192	188	4	538	183	355	730	371	359
		57. Middlemen, &c. (a) Brokers, &c.	358. Brokers, Agents, Dobash	161	161	...	465	171	294	626	332	294
			359. Auctioneers, Auditors, Actuaries, Notaries public, Appraisers, House-Agents, &c. ...	1	...	1	...	...	...	1	...	1
		57. Middlemen, &c. (b) Contractors and farmers.	360. Farmers of Tolls, ferries ...	119	119	...	213	69	144	332	188	144
			361. Farmers of liquor, opium, &c. ...	16	16	...	15	14	1	31	30	1
			362. Lessees and Superintendents of markets, stalls, &c. ...	1	1	...	...	...	...	1	1	...
			363. Contractors, otherwise unspecified	304	304	...	690	218	472	994	522	472
			364. Contractors for labour, Emigration Agents, &c.	1	1	...	4	...	4	5	1	4
			Carried over Class E ...	21,164	20,179	985	40,298	14,097	26,201	61,462	34,276	27,186

CENSUS 1891.

KASHMIR STATE.

TABLE XVII.—*Occupations.*—PART A.—(Continued).

Class.	Order.	Sub-order and Group.		Occupation.	Urban Population. Workers. Total.	Urban Workers. Males.	Urban Workers. Females.	Urban Dependents. Total.	Urban Dependents. Males.	Urban Dependents. Females.	Rural Population. Workers. Total.	Rural Workers. Males.	Rural Workers. Females.	Rural Dependents. Total.	Rural Dependents. Males.	Rural Dependents. Females.
				Brought forward Class E ...	3,625	3,586	39	7,891	2,800	5,091	17,539	16,593	946	32,407	11,297	21,110
CLASS E.—(Concluded.)	XIX.—Transport and Storage.	58. Railway ...	(b) Working Staff.*	371. Station Masters and Assistants, Inspectors, Overseers, &c. ...	25	25	...	12	12	...	...	...	...	22	...	22
		59. Road ...	(a) Cart, Carriage and Tramway owners and drivers.	375. Cart owners and drivers, carting Agents, &c.	...	...	...	...	...	...	10	10	...	25	9	16
				377. Drivers, stable-boys, &c., (*not private servants*)	10	10	...	12	8	4	...	...	...	...	...	...
				378. Palki, &c., owners, bearers, &c....	148	148	...	335	110	225	38	38	...	209	98	111
			(b) Carriers by pack animals.	379. Pack bullock owners, drivers, &c.	...	...	...	...	...	...	93	89	4	228	131	97
				380. Pack camel, elephant, mule, &c., owners and drivers ...	306	306	...	715	248	467	1,570	1,555	15	3,738	1,444	2,294
		60. Water ...	(b) Working Staff of vessels.	385. Boat and barge men ...	1,557	1,457	100	4,542	1,792	2,750	1,715	1,474	241	3,743	1,450	2,293
		61. Messages ...	(a) Post, &c. ...	390. Postal Directors, Postmasters and Clerks	48	48	...	109	38	71	93	93	...	33	16	17
				392. Messengers, (unspecified) ...	3	3	...	18	10	8	2	2	...	3	2	1
			(b) Telegraph and Telephone.	394. Signallers and messengers ...	...	...	...	...	...	...	4	4	...	...	...	...
		62. Storage and weighing ...		398. Porters (general) ...	8	8	...	35	15	20	...	...	...	...	...	...
				399. Weighmen and measurers ...	124	124	...	357	123	234	48	48	...	178	74	104
				400. Watchmen (not village) ...	...	...	...	...	...	...	455	451	4	1,745	694	1,051
				TOTAL CLASS E ...	5,854	5,715	139	14,026	5,156	8,870	21,567	20,357	1,210	42,331	15,215	27,116

* Excluding Police on Railway.

CENSUS 1891.

KASHMIR STATE.

TABLE XVII.—*Occupations.*—PART A—(Continued).

Class.	Order.	Sub-order and Group.		Occupation.	TOTAL. Workers. Total.	Workers. Males.	Workers. Females.	Dependents. Total.	Dependents. Males.	Dependents. Females.	Total. Total.	Total. Males.	Total. Females.
CLASS E.—*Concluded.*				*Brought forward Class E* ...	21,164	20,179	985	40,298	14,097	26,201	61,462	34,276	27,186
	XIX.—Transport and Storage,	58. Railway ...	(b) Working Staff.*	371. Station Masters and Assistants, Inspectors, Overseers, &c. ...	25	25	...	34	12	22	59	37	22
		59. Road ...	(a) Cart, Carriage, and Tramway owners and drivers.	375. Cart owners and drivers, carting Agents, &c.	10	10	...	25	9	16	35	19	16
				377. Drivers, stable boys, &c., (*not private servants*)	10	10	...	12	8	4	22	18	4
				378. Palki, &c., owners, bearers, &c. ...	186	186	...	544	208	336	730	394	336
			(b) Carriers by pack animals.	379. Pack bullock owners, drivers, &c.	93	89	4	228	131	97	321	220	101
				380. Pack camel, elephant, mule, &c., owners and drivers ...	1,876	1,861	15	4,453	1,692	2,761	6,329	3,553	2,776
		60. Water ...	(b) Working Staff of vessels.	385. Boat and barge men ...	3,272	2,931	341	8,285	3,242	5,043	11,557	6,173	5,384
		61. Messages ...	(a) Post, &c. ...	390. Postal Directors, Postmasters and Clerks	141	141	...	142	54	88	283	195	88
				392. Messengers, (unspecified) ...	5	5	...	21	12	9	26	17	9
			(b) Telegraph and Telephone.	394. Signallers and messengers ...	4	4	...	...	...	...	4	4	...
		62. Storage and weighing ...		398. Porters (general) ...	8	8	...	35	15	20	43	23	20
				399. Weighmen and measurers ...	172	172	...	535	197	338	707	369	338
				400. Watchmen (not village) ...	455	451	4	1,745	694	1,051	2,200	1,145	1,055
				TOTAL CLASS E ...	27,421	26,072	1,849	56,357	20,371	35,986	83,778	46,443	37,335

* Excluding Police on Railway.

CENSUS 1891.

KASHMIR STATE.

TABLE XVII.—*Occupations.*—PART A—(Continued).

Class.	Order.	Sub-order and Group.		Occupation.	Urban Population. Workers. Total.	Males.	Females.	Urban Population. Dependents. Total.	Males.	Females.	Rural Population. Workers. Total.	Males.	Females.	Rural Population. Dependents. Total.	Males.	Females.
CLASS F.—Professions.	XX.—Learned and Artistic Professions.	63. Religion ...	(a) Priests, Ministers, &c.	401. Priests, ministers, preachers, missionaries, &c.	2,257	2,118	139	5,059	1,698	3,361	6,018	5,516	497	13,019	4,634	8,385
				402. Catechists, readers, Zenana Mission service, &c.	69	65	4	168	59	109	7	7	...	31	14	17
			(b) Subsidiary religious services.	404. Religious mendicants, inmates of monasteries, convents, &c. ...	13	13	...	7	4	3	11	11	...	20	9	11
				405. Church, Temple, Masjid, Pagoda, ghat, burial or burning ground service, pilgrim conductors and undertakers	251	246	5	734	267	467	2,342	2,194	148	5,347	2,344	3,003
		64. Education	... ...	406. Administrative and inspecting officials	1	1	...	2	1	1	...	...	...	...	...	...
				407. Principals, Professors and Teachers in Colleges, &c., Schools, &c.	253	251	2	572	228	344	1,338	1,334	4	3,436	1,271	2,165
		65. Literature	... ...	409. Authors, Editors, Journalists, ballad-makers	75	75	...	221	68	153	60	60	...	229	85	144
				412. Public Scribes and Copyists ...	49	49	...	99	33	66	...	...	...	...	...	...
		66. Law ...	... ...	414. Barristers, Advocates and Pleaders	37	37	...	80	33	47	3	3	...	5	1	4
				418. Stamp-vendors	36	36	...	119	49	70	2	2	...	5	1	4
				419. Petition-writers	12	12	...	31	8	23	12	12	...	29	6	23
		67. Medicine ...	(a) Practitioners ...	241. Practitioner by Diploma ...	1	1	...	2	...	2	4	4	...	16	4	12
				422. Practitioner without Diploma (Baid, Hakim Kobiraj, &c. ...	223	219	4	728	290	438	355	342	13	906	348	558
			(b) Subsidiary Medical Service.	426. Midwifery	74	52	22	24	16	8	6	...	6	3	1	2
				428. Compounders, Nurses and Hospital, Asylum and Dispensary service	24	23	1	29	14	15	...	...	...	...	...	...
				Carried over Class F ...	3,375	3,198	177	7,875	2,768	5,107	10,153	9,485	668	23,046	8,718	14,328

CENSUS 1891.

KASHMIR STATE.

TABLE XVII.—*Occupations.*—PART A.—(Continued.)

Class.	Order.	Sub-order and Group.		Occupation.	TOTAL. Workers. Total.	Workers. Males.	Workers. Females.	Dependents. Total.	Dependents. Males.	Dependents. Females.	Total. Total.	Total. Males.	Total. Females.
CLASS F.—Professions.	XX.—Learned and Artistic Professions.	63. Religion ...	(a) Priests, Ministers, &c.	401. Priests, ministers, preachers, missionaries, &c.	8,270	7,634	636	18,078	6,332	11,746	26,348	13,966	12,382
				402. Catechists, readers, Zenana Mission, service &c.	76	72	4	199	73	126	275	145	130
			(b) Subsidiary religious services.	404. Religious mendicants, inmates of monasteries, convents, &c. ...	24	24	...	27	13	14	51	37	14
				405. Church, Temple, Masjid, Pagoda, ghat, burial or burning ground service, pilgrim conductors and undertakers	2,593	2,440	153	6,081	2,611	3,470	8,674	5,051	3,623
		64. Education		406. Administrative and inspecting officials	1	1	...	2	1	1	3	2	1
				407. Principals, Professors and Teachers, in Colleges, &c., Schools, &c.	1,591	1,585	6	4,008	1,499	2,509	5,599	3,084	2,515
		65. Literature		409. Authors, Editors, Journalists, ballad-makers	135	135	...	450	153	297	585	288	297
				412. Public Scribes and Copyists ...	49	49	...	99	33	66	148	82	66
		66. Law		414. Barristers, Advocates and Pleaders	40	40	...	85	34	51	125	74	51
				418. Stamp-vendors	38	38	...	124	50	74	162	88	74
				419. Petition-writers	24	24	...	60	14	46	84	38	46
		67. Medicine ...	(a) Practitioners...	421. Practitioner by Diploma ...	5	5	...	18	4	14	23	9	14
				422. Practitioner without Diploma (Baid, Hakim Kobiraj, &c.) ...	578	561	17	1,634	638	996	2,212	1,199	1,013
			(b) Subsidiary Medical Service.	426. Midwifery	80	52	28	27	17	10	107	69	38
				428. Compounders, Nurses and Hospital, Asylum and Dispensary service	24	23	1	29	14	15	53	37	16
				Carried over Class F ...	13,528	12,683	845	30,921	11,486	19,435	44,449	24,169	20,280

CENSUS 1891.

KASHMIR STATE.

TABLE XVII.—*Occupations.*—PART A.—(Continued.)

Class.	Order.	Sub-order and Group.	Occupation.	Urban Population. Workers. Total.	Urban Workers. Males.	Urban Workers. Females.	Urban Dependents. Total.	Urban Dependents. Males.	Urban Dependents. Females.	Rural Population. Workers. Total.	Rural Workers. Males.	Rural Workers. Females.	Rural Dependents. Total.	Rural Dependents. Males.	Rural Dependents. Females.
Class F.—*Concld.*			*Brought forward Class F* ...	3,375	3,198	177	7,875	2,768	5,107	10,153	9,485	668	23,046	8,718	14,328
	XX.—*Concld.* ...	68. Engineering & Surveying — (a) Engineers, Architects and Surveyors.	429. Administrative and Inspecting Staff	4	4	...	2	...	2	10	10	...	10	3	7
		68. Engineering & Surveying — (b) Subsidiary Staff	432. Draughtsmen and Operators in Survey Offices, Overseers, &c. ...	3	3	...	12	4	8	...	...	...	...	...	...
			433. Clerks, &c., in offices of the above,	3	3	...	5	2	3	10	10	...	...	...	...
		69. Other Sciences. — (b) Minor Sciences	437. Astrologers, Genealogists and Horoscopecasters	4	4	...	13	6	7	14	14	...	20	9	11
		71. Music, Acting, Dancing ...	444. Bandmasters and players (not Military)	19	19	...	58	24	34	97	90	7	238	78	160
			446. Actors, Singers and Dancers and their accompanists	66	61	5	55	9	46	113	107	6	262	85	177
	XXI.—Sport and Amusements.	72. Sport	448. Shikaris, Falconers, Birdcatchers,	9	9	...	30	13	17	65	65	...	250	105	145
		73. Exhibition & Games. — (b) Conjuring, fortune telling and other exhibitions.	453. Buffoons	2	2	...	4	2	2	319	316	3	1,077	432	645
			454. Story and Ballad reciters ...	...	...	...	...	...	...	2	2	...	2	1	1
		(c) Acrobatics and Athletics.	457. Tumblers, Acrobats, Wrestlers Professional cricketers, &c. ...	3	3	...	...	...	...	90	77	13	155	63	92
			TOTAL CLASS F ...	3,488	3,306	182	8,054	2,828	5,226	10,873	10,176	697	25,060	9,494	15,566

CENSUS 1891.

KASHMIR STATE.

Table XVII.—*Occupations.*—Part A.—(Continued.)

Class.	Order.	Sub-order and Group.		Occupation.	Total: Workers: Total.	Workers: Males.	Workers: Females.	Dependents: Total.	Dependents: Males.	Dependents: Females.	Total: Total.	Total: Males.	Total: Females.
				Brought forward Class F ...	13,528	12,683	845	30,921	11,486	19,435	44,449	24,169	20,280
Class F.—(*Concluded.*)	XX.—*Concld.* ...	68. Engineering & Surveying.	(a) Engineers, Architects and Surveyors.	429. Administrative and Inspecting Staff	14	14	...	12	3	9	26	17	9
			(b) Subsidiary Staff	432. Draghtsmen and Operators in Survey Offices, Overseers, &c. ...	8	8	...	12	4	8	15	7	8
				433. Clerks, &c., in offices of the above,	13	13	...	5	2	3	18	15	3
		69. Other Sciences.	(b) Minor Sciences.	437. Astrologers, Genealogists and Horoscopecasters ...	18	18	...	33	15	18	51	33	18
		71. Music, Acting, Dancing ...		444. Bandmasters and players (not Military)	116	109	7	296	102	194	412	211	201
				446. Actors, Singers and Dancers and their accompanists ...	179	168	11	317	94	223	496	262	234
	XXI.—Sport and Amusements.	72. Sport		448. Shikaris, Falconers Birdcatchers	74	74	...	280	118	162	354	192	162
		73. Exhibition & Games.	(b) Conjuring, fortune telling and other exhibitions.	453. Buffoons	321	318	3	1,081	434	647	1,402	752	650
				454. Story and Ballad reciters ...	2	2	...	2	1	1	4	3	1
			(c) Acrobatics and Athletics.	457. Tumblers, Acrobats, Wrestlers, Prossessional cricketers, &c. ...	93	80	13	155	63	92	248	143	105
				Total Class F ...	14,361	13,482	879	33,114	12,322	20,792	47,475	25,804	21,671

CENSUS 1891.

KASHMIR STATE.

Table XVII.—*Occupations.*—Part A.—(Continued.)

Class.	Order.	Sub-order and Group.		Occupation.	Urban Population. Workers. Total.	Urban Workers. Males.	Urban Workers. Females.	Urban Dependents. Total.	Urban Dependents. Males.	Urban Dependents. Females.	Rural Population. Workers. Total.	Rural Workers. Males.	Rural Workers. Females.	Rural Dependents. Total.	Rural Dependents. Males.	Rural Dependents. Females.
Class G.—Indefinite and Independent.	XXIII.—Indefinite	74. Unskilled, labour.	(a) Special branches	461. Well sinkers	43	43	...	117	38	79	10	10	...	48	22	26
				462. Tank diggers and excavators ...	1	1	...	1	1	...	10	10	...	...	...	...
				466. Rice-pounders and huskers ...	28	22	6	43	19	24	57	54	3	125	55	70
			(b) General ...	467. General labour	4,581	3,912	669	6,819	1,972	4,347	23,936	18,795	5,141	39,399	13,869	25,530
		75. Undefined, &c.		468. Undefined and disreputable means of livelihood	1,143	656	487	143	75	68	25,947	15,088	10,859	15	7	8
	XXIV.—Independent of work.	75. Property & alms.	(a) Property and allowances.	469. House-rent, shares, and other property not being land ...	1,095	1,091	4	3,416	1,342	2,074	88	83	5	126	40	86
			(b) Charity and endowment.	471. Educational or other endowments scholarship, &c. ...	500	487	13	481	173	308	1,064	925	139	1,743	676	1,067
				472. Mendicancy (not being affiliated to a religious order) ...	1,849	1,643	206	1,883	621	1,262	20,732	17,365	3,367	33,567	12,546	21,021
		77. Supported at the public charge.	(a) Pension ...	473. Pension, Civil Services ...	15	14	1	38	9	29	374	357	17	444	131	313
				474. Pension, Military Services ...	...	...	...	...	...	...	2	2	...	...	...	...
			(b) Prisoners ...	476. Prisoners, under trial ...	26	25	1	...	...	...	...	...	...	...	...	...
				477. Prisoners, for debt ...	1	1	...	...	...	...	...	...	...	...	...	...
				478. Prisoners, convicted or in Reformatories, &c.	233	221	12	...	...	...	...	...	...	...	...	...
				Total Class G ...	9,515	8,116	1,399	12,441	4,250	8,191	72,220	52,689	19,531	75,467	27,346	48,121

CENSUS 1891.

KASHMIR STATE.

TABLE XVII.—*Occupations*.—PART A.—(Continued.)

Class.	Order.	Sub-order and Group.		Occupation.	TOTAL. *Workers.* Total.	Males.	Females.	*Dependents.* Total.	Males.	Females.	*Total.* Total.	Males.	Females.
CLASS G.—Indefinite and Independent.	XXIII.—Indefinite	74. Unskilled, labour.	(a) Special branches	461. Well sinkers	53	53	...	165	60	105	218	113	105
				462. Tank diggers and excavators ...	11	11	...	1	1	...	12	12	...
				466. Rice-pounders and huskers ...	85	76	9	168	74	94	253	150	103
			(b) General ...	467. General labour	28,517	22,707	5,810	45,718	15,841	29,877	74,235	38,548	35,687
		75. Undefined &c.		468. Undefined and disreputable means of livelihood	27,090	15,744	11,346	158	82	76	27,248	15,826	11,422
	XXIV.—Independent of work.	76. Property & alms.	(a) Property and allowances.	469. House-rent shares, and other property not being land ...	1,183	1,174	9	3,542	1,382	2,160	4,725	2,556	2,169
			(b) Charity and endowment.	471. Educational or other endowments scholarship, &c.	1,564	1,412	152	2,224	849	1,375	3,788	2,261	1,527
				472. Mendicancy (not being affiliated to a religious order) ...	22,581	19,008	3,573	35,450	13,167	22,283	58,031	32,175	25,856
		77. Supported at the public charge.	(a) Pension ...	473. Pension, Civil Services ...	389	371	18	482	140	342	871	511	360
				474. Pension Military Services ...	2	2	...	...	...	...	2	2	...
			(b) Prisoners ...	476. Prisoners, under trial ...	26	25	1	...	...	...	26	25	1
				477. Prisoners, for debt ...	1	1	...	...	...	...	1	1	...
				478. Prisoners, convicted or in Reformatories, &c.	233	221	12	...	...	...	233	221	12
				TOTAL CLASS G ...	81,735	60,805	20,930	87,908	31,596	56,312	169,643	92,401	77,242

CENSUS 1891.

KASHMIR STATE.

TABLE XVII.—*Occupations.*—PART A.—(Concluded.)

Class.	Urban Population.						Rural Population.						Total.								
	Workers.			*Dependents.*			*Workers.*			*Dependents.*			*Workers.*			*Dependents.*			*Total.*		
	Total.	Males.	Females.	Total.	Males.	Females.	Total.	Males.	Females.	Total.	Males.	Females.	Total.	Males.	Females.	Total.	Males.	Females.	Total.	Males.	Females.
ABSTRACT.																					
Total Class A ...	11,986	11,912	74	14,686	5,251	9,435	15,383	14,936	447	26,680	10,385	16,295	27,369	26,848	521	41,366	15,636	25,730	68,735	42,484	26,251
Do. B ...	3,571	3,441	130	7,356	2,619	4,737	452,267	431,011	21,256	1,299,649	495,980	803,669	455,838	434,452	21,386	1,307,005	498,599	808,406	1,762,843	933,051	829,792
Do. C ...	7,316	6,835	481	11,498	4,041	7,457	26,699	23,842	2,857	39,260	15,255	24,005	34,015	30,677	3,338	50,758	19,296	31,462	84,773	49,973	34,800
Do. D ...	29,476	26,684	2,792	58,476	19,398	39,078	79,772	57,525	22,247	158,981	59,466	99,515	109,248	84,209	25,039	217,457	78,864	138,593	326,705	163,073	163,632
Do. E ...	5,854	5,715	139	14,026	5,156	8,870	21,567	20,357	1,210	42,331	15,215	27,116	27,421	26,072	1,349	56,357	20,371	35,986	83,778	46,443	37,335
Do. F ...	3,488	3,306	182	8,054	2,828	5,226	10,873	10,176	697	25,060	9,494	15,566	14,361	13,482	879	33,114	12,322	20,792	47,475	25,804	21,671
Do. G ...	9,515	8,116	1,399	12,441	4,250	8,191	72,220	52,689	19,531	75,467	27,346	48,121	81,735	60,805	20,930	87,908	31,596	56,312	169,643	92,401	77,242
GRAND TOTAL ...	71,206	66,009	5,197	126,537	43,543	82,994	678,781	610,536	68,245	1,667,428	633,141	1,034,287	749,987	676,545	73,442	1,793,965	676,684	1,117,281	2,543,952	1,353,229	1,190,723

JAMMU:
Dated 30th April 1892.

BHAG RAM,
Census Superintendent, Kashmir State.

CENSUS 1891.

KASHMIR STATE.

TABLE XVII.—PART B.—*Occupations.*

Class.	Order.	Sub-order and Group.	Occupation.	Workers. Total.	Workers. Males.	Workers. Females.	Dependents. Total.	Dependents. Males.	Dependents. Females.	Total. Total.	Total. Males.	Total. Females.	Remarks.
Class A.	I.—Administration	1. Service of the State ...	1. Maharaja and Rajas and their Families	3	3	...	77	1	76	80	4	76	
			2. Officers	171	171	...	231	104	127	402	275	127	
			3. Office Superintendents and Clerical Establishments. Police and Excise Inspectors, Sub-Registrars, &c.	16,799	16,436	363	30,019	11,522	18,497	46,818	27,958	18,860	
			4. Messengers, Constables, Bailiffs, Warders, Menials, &c. ...	1,303	1,302	1	1,232	462	770	2,535	1,764	771	
		2. Service of Local and Municipal Bodies.	5. Inspecting and Supervising Officials	1	1	...	4	1	3	5	2	3	
		3. Village Service	9. Accountants	665	665	...	2,630	1,125	1,505	3,295	1,790	1,505	
			11. Watchmen and other Menials ...	1,192	1,052	140	2,978	1,134	1,844	4,170	2,186	1,984	
	II.—Defence ...	4. Army	12. Officers	3	3	...	8	3	5	11	6	5	
			13. Non-Commissioned Officers and Privates	6,943	6,943	...	3,659	1,113	2,546	10,602	8,056	2,546	
	III.—Foreign and Feudatory State Service.	6. Administrative Service ...	20. Clerical Establishments and 21. Menials, &c.	281	264	17	506	165	341	787	429	358	
		7. Army and Marine	22. Officers	8	8	...	22	6	16	30	14	16	
			TOTAL CLASS A ...	27,369	26,848	521	41,366	15,636	25,730	68,735	42,484	26,251	

CENSUS 1891.

KASHMIR STATE.

TABLE XVII.—PART B.—*Occupations*.—(Continued.)

Class.	Order.	Sub-order and Group.		Occupation.	Workers.			Dependents.			Total.			Remarks.
					Total.	Males.	Females.	Total.	Males.	Females.	Total.	Males.	Females.	
Class B.	IV.—Live stock ...	8. Stock breeding and dealing.	(a.) Horses and horned cattle	25. Cattle breeders and dealers and Commissariat Farm Establishment	1,282	1,260	22	3,968	1,608	2,368	5,256	2,863	2,387	
				26. Herdsmen	1,898	1,840	58	7,144	3,054	4,090	9,042	4,894	4,148	
			(c.) Smallstock ...	31. Sheep and Goat breeders and dealers	5,747	5,131	616	9,521	3,858	5,663	15,268	8,989	6,279	
		9. Subsidiary services to stock.	(a.) Training and doctoring live stock...	34. Farriers and Gelders ...	45	45	...	128	41	87	173	86	87	
				35. Horse and Elephant breakers and trainers, &c.	71	71	...	153	52	101	224	123	101	
	V.—Agriculture ...	10. Interest in Land		37. Land occupants, not cultivating	36,631	35,292	1,339	125,754	47,384	78,370	162,385	82,676	79,709	
				38. Land occupants, cultivating ...	218,627	209,767	8,860	662,878	259,660	403,218	881,505	469,427	412,078	
				39. Lessees of Villages, &c. ...	1,470	1,380	90	4,663	1,854	2,809	6,133	3,234	2,899	
				41. Tenants and sharers, cultivating	189,525	179,187	10,338	491,715	180,691	311,024	681,240	359,878	321,362	
		12. Growers of special products and trees		44. Tea, Coffee and Cinchona Planters, Managers and Assistants	1	1	...	...	...	...	1	1	...	
				47. Waternut growers	64	40	24	89	33	56	153	73	80	
				52. Gardeners, seedsmen, &c. ...	345	306	39	786	311	475	1,131	617	514	
				54. Forest Officers	1	1	...	7	1	6	8	2	6	
				55. Forest Rangers, Guards, Peons ...	128	128	...	199	57	142	327	185	142	
		13. Agricultural training and supervision.		56. Directors of Agriculture and their Assistants	3	3	...	...	...	...	3	3	...	
				TOTAL CLASS B ...	455,8 38	434,452	21,386	1,307,005	498,599	808,406	1,762,843	933,051	829,792	

CENSUS 1891.

KASHMIR STATE.

TABLE XVII.—PART B.—*Occupations.*—(Continued.)

Class.	Order.	Sub-order and Group.	Occupation.	Workers. Total.	Workers. Males.	Workers. Females.	Dependents. Total.	Dependents. Males.	Dependents. Females.	Total. Total.	Total. Males.	Total. Females.	Remarks.
Class C.	VI.—Personal and household services.	14. Personal and domestic services ...	59. Barbers	4,160	4,160	...	11,388	4,136	7,252	15,548	8,296	7,252	
			63. Washermen (*sometimes also dyers*)	1,734	1,543	191	3,721	1,393	2,328	5,455	2,936	2,519	
			64. Water-carriers	1,646	1,340	306	2,938	1,030	1,908	4,584	2,370	2,214	
			65. Cooks	290	290	...	700	230	470	990	520	470	
			66. Indoor servants	25,090	22,426	2,664	29,531	11,499	18,032	54,621	33,925	20,696	
			67. Grooms, coachmen and dog-boys, &c.	69	69	...	34	8	26	103	77	26	
			68. Door-keepers, &c.	24	24	...	55	18	37	79	42	37	
		15. Non-domestic Establishment ...	70. Rest-house, Serai, Bath-house, &c., owners and Managers ...	157	154	3	714	311	403	871	465	406	
		16. Sanitation	74. Sweepers and scavengers ...	827	656	171	1,636	652	984	2,463	1,308	1,155	
			75. Dust and sweepings contractors	18	15	3	41	19	22	59	34	25	
			TOTAL CLASS C ...	34,015	30,677	3,338	50,758	19,296	31,462	84,773	49,973	34,800	
Class D.	Preparation and supply of material substances.	VII. Food & drink — 17. Animal Food	76. Cow and buffalo-keepers and milk and butter sellers ...	5,230	4,873	357	14,906	5,903	9,003	20,136	10,776	9,360	
			77. Ghee preparers and sellers ...	781	766	15	1,891	727	1,164	2,672	1,493	1,179	
			79. Butchers	953	946	7	2,517	913	1,604	3,470	1,859	1,611	
			81. Fishermen and fish curers (*many are also boatmen and palki bearers*)	402	389	13	1,460	619	841	1,862	1,008	854	
			Carried over Class D ...	7,366	6,974	392	20,774	8,162	12,612	28,140	15,136	13,004	

CENSUS 1891.

KASHMIR STATE.

TABLE XVII.—PART B.—*Occupations*.—(Continued.)

Class.	Order.	Sub-order and Group.		Occupation.	Workers. Total.	Workers. Males.	Workers. Females.	Dependents. Total.	Dependents. Males.	Dependents. Females.	Total. Total.	Total. Males.	Total. Females.	Remarks.
				Brought forward Class D ...	7,366	6,974	392	20,774	8,162	12,612	28,140	15,136	13.004	
Class D.—(*Continued.*)	Preparation and supply of material substances.—(*Contd*).	VII. Food & drink (*Contd*).	18. Vegetable Food.	83. Grain dealers	3,353	3,288	65	10,324	4,065	6,259	13,677	7,353	6,324	
				84. Grain parchers	78	60	18	89	36	53	167	96	71	
				86. Flour-mill service and management	2,131	1,921	210	3,510	1,206	2,304	5,641	3,127	2,514	
				87. Bakers	1.148	1,071	77	2,914	1,152	1,762	4,062	2,223	1,839	
				89. Vegetable sellers ...	1,081	949	132	2,371	862	1,509	3,452	1,811	1,641	
				90. Fruit sellers	588	517	71	1,460	560	900	2,048	,1,077	971	
				92. Confectioners and sweetmeat makers and sellers, and cooks who are also sometimes fishermen and water-carriers ...	417	412	5	778	280	498	1,195	692	503	
			19. Drink condiments and narcotics.	97. Country spirits distillers & sellers	37	35	2	20	8	12	57	43	14	
				105. Salt preparers and sellers ...	97	65	32	74	15	59	171	80	91	
				109. Grocers and general condiment dealers	190	181	9	371	106	265	561	287	274	
				112. Tobacco and snuff manufacturers and sellers	394	392	2	847	299	548	1,241	691	550	
				114. Opium, &c., manufacturers and sellers	1	1	...	...	...	...	1	1	...	
				115. Bhang, ganja, &c, preparers and sellers	15	15	...	25	7	18	40	22	18	
				Carried over Class D ...	16,896	15,881	1,015	43,557	16,758	26,799	60,453	32,639	27,814	

CENSUS 1891.

KASHMIR STATE.

TABLE XVII.—PART B.—*Occupations*.—(Continued.)

Class.	Order.	Sub-order and Group.	Occupation.	Workers. Total.	Workers. Males.	Workers. Females.	Dependents. Total.	Dependents. Males.	Dependents. Females.	Total. Total.	Total. Males.	Total. Females.	Remarks.
Class D.—(Continued.)			*Brought forward Class D* ...	16,896	15,881	1,015	43,557	16,758	26,799	60,453	32,639	27,814	
	VIII. Light, firing, and forage.	20. Lighting	116. Oil-pressers and sellers ...	3,026	2,879	147	9,193	3,622	5,571	12,219	6,501	5,718	
			119. Candle makers and sellers ...	2	2	...	1	...	1	3	2	1	
			120. Torch makers and sellers ...	16	16	...	54	19	35	70	35	35	
		21. Fuel and Forage	125. Firewood and grass gatherers and sellers	739	667	72	2,062	818	1,234	2,791	1,485	1,306	
			131. Hay, &c., contractors and dealers	10	10	...	2	2	...	12	12	...	
	IX. Buildings ...	22. Building materials	132. Brick and tile burners and sellers	97	90	7	243	85	158	340	175	165	
			133. Lime chunám and shell burners and sellers	73	73	...	245	91	154	318	164	154	
		23. Artificers in Buildings ...	136. Building contractors ...	200	200	...	505	213	292	705	413	292	
			137. Stone and marble workers ...	87	87	...	238	99	139	325	186	139	
			138. Masons	478	478	...	926	301	625	1,404	779	625	
	XI. Supplementary requirements.	27. Paper, &c.	153. Paper makers and sellers and palmleaf binders	147	147	...	409	150	259	556	297	259	
		28. Books and Prints, &c. ...	157. Press Proprietors, Lithographers and Printers	28	28	...	33	6	27	61	34	27	
			158. Book-binders	55	55	...	119	36	83	174	91	83	
			159. Book-sellers and publishers ...	2	2	...	...	...	...	2	2	...	
		29. Watches, Clocks and scientific instruments	163. Watch and Clock makers and sellers	16	16	...	29	10	19	45	26	19	
		30. Carving, engraving, &c. ...	172. Turners and lacquerers ...	43	43	...	136	46	90	179	89	90	
			173. Die-sinkers and seal, &c., engravers	95	95	...	159	43	116	254	138	116	
		31. Toys, curiosities &c.	178. Hukka stem makers and sellers ...	51	51	...	98	36	62	149	87	62	
			179. Papier-mache workers and sellers	242	240	2	484	131	353	726	371	355	
			Carried over Class D ...	22,303	21,060	1,243	58,483	22,466	36,017	80,786	43,526	37,260	

CENSUS 1891.

KASHMIR STATE.

TABLE XVII.—PART B.—*Occupations.*—(Continued.)

Class.	Order.	Sub-order and Group.	Occupation.	Workers. Total.	Workers. Males.	Workers. Females.	Dependents. Total.	Dependents. Males.	Dependents. Females.	Total. Total.	Total. Males.	Total. Females.	Remarks.
			Brought forward Class D ...	22,303	21,060	1,243	58,483	22,466	36,017	80,786	43,526	37,260	
CLASS D.—(*Continued.*)	XI. Supplementary requirements.—(*Concld.*)	32. Music and Musical Instruments ...	183. Music and Musical Instrument dealers	6	6	...	16	7	9	22	13	9	
		33. Necklaces, Bracelets, beads, sacred threads, &c.	185. Bangle makers and sellers in lac	223	212	11	450	134	316	673	346	327	
			194. Flower garland markers and sellers	5	5	...	12	3	9	17	8	9	
		35. Harness	201. Saddlery and Harness makers and sellers	280	280	...	417	121	296	697	401	296	
		36. Tools and Machinery ...	205. Knife and tool grinders ...	60	60	...	148	47	101	208	107	101	
		37. Arms and ammunition ...	210. Ammunition and Cap dealers ...	1	1	...	...	...	...	1	1	...	
			212. Fire-work makers and sellers ...	74	73	1	210	92	118	284	165	119	
			215. Bow and arrow makers and sellers	40	40	...	36	7	29	76	47	29	
	XII.—Textile Fabrics and dress ...	38. Wool and Fur	217. Carpet weavers and sellers ...	346	345	1	420	105	315	766	450	316	
			218. Shawl weavers and sellers ..	9,622	9,619	3	20,686	6,825	13,861	30,308	16,444	13,864	
			219. Felt and pashm workers and sellers	163	163	...	443	130	313	606	293	313	
			220. Blanket weavers and sellers (*often also shepherds*	4,544	4,506	38	13,000	4,915	8,085	17,544	9,421	8,123	
			221. Woollen cloth manufacturers and dealers	484	466	18	1,245	457	788	1,729	923	806	
			222. Woollen yarn spinners and sellers	21,743	83	21,660	5,084	1,945	3,139	26,827	2,028	24,799	
			223. Wool carders	188	188	...	538	177	361	726	365	361	
			224. Wool dyers	882	834	48	2,089	716	1,373	2,971	1,550	1,421	
			Carried over Class D ...	60,964	37,941	23,023	103,277	38,147	65,130	164,241	76,088	88,153	

CENSUS 1891.

KASHMIR STATE.

TABLE XVII.—PART B.—*Occupations.*—(Continued.)

Class.	Order.	Sub-Order and Group.	Occupation.	Workers. Total.	Workers. Males.	Workers. Females.	Dependents. Total.	Dependents. Males.	Dependents. Females.	Total. Total.	Total. Males.	Total. Females.	Remarks.
Class D.—(*Continued.*)			*Brought forward Class D* ...	60,964	37,941	23,023	103,277	38,147	65,130	164,241	76,088	88,153	
	XII.—*Concld.* ...	39. Silk	226. Silk-worm rearers and cocoon gatherers	94	94	...	266	91	175	360	185	175	
			229. Silk printers and dyers ...	10	10	...	25	10	15	35	20	15	
			230. Braid and ribbon makers and sellers	436	380	56	710	242	468	1,146	622	524	
		40. Cotton	231. Cotton cleaners, pressers and ginners	1,082	1,036	46	2,556	929	1,627	3,638	1,965	1,673	
			232. Cotton carpet and rug makers and sellers	45	45	...	105	29	76	150	74	76	
			234. Cotton weavers, Mill-owners and Managers	10,248	9,699	549	23,188	7,884	15,304	33,436	17,583	15,853	
			236. Calenderers, fullers and printers	91	91	...	248	91	157	339	182	157	
			237. Cotton dyers	18	18	...	69	14	55	87	32	55	
		41. Jute, flax, coir, &c.	241. Hemp rope makers and sellers ...	4	4	...	7	...	7	11	4	7	
			243. Sacking, tarpaulin and gunny makers and sellers ...	1	1	...	5	2	3	6	3	3	
		42. Dress	247. Tailors and darners	8,181	7,982	199	15,882	5,187	10,695	24,063	13,169	10,894	
			254. Embroiderers and lace and muslin-makers	412	409	3	623	184	439	1,035	593	442	
	XIII.—Metals and precious stones.	43. Gold, silver, and precious stones	260. Gold and silver workers ...	2,439	2,428	11	6,295	2,194	4,101	8,734	4,622	4,112	
			261. Gold beaters	4	4	...	24	12	12	28	16	12	
			262. Gold smiths' dust washers ...	10	10	...	33	10	23	43	20	23	
			265. Electro-platers	6	6	...	6	1	5	12	7	5	
			266. Gold and silver wire drawers, and braid makers	3	3	...	10	4	6	13	7	6	
			Carried over Class D ...	84,048	60,161	23,887	153,329	55,031	98,298	237,377	115,192	122,185	

CENSUS 1891.

KASHMIR STATE.

TABLE XVII.—PART B.—*Occupations.*—(Continued.)

Class.	Order.	Sub-order and Group.	Occupation.	Workers Total.	Workers Males.	Workers Females.	Dependents Total.	Dependents Males.	Dependents Females.	Total Total.	Total Males.	Total Females.	Remarks.
CESSAL D.—(*Continued.*)			*Brought forward Class D* ...	84,048	60,161	23,887	153,329	55,031	98,298	237,377	115,192	122,185	
	XIII.—*Concld.*	44. Brass, copper and bell metal ...	277. Brass pot makers and sellers ...	170	144	26	294	108	186	464	252	212	
			279. Copper workers and sellers ...	289	289	...	674	208	466	963	497	466	
		45. Tin, zinc, mercury and lead ...	284. Tin workers and sellers ...	146	146	...	435	152	283	581	298	283	
		46. Iron and steel	290. Blacksmiths	4,023	3,916	107	10,655	4,080	6,575	14,678	7,996	6,682	
	XIV.—Glass, pottery and stone ware.	47. Glass and Chinaware ...	297. Glass and Chinaware dealers ...	5	4	1	3	1	2	8	5	3	
		48. Earthen and stone ware ...	298. Potters and pot and pipe-bowl-makers and sellers. (*Some are brick and tile makers also*) ...	3,678	3,438	240	9,506	3,607	5,899	13,184	7,045	6,139	
			299. Grindstone and millstone makers, menders and sellers ...	5	5	...	12	3	9	17	8	9	
	XV.—Wood cane and leaves, &c.	49. Timber and wood	302. Timber and bamboo agents and dealers	671	635	36	1,460	544	916	2,131	1,179	952	
			303. Wood cutters and sawyers ...	321	321	...	934	367	567	1,255	688	567	
			304. Carpenters	5,043	5,043	...	12,816	4,659	8,157	17,859	9,702	8,157	
		50. Canework, matting and leaves &c.	306. Bamboo and rattan splitters, workers and sellers ...	736	672	64	1,826	676	1,150	2,562	1,348	1,214	
			307. Basket weavers and winnowing pan makers and sellers ...	510	442	68	1,057	411	646	1,567	853	714	
			308. Mat makers and sellers ...	207	87	120	162	55	107	369	142	227	
			310. Leaf-plate makers and sellers. (*Are also often temple servants*) ...	42	34	8	53	19	84	95	53	42	
			313. Brush and comb makers & sellers	32	32	...	75	24	51	107	56	51	
			315. Pith and bark collectors, workers and sellers ...	6	6	...	19	9	10	25	15	10	
			Carried over Class D ...	99,932	75,375	24,557	193,310	69,954	123,356	293,242	145,329	147,913	

CENSUS 1891.

KASHMIR STATE.

TABLE XVII.—PART B.—*Occupations.*—(Continued.)

Class.	Order.	Sub-order and Group.	Occupation.	Workers. Total.	Workers. Males.	Workers. Females.	Dependents. Total.	Dependents. Males.	Dependents. Females.	Total. Total.	Total. Males.	Total. Females.	Remarks.
			Brought forward Class D ...	99,932	75,375	24,557	193,310	69,954	123,356	293,242	145,329	147,913	
CLASS D.—(*Concluded.*)	XVI.—Drugs, gums, dyes, &c.	52. Drugs, dyes, pigments, &c. ...	324. Chemists and druggists ...	178	176	2	485	198	287	663	374	289	
			328. Soap makers and sellers ...	65	65	...	202	74	128	267	139	128	
			330. Indigo workers and dealers (not planters)	1	1	...	...	...	...	1	1	...	
			332. Ink-makers and sellers ...	26	26	...	84	27	57	110	53	57	
			337. Perfume preparers and sellers ...	14	14	...	9	3	6	23	17	6	
	XVII.—Leather, horns, bones, and grease.	53. Leather, &c.	338. Tanners, curriers and hide sellers (*many also shoe-makers*) ...	83	83	...	259	93	166	342	176	166	
			339. Shoe, sandals, boot-makers and sellers	8,912	8,432	480	23,043	8,497	14,546	31,955	16,929	15,026	
			340. Leather dyers	36	36	...	65	18	47	101	54	47	
			341. Water bag, well-bag, bucket and ghee pot makers and sellers ...	1	1	...	...	...	...	1	1	...	
			TOTAL CLASS D ...	109,248	84,209	25,039	217,457	78,864	138,593	326,705	163,073	163,632	

CENSUS 1891.

KASHMIR STATE.

Table XVII.—Part B.—*Occupations.*—(Continued.)

Class.	Order.	Sub-order and Group.		Occupation.	Workers.			Dependents.			Total.			Remarks.
					Total.	Males.	Females.	Total.	Males.	Females	Total.	Males.	Females	
Class E.—Commerce, Transport, Storage.	XVIII.—Commerce	54. Dealers in money and securities...		346. Bankers and Bank Managers ...	1,826	1,710	116	3,862	1,225	2,637	5,688	2,935	2,753	
				350. Money changers and testers ...	587	587	...	1,758	624	1,134	2,345	1,211	1,134	
		55. General Merchandise ...		352. General Merchants	4,872	4,618	254	8,222	2,780	5,442	13,094	7,398	5,696	
				353. Merchants' Managers, Accountants, Clerks, Assistants, &c. ...	25	25	...	129	62	67	154	87	67	
		56. Dealing unspecified		356. Shopkeepers, otherwise unspecified	13,059	12,449	610	24,402	8,751	15,651	37,461	21,200	16,261	
				357. Pedlars, Hawkers, &c. ...	192	188	4	538	183	355	730	371	359	
		57. Middlemen, &c.	(a) Brokers, &c.	358. Brokers, Agents, Dubash ...	161	161	...	465	171	294	626	332	294	
				359. Auctioneers, Auditors, Actuaries, Notaries public, Appraisers, House-Agents, &c. ...	1	...	1	...	...	...	1	...	1	
			(b) Contractors and farmers.	360. Farmers of Tolls, ferries ...	119	119	...	213	69	144	832	188	144	
				361. Farmers of liquor, opium, &c. ...	16	16	...	15	14	1	3	30	1	
				362. Lessees and Superintendents of markets, stalls, &c. ...	1	1	...	...	...	...	1	1	...	
				363. Contractors, otherwise unspecified	304	304	...	690	218	472	994	522	472	
				364. Contractors for labour, Emigration Agents, &c.	1	1	...	4	...	4	5	1	4	
	XIX.—Transport and Storage.	58. Railway ...	(b) Working Staff.*	371. Station Masters and Assistants, Inspectors, Overseers, &c. ...	25	25	...	34	12	22	59	37	22	
		59. Road ...	(a) Cart, Carriage and Tramway owners and drivers.	375. Cart owners and drivers, carting Agents, &c.	10	10	...	25	9	16	35	19	16	
				377. Drivers, stable-boys, &c., (*not private servants*)	10	10	...	12	8	4	22	18	4	
				378. Palki, &c., owners, bearers, &c....	186	186	...	544	208	336	730	394	336	
			(b) Carriers by pack animals.	379. Pack bullock owners, drivers, &c.	93	89	4	228	131	97	321	220	101	
				380. Pack camel, elephant, mule, &c., owners and drivers ...	1,876	1,861	15	4,453	1,692	2,761	6,329	3,553	2,776	
				Carried over Class E ...	23,364	22,360	1,004	45,594	16,157	29,437	68,958	38,517	30,441	

* Excluding Police on Railways.

CENSUS 1891.

KASHMIR STATE.

TABLE XVII.—PART B.—*Occupations*.—(Continued).

Class.	Order.	Sub-order and Group.	Occupation.	Workers. Total.	Workers. Males.	Workers. Females.	Dependents. Total.	Dependents. Males.	Dependents. Females.	Total. Total.	Total. Males.	Total. Females.	Remarks.
			Brought forward Class E ...	23,364	22,360	1,004	45,594	16,157	29,437	68,958	38,517	30,441	
CLASS E.—(*Concld.*)	XIX.—*Concld.* ...	60. Water ... (*b*) Working Staff of vessels.	385. Boat and barge men ...	3,272	2,931	341	8,285	3,242	5,043	11,557	6,173	5,384	
		61. Messages ... (*a*) Post, &c. ...	390. Postal Directors, Postmasters and Clerks	141	141	...	142	54	88	283	195	88	
			392. Messengers, (unspecified) ...	5	5	...	21	12	9	26	17	9	
		(*b*) Telegraph and Telephone.	394. Signallers and messengers ...	4	4	...	...	...	...	4	4	...	
		62. Storage and weighing ...	398. Porters (general)	8	8	...	35	15	20	43	23	20	
			399. Weighmen and measurers ...	172	172	...	535	197	338	707	369	338	
			400. Watchmen (not village) ...	455	451	4	1,745	694	1,051	2,200	1,145	1,055	
			TOTAL CLASS E ...	27,421	26,072	1,349	56,357	20,371	35,986	83.778	46,443	37,335	
CLASS F.—Professions.		63. Religion ... (*a*) Priests, Ministers, &c.	401. Priests, ministers, preachers, missionaries, &c.	8,270	7,634	636	18,078	6,332	11,746	26,348	13,966	12,382	
			402. Cathechists, readers, Zanana Mission service, &c. ...	76	72	4	199	73	126	275	145	130	
		(*b*) Subsidiary religious services.	404. Religious mendicants, inmates of monasteries, convents, &c. ...	24	24	...	27	13	14	51	37	14	
			405. Church, Temple, Masjid, Pagoda, ghat, burial or burning ground service, pilgrim conductors and undertakers	2,593	2,440	153	6,081	2,611	3,470	8,674	5,051	3,623	
		64. Education	406. Administrative and inspecting officials	1	1	...	2	1	1	3	2	1	
			407. Principals, Professors and Teachers in Colleges, &c., Schools, &c.	1,591	1,585	6	4,008	1,499	2,509	5,599	3,084	2,515	
	XX.—Learned and Artistic Professions.	65 Literature	409. Authors, Editors, Journalists, ballad-makers ...	135	135	...	450	153	297	585	288	297	
			412. Public Scribes and Copyists ...	49	49	...	99	33	66	148	82	66	
		66. Law	414. Barristers, Advocates and Pleaders	40	40	...	85	34	51	127	74	51	
			418. Stamp-vendors	38	38	...	124	50	74	162	88	74	
			419. Petition-writers	24	24	...	60	14	46	84	38	46	
			Carried over Class F ...	12,841	12,042	799	29,213	10,813	18,400	42,054	22,855	19.199	

CENSUS 1891.

KASHMIR STATE.

TABLE XVII.—PART B.—*Occupation.*—(Continued.)

Class.	Order.	Sub-order and Group.		Occupation.	Workers. Total.	Workers. Males.	Workers. Females	Dependents. Total.	Dependents. Males.	Dependents. Females.	Total. Total.	Total. Males.	Total. Females.	Remarks.
				Brought forward Class F ...	12 841	12,042	799	29,213	10,813	18,400	42,054	22,855	19,199	
CLASS F.—*Concld.*	XX.—*Concld.* ...	67. Medicine ...	(*a*) Practitioners ...	421. Practitioner by Diploma ...	5	5	...	18	4	14	23	9	14	
				422. Practitioners without Diploma (Baid, Hakim Kobiraj, &c.	578	561	17	1,634	638	996	2,212	1,199	1,013	
				426. Midwifery	80	52	28	27	17	10	107	69	38	
			(*b*) Subsidiary Medical Service.	428. Compounders, Nurses and Hospital, Asylum and Dispensary service	24	23	1	29	14	15	53	37	16	
		68. Engineering & Surveying	(*a*) Engineers, Architects and Surveyors.	429. Administrative and Inspecting Staff	14	14	...	12	3	9	26	17	9	
			(*b*) Subsidiary Staff	432. Draughtsmen and Operators in Survey Offices, Overseers, &c. ...	8	8	...	12	4	8	15	7	8	
				433. Clerks, &c., in offices of the above,	13	13	...	5	2	3	18	15	3	
		69. Other Sciences.	(*b*) Minor Sciences	437. Astrologers, Genealogists and Horoscopecasters	18	18	...	33	15	18	51	33	18	
		71. Music, Acting, Dancing ...		444. Bandmasters and players (not Military)	116	109	7	296	102	194	412	211	201	
				446. Actors, Singers and Dancers and their accompanists	179	168	11	317	94	223	496	262	234	
	XXI.—Sport and Amusements.	72. Sport		448. Shikaris, Falconers, Birdcatchers,	74	74	...	280	118	162	354	192	162	
		73. Exhibition & Games.	(*b*) Conjuring, fortune telling and other exhibitions.	453. Buffoons	321	318	3	1,081	434	647	1,402	752	650	
				454. Story and Ballad reciters ...	2	2	...	2	1	1	4	3	1	
			(*c*) Acrobatics and Athletics.	457. Tumblers, Acrobats, Wrestlers Professional cricketers, &c. ...	98	80	18	155	63	92	248	143	105	
				TOTAL CLASS F ...	14,361	13,482	879	33,114	12,322	20,792	47,475	25,804	21,671	

CENSUS 1891.

KASHMIR STATE.

TABLE XVII.—PART B.—*Occupations.*—(Continued.)

Class.	Order.	Sub-order and Group.		Occupation.	Workers. Total.	Workers. Males.	Workers. Females.	Dependents. Total.	Dependents. Males.	Dependents. Females.	Total. Total.	Total. Males.	Total. Females.	Remarks.
CLASS G.—Indefinite and Independent.	XXIII.—Indefinite	74. Unskilled, labour.	(a) Special branches	461. Well sinkers	53	53	...	165	60	105	218	113	105	
				462. Tank diggers and excavators ...	11	11	...	1	1	...	12	12	...	
				466. Rice-pounders and huskers ...	85	76	9	168	74	94	253	150	103	
			(b) General ...	467. General labour	28,517	22,707	5,810	45,718	15,841	29,877	74,235	38,548	35,687	
		75. Undefined, &c.		468. Undefined and disreputable means of livelihood	27,090	15,744	11,346	158	82	76	27,248	15,826	11,422	
	XXIV.—Independent of work.	76. Property & alms.	(a) Property and allowances.	469. House-rent, shares, and other property not being land ...	1,183	1,174	9	3,542	1,382	2,160	4,725	2,556	2,169	
			(b) Charity and endowment.	471. Educational or other endowments scholarship, &c. ...	1,564	1,412	152	2,224	849	1,375	3,788	2,261	1,527	
				472. Mendicancy (not being affiliated to a religious order) ...	22,581	19,008	3,573	35,450	13,167	22,283	58,031	32,175	25,856	
		77. Supported at the public charge.	(a) Pension ...	473. Pension, Civil Services ...	389	371	18	482	140	342	871	511	360	
				474. Pension, Military Services ...	2	2	...	...	...	...	2	2	...	
			(b) Prisoners ...	476. Prisoners, under trial ...	26	25	1	...	...	...	26	25	1	
				477 Prisoners, for debt	1	1	...	...	...	...	1	1	...	
				478 Prisoners, convicted or in Reformatories, &c.	233	221	12	...	...	...	233	221	12	
				TOTAL CLASS G ...	81,735	60,805	20,930	87,908	31,596	56,312	169,643	92,401	77,242	

CENSUS 1891

KASHMIR STATE.

TABLE XVII.—PART B.—*Occupations.*—(Concluded.)

Class.	Workers.			Dependents.			Total.			Remarks.
	Total.	Males.	Females.	Total.	Males.	Females.	Total.	Males.	Females.	
ABSTRACT.										
Total Class A	27,369	26,848	521	41,366	15,636	25,730	68,735	42,484	26,251	
Do. B	455,838	434,452	21,386	1,307,005	498,599	808,406	1,762,843	933,051	829,792	
Do. C	34,015	30,677	3,338	50,758	19,296	31,462	84,773	49,973	34,800	
Do. D	109,248	84,209	25,039	217,457	78,864	138,593	326,705	163,073	163,632	
Do. E	27,421	26,072	1,349	56,357	20,371	35,986	83,778	46,443	37,335	
Do. F	14,361	13,482	879	33,114	12,322	20,792	47,475	25,804	21,671	
Do. G	81,735	60,805	20,930	87,908	31,596	56,312	169,643	92,401	77,242	
GRAND TOTAL	749,987	676,545	73,442	1,793,965	676,684	1,117,281	2,543,952	1,353,229	1,190,723	

JAMMU:
Dated 9th February 1892.

BHAG RAM,
Census Superintendent, Kashmir State.

CENSUS 1891.

KASHMIR STATE.

TABLE XVII.—PART B.—*Occupations.—(Jammu Province.)*

Class.	Order.	Sub-order and Group.	Occupation.	Workers. Total.	Workers. Males.	Workers. Females.	Dependents. Total.	Dependents. Males.	Dependents. Females.	Total. Total.	Total. Males.	Total. Females.	Remarks.
Class A.	I.—Administration	1. Service of the State ...	1. Maharaja and Rajas and their Families	3	3	...	77	1	76	80	4	76	
			2. Officers	163	163	...	224	101	123	387	264	123	
			3. Office Superintendents and Clerical Establishments. Police and Excise Inspectors, Sub-Registrars, &c.	10,886	10,566	320	15,541	5,742	9,799	26,427	16,308	10,119	
			4. Messengers, Constables, Bailiffs, Warders, Menials, &c. ...	950	950	...	527	199	328	1,477	1,149	328	
		2. Service of Local and Municipal Bodies.	5. Inspecting and Supervising Officials	1	1	...	4	1	3	5	2	3	
		3. Village Service	9. Accountants	11	11	...	8	3	5	19	14	5	
			11. Watchmen and other Menials ...	729	603	126	1,389	484	905	2,118	1,087	1,031	
	II.—Defence ...	4. Army	12. Officers	3	3	...	8	3	5	11	6	5	
			13. Non-Commissioned Officers and Privates	5,463	5,463	...	2,418	718	1,700	7,881	6,181	1,700	
	III.—Foreign and Feudatory State Service,	6. Administrative Service ...	20. Clerical Establishments and 21. Menials, &c.	173	169	4	244	69	175	417	238	179	
			TOTAL CLASS A ...	18,382	17,932	450	20,440	7,321	13,119	38,822	25,253	13,569	

CENSUS 1891.

KASHMIR STATE.

TABLE XVII.—PART B.—*Occupations.*—(*Jammu Province.*)—(Continued.)

Class.	Order.	Sub-order and Group.	Occupation.	Workers. Total.	Workers. Males.	Workers. Females.	Dependents. Total.	Dependents. Males.	Dependents. Females.	Total. Total.	Total. Males.	Total. Females.	Remarks.
CLASS B.	IV.—Live stock ...	8. Stock breeding and dealing. (*c.*) Small stock ...	31. Sheep and Goat breeders and dealers	4,319	3,899	420	5,572	2,168	3,404	9,891	6,067	3,824	
		9. Subsidiary services to stock. (*d.*) Training and doctoring live-stock...	34. Farriers and Gelders ...	18	18	...	68	24	44	86	42	44	
			35. Horse and Elephant breakers and trainers, &c.	12	12	...	22	5	17	34	17	17	
	V.—Agriculture ...	10. Interest in Land	37. Land occupants, not cultivating	12,789	12,310	479	22,893	6,509	16,384	35,682	18,819	16,863	
			38. Land occupants, cultivating ...	135,289	127,808	7,481	326,927	115,343	211,584	462,216	243,151	219,065	
			39. Lessees of Villages, &c. ...	935	871	64	2,398	788	1,610	3,333	1,659	1,674	
			41. Tenants and sharers, cultivating	158,966	149,896	9,070	379,035	133,669	245,366	538,001	283,565	254,436	
		12. Growers of special products and trees	52. Gardeners, seedsmen, &c. ...	267	238	29	608	243	365	875	481	394	
			54. Forest Officers	1	1	...	4	1	3	5	2	3	
			55. Forest Rangers, Guards, Peons ...	128	128	...	199	57	142	327	185	142	
			TOTAL CLASS B ...	312,724	295,181	17,543	737,726	258,807	478,919	1,050,450	553,988	496,462	

CENSUS 1891.

KASHMIR STATE.

TABLE XVII.—PART B.—*Occupations.*—(*Jammu Province.*)—(Continued.)

Class.	Order.	Sub-order and Group.	Occupation.	Workers. Total.	Workers. Males.	Workers. Females.	Dependents. Total.	Dependents. Males.	Dependents. Females.	Total. Total.	Total. Males.	Total. Females.	Remarks.
CLASS C.	VI.—Personal and household services.	14. Personal and domestic services ...	59. Barbers	2,171	2,171	...	5,061	1,668	3,393	7,232	3,839	3,393	
			63. Washermen (*sometimes also dyers*)	1,079	948	131	2,045	746	1,299	3,124	1,694	1,430	
			64. Water-carriers	1,355	1,086	269	2,302	826	1,476	3,657	1,912	1,745	
			65. Cooks	24	24	...	59	20	39	83	44	39	
			66. Indoor servants	15,656	13,605	2,051	8,785	3,111	5,674	24,441	16,716	7,725	
			67. Grooms, coachmen and dog-boys, &c.	69	69	...	34	8	26	103	77	26	
			68. Door-keepers, &c.	16	16	...	37	13	24	53	29	24	
		15. Non-domestic Establishment ...	70. Rest-house, Serai, Bath-house, &c., owners and Managers ...	14	11	3	5	2	3	19	13	6	
		16. Sanitation	74. Sweepers and scavengers ...	725	575	150	1,514	599	915	2,239	1,174	1,065	
			TOTAL CLASS C ...	21,109	18,505	2,604	19,842	6,993	12,849	40,951	25,498	15,453	
CLASS D.	Preparation and supply of material substances.	VII. Food & drink — 17. Animal Food	76. Cow and buffalo-keepers and milk and butter sellers ...	2,535	2,298	237	5,564	1,993	3,571	8,099	4,291	3,808	
			77. Ghee preparers and sellers ...	781	766	15	1,891	727	1,164	2,672	1,493	1,179	
			79. Butchers	282	275	7	520	167	353	802	442	360	
			81. Fishermen and fish curers (*many are also boatmen and palki bearers*)	8	8	...	20	5	15	28	13	15	
			Carried over Class D ...	3,606	3,347	259	7,995	2,892	5,103	11,601	6,239	5,362	

CENSUS 1891.

KASHMIR STATE.

TABLE XVII.—PART B.—*Occupations.*—(*Jammu Province.*)—(Continued.)

Class.	Order.	Sub-order and Group.		Occupation.	Workers.			Dependents.			Total.			Remarks.
					Total.	Males.	Females.	Total.	Males.	Females.	Total.	Males.	Females.	
				Brought forward Class D ...	3,606	3,347	259	7,995	2,892	5,103	11,601	6,239	5,362	
CLASS D.—(*Continued.*)	Preparation and supply of material substances.—(*Contd*).	VII. Food & drink (*Contd*).	18. Vegetable Food.	83. Grain dealers	17	13	4	9	4	5	26	17	9	
				84. Grain parchers	46	36	10	32	13	19	78	49	29	
				86. Flour-mill service and management	1,870	1,670	200	2,791	931	1,860	4,661	2,601	2,060	
				87. Bakers	318	293	25	537	227	310	855	520	335	
				89. Vegetable sellers ...	308	268	40	526	176	350	834	444	390	
				90. Fruit sellers	15	13	2	18	7	11	33	20	13	
				92. Confectioners and sweetmeat makers and sellers, and cooks who are also sometimes fishermen and water-carriers ...	230	230	...	426	142	284	656	372	284	
			19. Drink condiments and narcotics.	97. Country spirits distillers & sellers	25	23	2	12	6	6	37	29	8	
				105. Salt preparers and sellers ...	97	65	32	74	15	59	171	80	91	
				109. Grocers and general condiment dealers	190	181	9	371	106	265	561	287	274	
				112. Tobacco and snuff manufacturers and sellers	33	32	1	71	22	49	104	54	50	
				114. Opium, &c., manufacturers and sellers	1	1	...	...	...	...	1	1	...	
				115. Bhang, ganja, &c, preparers and sellers	3	3	...	4	2	2	7	5	2	
				Carried over Class D ...	6,759	6,175	584	12,866	4,543	8,323	19,625	10,718	8,907	

CENSUS 1891.

KASHMIR STATE.

TABLE XVII.—PART B.—*Occupations.*—(*Jammu Province.*)—(Continued.)

Class.	Order.	Sub-order and Group.	Occupation.	Workers. Total.	Workers. Males.	Workers. Females	Dependents. Total.	Dependents. Males.	Dependents. Females	Total. Total.	Total. Males.	Total. Females.	Remarks.
Class D.—(*Continued.*)			*Brought forward Class D* ...	6,759	6,175	584	12,86	4,543	8,32	19,625	10,718	8,907	
	VIII. Light, firing, and forage.	20. Lighting	116. Oil-pressers and sellers ...	1,452	1,348	10	3,07	1,064	2,014	4,53	2,41	2,118	
			120. Torch makers and sellers ...	5	5	...	1	6	10	21	11	1	
		21. Fuel and Forage	125. Firewood and grass gatherers and sellers	373	313	6	651	226	425	1,02	539	48	
			131. Hay, &c., contractors and dealers	10	10	...	2	2	...	1	1	...	
	IX. Buildings ...	22. Building materials	182. Brick and tile burners and sellers	28	21	7	6	21	3	8	4	4	
		23. Artificers in Buildings ...	137. Stone and marble workers ...	72	72	...	18	78	11	26	150	11	
			138. Masons	237	237	...	46	159	30	7(0	396	304	
		28. Books and Prints, &c. ...	157. Press Proprietors, Lithographers and Printers	27	27	...	30	5	2	57	32	25	
			158. Book-binders	21	21	...	41	12	2	6	33	29	
			159. Book-sellers and publishers ...	2	2	...	...	...	...	2	2	...	
		29. Watches, Clocks and scientific instruments	163. Watch and Clock makers and sellers	5	5	...	6	4	2	11	9	2	
		30. Carving, engraving, &c. ...	172. Turners and lacquerers ...	15	15	...	55	21	34	7	36	34	
			173. Die-sinkers and seal, &c., engravers	2	2	...	...	...	...	2	2	...	
	XI. Supplementary requirements.	31. Toys, curiosities &c.	178. Hukka stem makers and sellers ...	28	28	...	43	17	26	71	45	26	
			179. Papier-mache workers and sellers	31	31	...	51	14	37	82	45	37	
			Carried over Class D ...	9,067	8,312	755	17,550	6,172	11,378	26,617	14,484	12,133	

CENSUS 1891.

KASHMIR STATE.

TABLE XVII.—PART B.—*Occupations.*—(*Jammu Province.*)—(Continued.)

Class.	Order.	Sub-order and Group.	Occupation.	Workers. Total.	Workers. Males.	Workers. Females.	Dependents. Total.	Dependents. Males.	Dependents. Females.	Total. Total.	Total. Males.	Total. Females.	Remarks.
Class D.—(*Continued.*)			*Brought forward Class D* ...	9,067	8,312	755	17,550	6,172	11,378	26,617	14,484	12,133	
	XI. Supplementary requirements.—(*Concld.*)	32. Music and Musical Instruments ...	183. Music and Musical Instrument dealers	4	4	...	10	4	6	14	8	6	
		33. Necklaces, Bracelets, beads, sacred threads, &c.	185. Bangle makers and sellers in lac	98	97	1	202	57	145	300	154	146	
		35. Harness	201. Saddlery and Harness makers and sellers	6	6	...	20	8	12	26	14	12	
		36. Tools and Machinery ...	205. Knife and tool grinders ...	28	28	...	47	12	35	75	40	35	
		37. Arms and ammunition ...	210. Ammunition and Cap dealers ...	1	1	...	...	...	...	1	1	...	
			212. Fire-work makers and sellers ...	27	27	...	77	27	50	104	54	50	
			215. Bow and arrow makers and sellers	40	40	...	36	7	29	76	47	29	
	XII.—Textile Fabrics and dress ...	38. Wool and Fur	217. Carpet weavers and sellers ...	7	7	...	5	3	2	12	10	2	
			218. Shawl weavers and sellers ..	74	71	3	135	50	85	209	121	88	
			219. Felt and pashm workers and sellers	2	2	...	9	4	5	11	6	5	
			221. Woollen cloth manufacturers and dealers	183	182	1	448	169	279	631	351	280	
			222. Woollen yarn spinners and sellers	2,633	35	2,598	1,058	431	627	3,691	466	3,225	
			224. Wool dyers	527	481	46	1,108	357	751	1,635	838	797	
			Carried over Class D ...	12,697	9,293	3,404	20,705	7,301	13,404	33,402	16,594	16,808	

CENSUS 1891.

KASHMIR STATE.

TABLE XVII.—PART B.—*Occupations.*—(*Jammu Province.*)—(Continued.)

Class.	Order.	Sub-Order and Group.	Occupation.	Workers. Total.	Workers. Males.	Workers. Females.	Dependents. Total.	Dependents. Males.	Dependents. Females.	Total. Total.	Total. Males.	Total. Females.	Remarks.
CLASS D.—(*Continued.*)			*Brought forward Class D* ...	12,697	9,293	3,404	20,705	7,301	13,404	33,402	16,594	16,808	
	XII.—*Concld.* ...	39. Silk	229. Silk printers and dyers ...	10	10	...	25	10	15	35	20	15	
			230. Braid and ribbon makers and sellers	111	98	13	174	65	109	285	163	122	
		40. Cotton	231. Cotton cleaners, pressers and ginners	481	448	33	857	279	578	1,338	727	611	
			234. Cotton weavers, Mill-owners and Managers	10,248	9,699	549	23,188	7,884	15,304	33,436	17,583	15,853	
			236. Calenderers, fullers and printers	21	21	...	32	7	25	53	28	25	
			237. Cotton dyers	18	18	...	69	14	55	87	32	55	
		41. Jute, flax, coir, &c.	241. Hemp rope makers and sellers ...	4	4	...	7	...	7	11	4	7	
			243. Sacking, tarpaulin and gunny makers and sellers ...	1	1	...	5	2	3	6	3	3	
		42. Dress	247. Tailors and darners	1,519	1,357	162	3,037	1,054	1,983	4,556	2,411	2,145	
			254. Embroiderers and lace and muslin-makers	3	...	3	5	...	5	8	...	8	
	XIII.—Metals and precious stones.	43. Gold, silver, and precious stones	260. Gold and silver workers ...	1,523	1,520	3	3,180	1,031	2,149	4,703	2,551	2,152	
			261. Gold beaters	2	2	...	5	2	3	7	4	3	
			262. Gold smiths' dust washers ...	9	9	...	22	6	16	31	15	16	
			265. Electro-platers	6	6	...	6	1	5	12	7	5	
			266. Gold and silver wire drawers, and braid makers	3	3	...	10	4	6	13	7	6	
			Carried over Class D ...	26,656	22,489	4,167	51,327	17,660	33,667	77,983	40,149	37,834	

CENSUS 1891.

KASHMIR STATE.

TABLE XVII.—PART B.—*Occupations.*—(*Jammu Province.*)—(Continued.)

Class.	Order.	Sub-order and Group.	Occupation.	Workers. Total.	Workers. Males.	Workers. Females.	Dependents. Total.	Dependents. Males.	Dependents. Females.	Total. Total.	Total. Males.	Total. Females.	Remarks.
			Brought forward Class D ...	26,656	22,489	4,167	51,327	17,660	33,667	77,983	40,149	37,834	
Class D.—(*Continued.*)	XIII.—*Concld.*	44. Brass, copper and bell metal ...	277. Brass pot makers and sellers ...	131	116	15	207	69	138	338	185	153	
			279. Copper workers and sellers ...	73	73	...	173	58	115	246	131	115	
		45. Tin, zinc, mercury and lead ...	284. Tin workers and sellers ...	140	140	...	418	149	269	558	289	269	
		46. Iron and steel	290. Blacksmiths	2,529	2,433	96	5,538	2,015	3,523	8,067	4,448	3,619	
	XIV.—Glass, pottery and stone ware.	47. Glass and Chinaware ...	297. Glass and Chinaware dealers ...	5	4	1	3	1	2	8	5	3	
		48. Earthen and stone ware ...	298. Potters and pot and pipe-bowl-makers and sellers. (*Some are brick and tile makers also*) ...	2,245	2,030	215	4,558	1,599	2,959	6,803	3,629	3,174	
			299. Grindstone and millstone makers, menders and sellers ...	5	5	...	12	3	9	17	8	9	
	XV.—Wood cane and leaves, &c.	49. Timber and wood ...	302. Timber and bamboo agents and dealers	668	632	36	1,451	540	911	2,119	1,172	947	
			303. Wood cutters and sawyers ...	3	3	...	4	...	4	7	3	4	
			304. Carpenters	2,830	2,830	...	5,546	1,766	3,780	8,376	4,596	3,780	
		50. Canework, matting and leaves &c.	306. Bamboo and rattan splitters, workers and sellers ...	298	261	37	603	207	396	901	468	433	
			307. Basket weavers and winnowing pan makers and sellers ...	454	386	68	905	353	552	1,359	739	620	
			308. Mat makers and sellers ...	7	7	...	10	2	8	17	9	8	
			310. Leaf-plate makers and sellers. (*Are also often temple servants*) ...	42	34	8	53	19	34	95	53	42	
			313. Brush and comb makers & sellers	32	32	...	75	24	51	107	56	51	
			Carried over Class D ...	36,118	31,475	4,643	70,883	24,465	46,418	107,001	55,940	51,061	

CENSUS 1891.

KASHMIR STATE.

TABLE XVII.—PART B.—*Occupations.*—(*Jammu Province.*)—(Continued.)

Class.	Order.	Sub-order and Group.	Occupation.	Workers.			Dependents.			Total.			Remarks.
				Total.	Males.	Females.	Total.	Males.	Females.	Total.	Males.	Females.	
			Brought forward Class D ...	36,118	31,475	4,643	70,883	24,465	46,418	107,001	55,940	51,061	
CLASS D.—(*Concluded.*)	XVI.—Drugs, gums, dyes, &c.	52. Drugs, dyes, pigments, &c. ...	324. Chemists and druggists ...	19	19	...	55	17	38	74	36	38	
			328. Soap makers and sellers ...	5	5	...	14	3	11	19	8	11	
			330. Indigo workers and dealers (not planters)	1	1	...	...	...	...	1	1	...	
			332. Ink-makers and sellers ...	4	4	...	5	2	3	9	6	3	
			337. Perfume preparers and sellers ...	13	13	...	9	3	6	22	16	6	
	XVII.—Leather, horns, bones, and grease.	53. Leather, &c.	338. Tanners, curriers and hide sellers (*many also shoe-makers*) ...	83	83	...	259	93	166	342	176	166	
			339. Shoe, sandals, boot-makers and sellers	6,361	5,916	445	14,375	4,928	9,447	20,736	10,844	9,892	
			340. Leather dyers	36	36	...	65	18	47	101	54	47	
			341. Water bag, well-bag, bucket and ghee pot makers and sellers ...	1	1	...	...	...	...	1	1	...	
			TOTAL CLASS D ...	42,641	37,553	5,088	85,665	29,529	56,136	128,306	67,082	61,224	

CENSUS 1891.

KASHMIR STATE.

TABLE XVII.—PART B.—*Occupations.*—(*Jammu Province*)—(Continued.)

Class.	Order.	Sub-order and Group.	Occupation.	Workers. Total.	Workers. Males.	Workers. Females.	Dependents. Total.	Dependents. Males.	Dependents. Females.	Total. Total.	Total. Males.	Total. Females.	Remarks.
Class E.—Commerce, Transport, Storage.	XVIII.—Commerce	54. Dealers in money and securities...	346. Bankers and Bank Managers ...	1,825	1,709	116	3,862	1,225	2,637	5,687	2,934	2,753	
			350. Money changers and testers ...	127	127	...	343	119	224	470	246	224	
		55. General Merchandise ...	352. General Merchants	4,591	4,345	246	7,358	2,395	4,963	11,949	6,740	5,209	
		56. Dealing unspecified	356. Shopkeepers, otherwise unspecified	11,578	10,986	592	20,548	7,200	13,348	32,126	18,186	13,940	
			357. Pedlars, Hawkers, &c. ...	96	96	...	286	83	203	382	179	203	
		57. Middlemen, &c. (a) Brokers, &c.	358. Brokers, Agents, Dubash ...	5	5	...	2	1	1	7	6	1	
		(b) Contractors and farmers.	360. Farmers of Tolls, ferries ...	107	107	...	174	53	121	281	160	121	
			361. Farmers of liquor, opium, &c. ...	16	16	...	15	14	1	31	30	1	
			362. Lessees and Superintendents of markets, stalls, &c. ...	1	1	...	...	...	...	1	1	...	
			363. Contractors, otherwise unspecified	301	301	...	681	215	466	982	516	466	
	XIX.—Transport and Storage.	58. Railway ... (b) Working Staff.*	371. Station Masters and Assistants, Inspectors, Overseers, &c. ...	25	25	...	34	12	22	59	37	22	
		59. Road ... (a) Cart, Carriage and Tramway owners and drivers.	375. Cart owners and drivers, carting Agents, &c.	7	7	...	25	9	16	32	16	16	
			377. Drivers, stable-boys, &c., (*not private servants*)	10	10	...	12	8	4	22	18	4	
		(b) Carriers by pack animals.	379. Pack bullock owners, drivers, &c.	93	89	4	228	131	97	321	220	101	
			380. Pack camel, elephant, mule, &c., owners and drivers ...	899	884	15	1,762	637	1,125	2,661	1,521	1,140	
			Carried over Class E ...	19,681	18,708	973	35,380	12,102	23,228	55,011	30,810	24,201	

* Excluding Police on Railways.

CENSUS 1891.

KASHMIR STATE.

TABLE XVII.—PART B.—*Occupations.—Jammu Province.*—(Continued).

Class.	Order.	Sub-order and Group.	Occupation.	Workers. Total.	Workers. Males.	Workers. Females.	Dependents. Total.	Dependents. Males.	Dependents. Females.	Total. Total.	Total. Males.	Total. Females.	Remarks.
			Brought forward Class E ...	19,681	18,708	973	35,330	12,102	23,228	55,011	30,810	24,201	
CLASS E.—(*Concld.*)	XIX.—*Concld.* ...	60. Water ... (*b*) Working Staff of vessels.	385. Boat and barge men ...	680	643	37	1,188	360	828	1,868	1,003	865	
		61. Messages ... (*a*) Post, &c. ...	390. Postal Directors, Postmasters and Clerks	140	140	...	134	52	82	274	192	82	
			392. Messengers, (unspecified) ...	2	2	...	3	2	1	5	4	1	
		(*b*) Telegraph and Telephone.	394. Signallers and messengers ...	4	4	...	...	...	...	4	4	...	
		62. Storage and weighing ...	399. Weighmen and measurers ...	1	1	...	3	1	2	4	2	2	
			TOTAL CLASS E ...	20,508	19,498	1,010	36,658	12,517	24,141	57,166	32,015	25,151	
CLASS F.—Professions.		63. Religion ... (*a*) Priests, Ministers, &c.	401. Priests, ministers, preachers, missionaries, &c.	5,537	5,006	531	10,686	3,538	7,148	16,223	8,544	7,679	
		(*b*) Subsidiary religious services.	405. Church, Temple, Masjid, Pagoda, ghat, burial or burning ground service, pilgrim conductors and undertakers	855	754	101	1,275	449	826	2,130	1,203	927	
		64. Education	406. Administrative and inspecting officials	1	1	...	2	1	1	3	2	1	
			407. Principals, Professors and Teachers in Colleges, &c., Schools, &c.	905	899	6	1,762	633	1,129	2,667	1,532	1,135	
	XX.—Learned and Artistic Professions.	66. Law	414. Barristers, Advocates and Pleaders	27	27	...	42	15	27	69	42	27	
			418. Stamp-vendors	13	13	...	19	6	13	32	19	13	
			419. Petition-writers	24	24	...	60	14	46	84	38	46	
			Carried over Class F ...	7,362	6,724	638	13,846	4,656	9,190	21,208	11,38[illegible]	9,82[illegible]	

CENSUS 1891.

KASHMIR STATE.

TABLE XVII.—PART B.—*Occupation.*—(*Jammu Province*).—(Continued.)

Class.	Order.	Sub-order and Group.		Occupation.	Workers. Total.	Workers. Males.	Workers. Females.	Dependents. Total.	Dependents. Males.	Dependents. Females.	Total. Total.	Total. Males.	Total. Females.	Remarks.
				Brought forward Class F ...	7,362	6,724	638	13,816	4,656	9,190	21,208	11,380	9,828	
CLASS F.—*Concld.*	XX.—*Concld.* ...	67. Medicine ...	(a) Practitioners ...	421. Practitioner by Diploma ...	3	3	...	15	4	11	18	7	11	
				422. Practitioners without Diploma (Baid, Hakim Kobiraj, &c.	271	257	14	519	194	325	790	451	339	
				426. Midwifery	6	...	6	3	1	2	9	1	8	
			(b) Subsidiary Medical Service.	428. Compounders, Nurses and Hospital, Asylum and Dispensary service	24	23	1	29	14	15	53	37	16	
		68. Engineering & Surveying	(a) Engineers, Architects and Surveyors.	429. Administrative and Inspecting Staff	1	1	...	5	2	3	6	3	3	
			(b) Subsidiary Staff	432. Draughtsmen and Operators in Survey Offices, Overseers, &c. ...	3	3	...	12	4	8	15	7	8	
				433. Clerks, &c., in offices of the above,	3	3	...	5	2	3	8	5	3	
		69. Other Sciences.	(b) Minor Sciences	437. Astrologers, Genealogists and Horoscopecasters	17	17	...	33	15	18	50	32	18	
		71. Music, Acting, Dancing ...		444. Bandmasters and players (not Military)	80	78	2	206	65	141	286	143	143	
				446. Actors, Singers and Dancers and their accompanists	160	151	9	250	62	188	410	213	197	
	XXI.—Sport and Amusements.	72. Sport		448. Shikaris, Falconers, Birdcatchers,	7	7	...	17	12	5	24	19	5	
		73. Exhibition & Games.	(b) Conjuring, fortune telling and other exhibitions.	453. Buffoons	22	19	3	44	26	18	66	45	21	
				454. Story and Ballad reciters ...	2	2	...	2	1	1	4	3	1	
			(c) Acrobatics and Athletics.	457. Tumblers, Acrobats, Wrestlers Professional cricketers, &c. ...	92	79	13	147	59	88	239	138	101	
				TOTAL CLASS F ...	8,053	7,367	686	15,133	5,117	10,016	23,186	12,484	10,702	

CENSUS 1891.

KASHMIR STAT

TABLE XVII.—PART B.—*Occupations.*—(*Jammu Province.*)—(Continued.)

Class.	Order.	Sub-order and Group.		Occupation.	Workers.			Dependents.			Total.			Remarks.
					Total.	Males.	Females.	Total.	Males.	Females.	Total.	Males.	Females.	
Class G.—Indefinite and Independent.	XXIII.—Indefinite	74. Unskilled, labour.	(a) Special branches	462. Tank diggers and excavators ...	11	11	...	1	1	...	12	12	...	
				466. Rice-pounders and huskers ...	85	76	9	168	74	94	253	150	103	
			(b) General ...	467. General labour	23,324	18,067	5,257	35,153	11,935	23,218	58,477	30,002	28,475	
		75. Undefined, &c.		468. Undefined and disreputable means of livelihood	6,143	3,474	2,669	66	42	24	6,209	3,516	2,693	
	XXIV.—Independent of work.	76. Property & alms.	(a) Property and allowances.	469. House-rent, shares, and other property not being land ...	66	57	9	52	15	37	118	72	46	
			(b) Charity and endowment.	471. Educational or other endowments scholarship, &c. ...	1,314	1,171	143	1,515	537	978	2,829	1,708	1,121	
				472. Mendicancy (not being affiliated to a religious order) ...	14,481	11,693	2,788	17,329	6,154	11,175	31,810	17,847	13,963	
		77. Supported at the public charge.	(a) Pension ...	473. Pension, Civil Services ...	375	358	17	447	131	316	822	489	333	
			(b) Prisoners ...	476. Prisoners, under trial ...	21	20	1	...	...	...	21	20	1	
				478. Prisoners, convicted or in Reformatories, &c.	111	105	6	...	...	...	111	105	6	
				TOTAL CLASS G ...	45,931	35,032	10,899	54,731	18,889	35,842	100,662	53,921	46,741	

CENSUS 1891.

KASHMIR STATE.

TABLE XVII.—PART B.—*Occupations.*—(*Jammu Province.*)—(Concluded.)

Class.	Workers.			Dependents.			Total.			Remarks.
	Total.	Males.	Females.	Total.	Males.	Females.	Total.	Males.	Females.	
ABSTRACT.										
Total Class A	18,382	17,932	450	20,440	7,321	13,119	38,822	25,253	13,569	
Do. B	312,724	295,181	17,543	737,726	258,807	478,919	1,050,450	553,988	496,462	
Do. C	21,109	18,505	2,604	19,842	6,993	12,849	40,951	25,498	15,453	
Do. D	42,641	37,553	5,088	85,665	29,529	56,136	128,306	67,082	61,224	
Do. E	20,508	19,498	1,010	36,658	12,517	24,141	57,166	32,015	25,151	
Do. F	8,053	7,367	686	15,133	5,117	10,016	23,186	12,484	10,702	
Do. G	45,931	35,032	10,899	54,731	18,889	35,842	100,662	53,921	46,741	
GRAND TOTAL	469,348	431,068	38,280	970,195	339,173	631,022	1,439,543	770,241	669,302	

JAMMU:
Dated 9th February 1892.

BHAG RAM,
Census Superintendent, Kashmir State.

CENSUS 1891.

KASHMIR STATE.

TABLE XVII.—PART B.—*Occupations.*—(*Kashmir Province.*)

Class.	Order.	Sub-order and Group.	Occupation.	Workers.			Dependents.			Total.			Remarks.
				Total.	Males.	Females.	Total.	Males.	Females.	Total.	Males.	Females.	
Class A.	I.—Administration	1. Service of the State ...	2. Officers	8	8	...	7	3	4	15	11	4	
			3. Office Superintendents and Clerical Establishments. Police and Excise Inspectors, Sub-Registrars, &c.	5,718	5,675	43	14,110	5,632	8,478	19,828	11,307	8,521	
			4. Messengers, Constables, Bailiffs, Warders, Menials, &c. ...	353	352	1	705	263	442	1,058	615	443	
		3. Village Service	9. Accountants	653	653	...	2,621	1,121	1,500	3,274	1,774	1,500	
			11. Watchmen and other Menials ...	462	448	14	1,589	650	939	2,051	1,098	953	
	II.—Defence ...	4. Army	13. Non-Commissioned Officers and Privates	1,097	1,097	...	1,122	363	759	2,219	1,460	759	
	III.—Foreign and Feudatory State Service.	6. Administrative Service ...	20. Clerical Establishments and 21. Menials, &c.	107	94	13	252	93	159	359	187	172	
		7. Army and Marine	22. Officers	8	8	...	22	6	16	30	14	16	
			TOTAL CLASS A ...	8,406	8,335	71	20,428	8,181	12,297	28,834	16,466	12,368	

CENSUS 1891.

KASHMIR STATE.

TABLE XVII.—PART B.—*Occupations.*—(*Kashmir Province.*)—(Continued.)

Class.	Order.	Sub-order and Group.		Occupation.	Workers.			Dependents.			Total.			Remarks.
					Total.	Males.	Females.	Total.	Males.	Females.	Total.	Males.	Females.	
Class B.	IV.—Live stock ...	8. Stock breeding and dealing.	(a.) Horses and horned cattle	25. Cattle breeders and dealers and Commissariat Farm Establishment	891	879	12	2,685	1,073	1,612	3,576	1,952	1,624	
				26. Herdsmen	1,898	1,840	58	7,144	3,054	4,090	9,042	4,894	4,148	
			(c.) Small stock ...	31. Sheep and Goat breeders and dealers	1,410	1,215	195	3,909	1,684	2,225	5,319	2,899	2,420	
		9. Subsidiary services to stock.	(a.) Training and doctoring live stock...	34. Farriers and Gelders ...	27	27	...	60	17	43	87	44	43	
				35. Horse and Elephant breakers and trainers, &c.	59	59	...	131	47	84	190	106	84	
	V.—Agriculture ...	10. Interest in Land		38. Land occupants, cultivating ...	83,329	81,950	1,379	335,901	144,298	191,603	419,230	226,248	192,982	
				39. Lessees of Villages, &c. ...	531	505	26	2,212	1,051	1,161	2,743	1,556	1,187	
				41. Tenants and sharers, cultivating	30,202	28,938	1,264	111,163	46,419	64,744	141,365	75,357	66,008	
		12. Growers of special products and trees		44. Tea, Coffee and Cinchona Planters, Managers and Assistants	1	1	...	...	...	...	1	1	...	
				47. Waternut growers	64	40	24	89	33	56	153	73	80	
				52. Gardeners, seedsmen, &c. ...	77	67	10	177	67	110	254	134	120	
				54. Forest Officers	...	...	...	3	...	3	3	...	3	
		13. Agricultural training and supervision.		56. Directors of Agriculture and their Assistants	3	3	...	...	...	...	3	3	...	
				TOTAL CLASS B ...	118,492	115,524	2,968	463,474	197,743	265,731	581,966	313,267	268,699	

CENSUS 1891.

KASHMIR STATE.

TABLE XVII.—PART B.—*Occupations.*—(*Kashmir Province*).—(Continued.)

Class.	Order.	Sub-order and Group.	Occupation.	Workers. Total.	Workers. Males.	Workers. Females.	Dependents. Total.	Dependents. Males.	Dependents. Females.	Total. Total.	Total. Males.	Total. Females.	Remarks.
Class C.	VI.—Personal and household services.	14. Personal and domestic services ...	59. Barbers	1,971	1,971	...	6,268	2,445	3,823	8,239	4,416	3,823	
			63. Washermen (*sometimes also dyers*)	648	588	60	1,648	633	1,015	2,296	1,221	1,075	
			64. Water-carriers	291	254	37	636	204	432	927	458	469	
			65. Cooks	266	266	...	641	210	431	907	476	431	
			66. Indoor servants	9,072	8,588	484	20,209	8,146	12,063	29,281	16,734	12,547	
			68. Door-keepers, &c.	8	8	...	18	5	13	26	13	13	
		15. Non-domestic Establishment ...	70. Rest-house, Serai, Bath-house, &c., owners and Managers ...	143	143	...	709	309	400	852	452	400	
		16. Sanitation	74. Sweepers and scavengers ...	102	81	21	122	53	69	224	134	90	
			75. Dust and sweepings contractors	18	15	3	41	19	22	59	34	25	
			TOTAL CLASS C ...	12,519	11,914	605	30,292	12,024	18,268	42,811	23,938	18,873	
Class D.	Preparation and supply of material substances.	VII. Food & drink — 17. Animal Food	76. Cow and buffalo-keepers and milk and butter sellers ...	2,695	2,575	120	9,342	3,910	5,432	12,037	6,485	5,552	
			79. Butchers	665	665	...	1,980	739	1,241	2,645	1,404	1,241	
			81. Fishermen and fish curers (*many are also boatmen and palki bearers*)	394	381	13	1,440	614	826	1,834	995	839	
			Carried over Class D ...	3,754	3,621	133	12,762	5,263	7,499	16,516	8,884	7,632	

CENSUS 1891.

KASHMIR STATE.

TABLE XVII.—PART B.—*Occupations.*—(*Kashmir Province.*)—(Continued.)

Class.	Order.	Sub-order and Group.		Occupation.	Workers.			Dependents.			Total.			Remarks.
					Total.	Males.	Females.	Total.	Males.	Females.	Total.	Males.	Females.	
CLASS D.—(*Continued.*)	Preparation and supply of material substances.—(*Contd*).	VII. Food & drink (*Contd*).		*Brought forward Class D* ...	3,754	3,621	133	12,762	5,263	7,499	16,516	8,884	7,632	
			18. Vegetable Food.	83. Grain dealers	3,336	3,275	61	10,315	4,061	6,254	13,651	7,336	6,315	
				84. Grain parchers	32	24	8	57	23	34	89	47	42	
				86. Flour-mill service and management	248	238	10	679	254	425	927	492	435	
				87. Bakers	826	775	51	2,374	925	1,449	3,200	1,700	1,500	
				89. Vegetable sellers ...	773	681	92	1,845	686	1,159	2,618	1,367	1,251	
				90. Fruit sellers	573	504	69	1,442	553	889	2,015	1,057	958	
				92. Confectioners and sweetmeat makers and sellers, and cooks who are also sometimes fishermen and water-carriers ...	187	182	5	352	138	214	539	320	219	
			19. Drink condiments and narcotics.	97. Country spirits distillers & sellers	12	12	...	8	2	6	20	14	6	
				112. Tobacco and snuff manufacturers and sellers	361	360	1	776	277	499	1,137	637	500	
				115. Bhang, ganja, &c, preparers and sellers	12	12	...	21	5	16	33	17	16	
				Carried over Class D ...	10,114	9,684	430	30,631	12,187	18,444	40,745	21,871	18,874	

CENSUS 1891.

KASHMIR STATE.

TABLE XVII.—PART B.—*Occupations.*—(*Káshmir Province.*)—(Continued.)

Class.	Order.	Sub-order and Group.	Occupation.	Workers. Total.	Workers. Males.	Workers. Females.	Dependents. Total.	Dependents. Males.	Dependents. Females	Total. Total.	Total. Males.	Total. Females.	Remarks.
CLASS D.—(*Continued.*)			*Brought forward Class D* ...	10,114	9,684	430	30,631	12,187	18,444	40,745	21,871	18,874	
	VIII. Light, firing, and forage.	20. Lighting	116. Oil-pressers and sellers ...	1,574	1,531	43	6,115	2,558	3,557	7,689	4,089	3,600	
			119. Candle makers and sellers ...	2	2	...	1	...	1	3	2	1	
			120. Torch makers and sellers ...	11	11	...	38	13	25	49	24	25	
		21. Fuel and Forage	125. Firewood and grass gatherers and sellers	361	350	11	1,391	591	800	1,752	941	811	
	IX. Buildings ...	22. Building materials	132. Brick and tile burners and sellers	69	69	...	183	64	119	252	133	119	
			133. Lime chunám and shell burners and sellers	73	73	...	245	91	154	318	164	154	
		23. Artificers in Buildings ...	136. Building contractors ...	199	199	...	502	210	292	701	409	292	
			137. Stone and marble workers ...	15	15	...	50	21	29	65	36	29	
			138. Masons	235	235	...	460	142	318	695	377	318	
		27. Paper, &c.	153. Paper makers and sellers and palmleaf binders	147	147	...	409	150	259	556	297	259	
		28. Books and Prints, &c. ...	157. Press Proprietors, Lithographers and Printers	1	1	...	3	1	2	4	2	2	
			158. Book-binders	34	34	...	78	24	54	112	58	54	
	XI. Supplementary requirements.	29. Watches, Clocks and scientific instruments	163. Watch and Clock makers and sellers	11	11	...	23	6	17	34	17	17	
		30. Carving, engraving, &c. ...	172. Turners and lacquerers ...	28	28	...	81	25	56	109	53	56	
			173. Die-sinkers and seal, &c., engravers	93	93	...	159	43	116	252	136	116	
			Carried over Class D ...	12,967	12,483	484	40,369	16,126	24,243	53,336	28,609	24,727	

CENSUS 1891.

KASHMIR STATE.

TABLE XVII.—PART B.—*Occupations.*—(*Kashmir Province.*)—(Continued.)

Class.	Order.	Sub-order and Group.	Occupation.	Workers. Total.	Workers. Males.	Workers. Females.	Dependents. Total.	Dependents. Males.	Dependents. Females.	Total. Total.	Total. Males.	Total. Females.	Remarks.
			Brought forward Class D ...	12,967	12,483	484	40,369	16,126	24,243	53,336	28,609	24,727	
Class D.—(Continued.)	XI. Supplementary requirements.—(*Concld.*)	31. Toys, curiosities &c.	178. Hukka stem makers and sellers ...	22	22	...	54	19	35	76	41	35	
			179. Papier-mache workers and sellers	211	209	2	433	117	316	644	326	318	
		32. Music and Musical Instruments ...	183. Music and Musical Instrument dealers	2	2	...	6	3	3	8	5	3	
		33. Necklaces, Bracelets, beads, sacred threads, &c.	185. Bangle makers and sellers in lac	125	115	10	248	77	171	373	192	181	
			194. Flower garland makers and sellers	5	5	...	12	3	9	17	8	9	
		35. Harness	201. Saddlery and Harness makers and sellers	274	274	...	397	113	284	671	387	284	
		36. Tools and Machinery ...	205. Knife and tool grinders ...	32	32	...	101	35	66	133	67	66	
		37. Arms and ammunition ...	212. Fire-work makers and sellers ...	47	46	1	133	65	68	180	111	69	
	XII.—Textile Fabrics and dress ...	38. Wool and Fur	217. Carpet weavers and sellers ...	339	338	1	415	102	313	754	440	314	
			218. Shawl weavers and sellers ..	9,491	9,491	...	20,317	6,674	13,643	29,808	16,165	13,643	
			219. Felt and pashm workers and sellers	161	161	...	434	126	308	595	287	308	
			220. Blanket weavers and sellers (*often also shepherds*)	4,423	4,385	38	12,714	4,818	7,896	17,137	9,203	7,934	
			221. Woollen cloth manufacturers and dealers	301	284	17	797	288	509	1,098	572	526	
			222. Woollen yarn spinners and sellers	19,110	48	19,062	4,026	1,514	2,512	23,136	1,562	21,574	
			Carried over Class D ...	47,510	27,895	19,615	80,456	30,080	50,376	127,966	57,975	69,991	

CENSUS 1891.

KASHMIR STATE.

TABLE XVII.—PART B.—*Occupations.*—(*Kashmir Province.*)—(Continued.)

Class.	Order.	Sub-Order and Group.	Occupation.	Workers. Total.	Workers. Males.	Workers. Females.	Dependents. Total.	Dependents. Males.	Dependents. Females.	Total. Total.	Total. Males.	Total. Females.	Remarks.
CLASS D.—(*Continued.*)			*Brought forward Class D* ...	47,510	27,895	19,615	80,456	30,080	50,376	127,966	57,975	69,991	
	XII.—*Concld.* ...	38 Concluded	223. Wool carders	188	188	...	538	177	361	726	365	361	
			224. Wool dyers	355	353	2	981	359	622	1,336	712	624	
		39. Silk	226. Silk-worm rearers and cocoon gatherers	94	94	...	266	91	175	360	185	175	
			230. Braid and ribbon makers and sellers	325	282	43	536	177	359	861	459	402	
		40. Cotton	231. Cotton cleaners, pressers and ginners	601	588	13	1,699	650	1,049	2,300	1,238	1,062	
			232. Cotton carpet and rug makers and sellers	45	45	...	105	29	76	150	74	76	
			236. Calenderers, fullers and printers	70	70	...	216	84	132	286	154	132	
		42. Dress	247. Tailors and darners	6,654	6,617	37	12,818	4,116	8,702	19,472	10,733	8,739	
			254. Embroiderers and lace and muslin-makers	409	409	...	618	184	434	1,027	593	434	
	XIII.—Metals and precious stones	43. Gold, silver, and precious stones ...	260. Gold and silver workers ...	881	881	...	3,017	1,124	1,893	3,898	2,005	1,893	
			Carried over Class D ...	57,132	37,422	19,710	101,250	37,071	64,179	158,382	74,493	83,889	

CENSUS 1891.

KASHMIR STATE.

TABLE XVII.—PART B.—*Occupations.*—(*Kashmir Province*).—(Continued.)

Class.	Order.	Sub-order and Group.	Occupation.	Workers. Total.	Workers. Males.	Workers. Females.	Dependents. Total.	Dependents. Males.	Dependents. Females.	Total. Total.	Total. Males.	Total. Females.	Remarks.
			Brought forward Class D ...	57,132	37,422	19,710	101,250	37,071	64,179	158,382	74,493	83,889	
CLASS D.—(*Continued.*)	XIII.—*Concld.*	44. Brass, copper and bell metal ...	277. Brass pot makers and sellers ...	39	28	11	87	39	48	126	67	59	
			279. Copper workers and sellers ...	213	213	...	480	142	338	693	355	338	
		45. Tin, zinc, mercury and lead ...	284. Tin workers and sellers ...	6	6	...	17	3	14	23	9	14	
		46. Iron and steel	290. Blacksmiths	1,443	1,432	11	4,938	1,995	2,943	6,381	3,427	2,954	
	XIV.—Glass, pottery and stone ware.	48. Earthen and stone ware ...	298. Potters and pot and pipe-bowl-makers and sellers. (*Some are brick and tile makers also*) ...	1,432	1,407	25	4,943	2,007	2,936	6,375	3,414	2,961	
	XV.—Wood cane and leaves, &c.	49. Timber and wood	302. Timber and bamboo agents and dealers	3	3	...	9	4	5	12	7	5	
			303. Wood cutters and sawyers ...	318	318	...	930	367	563	1,248	685	563	
			304. Carpenters	2,179	2,179	...	7,217	2,873	4,344	9,396	5,052	4,344	
		50. Canework, matting and leaves &c.	306. Bamboo and rattan splitters, workers and sellers ...	438	411	27	1,223	469	754	1,661	880	781	
			307. Basket weavers and winnowing pan makers and sellers ...	56	56	...	152	58	94	208	114	94	
			308. Mat makers and sellers ...	200	80	120	152	53	99	352	133	219	
			315. Pith and bark collectors, workers and sellers ...	6	6	...	19	9	10	25	15	10	
			Carried over Class D ...	63,465	43,561	19,904	121,417	45,090	76,327	184,882	88,651	96231	

CENSUS 1891.

KASHMIR STATE.

TABLE XVII.—PART B.—*Occupations.*—(*Kashmir Province.*)—(Continued.)

Class.	Order.	Sub-order and Group.	Occupation.	Workers. Total.	Workers. Males.	Workers. Females.	Dependents. Total.	Dependents. Males.	Dependents. Females.	Total. Total.	Total. Males.	Total. Females.	Remarks.
			Brought forward Class D ...	63,465	43,561	19,904	121,417	45,090	76,327	184,882	88,651	96,231	
Class D.—(*Concluded*).	XVI.—Drugs, gums, dyes, &c.	52. Drugs, dyes, pigments, &c. ...	324. Chemists and druggists ...	159	157	2	430	181	249	589	338	251	
			328. Soap makers and sellers ...	60	60	...	188	71	117	248	131	117	
			332. Ink-makers and sellers ...	22	22	...	79	25	54	101	47	54	
			337. Perfume preparers and sellers ...	1	1	...	...	...	...	1	1	...	
	XVII.—Leather, horns, bones, and grease.	53. Leather, &c.	339. Shoe, sandals, boot-makers and sellers	2,542	2,507	35	8,631	3,552	5,079	11,173	6,059	5,114	
			TOTAL CLASS D ...	66,249	46,308	19,941	130,745	48,919	81,826	196,994	95,227	101,767	
Class E.—Commerce, Transport, Storage.	XVIII.—Commerce,	54. Dealers in money and securities ...	346. Bankers and Bank Managers ...	1	1	...	...	...	...	1	1	...	
			350. Money changers and testers ...	460	460	...	1,415	505	910	1,875	965	910	
		55. General Merchandise ...	352. General Merchants	281	273	8	864	385	479	1,145	658	487	
			353. Merchants' Managers, Accountants, Clerks, Assistants, &c. ...	25	25	...	129	62	67	154	87	67	
			Carried over Class E ...	767	759	8	2,408	952	1,456	3,175	1,711	1,464	

CENSUS 1891.

KASHMIR STATE.

TABLE XVII.—PART B.—*Occupations.*—(*Kashmr Province.*)—(Continued.)

Class.	Order.	Sub-order and Group.	Occupation.	Workers. Total.	Workers. Males.	Workers. Females.	Dependents. Total.	Dependents. Males.	Dependents. Females.	Total. Total.	Total. Males.	Total. Females.	Remarks.
CLASS E.—Commerce, Transport, Storage.—(Contd.)			*Brought forward Class E* ...	767	759	8	2,408	952	1,456	3,175	1,711	1,464	
	XVIII.—Continued	56. Dealing unspecified	356. Shopkeepers, otherwise unspecified	1,419	1,401	18	3,765	1,505	2,260	5,184	2,906	2,278	
			357. Pedlars, Hawkers, &c. ...	93	89	4	248	100	148	341	189	152	
		57. Middlemen, &c. (a) Brokers, &c.	358. Brokers, Agents, Dubash ...	156	156	...	463	170	293	619	326	293	
			359. Auctioneers, Auditors, Actuaries, Notaries public, Appraisers, House-Agents, &c. ...	1	...	1	...	...	...	1	...	1	
		(b) Contractors and farmers.	360. Farmers of Tolls, ferries ...	12	12	...	39	16	23	51	28	23	
			363. Contractors, otherwise unspecified	3	3	...	9	3	6	12	6	6	
			364. Contractors for labour, Emigration Agents, &c.	1	1	...	4	...	4	5	1	4	
	XIX.—Transport and Storage.	59. Road ... (a) Cart, Carriage and Tramway owners and drivers.	375. Cart owners and drivers, carting Agents, &c.	3	3	...	...	...	...	3	3	...	
			378. Palki, &c., owners, bearers, &c....	186	186	...	544	208	336	730	394	336	
		(b) Carriers by pack animals.	380. Pack camel, elephant, mule, &c., owners and drivers ...	977	977	...	2,691	1,055	1,636	3,668	2,032	1,636	
			Carried over Class E ...	3,618	3,587	31	10,171	4,009	6,162	13,789	7,596	6,193	

CENSUS 1891.

KASHMIR STATE.

TABLE XVII.—PART B.—*Occupations.*—(*Kashmir Province.*)—(Continued).

Class.	Order.	Sub-order and Group.	Occupation.	Workers. Total.	Workers. Males.	Workers. Females.	Dependents. Total.	Dependents. Males.	Dependents. Females.	Total. Total.	Total. Males.	Total. Females.	Remarks.
			Brought forward Class E ...	3,618	3,587	31	10,171	4,009	6,162	13,789	7,596	6,193	
CLASS E.—(*Concld*).	XIX.—*Concld.* ...	60. Water ... (b) Working Staff of vessels.	385. Boat and barge men ...	2,592	2,288	304	7,097	2,882	4,215	9,689	5,170	4,519	
		61. Messages ... (a) Post, &c. ...	390. Postal Directors, Postmasters and Clerks	1	1	...	8	2	6	9	3	6	
			392. Messengers, (unspecified) ...	3	3	...	18	10	8	21	13	8	
		62. Storage and weighing ...	398. Porters (general)	8	8	...	35	15	20	43	23	20	
			399. Weighmen and measurers ...	171	171	...	532	196	336	703	367	336	
			400. Watchmen (not village) ...	455	451	4	1,745	694	1,051	2,200	1,145	1,055	
			TOTAL CLASS E ...	6,848	6,509	339	19,606	7,808	11,798	26,454	14,317	12,137	
CLASS F.—Professions.	XX.—Learned and Artistic Professions.	63. Religion ... (a) Priests, Ministers, &c.	401. Priests, ministers, preachers, missionaries, &c.	2,728	2,623	105	7,389	2,794	4,595	10,117	5,417	4,700	
			402. Cathechists, readers, Zanana Mission service, &c. ...	76	72	4	199	73	126	275	145	130	
		(b) Subsidiary religious services.	404. Religious mendicants, inmates of monasteries, convents, &c. ...	24	24	...	27	13	14	51	37	14	
			405. Church, Temple, Masjid, Pagoda, ghat, burial or burning ground service, pilgrim conductors and undertakers	1,177	1,172	5	4,092	1,679	2,413	5,269	2,851	2,418	
			Carried over Class F ...	4,005	3,891	114	11,707	4,559	7,148	15,712	8,450	7,262	

CENSUS 1891.

KASHMIR STATE.

TABLE XVII.—PART B.—*Occupation.*—(*Kashmir Province.*)—(Continued.)

Class.	Order.	Sub-order and Group.	Occupation.	Workers. Total.	Workers. Males.	Workers. Females.	Dependents. Total.	Dependents. Males.	Dependents. Females.	Total. Total.	Total. Males.	Total. Females.	Remarks.
			Brought forward Class F ...	4,005	3,891	114	11,707	4,559	7,148	15,712	8,450	7,262	
CLASS F.—*Concld.*	XX.—*Concld.* ...	64. Education	407. Principals, Professors and Teachers in Colleges, &c., Schools, &c.	677	677	...	2,218	854	1,364	2,895	1,531	1,364	
		65 Literature	409. Authors, Editors, Journalists, ballad-makers	135	135	...	450	153	297	585	288	297	
			412. Public Scribes and Copyists ...	49	49	...	99	33	66	148	82	66	
		66. Law	414. Barristers, Advocates and Pleaders	13	13	...	43	19	24	56	32	24	
			418. Stamp-vendors	25	25	...	105	44	61	130	69	61	
		67. Medicine ... (a) Practitioners ...	421. Practitioner by Diploma ...	1	1	...	2	...	2	3	1	2	
			422. Practitioners without Diploma (Baid, Hakim Kobiraj, &c.	300	297	3	1,107	443	664	1,407	740	667	
			426. Midwifery	74	52	22	24	16	8	98	68	30	
		68. Engineering & Surveying (a) Engineers, Architects and Surveyors.	429. Administrative and Inspecting Staff	12	12	...	6	1	5	18	13	5	
		71. Music, Acting, Dancing ...	444. Bandmasters and players (not Military)	27	23	4	68	30	38	95	53	42	
			446. Actors, Singers and Dancers and their accompanists	18	17	1	67	32	35	85	49	36	
	XXI.—Sport and Amusements.	72. Sport	448. Shikaris, Falconers, Birdcatchers,	46	46	...	169	70	99	215	116	99	
		73. Exhibition & Games. (b) Conjuring, fortune telling and other exhibitions.	453. Buffoons	299	299	...	1,037	408	629	1,336	707	629	
		(c) Acrobatics and Athletics.	457. Tumblers, Acrobats, Wrestlers Professional cricketers, &c. ...	1	1	...	8	4	4	9	5	4	
			TOTAL CLASS F ...	5,682	5,538	144	17,110	6,666	10,444	22,792	12,204	10,588	

CENSUS 1891.

KASHMIR STATE.

Table XVII.—Part B.—*Occupations.*—(*Kashmir Province.*)—(Continued.)

Class.	Order.	Sub-order and Group.		Occupation.	Workers.			Dependents.			Total.			Remarks.
					Total.	Males.	Females.	Total.	Males.	Females.	Total.	Males.	Females.	
Class G.—Indefinite and Independent.	XXIII.—Indefinite	74. Unskilled, labour.	(a) Special branches..	461. Well sinkers	53	53	...	165	60	105	218	113	105	
			(b) General ...	467. General labour	4,641	4,306	335	9,941	3,746	6,195	14,582	8,052	6,530	
		75. Undefined, &c.		468. Undefined and disreputable means of livelihood	4,175	2,154	2,021	92	40	52	4,267	2,194	2,073	
	XXIV.—Independent of work.	76. Property & alms.	(a) Property and allowances.	469. House-rent, shares, and other property not being land ...	1,117	1,117	...	3,490	1,367	2,123	4,607	2,484	2,123	
			(b) Charity and endowment.	471. Educational or other endowments scholarship, &c. ...	185	177	8	479	194	285	664	371	293	
				472. Mendicancy (not being affiliated to a religious order) ...	7,431	6,889	542	17,242	6,677	10,565	24,673	13,566	11,107	
		77. Supported at the public charge.	(a) Pension ...	473. Pension, Civil Services ...	14	13	1	35	9	26	49	22	27	
				474. Pension, Military Services ...	2	2	...	...	...	...	2	2	...	
			(b) Prisoners ...	476. Prisoners, under trial ...	5	5	...	...	...	...	5	5	...	
				477 Prisoners, for debt	1	1	...	...	...	...	1	1	...	
				478 Prisoners, convicted or in Reformatories, &c.	122	116	6	...	...	...	122	116	6	
				Total Class G ...	17,746	14,833	2,913	31,444	12,093	19,351	49,190	26,926	22,264	

CENSUS 1891

KASHMIR STATE.

TABLE XVII.—PART B.—*Occupations.*—(*Kashmir Province.*)—(Concluded.)

Class.	Workers.			Dependents.			Total.			Remarks.
	Total.	Males.	Females.	Total.	Males.	Females.	Total.	Males.	Females.	
ABSTRACT.										
Total Class A	8,406	8,335	71	20,428	8,131	12,297	28,834	16,466	12,368	
Do. B	118,492	115,524	2,968	463,474	197,743	265,731	581,966	813,267	268,699	
Do. C	12,519	11,914	605	30,292	12,024	18,268	42,811	23,938	18,873	
Do. D	66,249	46,308	19,941	130,745	48,919	81,826	196,994	95,227	101,767	
Do. E	6,848	6,509	339	19,606	7,808	11,798	26,454	14,317	12,137	
Do. F	5,682	5,538	144	17,110	6,666	10,444	22,792	12,204	10,588	
Do. G	17,746	14,833	2,913	31,444	12,093	19,351	49,190	26,926	22,264	
GRAND TOTAL	235,942	208,961	26,981	713,099	293,384	419,715	949,041	502,345	446,696	

JAMMU:
Dated 9th February 1892.

BHAG RAM,
Census Superintendent, Kashmir State.

CENSUS 1891.

KASHMIR STATE.

Table XVII.—Part B.—*Occupations.*—(*Ladakh.*)

Class.	Order.	Sub-order and Group.	Occupation.	Workers. Total.	Workers. Males.	Workers. Females.	Dependents. Total.	Dependents. Males.	Dependents. Females.	Total. Total.	Total. Males.	Total. Females.	Remarks.
Class A.	I.—Administration	1. Service of the State	3. Office Superintendents and Clerical Establishments. Police and Excise Inspectors, Sub-Registrars, &c.	78	78	...	121	34	87	199	112	87	
	II.—Defence ...	4. Army	13. Non-Commissioned Officers and Privates	163	163	...	62	20	42	225	183	42	
	III.—Foreign and Feudatory State Service.	6. Administrative Service ...	20. Clerical Establishment and 21. Menials, &c. ...	1	1	...	10	3	7	11	4	7	
			Total Class A ...	242	242	...	193	57	136	435	299	136	
Class B.	IV.—Live Stock ...	8. Stock breeding and dealing ... (a) Horses and horned cattle.	25. Cattle breeders and dealers and Commissariat Farm Establishment	347	337	10	1,089	439	650	1,436	776	660	
		(c) Small stock ...	31. Sheep and Goat breeders and dealers	6	5	1	17	2	15	23	7	16	
	V.—Agriculture ...	10. Interest in Land	37. Land occupants, not cultivating	4,783	4,202	581	18,397	7,105	11,292	23,180	11,307	11,873	
			38. Land occupants, cultivating ...	6	6	...	31	11	20	37	17	20	
			39. Lessees of Villages, &c. ...	1	1	...	4	...	4	5	1	4	
		12. Growers of special products and trees.	52. Gardners, seedsmen, &c. ...	1	1	...	1	1	...	2	2	...	
			Total Class B ...	5,144	4,552	592	19,539	7,558	11,981	24,683	12,110	12,573	
Class C.	VI.—Personal and household services.	14. Personal and domestic services ...	59. Barbers	5	5	...	18	8	10	23	13	10	
			63. Washermen (*sometimes also dyers*)	1	1	...	2	...	2	3	1	2	
			66. Indoor servants	92	70	22	166	80	86	258	150	108	
			Total Class C ...	98	76	22	186	88	98	284	164	120	

CENSUS 1891.

KASHMIR STATE.

TABLE XVII.—PART B.—*Occupations.*—(*Ladakh.*)—(Continued.)

Class.	Order.	Sub-order and Group.	Occupation.	Workers. Total.	Workers. Males.	Workers. Females.	Dependents. Total.	Dependents. Males.	Dependents. Females.	Total. Total.	Total. Males.	Total. Females.	Remarks.
Class D.	Preparation and supply of material substances.	VII.—Food and drink. 17. Animal Food ...	79. Butchers	4	4	...	10	4	6	14	8	6	
		18. Vegetable Food	86. Flour-mill service and management	1	1	...	3	1	2	4	2	2	
			87. Bakers	4	3	1	3	...	3	7	3	4	
	VIII.—Light, firing, and forage.	21. Fuel and Forage	125. Firewood and grass gatherers and sellers	2	1	1	2	1	1	4	2	2	
	IX.—Buildings ...	23. Artificers in Buildings ...	136. Building contractors ...	1	1	...	3	3	...	4	4	...	
	XI.—Supplementary requirements.	31. Toys, curiosities, &c.	178. Hukka-stem makers and sellers	1	1	...	1	...	1	2	1	1	
	XII.—Textile Fabrics and dress.	38. Wool and Fur	220. Blanket weavers and sellers (*often also shepherds*) ...	8	8	...	14	1	13	22	9	13	
		42. Dress	247. Tailors and darners	6	6	...	17	8	9	23	14	9	
	XIII.—Metals and precious stones.	43. Gold, silver, and precious stones ...	260. Gold and silver workers ...	23	15	8	32	13	19	55	28	27	
		46. Iron and steel	290. Blacksmiths	21	21	...	44	16	28	65	37	28	
	XV.—Wood cane and leaves, &c.	49. Timber and wood	304. Carpenters	12	12	...	11	3	8	23	15	8	
	XVII.—Leather, horns, bones and grease.	53. Leather, &c.	339 Shoe, sandals, boot-makers and sellers	2	2	...	4	3	1	6	5	1	
			TOTAL CLASS D ...	85	75	10	144	53	91	229	128	101	
Class E.	XVIII.—Commerce	56. Dealing unspecified	356. Shopkeepers, otherwise unspecified	50	50	...	41	28	13	91	78	13	
			TOTAL CLASS E ...	50	50	...	41	28	13	91	78	13	

CENSUS 1891.

KASHMIR STATE.

TABLE XVII.—PART B.—*Occupations*.—(*Ladakh*.)—(Continued.)

Class.	Order.	Sub-order and Group.	Occupation.	Workers. Total.	Workers. Males.	Workers. Females.	Dependents. Total.	Dependents. Males.	Dependents. Females.	Total. Total.	Total. Males.	Total. Females.	Remarks.
Class F.	XX—Learned and artistic Professions.	63. Religion ... (a) Priests, Ministers, &c.	401. Priests, ministers, preachers, missionaries, &c.	5	5	...	3	...	3	8	5	3	
		63. Religion ... (b) Subsidiary religious services.	405. Church, Temple, Masjid, Pagoda, ghat, burial or burning-ground service, pilgrim conductors and undertakers	561	514	47	714	483	231	1,275	997	278	
		67. Medicine ... (a) Practitioners	421. Practitioner by Diploma ...	1	1	...	1	...	1	2	1	1	
		67. Medicine ... (a) Practitioners	422. Practitioners without Diploma (Baid, Hakim Kobiraj, &c. ...	6	6	...	8	1	7	14	7	7	
		69. Other Sciences (b) Minor Sciences	437. Astrologers, Genealogists and Horoscopecasters	1	1	...	...	...	...	1	1	...	
		71. Music, Acting, Dancing ...	444. Bandmasters and players (not Military	3	2	1	...	...	...	3	2	1	
	XXI.—Sport and amusements.	72. Sport	448. Shikaris, Falconers, Birdcatchers	1	1	...	7	3	4	8	4	4	
			TOTAL CLASS F ...	578	530	48	733	487	246	1,311	1,017	294	
Class G.—Indefinite & Independent.	XXIII.—Indefinite	74. Unskilled, labour (b) General ...	467. General labour	308	167	141	441	120	321	749	287	462	
		75. Undefined, &c.	468. Undefined and disreputable means of livelihood ...	8	7	1	...	...	...	8	7	1	
	XXIV.—Independent of work.	76. Property and alms. (b) Charity and endowment.	471. Educational or other endowments scholarship, &c.	17	16	1	9	7	2	26	23	3	
			472. Mendicancy (not being affiliated to a religious order) ...	225	140	85	233	97	136	458	237	221	
			TOTAL CLASS G ...	558	330	228	683	224	459	1,241	554	687	

CENSUS 1891.

KASHMIR STATE.

TABLE XVII.—PART B.—*Occupations.*—(*Ladakh.*)—(Concluded.)

Class.	Workers.			Dependents.			Total.			Remarks.
	Total.	Males.	Females.	Total.	Males.	Females.	Total	Males.	Females.	
ABSTRACT.										
Total Class A	242	242	...	193	57	136	435	299	136	
Do. B	5,144	4,552	592	19,539	7,558	11,981	24,683	12,110	12,573	
Do. C	98	76	22	186	88	98	284	164	120	
Do. D	85	75	10	144	53	91	229	128	101	
Do. E	50	50	...	41	28	13	91	78	13	
Do. F	578	530	48	733	487	246	1,311	1,017	294	
Do. G	558	330	228	683	224	459	1,241	554	687	
GRAND TOTAL	6,755	5,855	900	21,519	8,495	13,024	28,274	14,350	13,924	

JAMMU:
Dated 9th February 1892.

BHAG RAM,
Census Superintendent, Kashmir State.

CENSUS 1891.

KASHMIR STATE.

Table XVII.—Part B.—*Occupations.*—(*Skardu.*)

Class.	Order.	Sub-order and Group.	Occupation.	Workers. Total.	Workers. Males.	Workers. Females.	Dependents. Total.	Dependents. Males.	Dependents. Females.	Total. Total.	Total. Males.	Total. Females.	Remarks.
Class A.	I.—Administration	1. Service of the State	3. Office Superintendents and Clerical Establishments. Police and Excise Inspectors, Sub-Registrars, &c. ...	117	117	...	247	114	133	364	231	133	
		3. Village Service	9. Accountants	1	1	...	1	1	...	2	2	...	
	II.—Defence ...	4. Army	13. Non-Commissioned Officers and Privates	220	220	...	57	12	45	277	232	45	
			Total Class A ...	338	338	...	305	127	178	643	465	178	
Class B.	IV.—Live stock ...	8. Stock breeding and dealing ... (a) Horses and horned cattle.	25. Cattle breeders and dealers and Commissariat Farm Establishment	44	44	...	194	91	103	238	135	103	
		(c) Small stock...	31. Sheep and Goat breeders and dealers	12	12	...	23	4	19	35	16	19	
	V.—Agriculture ...	10. Interest in Land	37. Land occupants, not cultivating	19,058	18,779	279	84,464	33,770	50,694	103,522	52,549	50,973	
			38. Land occupants, cultivating ...	3	3	...	19	8	11	22	11	11	
			39. Lessees of Villages, &c. ...	3	3	...	49	15	34	52	18	34	
			41. Tenants and sharers, cultivating	357	353	4	1,517	603	914	1,874	956	918	
			Total Class B ...	19,477	19,194	283	86,266	34,491	51,775	105,743	53,685	52,058	
Class C.	VI.—Personal and household services,	14. Personal and domestic services ...	59. Barbers	13	13	...	41	15	26	54	28	26	
			63. Washermen (*Sometimes also dyers*)	6	6	...	26	14	12	32	20	12	
			66. Indoor servants	259	152	107	371	162	209	630	314	316	
			Total Class C ...	278	171	107	438	191	247	716	362	354	

CENSUS 1891.

KASHMIR STATE.

TABLE XVII.—PART B.—*Occupations.*—(*Skardu*).—(Continued.)

Class.	Order.	Sub-order and Group.	Occupation.	Workers. Total.	Workers. Males.	Workers. Females.	Dependents. Total.	Dependents. Males.	Dependents. Females.	Total. Total.	Total. Males.	Total. Females.	Remarks.
Class D.	Preparation and supply of material substances.	VII. Food & drink. 17. Animal Food	79. Butchers	2	2	...	7	3	4	9	5	4	
		VII. Food & drink. 18. Vegetable Food.	86. Flour-mill service and management	12	12	...	37	20	17	49	32	17	
	VIII. Light, firing, and forage.	21. Fuel and Forage	125. Firewood and grass gatherers and sellers	3	3	...	8	...	8	11	3	8	
	XII. Textile Fabrics and dress.	38. Wool and Fur	218. Shawl weavers and sellers ...	57	57	...	234	101	133	291	158	133	
			220. Blanket weavers and sellers (*often also shepherds*) ...	113	113	...	272	96	176	385	209	176	
		42. Dress	247. Tailors and darners ...	2	2	...	10	9	1	12	11	1	
	XIII.—Metals and precious stones.	43. Gold, silver, and precious stones,	260. Gold and silver workers ...	12	12	...	66	26	40	78	38	40	
			261. Gold beaters	2	2	...	19	10	9	21	12	9	
			262. Goldsmiths' dust washers ...	1	1	...	11	4	7	12	5	7	
		44. Brass, copper and bell metal ...	279. Copper workers and sellers ...	3	3	...	21	8	13	24	11	13	
		46. Iron and steel	290. Blacksmiths	30	30	...	135	54	81	165	84	81	
	XIV.—Glass, pottery and stone ware.	48. Earthen and stone ware ...	298. Potters and pot and pipe-bowl makers and sellers	1	1	...	5	1	4	6	2	4	
	XV.—Wood cane and leaves, &c.	49. Timber and wood	304. Carpenters	16	16	...	42	17	25	58	33	25	
	XVII.—Leather, horns, bones & grease.	53, Leather, &c.	339. Shoe, sandals, boot makers and sellers	7	7	...	33	14	19	40	21	19	
			TOTAL CLASS D ...	261	261	...	900	363	537	1,161	624	537	

CENSUS 1891.

KASHMIR STATE.

TABLE XVII.—PART B.—*Occupations.*—(*Skardu.*)—(Continued.)

Class.	Order.	Sub-order and Group.	Occupation.	Workers. Total.	Workers. Males.	Workers. Females.	Dependents. Total.	Dependents. Males.	Dependents. Females.	Total. Total.	Total. Males.	Total. Females.	Remarks.
Class E.—Commerce, transport storage.	XVIII.—Commerce	56. Dealing unspecified ...	356. Shopkeepers, otherwise unspecified	12	12	...	48	18	30	60	30	30	
			357. Pedlars, Hawkers, &c. ...	3	3	...	4	...	4	7	3	4	
			TOTAL CLASS E ...	15	15	...	52	18	34	67	33	34	
Class F.—Professions.	XX.—Learned and artistic Professions.	64. Education	407. Principals, Professors and Teachers in Colleges, &c., Schools, &c.	9	9	...	28	12	16	37	21	16	
		67. Medicine ... (a) Practitioners ...	422. Practitioners without Diploma (Baid, Hakim Kobiraj, &c. ...	1	1	...	...	...	...	1	1	...	
		71. Music, Acting, Dancing ...	444. Bandmasters and players (not Military)	6	6	...	22	7	15	28	13	15	
			446. Actors, Singers and Dancers and their accompanists	1	...	1	...	...	...	1	...	1	
	XXI.—Sport and amusements.	72. Sport	448. Shikaris, Falconers, Birdcatchers	20	20	...	87	33	54	107	53	54	
			TOTAL CLASS F ...	37	36	1	137	52	85	174	88	86	
Class G.—Indefinite and Independent.	XXIII.—Indefinite	74. Unskilled labour. (b) General ...	467. General labor ...	130	53	77	183	40	143	313	93	220	
		75. Undefined, &c.	468. Undefined and disreputable means of livelihood	149	64	85	...	...	...	149	64	85	
	XXIV.—Independent of work.	76. Property & alms. (b) Charity and endowment.	471. Educational or other endowments scholarship, &c. ...	48	48	...	221	111	110	269	159	110	
			472. Mendicancy (not being affiliated to a religious order) ...	444	286	158	646	239	407	1,090	525	565	
			TOTAL CLASS G ...	771	451	320	1,050	390	660	1,821	841	980	

CENSUS 1891.

KASHMIR STATE.

TABLE XVII.—PART B.—*Occupations*.—(*Skardu*.)—(Concluded.)

Class.	Workers.			Dependents.			Total.			Remarks.
	Total.	Males.	Females.	Total.	Males.	Females.	Total.	Males.	Females.	
ABSTRACT.										
Total Class A	338	338	...	305	127	178	643	465	178	
Do. B	19,477	19,194	283	86,266	34,491	51,775	105,743	53,685	520,58	
Do. C	278	171	107	438	191	247	716	362	354	
Do. D	261	261	...	900	363	537	1,161	624	537	
Do. E	15	15	...	52	18	34	67	33	34	
Do. F	37	36	1	137	52	85	174	88	86	
Do. G	771	451	320	1,050	390	660	1,821	841	980	
GRAND TOTAL	21,177	20,466	711	89,148	35,632	53,516	110,325	56,098	54,227	

JAMMU:
Dated 9th February 1892.

BHAG RAM,
Census Superintendent, Kashmir State.

CENSUS 1891.

KASHMIR STATE.

TABLE XVII.—PART B.—*Occupations.*—(*Gilgit.*)

Class.	Order.	Sub-order and Group.	Occupation.	Workers. Total.	Workers. Males.	Workers. Females.	Dependents. Total.	Dependents. Males.	Dependents. Females.	Total. Total.	Total. Males.	Total. Females.	Remarks.
Class A.	I.—Administration	3. Village Service	11. Watchmen and other Menials ...	1	1	...	...	...	...	1	1	...	
			Total Class A ...	1	1	...	...	...	...	1	1	...	
Class B.	V.—Agriculture ...	10. Interest in Land	37. Land occupants, not cultivating.	1	1	...	...	...	...	1	1	...	
			Total Class B ...	1	1	...	...	...	...	1	1	...	
Class C.	VI.—Personal and household services.	14. Personal and domestic services ...	66. Indoor servants ...	11	11	...	...	...	...	11	11	...	
			Total Class C ...	11	11	...	...	...	...	11	11	...	
Class D.	IX.—Buildings ...	23. Artificers in Buildings ...	138. Masons ...	6	6	...	3	...	3	9	6	3	
	XV.—Wood cane and leaves, &c.	49. Timber and wood	304. Carpenters ...	6	6	...	...	...	...	6	6	...	
			Total Class D ...	12	12	...	3	...	3	15	12	3	
Class F.—Profession.	XX.—Learned and artistic Professions.	68. Engineering & Surveying. (a) Engineers, Architects and Surveyors.	429. Administrative and Inspecting Staff ...	1	1	...	1	...	1	2	1	1	
		(b) Subsidiary Staff.	433. Clerks, &c., in offices of the above	10	10	...	...	...	...	10	10	...	
			Total Class F ...	11	11	...	1	...	1	12	11	1	
Class G.—Indefinite & Independent.	XXIII.—Indefinite	74. Unskilled, labour. (b) General ...	467. General labour ...	114	114	...	...	...	...	114	114	...	
		75. Undefined, &c.	468. Undefined and disreputable means of livelihood ...	16,615	10,045	6,570	...	...	...	16,615	10,045	6,570	
			Total Class G ...	16,729	10,159	6,570	...	...	...	16,729	10,159	6,570	

CENSUS 1891.

KASHMIR STATE.

TABLE XVII.—PART B.—*Occupations.*—(*Gilgit.*)—(Concluded.)

Class.	Workers.			Dependents.			Total.			Remarks.
	Total.	Males.	Females.	Total.	Males.	Females.	Total.	Males.	Females.	
ABSTRACT.										
Total Class A	1	1	...	...	...	...	1	1	...	
Do. B	1	1	...	...	...	...	1	1	...	
Do. C	11	11	...	...	...	...	11	11	...	
Do. D	12	12	...	3	...	3	15	12	3	
Do. E	...	...	...	...	...	...	...	...	...	
Do. F	11	11	...	1	...	1	12	11	1	
Do. G	16,729	10,159	6,570	...	...	...	16,729	10,169	6,570	
GRAND TOTAL	16,765	10,195	6,570	4	...	4	16,769	10,195	6,574	

JAMMU:
Dated 9th February 1892.

BHAG RAM,
Census Superintendent, Kashmir State.

CENSUS 1891.

KASHMIR STATE.

TABLE XVII.—PART B.—*Occupations.*—(*Jammu Town.*)

Class.	Order.	Sub-order and Group.	Occupation.	Workers.			Dependents.			Total.			Remarks.
				Total.	Males.	Females.	Total.	Males.	Females.	Total.	Males.	Females.	
Class A.	I.—Administration	1. Service of the State ...	1. Maharaja and Rajas and their Families	3	3	...	77	1	76	80	4	76	
			2. Officers	160	160	...	224	101	123	384	261	123	
			3. Office Superintendents and Clerical Establishments. Police and Excise Inspectors, Sub-Registrars, &c.	3,129	3,112	17	3,621	1,287	2,334	6,750	4,399	2,351	
			4. Messengers, Constables, Bailiffs, Warders, Menials, &c. ...	670	670	...	246	74	172	916	744	172	
		2. Service of Local and Municipal Bodies.	5. Inspecting and Supervising Officials	1	1	...	4	1	3	5	2	3	
	II.—Defence ...	4. Army	12. Officers	3	3	...	8	3	5	11	6	5	
			13. Non-Commissioned Officers and Privates	3,313	3,313	...	839	254	585	4,152	3,567	585	
	III.—Foreign and Feudatory State Service.	6. Administrative Service ...	20. Clerical Establishments and 21. Menials, &c.	1	1	...	...	...	...	1	1	...	
			TOTAL CLASS A ...	7,280	7,263	17	5,019	1,721	3,298	12,299	8,984	3,315	

CENSUS 1891

KASHMIR STATE.

TABLE XVII.—PART B.—*Occupations.*—(*Jammu Town.*)—(Continued.)

Class.	Order.	Sub-order and Group.	Occupation.	Workers.			Dependents.			Total.			Remarks.
				Total.	Males.	Females.	Total.	Males.	Females.	Total.	Males.	Females.	
Class B.	IV.—Live stock ...	8. Stock breeding and dealing. (c.) Small stock...	31. Sheep and Goat breeders and dealers	7	7	...	16	2	14	23	9	14	
		9. Subsidiary services to stock. (a.) Training and doctoring live stock...	34. Farriers and Gelders ...	1	1	...	...	...	...	1	1	...	
			35. Horse and Elephant breakers and trainers, &c.	4	4	...	12	3	9	16	7	9	
	V.—Agriculture ...	10. Interest in Land	38. Land occupants, cultivating ...	198	194	4	95	74	21	293	268	25	
			39. Lessees of Villages, &c. ...	19	18	1	15	10	5	34	28	6	
			41. Tenants and sharers, cultivating	24	13	11	22	7	15	46	20	26	
		12. Growers of special products and trees	54. Forest Officers	1	1	...	4	1	3	5	2	3	
			55. Forest Rangers, Guards, Peons	10	10	...	14	5	9	24	15	9	
			TOTAL CLASS B ...	264	248	16	178	102	76	442	350	92	

CENSUS 1891.

KASHMIR STATE.

TABLE XVII.—PART B.—*Occupations.*—(*Jammu Town.*)—(Continued.)

Class.	Order.	Sub-order and Group.	Occupation.	Workers. Total.	Workers. Males.	Workers. Females.	Dependents. Total.	Dependents. Males.	Dependents. Females.	Total. Total.	Total. Males.	Total. Females.	Remarks.
CLASS C.	VI.—Personal and household services.	14. Personal and domestic services ...	59. Barbers	70	70	...	145	48	97	215	118	97	
			63. Washermen (*sometimes also dyers*)	85	76	9	149	51	98	234	127	107	
			64. Water-carriers	97	79	18	142	41	101	239	120	119	
			65. Cooks	15	15	...	21	8	13	36	23	13	
			66. Indoor servants	1,524	1,442	82	1,127	375	752	2,651	1,817	834	
			68. Door-keepers, &c.	15	15	...	30	12	18	45	27	18	
			TOTAL CLASS C ...	1,806	1,697	109	1,614	53[illegible]	1,079	3,420	2,232	1,188	
CLASS D.	Preparation and supply of material substances.	VII. Food & drink — 17. Animal Food	77. Ghee preparers and sellers ...	34	34	...	12	[illegible]	8	46	38	8	
			79. Butchers	81	79	2	160	5[illegible]	108	241	131	110	
			81. Fishermen and fish curers (*many are also boatmen and palki bearers*)	2	2	...	5	2	3	7	4	3	
			Carried over Class D ...	117	115	2	177	[illegible]	119	294	173	121	

CENSUS 1891.

KASHMIR STATE.

TABLE XVII.—PART B.—*Occupations.*—(*Jammu Town.*)—(Continued.)

Class.	Order.	Sub-Order and Group.	Occupation.	Workers. Total.	Workers. Males.	Workers. Females.	Dependents. Total.	Dependents. Males.	Dependents. Females.	Total. Total.	Total. Males.	Total. Females.	Remarks.
			Brought forward Class D ...	117	115	2	177	58	119	294	173	121	
Class D.—(*Continued.*)	Preparation and supply of material substances.—(*Contd*).	VII. Food & drink (*Contd*). 18. Vegetable Food.	84. Grain parchers	6	6	...	6	2	4	12	8	4	
			86. Flour-mill service and management	67	59	8	124	50	74	191	109	82	
			87. Bakers	116	104	12	164	80	84	280	184	96	
			89. Vegetable sellers ...	26	23	3	63	20	43	89	43	46	
			90. Fruit sellers	14	12	2	15	6	9	29	18	11	
			92. Confectioners and sweetmeat makers and sellers, and cooks who are also sometimes fishermen and water-carriers ...	141	141	...	215	82	133	356	223	133	
		19. Drink condiments and narcotics.	97. Country spirits distillers & sellers	14	12	2	4	3	1	18	15	3	
			109. Grocers and general condiment	61	57	4	108	31	77	169	88	81	
			112. Tobacco and snuff manufacturers and sellers	24	24	...	38	12	26	62	36	26	
			114. Opium, &c., manufacturers and sellers	1	1	...	...	...	...	1	1	...	
			115. Bhang, ganja, &c, preparers and sellers	3	3	...	4	2	2	7	5	2	
			Carried over Class D ...	590	557	33	918	346	572	1,508	903	605	

CENSUS 1891.

KASHMIR STATE.

TABLE XVII.—PART B.—*Occupations.*—(*Jammu Town.*)—(Continued.)

Class.	Order.	Sub-order and Group.	Occupation.	Workers. Total.	Workers. Males.	Workers. Females.	Dependents. Total.	Dependents. Males.	Dependents. Females.	Total. Total.	Total. Males.	Total. Females.	Remarks.
			Brought forward Class D ...	590	557	33	918	346	572	1,508	903	605	
Class D.—(*Continued.*)	VIII. Light, firing, and forage.	20. Lighting	116. Oil-pressers and sellers ...	2	1	1	1	...	1	3	1	2	
		21. Fuel and Forage	125. Firewood and grass gatherers and sellers	35	26	9	55	20	35	90	46	44	
	IX. Buildings ...	22. Building materials	132. Brick and tile burners and sellers	4	4	...	11	2	9	15	6	9	
		23. Artificers in Buildings ...	137. Stone and marble workers ...	31	31	...	52	16	36	83	47	36	
			138. Masons	156	156	...	286	109	177	442	265	177	
	XI. Supplementary requirements.	28. Books and Prints, &c. ...	157. Press Proprietors, Lithographers and Printers	27	27	...	30	5	25	57	32	25	
			158. Book-binders	12	12	...	21	7	14	33	19	14	
		29. Watches, Clocks and scientific instruments	163. Watch and Clock makers and sellers	5	5	...	6	4	2	11	9	2	
		30. Carving, engraving, &c. ...	172. Turners and lacquerers ...	9	9	...	16	7	9	25	16	9	
			173. Die-sinkers and seal, &c., engravers	2	2	...	...	...	...	2	2	...	
			Carried over Class D ...	873	830	43	1,396	516	880	2,269	1,346	923	

CENSUS 1891.

KASHMIR STATE.

TABLE XVII.—PART B.—*Occupations.*—(*Jammu Town.*)—(Continued.)

Class.	Order.	Sub-order and Group.	Occupation.	Workers. Total.	Workers. Males.	Workers. Females.	Dependents. Total.	Dependents. Males.	Dependents. Females	Total. Total.	Total. Males.	Total. Females.	Remarks.
			Brought forward Class D ...	873	830	43	1,396	516	880	2,269	1,346	923	
CLASS D:—(*Continued.*)	XI. Supplementary requirements.—(*Concld.*)	31. Toys, curiosities &c. ...	178. Hukka stem makers and sellers ...	23	23	...	30	13	17	53	36	17	
			179. Papier-mache workers and sellers	17	17	...	35	14	21	52	31	21	
		32. Music and Musical Instruments ...	183. Music and Musical Instrument dealers	4	4	...	10	4	6	14	8	6	
		36. Tools and Machinery ...	205. Knife and tool grinders ...	11	11	...	14	4	10	25	15	10	
		37. Arms and ammunition ...	210. Ammunition and Cap dealers ...	1	1	...	...	...	...	1	1	...	
			212. Fire-work makers and sellers ...	13	13	...	36	19	17	49	32	17	
	XII.—Textile Fabrics and dress ...	38. Wool and Fur ...	217. Carpet weavers and sellers ...	6	6	...	2	2	...	8	8	...	
			218. Shawl weavers and sellers ...	11	8	3	4	...	4	15	8	7	
			219. Felt and pashm workers and sellers	2	2	...	9	4	5	11	6	5	
			221. Woollen cloth manufacturers and dealers	71	70	1	174	57	117	245	127	118	
			222. Woollen yarn spinners and sellers	61	21	40	86	34	52	147	55	92	
			Carried over Class D ...	1,093	1,006	87	1,796	667	1,129	2,889	1,673	1,216	

CENSUS 1891.

KASHMIR STATE.

TABLE XVII.—PART B.—*Occupations.*—(*Jammu Town.*)—(Continued.)

Class.	Order.	Sub-order and Group.	Occupation.	Workers. Total.	Workers. Males.	Workers. Females.	Dependents. Total.	Dependents. Males.	Dependents. Females.	Total. Total.	Total. Males.	Total. Females.	Remarks.
CLASS D.—(*Continued.*)			*Brought forward Class D* ...	1,093	1,006	87	1,796	667	1,129	2,889	1,673	1,216	
	XII.—*Concld.* ...	38 Concluded	224. Wool dyers	76	72	4	137	46	91	213	118	95	
		39. Silk	230. Braid and ribbon makers and sellers	88	76	12	123	45	78	211	121	90	
		40. Cotton	231. Cotton cleaners, pressers and ginners	12	11	1	8	3	5	20	14	6	
			234. Cotton weavers, Mill-owners and Managers	50	44	6	81	21	60	131	65	66	
			236. Calenderers, fullers and printers	2	2	...	3	...	3	5	2	3	
		42. Dress	247. Tailors and darners	215	194	21	429	172	257	641	366	278	
	XIII.—Metals and precious stones.	43. Gold, silver, and precious stones ...	260. Gold and silver workers ...	180	177	3	305	106	199	485	283	202	
			Carried over Class D ...	1,716	1,582	134	2,882	1,060	1,822	4,598	2,642	1,956	

CENSUS 1891.

KASHMIR STATE.

TABLE XVII.—PART B.—*Occupations.*—(*Jammu Town.*)—(Continued).

Class.	Order.	Sub-order and Group.	Occupation.	Workers. Total.	Workers. Males.	Workers. Females.	Dependents. Total.	Dependents. Males.	Dependents. Females.	Total. Total.	Total. Males.	Total. Females.	Remarks.
CLASS D.—(*Continued.*)			*Brought forward Class D* ...	1,716	1,582	134	2,882	1,060	1,822	4,598	2,642	1,956	
	XIII.—*Concld.*	44. Brass, copper and bell metal ...	277. Brass pot makers and sellers ...	17	17	...	64	25	39	81	42	39	
		45. Tin, zinc, mercury and lead ...	284. Tin workers and sellers ...	6	6	...	5	2	3	11	8	3	
		46. Iron and steel	290. Blacksmiths	53	53	...	88	29	59	141	82	59	
	XIV.—Glass, pottery and stone ware.	48. Earthen and stone ware ...	298. Potters and pot and pipe-bowl-makers and sellers. (*Some are brick and tile makers also*) ...	26	23	3	91	24	67	117	47	70	
	XV.—Wood cane and leaves, &c.	49. Timber and wood	302. Timber and bamboo agents and dealers	4	4	...	5	...	5	9	4	5	
			304. Carpenters	230	230	...	226	87	139	456	317	139	
		50. Canework, matting and leaves &c.	307. Basket weavers and winnowing pan makers and sellers ...	29	29	...	20	5	15	49	34	15	
			308. Mat makers and sellers ...	6	6	...	5	...	5	11	6	5	
			310. Leaf-plate makers and sellers. (*Are also often temple servants.*)	1	1	...	4	...	4	5	1	4	
			Carried over Class D ...	2,088	1,951	137	3,390	1,232	2,158	5,478	3,183	2,295	

CENSUS 1891.

KASHMIR STATE.

TABLE XVII.—PART B.—*Occupations.*—(*Jammu Town.*)—(Continued.)

Class.	Order.	Sub-order and Group.	Occupation.	Workers. Total.	Workers. Males.	Workers. Females.	Dependents. Total.	Dependents. Males.	Dependents. Females.	Total. Total.	Total. Males.	Total. Females.	Remarks.
			Brought forward Class D ...	2,088	1,951	137	3,390	1,232	2,158	5,478	3,183	2,295	
Class D.—(*Concluded.*)	XVI.—Drugs, gums, dyes, &c.	52. Drugs, dyes, pigments, &c. ...	330. Indigo workers and dealers (not planters)	1	1	...	...	...	...	1	1	...	
			332. Ink-makers and sellers ...	4	4	...	5	2	3	9	6	3	
			337. Perfume preparers and sellers ...	12	12	...	9	3	6	21	15	6	
	XVII.—Leather, horns, bones, and grease.	53. Leather, &c.	338. Tanners, curriers, and hide sellers (*many also shoe-makers*) ...	4	4	...	7	3	4	11	7	4	
			339. Shoe, sandals, boot-makers and sellers	173	168	5	361	115	246	534	283	251	
			340. Leather dyers	13	13	...	25	8	17	38	21	17	
			TOTAL CLASS D ...	2,295	2,153	142	3,797	1,363	2,434	6,092	3,516	2,576	
Class E.—Commerce, Transport, Storage.	XVIII.—Commerce,	54. Dealers in money and securities ...	346. Bankers and Bank Managers ...	188	181	7	238	87	151	426	268	158	
			350. Money changers and testers ...	44	44	...	125	55	70	169	99	70	
		55. General Merchandise ...	352. General Merchants	44	44	...	63	31	32	107	75	32	
			Carried over Class E ...	276	269	7	426	173	253	702	442	260	

CENSUS 1891.

KASHMIR STATE.

TABLE XVII.—PART B.—*Occupations.*—(*Jammu Town.*)—(Continued).

Class.	Order.	Sub-order and Group.	Occupation.	Workers. Total.	Workers. Males.	Workers. Females.	Dependents. Total.	Dependents. Males.	Dependents. Females.	Total. Total.	Total. Males.	Total. Females.	Remarks.
Class E.—Commerce, Transport, Storage.—(*Contd.*)			*Brought forward Class E* ...	276	269	7	426	173	253	702	442	260	
	XVIII.—Continued	56. Dealing unspecified	356. Shopkeepers, otherwise unspecified	1,134	1,111	23	1,637	578	1,059	2,771	1,689	1,082	
			357. Pedlars, Hawkers, &c. ...	23	23	...	123	27	96	146	50	96	
		57. Middlemen, &c. (a) Brokers, &c....	358. Brokers, Agents, Dubash ...	1	1	...	...	...	...	1	1	...	
		(b) Contractors and farmers.	360. Farmers of Tolls, ferries ...	52	52	...	62	25	37	114	77	37	
			363. Contractors, otherwise unspecified	119	119	...	226	77	149	345	196	149	
	XIX.—Transport and Storage.	58. Railway ... (b) Working Staff*	371. Station Masters and Assistants, Inspectors, Overseers, &c. ...	25	25	...	12	12	...	37	37	...	
		59. Road ... (a) Cart, Carriage and Tramway owners and drivers.	377. Drivers, stable-boys, &c., (*not private servants*)	10	10	...	12	8	4	22	18	4	
		(b) Carriers by pack animals.	380. Pack camel, elephant, mule, &c., owners and drivers ...	31	31	...	65	26	39	96	57	39	
			Carried over Class E ...	1,671	1,641	30	2,563	926	1,637	4,234	2,567	1,667	

* Excluding Police on Railway.

CENSUS 1891.

KASHMIR STATE.

TABLE XVII.—PART B.—*Occupations.*—(*Jammu Town.*)—(Continued.)

Class.	Order.	Sub-order and Group.	Occupation.	Workers. Total.	Workers. Males.	Workers. Females	Dependents. Total.	Dependents. Males.	Dependents. Females.	Total. Total.	Total. Males.	Total. Females.	Remarks.
			Brought forward Class E ...	1,671	1,641	30	2,563	926	1,637	4,234	2,567	1,667	
CLASS E.—(*Concld.*)	XIX.—*Concld.* ...	60. Water ... (b) Working Staff of vessels.	385. Boat and barge men ...	1	1	...	...	...	...	1	1	...	
		61. Messages ... (a) Post, &c. ...	390. Postal Directors, Postmasters and Clerks	47	47	...	101	36	65	148	83	65	
			TOTAL CLASS E ...	1,719	1,689	30	2,664	962	1,702	4,383	2,651	1,732	
CLASS F.—Professions.	XX.—Learned and Artistic Professions.	63. Religion ... (a) Priests, Ministers, &c.	401. Priests, ministers, preachers, missionaries, &c.	319	282	37	522	163	359	841	445	396	
		63. Religion ... (b) Subsidiary religious services.	405. Church, Temple, Masjid, Pagoda, ghat, burial or burning ground service, pilgrim conductors and undertakers	1	1	...	2	1	1	3	2	1	
		64. Education	406. Administrative and inspecting officials	1	1	...	2	1	1	3	2	1	
			Carried over Class F ...	321	284	37	526	165	361	847	449	398	

CENSUS 1891.

KASHMIR STATE.

TABLE XVII.—PART B.—*Occupations.*—(*Jammu Town.*)—(Continued.)

Class.	Order.	Sub-order and Group.	Occupation.	Workers. Total.	Workers. Males.	Workers. Females.	Dependents. Total.	Dependents. Males.	Dependents. Females.	Total. Total.	Total. Males.	Total. Females.	Remarks.
			Brought forward Class F ...	321	284	37	526	165	361	847	449	398	
Class F.—*Concld.*	XX.—*Concld.* ...	64. Education	407. Principals, Professors and Teachers in Colleges, &c., Schools, &c.	86	85	1	84	32	52	170	117	53	
		66. Law	414. Barristers, Advocates and Pleaders	21	21	...	22	8	14	43	29	14	
			418. Stamp-vendors	11	11	...	14	5	9	25	16	9	
			419. Petition-writers	8	8	...	22	5	17	30	13	17	
		67. Medicine ... (a) Practitioners ...	422. Practitioners without Diploma (Baid, Hakim Kobiraj, &c.	37	36	1	78	32	46	115	68	47	
		(b) Subsidiary Medical Service.	428. Compounders, Nurses and Hospital, Asylum and Dispensary service	24	23	1	29	14	15	53	37	16	
		68. Engineering & Surveying (b) Subsidiary Staff.	432. Draughtsmen and Operators in Survey Offices, Overseers, &c. ...	3	3	...	12	4	8	15	7	8	
			433. Clerks, &c., in offices of the above	3	3	...	5	2	3	8	5	3	
		69. Other Sciences. (b) Minor Sciences ...	437. Astrologers, Genealogists and Horoscopecasters ...	4	4	...	13	6	7	17	10	7	
		71. Music, Acting, Dancing ...	444. Bandmasters and players (not Military)	1	1	...	5	5	...	6	6	...	
			446. Actors, Singers and Dancers and their accompanists	29	28	1	33	4	29	62	32	30	
	XXI—Sport and Amusements.	73. Exhibition & Games. (c) Acrobatics and Athletics.	457. Tumblers, Acrobats, Wrestlers, Professional cricketers, &c. ...	3	3	...	...	...	...	3	3	...	
			TOTAL CLASS F ...	551	510	41	843	282	561	1,394	792	602	

CENSUS 1891.

KASHMIR STATE.

TABLE XVII.—PART B.—*Occupations*.—(*Jammu Town.*)—(Continued.)

Class.	Order.	Sub-order and Group.		Occupation.	Workers. Total.	Workers. Males.	Workers. Females.	Dependents. Total.	Dependents. Males.	Dependents. Females.	Total. Total.	Total. Males.	Total. Females.	Remarks.
Class G.—Indefinite and Independent.	XXIII.—Indefinite	74. Unskilled, labour.	(a) Special branches..	466. Rice-pounders and huskers ...	28	22	6	43	19	24	71	41	30	
			(b) General ...	467. General labour	2,240	1,766	474	2,139	715	1,424	4,379	2,481	1,898	
		75. Undefined, &c.		468. Undefined and disreputable means of livelihood	380	262	118	47	31	16	427	293	134	
	XXIV.—Independent of work.	76. Property & alms.	(a) Property and allowances.	469. House-rent, shares, and other property not being land ...	52	48	4	44	14	30	96	62	34	
			(b) Charity and endowment.	471. Educational or other endowments scholarship, &c. ...	413	413	...	246	95	151	659	508	151	
				472. Mendicancy (not being affiliated to a religious order) ...	473	401	72	258	101	157	731	502	229	
		77. Supported at the public charge.	(a) Pension ...	473. Pension, Civil Services ...	2	2	...	15	6	9	17	8	9	
			(b) Prisoners ...	476. Prisoners, under trial ...	21	20	1	...	...	...	21	20	1	
				478 Prisoners, convicted or in Reformatories, &c.	111	105	6	...	...	...	111	105	6	
				TOTAL CLASS G ...	3,720	3,039	681	2,792	981	1,811	6,512	4,020	2,492	

CENSUS 1891.

KASHMIR STATE.

TABLE XVII.—PART B.—*Occupations.*—(*Jammu Town.*)—(Concluded.)

Class.	Workers.			Dependents.			Total.			Remarks.
	Total.	Males.	Females.	Total.	Males.	Females.	Total	Males.	Females.	
ABSTRACT.										
Total Class A	7,280	7,263	17	5,019	1,721	3,298	12,299	8,984	3,315	
Do. B	264	248	16	178	102	76	442	350	92	
Do. C	1,806	1,697	109	1,614	535	1,079	3,420	2,232	1,188	
Do. D	2,295	2,156	139	3,797	1,363	2,434	6,092	3,516	2,576	
Do. E	1,719	1,689	30	2,664	962	1,702	4,383	2,651	1,732	
Do. F	551	510	41	843	282	561	1,394	792	602	
Do. G	3,720	3,039	681	2,792	981	1,811	6,512	4,020	2,492	
GRAND TOTAL	17,635	16,599	1,036	16,907	5,946	10,961	34,542	22,545	11,997	

JAMMU:
Dated 9th February 1892.

BHAG RAM,
Census Superintendent, Kashmir State.

CENSUS 1891.

KASHMIR STATE.

TABLE XVII.—PART B.—*Occupations.*—(*Srinagar Town.*)

Class.	Order.	Sub-order and Group.	Occupation.	Workers. Total.	Workers. Males.	Workers. Females.	Dependents. Total.	Dependents. Males.	Dependents. Females.	Total. Total.	Total. Males.	Total. Females.	Remarks.
CLASS A.	I.—Administration	1. Service of the State ...	2. Officers	7	7	...	7	3	4	14	10	4	
			3. Office Superintendents and Clerical Establishments. Police and Excise Inspectors, Sub-Registrars, &c.	1,936	1,912	24	5,751	2,193	3,558	7,687	4,105	3,582	
			4. Messengers, Constables, Bailiffs, Warders, Menials, &c. ...	268	267	1	549	197	352	817	464	353	
		3. Village Service	9. Accountants	42	42	...	172	73	99	214	115	99	
			11. Watchmen and other Menials ...	86	79	7	225	85	140	311	164	147	
	II.—Defence ...	4. Army	13. Non-Commissioned Officers and Privates	443	443	...	721	231	490	1,164	674	490	
	III.—Foreign and Feudatory State Service.	6. Administrative Service ...	20. Clerical Establishments and 21. Menials, &c.	82	69	13	163	50	113	245	119	126	
		7. Army and Marine	22. Officers	8	8	...	22	6	16	30	14	16	
			TOTAL CLASS A ...	2,872	2,827	45	7,610	2,838	4,772	10,482	5,665	4,817	

CENSUS 1891

KASHMIR STATE.

TABLE XVII.—PART B.—*Occupations.*—(*Srinagar Town.*)—(Continued.)

Class.	Order.	Sub-order and Group.	Occupation.	Workers. Total.	Workers. Males.	Workers. Females	Dependents. Total.	Dependents. Males.	Dependents. Females	Total. Total.	Total. Males.	Total. Females.	Remarks.
Class B.	IV.—Live stock ...	8. Stock breeding and dealing. (a.) Horses and horned cattle.	25. Cattle breeders and dealers and Commissariat Farm Establishment	195	192	3	769	261	508	964	453	511	
			26. Herdsmen	43	42	1	20	9	11	63	51	12	
		9. Subsidiary services to stock. (a.) Training and doctoring live stock...	34. Farriers and Gelders ...	26	26	...	60	17	43	86	43	43	
			35. Horse and Elephant breakers and trainers, &c.	7	7	...	23	8	15	30	15	15	
	V.—Agriculture ...	10. Interest in Land	38. Land occupants, cultivating ...	287	272	15	927	329	598	1,214	601	613	
			39. Lessees of Villages, &c. ...	26	26	...	139	71	68	165	97	68	
			41. Tenants and sharers, cultivating	123	116	7	254	89	165	377	205	172	
		12. Growers of special products and trees	47. Waternut growers	61	37	24	78	28	50	139	65	74	
			52. Gardeners, seedsmen, &c. ...	69	59	10	133	47	86	202	106	96	
			54. Forest Officers	...	...	...	3	...	3	3	...	3	
		13. Agricultural training and supervision	56. Directors of Agriculture and their Assistants	3	3	...	...	...	...	3	3	...	
			TOTAL CLASS B ...	840	780	60	2,406	859	1,547	3,246	1,639	1,607	

CENSUS 1891.

KASHMIR STATE.

TABLE XVII.—PART B.—*Occupations.*—(*Srinagar Town.*)—(Continued.)

Class.	Order.	Sub-order and Group.	Occupation.	Workers. Total.	Workers. Males.	Workers. Females.	Dependents. Total.	Dependents. Males.	Dependents. Females.	Total. Total.	Total. Males.	Total. Females	Remarks.
Class C.	VI.—Personal and household services.	14. Personal and domestic services ...	59. Barbers	390	390	...	813	282	531	1,203	672	531	
			63. Washermen (*sometimes also dyers*)	309	274	35	579	205	374	888	479	409	
			64. Water-carriers	205	177	28	420	134	286	625	311	314	
			65. Cooks	199	199	...	442	139	303	641	338	303	
			66. Indoor servants	2,826	2,626	200	5,282	1,854	3,428	8,108	4,480	3,628	
			68. Door-keepers, &c.	7	7	...	17	5	12	24	12	12	
		15. Non-domestic Establishment ...	70. Rest-house, Serai, Bath-house, &c., owners and Managers ..	16	16	...	22	4	18	38	20	18	
		16. Sanitation	74. Sweepers and scavengers ...	49	38	11	25	14	11	74	52	22	
			75 Dust and sweepings contractors...	18	15	3	41	19	22	59	34	25	
			TOTAL CLASS C ...	4,019	3,742	277	7,641	2,656	4,985	11,660	6,398	5,262	
Class D.	Preparation and supply of material substances.	VII. Food & drink — 17. Animal Food	76. Cow and buffaloe-keepers and milk and butter sellers ...	801	736	65	1,800	639	1,161	2,601	1,375	1,226	
			79. Butchers	401	401	...	1,031	368	663	1,432	769	663	
			81. Fishermen and fish curers (*many are also boatmen and palki bearers*)	58	52	6	170	58	112	228	110	118	
			Carried over Class D ...	1,260	1,189	71	3,001	1,065	1,936	4,261	2,254	2,007	

CENSUS 1891.

KASHMIR STATE.

TABLE XVII.—PART B.—*Occupations.*—(*Srinagar Town.*)—(Continued.)

Class.	Order.	Sub-Order and Group.		Occupation.	Workers. Total.	Workers. Males.	Workers. Females.	Dependents. Total.	Dependents. Males.	Dependents. Females	Total. Total.	Total. Males.	Total. Females	Remarks.
				Brought forward Class D ...	1,260	1,189	71	3,001	1,065	1,936	4,261	2,254	2,007	
CLASS D.—(*Continued.*)	Preparation and supply of material substances.—(*Contd*).	VII. Food & drink (*Contd*).	18. Vegetable Food.	83. Grain dealers	1,026	993	33	2,411	857	1,554	3,437	1,850	1,587	
				84. Grain parchers	32	24	8	57	23	34	89	47	42	
				86. Flour-mill service and management	15	15	...	58	21	37	73	36	37	
				87. Bakers	349	327	22	831	304	527	1,180	631	549	
				89. Vegetable sellers ...	622	543	79	1,437	527	910	2,059	1,070	989	
				90. Fruit sellers	419	364	55	929	347	582	1,348	711	637	
				92. Confectioners and sweetmeat makers and sellers, and cooks who are also sometimes fishermen and water-carriers ...	161	156	5	303	121	182	464	277	187	
			19. Drink condiments and narcotics.	97. Country spirits distillers & sellers	9	9	...	8	2	6	17	11	6	
				112. Tobacco and snuff manufacturers and sellers	304	303	1	641	225	416	945	528	417	
				115. Bhang, ganja, &c, preparers and sellers	12	12	...	20	5	15	32	17	15	
				Carried over Class D ...	4,209	3,935	274	9,696	3,497	6,199	13,905	7,432	6,473	

CENSUS 1891.

KASHMIR STATE.

TABLE XVII.—PART B.—*Occupations.*—(*Srinagar Town.*)—(Continued.)

Class.	Order.	Sub-order and Group.	Occupation.	Workers. Total.	Workers. Males.	Workers. Females.	Dependents. Total.	Dependents. Males.	Dependents. Females.	Total. Total.	Total. Males.	Total. Females.	Remarks.
CLASS D.—(*Continued.*)			*Brought forward Class D* ...	4,209	3,935	274	9,696	3,497	6,199	13,905	7,432	6,473	
	VIII. Light, firing, and forage.	20. Lighting	116. Oil-pressers and sellers ...	137	120	17	305	113	192	442	233	209	
			119. Candle makers and sellers ...	2	2	...	1	...	1	3	2	1	
			120. Torch makers and sellers ...	10	10	...	33	11	22	43	21	22	
		21. Fuel and Forage	125. Firewood and grass gatherers and sellers ...	222	213	9	855	341	514	1,077	554	523	
	IX. Buildings ...	22. Building materials	132. Brick and tile burners and sellers	69	69	...	183	64	119	252	133	119	
		23. Artificers in Buildings ...	136. Building Contractors ...	52	52	...	217	85	132	269	137	132	
			138. Masons	193	193	...	425	127	298	618	320	298	
	XI. Supplementary requirements.	27. Paper, &c.	153. Paper makers and sellers' and palmleaf binders	145	145	...	398	147	251	543	292	251	
		28. Books and Prints, &c. ...	157. Press Proprietors, Lithographers and Printers	1	1	...	3	1	2	4	2	2	
			158. Book-binders	32	32	...	69	22	47	101	54	47	
		29. Watches, Clocks and scientific instruments	163. Watch and Clock makers and sellers	11	11	...	23	6	17	34	17	17	
		30. Carving, engraving, &c. ...	172. Turners and lacquerers ...	28	28	...	81	25	56	109	53	56	
			173. Die-sinkers and seal, &c., engravers	89	89	...	150	40	110	239	129	110	
			Carried over Class D ...	5,200	4,900	300	12,439	4,479	7,960	17,639	9,379	8,260	

CENSUS 1891.

KASHMIR STATE.

TABLE XVII.—PART B.—*Occupations.*—(*Srinagar Town.*)—(Continued.)

Class.	Order.	Sub-order and Group.	Occupation.	Workers. Total.	Workers. Males.	Workers. Females.	Dependents. Total.	Dependents. Males.	Dependents. Females.	Total. Total.	Total. Males.	Total. Females.	Remarks.
CLASS D.—(*Continued.*)			*Brought forward Class D* ...	5,200	4,900	300	1,2439	4,479	7,960	17,639	9,379	8,260	
	XI. Supplementary requirements.—(*Concld.*)	31. Toys, curiosities, &c. ...	178. Hukka stem makers and sellers ...	22	22	...	54	19	35	76	41	35	
			179. Papier-mache workers and sellers	208	208	...	423	108	315	631	316	315	
		32. Music and Musical Instruments ...	183. Music and Musical Instrument dealers	2	2	...	6	3	3	8	5	3	
		33. Necklaces, Bracelets, beads, sacred threads, &c.	185. Bangle makers and sellers in lac	85	77	8	145	43	102	230	120	110	
			194. Flower garland makers and sellers	2	2	...	10	3	7	12	5	7	
		35. Harness	201. Saddlery and Harness makers and sellers	249	249	...	339	80	259	588	329	259	
		36. Tools and Machinery ...	205. Knife and tool grinders ...	8	8	...	24	8	16	32	16	16	
		37. Arms and ammunition ...	212. Fire-work makers and sellers ...	14	14	...	31	13	18	45	27	18	
	XII.—Textile Fabrics and dress ...	38. Wool and Fur	217. Carpet weavers and sellers ...	332	331	1	408	101	307	740	432	308	
			218. Shawl weavers and sellers ..	5,148	5,148	...	9,989	2,937	7,052	15,137	8,085	7,052	
			219. Felt and pashm workers and sellers	161	161	...	434	126	308	595	287	308	
			220. Blanket weavers and sellers (*often also shepherds*)	440	440	...	949	312	637	1,389	752	637	
			221. Woollen cloth manufacturers and dealers	279	262	17	686	243	443	965	505	460	
			222. Woollen yarn spinners and sellers	1,543	11	1,532	701	271	430	2,244	282	1,962	
			Carried over Class D ...	13,693	11,835	1,858	26,638	8,746	17,892	40,331	20,581	19,750	

CENSUS 1891

KASHMIR STATE.

TABLE XVII.—PART B.—*Occupations.*—(*Srinagar Town.*)—(Continued.)

Class.	Order.	Sub-order and Group.	Occupation.	Workers. Total.	Workers. Males.	Workers. Females.	Dependents. Total.	Dependents. Males.	Dependents. Females.	Total. Total.	Total. Males.	Total. Females.	Remarks.
CLASS D.—(*Continued.*)			*Brought forward Class D* ...	13,693	11,835	1,858	26,638	8,746	17,892	40,331	20,581	19,750	
	XII.—*Concld.* ...	38 Concluded	223. Wool carders	188	188	...	538	177	361	726	365	361	
			224. Wool dyers	226	226	...	480	156	324	706	382	324	
		39. Silk	226. Silk-worm rearers and cocoon gatherers	26	26	...	76	23	53	102	49	53	
			230. Braid and ribbon makers and sellers	267	224	43	400	120	280	667	344	323	
		40. Cotton	231. Cotton cleaners, pressers and ginners	90	90	...	201	66	135	291	156	135	
			232. Cotton Carpet and rug makers and sellers	45	45	...	105	29	76	150	74	76	
		42. Dress	247. Tailors and darners	4,868	4,848	20	8,249	2,417	5,832	13,117	7,265	5,852	
			254. Embroiderers and lace and muslin makers	409	409	...	618	184	434	1,027	593	434	
	XIII.—Metals and precious stones.	43. Gold, silver, and precious stones ...	260. Gold and silver workers ...	482	482	...	1,345	436	909	1,827	918	909	
			Carried over Class D ...	20,294	18,373	1,921	38,650	12,354	26,296	58,944	30,727	28,217	

CENSUS 1891.

KASHMIR STATE.

TABLE XVII.—PART B.—*Occupations.*—(*Srinagar Town.*)—(Continued).

Class.	Order.	Sub-order and Group.	Occupation.	Workers. Total.	Workers. Males.	Workers. Females.	Dependents. Total.	Dependents. Males.	Dependents. Females.	Total. Total.	Total. Males.	Total. Females.	Remarks.
			Brought forward Class D ...	20,294	18,373	1,921	38,650	12,354	26,296	58,944	30,727	28,217	
Class D.—(*Continued.*)	XIII.—*Concld.*	44. Brass, copper and bell metal ...	277. Brass pot makers and sellers ...	38	27	11	87	39	48	125	66	59	
			279. Copper workers and sellers ...	194	194	...	412	116	296	606	310	296	
		45. Tin, zinc, mercury and lead ...	284. Tin workers and sellers ...	6	6	...	17	3	14	23	9	14	
		46. Iron and steel	290. Blacksmiths	306	306	...	614	190	424	920	496	424	
	XIV.—Glass, pottery and stone ware.	48. Earthen and stone ware ...	298. Potters and pot and pipe-bowl-makers and sellers. (*Some are brick and tile makers also*) ...	91	91	...	255	94	161	346	185	161	
	XV.—Wood cane and leaves, &c.	49. Timber and wood	303. Wood cutters and sawyers ...	127	127	...	271	77	194	398	204	194	
			304. Carpenters	405	405	...	911	290	621	1,316	695	621	
		50. Canework, matting and leaves &c.	306. Bamboo and rattan splitters, workers and sellers	63	51	12	96	32	64	159	83	76	
			308. Mat makers and sellers ...	63	17	46	56	16	40	119	33	86	
			Carried over Class D ...	21,587	19,597	1,990	41,369	13,211	28,158	62,956	32,808	30,148	

CENSUS 1891.

KASHMIR STATE.

TABLE XVII.—PART B.—*Occupations.*—(*Srinagar Town.*)—(Continued.)

Class.	Order.	Sub-order and Group.	Occupation.	Workers. Total.	Workers. Males.	Workers. Females.	Dependents. Total.	Dependents. Males.	Dependents. Females.	Total. Total.	Total. Males.	Total. Females.	Remarks.
			Brought forward Class D ...	21,587	19,597	1,990	41,369	13,211	28,158	62,956	32,808	30,148	
CLASS D.—(*Concluded.*)	XV.—*Concld.* ...	50. Concluded	315. Pith and bark collectors, workers and sellers	6	6	...	19	9	10	25	15	10	
	XVI.—Drugs, gums, dyes, , &c.	52. Drugs, dyes, pigments, &c. ...	324. Chemists and druggists ...	155	153	2	402	172	230	557	325	232	
			328. Soap makers and sellers ..	33	33	...	117	44	73	150	77	73	
			332. Ink-makers and sellers ...	22	22	...	79	25	54	101	47	54	
	XVII.—Leather, horns, bones, and grease.	53. Leather, &c.	339. Shoe, sandals, boot-makers and sellers	456	450	6	1,150	410	740	1,606	860	746	
			TOTAL CLASS D ...	22,259	20,261	1,998	43,136	13,871	29,265	65,395	34,132	31,263	
CLASS E.—Commerce, Transport, Storage.	XVIII.—Commerce,	54. Dealers in money and securities ...	346. Bankers and Bank Managers ...	1	1	...	...	...	...	1	1	...	
			350. Money changers and testers ...	432	432	...	1,327	468	859	1,759	900	859	
		55. General Merchandise ...	352. General Merchants	103	98	5	331	136	195	434	234	200	
			353. Merchants' Managers, Accountants, Clerks, Assistants, &c. ...	25	25	...	129	62	67	154	87	67	
			Carried over Class E ...	561	556	5	1,787	666	1,121	2,348	1,222	1,126	

CENSUS 1891.

KASHMIR STATE.

TABLE XVII.—PART B.—*Occupations.*—(*Srinagar Town.*)—(Continued).

Class.	Order.	Sub-order and Group.	Occupation.	Workers. Total.	Workers. Males.	Workers. Females.	Dependents. Total.	Dependents. Males.	Dependents. Females.	Total. Total.	Total. Males.	Total. Females.	Remarks.
Class E.—Commerce, Transport, Storage.—(Concld.)			*Brought forward Class E* ...	561	556	5	1,787	666	1,121	2,348	1,222	1,126	
	XVIII.—Concld. ...	56. Dealing unspecified ...	357. Pedlars, Hawkers, &c. ...	76	72	4	196	77	119	272	149	123	
		57. Middlemen, &c. (a) Brokers, &c. ...	358. Brokers, Agents, Dubash ...	143	143	...	419	148	271	562	291	271	
		57. Middlemen, &c. (b) Contractors and farmers.	360. Farmers of Tolls, ferries ...	12	12	...	39	16	23	51	28	23	
			364. Contractors for labour, Emigration Agents, &c. ...	1	1	...	4	...	4	5	1	4	
	XIX.—Transport and Storage.	59. Road ... (a) Cart, Carriage and Tramway owners and drivers.	378. Palki, &c., owners, bearers, &c. ...	148	148	...	335	110	225	483	258	225	
		59. Road ... (b) Carriers by pack animals.	380. Pack camel, elephant, mule, &c., owners and drivers ...	141	141	...	371	122	249	512	263	249	
		60. Water ... (b) Working Staff of vessels.	385 Boat and barge men... ...	1,036	943	93	2,546	915	1,631	3,582	1,858	1,724	
		61. Messages ... (a) Post, &c. ...	390. Postal Directors, Postmasters and Clerks	1	1	...	8	2	6	9	3	6	
			392. Messengers (unspecified) ...	3	3	...	18	10	8	21	13	8	
		62. Storage and Weighing ...	399. Weighmen and measurers ...	120	120	...	344	117	227	464	237	227	
			TOTAL CLASS E. ...	2,242	2,140	102	6,067	2,183	3,884	8,309	4,323	3,986	

CENSUS 1891.

KASHMIR STATE.

Table XVII.—Part B.—*Occupations.*—(*Srinagar Town.*)—(Continued.)

Class.	Order.	Sub-order and Group.		Occupation.	Workers.			Dependents.			Total.			Remarks.
					Total.	Males.	Females.	Total.	Males.	Females.	Total.	Males.	Females.	
Class F.—Professions.	XX.—Learned and Artistic Professions.	63. Religion ...	(a) Priests, Ministers, &c.	401. Priests, ministers, preachers, missionaries, &c.	1,672	1,585	87	3,907	1,317	2,590	5,579	2,902	2,677	
				402. Catechists, readers, Zanana Mission service, &c. ...	68	64	4	160	55	105	228	119	109	
			(b) Subsidiary religious services.	404. Religious mendicants, inmates of monasteries, convents, &c. ...	13	13	...	7	4	3	20	17	3	
				405. Church, Temple, Masjid, Pagoda, ghat, burial or burning ground service, pilgrim conductors and undertakers	173	168	5	519	189	330	692	357	335	
		64. Education		407. Principals, Professors and Teachers in Colleges, &c., Schools, &c.	130	130	...	401	155	246	531	285	246	
		65. Literature		409. Authors, Editors, Journalists, ballad-makers	53	53	...	153	46	107	206	99	107	
				412. Public Scribes and Copyists ...	49	49	...	99	33	66	148	82	66	
		66. Law		414. Barristers, Advocates and Pleaders	10	10	...	38	18	20	48	28	20	
				418. Stamp-vendors	25	25	...	105	44	61	130	69	61	
				Carried over Class F ...	2,193	2,097	96	5,389	1,861	3,528	7,582	3,958	3,624	

CENSUS 1891.

KASHMIR STATE.

TABLE XVII.—PART B.—*Occupations.*—(*Srinagar Town.*)—(Continued.)

Class.	Order.	Sub-order and Group.		Occupation.	Workers. Total.	Workers. Males.	Workers. Females	Dependents. Total.	Dependents. Males.	Dependents. Females	Total. Total.	Total. Males.	Total. Females.	Remarks.
				Brought forward Class F ...	2,193	2,097	96	5,389	1,861	3,528	7,582	3,958	3,624	
Class F.—*Concld.*	XX.—*Concld.* ...	67. Medicine ...	(*a*) Practitioners ...	421. Practitioner by Diploma ...	1	1	...	2	...	2	3	1	2	
				422. Practitioners without Diploma (Baid, Hakim Kobiraj, &c.)	144	141	3	494	194	300	638	335	303	
				426. Midwifery	73	52	21	24	16	8	97	68	29	
		68. Engineering & Surveying	(*a*) Engineers, Architects and Surveyors.	429. Administrative and Inspecting Staff.	4	4	...	2	...	2	6	4	2	
		71. Music, Acting, Dancing ...		444. Bandmasters and players (not Military)	2	2	...	3	...	3	5	2	3	
	XXI.—Sport and Amusements.	72. Sport		448. Shikaris, Falconers, Birdcatchers	9	9	...	30	13	17	39	22	17	
		73. Exhibition and games.	(*b*) Conjuring, fortune telling and other exhibitions.	453. Buffoons	1	1	...	...	...	...	1	1	...	
				TOTAL CLASS F ...	2,427	2,307	120	5,944	2,084	3,860	8,371	4,391	3,980	

CENSUS 1891.

KASHMIR STATE.

TABLE XVII.—PART B.—*Occupations.*—(*Srinagar Town.*)—(Continued.)

Class.	Order.	Sub-order and Group.		Occupation.	Workers.			Dependents.			Total.			Remarks.
					Total.	Males.	Females.	Total.	Males.	Females.	Total.	Males.	Females.	
Class G.—Indefinite and Independent.	XXIII.—Indefinite	74. Unskilled, labour.	(a) Special branches..	461. Well sinkers	31	31	...	73	21	52	104	52	52	
			(b) General ...	467. General labour	1,722	1,635	87	3,303	977	2,326	5,025	2,612	2,413	
		75. Undefined, &c.		468. Undefined and disreputable means of livelihood	293	163	130	80	35	45	373	198	175	
	XXIV.—Independent of work.	76. Property & alms.	(a) Property and allowances.	469. House-rent, shares, and other property not being land ...	1,034	1,034	...	3,367	1,327	2,040	4,401	2,361	2,040	
			(b) Charity and endowment.	471. Educational or other endowments scholarship, &c. ...	38	31	7	149	49	100	187	80	107	
				472. Mendicancy (not being affiliated to a religious order) ...	619	552	67	635	184	451	1,254	736	518	
		77. Supported at the public charge.	(a) Pension ...	473. Pension, Civil Services ...	11	10	1	14	1	13	25	11	14	
			(b) Prisoners ...	476. Prisoners, under trial ...	5	5	...	...	...	...	5	5	...	
				477. Prisoners, for debt	1	1	...	...	...	...	1	1	...	
				478 Prisoners, convicted or in Reformatories, &c.	122	116	6	...	...	...	122	116	6	
				TOTAL CLASS G ...	3,876	3,578	298	7,621	2,594	5,027	11,497	6,172	5,325	

CENSUS 1891.

KASHMIR STATE.

TABLE XVII.—PART B.—*Occupations.*—(*Srinagar Town.*)—(Concluded.)

Class.	Workers.			Dependents.			Total.			Remarks.
	Total.	Males.	Females.	Total.	Males.	Females.	Total.	Males.	Females.	
ABSTRACT.										
Total Class A	2,872	2,827	45	7,610	2,838	4,772	10,482	5,665	4,817	
Do. B	840	780	60	2,406	859	1,547	3,246	1,639	1,607	
Do. C	4,019	3,742	277	7,641	2,656	4,985	11,660	6,398	5,262	
Do. D	22,259	20,261	1,998	43,136	13,871	29,265	65,395	34,132	31,263	
Do. E	2,242	2,140	102	6,067	2,183	3,884	8,309	4,323	3,986	
Do. F	2,427	2,307	120	5,944	2,084	3,860	8,371	4,391	3,980	
Do. G	3,876	3,578	298	7,621	2,594	5,027	11,497	6,172	5,325	
GRAND TOTAL	38,535	35,635	2,900	80,425	27,085	53,340	118,960	62,720	56,240	

JAMMU:
Dated 9th February 1892.

BHAG RAM,
Census Superintendent, Kashmir State.

TABLE XVII.—Part B.

Occupations by Age, (Europeans and Eurasians), (Kashmir State.)

CENSUS

KASHMIR

TABLE XVII.—PART B.—*Occupations by Age, (Kashmir*

Class.	Order.	Sub-order and Group.	Occupation.
CLASS A.	I.—Administration ...	1. Service of the State	2. Officers ... ...
		2. Service of Local and Municipal Bodies ...	5. Inspecting and Supervising Officials ...
	II.—Defence ...	4. Army	12. Officers ... ...
	III.—Foreign Service (British.)	7. Army and Marine	22. Officers ... ...
			TOTAL CLASS A ...
CLASS B.	V.—Agriculture ...	12. Growers of Special products and trees	44. Tea, Coffee and Cinchona Planters, Managers and Assistants ...
			54. Forest Officer ... ...
		13. Agricultural training and supervision ...	56. Directors of Agriculture and their Assistants ... ...
			TOTAL CLASS B ...
CLASS C.	VI.—Personal and household services.	14. Personal and Domestic services ...	66. Indoor Servants ... ...
CLASS E.	XVIII.—Commerce ...	54. Dealers in money and securities ...	346. Bankers and Bank Managers ...
		55. General Merchandise	352. General Merchants (unspecified) ...
		57. Middlemen, &c. (a) Brokers, &c. ...	359. Auctioneers, Auditors, Actuaries, Notaries, Public Appraisers, House Agents, &c. ... ...
	XIX.—Transport and Storage.	61. Messages (a) Posts, &c. ...	390. Postal Directors, Postmasters & Clerks,
			TOTAL CLASS E ...
CLASS F.	XX.—Learned and artistic professions.	63. Religion (a) Priests, Ministers, &c.	401. Priests, Ministers, Preachers, Missionaries, &c. ... ...
		66. Law	414. Barristers, Advocates and Pleaders ...
		68. Engineering and Surveying. (a) Engineers, Architects and Surveyors.	429. Administrative and Inspecting Staff ...
		(b) Subsidiary Staff,	433. Clerks, &c., in offices of the above ...
			TOTAL CLASS F ...
CLASS G.	XXIII.—Indefinite ...	75. Unspecified, &c.	468. Undefined and disreputable means of livelihood ... ...
	XXIV.—Independent of work.	76. Property and alms (a) Property and allowance.	469. House-rent, shares, and other property, not being land ... ...
		77. Supported at the public charge. (a) Pension ...	473. Pension, Civil Services ... ...
			474. " Military Services ... ...
			TOTAL CLASS G ...
			GRAND TOTAL ...

1891.

STATE.

State.)—(Europeans and Eurasians.)

Workers.											
Total.				Males.				Females.			
Total.	0–4.	5–14.	15 and over.	Total.	0–4.	5–14.	15 and over.	Total.	0–4.	5–14.	15 and over.
1	...	...	1	1	...	...	1	...	...	...	...
1	...	...	1	1	...	...	1	...	...	...	...
3	...	...	3	3	...	...	3	...	...	...	...
8	...	...	8	8	...	...	8	...	...	...	...
13	...	...	13	13	...	...	13	...	...	...	...
1	...	...	1	1	...	...	1	...	...	...	...
...	...	...	...	...	...	...	...	...	...	...	...
3	...	...	3	3	...	...	3	...	...	...	...
4	...	...	4	4	...	...	4	...	...	...	...
5	...	...	5	...	...	...	...	5	...	...	5
1	...	...	1	1	...	...	1	...	...	...	...
2	...	...	2	2	...	...	2	...	...	...	...
1	...	...	1	...	...	...	...	1	...	...	1
1	...	...	1	1	...	...	1	...	...	...	...
5	...	...	5	4	...	...	4	1	...	...	1
12	...	...	12	7	...	...	7	5	...	...	5
1	...	...	1	1	...	...	1	...	...	...	...
14	...	...	14	14	...	...	14	...	...	...	...
2	...	...	2	2	...	...	2	...	...	...	...
29	...	...	29	24	...	...	24	5	...	...	5
4	...	...	4	...	...	...	...	4	...	...	4
4	...	...	4	2	...	...	2	2	...	...	2
1	...	...	1	...	...	...	...	1	...	...	1
2	...	...	2	2	...	...	2	...	...	...	...
11	...	...	11	4	...	...	4	7	...	...	7
67	...	...	67	49	...	...	49	18	...	...	18

CENSUS

KASHMIR

TABLE XVII.—PART B.—*Occupations by Age, (Kashmir*

Class.	Order.	Sub-order and Group.	Occupation.
CLASS A.	I.—Administration ...	1. Service of the State	2. Officers ... ...
		2. Service of Local and Municipal Bodies ...	5. Inspecting and Supervising Officials ...
	II.—Defence ...	4. Army	12. Officers ... ...
	III.—Foreign Service (British.)	7. Army and Marine	22. Officers ... ...
			TOTAL CLASS A ...
CLASS B.	V.—Agriculture ...	12. Growers of Special products and trees	44. Tea, Coffee and Cinchona Planters, Managers and Assistants ...
			54. Forest Officer ... ...
		13. Agricultural training and supervision ...	56. Directors of Agriculture and their Assistants ... ...
			TOTAL CLASS B ...
CLASS C.	VI.—Personal and household services.	14. Personal and Domestic Services ...	66. In-door Servants ... ...
CLASS E.	XVIII.—Commerce ...	54. Dealers in money and securities ...	346. Bankers and Bank Managers ...
		55. General Merchandise	352. General Merchants (unspecified) ...
		57. Middlemen &c. (a) Brokers, &c. ...	359. Auctioneers, Auditors, Actuaries, Notaries Public, Appraisers, House Agents, &c. ... ...
	XIX.—Transport and Storage.	61. Messages (a) Posts, &c. ...	390. Postal Directors, Postmasters & Clerks
			TOTAL CLASS E ...
CLASS F.	XX.—Learned and Artistic Professions.	63. Religion (a) Priests, Ministers, &c.	401. Priests, Ministers, Preachers, Missionaries, &c. ... ...
		66 Law	414. Barristers, Advocates and Pleaders ...
		68. Engineering and Surveying. (a) Engineers, Architects and Surveyors.	429. Administrative and Inspecting Staff ...
		68. Engineering and Surveying. (b) Subsidiary Staff,	433. Clerks, &c., in offices of the above ...
			TOTAL CLASS F ...
CLASS G.	XXIII.—Indefinite ...	75. Unspecified, &c.	468. Undefined and disreputable means of livelihood ... ...
	XXIV.—Independent of work.	76. Property and alms (a) Property and allowance.	469. House rent, shares, and other property not being land ... ...
		77. Supported at the public charge. (a) Pension ...	473. Pension, Civil Services ... ...
			474. Pension, Military Services ... ...
			TOTAL CLASS G ...
			GRAND TOTAL ...

1891.

STATE.

State.)—(*Europeans and Eurasians.*)—(Continued.)

Dependents.											
Total.				*Males.*				*Females.*			
Total.	0—4.	5—14.	15 and over.	Total.	0—4.	5—14.	15 and over.	Total.	0—4.	5—14.	15 and over.
2	1	...	1	1	1	...	...	1	...	...	1
4	3	...	1	1	1	...	...	3	2	...	1
8	4	...	4	3	2	...	1	5	2	...	3
22	6	6	10	6	3	3	...	16	3	3	10
36	14	6	16	11	7	3	1	25	7	3	15
...	...	...	...	...	...	...	...	...	...	...	...
3	1	...	2	...	...	...	...	3	1	...	2
...	...	...	...	...	...	...	...	...	...	...	...
3	1	...	2	...	...	...	...	3	1	...	2
...	...	...	...	...	...	...	...	...	...	...	...
...	...	...	...	...	...	...	...	...	...	...	...
2	1	...	1	...	...	...	...	2	1	...	1
...	...	...	...	...	...	...	...	...	...	...	...
8	2	4	2	2	...	2	...	6	2	2	2
10	3	4	3	2	...	2	...	8	3	2	3
5	1	2	2	2	1	1	...	3	...	1	2
2	...	...	2	1	...	...	1	1	...	...	1
12	3	4	5	3	1	2	...	9	2	2	5
3	1	1	1	1	1	...	...	2	...	1	1
22	5	7	10	7	3	3	1	15	2	4	9
...	...	...	...	...	...	...	...	...	...	...	...
1	...	...	1	...	...	...	...	1	...	...	1
...	...	...	...	...	...	...	...	...	...	...	...
...	...	...	...	...	...	...	...	...	...	...	...
1	...	...	1	...	...	...	...	1	...	...	1
72	23	17	32	20	10	8	2	52	13	9	30

CENSUS

KASHMIR

TABLE XVII.—PART B.—*Occupations by Age, (Kashmir*

Class.	Order.	Sub-order and Group.	Occupation.
CLASS A.	I.—Administration ...	1. Service of the State	2. Officers ... ...
		2. Service of Local and Municipal Bodies ...	5. Inspecting and supervising officials ...
	II.—Defence ...	4. Army	12. Officers ... ...
	III.—Foreign Service (British.)	7. Army and Marine	22. Officers ... ...
			TOTAL CLASS A ...
CLASS B.	V.—Agriculture ...	12. Growers of Special products and trees	44. Tea, Coffee and Cinchona Planters, Managers and Assistants ...
			54. Forest Officer ... ...
		13. Agricultural training and supervision ...	56. Directors of Agriculture and their Assistants ... ...
			TOTAL CLASS B ...
CLASS C.	VI.—Personal and household services.	14. Personal and Domestic Services ...	66. In-door Servants ... ...
CLASS E.	XVIII.—Commerce ...	54. Dealers in money and securities ...	346. Bankers and Bank Managers ...
		55. General Merchandise	352. General Merchants (unspecified) ...
		57. Middlemen, &c. (a) Brokers, &c. ..	359. Auctioneers, Auditors, Actuaries, Notaries, Public Appraisers, House Agents, &c. ... ...
	XIX.—Transport and Storage.	61. Messages (a) Posts, &c. ...	390. Postal Directors, Postmasters & Clerks,
			TOTAL CLASS E ...
CLASS F.	XX.—Learned and Artistic Professions.	63. Religion (a) Priests, Ministers, &c.	401. Priests, Ministers, Preachers, Missionaries, &c. ... ...
		66. Law	414. Barristers, Advocates, and Pleaders ...
		68. Engineering and Surveying. (a) Engineers, Architects and Surveyors.	429. Administrative and Inspecting Staff ...
		(b) Subsidiary Staff,	433. Clerks, &c., in offices of the above ...
			TOTAL CLASS F ...
CLASS G.	XXIII.—Indefinite ...	75. Unspecified, &c.	468. Undefined and disreputable means of livelihood ... ...
	XXIV.—Independent of work.	76. Property and alms (a) Property and allowance.	469. House-rent, shares, and other property not being land ... ...
		77. Supported at the public charge. (a) Pension ...	473. Pension, Civil Services ... ...
			474. Pension, Military Services... ...
			TOTAL CLASS G ...
			GRAND TOTAL ...

JAMMU :
Dated 17*th December* 1891.

1891.

STATE.

State.)—(*Europeans and Eurasians.*)—(Concluded.)

TOTAL.											
Total.				*Males.*				*Females.*			
Total.	0—4.	5—14.	15 and over.	Total.	0—4.	5—14.	15 and over.	Total.	0—4.	5—14.	15 and over.
3	1	...	2	2	1	...	1	1	...	...	1
5	3	...	2	2	1	...	1	3	2	...	1
11	4	...	7	6	2	...	4	5	2	...	3
30	6	6	18	14	3	3	8	16	3	3	10
49	14	6	29	24	7	3	14	25	7	3	15
1	...	...	1	1	...	...	1	...	...	...	...
3	1	...	2	...	...	...	...	3	1	...	2
3	...	...	3	3	...	...	3	...	...	...	...
7	1	...	6	4	...	...	4	3	1	...	2
5	...	...	5	...	...	...	...	5	...	...	5
1	...	...	1	1	...	...	1	...	...	...	...
4	1	...	3	2	...	...	2	2	1	...	1
1	...	...	1	...	...	...	...	1	...	...	1
9	2	4	3	3	...	2	1	6	2	2	2
15	3	4	8	6	...	2	4	9	3	2	4
17	1	2	14	9	1	1	7	8	...	1	7
3	...	...	3	2	...	...	2	1	...	...	1
26	3	4	19	17	1	2	14	9	2	2	5
5	1	1	3	3	1	...	2	2	...	1	1
51	5	7	39	31	3	3	25	20	2	4	14
4	...	...	4	...	...	...	...	4	...	...	4
5	...	...	5	2	...	...	2	3	...	...	3
1	...	...	1	...	...	...	...	1	...	...	1
2	...	...	2	2	...	...	2	...	...	...	...
12	...	...	12	4	...	...	4	8	...	...	8
139	23	17	99	69	10	8	51	70	13	9	48

BHAG RAM,

Census Superintendent, Kashmir State.

CENSUS

KASHMIR

TABLE XVII.—PART B.—*Occupations by Age, (Jammu*

Class.	Order.	Sub-order and Group.	Occupation.
CLASS A.	I.—Administration ...	2. Service of Local and Municipal Bodies ...	5. Inspecting and Supervising officials ...
	II.—Defence ...	4. Army	12. Officers ... ...
			TOTAL CLASS A ...
CLASS C.	VI.—Personal and household services.	14. Personal and domestic services ...	66. In-door servants ... ...
CLASS E.	XX.—Learned & artistic professions.	68. Engineering and Surveying. (a) Engineers, architects and Surveyors.	429. Administrative and Inspecting Staff ...
		(b) Subsidiary Staff	433. Clerks, &c., in offices of the above ...
			TOTAL CLASS E ...
			GRAND TOTAL ...

1891.

STATE.

Province.)—*(Europeans and Eurasians.)*—(Continued.)

Workers.											
Total.				*Males.*				*Females.*			
Total.	0—4.	5—14.	15 and over.	Total.	0—4.	5—14.	15 and over.	Total.	0—4.	5—14.	15 and over.
1	...	...	1	1	...	...	1	...	...	...	...
3	...	...	3	3	...	...	3	...	...	...	...
4	...	...	4	4	...	...	4	...	...	...	...
1	...	...	1	...	...	...	...	1	...	...	1
1	...	...	1	1	...	...	1	...	...	...	...
2	...	...	2	2	...	...	2	...	...	...	...
3	...	...	3	3	...	...	3	...	...	...	...
8	...	...	8	7	...	...	7	1	...	...	1

CENSUS

KASHMIR

TABLE XVII.—PART B.—*Occupations by Age, (Jammu*

Class.	Order.	Sub-order and Group.	Occupation.
CLASS A.	I.—Administration ...	2. Service of Local and Municipal Bodies ...	5. Inspecting and Supervising officials ...
	II.—Defence ...	4. Army	12. Officers ... ...
			TOTAL CLASS A ...
CLASS C.	VI.—Personal and household services.	14. Personal and domestic services ...	66. Indoor servants ... ...
CLASS E.	XX.—Learned & artistic professions.	68. Engineering and Surveying. (a) Engineers, architects and Surveyors.	429. Administrative and Inspecting Staff ...
		(b) Subsidiary Staff	433. Clerks, &c., in offices of the above ...
			TOTAL CLASS E ...
			GRAND TOTAL ...

1891.

STATE.

Province.)—(*Europeans and Eurasians.*)—(Continued.)

Dependents.											
Total.				*Males.*				*Females.*			
Total.	0—4.	5—14.	15 and over.	Total.	0—4.	5—14.	15 and over.	Total.	0—4.	5—14.	15 and over.
4	3	...	1	1	1	...	...	3	2	...	1
8	4	...	4	3	2	...	1	5	2	...	3
12	7	...	5	4	3	...	1	8	4	...	4
...	...	...	...	...	...	...	...	...	...	...	...
5	2	1	2	2	1	1	...	3	1	...	2
3	1	1	1	1	1	...	...	2	...	1	1
8	3	2	3	3	2	1	...	5	1	1	3
20	10	2	8	7	5	1	1	13	5	1	7

CENSUS

KASHMIR

TABLE XVII.—PART B.—*Occupations by Age, (Jammu*

Class.	Order.	Sub-order and Group.	Occupation.
CLASS A.	I.—Administration ...	2. Service of Local and Municipal Bodies ...	5. Inspecting and Supervising officials ...
	II.—Defence ...	4. Army	12. Officers ... ...
			TOTAL CLASS A ...
CLASS C.	VI.—Personal and household services.	14. Personal and domestic services ...	66. In-door servants ... ...
CLASS E.	XX.—Learned & artistic professions.	68, Engineering and Surveying. (a) Engineers, architects and Surveyors.	429. Administrative and Inspecting Staff ...
		(b) Subsidiary Staff	433. Clerks &c., in offices of the above ...
			TOTAL CLASS E ...
			GRAND TOTAL ...

JAMMU :
Dated 17th December 1891.

1891.

STATE.

Province.)—(Europeans and Eurasians.)—(Concluded.)

Total.											
Total.				*Males.*				*Females.*			
Total.	0—4.	5—14.	15 and over.	Total.	0—4.	5—14.	15 and over.	Total.	0—4.	5—14.	15 and over.
5	3	...	2	2	1	...	1	3	2	...	1
11	4	...	7	6	2	...	4	5	2	...	3
16	7	...	9	8	3	...	5	8	4	...	4
1	...	...	1	...	...	...	...	1	...	...	1
6	2	1	3	3	1	1	1	3	1	...	2
5	1	1	3	3	1	...	2	2	...	1	1
11	3	2	6	6	2	1	3	5	1	1	3
28	10	2	16	14	5	1	8	14	5	1	8

BHAG RAM,

Census Superintendent, Kashmir State.

CENSUS

KASHMIR

TABLE XVII.—PART B.—*Occupations by Age, (Kashmir*

Class.	Order.	Sub-order and Group.		Occupation.
CLASS A.	I.—Administration ...	1. Service of the State		2. Officers ... ...
	II.—Defence ...	4. Army		12. Officers ... ...
				TOTAL CLASS A ...
CLASS B.	V.—Agriculture ...	12. Growers of Special products and trees		44. Tea, Coffee and Cinchona Planters, Managers and Assistants ...
				54. Forest Officers ... ...
		13. Agricultural training and supervision ...		56. Directors of Agriculture and their Assistants ... ...
				TOTAL CLASS B ...
CLASS C.	VI.—Personal and household services.	14. Personal and Domestic services ...		66. Indoor Servants ... ...
CLASS E.	XVIII.—Commerce ...	54. Dealers in money and securities ...		346. Bankers and Bank Managers ...
		55. General Merchandise		352. General Merchants (unspecified) ...
		57. Middlemen, &c.	(a) Brokers, &c. ...	359. Auctioneers, Auditors, Actuaries, Notaries, Public Appraisers, House Agents, &c. ... ...
	XIX.—Transport and Storage.	61. Messages	(a) Posts, &c. ...	390. Postal Directors, Postmasters & Clerks,
				TOTAL CLASS E ...
CLASS F.	XX.—Learned and Artistic Professions.	63. Religion	(a) Priests, Ministers, &c.	401. Priests, Ministers, Preachers, Missionaries, &c. ... ...
		66. Law		414. Barristers, Advocates and Pleaders ...
		68. Engineering and Surveying.	(a) Engineers, Architects and Surveyors.	429. Administrative and Inspecting Staff ...
				TOTAL CLASS F ...
CLASS G.	XXIII.—Indefinite ...	75. Unspecified, &c.		468. Undefined and disreputable means of livelihood ... ...
	XXIV.—Independent of work.	76. Property and alms	(a) Property and allowance.	469. House-rent, shares, and other property, not being land ... ...
		77. Supported at the public charge.	(a) Pension ...	473. Pension, Civil Services ... ...
				474. " Military Services ... ...
				TOTAL CLASS G ...
				GRAND TOTAL ...

1891.

STATE.

Province.)—(Europeans and Eurasians.)

Workers.											
Total.				*Males.*				*Females.*			
Total.	0–4.	5–14.	15 and over.	Total.	0–4.	5–14.	15 and over.	Total.	0–4.	5–14.	15 and over.
1	...	...	1	1	...	...	1	...	...	...	...
8	...	...	8	8	...	...	8	...	...	...	...
9	...	...	9	9	...	...	9	...	...	...	...
1	...	...	1	1	...	...	1	...	...	...	...
...	...	...	...	...	...	...	...	...	...	...	...
3	...	...	3	3	...	...	3	...	...	...	...
4	...	...	4	4	...	...	4	...	...	...	...
4	...	...	4	...	...	...	...	4	...	...	4
1	...	...	1	1	...	...	1	...	...	...	...
2	...	...	2	2	...	...	2	...	...	...	...
1	...	...	1	...	...	...	...	1	...	...	1
1	...	...	1	1	...	...	1	...	...	...	...
5	...	...	5	4	...	...	4	1	...	...	1
8	...	...	8	3	...	...	3	5	...	...	5
1	...	...	1	1	...	...	1	...	...	...	...
12	...	...	12	12	...	...	12	...	...	...	...
21	...	...	21	16	...	...	16	5	...	...	5
4	...	...	4	...	...	...	...	4	...	...	4
4	...	...	4	2	...	...	2	2	...	...	2
1	...	...	1	...	...	...	...	1	...	...	1
2	...	...	2	2	...	...	2	...	...	...	...
11	...	...	11	4	...	...	4	7	...	...	7
54	...	...	54	37	...	...	37	17	...	...	17

KASHMIR

TABLE XVII.—PART B.—*Occupations by Age, (Kashmir*

Class.	Order.	Sub-order and Group.	Occupation.
CLASS A.	I.—Administration ...	1. Service of the State	2. Officers ... ...
	II.—Defence ...	4. Army	12. Officers ... ...
			TOTAL CLASS A ...
CLASS B.	V.—Agriculture ...	12. Growers of Special products and trees	44. Tea, Coffee and Cinchona Planters, Managers and Assistants ...
			54. Forest Officers ... ...
		13. Agricultural training and supervision ...	56. Directors of Agriculture and their Assistants ... ...
			TOTAL CLASS B ...
CLASS C.	VI.—Personal and household services.	14. Personal and Domestic Services ...	66. Indoor Servants ... ...
CLASS E.	XVIII.—Commerce ...	54. Dealers in money and securities ...	346. Bankers and Bank Managers ...
		55. General Merchandise	352. General Merchants (unspecified) ...
		57. Middlemen &c. (a) Brokers, &c. ...	359. Auctioneers, Auditors, Actuaries, Notaries Public, Appraisers, House Agents, &c. ... ...
	XIX.—Transport and Storage.	61. Messages (a) Posts, &c. ...	390. Postal Directors, Postmasters & Clerks
			TOTAL CLASS E ...
CLASS F.	XX.—Learned and Artistic Professions.	63. Religion (a) Priests, Missionaries, &c.	401. Priests, Ministers, Preachers, Missionaries, &c. ... ...
		66 Law	414. Barristers, Advocates and Pleaders ...
		68. Engineering and Surveying. (a) Engineers, Architects and Surveyors.	429. Administrative and Inspecting Staff ...
			TOTAL CLASS F ...
CLASS G.	XXIII.—Indefinite ...	75. Unspecified, &c.	468. Undefined and disreputable means of livelihood ... ...
	XXIV.—Independent of work.	76. Property and alms (a) Property and allowance.	469. House rent, shares, and other property not being land ... ...
		77. Supported at the public charge. (a) Pension ...	473. Pension, Civil Services ... ...
			464. Do. Military do. ... ...
			TOTAL CLASS G ...
			GRAND TOTAL ...

1891.

STATE.

Province.)—(*Europeans and Eurasians.*)—(Continued.)

DEPENDENTS.											
Total.				*Males.*				*Females.*			
Total.	0–4.	5–14.	15 and over.	Total.	0–4.	5–14.	15 and over.	Total.	0–4.	5–14.	15 and over.
2	1	...	1	1	1	...	...	1	...	...	1
22	6	6	10	6	3	3	...	16	3	3	10
24	7	6	11	7	4	3	...	17	3	3	11
...	...	...	...	...	...	...	...	...	...	...	...
3	1	...	2	...	...	...	...	3	1	...	2
...	...	...	...	...	...	...	...	...	...	...	...
3	1	...	2	...	...	...	...	3	1	...	2
...	...	...	...	...	...	...	...	...	...	...	...
...	...	...	...	...	...	...	...	...	...	...	...
2	1	...	1	...	...	...	...	2	1	...	
...	...	...	...	...	...	...	...	...	...	...	...
8	2	4	2	2	...	2	...	6	2	2	2
10	3	4	3	2	...	2	...	8	3	2	3
2	1	1	...	2	1	1	...	...	...	...	...
2	...	...	2	1	...	...	1	1	...	...	1
6	1	3	2	1	...	1	...	5	1	2	2
10	2	4	4	4	1	2	1	6	1	2	3
...	...	...	...	...	...	...	...	...	...	...	...
1	...	...	1	...	...	...	...	1	...	...	1
...	...	...	...	...	...	...	...	...	...	...	...
...	...	...	...	...	...	...	...	...	...	...	...
1	...	...	1	...	...	...	...	1	...	...	1
48	13	14	21	13	5	7	1	35	8	7	20

CENSUS

KASHMIR

TABLE XVII.—PART B.—*Occupations by Age, (Kashmir*

Class.	Order.	Sub-order and Group.	Occupation.
CLASS A.	I.—Administration ...	1. Service of the State	2. Officers ... ...
	II.—Defence ...	4. Army	12. Officers ... ...
			TOTAL CLASS A ...
CLASS B.	V.—Agriculture ...	12. Growers of Special products and trees	44. Tea, Coffee and Cinchona, Planters, Managers and Assistants ...
			54. Forest Officers ... ...
		13. Agricultural training and supervision ...	56. Directors of Agriculture and their Assistants ... ...
			TOTAL CLASS B ...
CLASS C.	VI.—Personal and household services.	14. Personal and Domestic Services ...	66. Indoor servants ... ...
CLASS E.	XVIII.—Commerce ...	54. Dealers in money and securities ...	346. Bankers and Bank Managers ...
		55. General Merchandise	352. General Merchants (unspecified) ...
		57. Middlemen &c, (a) Brokers, &c. ...	359. Auctioneers, Auditors, Actuaries, Notaries Public Appraisers, House Agents, &c. ... ...
	XIX.—Transport and Storage.	61. Messages (a) Posts, &c. ...	390. Postal Directors, Postmasters and clerks.
			TOTAL CLASS E ...
CLASS F.	XX.—Learned and Artistic Professions.	63. Religion (a) Priests, Missionaries, &c. ...	401. Priests, Ministers, Preachers, Missionaries, &c. ... ...
		66. Law	414. Barristers, Advocates and Pleaders ...
		68. Engineering and Surveying. (a) Engineers, Architects and Surveyors.	429. Administrative and Inspecting Staff ...
			TOTAL CLASS F ...
CLASS G.	XXIII.—Indefinite ...	75. Unspecified, &c.	468. Undefined and disreputable means of livelihood ... ...
	XXIV.—Independent of work.	76. Property and alms. (a) Property and allowances ...	469. House rent shares and other property not being land ... ...
		77. Supported at the public charge. (a) Pension ...	473. Pension, Civil Services ... ...
			474. Do., Military do. ... ...
			TOTAL CLASS G ...
			GRAND TOTAL ...

JAMMU;
Dated the 17*th December* 1891.

1891.

STATE.

Province.)—(*Europeans aud Eurasians.*)—(Concluded.)

TOTAL.											
Total.				*Males.*				*Females.*			
Total.	0—4.	5—14.	15 and over.	Total.	0—4.	5—14.	15 and over.	Total.	0—4.	5—14.	15 and over.
3	1	...	2	2	1	...	1	1	...	...	1
30	6	6	18	14	3	3	8	16	3	3	10
33	7	6	20	16	4	3	9	17	3	3	11
1	...	...	1	1	...	...	1	...	...	...	...
3	1	...	2	...	...	...	...	3	1	...	2
3	...	...	3	3	...	...	3	...	...	...	...
7	1	...	6	4	...	...	4	3	1	...	2
4	...	...	4	...	...	...	...	4	...	...	4
1	...	...	1	1	...	...	1	...	...	...	...
4	1	...	3	2	...	...	2	2	1	...	1
1	...	...	1	...	...	...	...	1	...	...	1
9	2	4	3	3	...	2	1	6	2	2	2
15	3	4	8	6	...	2	4	9	3	2	4
10	1	1	8	5	1	1	3	5	...	...	5
3	...	...	3	2	...	...	2	1	...	...	1
18	1	3	14	13	...	1	12	5	1	2	2
31	2	4	25	20	1	2	17	11	1	2	8
4	...	...	4	...	...	...	...	4	...	...	4
5	...	...	5	2	...	...	2	3	...	...	3
1	...	...	1	...	...	...	...	1	...	...	1
2	...	...	2	2	...	...	2	...	...	...	...
12	...	...	12	4	...	...	4	8	...	...	8
102	13	14	75	50	5	7	38	52	8	7	37

BHAG RAM,

Census Superintendent, Kashmir State.

TABLE XVII.—PART B.—*Occupations by Age,*

Class.	Order.	Sub-order and Group.	Occupation.
CLASS F.	XX.—Learned and Artistic Professions.	63. Religion ... (a) Priests, Ministers, &c.	401. Priests, Ministers, Preachers, Missionaries, &c. ... ...

1891.

STATE.

(*Ladakh.*)—(*Europeans and Eurasians.*)

Workers.											
Total.				*Males.*				*Females.*			
Total.	0—4.	5—14.	15 and over.	Total.	0—4.	5—14.	15 and over.	Total.	0—4.	5—14.	15 and over.
4	...	...	4	4	...	...	4	...	...	...	...

TABLE XVII.—PART B.—*Occupations by Age,*

Class.	Order.	Sub-order and Group.	Occupation.
CLASS F.	XX.—Learned & Artistic Professions. ...	63. Religion ... (a) Priests, Ministers, &c. ...	401. Priests, Ministers, Preachers, Missionaries, &c. ... ...

1891.

STATE.

(*Ladakh.*)—(*Europeans and Eurasians.*)—(Continued.)

Workers.											
Total.				*Males.*				*Females.*			
Total.	0—4.	5—14.	15 and over.	Total.	0—4.	5—14.	15 and over.	Total.	0—4.	5—14.	15 and over.
3	...	1	2	...	...	...	...	3	...	1	2

CENSUS

KASHMIR

TABLE XVII.—PART B.—*Occupations by Age.*

Class.	Order.	Sub-order and Group.	Occupation.
CLASS F.	XX.—Learned and Artistic Professions.	63. Religion ... (*a*) Priests, Ministers, &c.	401. Priests, Ministers, Preachers, Missionaries, &c. ... ...

JAMMU :

Dated the 17*th December* 1891.

1891.

STATE.

(*Ladakh.*)—(*Europeans and Eurasians.*)—(Concluded.)

TOTAL.											
Total.				*Males.*				*Females.*			
Total.	0—4.	5—14.	15 and over.	Total.	0—4.	5—14.	15 and over.	Total.	0—4.	5—14.	15 and over.
7	...	1	6	4	...	...	4	3	...	1	2

BHAG RAM,

Census Superintendent, Kashmir State.

TABLE XVII.—PART B.—*Occupations by Age, (Gilgit*

Class.	Order.	Sub-order and Group.		Occupation.
CLASS F.	XX.—Learned & Artistic Professions.	68. Engineering and Surveying.	(a) Engineers, Architects and Surveyors.	429. Administrative and Inspecting Staff ...

1891.

STATE.

Road.)—(*Europeans and Eurasians.*)

Workers.											
Total.				*Males.*				*Females.*			
Total.	0—4.	5—14.	15 and over.	Total.	0—4.	5—14.	15 and over.	Total.	0—4.	5—14.	15 and over.
1	...	...	1	1	...	...	1	...	...	...	...

TABLE XVII.—PART B.—*Occupations by Age, (Gilgit*

Class.	Order.	Sub-order and Group.		Occupation.
CLASS F.	XX.—Learned & Artistic Professions.	68. Engineering and Surveying.	(a) Engineers, Architects and surveyors.	429. Administrative and Inspecting Staff ...

1891.

STATE.

Road.)—(*Europeans and Eurasians.*)—(**Continued.**)

Dependents.											
Total.				*Males.*				*Females.*			
Total.	0—4.	5—14.	15 and over.	Total.	0—4.	5—14.	15 and over.	Total.	0—4.	5—14.	15 and over.
1	...	...	1	...	...	...	...	1	...	...	1

CENSUS

KASHMIR

TABLE XVII.—PART B.—*Occupations by Age, (Gilgit*

Class.	Order.	Sub-order and Group.		Occupation.
CLASS F.	XX.—Learned & Artistic Professions.	68. Engineering and Surveying.	(a) Engineers, Architects and Surveyors.	429. Administrative and Inspecting Staff ...

JAMMU;

Dated the 17th December 1891.

1891.

STATE.

Road)—(*Europeans and Eurasians.*)—(Concluded).

TOTAL.											
Total.				*Males.*				*Females.*			
Total.	0—4.	5—14.	15 and over.	Total.	0—4.	5—14.	15 and over.	Total.	0—4.	5—14.	15 and over.
2	...	...	2	1	...	...	1	1	...	...	1

BHAG RAM,

Census Superintendent, Kashmir State.

SUPPLEMENTARY TABLES.

CENSUS 1891.

KASHMIR STATE.

TABLE A.—PART I.—*Christians by Sect and Race.*

Province.	Total Christians.			Distribution by Sect.																							
				Church of England.								Roman Catholic.								Unsectarian.							
				Total.		*Foreign.*		*Eurasian.*		*Native.*		*Total.*		*Foreign.*		*Eurasian.*		*Native.*		*Total.*		*Foreign.*		*Eurasian.*		*Native.*	
	Total.	Males.	Females.	Males.	Females.	Males.	Females.	Males.	Females.	Males.	Females.	Males.	Females.	Males.	Females.	Males.	Females.	Males.	Females.	Males.	Females.	Males.	Females.	Males.	Females.	Males.	Females.
Jammu	46	24	22	19	20	7	9	2	3	10	8	5	2	5	2	...	...	...	...	...	...	...	...	...	...	...	...
Kashmir	145	77	68	65	60	38	44	...	...	27	16	4	2	4	2	...	...	...	...	3	1	3	1	...	...	...	...
Ladakh	25	11	14	7	11	...	...	...	...	7	11	2	...	2	...	...	...	...	...	...	...	...	...	...	...	...	...
Skardu	...	...	...	...	...	...	...	...	...	...	...	...	...	...	...	...	...	...	...	...	...	...	...	...	...	...	...
Gilgit Road	2	1	1	...	...	...	...	...	...	...	...	...	...	...	...	...	...	...	...	...	...	...	...	...	...	...	...
TOTAL ...	218	113	105	91	91	45	53	2	3	44	35	11	4	11	4	...	...	...	...	3	1	3	1	...	...	...	...

CENSUS 1891.

KASHMIR STATE.

TABLE A.—PART I.—*Christians by Sect and Race.*—(Concluded.)

Province.	Total Christains.			Distribution by Sect.																							
				Presbyterian.								Moravian.								Unspecified.							
				Total.		*Foreign.*		*Eurasian.*		*Native.*		*Total.*		*Foreign.*		*Eurasian.*		*Native.*		*Total.*		*Foriegn.*		*Eurasian.*		*Native.*	
	Total.	Males.	Females.	Males.	Females.	Males.	Females.	Males.	Females.	Males.	Females.	Males.	Females.	Males.	Females.	Males.	Females.	Males.	Females.	Males.	Females.	Males.	Females.	Males.	Females.	Males.	Females.
Jammu	46	24	22	...	...	...	...	...	...	...	...	...	...	...	...	...	...	...	...	...	...	...	...	...	...	...	...
Kashmir	145	77	68	3	1	3	1	...	...	...	...	...	...	...	...	...	...	...	...	2	4	2	4	...	...	...	...
Ladakh	25	11	14	...	...	...	...	...	...	...	...	2	3	2	3	...	...	...	...	...	...	...	...	...	...	...	...
Skardu	...	...	...	...	...	...	...	...	...	...	...	...	...	...	...	...	...	...	...	...	...	...	...	...	...	...	...
Gilgit Road	2	1	1	...	...	...	...	...	...	...	...	...	...	...	...	...	...	...	...	1	1	1	1	...	...	...	...
TOTAL ...	218	113	105	3	1	3	1	...	...	...	...	2	3	2	3	...	...	...	...	3	5	3	5	...	...	...	...

JAMMU:

Dated the 17th December 1891.

BHAG RAM,

Census Superintendent, Kashmir State.

CENSUS 1891.

KASHMIR STATE.

TABLE A.—PART II.—*Races Christians*).

Province.	Total Christians.			Distribution by Race.																													
				Foreign.															Eurasian.														
				Total.			*Church of England.*		*Roman Catholic.*		*Unsectarian.*		*Presbyterian.*		*Moravian.*		*Unspecified.*		*Total.*			*Church of England.*		*Roman Catholic.*		*Unsectarian.*		*Presbyterian.*		*Moravian.*		*Unspecified.*	
	Total.	Males.	Females.	Total.	Males.	Females.	Males.	Females.	Males.	Females.	Males.	Females.	Males.	Females.	Males.	Females.	Males.	Females.	Total.	Males.	Females.	Males.	Females.	Males.	Females.	Males.	Females.	Males.	Females.	Males.	Females.	Males.	Females.
Jammu	46	24	22	23	12	11	7	9	5	2	...	...	...	...	...	...	...	...	5	2	3	2	3	...	...	...	...	...	...	...	...	...	...
Kashmir	145	77	68	102	50	52	38	44	4	2	3	1	3	1	...	...	2	4	...	...	...	...	...	...	...	...	...	...	...	...	...	...	...
Ladakh	25	11	14	7	4	3	...	...	2	...	...	...	...	...	2	3	...	...	...	...	...	...	...	...	...	...	...	...	...	...	...	...	...
Skardu	...	...	...	...	...	...	...	...	...	...	...	...	...	...	...	...	...	...	...	...	...	...	...	...	...	...	...	...	...	...	...	...	...
Gilgit Road	2	1	1	2	1	1	...	...	...	...	...	...	...	...	...	...	1	1	...	...	...	...	...	...	...	...	...	...	...	...	...	...	...
TOTAL ...	218	118	105	134	67	67	45	53	11	4	3	1	3	1	2	3	3	5	5	2	3	2	3	...	...	...	...	...	...	...	...	...	...

CENSUS 1891.

KASHMIR STATE.

TABLE A.—PART II.—*Races* (*Christians*).—(Concluded).

Province.	Total Christians.			Distribution by Race.																
				Native.																
				Total.			*Church of England.*		*Roman Catholic.*		*Unsectarian.*		*Presbyterian.*		*Moravian.*		*Unspecified.*			
	Total.	Males.	Females.	Total.	Males.	Females.	Males.	Females.	Males.	Females.	Males.	Females.	Males.	Females.	Males.	Females.	Males.	Females.		
Jammu	46	24	22	18	10	8	10	8	...	...	...	...	...	...	...	...	...	...		
Kashmir	145	77	68	43	27	16	27	16	...	...	...	...	...	...	...	...	...	...		
Ladakh	25	11	14	18	7	11	7	11	...	...	...	...	...	...	...	...	...	...		
Skardu	...	...	...	...	...	...	...	...	...	...	...	...	...	...	...	...	...	...		
Gilgit	2	1	1	...	...	...	...	...	...	...	...	...	...	...	...	...	...	...		
Total ...	218	113	105	79	44	35	44	35	...	...	...	...	...	...	...	...	...	...		

JAMMU :
Dated the 17*th December* 1891.

BHAG RAM,
Census Superintendent, Kashmir State.

CENSUS 1891.

KASHMIR STATE.

TABLE B.—*Christians by Race and Age.*

Province.	Total.			Non-Asiatics.											Eurasians.										
				All ages.			0—14.		15—34.		35—49.		50 and over		All ages.			0—14.		15—34.		35—49.		50 and over.	
	Total.	Males.	Females.	Total.	Males.	Females.	Males.	Females.	Males.	Females.	Males.	Females.	Males.	Females.	Total.	Males.	Females.	Males.	Females.	Males.	Females.	Males.	Females.	Males.	Females.
Jammu	46	24	22	23	12	11	5	4	3	6	4	...	...	1	5	2	3	1	2	1	1	...	...	...	...
Kashmir	145	77	68	102	50	52	12	15	18	20	13	15	7	2	...	...	...	...	...	...	...	...	...	...	...
Ladakh	25	11	14	7	4	3	...	1	3	1	...	1	1	...	...	...	...	...	...	...	...	...	...	...	...
Skardu	...	...	...	...	...	...	...	...	...	...	...	...	...	...	...	...	...	...	...	...	...	...	...	...	...
Gilgit Road	2	1	1	2	1	1	...	...	...	...	1	1	...	...	...	...	...	...	...	...	...	...	...	...	...
TOTAL ...	218	113	105	134	67	67	17	20	24	27	18	17	8	3	5	2	3	1	2	1	1	...	...	...	...

CENSUS 1891.

KASHMIR STATE.

TABLE B.—*Christians by Race and Age.*—(Concluded.)

Province.	Total.			Native.											
				All ages.			0—14.		15—34.		35—49.		50 and over.	
	Total.	Males.	Females.	Total.	Males.	Females.	Males.	Females.	Males.	Females.	Males.	Females.	Males.	Females.
Jammu	46	24	22	18	10	8	3	...	3	5	4	3	...	...
Kashmir	145	77	68	43	27	16	11	5	11	9	5	1	...	1
Ladakh	25	11	14	18	7	11	3	6	1	2	2	2	1	1
Skardu	...	...	...	...	...	...	...	...	...	...	...	...	...	...
Gilgit Road	2	1	1	...	...	...	...	...	...	...	...	...	...	...
TOTAL ...	218	113	105	79	44	35	17	11	15	16	11	6	1	2

JAMMU:
Dated the 17th December 1891.

BHAG RAM,
Census Superintendent, Kashmir State.

CENSUS 1891

KASHMIR STATE.

TABLE C.—*Literate by language known (Europeans and Eurasians).*

Province.	Total Literate.			Languages known.																				
				English.			*English and Vernacular.*			*English and French.*			*Italian.*			*English, French, Italian, Kashmiri and Hindustani.*			*Dutch.*			*German.*		
	Total.	Males.	Females.	Total.	Males.	Females.	Total.	Males.	Females.	Total.	Males.	Females.	Total.	Males.	Females.	Total.	Males.	Females.	Total.	Males.	Females.	Total.	Males.	Females.
Jammu ...	16	8	8	16	8	8	...	...	...	...	...	...	...	...	...	...	...	...	...	...	...	...	...	...
Kashmir ...	79	40	39	72	34	38	1	1	...	2	2	...	2	2	...	2	1	1	...	...	...	...	...	...
Ladakh ...	7	4	3	1	1	...	...	...	...	...	...	...	...	...	...	...	...	...	1	1	...	5	2	3
Skardu ...	...	...	...	...	...	...	...	...	...	...	...	...	...	...	...	...	...	...	...	...	...	...	...	...
Gilgit Road ...	2	1	1	2	1	1	...	...	...	...	...	...	...	...	...	...	...	...	...	...	...	...	...	...
TOTAL ...	104	53	51	91	44	47	1	1	...	2	2	...	2	2	...	2	1	1	1	1	...	5	2	3

JAMMU :
Dated the 17th December 1891.

BHAG RAM,
Census Superintendent, Kashmir State.